T0381348

DEVOTIONAL JOURNAL LIVING

Nuggets of Wisdom for
Practical Living; Scrolling
Through Sermons from My
Daily Posting

Pastor
Stephen Kyeyune

authorHOUSE®

AuthorHouse™
1663 Liberty Drive
Bloomington, IN 47403
www.authorhouse.com
Phone: 1 (800) 839-8640

Published by AuthorHouse   05/07/2015

ISBN: 978-1-5049-1049-1 (sc)
ISBN: 978-1-5049-1055-2 (e)

Library of Congress Control Number: 2015907020

Print information available on the last page.

Acknowledgment

Special thanks to Brother Godfery E N Nsubuga and Sister Valtrude Mujawumukiza for birthing the idea of putting together a book consisting of sermons on my postings.

About the Author

Pastor Stephen Kyeyune is currently the senior pastor of the Multicultural Family Fellowship Church at South Bend Indiana, USA. He is the author of several books including The New Generation of Worshipers; The Spirit is the Crown of the heart; The Acts of the Holy Spirit; When God Calls a Man; The Legacy of a Hero; A Miracle at Prairie Avenue; A series of books> Shaping the Society.

You may contact me on the address below:

Pastor Stephen Kyeyune
2029 South Michigan Street
South Bend Indiana 466613
<stephkyeyu@hotmail.com>

From my Desk: I usually begin writing my books by thanking all of my friends who contributed directly and indirectly to the work of putting together my books. I just want to use this avenue to say how honored and grateful I am to my Facebook friends. Thanks a lot. You are not just friends but we are a family. You guys rock my world. I love you all. We have been fairly homogeneous group and we shall continue that way. I will continue to treasure the unique relationship I have with each of you.

It is not easy to write a book that is appealing to all classes of people without engaging people. That is why it is necessary to express my sincere appreciations to those who have helped me to accomplish this task in particular my friends on the social media. You have been a valuable untapped part of my network. You have been such great mentors. You literally zapped me from my comfort zone and jump-started this work with minimum stress on my side in spite of irritating and unpleasant circumstances. You positioned and equipped me to leverage in the future.

When Facebook was launched over a decade ago, it was nothing more than messaging and chats. Not anymore. Suddenly, Facebook has become an integral part of daily modern living, where business is made, where some marriages incubate and where serious activism goes on. From spiritual nourishment offered by different Church organizations to breaking news to making headlines, Facebook is the trendsetter for much of what we do today.

Freedom of speech has been overstretched. With social media's limitless freedom of expression, political leaders are on the receiving end of an avalanche of ridicule, all sorts of critics taking a swipe at what they consider to be good governance.

One of the side effects of the social media is the dramatic decrease in intimacy. Physical contact between people is at its lowest. Technology has made it possible for our devices to produce all kinds of destructive noises (beeping, buzzes, flashes and etc.) all intended to entice us. People are having significantly less sex and the birth of the internet may be the reason, a leading statistician has suggested, the Independent reported yesterday. According to the newspaper, Professor David Spiegelhalter, of Cambridge University, found that the number of times the average

1

heterosexual couple in the UK makes love has fallen from four times a month in 2000 to three times a month now. The figure in 1990 was five times a month. The Independent a UK based news paper said that speaking on BBC Radio 4's Woman's Hour, he said it was hard to identify the reasons behind the decline but suggested that being connected to the world all the time by mobile devices meant that people perhaps had less time for each other.

The world is changing, and it's changing fast. Technology makes information more accessible every day. This changing digital scene brings with it new challenges to maintaining purity as a Christian— for singles, for couples, and for families as a whole, including children. Christians are called to guard their hearts.

Given the fact, Facebook (FB) is a goldmine in terms of valuable information. It is fair to say that we are swimming in the pool of data whereby you can access information at the click of the mouse at your fingertips. Social media presents to us a golden opportunity to easily interact with each other while dining in our sitting rooms. For better understanding, social media is the practice of gaining and garnering attention through the use of social networking websites and platforms like Facebook, Twitter, Instagram, Google+, WhatsApp, LinkedIn and several others. This kind of attention creates content that attracts and encourages readers to share across their networks. As Patrica Kahill insinuated, "The benefits of social media and why you need it are no longer relevant questions. What matters is how, when and with who do you have to do it."

This is the age of knowledge whereby we cannot ignore the impact of social media. This is a good way for us to express ourselves and to learn from others on a large scale. You don't have to go to the library to do intensive research in volumes of books in search for knowledge; you don't have to change your daily routines because all the information you need is available at the click of a mouse or button. Given the advantages, according to survey, some pastors for some reasons feel uncomfortable associating themselves with the online reputation. The fear of miss-communication going viral can be at the top of their minds.

Personally, I think that people ignore the Social media for other reasons in particular for the sake of privacy and out of fear to publicly express their views on various social and political issues affecting the masses. There is the need for Christians to break the "spiral of silence" when it comes to hot-button social issues. The term "spiral of silence" refers to the desire we all have to avoid reprisal or isolation in public settings, and so people generally go along with what they think is the popular opinion—even if they object to that opinion themselves. So instead of speaking up, they remain silent.

It is true that the vast majority of Facebook users primarily use the forum for chatting, gossip and posting photographs for which a new term, selfie, has evolved. At the same time it is true that the social media provides a platform where vital matters in all circles of life are discussed. According to Break Point Commentaries, now advocates of social media often suggest that online communication tools combat the spiral of silence. Because social media platforms such as Facebook and Twitter provide more options for those with minority views, they should feel freer to say what they really think and thus break the spiral of silence. But it hasn't worked out that way. In fact, social media may have made the spiral of silence even worse.

According to Pew Research, 86 percent of Americans are willing to have an in-person conversation about a controversial public issue, but just 42 percent of Facebook and Twitter users are willing to post about it on those platforms. And of the 14% of Americans who were unwilling to discuss the story face to face with others, only 0.3% were willing to post about it on social media. The findings add statistical backing to anecdotal evidence for a link between gossiping and social media. Now perhaps you're thinking, "Well, social media isn't usually the best place to have these discussions." And I would agree. Often it's not. But the study also suggested that "social media users were less willing to share their opinions in face-to-face settings." In other words, their hesitancy to express their opinions on social media made them less likely to do it in other social settings too.

Social media presents to us opportunities to reach-out to multitudes of people whom we have never even met. No wonder Facebook and Twitter, within in a moment of time have become like a blooming flower laden with nectar. Naturally, all manner of insects; bees and wasps alike are attracted to it. The difference is that while some insects perch to pick nectar, others land to deplete the flower of its life. Certainly there are the positive and negative aspects of the social media. One of the negatives is that the social media has enabled the spirit of the age to become the spirit of the Church. In this book I try to see the positive in negative events because God never ends anything on a negative; God always ends on a positive. I can say with confidence that the positives outweigh the negatives. One of the advantages of the social media is that many people have discovered their potential talents to write and publish articles. I am amazed at the creativity of many friends by reading their postings on Facebook. Not ignoring the fact that it is on this site, where strangers and sophomores share their weirdest experiences.

Whether you acknowledge it or not, creation is the central theme of your life. Not creation in such a way of bringing something out of nothing because God alone can do that, but being creative involving utilizing effectively the opportunities that God has put at our finger tips. The posted messages and the manner they are presented to us in artistic form is stirring. Perhaps it is fit to say that we have reaped shoves from the creativity of the Artists. The first thing that attracts anyone to a product is the way its hardware is designed not the inner workings of the product no matter how fantastic that may be. So the creativity of the artist/designers is important in any form of successful production including packaging. It is stipulated that what has made apple the wealthiest company is the art work of the company designers as shown in their beautiful products. The big cities like Milan, Florence in Italy and Paris in France became magnets of design. Art and creativity go hand in hand. You don't necessarily have to be an artist or writer, but you can be creative in your own way.

Arts subjects are studies of humanities. Culture is the expression of our talents and the product we generate as statement of our talents. All cultures are constructed of a blend of the arts & the sciences. The more successful & prosperous cultures are those that have achieved a good synergy between the two. Technological involves innovation implying a combination of "scientific" knowledge (understanding systems) and creative thought (innovating). Then there's also the role of advertising, which is inherently a creative field. Creative people are thinkers and they are doers as well. There are plenty of creative ideas in your head clamoring to be expressed. Why not give it a try? You have nothing to lose, and you may be astonished by what you're able to accomplish.

Every person can write. One writer said that "A story of one of us in some measure is a story for all." He meant that if you are able to tell your story well there is a good chance that your story is going to intercept with the people in your audience. Your story is unique but people are going to relate to you by reading what you shared in your story. Each one of us has skeletons of the past mistakes and pain in our closets. "We carry our scars where our story is". Again, it is important to write your own story or else others will write a different story about you.

You can even write you future life story by examining your past and present. Start from the age you are just now and start writing your future life story as you'd like it to be. Be as outrageous as you want and just write about your ideal life and how you interact with it. Improve your story by reading stimulating blog posts; anything no matter how little it is will help disciplining your minds and will add a little bit to make your story interesting. Remember that words on paper are powerful and can help shape your goals.

We are not the main characters of our stories but Jesus is. Stories—true stories—of the patriarchs, the kings of Israel, Jesus, and His apostles make up a large portion of the Bible. But the Bible (with many stories) is summarized in one story of Jesus who gave up His life to save the world.

Indeed, stories shape our way of looking at the world, and this is true also of fictional literature. As a Christian author, my understanding of the Holy Spirit impacts my writing. I hope you will be empowered by the Holy Spirit too. Also, I have benefited much by reading other writers' articles and postings. Some of you the reach of your vocabulary is well-nigh inexhaustible—and this is the more instructive, as we so seldom meet today with displays of wordcraft that send us, fascinated, to the dictionary. You have been instrumental to sustain my vision where it is supposed to be.

Writers, it has been well said, write. They embrace the disciplines of writing. But so too, if they are wise, they sit at the feet of other writers, and learn. As the saying goes, "Iron sharpens iron". I want to say that writing and reading are compared to the two wings of the plane; you need both wings in order to fly. You cannot afford to miss one wing.

It was not my prior intention to write this book. I started by keeping journal of my daily blessings to thank God for his daily blessings. Blessings are supposed to be redistributed. That is why I resolved to share them with my friends on social media. The response from the four corners of the earth was very encouraging. Eventually, I decided to crack open my journals and start writing this book for you so that you could share in the same blessings. The good part of it is that most of my friends claimed to be believers. Discussion is smooth with someone who claims to seek the truth, and is obsessed with achieving or utmost who has already possessed it.

Although writing a book was not my prior intention, I am excited about the procedures. It adds value because messages in books cannot be easily deleted and lost. After all, for the most part to confide in one's self, and become something of worth and value is the safest course. One pastor insinuated that the grave yard is full of un-written books. He was talking about those people who die without writing down their stories. "Without words, without writing and without books there would be no history, there could be no concept of humanity" - Hermann Hesse

Given the fact, I am careful not to boast in my own accomplishment but in God's accomplishments. Jeremiah warned that, "Let not a wise man boast of his wisdom, and let not the mighty man boast of his might, let not a rich man boast of his riches; but let him who boasts boast of this, that he understands and knows Me, that I am the LORD who exercises lovingkindness, justice and righteousness on earth; for I delight in these things," declares the LORD.… (Jeremiah 9:23-24). This book points to the only book that is inspired and written by God (the Bible). The Bible is my point of reference in all my writings. This book is therefore not a substitute for the Bible. I encourage you to read the Bible regularly.

Putting together this book was stirring. It was not necessary for me to edit my journal. I did not have to concoct my language. C.S. Lewis warned that, "Don't use words too big for the subject. Don't say "infinitely" when you mean "very"; otherwise you'll have no word left when you want to talk about something really infinite."

When I embarked on this task everything was in its right place. I did not write to criticize or challenge somebody. After-all, I have always shunned being judgmental. Modern writing is beyond that echelon. I just got my message out in its simplicity and presented it to you the way it is. One great use of words is to hide our thoughts but at the same time words have no power to impress the mind without the exquisite horror of their reality. Voltaire Henry Wadsworthy said that "In character, in manner, in style, in all things, the supreme excellence is simplicity." I like this comment by Nathaniel Hawthorne: "Words – so innocent and powerless as they are, as standing in a dictionary, how potent for good and evil they become in the hands of one who knows how to combine them".

I began putting together this journal with a positive attitude and with good motives. My objective is to plant the seed of success in the mind of somebody. Albert Einstein insinuated, "Three rules Work: Out of clutter find simplicity; From discord find harmony; In middle of difficulty lies opportunity."

I want to say that it has been real exciting to write this book. It involved keeping daily journals for a couple of years and knitting them into presentable manuscripts in anticipation of solving some of the puzzles of life. It would be a blunt lie to say that I addressed all of the puzzles of life. Afterall even if I inked my pen in the ocean to write them down it won't be enough! But I can assure you that by scrolling through my sermons attentively you will find an answer to your pending problem. I have left no stone un-turned when addressing various issues of life. There is an adage saying that, "Hearts are often confused and broken by thoughtful words left unspoken."

I believe that somebody at the other end of the world is anxiously searching for an answer that is highlighted in my manuscripts. My prayer is to touch a soul somewhere in the echelons of power whose candle of hope struggles to light. "I can't hope to convey the full effect of the embraces and avowals, but I can perhaps offer a crumb of counsel." If there is anybody known to you who might benefit from my manuscript, please make them available to him or her. Do not let that opportunity pass. The difference made will certainly be more than your imagination.

I am in particular thrilled by religious and spiritual postings flashing on almost every home page on Facebook. It is often tempting to believe that almost all friends on Facebook are born again believers. It is not given to me to judge who is born again and who is not. All I can say is that posting religious or spiritual messages on socials sites has become a prevalent phenomenon. Whereas it is a good habit, there is also the risky part of it. We find so much solace in outward revelations of our commitment and devotion to godly events. Without proper concentration, the whole lot could just be a dangerous catharsis that placates our hearts and tucks away our guilty consciences so that in and after moments of the resultant amnesia, we finally believe our names have been written in the Book of Life.

True change must come from a transformed heart and expressed externally. God is the God of hearts. He demands total commitment from inside to the outside. He watches every step we make, every word we utter and every thought we conceive. Those that aren't posted on social sites like Facebook, but are keenly observed within the scopes of our consciences are the ones that determine our place in God's kingdom. But, yet, even those that we extol publicly have their own fair share of aligning us with or exempting us from His grace.

God won't teach us to observe his commands simply because we have posted a 'relevant' request on social sites. The post may not even transcend the physical, human realm if its actual conviction is stuck on the hand that posted it. If it must break through the firm blockade of transcendental qualification, it must emanate from the deep recesses of our hearts. To be specific, it must come from a conscience that is cleaned by the blood of Jesus.

I want to take this opportunity to thank most of my friends on social media for conducting yourselves appropriately. I encourage you to continue conducting yourselves with dignity. I want to highlight another area where the score is high. It is the field of encouragement. It is important to complement each other but read carefully the message before complementing. There is a tendency of clicking on "like" just to impress somebody without even reading through their messages.

There are a lot of junk messages and images from cold-hearted people piled on our home pages. I mean people who take delight in profanity. "Some people tend to live 'double' lives. In the physical world they are more restrained. But when it comes to online, they just become someone else spewing all sorts of things in all sorts of language..." Please immediately delete those messages that do not glorify God. At times it is better to de- friend immoral characters. Simplifying your life means putting your life together in accordance to God's will, plan and provision, "As you simplify your life, the laws of the universe will be simpler; solitude will not be solitude, poverty will not be poverty, nor weakness" - Henry David Thoreu

As we are actively engaged in using different social media platforms, it is advisable to be cautious so as to avoid being victims of cybercrime which is on a marked rise in the world today. Cybercrime especially email address hacking, website hacking and cyber stacking are on the rise. Musana says that, "These cyber criminals, disguised as friends on Facebook and other social networks, initially befriend the victim and thereafter persuade them to share crucial personal information like one's password, pin code, credit card information. This is what is happening even right now. With such information at their disposal, they can easily wire the victim's money to their bank accounts elsewhere; disorganize business proceedings, thereafter crashing their illegal software together with the victim's data system once they have no more use of it so as to avoid being tracked. This is how some people have lost out on their businesses.

Internet users must be cautious especially parents with youth in possession of smart phones, laptops and other internet accessing devises, and parents should install monitoring software on their children gadgets so as to keep track of the internet sites they regularly access to avoid being victims of cybercrime. Not forgetting the murky waters of revenge porn.

Dorothy Okello of Women of Uganda Network (WOUGNET) notes that whereas communications surveillance and cyber security monitoring is necessary; the state has to ensure that the collected data is safely guarded against abuse and misuse.

Whether with state surveillance or not, individuals should exercise personal responsibility to live normal lives. And, if anything, online users should even be more careful in cyberspace as most of the online platforms do surveillance themselves, argues Lillian Nalwoga of International ICT Policy in East and Southern Africa (CIPESA).

And it seems like the online platforms like Facebook, Twitter, etc, have realized this and somewhat loosened up on their data protection policies. It is now possible to request them [online platforms] to delete your previous comments. This may come in handy especially now in the era where job/tender applications are followed with a quick search to see the online activity of the applicant.

Given the fact, the governments and the online platforms cannot substitute for good parenting. There is a saying that "When the going gets tough, the tough get going". One way to do the job not perfectly but as best as we can is for the parents to be authoritarians. Authoritative parenting is a parenting style characterized by strict rules, harsh punishments and little warmth. Such parent has a will to say no to what is good for their children. In this case not only should the parents know the people whom their children befriend but should also watch and control the circles of their own friends. While parents innocently and for good reason are friends with their children on online platforms, they ought to know the kind of online circles they are in– as their children might end up consuming material that was never intended for their age group.

We should not only regulate the Internet but we should use it effectively for our advantage. The Internet has become a crucial battleground in the fight against immoral propaganda. The Christians need to step up their efforts to countering the radical and immoral groups like the homosexuals that have the branding and marketing department on the social media. So far the think tank has carried out several experiments using Google Ideas, Twitter and Facebook to try to directly engage with potential recruits -- and dissuade them from joining these depraved movements.

Dan Levy, Facebook's vice president for global marketing and small business, said Facebook has boosted the number of advertisers on the social network to two million as it launched a mobile app for those managing their commercial pitches. The number of advertisers has doubled over the past year and a half.

Pastors need not to stand on sideline watching; they can participate in creating value for their communities. I want to encourage the pastors never to be afraid to be on social media. This is the right place to document our thoughts on sensitive national issues. Social media provides platform to address today's challenges. We can be today's solutions for today's challenges.

The fact that people look at pastors as the cream of cream, it is not easy for some pastors to participate in various social activities. To be a pastor is like being caught up between the horns and trumpet whereby you are left with no option but to feel the noise and bear accordingly. The calling of a pastoral ministry is a calling to step in the shoes of the Chief-shepherd (Jesus Christ). It is tough because people are intensively gazing at you, sniffing for any inappropriate behavior ignoring the fact that you are a mortal man too. It has nothing to do with profiling but simply "objectifying" and scrutinizing of preachers for the sake of criticism and self-justification. It is scaring taking into account that the public has better peripheral vision than we do.

I advise the pastors never to be afraid to fail. Allow failure to be your friend. Allow both positive and negative criticism. Remember that a word of encouragement after failure is worth more than an hour of praise after success. A pastor must let his congregation know that he is a human being who is subject to flaws. He should not accord himself a super-human status. You are not a good man because you are a good pastor; you are a good pastor because you are first a good man. Many preachers pretend to be holier than they are in an attempt to absolve themselves from the responsibilities of their actions. They end up hurting themselves than helping themselves. I want to appeal to my audience to pray for your pastors always because they are the custodians for their and your souls.

Contents / page numbers:

January:	Preparation to prosper	13
February:	Spiritual growth	60
March:	Resurrection	122
April:	Overcoming Temptation	142
May:	Apologetics	177
	Memorial	258
June:	Celebration of family	278
	Humor	348
July:	Freedom / Liberty	365
August:	Evangelism	438
September:	Resting in Christ	467
	Laboring / Harvest	488
October:	Halloween	503
November:	Praying	505
	Thanksgiving	531
December:	First / Second Coming of Christ	537
	Seeking wisdom	564

1ˢᵗ January (New Year) Month of Preparation:

January is saturated with messages about entering the New Year. A new year represents the new beginning. The New Year has always been an inspiration for most people to set "New Year's Resolutions." It gives everyone an opportunity to start-over, try new things, and make whatever improvements we feel is necessary in our lives. Whenever I hear the New Year's resolutions, I often wonder whether they worked on implementing the same resolutions way behind in the past year. The best way to predict the future is by creating it. I believe that resolutions can only work if you put in work. "It is better done than better said". Action separates reality from fiction. If you put in work results will definitely come. "Big results require big ambitions" ~ Heraclitus.

According to Angela Huffmon the reason most New Year's Resolutions fail is because most people don't make a plan to succeed ahead of time. Dramatic changes to your routine should not be expected to happen suddenly. It's important to remember that any changes must be taken in small gradual steps. There's a quote by Cicero that says, "The beginnings of all things are small." I agree with her but I want to add that we (Christians) focus primarily on God's accomplishments in and through us as opposed to our own accomplishments. As a child of God you do not have your own plans apart from the plans of God. God has a plan and purpose for your life. Seek His plans and apply godly wisdom to implement them. Excel in everything pertaining to the divine will and purpose for your life. Success is walking strictly in accordance to the divine calling.

A season is a subdivision of the year, marked by changes in weather, ecology, and hours of daylight. Every season comes up with different changes. It ensures a paradigm shift in everything, and a complete turn of events. Seasons change and are at times unpredictable but we can count on the unchanging character of God. When He instructs you to do something do not hesitate even when His instructions defy logic. Go ahead and jump with your eyes closed rather than resisting with your eyes open. At times certain occurrences take us by surprise and if we are not careful it is easy to be frustrated. On the positive side, when we exercise our faith the unpredictability of the season become exciting. For example Abraham went on the mountain to sacrifice

13

his son most probably a sad man but walked down the mountain the happiest man. Keep up the faith of the walk and the walking by faith. "Life is like riding a bicycle - in order to keep your balance, you must keep moving" - Albert Einstein.

Ask God of the main reason for the season then join up in happiness of the season. There is always something to celebrate. Celebrate the gift of life. Life is the greatest gift from God. The Bible says that, "For with you is the fountain of life" (Psalms 36:9). Age is a gift because there are many people who died and did not get a chance to see what you are seeing. Every year that passes we grow old. Claim your promise for old age: "Even to your old age and gray hairs I am he, I am he who will sustain you. I have made you and I will carry you; I will sustain you and I will rescue you" (Isaiah 46:4). Every single day you are alive it is because of the grace of God. Grace is the air (oxygen) that you need to breathe in and out.

The past year is gone without a possibility of recuperation and so is our age. We cannot deny that the New Year comes with old age. As I mentioned, it is your attitude towards age that makes a difference. The National Opinion Research Center at the University of Chicago has found that nearly 40 percent of Americans aged 65 and older described themselves as "very happy," compared with just 33 percent of those between 35 and 49. The accumulation of years can help us not take ourselves so seriously. And then there's the acquired wisdom of responding to competing demands. Virtue is the mark of a life well lived, and it takes a lifetime to cultivate. Christians, whatever our age, are supposed to seek the wisdom that only God can provide. Happiness is not the mere pursuit of good experiences or feelings, but the classically understood "good life", or the deliberate acquisition of virtue; wisdom, ultimately, comes from the Lord.

There is no possibility of regaining our lost youthful age. The adage goes, "You can't put the corn back on the cob". Therefore, look forward for the best in the future. Certainly nobody has control over time because it is running faster than our schedules. But do not make time your enemy; make time your best friend so that you can always accomplish something. Remember that faith is not limited by time. Also, a great blessing is worthy a great sacrifice. The people of the world are busy making resolutions for the coming year. But we (believers) find our life in Christ, and the biblical way for us is not to make resolutions of what we are going to accomplish but to focus on what God is going to accomplish on our behalf.

Time is a very misleading thing. Don't dwell in the past. All there is ever, is the now and future. The past year is gone. We have only the New Year. Let us begin afresh. Definitely, the past year had its setbacks. But you can't rewind the past, likewise you can't stop the future, but you can press on the present. Don't focus on the past failures. It is like spending time beating on a wall, hoping to transform it into a door. Focus on the doors opened in the New Year. You can learn from the past, and then move on. The past year's experiences should not deter you but should rather motivate you to excel. "Life can only be understood backwards; but it must be lived forwards."

I predict 2015 to be a year of exuberance. Don't worry about hindrances trying to stop you because God gave us potentiality to overcome the huddles of life. So the side shows are not there for distraction but may just be illuminating your path to reach your intended destiny. Remember that the future belongs to those who believe in the beauty of their dreams and who are committed to take the high way. Inferiority complex is a worm that tends to deny us our abilities to excel.

Working together we can beat the huddles of life. God deals with us as a unit entity (His body or Church). It is therefore imperative that we work together uplifting one another. No man is an island to himself. We need each other. "If the mountain had no pointed rocks and crevices you wouldn't have anything to grip on and to step on as you climb to conquer the heights of triumph!"

2014 is history. "To put the past behind you, you must accept that you've moved beyond it." The New Year signifies marching forward; it means yet another distance to go faced with the same tasks including impediments: More trials, more joys; more temptations, more triumphs; more prayers, more answers; more toils, more strength; more fights, more victories; and also not ignoring the misery of life like sickness, old age and of course death. The Bible says that, "And we know that all things work together for good to those who love God, to those who are the called according to his purpose." (Rom 8:28).

The negatives of life should not obstruct us from our ultimate goal. The trials of life are intended to make us more sincere, more earnest, more spiritual, more heavenly-minded and more convinced that the Lord Jesus can alone bless and comfort our souls. Jesus is the anchor in life's storms! Do you have Him in Your boat? Is He the firm and secure "Anchor" for your soul? Our hope is neither in creative philosophy nor in positive thinking but in Christ. The gospel is about God coming down to the earth to navigate our lives to where He is (at the right hand of the Father). The New Year is a step closer to His return. It is imperative that you believe in Jesus, if you do not intend to miss out on the divine purpose for your life (the benevolence of salvation).

For many 2014 has ended with unfulfilled dreams leading to frustration and despair. A desperate person is most likely to cling on anything. Then the New Year shoves in lots of excitements. Every person is emotionally stimulated. In our humanity, we are most likely to make decisions emotionally to fill the huge emotional void in our lives. Given the fact, most people treat their emotions as though they're purely incidental and sometimes even a hindrance in life. Consequently, emotions are often side-lined as impulsive and troublesome parts of ourselves that have to be controlled and are of little value to us. Actually, our emotions, both negative and positive, are all perfectly safe and healthy and serve us in incredible ways, especially when it comes to making important life decisions as long as the decisions we make line up with the Scriptures. As a tip to you, never make a promise when you are excited. Never take a decision when you are angry. Control your tongue. "If your foot slips, you can recover your balance. But if your tongue slips, you can never recall your words."

The past year has been characterized with challenges, struggles and new opportunities. Given the fact, generations look for sanity in the past times. You often hear them using the term "I am missing the past old days". There has never been an age that did not applaud the past and lament the present. The future may be scary too and unpredictable but you can't keep running to the past just because it seems familiar.

Trusting in the God of tomorrow is the key to fulfillment. Wonder is the perception and curiosity of how big God is. Your God owns all the cattle and the mountains. Everything was made for your inheritance.

The universe was not made for us because it is too big for us. But it was made to manifest the glory of God that is much bigger and greater than this universe. The glory of God is ultimate joy that we regain through Jesus Christ. You are an over-comer because Jesus Christ who overcame the world dwells in you. You have the life of God in you. "In the end, it's not the years in your life that count. It's the life in your years." You were not meant for a mundane or mediocre life! As I said, you are the child of God. You must believe as one and act as one.

"How we see ourselves in Christ Jesus will always decide how much of Jesus we will be able to exhibit to others around us. Never forget saints, In Him we live and move and have our being! So see yourself as God sees you in Christ Jesus." — Abraham Israel

God uses weak vessels so that He may get the glory. Look at the calling of Moses: But Moses responds with a question: But Moses said to God, "Who am I, that I should go to Pharaoh, and that I should bring the sons of Israel out of Egypt?" Good question: Who am I? I'm a nobody, and how is it that I am supposed to go out and tell people that I am here to save them, because God has spoken to me? Who am I, after all? And God responded by not telling him who he was: And He said, "Certainly I will be with you, and this shall be the sign to you that it is I who have sent you: when you have brought the people out of Egypt, you shall worship God at this mountain."

Notice two things: First, who Moses was didn't matter, because God would be with him, and that's the deciding factor, no matter who Moses is or who we are. Second, the "sign" God gives does not precede his obedience. Moses has to step out in obedience first, and then God honors his obedience by the manifestation of the miracle. We are not supposed to seek the miracles or the blessings of God but we are called to obey His ordinances. Success follows those who obey.

Scrolling through my sermons on prosperity/success:

It is the end of 2014 and the beginning of 2015. We cannot roll time back but we can comb the corners of our memory to delete all the past negative experiences and move on with life. Otherwise, putting one leg in the past year and one leg in the New Year may result into getting stranded. Paul said that, "But this one thing I do, forgetting those things which are behind, and reaching forth unto those things which are before, I press toward the mark for the prize of the high calling of God in Christ Jesus" (Philippians 3:13-14). Until you know where you want to go, you settle anywhere and end up going nowhere. Never limit your view of life by any past experience. May the bridges you burn today light the way for a better tomorrow.

****

2014 is meandering towards the close. It is time to take inventory regarding your performances throughout the year. If you achieved nothing, you just missed golden opportunities that could have changed your story in life, but you don't need to give up in despair: "For thus saith the Lord of hosts; Yet once, it is a little while, and I will shake the heavens, and the earth, and the sea, and the dry land" (Haggai 2:6). God is about to create another chance for you. In the New Year, He is already shaking the heavens, just to have some blessings drop down for you. Just position yourself to receive. May your rivers flow without end, meandering through pastoral valleys tinkling with bells of hope in 2015.

****

2014 has been a very tough year to some of us and 2015 is not exceptional either. Life is short, sweet and tough but we must learn to be comfortable with the uncomfortable. Given the fact, there is a reason to rejoice. "Life is at its best when everything has fallen out of place, and you decide that you're going to fight to get them right, not when everything is going your way and everyone is praising you." The challenged life is the best therapist. Nothing is more beautiful than a real smile that has struggled through tears! Congratulation graduates.

****

As the years come and go so does this earthly life evaporates in thin air. Old age is inevitable and scaring too. In the U.S. and in scores of countries, young adults tend to rate themselves as very happy, but the older they get, up to age 50, the less happy they become. However, the

National Opinion Research Center at the University of Chicago has found that nearly 40 percent of Americans aged 65 and older described themselves as "very happy," compared with just 33 percent of those between 35 and 49. New York Times columnist David Brooks says that many psychologists attribute this boost in well-being to natural changes in the brain. And while there may be some truth to this, I agree with Brooks' opinion, "that elder happiness is an accomplishment, not a condition, that people get better at living through effort, by mastering specific skills." Certainly, there are advantages of old age. Age is wisdom, and wisdom involves the duration of time invested in learning. Yes, some of us learn when we are too old, but life goes on… The Bible instructs us to number our days; it means seeking to know God's purpose for you every single time you are breathing. It is planning your future by applying godly wisdom to your days, the opposite of which is suicidal!

****

The end of 2014 does not mean the end of the journey, but the beginning of the next great voyage. We are about to start navigating 2015. I can't promise that it will be milk and honey. Difficult and painful as it may appear, we must walk on in the days ahead with an audacious faith in the future. As Edward Kennedy said, "We know the future will outlast all of us, but I believe that all of us will live on in the future we make."

In order to break out of the bracket, you need a daring heart. When Jesus bade Peter "come" on the stormy high sea, it was the worst risk ever, to be attempted by man; but he saw an invisible bridge. That is faith! Each time you seem compelled by situations to do what others can't and won't dare, just realize that you are denying God an opportunity to make a Star out of you. The storms of life are not there to deter you but to connote victory. "When our days become dreary with low-hovering clouds of despair, and when our nights become darker than a thousand midnights, let us remember that there is a creative force in this universe, working to pull down the gigantic mountains of evil, a power that is able to make a way out of no way and transform dark yesterdays into bright tomorrows."

****

2015 is your year. Aim high and swing into action. Remember that opportunities dance with those who are already on the dance floor. Your future life is your autobiography. It is important to write down your vision for 2015. The vision is intended to illuminate your path to which God wants you to tread and things that God wants you to achieve. Sometimes in life, a fog sets in and you don't know which way is the right direction. The vision helps you to focus and at the same time avoid to be pulled away in different directions. It helps you to stick to your guns by leaning on the integrity and sovereignty of God. It is a pledge that senility has not the last say in everything but God does (Isaiah 40:7-8).

****

I predict 2015 to be a prosperous year. All of us potentially have unlimited opportunities to excel. However, the blessings of God come to us in form of investment. When the blessings spring to you from God, you must be creative enough to diversify them into different channels of blessing in the lives of others. As at creation, a river sprang from Eden to water the Garden, but right there, it was redistributed into four other tributaries (rivers) (Genesis.2:10-14). The blessings of God should not be hoarded, but redistributed. You are that distributing agent rather than a consumer!

****

I predict 2015 a year with a thick business muscle to reckon with, for those who exude a character identified with the business and entrepreneurial world. Arm yourself with a sharp sense of foresight. See the unusual opportunity to drink from the New Year's gourd of business acumen. Search for financially liberating opportunities where they do not seem obvious. Take advantage of the given opportunity at the earliest moment. Don't wait too long before you swing into action. "I was seldom able to see an opportunity until it had ceased to be one" -Mark Twain

****

As we are putting behind 2014 and welcoming 2015, I want to elaborate on some of the menaces that transpired in 2014. Immorality has been an acceptable way of life. Like a tsunami, the so-called gay marriage has swept aside just about every obstacle in its path, creating a very different cultural landscape. Same-sex marriage isn't the start of the problem; it's the fruit of a long-going sexual revolution. There has been swift embrace of all kinds of immorality. Bedroom privacy has been aggressively violated - Pornography and 'nude bedroom photos' frequently flashing on the front pages of the public magazines and social media. The family institution has been hit worst. Sociologist David Popenoe said that no civilization ever survived after its family life deteriorated. G.K. Chesterton insinuated that, "This triangle of truisms, of father, mother and child, cannot be destroyed; it can only destroy those civilizations which disregard it." In 2015 we can work together to make a difference. The grace of God ignores the missed marks but requires obedient to God and demands spiritual maturity too.

****

Making resolutions has become a must-do activity at the beginning of every New Year. However, the test is the end of year review. If it has not worked in 2014, how do you expect to come through in 2015? By now, you should have reviewed the year 2014 to get your current financial position. This entails computing your current level of assets and liabilities. Knowing the assets you have including savings, investments and loans gives you an accurate financial position as opposed to only looking at your current income. Just like in all aspects of your life, the New Year is a good time to make commitments in the area of personal financial management. To do things differently this time around, think of it as an action plan from 2015 and beyond. Plan how to reduce your debt either through increasing repayments (if you have room) or get other sources of income to help clear it. Critical to your action plan, is figuring out how to reduce the risk of being one pay check away from poverty. Learn to prioritize your expenditure. For example, you would be irresponsible if you spent all the money on entertainment today yet you have tuition to pay. Avoid anxiety by managing expectations in your household through giving them a clear position of what priorities should be in line with available resources. (Sylvia Juuko)

****

Why I don't make resolutions outside the promises of God: I learnt the hard way never to make promises to God because I find myself often failing to keep the same promises. Jesus said that the spirit is willing but the body is weak (Matthew 26:41). Paul said that "For that which I do I allow not: for what I would, that do I not; but what I hate, that do I" (Romans 7:15). Therefore, I decided to depend on the promises of God rather than making promises to God because God will never back out on His promises. He said that "My covenant will I not break, nor alter the thing that is gone out of my lips" (Psalms 89:34).

****

You can rewind the clock, but you cannot reverse the time. The future is where we are all headed to; the fact is that we can remember the past but we can never live in the past anymore. We may try to forget the past but at times the things we forget are as important as those we remember! Think about it.

****

Then the LORD said, "My Spirit will not contend with humans forever, for they are mortal; their days will be a hundred and twenty years" (Genesis 6:3). Before God judged the world by the floods people used to live beyond five hundred years. When sin mounted, God shortened life expectancy up to 120. According to the recent survey carried out, less than 50% of the people who participated expressed desire to live up to 120 years because of the burdens associated with old age. A friend of mine said that he never celebrates the New Year because it means growing old. "Your spiritual destination is by far the most important decision you will ever have to face and make. If you think that this earthly life is miserable or long, eternity is over a million times longer than 120 years!" ~ Legacy of Hero by Pastor Stephen Kyeyune

****

Proverbs 9:10 - Knowing God is the beginning of wisdom. The beginning stands for the solid foundation upon which all truth must be established. There is always room to know more than what is already known! God wants us to prosper in all aspects of life but above all things He wants our soul to prosper. That is why He has revealed to us everything we need to know in order to be saved and to stay saved.

****

The value you place on a thing determines how much time you spend on it or with it. Spending time with your Bible shows you value the Word. "When you know what God prefers, and you do what He prefers, God makes you the preferred." A dynamic life is always fired by the vision, the vision built on the Word of God. The Word helps us to see things from the prospective of God. It is important to see distant things as if they were close and to take a distanced view of close things. "A blind man's world is bounded by the limits of his touch, an ignorant man's world by the limits of his knowledge, and a great man's world by the limit of his vision" ~ Paul Harvey

****

Believe in what God can accomplish in you and through you. Philippians 4:13 – I can do all things through Christ that strengthens me. Strength is conceived in the atmosphere of passion, hatched in the face of commitment, exercise in place of challenge, showcased in prodigy, triumphs in tenacity, resourceful in resilience, comforts in brevity, rests in hope, maximizes in dreams, exploits in targets, drives with patience, accelerates in faith, conquers in purpose, celebrates in confidence. Go for strength, maximize your moments and win your struggles. In Christ Jesus you have strength to win your battles.

****

Challenges are what make life interesting. Overcoming them is what makes life meaningful. Ordinary people believe only in the possible. Extraordinary people visualize not what is possible or probable, but rather what is impossible. And by visualizing the impossible, they begin to see it as possible. -- Cherie Carter-Scott

****

Begin this year with a vision. The Bible says that "Where there is no vision, the people perish" (Proverbs 29:18). Your eye is the window to your soul. The heart pursues what your eyes behold. An African proverb projects that, "Toddlers cry for the very things exposed to their sight." Your physical eyes need the light to see in the same manner your spiritual eyes need a revelation to perceive. It is only the spiritually enlightened that can perceive things from the divine prospective. Spiritual illumination unveils the divine vision for your life. Spiritually alive people have a sense of expectation that God will act, and will let people be aware of the continuing divine involvement in their lives. When your spiritual eyes are open you can share the pleasures of divine company. With spiritual vision, you can figure out where God is headed and where you belong in it. The visionary people trust the Holy Spirit to pull them and others out of whatever holes they may have dug for themselves. They can see the course ahead with a clearer spiritual vision. The vision actualizes what you see in future giving you direction to your destiny. It controls and propels you to move in the center of God's will for your life, gloriously fulfilling your divine purpose in Him.

****

Today's prayer: Immortal God everlasting father. I thank you for adding another year to my year today. You were my anchor during the stormy weather of my life. You were my shield during the turbulent period of my life. You did it before and can do it again. Even if you don't do it you are my God & you will remain my God forever. I know my best song is yet to be sung; my best story is yet to be told; my chapter is yet to be written & my best years still lies ahead.

****

What lies behind us and what lies before us are tiny matters compared to what lies within us. The vision is perceived by faith. The vision begins from within. The Eye of Faith is the strength of Faith. It is what you can see ahead of you that strengthens your Faith! Faith sees beyond natural. You cannot get to where you cannot see. The promise is always as far as your spiritual eyes can see. (Gen. 13:14).

****

A vision is an imagination is the perceptive part of you that cannot be seen by natural eyes. It is not fantasy but it is seeing the future reality in the present. Manifestation does not surprise a visionary person because he had already seen the image painted in the inside long time before it manifested in the physical.

****

Any vision involves people. You need people to implement your vision. See the people as your assets rather than liabilities. It does not mean all people that come to you are God sent but it means that you are sent to all of them. Exercise the gift of discernment in your dealing with people. We are a community of grazers and opportunists. Some are just picking up the early green shoots, anything that is left over. That is what they are doing, just feeding and they move around a lot as they go. One columnist said that, we are either motivated by some returns or we are that abrasive because we are yet to get into those positions of poor. We engage to profile ourselves for a bigger calling that we have strategically positioned ourselves to achieve. We use what we know against the naivety of the community to get what we want. This is what has made community development colorless and tasteless.

****

Mobilization is the ability to move people in the direction of a goal. In order to achieve your dreams, leverage on the power of quality relationships. The truth is that no matter how lofty and exciting your dreams are, you cannot achieve it alone without engaging people. Assets and other resources without human resources end in stagnation and frustration. You need both (resources/human resources) in order to excel.

****

Setting goals is the first step in turning the invisible into the visible. One way to keep momentum going is to have constantly greater goals. Setting goals allows you to stay focused on your vision, and going after it by moving toward your goals. How to visualize your goals is made easy when you use a vision board. Visualizing your goals involves firstly writing out a clear list of everything that you would like to achieve and then putting a time frame on each of these goals. Visualizing your goals and actually forming a mental picture of that which you wish to attract into your life on a sub conscious level, is affirming to yourself that what you want is possible and that it will happen. It is a spiritual drive involving making right turns based on biblical moral principals at key intersections.

****

Wade Ryan gives advises concerning setting goals. He says that it is important to remember that most of these desires and goals, in order to be achieved, will require some sought of action on your part. As you are feeling the feelings of manifesting these desired goals into your life, you will feel impulses to take some form of action. When this happens you must take action quickly, because the universe likes speed. The more powerful your vision, the quicker they will be manifested. But specify your underlying feelings of having your goals now. Hit the nail while it is still hot. As fast as each opportunity presents itself, use it! Act fast but precisely in order to avoid disappointment: compared to climbing a ladder and after reaching at the top you realize that it is leaning on the wrong wall.

****

The most desired things are often not the ones we achieve at the first try but after times of persistence and dogged tenacity; but in the end we are capable of achieving the desired goals. What hurts you today makes you stronger tomorrow. Therefore never give up on your dreams. "A real dream is your experience when awake that let you sleep but that will keep you awake in bed."

****

Success is about a whole life approach to achieving noble & worthwhile goals/dreams. A great blessing is worthy a great sacrifice. "When it is obvious that the goals cannot be reached, don't adjust the goals, adjust the action steps" ~ Confucius

****

You must discover and live life through your passion. Passion makes the world go round. The great entrepreneurs are men of passion. Their work reflects the passion, the desire and the fire in them. With passion in their hearts and fire in their souls they become masters in their field of work. "If passion drives you, let reason hold the reins." ~ Benjamin Franklin

****

God never asks us to do something big for Him. He asks us to take small steps of faith so He can do something Big in us. "A pessimist sees the difficulty in every opportunity; an optimist sees the opportunity in every difficulty" ~ Winston Churchill

****

Expectations are real. Expectation usually creates anticipation for something that has not yet entered our personal space or domain. As a tree loses leaves and even the whole branches with the onslaught of strong winds and storms, so shall our expectations die, and are reborn. We cannot curb them, as the tree could not stop new leaves and branches from forming. But while they are with us, we must avoid being over demanding. The hustle for superiority is passionately engraved on the hearts of many and its pursuits often skip steps which will always demand to be revisited… Our expectation of others is so great such that it has become the major cause of sadness and disappointment. Greater expectation that is focused on how we think others should conduct themselves, take on their assigned responsibilities and etc., will only bring abject sinking and disintegration. It is for the same reason some who can't stand pressure end up quitting prematurely. Never be coerced to perform simply to please them because they will leave you regardless. "When people walk away from you, let them go. Your destiny is never tied to anyone who leaves you" ~ Marilyn Monroe

****

Regarding any project there is always going to be adversity. Avoiding danger is no safer in the long run than outright exposure. "To win without risk is to triumph without glory." Great achievers are risk takers. They invest wisely but without fear. Patton, Jr. says that the time to take counsel of your fears is before you make an important battle decision. That's the time to listen to every fear you can imagine! When you have collected all the facts and fears and made your decision, turn off all your fears and go ahead! "Living at risk is jumping off the cliff and building your wings on the way down" ~ Ray Bradbury

****

The road to victory begins with your characters. Brother Lamont Coakley says that, "When character does not collaborate with your blessing; your blessing becomes a curse." God's blessings come in form of massive opportunities without limitation but there is a need for spiritual and emotional preparation to sustain the availed blessings. Opportunity is often difficult to recognize. Claude McDonald said that, "Opportunity is a bird that never perches." It is possible not to see an opportunity until it has ceased to be one. It is therefore advisable to jump at every small opportunity available in bid to get to your intended destiny. But without characters opportunities become purposeless and abuse is inevitable. Your characters define who you are. Irrespective of your status in life, no one can place a value on you far greater than you place on yourself. "We can't change the whole world at one time but we can change the way we live in it one subscriber at a time, beginning with you!"

****

The people you admire worked hard to be what they are. You have the same capabilities to make it to the top. It is the coward and sluggish in you that demands that you sleep early in the morning every day when everybody else seems to be going to work. This is a reverse psychology that has baffled friends and foes alike. According to a new study published in the journal Social Indicator, lazy people don't necessarily remain lazy for the rest of their lives. According to Ifeanyi Onuegbu, weakness is not always a trait traced to parentage; but most times an unfortunate demeanor, developed and capped in the atmosphere of fantasy, futility, illusion and despondency; a migration from doggedness, tenacity and resilience to the world of procrastination, a sticking to pessimism rather than optimism; subscribing to trivialities that threaten our capped and latent possibilities.

****

"The bravest know fear but they do not yield to it...the world owes its progress to the men who have dared...Men erect no monuments and weave no laurels for those who fear to do what they can".

****

According to Sylvia Juuko, while we may not care to admit, family background could have inevitably shaped the way we think about money. Some of your current money habits could be shaped by your upbringing. Some of these habits boost our financial well-being and should be consolidated. There are a number of people from privileged backgrounds, who have struck out on their own and built wealth. However, there are cases where a privileged background fostered a sense of entitlement that has become a stumbling block towards efforts to manage money prudently. If your family has generational wealth, how has this shaped your views about money? Do you spend money indiscriminately because you are assured that you can always get bailed out by family? Problems arise if you lack the income to match the kind of luxury you are used to. To make matters worse, if you start earning income, you will probably desire to be highly paid without any change in your work ethic.

****

We are different and God called us to do different things because He is the God of varieties. Disciplining yourself to do what you know is right and important, although difficult, is the highroad to pride, self-esteem, and personal satisfaction - Thatcher

****

The only difference between you and the people you admire is their perspective. Be yourself. "Putting out the other fellow's candle never brightens your own" - Kenneth E Hagin

****

God's blessings are passed on to generations. "For I will pour water on him who is thirsty, And floods on the dry ground; I will pour My Spirit on your descendants, And My blessing on your offspring" (Isaiah 44:3 NKJV)

****

They say that time is money but I say that time is life. Every moment you invest into others you invest your life into them. You impact their lives by giving them your time. The world is compared to a drowning person that needs your CPR to revive it. Candidly consider yourself to be on a rescue mission with assignment to save life.

****

You and God is the majority. Be anxious to know things and to do the right thing. Be proud in the little accomplishment registered. "Why do we love and get mesmerized by the strength and might of others but we are indifferent to building our own."

****

It is more important to live what we believe than to just talk about it, because what we talk might be impressive but how we live of what we talk will make an eternal impact for Jesus. As Jesus Himself said that without partnership with Himself in the intimacy of our spirit-man inside us, we can do nothing eternally worthwhile for the Glory of God. "Lives are changed eternally when we actually walk the talk and then talk the walk!" ~ Abraham Israel

****

Gambling is a game and a job to some. Each and every gambler knows that the secrete to survival is knowing what to throw and knowing what to pick. But there is no such a thing as lottery Faith in God. The holy God (YHWH) neither gambles nor does lottery. He is the perfect Judge that rewards faithfully. His rewarding is not emotionally motivated; it is not guess work; it is not a trial & error. Next time when somebody asks you to sow a seed of one hundred dollars into him so that you may receive one thousand, ask him to sow a seed of one thousands in you so that he may receive ten thousand.

****

Many of us base our self-confidence on what other people think, so we work hard at being accepted. We buy things, we wear things, we join things -- all just for the benefit of trying to be accepted by our friends, family, co-workers and peers. Does God say you have to earn acceptance? That you could ever deserve it? No. The Bible says that God has accepted you. Come with all your burdens to Him.

****

"God made man. Man made money. Money made man mad". The human body has billions of nerves. But the most important nerve to the natural man is the artificial nerve that runs from the heart to the pocket. Show me where you spend your money and I will define your characters.

****

Neither does God condemn material prosperity nor does He equate it with piety. Likewise, we should never equate material prosperity with spirituality. If material prosperity was a reward for spirituality the twelve Apostles chosen by Christ could have been billionaires. But Peter, when speaking on behalf of the Apostles lamented that, "Sliver and gold I have not" (Acts 3:6).

****

A lady was going on mission to Africa, one of the elders handed her a sealed envelope and instructed her to open it only when she reaches a point when she has no body to turn to. The lady spent thirty years on mission in Africa and returned with a sealed envelope. She then gave a testimony that for thirty years there was no point of time when she had no body to turn to because Jesus was ever there for her to turn to.

****

Tithing is making a covenant with God involving your finances. Tithing is dotted throughout the Old Testament. Abraham tithed (Genesis 14:20); Jacob tithed (Genesis 28:22); Moses tithed (Leviticus 27:30-33). Tithing was a command for God's covenant people to set aside one tenth of all their produce (crops and animals) as an offering to God. If an Israelite lived too far away from the Temple to bring his tithes to it, he could exchange the goods for money and send money, but the norm was for all the produce to be brought to Jerusalem at set times in the calendar. This was an act of faith - showing trust in God providing and honoring God with their produce. It also provided the priests and Levites a means of living, for they were not given land as their inheritance. They depended on the tithes for their portion, and out of their portion, they also had to tithe! (Leviticus 27:30, Deuteronomy 12:17).

In the New Testament, Jesus scolds the Pharisees for tithing on spices but disregarding "justice and the love of God. Jesus says "they should have done [the tithing] without neglecting the other...." (Luke 11:42-44). The Temple was still functioning, but Jesus warned that it would be utterly destroyed, and so it was, in AD 70. That put an end to tithing on crops and animals. So Christians no longer did that. Instead, they set aside a tenth of their income to give to the newly established Christian Church which did a great work of giving to the poor (they had no buildings to maintain, or salaries to pay back then!). Tithes should be brought to the Church that feeds you to do the work of God. Remember that God does not need your money but needs you and your obedience.

****

Many of us wait until others succeed before we believe we can succeed and when they fail we think we will also fail. Unknowing to us, it is determination that makes the difference between success and failure. Deciding which steps to take can be difficult, but if you weigh your choices carefully, you can take "great strides". Determination and commitment are the keys you need to unlock your victory. The hurdles in your way are not there to stop you but to enhance your ambition to put your best foot forward. Thomas Calyle once said "The block of granite, which was an obstacle in the pathway of the weak, became a stepping-stone in the pathway of the strong". Be the pacesetter and let others follow!

****

Try new things and adopt new ways. According to Henry Miller, a new world is not made simply by trying to forget the old. A new world is made with a new spirit, with new values. Our world may have begun that way, but today it is caricature. Our world is a world of things. What we dread most, in the face of the impending debacle, is that we shall be obliged to give up our gewgaws, our gadgets, all the little comforts that have made us so uncomfortable. We are not peaceful souls; we are smug, timid, queasy and quaky.

****

C.S. Lewis insinuated that, "Nothing is yet in its true form because things are subject to change." The winds of God are always blowing, but you must set the sails. Remember that nothing is interesting, if you're not interested. "The wheel of change moves on, and those who were down go up and those who were up go down."

****

The environment can be a hindrance to the success of many. For example in East Africa the economic empire and wealth of the most privileged is hereditary. It is tough for a poor disadvantaged person with basic education, to raise capital and rise above the challenges of a non-entity with no one to lean on, to move towards economic emancipation. In most of East Africa education seems to brainwash people away from business, leaving the half-baked middle class to dominate, and perhaps, this has restricted us to small scale businesses that do not expand and collapse with the demise of the sole proprietor.

****

"The fastest runner doesn't always win the race, and the strongest warrior doesn't always win the battle. The wise sometimes go hungry, and the skillful are not necessarily wealthy. And those who are educated don't always lead successful lives. It is all decided by being in the right place at the right time" ~ King Solomon (RKJV)

****

Begin this week with an attitude of gratitude. The will of God will never take you where the grace of God will not protect you. Never let the bad attitudes of others come in and destroy the greatness that's on the inside of you. "A hero is someone who collects stones thrown to him by the crowd and instead of throwing them back to the crowd; uses those stones to build a castle for himself."

****

Never be over-exited and never panic in times of crisis. High-pressure situations are common in the business world. Things almost never go according to plan and often times they go terribly wrong. If you can't override your adrenaline response and remain calm in a crisis, you're sort of screwed.

****

Fanaticism: Passion is a big success driver, but when you cross that line and become over-the-top fanatical, that works against you. I've seen it time and again. It leads to a skewed perception of reality, flawed reasoning, and bad decision-making.

****

Passionate is a good pay-master. Child of God, what fully enchants you to remain in a pit when you may sit on a throne? Do not live in the lowlands of bondage now that mountain liberty is conferred upon you. Do not be satisfied any longer with your tiny attainments, but press forward to things more sublime and heavenly. Aspire to a higher, a nobler, a fuller life.

****

Pharaoh couldn't stop Moses, Saul couldn't stop David from the Throne, Satan couldn't stop Jesus, May no obstacle Stop you this week In Jesus name. Winners are never quitters. Sometimes walking away has nothing to do with weakness, but everything to do with strength. We walk away not because we want others to realize our worth and value, but because we finally realize our own. ~ Robert Tew

****

The power of unity cannot be underestimated. "When we dream alone it is only a dream, but when many dream together it is the beginning of a new reality" ~ Friedensreich Hundertwasser

****

Business philosophy: If you want to grow very fast in business, go alone, but if you want to go far please go with your family. You will achieve a bigger goal since the whole family is growing. When everyone succeeds, the family succeeds.

****

The things we own should never own us. There is nothing wrong with money but the love of money. "Although gold dust is precious, when it gets in your eyes it obstructs your vision." His-Tang Chih Tsang

****

Right is never defined in terms of self-interest or expediency. "Do the right thing" is the best legacy anyone can leave.

****

The problem is not getting new, innovative ideas into our minds but getting the old ones out.

****

I will be somewhere and not everywhere; I will do something and not everything. That is what I live for and I am enjoying it.

****

The roads we take are more important than the goals we announce. Decisions determine destiny. - Frederick Speakman

About success:

In times of trouble we run to God to restore our strength. The book of Psalms is the most quoted book in the New Testament. Jesus (the suffering servant) quoted the book of Psalms more than any other book. Calvin and the Puritans felt convicted to sing psalms in public worship and loved doing so. Yet the Puritans called the book of Psalms the book covered with tears because most believers who are in pain open and read this book covering its pages with tears. The Psalms are theological as well as doxological; they teach us about God and help to develop His character in us in times of trouble.

Success is achieving something that you been passionately pursuing. Success is most times measured in material gains because we live in the material world with real material needs like food, shelter, transportation, communication, good health and etc. Jesus used money in his teachings more than any other object. In fact He talked about money more than He did Heaven and Hell combined. Jesus talked about money more than anything else except the Kingdom of God. 11 of 39 parables talk about money. One of every 7 verses in the Gospel of Luke talk about money. The Word Money is actually used in connection with Jesus (whether He uses the word or it is used in connection with Him) approximately 25 times throughout the 4 Gospel accounts of Matthew, Mark, Luke and John. Jesus also speaks of treasure and wealth a handful of time in those books. But the kingdom of God is central to His teaching. Jesus said that "For where your treasure is, there will your heart be also" (Matthew 6:21). What you spend your money on is most likely to be the most important thing to you because money is time. A believer is supposed to spend most of his or her money on extending the kingdom of God to the uttermost ends of the earth.

I want to emphasize that money is not the reason for happiness. The Bible warns that, "In the house of the righteous is much treasure: but in the revenues of the wicked is trouble" (Proverbs 15:6). The meaning is that great wealth is in the house of the righteous, but trouble is in the income of the wicked. I know many rich people who do not have peace because they are ever worried about their riches. Yet there are many poor people who are fulfilled and happy in spite of lacking some essential commodities.

Success has multiple interpretations depending on whom you ask. We (Christians) look for interpretations from the biblical prospective. According to Christianity, success does not erode sufferings. Jesus suffered for our sake yet He was perfect. The Bible says that God blesses the just and the unjust. "He makes His sun rise on the evil and on the good, and sends rain on the just and on the unjust." (Matthew 5:45). Christians have absolute victory in the future heaven coming on earth. We are seeker sensitive people. We seek God, the Holy Spirit, the kingdom of God and love.

True love for God is trusting God and believing Him when expecting nothing from Him. We love Him because of who He is but not because of what He can do for us. Satan challenged God that Job loved Him because of the blessings that God had given him. Job was one of the wealthiest men in the world at that time, so Satan wanted to test Job to prove to God that humans would turn their back on God if they lost all their material possessions. Satan is in Heaven arrogantly and disrespectfully challenging humans' motive for serving and worshiping God. Satan claimed that humans only love God because of the blessings that God has given them. We have the responsibility to live our lives in a way that proves we will not abandon righteous principles when tested. We uphold God's right to determine what is good and bad each time we make a choice or decision based on God's righteous standards instead of our own selfish desires!

'Success' is pursued by all. Yet not all of people do what it takes to succeed. The first step should be developing the passion to succeed. Success comes to those who dare to live out their passion, no matter how much obstacle and challenges try to deter them. "The energy and intensity it takes for long term success comes from putting your passion to work. This is the essence of passion capital." Passion is restrained eagerness with persistence and focusing as opposed to selfishness and greedy. Success and the passion to succeed are as important as eating and drinking whereby we ought to allow the one appetite to be satisfied with as little restraint or false modesty as the other. Passionate people enjoy what they do in spite of the obstacles. When you do something with a lot of honesty, appetite and commitment, the input reflects the output. Noblesse Oblige said that, "Hungry people follow the scent of a good meal while those who do not worry about their next meal can afford to question the status quo."

Big things begin small. An African proverb says the rooster crowing in the morning was once an age. A decade is a period of ten years. The word is derived (via French) from the Ancient Greek *dekas* which means ten. Interestingly, the decade began as a second, then minute, hour, day, week, month and year. Maturity is not when we start speaking big things...it is when we start understanding small things. For example in order to understand the human body, you must know the tinny cells making up the human body, then the nucleus, atoms and molecules making up the cell. Learn to appreciate little things because big things begin small. The Bible says that, "One who is faithful in a very little is also faithful in much--" (Luke 16:10).

A regenerated person has confidence in God and will go an extra mile to find the purpose of God for him or her. Achievement is reached by responsible people. Accepting responsibility for your life means understanding that you are responsible for creating the life you want to live. If you don't do it, who else will? This is a tremendously empowering realization, or at least it was for me. When I realized I was responsible for myself, I stopped making excuses and I stopped waiting for others to help me. Instead, I started changing my life. I'll say it again: You can decide what you want your life to be about. The choice is yours.

Virtue distinguishes the men from boys, managers from subordinates, the outstanding from mediocre. In order to be a man and gentleman as well, do what is right regardless of the people's opinions. When you please others in hopes of being accepted, you lose your self-worth in the process. "I prefer to be true to myself, even at the hazard of incurring the ridicule of others, rather than to be false, and to incur my own abhorrence." ~ Frederick Douglass

****

The wisdom of man is the ability to put things apart (dismantle). The wisdom of God put the broken pieces together. The cross is the greatest display of the wisdom of God. This is the place where the broken pieces of our lives are reassembled and our lives fixed.

****

Solomon is the Old Testament prodigal son. He took all the wisdom his Father gave him and squandered it recklessly on the pleasures of life. He married in non-restrained manner and had three hundred concubines. The floor and walls of his palace were covered with gold. He wrote the journal for his reckless life in Ecclesiastes. At the end of the day he recounted that everything is vanity.

****

When blessings spring to you from God, you must be creative enough to diversify them into different channels of blessing in the lives of others. As usual, a river sprang from Eden to water the Garden, but right there, it was redistributed into four other channels. The blessings of God should not be hoarded, but redistributed Genesis.2:10-14. You are that distribution center from today, in Jesus name!

****

The successful man is focused! Mediocrity is the result of living a distracted life. Lack of direction, not lack of time, is the major problem we have. Stay focused on the solution and not the problem. Focus on the journey, not the destination.

****

Desire is what gives birth to a vision. Desire inspires and motivates. It was desire that inspired the Wright Brothers to fly. The proof of desire is pursuit irrespective of the unfavorable conditions. What you pursue says a lot about you. Hope and wish are different from definite desire.

****

Successful people make good choices. Healthy choices are godly choices. God's choices for us sometimes do not make sense because they are spiritually discerned. Godly choices do not necessarily appeal to our emotional desires but they are the best choices for us. Sometimes you have to do the things you don't want in order to get the things you want. It's not hard to make good decisions when you know what your values are. Decisions become easier when your will to please God outweighs your will to please the world "Life is the sum of all your choices." ~ Albert Camus

****

Contentment is the key to success. "Consider your ways. Ye have sown much, and bring in little; ye eat, but ye have not enough; ye drink, but ye are not filled with drink; ye clothe you, but there is none warm; and he that earneth wages earneth wages to put it into a bag with holes. Thus saith the LORD of hosts; Consider your ways" (Haggai 1:7-8).

****

Persistence is the state or quality of being persistent. It is making every second the most valuable second of your life. Being non-productive in the past second, makes the journey difficult, but definitely not impossible. Persistence never loses hope but keeps up the good fight. "Nothing in the world can take the place of persistence. Talent will not; nothing is more common than unsuccessful men with talent. Genius will not; unrewarded genius is almost a proverb. Education will not; the world is full of educated derelicts. Persistence and determination alone are unique" Persistence is therefore a virtue. Never give up. Remember that the journey of the thousand miles begins with a single step. Continue to water that tree until it bears fruits. Then shake it until it releases its fruits into your hands. Have a blessed week!

****

Happiness does not depend in material possessions. "Just remember there is someone out there that is more happier than you with less than what you have".

****

Success is sweet. But the road to success is very bitter, bumpy and is paved with failures. There are Intersections, By-passes, Round-about and etc., but no U-Turn. The road less traveled is sometimes littered with barricades bumps and uncharted terrain, but it is on that street on which the address Success is! Failure is staged at various junctions on the high way not to deter you but to train your character into perseverance so that you might come out of it strong. "Failure is success if we can learn from it." In order to sprint to success you must be ready to admit that your problems are due to your own poor judgment. You do not blame them on your mother, the ecology, or the president. Success does not knock at the doors of irresponsible people. You must realize that you control your own destiny. "You are today a summation of your past choices. You will be tomorrow and into the future what you choose to do now. Lead Yourself First." - David Bernard-Stevens

****

Successful people are good planners. You don't need a fortune in order to invest; you need a plan. Good planning is sensitive to the surroundings. Before you journey, observe the wind carefully, detect its direction, and then follow it. You will get to your destination twice as fast with half the effort. Good planning allows you to tackle even risky projects with minimum problems. It is well known that "problem avoidance" is an important part of problem solving. Instead of solving the problem you go upstream and alter the system so that the problem does not occur in the first place.

****

Long term goals will keep me from the frustrations of short term failures and disappointments. But I am open to new ideas. "He that never changes his opinions, never corrects his mistakes, and will never be wiser on the morrow than he is today"

****

"Success is neither magical nor mysterious. Success is the natural consequence of consistently applying the basic fundamentals." Basic techniques of success never change. Therefore don't try to re-invent success. In order to succeed learn from people that succeeded and if necessary partner with them. But choose intelligently your partners. One person with passion is better than forty people who are merely interested.

****

Successful people are initiators and inventors. Do not seek to do what others are already doing. Successful people are normally innovators of ideas. They do things that no one else has ever done; by the time others learn what they are doing, they are already far away beyond reach. Therefore, in order to be an achiever, you have to think radically irrational; to look where everyone else has looked, but to see what no one else has seen.

****

Successful people are specialists. Arthur Miller said that, "You specialize in something until one day you find it is specializing in you." Specialization is the unrestricted access to knowledge, involving proper planning. "The kinds of nets we know how to weave determine the kinds of nets we cast. These nets, in turn, determine the kinds of fish we catch.." — Elliot Eisner, Cognition and Curriculum

****

Jesus paid the wages for our sins but not for His sins. He put others' needs above His needs. Successful people are measured by the things they do for others. There are at least four things you can do with your hands. You can wring them in despair; you can fold them in idleness; you can clench them in anger; or you can use them to help someone. Success is measured in what you do for others rather than for yourself. "A kind gesture can reach a wound that only compassion can heal." ~ Steve Maraboli

****

Begin this week with enthusiasm to succeed. Your living is determined not so much by what life brings to you as by the attitude you bring to life. Napoleon Hill said, "Remember, the thoughts that you think and the statements you make regarding yourself determine your mental attitude. If you have a worthwhile objective, find the one reason why you can achieve it rather than hundreds of reasons why you can't. Think positive about yourself even if it means cutting off negative people around you.

****

If you want to succeed in life be a man of value. When you make a one step of trust and integrity, God will accompany you to the next step... Life must be lived by convictions not consensus.

****

"If some people hustled as hard as they hated they'd be millionaires. Too much talking without action will leave you with no respect or influence. Seriously, successful people worry about their business, and nobody else's" ~ Zarinah Tlale

****

A business strategy lays out the plans for the direction of your company, including the goals you plan to achieve within the business. The strategy serves as your guide to making business decisions in order to develop and grow the company. Developing your business strategy takes more than simply writing down your wishes for the company. Thorough research and concrete, realistic goals make the business strategy more effective.

****

Success means finishing well. Every person has goals to archive. Reaching the same goals becomes the finishing line that must be crossed in lifetime in order to be successful. The road to success is compared to running a race. Runners just do it. They run for the finish line even if someone else has reached it first. "Running is a road to self-awareness and reliance ...you can push yourself to extremes and learn the harsh reality of your physical and mental limitations or coast quietly down a solitary path watching the earth spin beneath your feet." Physical fitness is crucial. It involves putting off unwanted loads of weights so that you can sprint fast to the finish line. Each of us has a sack packed with unwanted rocks on our shoulders. I mean baggage of past experiences like rejection, low esteem, abuse and etc. Your shoulders are too weak to sustain these baggage. Jesus came to unload you of these baggage so that you can run fast to the finish line. What is important is not what you do for yourself, but what you let God do on your behalf. You can be as good a runner as you let Him be who He is in your life!

****

Nobody was predestined to be a failure in life. You have the same potentiality to make it or not. You may have a fresh start any moment you choose. For this thing that we call 'failure,' it is not the falling down, but the staying down. "If you can't fly, then run, if you can't run, then walk, if you can't walk, then crawl, but you have to keep moving forward" ~ Martin Luther Jr.

****

In our Christian walk there are disruptive moments. Such are bumps in the road which can be avoided but not all times do we succeed in avoiding them because they are there for a reason. As long as you are moving chances are you will stumble on something, perhaps when you are least expecting it. Just keep on going without fear of stumbling. I have never heard of anyone stumbling on something when sitting down!

****

Success is a journey and not a destination. The mistake most people make is aligning money with success. Money is only a medium of exchange and can never be measured side-by-side with success. Our greatest lack is not money for undertaking, but ideas; if ideas are good, cash will naturally flow to where it is needed. Money is like flowing water that always finds its way to flow.

****

Make an effort to constantly think positive, no matter what the situation is. High achievers will gain the most out of situations where the probability of success is relatively low and that success becomes a challenge. However a low achiever may see losing in such a scenario as one that promotes a feeling of personal shame from a loss. "The truth of the matter is that you always know the right thing to do. The hard part is doing it" ~ Norman Schwarzkopf

****

Don't confuse your path with your destination, just because it's stormy now, doesn't mean you aren't headed for sunshine. The fact is that there are things in life that aren't meant to stay. God can use your past and current miseries as tomorrow's testimony. That is when your past pain becomes your preview of life's lesson. "The only mistake in life is the lesson not learned." — Albert Einstein

****

Success is not measured in terms of material gains alone. Material riches can be either a blessing or a curse depending on your priorities. The Bible says that "But first, be concerned about his kingdom and what has his approval. Then all these things will be provided for you" (Matthew 6:33). What we see as winning in the physical realm isn't always victory in the spiritual realm, and what we consider to be losing isn't always defeat. Jesus made all believers winners. The ground beneath the cross is leveled. There is no superior and inferior because all of us stand evenly before God. The Bible says that, "All praise to God, the Father of our Lord Jesus Christ, who has blessed us with every spiritual blessing in the heavenly realms because we are united with Christ" (Ephesians 1:3). Success is manifesting what God has already treasured in you and has equipped you to do through Christ.

****

People are more likely to cry out to God when they are in need than when they have plenty. Too often, the wealthy become complacent and self-satisfied and ascribe their riches to their own efforts instead of acknowledging that every good gift comes from God. The easier our lives become, the more enjoyment we derive from our wealth, the greater the temptation to store up treasures on earth, instead of in heaven. Whenever we focus on earthly things like material wealth and possessions, we fail to give God the glory and worship He deserves. We are called to choose to serve God rather than the riches of the world (Proverbs 23:4).

****

Good things come to people who wait, but better things come to those who go out and get them...while the best are reserved for those who while striving and seeking, understand the fickleness of their own strength and rely on the awesomeness of their Creator's might.

****

Isaiah 3:10 - Tell the righteous that it shall be well with them in spite of the circumstances. God will never forsake the righteous. But often we tend to focus on the circumstances as opposed to the promises of God. Before long we complicate ourselves into paralysis. Instead of sticking to what we are given to know in the Scriptures, we resort to searching for the forbidden knowledge about God. But we simply cannot know all that God is doing "under the radar." The Bible says that, "The secret things belong unto the LORD our God: but those things which are revealed belong unto us and to our children for ever, that we may do all the words of this law" (Deut. 29:29). God will be trusted for who He is, not what He can prove. The culprits end up frustrated because they can't know everything about God they don't do anything.

****

"Your gift can take you where your character cannot sustain you. When your gift out- weighs your character it becomes a curse" ~ Lomont Coakley

****

"There are at least four things you can do with your hands. You can wring them in despair; you can fold them in idleness; you can clench them in anger; or you can use them to help someone." Begin this week with a kingdom mentality yearning to uplift somebody. When we seek to discover the best in others, we somehow bring out the best in ourselves. "Cast thy bread upon the waters; for thou shalt find it after many days." (Ecclesiastes 11:1). Throwing your bread in water is not exceptional but it requires a miracle to find it after many days. The beauty of serving God is that whatever we do to the needy is treasured in eternity. We are stewards called to invest into others the things we have including gifts. Do not look mournfully into what you gave away, for it will come back to you a hundred folds. Invest wisely so that you can go forth to meet the shadowy future with hope.

****

A "Mistake" is when something is done once, and learned upon... If repeated consistently, it's a "Habit"; a "Failure" is nothing more than a habitual mistake!!

****

We have each heard some flash-in-the-pan success stories; tales of people and businesses that skyrocket to fame and fortune, only to plummet back into the pit of nothingness just as quickly as they had emerged from it. Never let other people's failures be a hindrance to you; better try and fail than not trying at all. Risk is a part of any great adventure, discovery, and successful venture. If it is God's will, don't be afraid of taking risk.

****

Success never rests. To achieve the impossible, one must think the absurd; at times you need to embrace what others call madness and see life as it is and not as it should be.

****

The roads we take are more important than the goals we announce. Decisions determine destiny ~ Frederick Speakman

****

"Time is a great teacher, but unfortunately it kills all its pupils." Procrastination is a thief of time. Tomorrow is an old deceiver; his cheat does not grow stale... "I've never met a poor man who puts value on his time. I've never met a rich man who did not" ~ Dr. Mike Murdock

****

Dream big time and pursue your dreams with passion. A dream, backed by an unrelenting will to attain it, is truly a reality with an imminent arrival.

****

"Your vision will become clear only when you look into your heart. Who looks outside, dreams. Who looks inside, awakens." ~ Carl Gustav Jung

****

The power of priotizing: "I will be somewhere and not everywhere; I will do something and not everything. That is what I live for and I am enjoying it."

****

It is more blessed to give than to receive. Generosity does not depend on how much a person has. For the sake of consistency and conceptual clarity, the concept "selflessness" has nothing to do with being either rich or poor. Today, posses your possessions by blessing somebody!

****

Every relationship is one of give and take. Giving engenders receiving, and receiving engenders giving. What goes up must come down; what goes out must come back. In reality, receiving is the same thing as giving, because giving and receiving are different aspects of the flow of energy in the universe. And if you stop the flow of either, you interfere with nature's intelligence

****

You cannot win a game without practicing. Practice makes perfect. After a long time of practicing, your work becomes natural, skillful, swift, and steady. "There is no exercise better for the heart than reaching down and lifting people up." The muscles of the receiving hand are built up when you exercise them by giving. You can give without loving but you cannot love without giving. Generosity is giving more than you can afford; it is a decision to be a blessing to others instead of blessing yourself.

****

"Hit the iron while still hot." Procrastination is the lead cause of regrets. Do what you ought to do whenever opportunity avails, this applies to relationships, work, studies, name it...

****

Opportunity often comes disguised in the form of misfortune, or temporary defeat. "Opportunity is missed by most people because it is dressed in overalls and looks like work..." An enterprising person is one who sees opportunity in all areas of life.

****

"It is the characteristic of the magnanimous man to ask no favor but to be ready to do kindness to others" ~ Aristotle

****

"Little things are indeed little; they can never be recognized among the great ones. But to be faithful and be trusted in those little things is a great thing."

****

"Generosity is giving more than you can, and pride is taking less than you need" ~ Khalil Gibran

****

The happiest people don't have the best of everything; they make the best of everything. A person wants three things to be happy in this world: someone to love, something to do, and something to hope for. But what we want is not truly what we need. You will never be happy if you continue to search for happiness outside what happiness consists of. True happiness is contained in the person of Jesus Christ; it is not discovered but it is revealed and received. Christians are called to rejoice regardless of the situation because God predetermined the end to work in their favor. "And we know that in all things God works for the good of those who love him, who have been called according to his purpose" (Romans 8:28).

****

Statistics show that the people who have the most live the longest. No man can sincerely try to help another without helping himself first. Given the fact, sharing with the needy is a virtue. Remember that you only keep what you give away. You can give without loving, but you can't love without giving. There are three kinds of givers -- the flint, the sponge and the honeycomb. To get anything out of a flint you must hammer it. And then you get only chips and sparks. To get water out of a sponge you must squeeze it, and the more you use pressure, the more you will get. But the honeycomb just overflows with its own sweetness. Which kind of giver are you? "We make a living by what we get but we make life by what we give" ~ Winston Churchill

****

Everyone needs somebody in order to sail in the turbulent waters of life. If I have seen farther than others, it is because I was standing on the shoulder of giants.

****

Over- reliance on others is risky. The danger of depending on someone is the possibility of not being there when you really need them. Don't depend on anyone in this world, even your own shadow leaves you when you are in the darkness

****

"In times of prosperity we are apt to forget God; we imagine it does not matter whether we recognize Him or not. As long as we are comfortably clothed and fed and looked after, our civilization becomes an elaborate means of ignoring God" ~ Oswald Chambers

****

The tormenting problem you have demands a solution. Without a problem there can be no solution. Likewise, without a defect there can be no anticipation for a miracle. The need in your life necessitates the provision. Don't focus on the demand of the problem but focus on the possibilities available to overcome. See the problem as a challenge to triumph. Start by getting the right diagnoses in order to avoid putting bandages on headaches. If you can, position yourself in the closest range in order to solve your problem instead of solving it from a long distance.

****

Don't underestimate the power of thoughts and words. What you tell yourself every morning will set your mind and life on that path. Talk success, victory, happiness and blessings over your destiny. ~ Nina Bolivares

****

Be encouraged to begin this season with enthusiasm. Courage is not the absence of fear, but rather the judgment that something else is more important than fear.... Courage is what it takes to stand up for your rights; to stand up and speak; courage is also what it takes to sit down and listen. "Courage is like love, it must have hope for nourishment." ~ Napoleon Bonaparte.

****

If it is not raining yet, it's because your cloud is not yet full. Keep filling it. You may be looking for a shower to water your plants but God may be thinking of a flood to give you a new start. At the end it will be just you and God.

****

God's promises are Yes and Amen! We can't give up on the things that we know belong to us, no matter how tough the battle is. Sometimes, you have to get knocked down lower than you have ever been in order to stand up taller than you have ever been. We have assurance, as children of God, that we are destined to win. "Those who leave everything in God's hand will see God's hand in everything".

****

"Ability is what you're capable of doing. Motivation determines what you do. Attitude determines how well you do it." ~ Lou Holtz.

****

"I never thought of losing, but now that it has happened, the only thing is to do it right. That's my obligation to all the people who believe in me. We all have to take defeats in life." ~ Muhammad Ali

****

"Be careful who you share your weaknesses with. Some people can't wait for the opportunity to use them against you."

****

"You have to learn the rules of the game. And then you have to play better than anyone else."

****

Do not go where the path may lead, go instead where there is no path and leave a trail ~ Ralph Wald Emerson

****

If you want to excel do something that somebody has never done before. You shall be distinguished for your creativity and novelty. "Wealth does not know its owner, it only knows stake holders."

****

Everything that God made valuable in the world is covered and hard to get to. Where do you find gold and diamonds? Deep down in the ground, covered and protected with layers and layers of rock. You've got to work hard to get to them. Where do you find pearls? Deep down at the bottom of the ocean, covered up and protected in a beautiful shell ~ Mohammad Ali

****

"Your living is determined not so much by what life brings to you as by the attitude you bring to life; not so much by what happens to you as by the way your mind looks at what happens." ~ Kahlil Gibran

****

"The odds will always favor the man with a plan." But it is the favor of God that will take you where nothing else can. Favor is not achieved, it is a divine flavor bestowed on you. "One day of favor is worth of thousand years of labor" ~ Dr Mike Murdock

****

"It is the characteristic of the magnanimous man to ask no favor but to be ready to do kindness to others" ~ Aristotle

****

"As a single footstep will not make a path on the earth, so a single thought will not make a pathway in the mind. To make a deep physical path, we walk again and again. To make a deep mental path, we must think over and over the kind of thoughts we wish to dominate our lives" ~ Henry David Thoreau

****

A beautiful day begins with a positive mindset. Take a moment to think about how privileged you are to be alive, the moment you start acting like life is blessing, I assure you it will start to feel like one. It comes in

53

full circle, feeling blessed, feeling grateful and wanting to do more and feeling happier. You begin to see and feel how precious life is and feel know that time spent living is time worth appreciating.

****

You are the apple of God's eye; the ultimate design of His purpose and His workmanship. Do not look at how big your problem is, but at how Big your God is. No matter how tight your situation is, no matter how scorching your fire might be, just do one thing - Praise God. Remember that the God of the mountain is still the God of the valley. When things go wrong He will make them right. "Life is 10% what happens to you and 90% how you react to it." ~ Charles Swindoll

****

"Anything under God's control is never out of control". When you have nothing left but God, you have more than enough. You can succeed where you thought it is not possible with Him. "In the kingdom of the world, money is the principle but in the kingdom of God, Christ is the principle".

****

The secret of success is working hard plus contentment. Be ready to seize the opportunity when it comes. Contentment is the key to ultimate happiness and peace. When you get little, you want more. When you get more, you desire even more. But when you lose everything, you realize little was enough...always remember, greed will bring you nowhere in life.

****

Never underestimate the distance that one simple act of kindness can carry you.

****

Life is a basket of choices. Choose to be a blessing in order to be blessed. Make a concerted effort to be kind, generous and considerate.

****

No pain no gain. There is an ancient tribal proverb I once heard in India. It says that before we can see properly we must first shed our tears to clear the way.
— Libba Bray

****

Sometimes the grass is greener on the other side because you aren't watering your side enough.

****

"If money and material things become the centre of our lives, they seize us and make us slaves" ~ Pope Francis

****

There is nothing as powerful as an idea whose time has come.

****

Noblesse Oblige said that, "Hungry people follow the scent of a good meal while those who do not worry about their next meal can afford to question the status quo."

****

"Do not spoil what you have by desiring what you have not; remember that what you now have was once among the things only hoped for."

****

How much you save is as important as how much you labor. China's richest man with a worth of US $21.8 billion, Zong Qinghou, eats the same meals as his workers and lives on only $20 a day!

****

"Don't be afraid if things seem difficult in the beginning. That's only the initial impression. The important thing is not to retreat; you have to master yourself." ~ Olga Korbutu

****

"If someone feels that they had never made a mistake in their life, then it means they had never tried a new thing in their life". A life spent making mistakes is not only more honorable, but more useful than a life spent doing nothing. ~ George Bernard Shaw

****

If you want to excel do something that somebody has never done before. You shall be distinguished for your creativity and novelty. "Wealth does not know its owner, it only knows stake holders."

****

Successful people exploit good management. Failing organizations are usually over-managed and under-led. Management stands for orderliness as opposed to confusion. There is order in the universe, because God is orderly. The beauty of God's orderliness is reflected in His creation, in particular in the Physical laws governing the universe and the Moral laws governing the conducts of the people. When Jesus is central to your life, God puts everything in its right order in accordance to the divine plan. Orderliness is having a sense of where things belong and how they relate to each other, and keeping them organized accordingly.

****

Successful people exploit good management. Failing organizations are usually over-managed and under-led. When things are bad, it's the best time to reinvent yourself. You don't reinvent yourself; you get better with what you do. There are two ways of being creative. One can sing and dance. Or one can create an environment in which singers and dancers flourish. "People who cannot invent and reinvent themselves must be content with borrowed postures, secondhand ideas, fitting in instead of standing out" ~ Warren G. Bennis

****

Success stalks those who strictly exercise direct supervision (Micromanagement). The road to success is compared to driving on our streets whereby taking precaution is inevitable. Accidents are caused by your mistakes and other drivers' recklessness. It is advisable when you are driving not only to watch out for your driving but also for others' driving in order to prevent other people's mistakes to be your problem. Basically you have to keep your eyes open for everything and never expect anyone to do what they're supposed to do. Regarding any project, if you keep a close eye on your employees and how they work, they are more likely to perform tasks precisely the way you want. Micromanaging is a profoundly hands-on leadership style that gives you direct control over tasks that employees might do on their own.

****

Nobody is always an effective communicator. You may be more assertive with strangers, or casual acquaintances, but find it harder to do so with loved ones and co-workers. There are times when it is good to be aggressive in your communication. For example, if your life or property is in danger, it might not be the best time to practice assertive communication.

****

Aggressive Communication Style: People will never push me around. I always get my way even if I have to hurt or offend people to get it. I use my position, power, and harsh or manipulative words. I don't care if I offend people. I speak in a loud voice. I can be abusive, and I really like to get even with people.

****

Passive Aggressive Communication Style: I protect myself by avoiding problems and try not to take any risks. I'm sly, sarcastic, and subtly insulting. I deliberately ruin other people's plans or projects. I talk about other people in negative ways. I dress however I want to regardless of the situation. I often fail at school or work. I feel like a victim and never like to take responsibility. I feel jealous and resentful of others achievements.

****

Assertive Communication Style: I often get what I want without offending other people or making them angry. I am clear and direct when I communicate, and I'm able to express my thoughts, feelings, and wants directly. I am honest, and show my confidence without being aggressive about it.

****

Identify Your Problems Solving Style: You may have no problem with general communication, but tend to be passive or aggressive when it comes to solving problems. Use the examples above to identify what communication style do you use while problem solving.

****

Learn Your Legitimate Rights: You learn a set of rules or beliefs early in your life that affect your behavior. These are a set of rules about "good" and "bad" ways to act, as they were taught to you by your parents and other role models. These beliefs may have helped you get along with the people you grew up with, they are not set in stone, and you can decide to behave differently now. The Bible has the ultimate standard by which to adjust values.

****

"The art of listening is an entrepreneur's bridge to success. Listen. Adapt. Launch. Deliver. Entrepreneurship is about changing lives" ~ David Opito

****

Are there any quick ways to succeed in business without spending a huge amount of money on marketing?

Answer: Unfortunately, there is no shortcut or magic recipe to success - or if there is, I haven't found it yet. Creating a successful and profitable business takes time, since you build your reputation as customers learn to trust and rely on you, one by one.

Also, there's no guarantee that spending a huge amount of money on marketing will slingshot your business forward. If you spend your time looking for shortcuts, you will find one - right out of business. While there are no set rules for succeeding in business, over my 40 years as an entrepreneur, I have embraced some rough guidelines that can be very helpful:

Create a useful product or service. It's important to create something of use that is going to benefit society as a whole. If you do something you truly care about, you will be in a much better position to find customers, connect with them, and keep them coming back.

Simplify your message. Customers don't just shop for a brand and its products, but also identify with its core values. Ask yourself, why did I start my business? Be honest - this will help you establish an authentic value and voice. Then distill your message into something simple.

Marketing is a powerful tool, but it doesn't have to be expensive. According to Sir Freddie Laker, a man who had started a company to challenge British Airways on their home turf, acknowledging that you can't match the more established airlines in terms of marketing budget is important. "Drive the publicity yourself: Use yourself. Make a fool of yourself. Otherwise you won't survive." Take his advice and begin thinking up fun ways to stand out from the crowd and draw the media's attention to your company. The outcome is promising - from breaking world records to pulling pranks. It is not necessary to have the same preferences. Find your tone, know your brand, do things your own way, and create waves. The free advertising will follow. Embrace social media - Tools like Twitter and Facebook are wonderful ways to get your message out to a wide audience. Social media is not only more cost-efficient than advertising, but it also offers great opportunities for innovative engagement with your customers. Use it to your advantage.

Keep on enjoying what you do. If you genuinely love and believe in what you do, others will take notice and share your enthusiasm. Switch from operations to management, move on, expand into new territories, anything that interests you. To find success, you need to be fully committed or your work will show it.

February for Spiritual Growth

God is holy and He calls His children to be sanctified by His Word and Spirit. According to Webster's 1828 Dictionary, holiness means, "The state of being holy; purity or integrity of moral character; freedom from sin; sanctity." Furthermore, Webster states, "Applied to human beings, holiness is purity of heart or dispositions; sanctified affections; piety; moral goodness, but not perfect." The above definitions are in complete agreement with the use of the word holy or holiness throughout both the Old and New Testaments.

In the Old Testament the Hebrew word most commonly translated as holiness or holy is *qodesh*, which means apartness, holiness, sacredness, or separateness. *Qodesh* comes from the root word *qadash*, which means to consecrate, sanctify, prepare, dedicate, be hallowed, be holy, be sanctified, or be separate. Other English translations of *qadash* include sanctify, hallow, dedicate, and consecrate. Some derivative of these two Hebrew words is used in the Old Testament some 640 times.

In the New Testament the Greek word most frequently translated as holiness or holy is *hagios,* which means most holy thing or a saint. This word is translated as holy 161 times and as saints 61 times. The root word from which *hagios* is derived and where it gets its meaning is *hagnos*, which is defined as pure from every fault, immaculate. Thus, *hagnos* is translated as pure, chaste, or clear throughout the New Testament. It is interesting to note that in the Septuagint the Greek word *hagios* stands for the Hebrew word *qodosh*. Other translations of this Greek word group include sanctification, godliness, sanctuary, and holy place (*Part of the above information is taken from the New Strong's Exhaustive Concordance, the Webster's New Practical dictionary and encyclopedia).*

To fully comprehend and understand what holiness means, it is imperative to know what the Bible teaches regarding the holiness of

God, because it is His standard of holiness by which all men shall be judged. God's holiness is proven by His hatred for sin and His delight in righteousness. He separates a sinner from Himself unless that sinner accepts His provision for an infinite sacrifice to be saved. He rewards the wages of sin with death. At the cross Jesus became a substitute Lamb that died for all sinners that put their faith in Him.

God imputes to us His own holiness through Jesus Christ. One must be deemed holy as God in order to enter into the presence of God. This kind of holiness cannot be merited by any human being; it is imputed to us when we invest our faith in Christ. Without His holiness a person is unholy and they are destined to an eternity in the lake of fire. The Bible says that, "The wrath of God is revealed from heaven against all ungodliness and unrighteousness of men" (Romans 1:18). There is going to be retribution of every sin that is not confessed to Christ. The future retribution is one aspect of the natural consequence of sin, yet it is also in another aspect the positive infliction of divine wrath. It is shown to be the natural outcome of sin in such passages as "Whatsoever a man soweth, that shall he also reap" (Galatians 6:7); "He that soweth unto his own flesh shall of the flesh reap corruption" (Galatians 6:8). It is not without suggestiveness that the Hebrew word `awon means both iniquity and punishment, and when Cain said "My punishment is greater than I can bear" (Genesis 4:13), he really said "My iniquity is greater than I can bear"; his iniquity became his punishment. A due consideration of this thought goes a long way toward meeting many of the objections brought against the doctrine of future punishment. The fact that remains true and that must be emphasized is that there is an actual infliction of divine wrath. All the great statements about the divine judgment imply this, and while it is wrong not to take account of the natural working out of sin in its terrible consequences, it is equally wrong, perhaps more so, to refuse to recognize this positive divine infliction of punishment.

Jesus paid the ultimate price for the sins of the world. That does not mean that all men will repent of their sins and be reconciled to God, but that God has provided the means for it to happen. Those who have been declared to be holy must prove that they are holy by living as Jesus lived. The holiness of God becomes the standard for the believer's life and conduct. 1 Peter 1:15, 16 says, "But as he which hath called you is holy, so be ye holy in all manner of conversation; Because it is written, Be ye holy; for I am holy." Elsewhere, Paul writes, "Having therefore these promises, dearly beloved, let us cleanse ourselves from all filthiness of the flesh and spirit, perfecting holiness in the fear of God" (2 Corinthians 7:1). It is this perfecting of holiness that must be dealt with after salvation.

We live the life of Christ by faith. Each person is given a measure of faith. The saving faith is supernaturally activated when the gospel is preached. God reveals Himself through Jesus Christ to save a sinner. Faith is the positive response to the revelation. We should not confuse belief with faith. Belief is purely natural mind oriented; it is our natural capability to figure out something and believe it. Belief is subject to error, serious error. Just like any scientist. But real faith is a gift from God. It is the supernatural enlightenment of the soul. Faith comes (grows) in the heart as the soul grows in response to our spiritual yearnings. Faith is not subjected to error. Jesus recommended the little faith that can grow (Matthew 17:20).

Spiritual growth is detailed in 2 Peter 1:3-8, "His divine power has given us everything we need for life and godliness through our knowledge of him who called us by his own glory and goodness. Through these he has given us his very great and precious promises, so that through them you may participate in the divine nature and escape the corruption in the world caused by evil desires. For this very reason, make every effort to add to your faith goodness; and to goodness, knowledge; and to knowledge, self-control; and to self-control, perseverance; and to perseverance, godliness; and to godliness, brotherly kindness; and to brotherly kindness, love. For if you possess these qualities in increasing measure, they will keep you from being ineffective and unproductive in your knowledge of our Lord Jesus Christ."

So, spiritual growth includes: (1) increasing in your knowledge and understanding of God's Word, (2) decreasing in your frequency and severity of sin, (3) increasing in your practice of Christ-like qualities, and (4) increasing in your faith and trust in God. Perhaps the best summary of spiritual growth is becoming more like Jesus Christ. In 1 Corinthians 11:1, Paul says, "Follow my example, as I follow the example of Christ." Jesus Christ is the ultimate example of what it truly means to be spiritual.

I am going to outline some tips toward spiritual growth: Read your Bible daily. Find a Bible reading plan that's right for you. A plan will keep you from missing anything God has written in His Word. Also, if you follow the plan, you'll be on your way to reading through the Bible once every year! The easiest way to truly "grow up" in the faith is to make Bible reading a priority. God speaks to us in the Scriptures. Rightly divide the Scriptures and apply the truth to your life in order to benefit from the written Word.

Meet together with other believers regularly. The reason we attend church or gather with other believers regularly (Hebrews 10:25) is for teaching, fellowship, worship, communion, prayer and to build one another up in the faith (Acts 2:42-47). Participating in the body of Christ is fundamental to spiritual growth. If you're having trouble finding a church, check out these resources on how to find a church that's right for you. I mean the church that teaches the full gospel.

Pray daily. Prayer is simply talking to God. You don't have to use big fancy words. There are no right and wrong words. Just be yourself. Give thanks to the Lord daily for your salvation. Pray for others in need. Pray for direction. Pray for the Lord to fill you daily with His Holy Spirit. There is no limit to prayer. Praying includes praising and worshiping. We praise God because He is able to do exceedingly great things than we can do for ourselves. We worship Him because of who He is.

We are in a spiritual warfare. Throughout World War I, music was a prominent feature on the home fronts and the battlefields. Most homes had a piano, and at least one member of each family knew how to play it, providing a common form of entertainment and socialization. Popular music, therefore, saturated the citizenry and reached into all of its corners, forming a great medium for conveying messages. Recognizing this capability, governments often used it as an effective means for inspiring fervor, pride, patriotism, and action in the citizens in order to gain manpower, homeland support, and funds. Dramatic graphics and additional messages printed on sheet music provided extra inspiration to the messages expressed by the lyrics and melodies, markedly increasing their capabilities as propaganda vehicles. Basically, music during World War I was often used to inspire passion and voluntary compliance in the listeners and, occasionally, shame in those who didn't support the war. God anoints us to sing praising, worshiping and gospel songs in our warfare. The gospel songs draw the lost world towards God and strengthen us (who are already born again). The praising and worshiping songs usher us into the presence of God. There is that joy of being in His presence. True pleasure comes from knowing God. Our worshiping is not just a song of the mouth but it is a song of the transformed heart.

The Christian life is not always an easy road. In fact Jesus called it a narrow way that is not comfortable to the natural man. We need each other to walk this tight way. The Bible calls upon believers to encourage others (our brothers and sisters in Christ) daily so that no one turns away from the living God. Backsliding is a process that grows gradually till you are completely off-track. Sometimes we start getting off track unaware. If you cease to do what God called you to do or to seek God by praying and reading the Bible, you are backsliding or drifting away from the Lord.

In case of sin we need to return to God rather than running away from Him. God loves us unconditionally, therefore we should never let our desire to be in His presence diminish. Come to God daily for forgiveness and cleansing. If we confess our sins, he is faithful and just and will forgive us our sins and purify us from all unrighteousness (1 John 1:9).

Sanctification is a process. Jesus washing of the feet of His disciples was symbolic of His sanctifying work (John 13:1-17). "He came to Simon Peter, who said to him, "Lord, are you going to wash my feet?" Jesus replied, "You do not realize now what I am doing, but later you will understand." "No," said Peter, "you shall never wash my feet." Jesus answered, "Unless I wash you, you have no part with me." We need to be washed once to be justified and occasionally because we get dirty by walking in the corrupt world. Justification is the grace extended to all believers who accept the atoning work of the blood of Jesus. Sanctification is the cleansing of our minds to get rid of sin. Glorification is the putting on the incorruptible bodies that need not to be sanctified. Growing in the Spirit is experiencing the sanctifying power of the Holy Spirit momentarily. It is growing in His grace.

During His earthly ministry, Jesus washed the feet of His disciples and served them at the Last Supper. But that was then and this is now! By then His glory was veiled in human flesh. The scripture below insinuates that He will wait on His faithful servants at table when He is in His utmost glory: "Blessed are those servants, whom the lord will find watching when he comes. Most assuredly I tell you, that he will gird himself, and make them recline, and will come and serve them" (Luke 12:37). The degree of the glory makes it fascinating; it makes me addicted to serving. And the Bible says "The Glory of your latter days shall be greater than the Glory of your former". Let your past be history and strive towards the prize that is ahead!

Spiritual maturity is measured not just in the manifestations of the gifts of the Holy Spirit but in a believer's capability to love (Agape love). The Bible says that, "If I speak with the tongues of men and of angels, but do not have love, I have become a noisy gong or a clanging cymbal. If I have the gift of prophecy, and know all mysteries and all knowledge; and if I have all faith, so as to remove mountains, but do not have love, I am nothing" (1 Corinthians 13:1-2). Also, "Beloved, let us love one another, for love is from God; and everyone who loves is born of God and knows God. The one who does not love does not know God, for God is love" (1 John 4:8). Agape love is expressed emotionally but it is not emotional. Feelings are like chemicals; the more you analyze them the worse they smell. Agape love never loses value; it is sacrificial, unconditional and spiritual. It involves commitment to love in spite of the response of the person you love.

Spiritual growth is manifested in our willingness to serve. God calls us and anoints us to serve. I am going to use the story of Elijah and Elisha as example: At the end of Elijah's lifework, a spiritual revival, however small it seemed, had begun. As Elijah was nearing the end of his ministry, God directed him to anoint a younger man named Elisha to take his place. Elisha, son of Shaphat, was from Abel Meholah, of the Jordan Valley (1 Kings 19:16). Elisha was an Old Testament prophet who lived around 800 B.C., a time when God involved Himself in a very direct way with the people and the leadership of ancient Israel.

Elisha began his ministry as Elijah's student and personal attendant. The young man would first prove himself faithful in small things, such as the humble duty of pouring water on the hands of Elijah (2 Kings 3:11). Elisha's training under Elijah would gradually prepare him for a work that he would one day take up alone. Around this period, God sent at least 30 prophets, between the northern kingdom of Israel and the southern kingdom of Judah, in an effort to turn their citizens away from idolatry and other sins. The Bible mentions both Elijah and Elisha visiting centers of religious learning in Israel that were attended by groups of men called "the sons of the prophets" (for example, see 1 Kings 20:35; 2 Kings 2:3, 5, 7, 15).

On the day that the prophet Elijah understood his ministry was coming to a close and that Elisha would take his place, Elijah said to Elisha, "'Ask! What may I do for you, before I am taken away from you?' Elisha said, 'Please let a double portion of your spirit be upon me'" (2 Kings 2:9). "The 'double portion' is that which denotes the proportion of a father's property which was the right of an eldest son (Deuteronomy 21:17). Elisha therefore asked for twice as much of Elijah's spirit as should be inherited by any other of the 'sons of the prophets.' He wished to be acknowledged as Elijah's 'firstborn spiritual son'" (Albert Barnes' Notes on the Bible, 2 Kings 2:9). Elisha didn't ask for worldly honor or for a high place among men. What he really desired was a large measure of the Holy Spirit that God had so freely placed upon the prophet Elijah. He knew that He needed God's Holy Spirit to equip him for the responsibilities that lay ahead. Elijah then answered, "You have asked a hard thing. Nevertheless, if you see me when I am taken from you, it shall be so for you; but if not, it shall not be so" (2 Kings 2:10). The Hebrew words in this verse mean that if Elisha would be given the privilege of seeing the miraculous way God would take Elijah away, then it would be a sign that his request would be granted.

Elisha performed more miracles than any other Old Testament prophet. Elisha's prophetic ministry included works of healing and restoration. The biblical record also shows Elisha bringing joy to people through miracles from God. His gentle spirit enabled him to have a positive influence on the lives of many in Israel and is revealed in several illustrations in 2 Kings 4-6. Elijah's ministry began by shutting up the heavens for three and a half years, whereas Elisha's ministry began by healing a spring of water near Jericho (2 Kings 2:19-22).

Elisha's second recorded miracle granted an impoverished family of faith a financial blessing. A student of one of the religious training centers died and his wife became a widow. She was very poor and owned just one marketable item of value, a jar of olive oil. She had two sons to care for, and she asked Elisha to help her as she feared her sons would be taken away to pay a debt. Elisha instructed her to go to all her neighbors and borrow as many empty jars as she could. A miracle was going to occur that would allow her to fill every empty jar to the top by pouring from her one jar of olive oil. The one jar of oil was multiplied miraculously, and she was able to sell enough of the valuable oil to pay off her debt and live off the remainder (2 Kings 4:1-7). God's miraculous provision was unlimited as long as there were empty jars to be filled. Olive oil is symbolic of the anointing power of the Holy Spirit. God's refilling bottle is without limit and without bottom; it is ever flowing looking for empty vessels to fill. But our bottles are often limited with bottoms such that we thwart the provision of the grace of God!

Scrolling through my sermons on spiritual growth:

The term religiosity is in reference to an attitude of doing things in a ritualistic manner without the sincerity of a clean and transformed heart. Christianity is not a religion but faith in God's provision for the salvation of man. We are all born with the same malady. Love for God (affection for Christ) is not natural to us but it is born into us. We are born loving the corrupt world and the corrupt 'self' more than the creator. Our love is naturally reserved for other gods other than Jehovah. The love of one true God is lacking in every person until they are regenerated. God turns the hearts of stone into hearts of flesh. The prophetic words say that, "I will give you a new heart and put a new spirit in you; I will remove from you your heart of stone and give you a heart of flesh" (Ezekiel 36:26). It means acquiring a new heart that pulsates with life and affection for God. This is what it means to be "Born again". It is the change of heart by transformation (Spirit) and conversion involving the Christ-like characters (holiness). The old corrupt nature can neither be improved on nor recycled but must die in order to allow space for the new nature that is born into us and that is only acceptable to God.

Man is a triune being because he is created in the image of God. "God said, Let us make man in Our image" (Genesis 1:26). We know that God is a Trinity. The Holy Trinity is clearly set forth in the Apostle Paul's benediction that closed his Second Corinthian Epistle: "The grace of the Lord Jesus Christ, and the love of God, and the communion of the Holy Ghost, be with you all. Amen" (2 Corinthians 13:14). Our Lord Himself said, in what we call "The Great Commission": "Go ye therefore, and teach all nations, baptizing them in the name of the Father, and of the Son, and of the Holy Ghost" (Matthew 28:19). Created in the image of God, man is likewise a trinity. He has a spiritual nature that is separate and distinct from the body in which it dwells. The threefold nature of man might be illustrated in several ways.

Dr. Clarence Larkin uses three circles. The outer circle stands for the body of man, the middle circle for the soul, and the inner for the spirit (Rightly Dividing The Word, page 86). At this point it will be well to quote a portion from Dr. Larkin's book: In the outer circle the 'Body' is shown as touching the Material world through the five senses of 'Sight,' 'Smell,' 'Hearing,' 'Taste' and 'Touch.' The Gates to the 'Soul' are 'Imagination,' 'Conscience,' 'Memory,' 'Reason' and the 'Affections.' The "Spirit" receives impressions of outward and material things through the soul. The spiritual faculties of the 'Spirit' are 'Faith,' 'Hope,' 'Reverence,' 'Prayer' and 'Worship.'

****

Repentance is the changing of our mindset and attitude, and adopting the mindset and attitude of God. Basically, repentance is turning from "self" to Christ. Faith is activated upon repentance. Yet it is not the strength of your faith that saves you but it is the strong Savior that saves you. Faith connects us to the Savior. Faith is an endless journey traveled in this world; after we are saved, we are required to continue walking in faith. That is when the character of our Lord and Savior becomes the character of our walk.

****

John 3:7 - "The wind blows where it wishes, and you hear its sound, but you do not know where it comes from or where it goes. So it is with everyone who is born of the Spirit." To be born again is to be born from above or heaven. It is to be born of the Father in His very nature (spirit). Being "born again" is a matter so mysterious that human words cannot describe it. Nevertheless, it is a change that is known and felt--known by works of holiness and felt by a gracious experience. This great work is supernatural. It is not an operation that a man performs for himself because a natural man cannot work against his very nature. The new nature comes with new desires that are in contradiction to the old. A new principle is infused that works in the heart, renews the soul, and affects his whole life. God repeatedly gives us the assurance of our salvation in His word the Bible. However, the Bible instructs us to have assurance of our salvation (2 Peter 1:10).

****

A tree is known and recognized by its fruit. The maturity of a tree is determined by its capability to produce the fruits. Likewise, spiritual maturity depends on a believer's ability to manifest the fruit of the Spirit. The deeper you are rooted in the Word the more you manifest the fruit of the Spirit.

****

The idiom "virtue is its own reward" means that a good deed is its own reward. The dictionary defines virtue as the conformity to the standard of right: morality. Moral excellency; beneficial quality, strength and courage and the capacity to act: potency. Spiritually, virtue is to excel in godliness. The Christian virtues of faith, hope, love, wisdom, temperance, joy, courage, faithfulness, peace, humility, gentleness, and whatever other virtue there is, are learned in relationships with God (and the circumstances He brings into our lives) and others. It is the obligation of a believer to perpetually manifest virtue. Virtue is the application of being good from both the conscious will to do what is right from God's revealed Word and from personal responsibility. We acquire Virtue by our faith but manifest virtue by our obedience to Christ and by being persistent in Him. A virtuous person must actively get involved in the following activities: Listening to God (reading Bible);

talking to God (praying); talking to others about God (preaching the gospel).

****

The Bible calls us to have assurance of our salvation: "And beside this, giving all diligence, add to your faith virtue; and to virtue knowledge; and in your knowledge, self-control, and in your self-control, perseverance, and in your perseverance, godliness,....Therefore, brothers, make every effort to confirm your calling and election, because if you do these things you will never stumble" (2 Peter 1:5-10). The word 'add' means constant growth or to excel. "If something ceases to be better, it ceases to be good!"

****

The word "doctrine" comes from the old Latin noun *doctrina* which simply meant "teaching", "instruction". That was connected to the verb *doceo,* "to teach", and the noun doctor which meant "teacher", "master". Doctrine is absolutely essential to our Christian faith. Without doctrine, we'd have nothing to believe. We are products of what we believe. "You can have good doctrine and still be lost, but there are some doctrines without which you will not be found." In order to have eternal life, the doctrine of salvation by faith in the finished works of Jesus Christ must not be ignored. Also the nature of Jesus Christ (truly God/truly man) and His sinless character must be apprehended.

The Bible says that, "And they were astonished at his doctrine: for his word was with power" (Luke 4:32). Satan diminishes the power of the true doctrine by twisting the Scriptures. Paul warned of the danger of the false doctrines: "Preach the word; be ready in season and out of season; reprove, rebuke, exhort, with great patience and instruction. For the time will come when they will not endure sound doctrine; but wanting to have their ears tickled, they will accumulate for themselves teachers in accordance to their own desires" (2 Timothy 4:1-3). The false teachers have a reputation of adding and subtracting from the Scriptures, ending up with false doctrines. The end time deception is evidently seen in the blossoming of the false teachers and the false believers. Arrogance is the key to deception. The people that are lost see no need to know more than what they already know! "Nothing is arrogant as ignorance, unless it is puffed up with knowledge".

****

Today's scripture: "Faith comes by hearing and hearing the word of God" (Romans 10:17). The Bible says that today if you hear His voice, do not harden your hearts (Hebrews 3:15). It means reading the Word, believing the Word and acting on the truth believed. "Life does not come from works but works are evidence of life. Good works come from a living person to sustain the eternal life that is already in place"

****

The persecution by Satan is intended to take away the praises of God from your lips. Whenever you experience persecution, continue to praise God even more than before because that is what Satan hates. This is the only way to stop him from persecuting you.

****

Fulfillment is ultimate satisfaction. The secret of fulfillment is not in finding a god that can supply all of your earthly wants. True fulfillment is God finding you and giving Himself to you. Fulfillment is therefore receiving God as opposed to receiving material things. The Bible says that as many as received Jesus to them He gave them power to become sons of God (John 1:12). Jesus means Yahweh Saves. The name of Jesus is Immanuel,' which is translated, 'God with us' (Isaiah 7:14; Matthew 1:23). Jesus being born in the flesh as a man gives us the ultimate fulfillment of "God with us" as it was indeed "Yahweh". Yahweh (the eternal I AM) introduced Himself in the beginning as Elohim (God) that created the heaven and the earth (Gen. 1:1). 'Elohim' is in the plural: "Let Us make man in Our image, after Our likeness…" (Gen.1:26-27). The Triune God created, and the Triune God saves: "I have given them the glory that you gave me, that they may be one as We are one" (John 17:22).

****

When a believer is adopted into the Lord's family, his relationship to the old nature (old Adam) is severed. He is a new creature under a new covenant. Believer, you are God's child; it is your first duty to obey your heavenly Father. A servile spirit you have nothing to do with: You are a child of God and a bond slave to the new Master that saves you. As much as you are a beloved child, you are bound to obey your Father by doing His will, even the least intimation of His will. He fulfilled the sacred ordinances for your sake. You are called to manifest His life by living as He lived. You can neglect it at your peril.

****

This world (cosmos) is our father's property. Yet this world is not our home. The Apostle John warns us not to love the world (1 John 1:15). He is not talking about the physical world (cosmos) but the corrupt and fallen nature or system that is in subjection to the evil one. "Worldly" (kosmikos) is a moral and religious sphere of evil that captivates the minds of those who have no interest in honoring God. It is the whole realm of "this-world" interests, involving things that are hollow, frail, and fleeting. Our fallen tendency to view the world as an ultimate end must be crucified. We are called to "Deny" (arneomai, to repudiate, renounce) what the system of the world has to offer or impose on us. We should answer with a resounding "No". We must fight against our dark inclinations to set our hearts on this age and its pleasures. Worldliness embraces that which is devilish and seductive. It has to do with matters that are obstacles to the service of God, and in many cases, lure men away from interest in Christ altogether. John wrote: "For all that is in the world, the lust of the flesh and the lust of the eyes and the vainglory of life, is not of the Father, but is of the world" (1 John 2:16). But God created the world to glorify Himself, and as we make Him our ultimate end, we can identify the sins that manifest our love for the world and enjoy the Lord's creation in an appropriate way. The love of the Father in us is given to fight off the evil desires; to hate what God hates and to love what God loves. For example in course of pursuing the light of God, we can identify and fight against sin in the world while loving our enemies and blessing those who curse us.

****

How do you choose a good home Church? A good Church must be full gospel Bible teaching Church. The pastor must teach the Bible book by book, verse by verse, line by line. According to Isaiah 28:10-13 - For precept must be upon precept, line upon line, here a little, and there a little. Expository book by book teaching is the most preferred method in order for God to bring glory and beauty to His people. Intriguingly, according to survey, most people look for Mega Churches as proof for a good Church. Whereas there are some good Mega Churches, I think Church attendance should not be the determining factor when choosing a home Church. Remember that Jesus did not look for a big congregation. When He told His audience to partake of His body and blood the response was devastating. They responded that, "This is a hard teaching. Who can accept it?" They left! Jesus did not change his message or try to make it more "user-friendly" to attract them. Instead, Jesus confronted the twelve by asking: "Does this offend you? Do you also want to go?" Peter answered that, "Lord to whom shall we go? You have the words of eternal life (John 6:53- 68). Jesus had multitudes of followers. At one time He fed 5000 people. But at the end of the day, His congregation consisted of just 120 who faithfully waited in the upper room for the Promise of the Holy Spirit. "Whether big or small congregation, finding your niche in the Body of Christ requires the leading of the Holy Spirit. Choosing where you and your children will learn the things of God and serve the Lord Jesus Christ has eternal ramifications."

****

The value you place on a thing determines how much time you spend on it or with it... Spend time with your Bible it shows you value the Word... We are followers of Christ called to obey His Word in its fullness. God is the author of the Bible, and we are not called to edit what He wrote but take it as He wrote it.

****

In times of trouble we run to God to restore our strength. The book of Psalms is the most quoted book in the New Testament. Jesus (the suffering servant) quoted the book of Psalms more than any other book of the Old Testament. Calvin and the Puritans felt convicted to sing the

Psalms in public worship and loved doing so. Yet the Puritans called the book of Psalms the book covered with tears because most believers who are in pain open and read this book covering its pages with their tears. The Psalms are theological as well as doxological; they teach us about God and they help in developing His character in us in times of trouble.

****

Psalm 23 ... your rod and your staff, they comfort me. Thy rod and thy staff – שבטך *shibtecha*, thy scepter, rod, ensign of a tribe, staff of office. It signifies the shepherd's rod or crook which the shepherds might carry with them to defend his sheep, and with it lay hold of their horns or legs to pull them out of thickets, pits, or waters. We are not to suppose the rod is meant for correction or chastisement: there is no idea of this kind either in the text, or in the original word; nor has it this meaning in any part of Scripture. Besides, correction and chastisement do not comfort; they are not for joyous but grievous; nor can any person look forward to them with comfort. 'Your rod comforts me' is therefore symbolic of God's protecting hand pulling back the sheep that has blindly walked astray. This is the mindset to imbibe!

****

Psalms 23:5 -You prepare a table before me in the presence of my enemies. The Hebrew translation says a table against my enemies. God has defeated our enemies by bridging the gap between us and Him. The table of protection is symbolic of an escape route for us through reconciliation. It is a table of triumph and acknowledgement (rewarding). In our world, reward systems are designed to recognize people who distinguish themselves in a particular field of human Endeavor. Nobel Prizes winners and Oscars are rewarded after specifying the niche. At the judgment seat there are promises of rewards (crowns) to be handed out to the over-comers in various fields. But this is the most humbling promise in the Scripture: "Blessed are those servants, whom the lord when he comes shall find watching: truly I say to you, that he shall gird himself, and make them to sit down to meat, and will come forth and serve them" (Luke 12:37). In His utmost glory, Jesus will wait on His faithful servants at table as a gesture of appreciation. All of the pains and sufferings that we encounter in this world can be rubbed out by reflecting on that gorgeous moment: "Eternal beauty for ashes and eternal joy for mourning"

****

Psalm 23:5 - "You anoint my Head with Oil; My Cup Runs Over." David speaks of an additional blessing that God bestows on those who faithfully submit to His' purpose and will. The word 'anointment' means rubbing on; Jesus the perfect God and the perfect man rubbing on us. Unlike the old covenant, the new covenant is forever because it was made between the perfect God and the perfect man. The essence of the messianic ministry is God in union with man. We are the anointed ones. But anointing was also a representation of setting someone or something aside for the Service of God. We as believers and followers of Christ must indeed be separated for the service of God: Living in this world but not of this world. The anointing breaks the yoke. It is God's power over sin and sicknesses. James 5:14 proposes that if any one amongst us is sick they should call for the elders of the church and through prayer and the anointing of oil pray for healing. The anointment is for the healing of nations and much more, the body of Christ needs healing too because the enemy is constantly buzzing around our heads and we are sick and tired of our flesh. God wants our cup to run over (over flowing with the Holy Spirit).

****

Psalms 23:6 - Surely goodness and mercy shall follow me all the days of my life: and I will dwell in the house of the LORD forever. Goodness and mercy are attributes of God. God told Moses that, "I will make all my goodness pass before thee, and I will proclaim the name of the LORD before thee; and will be gracious to whom I will be gracious, and will shew mercy on whom I will shew mercy" (Exodus 33:19). It is an utter impossibility for God's goodness and mercy to fail us (Romans 2:4, Ephesians 2:4). With the Lord (shepherd) in charge, the twin blessings of goodness and mercy hunt the flock from the rear, front and sides. Our perpetual confidence depends on the conviction that "goodness" meets all our needs, and "mercy" meets all our faults. With such boldness we walk before the throne of God without fear and guilty;

our Father's place is our house for ever; our bodies are His dwelling place forever. It cannot be more intimate than this!

****

Faith is triumphant in trial. Triumphant faith is not "instant" faith; sometimes it takes a long time, but it always wins in the long run. The Psalmist said that I will always sing of your steadfast love and justice (Psalms 101:1). When reason has her feet fastened in the stocks of the inner prison, faith makes the dungeon walls ring with her happy notes as she cries, "I will sing of steadfast love and justice; to you, O LORD, I will make music." Faith pulls the dark mask from the face of trouble and discovers the angel beneath. Faith looks up at the cloud and sees that "It is big with mercy------ the trial is not as difficult as it might have been; next, the trouble is not as severe as we deserved; and our affliction is not as crushing as the burden that others have to carry. Faith sees that in her deepest sorrow there is no punishment. There is not a drop of God's wrath in it; it is all sent in love. Faith finds love gleaming like a jewel on the breast of an angry God. Faith wears her grief "like a badge of honor" and sings of the sweet result of her sorrows, because they work for her spiritual good. Faith says, "For this slight momentary affliction is preparing for us an eternal weight of glory beyond all comparison." So faith rides out in victory, trampling down earthly wisdom and carnal knowledge, and singing songs of triumph where the battle rages.

****

Psalms 1:1-2 - Blessed is the man who does not walk in the counsel of the wicked or stand in the way of sinners or sit in the seat of mockers. But his delight is in the law of the LORD, and on his law he meditates day and night" A godly man neither seeks the company of the ungodly people nor is influenced by them. He seeks the counsel of the godly people. A godly man is firmly planted in Christ. He delights in God's laws.

****

Hebrews 12:7 – "Endure hardship as discipline; God is treating you as His children. For what children are not disciplined by their father? 8

If you are not disciplined—and everyone undergoes discipline—then you are not legitimate, not true sons and daughters at all. 9 Moreover, we have all had human fathers who disciplined us and we respected them for it. How much more should we submit to the Father of spirits and live! 10 They disciplined us for a little while as they thought best; but God disciplines us for our good, in order that we may share in His holiness. 11 No discipline seems pleasant at the time, but painful. Later on, however, it produces a harvest of righteousness and peace for those who have been trained by it."

****

Philippians 2:5-7 – "In your relationships with one another, have the same mindset as Christ Jesus: Who, being in very nature[a] God, did not consider equality with God something to be used to his own advantage; rather, he made himself nothing by taking the very nature of a servant, being made in human likeness". We are called to imitate the attitude of Jesus who did not use His deity for His own advantage but for the advantage of others.

****

You can count on God's goodness and mercy. It has been pointed out that there is no danger of either goodness or mercy becoming exhausted, because God's Word tells us of the "riches of His goodness" in (Romans 2:4), and that He is also "rich in mercy" (Ephesians 2:4). God's riches would have to fail—an utter impossibility!—for goodness and mercy to give up their chase.

****

There is a saying that the strength of the chain of the bicycle depends on its softness after it is lubricated with oil. Humility is the evidence of a strong Christian. The key to the anointment is brokenness. God's power works in our weaknesses but not apart from our weaknesses. God does not use the mighty but the humble. Never be disillusioned when people fault you. God sees beauty in your humbleness and humility rather than failure. "God opposes the proud" (James 4:6).

****

Humility is the proof of spiritual maturity. Examine the attitude of James. He was the brother of Jesus: "Is not this the carpenter, the son of Mary, the brother of James, and Joses, and of Juda, and Simon? and are not his sisters here with us?" (Mark 6:3). James' humility is evidently seen by the way he saw himself when he wrote his epistle some 30 years later: "James, a servant of God and of the Lord Jesus Christ" (James: 1:1). James identified himself as the servant of Jesus rather than as a close relative of the Savior.

****

Growing in faith is growing in the grace. The Bible says that, "All things are possible for one who believes" (Mark 9:23). Faith is trusting in God's abilities other than your own abilities. Great men in the Bible were men of great faith. But there is nothing that one saint was that you may not be. There is no elevation of grace, no attainment of spirituality, no clearness of assurance, no place of duty that is not open to you if you exercise the power of believing in God's Word. Lay aside your sackcloth and ashes, and rise to the dignity of your true position; you are impoverished not because you have to be but because you want to be.

****

We become like what we believe. It is better to have small faith in the Great God than having great faith in a small god. Today we have gods (idols) not necessarily made by human hands but made by minds. We make up god in our minds that fits our desires. This is the ultimate futility!

****

I often hear some men saying "i am what i am." When the same words are used in reference to God they drastically change the meaning. Man's will thinks and says "I will be"...God's will thinks and says "I am". God shows his superiority as one who must be accepted as He is, an unchanging entity. "I am who I am" means that God will be faithful to His Word. "I WILL BE THAT I AM" regardless of time. I appeal to you to enter the state of what you desire to be in the power of God. God put on the human flesh so that by sharing Himself with us we might want to share ourselves with Him. Jesus died on the cross to reconcile us to God. He created a place for us to crucify our old nature (flesh or corrupt selfish nature that does not glorify God) so that we might manifest His very nature and character (John 14:20). "Before the truth can set you free you need to realize which lie is holding you Hostage" ~ Angisho

****

"You have magnified your word above all your name" (Psalms 138:2). We are more privileged than Moses who spoke face to face (directly) to God because we have the indwelling Spirit of God and the full revelation of the Word of God (Bible). No wonder Jesus said that "Among those that are born of women there is not a greater prophet than John the Baptist: but he that is least in the kingdom of God is greater than he" (Luke 7:28). Unlike the Old Testament prophets, John the Baptist did not point to the future coming of the Messiah but he introduced the Messiah by baptizing Him. He pointed to Him saying "Behold the Lamb of God that takes away the sins of the world" (John 1:29). Jesus said that John is the greatest among the natural men; yet the least of the born again believer (spiritual man) is greater than John the Baptist. On Pentecost, God came down to dwell in us and make us His dwelling place (home). We who have experienced transformation are greater than any of the Old Testament prophet. Jesus emphasized this very fact that many of us tend to ignore!

****

Cor. 6:1-13 - Don't receive God's Grace in Vain. The general gist of what I gained is that we can't behave in any manner that contradicts the commitment to live a life for God regardless of the difficulties life or people present. To do so will render receiving God's grace in vain. If we act like we don't know Christ and the power of the Holy Spirit to transform our lives, it nullifies, in the minds of onlookers, the life of Christ we received. By refusing to hear the admonition of Paul, the Corinthians were in danger of rejecting the grace offered to them. They were choosing comfort over conviction, rhetoric over repentance, and wealth over wisdom. They placed more value in immediate appearances than eternal priorities. Faith is knowing the Word of God and knowing the God of the Word.

****

In the same manner, we find Jesus articulating the three pillars of His faith. In Matthew 6:1–18, Jesus outlines three spiritual disciplines: righteousness (alms-giving), prayer, and fasting (repentance). With each practice, He warns not to practice before people, but rather before "your Father, who sees what is done in secret" (verses 4, 6, 18), who is the one who rewards: "Be careful not to do your acts of righteousness before men (verse 1). ... But, when you give to the needy. ... Then your Father, who sees what is done in secret, will REWARD you (verses 3, 4). And when you pray. ... But when you pray. ... Then your Father, who sees what is done in secret, will reward you (verses 5, 6). ... When you fast. ... But when you fast ... and your Father, who sees what is done in secret, will reward you" (verses 16–18). Sincere believing does not constitute just external performance but it involves internal transformation manifested in external works.

****

John 15:15 – "I no longer call you servants, because a servant does not know his master's business. Instead, I have called you friends, for everything that I learned from my Father I have made known to you." Jesus made this stunning statement to His disciples who followed Him during His earthly ministry in the land of the Bible. He elevated their status to friends. Friendship is inclusive and expanding relationship that includes the friends of your friends. When you become a friend of Jesus, you must be ready to engage all of His friends, their friends and their friends' friends into an ever enlarging and unlimited circle of friendship (akin to Facebook friends). This is the discipline of Christian living.

****

Yes, a believer has the personal relationship with God. Yes, God calls us His friends. But the presence of God should not be approached in a casual manner. There is the need of consecration. Consecration is the basis for every spiritual experience. The Word consecrate means holiness, sanctification, cleanness, dedication and setting apart. The blood of Jesus cleans us and sets us apart for God but there is a need for us to consecrate ourselves: Paul instructed that, "I beseech you therefore, brethren, by the mercies of God, that you present your bodies a living sacrifice, holy, acceptable to God, which is your reasonable service" (Romans 12:1). Peter warned that, "Therefore gird up the loins of your mind, be sober, and rest your hope fully upon the grace that is to be brought to you at the revelation of Jesus Christ; as obedient children, not conforming yourselves to the former lusts, as in your ignorance; but as He who called you is holy, you also be holy in all your conduct, because it is written, "Be holy, for I am holy" (1 Peter 1:13-16).

****

Galatians 3:13 – "Christ hath redeemed us from the curse of the law, being made a curse for us: for it is written, Cursed is every one that hangs on a tree". This scripture does not exempt us from observing the commandments of God. It means that Christ redeemed us from the consequences of breaking God's Law. By law no one is redeemed but by the grace all believers are redeemed. No one can observe all the laws without breaking one; breaking one is alternatively breaking all because God demands perfect obedience. The Law was therefore a curse to all mankind because it condemns all to death (curse of breaking the Law). Those who received Christ as Lord and Savior live in Him and for Him; they are protected by the Umbrella of Christ because He was judged and condemned in their place. They will not face spiritual death (separation from God). They become partakers of the righteousness of Christ.

****

Jesus fulfilled the Law in three ways: By living a sinless life without breaking the Law; by righteously interpreting the Law for us to observe; by paying the penalty for breaking the Law on our behalf.

****

The word sin and its cognates are used 786 times in the New International Version of the Bible. Sin means "to miss the mark." It can refer to doing something against God or against a person (Exodus 10:16), doing the opposite of what is right (Galatians 5:17), doing something that will have negative results (Proverbs 24:33-34), and failing to do something you know is right (James 4:17). Sin is basically breaking the Law of God. The Bible says that "Everyone who sins breaks the law; in fact, sin is lawlessness" (1 John 3:4). The Moral Law (Ten Commandments) reflects the holiness of God. A born again believer does not deliberately break the Law. His new nature loves to observe the statutes and ordinances of God. Whenever he or she breaks the law it is called trespassing (walking where he is not supposed to walk). He repents and the blood of Jesus washes him clean. Repenting is not just feeling sorry but it is changing of attitude and mind from wrong doing towards the righteousness of God.

****

Until you get the right view of who God really is, you will never connect with God. You must understand the depth of your depravity in order to see the need of God. Most people do not accept God's free gift of the grace because they see no need to be saved. The reason they don't see the need for the atoning death of Christ is because they don't have the concept of sin. Not until they have the concept of sin, as offensive and utterly repulsive before God and acknowledge their inability to untangle themselves from it, will they see the need for the Savior. Pastor Gram said that, "One question I'm often asked is why I preach so much about the ugliness of sin. And the answer is that if we don't have a right idea of what sin is, then we can never truly understand the Gospel and the grace of God." Our sin is repulsive to God. A non-repented sinner is alienated from God by his or her sin; He or she is completely separated from God. The Bible says that, "But your iniquities have separated you from your God; your sins have hidden his face from you, so that he will not hear" (Isaiah 59:2).

****

In Psalms 32:5, the psalmist says, "I acknowledged my sin to you and did not cover up my iniquity. I said, 'I will confess my transgressions to the LORD.'" In this one verse, "sin," "iniquity," and "transgression" are all mentioned. Basically, the three words communicate the same idea: evil and lawlessness, as defined by God (see 1 John 3:4). However, upon closer examination, each word also carries a slightly different meaning.

Transgression destroys the peace of mind, obscures fellowship with Jesus, hinders prayer, brings darkness over the soul; therefore do not be the serf and slave of sin. Jesus died for the transgressions against you and your transgressions against others. The grace of God eradicates the consequences of ours sins but also teaches us to be holy. Grace and truth meet in Jesus. Embracing grace without embracing truth is hypocrisy.

****

Iniquity is more deeply rooted. Iniquity means "premeditated choice, continuing walking in the generation sins without repentance." David's sin with Bathsheba that led to the killing of her husband, Uriah, was iniquity (2 Samuel 11:3-4; 2 Samuel 12:9). In David's psalm of repentance, he cries out to God, saying, "Wash away all my iniquity and cleanse me from my sin". Micah 2:1 says, "Woe to those who plan iniquity, to those who plot evil on their beds! At morning's light they carry it out because it is in their power to do it." God forgives iniquity, as He does any type of sin when we repent (Jeremiah 33:8; Hebrews 8:12). However, iniquity left unchecked leads to a state of willful sin with no fear of God. The build-up of unrepentant sin is sometimes pictured as a "cup of iniquity" being filled to the brim (Revelation 17:4; Genesis 15:16). This often applies to nations who have forsaken God completely.

****

The biblical writers used different words to refer to sin in its many forms. However, regardless of how depraved a human heart may become, Jesus' death on the cross was sufficient to cover all sin (John 1:29; Romans 5:18). Psalms 32:5 ends with these words: "And you forgave the guilt of my sin." The only sin that God cannot forgive is the final rejection of the Holy Spirit's drawing to repentance—the ultimate fruit of a reprobate mind (Matthew 12:32; Luke 12:10).

****

No matter how spiritually mature you become you will never outgrow temptation. When you conquer it on one front it attacks you on the other. And the closer you get to God the more Satan will try to tempt you. That is the general challenge for everyone on the earth. The reality is that sin attracts demons like garbage attracts rats. That is why we need the divine protection through prayers. As much as we are called to pray, without the intercessory prayer of our Lord we are left desolate. The Bible says that, "Christ Jesus, who died-more than that, who was raised to life-is at the right hand of God and is also interceding for us" (Romans 8:34). Therefore the more intimate we are with Him, the more powerful our lives will be. He turns the temptations of Satan into tests for promotion.

****

Sin is the missing of the mark. "If you would hit the mark, you must aim a little above it. Every arrow that flies feels the attraction of earth." ~ H. Wadsworth Longfellow

****

Doubt is not the opposite of faith. Unbelief is the opposite of faith. Unbelief is refusing to believe what God said. It is putting the traditions of man and religion above the Word of God.

****

Faith does not suspend our sense of good judgment; it reinforces it. Faith is trusting in the integrity of the perfect God. If at all we understood this shocking fact, there wouldn't be a need of the hassle and worry that comes with mistrust.

****

Jesus left to us nothing tangible to trust in - The empty cross; the empty tomb; the empty altars of our sanctuaries with no tangible idols and etc. The most supreme name in all of history, honored by millions, is ultimately faceless to us. Artists have drawn pictures, painted canvasses, and sculpted images of Jesus as they imagine Him. But I still find it odd, that the most revered personality in whose birth is the point of reference for our Calendar and who is described as "the greatest story ever told," has left us no picture of himself. Only faith remains for us to believe and be blessed. "Faith blinds the physical eyes and opens the spiritual eyes. The eyes of the heart need the light of the Son rather than the light of the sun to behold" ~ Stephen Bamutungire

****

Patience is a virtue. History projects some biblical characters who waited and never gave up. Abraham waited for 25 years. Joseph waited for 15 years. Moses waited for 40 years. Jesus waited for 30 years.

****

Oswald Chambers says that in learning to walk with God, there is always the difficulty of getting into His stride. As soon as we start walking with Him we find that He has different ways of doing things, and we have to be trained and disciplined in His ways. If at all we are going to get into God's stride there is the need of intimate oneness with Him. This is a day to day struggle that involves patience and perseverance. If you don't give up you will discover your new vision and purpose.

****

Faith sends expectant hope. Faith is quickened to plead more fervently with her God. Faith is humbled but not crushed. The groans of faith are deeper, and the sighings of faith are more vehement. Faith is not the clinging to a shrine but an endless pilgrimage of the heart. Faith never relaxes but holds on God.

****

It happens every five minutes. On average, a Christian is martyred every five minutes — killed because of their faith. Introvigne told the conference gathered near Budapest the number of Christians killed every year for their faith is about 105,000. And these are only those who were put to death because they were Christians. It does not include those killed as victims of war. Martyrdom is a gift from God to those who die because of their faith. However not all of us are called to die because of our faith but all of us are called to live our faith. Living for Christ is manifesting His sinless life by faith. It is only our faith that pleases God (Hebrews 11:6). The faith that saves is a faith that brings grace; it is a life transforming empowerment that enables a man to live uprightly and even holy before God.

****

Matthew 10:36 - "A man's enemies will be the members of his own household". Jesus is saying that when you lead your life His way, you will find that even members of your own family may turn against you because they prefer that you lived in their own sinful ways. We are fighting a spiritual warfare. We are vulnerable because our enemy is behind the obvious - among family members, relatives and close friends. But we do not fight against flesh and blood. "For our struggle is not against flesh and blood, but against the rulers, against the authorities, against the powers of this dark world and against the spiritual forces of evil in the heavenly realms" (Ephesians 6:12). We cannot avoid suffering for Christ's sake because God uses our pain to open our eyes to the spiritual warfare. We must therefore be ready to pay the price. Unfortunately in America we have the foggy notion regarding what it means paying the ultimate price for the sake of our faith. We are blind to the fact that there is more persecution taking place right now than ever before in the history of the Church!

****

1 Samuel 13:13-14 - God called David a man after His own heart, yet like any other human being David was not perfect. David had a unique devotion to the Lord. God looks at the heart of man while man foolishly tries to work his way into favor with God. God reads the hearts or the inner most thoughts and desires of all humans. In spite of the flaws, David had the passion and the hunger for God. He always desired to please and bring honor to his God. The same applies to other biblical character that found favor with God: Rehab was definitely from the wrong side of the tracks. She was a Gentile and a prostitute but she was used by God and saved because of her hunger for God (Joshua 2:15-24). Cornelius, a Gentile without the Law was a devout man with hunger for God. He became the first Gentile to have the Pentecost experience of

receiving the Holy Spirit (Acts 10). God alone is perfect, and He accepts us on condition of His perfection through Jesus Christ. Jesus said that He is the vine and we are branches. The fruit we produce hangs on the branch but belongs to the vine (Christ). God can use us if only we can develop and exhibit the passion and hunger for Him and manifest His fruit (the godly characteristics of Christ).

****

Until you are broken, you don't know what you're made of. The future belongs to the people of conviction. You are destined to become what you decide to be.

****

This year we had a glimpse at the rare hybrid solar eclipse. Some nice experiences in life are as infrequent as the rare hybrid solar eclipse. We take long waiting for them to occur but when they come, they offer a momentary eclipse to our other hurting side. "This is the typical reflection of the fleeting of our lives here on earth. Unless a life is hinged in God, it can never fill up the vacuum of the excitement that is left behind after the short-lived occurrence of a time of relief" ~ Godfrey E Nsubuga

****

Today, there are a lot of counterfeit merchandises flooding the market. Some Africans nicknamed them 'Chinese-made.' There is a need to properly scrutinize before buying. Likewise, there is a need of self-examination spiritually. You want to make it to heaven? Get real with yourself! It is possible to go to Church, preach the best sermons, cast out demons, contribute your money to Church and etc., without a possibility of graduating to heaven. The Bible is a good reality check. It makes you aware of your pending destiny. Jesus warned that, "Not everyone that saith unto me, Lord, Lord, shall enter into the kingdom of heaven; but he that doeth the will of my Father which is in heaven. Many will say to me in that day, Lord, Lord, have we not prophesied in thy name? and in thy name have cast out devils? and in thy name done many wonderful works? And then will I profess unto them, I never knew you: depart from me, ye that work iniquity" (Matthew 7:21-23). The sheep of Jesus have the following characteristics: They hear the voice of their Master and their Master knows them (John 10:27). "Human good works at their best, without Christ, are equated to iniquities". Have a blessed weekend!

****

Dwight L Moody asked his audience the safest way to suck air from a glass pitcher. One man answered that by pumping it out. Moody answered that using a powerful pump will shatter the glass. He added that the safest way to do it is by filling the glass pitcher with water. The force of the atmosphere pushing the water in the glass pitcher is higher than the force of air inside the pitcher forcing the air out. He used this analogy to explain why there is a need to be filled with the Holy Spirit. Satan is more powerful than any of us but he is no match to God's power in Christ. God fills our hearts with the Holy Spirit to empty us of Satan. Jesus said that, "how can one enter a strong man's house and plunder his goods, unless he first binds the strong man? Then indeed he may plunder his house" (Matthew 12:29). We receive the Holy Spirit one time when we are born again. But to be filled with the Holy Spirit is a choice we make by emptying ourselves of carnality. The filling is given in excess (overflowing) to allow others to partake of Christ flowing in and through us. Be that vessel which Jesus can clean and fill to use for His glory by responding to the gospel and by acting on the truth in the Word. Jesus said that "The words I speak to you are Spirit, and are life" (John 6:63). It doesn't matter what man says; what matters is what God says.

****

Yes, a believer has the personal relationship with God. Yes, God calls us His friends. But the presence of God should not be approached in a casual manner. There is the need of consecration. Consecration is the basis for every spiritual experience. The Word consecrate means holiness, sanctification, cleanness, dedication and setting apart. The blood of Jesus cleans us and sets us apart for God but there is a need for us to consecrate ourselves: Paul instructed that, "I beseech you therefore, brethren, by the mercies of God, that you present your bodies a living sacrifice, holy, acceptable to God, which is your reasonable service" (Romans 12:1). Peter warned that, "Therefore gird up the loins of your mind, be sober, and rest your hope fully upon the grace that is to be brought to you at the revelation of Jesus Christ; as obedient children, not conforming yourselves to the former lusts, as in your ignorance; but as He who called you is holy, you also be holy in all your conduct, because it is written, "Be holy, for I am holy" (1 Peter 1:13-16).

****

The three Pillars in the Christian life are Grace, Faith and Love. These are the three supernatural and spiritual practices which are essential for a Christian. Grace is God's acceptance of us. Faith is our acceptance of God's acceptance. Love is our acceptance of others. Grace connects God to us. Faith connects us to God. Love connects us to others.

****

Faith, hope, and love are three personal spiritual virtues that every believer in Christ has the privilege of developing and applying. Faith (pisti-, pistis; pisteuw, pisteuo) is the conviction, the acceptance, the belief that what God has said is true; it is trusting in God's capabilities other than human capabilities. Hope (elpi-, elpis; elpizw, elpizo) is the confident expectation that something that God has promised to happen will happen. Love (agaph, agape; agapaw, agapao) that God wants believers to have and apply is his unconditional love poured into us and then demonstrated through us to others.

****

Faith is not an assumption that something will happen, but a conviction that something has already happened.

****

Faith drives away fear. "We are troubled on every side, yet not distressed..." (2 Cor.4:8-9). We are kept within the faith domain, despite all we've been through.

****

They said it but it is not true: "Reason is the enemy of faith" (Martin Luther). "Faith means making a virtue out of not thinking" (Bill Maher). "The way to see by faith is to shut the eye of reason." (Ben). It is a wrong teaching that faith has absolutely nothing to do with any kind of reasoning and knowledge. You cannot believe and obey what you don't understand. For example you cannot love Agape unless you understand the meaning of Agape love. Faith and reason go hand in hand. "Reason is our soul's left hand, Faith her right" ~ John Donne

****

Faith and believing have the same essential element of trusting in God. God will deliver as He promised. Faith brings hope. Hope is not mere wishing but it is real expectation. It is a receipt at your figure tips as proof of the purchase ready to be delivered. "Hope is like the sun, when you march towards it the shadow you are burdened with will be left behind".

****

Growing in faith is growing in grace. The need of great faith corresponds with the great grace provided. The Bible says that, "All things are possible for one who believes" (Mark 9:23). Great men in the Bible were men of great faith. But you are equally a saint as them because there is nothing that one saint was that you may not be. There is no elevation of grace, no attainment of spirituality, no clearness of assurance, no place of duty that is not open to you if you believe in God's Word. "Lay aside your sackcloth and ashes, and rise to the dignity of your true position; you are impoverished not because you have to be but because you want to be."

****

Hebrews 11:1 – "Now faith is the substance of things hoped for, the evidence of things not seen." Faith is not escapism. 'Faith is the substance' - stands for reality proven and experienced in a tangible manner. 'Faith is evidence' - stands for legally approved.

****

Weakness of attitude automatically becomes weakness of character. "A cynic is a man who knows the price of everything, and the value of nothing." Cynicism masquerades as wisdom, but it is the farthest thing from it. Because cynics don't learn anything, and because cynicism is a self-imposed blindness, it is a one-way path and once taken the possibility of finding your way back is lost. Every ounce of cynicism is supported by human ego. Cynicism is a rejection of the grace of God and doubting everything about God.

****

Life is a pilgrimage. A good traveler is the one that plans his trip by faith but at the same time who knows how to travel with the sound mind (good planning). Faith travels nowhere without God. Faith waits patiently to follow God. Contemplation is the luxury that costs nothing but faith. The Holy Spirit works with us through contemplation. God cannot be rushed to meet our schedule because He works on His own schedule. But we can count on His integrity that He is never late; He is always on time.

****

Everything was done so that you may be saved. God saves us and sustain us in salvation. Justification is God's act on the human soul. Sanctification is God jointly working with you all the way to glorification. The key to unlock the door to your destination is acquired in this life. Open up your heart to receive what is unfolding. It is not what you do but what God can do. Check your ego at the door and listen to the possibilities not the limitations. The Holy Spirit is whom you need to accomplish everything spiritually. Jesus said that, "----------
If you then, being evil, know how to give good gifts unto your children, how much more shall your heavenly Father give the Holy Spirit to them that ask Him?" (Luke 11:13). The promise of the Holy Spirit was given on Pentecost. He is the Spirit of the Father and the Son. He indwells those who ask Jesus to be their Lord and Savior. In the person of Jesus we have the fullness of God: "On that day you will realize that I am in my Father, and you are in me, and I am in you" (John 14:20). The choice is yours to get rid of your carnality (die to your flesh or old nature) so that He can work in you and through you. Spiritual transformation and

conversion are possible to those who are truly sincere, committed and willing to surrender and persevere.

****

Jesus called the Apostles to follow Him. While they made great sacrifices to follow this seemingly rabble-rouser who shattered years of Jewish tradition, they had at least His physical presence with them. After Jesus ascended, they depended entirely on their faith. In fact they were called followers of the way (without a visible Rabbi to follow). They, like Jesus, when confronted by the Sanhedrin they never departed from their convictions even when it threatened their survival. They planted a seed that is still thriving and growing today. Like the disciples of the first century, we are without the physical presence of Jesus -- even though we have His presence in the person of the Holy Spirit, still in our humanity we are often let down by our faith and feel vulnerable. In such situation we are encouraged by His promise that He will never forsake us but He will be with us up to the utmost ends of the world.

****

All our actions; failures and successes are as a result of our mindset. How you change it is how your destiny will be. "One's destination should never be a place, but rather a new way of seeing things" ~ Henry Miller.

****

"Remember that there is meaning beyond absurdity. Know that every deed counts, that every word is power...Above all, remember that you must build your life as if it were a work of art."
~ Abraham Joshua

****

Hell is a doctrine which the heart revolts from and struggles against. The doctrine of hell is a doctrine to which the heart submits only under the stress of authority. The Church believes the doctrine of hell because it must believe it or renounce faith in the Bible and thereby give up all the hopes founded upon its promises.

****

Fallen flowers can't grow back on the tree, but if the root is strong new flowers certainly can. Nothing is permanent in this world, not even our troubles and challenges. You can have a new beginning if you are rooted in Christ. A catalyst is an agent of change. God's grace is the catalyst of change that can bring about hope in a hopeless situation.

****

The lowest degree of grace is superior to the noblest development of unregenerate nature. Where the Holy Spirit implants divine life in the soul, there is a precious deposit that none of the refinements of education can equal - Alistair Begg

****

The law of success & progress says that change automatically comes to people even those who don't want it. But Christians believe that we cannot change our divine destiny unless we embrace the divine plan of salvation. We are not biological substances but spiritual entities. Don't gamble on your future by trying to Change your life. Life isn't about creating yourself but finding your image in Christ. You are not the masterpiece of your own life but Christ is. The required change is exchanging your will with the will of God. The will of God will never take you where the Grace of God will not sustain you. "You were born an original. Don't die a copy" - John Mason

****

The end times is characterized with tribulations. John introduced himself as our brother, and companion in tribulation, and in the kingdom and patience of Jesus Christ (Revelation 1:9). The spirit of deception is the spirit of confusion aimed at bringing despair and discouragement but the Spirit of Christ is that of inspiration and encouragement. Jesus sent John to give us the following promise: "He who overcomes, I will grant to him to sit down with Me on My throne, as I also overcame and sat down with My Father on His throne. He who has an ear, let him hear what the Spirit says to the churches" (Revelation 3:21-22). In other words the ordinances of God are pure and edifying therefore put them in practice. "If the shoe fits, wear it!"

****

There are two types of Christians: The thermostat and thermometer Christians. A thermostat Christian is the one that changes with circumstances. A thermometer Christ is the one who does not change regardless of the external circumstances.

****

The world today is looking for something real. It is tired of counterfeit spirituality: Exiting messages of preachers for itching ears; empty words of politicians. I mean lifeless formulas that don't really work but just appealing to our emotions. Life is a shadow of what you believe. If you want something, create it by your practical living. Jesus did not preach something He couldn't do. Any religious gathering of people of which Christ is not the center is not a Church but a mere conference. "A conference is a gathering of important people who singly can do nothing, but together can decide that nothing can be done" ~ Fred Allen, American comedian

****

The term religiosity is in reference to an attitude of doing things in a ritualistic manner without the sincerity of a clean and transformed heart. Christianity is not a religion but faith in God's provision for the salvation of man. We are all born with the same malady. Love for God (affection for Christ) is not natural to us but it is born into us. We are born loving the corrupt world and the corrupt 'self' more than the creator. Our love is naturally reserved for other gods other than Jehovah. The love of one true God is lacking in every person until they are regenerated. God turns the hearts of stone into hearts of flesh. The prophetic words say that, "I will give you a new heart and put a new spirit in you; I will remove from you your heart of stone and give you a heart of flesh" (Ezekiel 36:26). It means acquiring a new heart that pulsates with life and affection for God. This is what it means to be "Born again". It is the change of heart by transformation (Spirit) and conversion involving the Christ-like characters (holiness). The old corrupt nature can neither be improved on nor recycled but must die in order to allow space and prominence to the new nature that is born into us and that is only acceptable to God.

****

"A brute at work may be a brute at home." Our archenemy (Satan) comes disguising to be anything appealing to our emotions purposely to snatch our faith. Jesus (our Master) does not take lightly our unbelief as we do. He gave to us the 66 caliber rifle (66 books of the Bible) to shot down the adversary in whatever form he comes. Even if he comes as your closest family member - shoot him in the head and stomach. Do whatever it takes to live in harmony with everybody (Romans 12:16) but stand warned that there are certain situations which must die in order for you live. Jesus said if your right arm causes to stumble cut it off. It is better for you be in this life maimed or crippled than to have two hands or two feet and be thrown into eternal fire (Matthew 5:30). It is a calling to amputate everything that regularly trip you up in your relationship with God. Nothing in this world is worthy losing eternity in heaven (Matthew 16:26). But Satan has lulled people into a state of complacency. The culprits blindly follow the pleasures of this world ending up missing the eternal blessings in heaven. Please be diligent to make your calling and election sure (2 Peter 1:10).

****

The social gospel appeals to the temporally things of the world as opposed to the eternal benevolences. The Christians of the early Church were able to resist the cocktail of religious mixtures, cynicism and the effects of the weakness of Roman culture. They refused to settle into a depressing pattern of ethnic upheavals. They were a unique and peculiar community because they were kingdom minded. Unfortunately, today Satan has lulled people into a state of complacency. Let's make sure that we avoid Hell and that we go to Heaven. We must be "even more diligent to make your calling and election sure" (2 Peter 1:10).

****

Songs of Solomon 5:2 – "I slept, but my heart was awake" Paradoxes abound in Christian experience, and here is one: The spouse was asleep, and yet she was awake. The only one who can read the believer's riddle is he who has lived through this experience. The two points in this evening's text are: a mournful sleepiness and a hopeful wakefulness. "I slept." Through sin that dwells in us we may become lax in holy duties, lazy in religious exercises, dull in spiritual joys, and completely indolent and careless. This is a shameful state for one in whom the quickening Spirit dwells; and it is dangerous in the highest degree. Even wise virgins sometimes slumber, but it is high time for all to shake off the chains of idleness. It is to be feared that many believers lose their strength as Samson lost his hair, while sleeping on the lap of carnal security. Alastair Begg warns against the danger of sleeping while the world around us is perishing. With eternity so close at hand sleeping is irresponsible and cruel. In reality none of us is as awake as we should be. Just a little bit of calamity can badly shake us up. Challenges may come in form of war or disease or personal bereavements and loss. "May we leave forever the couch of fleshly ease, and go out with flaming torches to meet the coming Bridegroom!" ~ Alastair Begg

****

Good things happen when you get your priorities straight. Establish your priorities. Decide what you want, decide what you are willing to exchange for it. Have your priorities right. A little girl Christian girl became sick with cancer. Her father that was a non-believer tried in vain all kinds of treatment to improve her condition. Out of despair he eventually turned to God for divine healing. He started praying for her daughter. One day he whispered to her daughter that he wishes her to be well. The daughter whispered back that "It is my sickness that has drawn you close to God. If it is my sickness that keeps you closer to God, I pray that I stay sick because my life is not more important than your relationship with God".

****

When an egg is broken by an outward force, life ends. If broken by an inward force, Life Begins! True character begins from within to outside. The enemy from outside cannot be defeated without defeating the enemy from within. God pulls down the strongholds of Satan erected from within in order to defeat the enemy from outside. In Galatians 5:19-21, Paul said that the strongholds of Satan are "manifested" which means "apparent, evident, or known" in the works of the flesh. God defeats your enemy by turning your internal weaknesses into strength. The naked truth is that anything done from outside without beginning from inside is considered to be hypocrisy. Hypocrisy means acting to be something that you are not. Hollywood actors are paid lots of money for acting to be something they are not. This weekend try to be real and sincere even in your worshiping. Don't display fake things from outside that do not originate from your heart. "Real hellos are not actors but are real hellos in real life."

****

"We are surprised at our own versatility in being able to fail in so many different ways but God is not surprised at all when we fail." Don't be frustrated whenever you fail living to the required biblical standards. The blood of Jesus cleanses our conscience. God rewards our intents as opposed to our works. When our intents are clean, our works are rendered to be clean in spite of the flaws. Paul said that "-- for I am not practicing what I would like to do, but I am doing the very thing I hate" (Romans 7:16). Born again believers aim high for the righteousness of God but it does not mean they are not going to fail. When we fail it is considered to be missing our intended mark (target) as opposed to deliberate intentions to sin. In such cases we do not delight in our sins but we repent. God extends His grace to us without limits to rectify our failures. Heaven is for guilty people who are forgiven and cleaned by the blood of Jesus. Our perfection is of Christ.

****

The storms of life are part of life yet none of us knows how to handle them. A thunder storm may come in the form of war or disease or personal bereavements and loss. Unless we stir up our faith we are most likely to be caught off-guard. "It is better to be in the midst of storms with Jesus Christ than to be at the shore where it is calm but without Christ."

****

Luke 23:31 - "For if they do these things in a green tree, what shall be done in the dry?" The difference between dry wood and green wood, especially when it comes to fire is that dry wood burns more easily. If you are a follower of Jesus and maintain a consistent, Christlike walk and behavior, you are not exempted from persecution and rejection. Your Christian testimony will be examined, scrutinized and criticized. You will be rejected as Jesus was rejected. The pagan world will not admire your Christlike characters and virtues. "If they did not prize the polished gem, do you think that they will esteem the rough cut jewel? If they have referred to Jesus as Satan, how much more will they denigrate the teacher's disciples?" - Alistair Begg

****

The greatest sermon is preached when we are going through trials. By the way, your non-Christian friends are very interested in this as well. Most of the times your non-Christian friends care less about the doctrines of the Christian faith that you hold; they're not interested in listening to what you say either. But if they see you going through the tragedies or difficulties of life and realize that you are able to triumph over these problems, with the peace of the minds that surpasses understanding and logic, then they will want to know, how you do that. The reason they want to know is simple. Your non-Christian friends are unhappy and frustrated. They're uncertain and fearful because of the difficulties they face every day. If they see that you have peace and calmness, quietness, then they are apt to say, "Hey, tell me, what your secret is? How do you have such great peace?"

****

The Scripture says in 1 Peter 4:12, "Don't think it strange when you face fiery trials." Sometimes you face challenges not because you're doing something wrong but because you're doing something right. Satan does not hang out at grave yards. Learn how to declare God's promises over your life and become what you are saying. Here is His promise for you: "Although you have been forsaken and hated, with no one traveling through, I will make you the everlasting pride and the joy of all generations" (Isaiah 60:15).

****

Confidence is not the absence of fear but the mastery of it. Confident people are candidates of good managers because they make solid decisions not based on emotions. On the other hand desperateness is the recipe of wrong decisions.

****

Jesus said, "Whoever has ears to hear, let them hear." He was appealing to those who have the spiritual antenna to grasp the spiritual meaning from His teachings. He was not appealing to the elites. Certainly, He didn't say that let him who has a brain, let him reason. Spiritual things are supernaturally revealed and discerned by the transformed heart and renewed minds. But it also involves the discipline of the minds. The disciplined minds hear the words of Jesus and let them influence their obedience. To truly hear you must quite the mind, discard the prior knowledge and allow the greatest teacher (Holy Spirit) to minister to you. "It is only when we stop our learning that we begin to know" - Albert Shcheitzer

****

Junk food is not good for our bodies as junk stuff are not good for our minds. "Do not read, as children do, to amuse yourself, or like the ambitious, for the purpose of instruction. No, read in order to live" - Gustave Flaubert

****

The disciplined mind is reflected in humility. It is silence in submission. Talking too much ends up in murmuring. We can speak louder without murmuring.

****

God is moved by His compassion, and His compassion is drawn to humility. Like a river of love, God's compassion flows to the lowest situation in your life, your greatest need, your greatest weakness, and your greatest failures. Whatever you lay low before the Lord He will be drawn to that area of your life. God gives grace to the humble, and His strength is made perfect in your weakness. God says to you "I live in a high and holy place, but also with him who is contrite and lowly in spirit, to revive the spirit of the lowly and to revive the heart of the contrite." Jesus says, "It is not the healthy who need a doctor, but the sick." His mission on earth is to seek the lost and to set free those who are oppressed. "The Son of God appeared for this purpose, to destroy the works of the devil" (1 John 3:8).

****

The best of people make mistakes; it's how you gain knowledge and develop character. The Bible says, 'If you think you are too important to help...you are only fooling yourself.' Sometimes you're called to serve upward to those in authority; other times you're called to serve downward to those in need. Either way, you're serving God only when you're willing to do what's required.

****

A healthy Church is the best witness to a hurtling world. Christians are supposed to be the mirrors at which people look at and they are convicted. Our godliness (inward devotion, relentless optimism and resilient persistence) gives the world a reason to want what we have. But it is a terrible trend when the Church fails to be the kind of witness God wants her to be. Her light becomes dimmer and dimmer instead of shining very brightly in this dark world, and finally is put out. The terrible effect of the lukewarm Church is drawing people away from God instead of towards God. The Church can be neither cold nor warm (lukewarm) whenever we yield to inordinate attachment to this world, resulting into waning love (Revelation 3:15, 16). Jesus warned that in the end times the love of many will wax "cold" (Matthew 24:12). Coldness is the freezing point involving concrete hardening of the hearts. In such condition the Holy Spirit has no impact. "Take away the Holy Spirit from the lukewarm Church and people won't notice the difference because His presence and His absence among the lukewarm believers is the same."

****

Life is a pilgrimage. We wonder from place to place in search for pleasure. "We go after much company, and seek out new excitements, but we are not acquainted with peace; in divers paths of pleasure we search for happiness, but we do not come to rest; through divers ways of laughter and feverish delirium we wander after gladness and life, but our tears are many and grievous, and we do not escape death. "Drifting upon the ocean of life in search of selfish indulgences, we are caught in its storms, and only after many tempests and much privation do we fly to the Rock of Refuge which rests in the deep silence of our own being" ~ James Mwabbs

****

Jesus said that the greatest in His kingdom is the servant. The only significant problem that mankind faces today is the hustle for superiority. It is passionately engraved on the hearts of many and its pursuits often skip steps which will always demand to be revisited...

****

It is weird to yearn for something that you won't have. Commitment to the revealed truth is the niche of those who are sincere and faithful. Some people claim that they want to go to heaven but in reality they are walking in the opposite direction. Plant your feet in the direction where your heart want to be. To gain that which is worth having, it may be necessary to lose everything else that matters to you. "The price of excellence is discipline. The cost of mediocrity is disappointment" ~William Arthur Ward

****

"When I consider Your heavens, the work of Your fingers, The moon and the stars, which You have ordained; What is man that You take thought of him, And the son of man that You care for him?" (Psalms 9:3-5). Man is God's greatest possession and greatest creation. God created man with special responsibility to be a steward of the rest of the creations on the earth. God attached His will to the center of man's will and gave him dominion over the whole earth. Man is a living soul with the very breathe (life) of God. The central command of man's soul is his mind, will, and intellect. The soul was created to be servant to the spirit. The greatest enemy to man is the pride of life, lust of the eye, and the lust of self (flesh). Man without Christ seeks fulfillment elsewhere instead of drawing from God and his will.

****

Luke 11:4 – "Forgive us our sins, for we also forgive everyone who sins against us." At another occasion Jesus said that, "For if you forgive others for their transgressions, your heavenly Father will also forgive you. But if you do not forgive others, then your Father will not forgive your transgressions" (Matthew 6:14-15). Forgiving others is not a condition of receiving the grace of God because the grace of God is given unconditionally but forgiving others is a condition for the smooth communication with God.

****

Spiritual mutuality is manifested in submission. Exodus 20:12 - "Honor your father and your mother, so that you may live long in the land the LORD your God is giving you". Leviticus 19:3 – "You shall fear every man his mother, and his father, and keep my sabbaths: I am the LORD your God. Listen to your father, who gave you life, and do not despise your mother when she is old". Proverbs 23:22 – "Listen to your father, who gave you life, and do not despise your mother when she is old". Love of the parents is unconditional; it is a calling to pursue the love even when it is an insult to the pursuer.

Obey your spiritual leaders and submit to them, for they keep watch over your souls as those who will give an account. Let them do this with joy and not with grief, for this would be unprofitable for you. (Hebrews 13:17). Political leaders rise to power only through the will of God. Daniel 2:21 says that the Lord "changes the times and the epochs; He removes kings and establishes kings." Read Daniel 5:1-31. We are instructed to obey the authorities until the authorities tell us to disobey the authorities above them.

****

I believe that peace is the number one beautiful ornament you can wear. You can always wear a smile without necessarily looking stupid. Always carry peace with you wherever you go. If you seek peace then peace will find you. Be a peacemaker because it makes your heart beautiful and it makes you look beautiful, too. "You want to have perfect physical posture when you stand, sit, and walk, and peace is the perfect posture of the soul, really. Try perfect posture outside as well as inside. Peace creates grace and grace gives peace." ~ C. JoyBell C.

****

I pray God your whole spirit and soul and body be preserved blameless unto the coming of our Lord Jesus Christ (1 Thessalonians 5:23). It is God's will that we prosper in the total man (spirit, soul and body). Some personal behaviors affect the brain negatively. For example, if one drinks alcohol every day (year in, year out), this is bound to affect the brain negatively irrespective of whatever else one does. Science says that getting angry and flexing our facial muscles, makes us look haggard and old. And social philosophy tells us that "old age is wisdom". So, science, social wisdom and social philosophy all converge at one point, that an active brain outlives an aging body and because the brain can't operate outside the body, it makes up for the sustenance of its house, the body.

****

Self-will deludes us into believing we can renew and transform ourselves. Thus it is preventive of real spiritual renewal and transformation that is possible by God alone. For the most part, self exaltation is vain phantom; it is not worthy to pretend to be something of worth and value but that is not acceptable to God. God accepts His worthiness in us that cannot be archived by any natural means but it is a gift from God.

****

Your living is determined not so much by what life brings to you as by the attitude you bring to life; not so much by what happens to you as by the way your mind looks at what happens. Someone said - life is turn by turn. To change is to live and to live is to keep on changing. The truth is that each one of us has the potentiality to change. Life would be a whole lot easier if only we can accept each other not for who we are but for the persons we would want to become. "If you want to get the best out of a person you must look for the best that is in him" ~ Mr. Iceman

****

The best way to find yourself is to lose yourself in the service of others and only a life lived in the service to others is sacrificial. The trinity of the fallen nature of humanity is "I" "Me" & "Myself". Believers change their attitudes by acquiring the minds of Christ and by crucifying their ego. They are required to put others' needs above theirs. Ironically, the virtues we exude become our expectations of others. For example the need to be appreciated is among the deepest cravings of human nature. You have the need, but don't forget that others have it too. Receive it in anticipation of passing it on. What we give out has a way of coming back to us. Respect begets respect, Love begets love, Trust begets trust… The reality is that none of these principles has any meaning except the meaning we give it by virtue of demonstration. Jesus is our point of reference; He practically demonstrated in His life everything He taught.

****

In the first century every person within the Roman Empire had to confess that Caesar is Lord. To confess that Jesus is Lord was considered to be an act of treason. Alistair Begg says concerning the Christians of the early Church that they fought a good fight of faith because the love of Christ constrained them. "In those grand old ages, which are the heroic periods of the Christian religion, this double mark was clearly seen in all believers in Jesus; they were men who knew the love of Christ and rested upon it as a man leans upon a staff whose trustfulness he has proved." The love that they felt toward the Lord was not a quiet emotion that they hid within themselves in the secret place of their souls and that they only spoke about in private or when they met on the first day of the week and sang hymns in honor of Christ Jesus the crucified; it was a passion with them of such a vehement and all-consuming energy that it was visible in all their actions, evident in their conversation, and seen in their eyes, even in their casual glances. Love for Jesus was a flame that fed upon the core and heart of their being and therefore by its own force burned its way into their demeanor and shone there. Zeal for the glory of King Jesus was the seal and mark of all genuine Christians; and it will always be.

****

The only difference between you and the people you admire is their perspective. Be yourself. "Putting out the other fellow's candle never brightens your own" - Kenneth E Hagin

****

Christians have been despised, mocked and labeled as ignorant. Never be afraid to express your faith. "If people are trying to bring you down, it only means that you are above them."

****

Beautiful pictures are developed from negatives in dark room. So, if you are a believer, any time you see darkness in your life, it means God is developing a beautiful future for you.

****

Hebrews 3:1 - "You who share in a heavenly calling". "Heavenly calling" means a call from heaven. If your call comes from man alone, you are uncalled. Is your calling from God? Is it a call to heaven as well as from heaven? Abraham looked forward to the city with foundations, whose architect and builder is God (Hebrews 11:10). Unless you are a stranger here, and heaven is your home, you have not been called with a heavenly calling, for those who have been called from heaven declare that they look for a city that has foundations, whose builder and maker is God, and they find themselves strangers and pilgrims on the earth. Is your calling holy, high, heavenly? Then, beloved, you have been called of God, for such is the calling by which God calls His people.

****

The glory belongs to God. We are not manufacturers of His glory but distributors. We are called to reflect His glory in everything we do. Manifesting the glory of God is our security on earth. God's man at the center of God's will is immortal as long as God is not done with him.

****

Some people claim that they want to go to heaven but in reality they are walking in the opposite direction. Plant your feet in the direction where your heart want to be. "It is easier to cry over one thousand sins of others than to kill one of your own."

****

When the religious leaders challenged Jesus to silence His disciples, He replied that, "I tell you, if they keep quiet, the stones will cry out" (Luke 19:40). Jesus was most probably referring to the temple stones. If the stones were to speak, they could tell of their breaker, how he took them from the quarry and made them fit for the temple. In the same manner we are called not to be silent but to proclaim our Maker. The Bible says that we are the living stones making up the true Temple of God (1 Peter 2:5). We are created for good works to testify of the handiwork of God who made us in His very righteousness. We are called to know Him and to make Him known!

****

Order in our sanctuaries: Psychology dictates that toys are mind-sharpening tools at the fingertips of our kids. If that is true we had an upper during our times because we invented and made our toys. Today there are numerous toys commercialized in the media circulated environment to engage our children. Recent statics show that Americans spend twenty two billion dollars a year on toys. If you don't have the toys they want the neighbors have them. Thank God for the video games with biblical stories of inspiration. On the negative side, toys are a gate way to addiction such that our kids can't keep their hands on themselves (idle). I regularly see them in Church tossing bibles in form of toys. Gone are the days when kids humbled themselves in the sanctuaries with their fingers crossed in reverence to God. For sometime parents have allowed kids unfettered access to toys, and now I think it is time for you to reciprocate that gesture!

****

God's dwelling place is called the temple because there is no place that can contain Him (1 King 8:27). In heaven there is no sun because God is the light to the heavenly temple: "And there shall be no night there; and they need no lamp, neither light of the sun; for the Lord God gives them light: and they shall reign forever and ever" (Revelation 22:5). Today we manifest God's glory by manifesting the fruit of the Spirit (Galatians 5:22). In heaven we are going to shine in God's glory in its fullness by reflecting His light.

****

Lord keep my cup overflowing with your joy; do not let my fountain dry up so that others may drink from me. "Nothing else in all life is such a maker of joy and cheer as the privilege of doing good" - J.R. Miller

****

Habakkuk 3:17-18 - "Though the fig tree should not blossom, nor fruit be on the vines, the produce of the olive fail and the fields yield no food, the flock be cut off from the fold and there be no herd in the stalls, yet I will rejoice in the LORD; I will take joy in the God of my salvation." Job said that "God, my Maker, who gives songs in the night" (Job 35:10). So, since our Maker gives "songs in the night," let us wait upon Him for the music. He changes water into wine. He replaces sorrow with joy. The joy of the Lord is placed in the eternity of our hearts for the sake of praising. Let us not remain songless because we face affliction, but tune our lips to the melody of thanksgiving. "Any man can sing during the day when his or her cup is full but can you sing at night when you are in the shadow of darkness?" - Alistair Begg

****

Friendly fire is an attack by a military force on friendly forces while attempting to attack the enemy, either misidentifying the target as hostile, or due to errors or inaccuracy. Such attacks often cause injury or death. The term friendly fire was originally adopted by the United States but it is not foreign to the Church. There are many believers out there who are mistakenly targeted by other fellow believers. They are deeply wounded and offended. Intriguingly, at times we are more worried of the believers who confessed Jesus Christ than the people of the world who sold their souls to the Dragon (Satan). We have lost that place of comfort and security such that people run away from us instead of towards us. Today, many run to the social media to express their emotions instead of running to us. I want to challenge every believer to be considerate of others by putting your neighbor's interests above yours. God calls us to a higher standard of discipline whether it involves your speech, your inner thoughts, your actions, or anything else. To those who have been offended I want to remind you that love is patient. A believer is a bond-slave of Christ that has no right to run away. The Bible says that "Wounds from a friend can be trusted" (Proverbs 27:6).

****

Don't take what others do as your standard — whether it involves your speech, your inner thoughts, your actions, or anything else. God calls us to a higher standard because He calls us to be like Christ and to put Him first in our lives. The Bible says, "Do not conform to the pattern of this world, but be transformed by the renewing of your mind" (Romans 12:2). Be grateful that you now belong to Christ. Now make it your goal to live for Him every day — not in your own strength, but with the strength He will give you as you turn to Him. The Bible says, "Put on the new self, created to be like God in true righteousness and holiness" (Ephesians 4:24).

****

The Bible addresses our influence in the world. Biblical themes such as justice, compassion, reconciliation and peace (shalom) must be a part of our daily spiritual reflection. "The Church must be reminded that it is not the master or servant of the state, but rather the conscience of the

state. It must be the guide and the critic of the state, and never its tool"
~ Martin Luther King Jr.

****

Matthew 16:18: "I will build my church, and the gates of Hades will not overcome it." The heart may lose its strength to beat, but never lose its power to glow. The blessed hope is that the spirit of the redeemed person lives beyond the grave.

****

The Holy Spirit is often pleased, in a most gracious manner, to witness with our spirits to the love of Jesus. He takes the things of Christ and reveals them to us. No voice is heard from the clouds, and no vision is seen in the night, but we have a testimony more certain than either of these. "Withhold no part of the precious truth, but speak what you know and declare what you have seen. Do not allow the toil or darkness or possible unbelief of your friends to dissuade you. Let us rise and march to the place of duty, and there declare what great things God has shown to our soul."

****

Solitude begins when a man silences the competing voices of the market and mass, and listens to the dictates of his own heart. The mood of our contemporary culture is reflected in fast and easy means (short-cuts). Be patience toward all that is unresolved in your heart is rewarding. Try to love the mysteries of life for which you have no answers. Compare them to locked rooms of treasures or books that are written in a foreign tongue which access is difficult but inevitable.

****

On this day February 2nd - Just want to thank all of you who wished me a great day on this birthday. The most evident token and apparent sign of true wisdom is a constant and unconstrained rejoicing with those who are rejoicing. Thanks for celebrating with me. I am consecutively celebrating the birthday as well as the happiness that friends like you are giving. "The more you praise and celebrate your life, the more there is in life to celebrate" ~ Oprah Winfrey

****

I want to appreciate everyone for the goodwill messages via various social platforms. I am deeply overwhelmed with your heartfelt wishes on my birthday. My profound appreciation in particular goes to my friends on Facebook. You are a unique family to me. Thanks for your messages, prayers and sweet wishes on this special day as I am adding a year to my pilgrimage on this universe while at the same time subtracting a year from my life span. "Life is sweet and short. Only those who impart others will ride on the path of history and will be remembered by generations."

****

Mid February 15th Month of Igniting Romance:

Valentine week is about expressing love romantically. We are the bride of Christ. If Jesus could exchange His elect bride for all the queens and empresses of earth, or even for the angels in heaven, He would not, for He puts her first and foremost! Like the moon she far outshines the stars. Nor is this an opinion that He is ashamed of, for He invites all men to hear it. He sets a "behold" before it, a special note of exclamation, inviting and arresting attention. "Behold, you are beautiful, my love, behold, you are beautiful!" (Song of Sol. 4:1). The romantic Songs of Solomon reflect the romantic love of Christ for His bride (Church). The songs establish a living, sensible, and delightful union that produces streams of love, confidence, sympathy, contentment, and joy, from which both the bride and Bridegroom love to drink. When the soul can clearly see this oneness between itself and Christ, the pulse may be felt as beating for both, and the one blood as flowing through the veins of each. Then the heart is as near heaven as it can be on earth and is prepared for the enjoyment of the most sublime and spiritual kind of fellowship.

No man is an island to himself. All societies around the globe have something they lack and the need to learn from other cultures. African people are more sincere lovers than the people from the West. Yet, African men are lagging behind in the area of romance. Romance placed in African context is like the rough diamond that must be polished, or the luster of it will never appear. This is a distinct week for igniting romance in your relationship. I want to warn that as much as we need some nuggets from the Western culture to polish our romance we must not drop our guards and allow the sewage of the insidious erotic behaviors from the West to be dumped in our culture. We must be selective regarding what to implement. The mentality that 'whatever style the West rocks, I can rock better is delusive. As Alfred said that 'we are living in a world today where lemonade is made from artificial flavors and furniture polish is made from real lemon'.

****

Look at the awful romantic love of Jesus for His bride (Church): "I put an embroidered dress on you and fine leather sandals on your feet. I dressed you in fine linen and covered you with silk. I gave you jewelry. I put bracelets on your wrists and a necklace around your neck. I put a ring in your nose, earrings on your ears, and a beautiful crown on your head." (Ezekiel 16:10-12.). The Lord Jesus expresses His love thoughts towards the Church. He does not consider it sufficient to declare them behind her back, but in her very presence He says, 'Behold, you are beautiful, my love.' "The Lord is a wise lover and knows when to hold back the intimation of love and when to declare it; but there are times when He will make no secret of it, times when He will put it beyond all dispute in the souls of His people" (R. Erskine's Sermons).

****

It is important to know that Christ delights in the beauty of His bride (the Church); He delights to look upon His glory on her. "As the bird returns often to its nest, and as the traveler hurries to his home, so the mind continually pursues the object of its choice." Too often we desire to look upon the face we love; we continually desire to have what is precious to us. This is also true with our Lord Jesus. From all eternity He delighted in the children of man. He stepped into time and space to become like one of us. Many a time before His incarnation, He descended to this lower earth in the similitude of a man-on the plains of Mamre (Gen. 18). The Son of Man visited His people. Because His soul delighted in them, He could not stay away from them, for His heart longed for them. They were never absent from His heart, for He had written their names upon His hands and had graven them upon His side. As the breastplate containing the names of the tribes of Israel was the most brilliant ornament worn by the high priest, so the names of Christ's elect were His most precious jewels that glittered on His heart. We may often forget to meditate upon the perfections of our Lord, but He never ceases to remember us. Let us chide ourselves for past forgetfulness, and pray for grace that we might constantly and fondly remember Him. Lord, paint upon the eyeballs of my soul the image of Your Son. (Proverbs 8:21-31).

****

Our Father's Son, Jesus Christ, was literally impaled in His feet- and Hands with very large crude nails. He, the Lamb of God-- our Father's "Isaac" had His hands "graven" that way, and what He experienced, you can be sure His Father in Heaven experienced WITH Him. At Golgatha, we were engraved in the palm of Jesus' hands. On that Day that Jesus Christ, our King, returns we will see the scars in His hands-- scars revealing His intense Love for His Bride!

****

Valentine died for love, Romeo also died for love, Jack in Titanic died for love, Samson in the Bible died for love, Greek heroes Hercules & Archilles died for love ... & even Jesus Christ died for love! Where are the women? Don't buy any woman a Valentine gift this year until she gives you at least 5 names of women who died for love. Send this to all the males you know and let's boycott this Valentine brouhaha. Lol! ~ Okafor Erasmus

****

There comes Valentine weekend. To somebody that is stressed out as a result of lost love. Lost love is at times more tormenting than lost life. The reason is because the dead person disappears from sight but the person whom you loved interacts with you occasionally bringing back past memories. Their presence is like an itching scrap at your back that you cannot scratch.

****

Valentine is all about love, sacrifice and giving. It is not about booze, drugs and sex. Please go out there tomorrow and make somebody genuinely happy. Go to the less privileged like the motherless, homeless, widows and disabled. All of these people need your love. Show them that they are human being like any of us rather than outcasts. Happy Valentine Day to you all.

****

Every woman wants a man who respects her for her values, virtues and ethics. She wants a man who is proud of her strong character and her unique personality. A man who can support her unconditionally and stay connected to her soul fully.

****

To ladies on this Valentine Day - Romance is a two-way street. What's good for the goose is good for the gander. This comes from an earlier proverb, "What's sauce for the goose is sauce for the gander. What is good for a man is equally good for a woman; or, what a man can have or do, so can a woman have or do. Men cherish emotional closeness with their wives. When you display those romantic qualities like; telling him to help you scrub your back. It makes him happy. But don't forget to ask him to scrub his too!

****

Hope you had a good romantic Valentine night. They say that an ounce of performance is worth pounds of promises. The moment romance lacks sincere love, trust (honesty) and respect; it is reduced to mere performance with dashed expectations. Love today is for the most part a bag of empty promises and vain phantom. In most romantic moods, lust disguising as love is served on the menu, shrinking commitment to life time relationship. Both of you (husband/wife) have a vital role to play to improve on your relationship to make it enjoyable and lasting.

Realizing that your body belongs to your spouse (1 Cor. 7:4) is the driving force and the best and safest course; it makes us good stewards of each other's interests.

****

We have been well educated by books, movies, songs and friends that once you find that special someone they will love you 'till the end of time. And when they don't, or at least not in the way that we want/ expect them to, our dreams get crushed and we find ourselves out of love. Then we struggle, fight, cheat or settle because life is life and that's the way it is. But it doesn't have to be! Fact is that love is not external! The affection and closeness you desire cannot be found in the arms of another. Your expectations of the way you should be loved can never fully be met by your partner. Love comes from within! Of course we want others to appreciate us for who we are, but who we are changes drastically depending on whether we actually love and respect ourselves.

****

Roses are red, Violets are blue. Love never crossed my mind until the day I met you.

****

To love a person is to learn the song that is in their heart, and to sing it to them when they have forgotten.

****

Anyone can catch your eye, but it takes someone special to catch your heart -Author Unknown

****

To the love of my heart: "Some things can be left undone. Some words can be left unsaid. Some feelings can be left unexpressed. But someone like you can never be left unremembered."

****

It hurts when you have someone in your heart but can't have in your arms.

****

No sunset outshines the light of your face, no stars twinkles more than your eyes, no moon will ever have your mysterious charm and never will the sun be more radiant than you; you are simply the best.

****

Some things can be left undone. Some words can be left unsaid. Some feelings can be left unexpressed. But someone like you can never be left unremembered

****

When everything seems to be unfair to you; when all that you do is not appreciated, I'll take your hand, wipe away your tears, take you for a walk and remind you how special you are. Not for the sake of the public but for my sake.

****

On this Valentine Day, to the love of my heart: "May the Lord grant you a long life, punctuated by good health, wisdom and fruitfulness" - With love from the deepest of my heart.

****

It is Valentine's Day. Enjoy all the special feelings of being in love. True love happens once in a lifetime…embrace it with open arms…let the magic of love work on you.….cherish those butterflies in your stomach and goose bumps on your skin. Let the purity of love touch your heart and awaken your soul.

****

"Deep feelings are expressed in words and deeds. I won't say I love you; I will make you feel "I Do". Falling in love is easy but staying in love is a challenge. Couples would be more intimate if only they adhered to this simple rule: "The ingredients of patience and commitment keep the flame of love alive." But when you realize you want to spend the rest of your life with somebody, you want the rest of your life to start as soon as possible!"

****

Please accept to be my best friend ever. It is one thing to turn a friend into a lover, but it's completely different to try to turn a lover into a friend.

****

"I'm in love with you, and I'm not in the business of denying myself the simple pleasure of saying true things. I'm in love with you, and I know that love is just a shout into the void, and that oblivion is inevitable, and that we're all doomed and that there will come a day when all our labor will be turned into dust, and I know the sun will swallow the only earth we'll ever have to share, and I am in love with you."

****

If you love(d) someone, their name is permanently tattooed in your heart. No matter how hard you try to erase it, it'll always remain there.

****

"You can't force love, I realized. It's there or it isn't. If it's not there, you've got to be able to admit it. If it is there, you've got to do whatever it takes to protect the ones you love." ~ Richelle Mead, Frostbite

****

Romance is necessary for love making but it is not all that love is. Avoid making love decisions in a rushing manner. Avoid falling in love without measuring the risks. See the best in everyone but never assume that everyone is emotionally capable of reaching their highest potential. "I have fallen in love more times than I care to count with the highest potential of a man, rather than with the man himself, and I have hung on to the relationship for a long time (sometimes far too long) waiting for the man to ascend to his own greatness. Many times in romance I have been a victim of my own optimism" ~ Elizabeth Gilbert

****

Fifteen ways to make a girl smile on this Valentine Day:

1. Tell her she's BEAUTIFUL. Not hot or Sexy.
2. Hold her hand, just because you love her.
3. Leave her voice messages to wake up to.
4. Wrestle with her, and let her win.
5. Hug her from behind.
6. Don't hang out with your ex when she's not around. It kills her inside.
7. If you talk to another girl, walk over to her after you're done and kiss her.
8. Write her notes or call her just to say I love you.
9. Introduce her to your friends, as your girlfriend.
10. Play with her hair.
11. Pick her up, even when she says no.
12. Get upset if she gets unwanted contact from someone else.
13. Make her laugh, just because you love to see her smile.
14. Let her fall asleep in your arms.
15. If she's mad at you, kiss her, don't fight back.

Single life:

When we think of our ancestors in the Bible, we often think in pairs. Famous couples leap to mind: Adam and Eve, Abraham and Sarah, Mary and Joseph. But there are single people in the Bible as well. The one who comes most easily to mind is, of course, Jesus. But many of Jesus' friends and disciples were also single: Mary Magdalene, Mary and Martha, and Lazarus. The apostle Paul was very vocal about the advantages of being single. There are also single people in the Hebrew Scriptures. Miraim, Moses' sister, was single, and so were some of the prophets, such as Jeremiah and Elijah.

I see the Bible as the book where most of the wisdom to lead our lives can be found. And so it is possible to find in Scripture clues and suggestions for the single life. Look at the virtues modeled by singles: the initiative of Paul as he traveled through the Roman Empire. Or the wonderful courage of Miriam, who, as a young girl, found a nurse for Moses, and then helped Moses lead the people from Egypt; the generosity of the poor widow who gave most of what she had; the leadership of Lydia who began the church at Philippi. From Jesus, perhaps the most famous single person in the Bible, we can learn about a life of love, healing, and sacrifice that we, too, can imitate. All these and more models for us the productive, meaningful lives and ministries we can have as single people.

Sexual purity is the key to engaging God in your future plans and laying a strong foundation for your future marriage. Temptation is real, and nobody is beyond temptation. Therefore avoid making yourself vulnerable. Know your limits when dealing with the opposite sex. Remember that it is risky to put fire next to gas. Given the fact, you should take risk to known your partner but with precaution.

Singles people at times feel inferior and shunned in the Church. Eric Metaxas mentioned recently on BreakPoint that 63 percent of single Christians in one survey said they would have sex before marriage. I wonder how that statistic could change by Christ's Church reaching out and caring for single Christians. If the problem is relational, it's likely the solution is relational as well.

There are singles out there who whether explicitly or implicitly, have gotten the message that marriage is a requirement for full participation in the life of the Church. On the contrary, concerning the completeness and health of the Church, Paul requires the involvement and participation of all of its members, married or not. Singleness allows freedom from the duties of family life; can permit us to spend more time developing our relationship with God and serving the Church. It also frees us from falling into the trap of relying on a [spouse] to fulfill our deepest needs. Only God can do that, and when we are single, we are faced with that reality. There is no hiding behind a marriage. There is only God.

To all my friends who are still single but are looking forward to get married: We marry people to stay together for life in good and bad times. Marital problems cannot be evaded because they are part of married life. But they must be solved in a descent manner whenever they come. That is why the personality of your spouse matters. The most difficult part of marriage is the most important part of it, and it is the very first step in marriage: It is choosing the right person to marry. If you fail the first step there is no counseling that will rectify the enormity. The key to the happiness of your future marriage is in your pocket; use it effectively rather than emotionally. Take your time to do it right the first time, so that you won't do it over and over.

What does the Bible says about being single?

1 Corinthians 7:8-9: "Now to the unmarried and the widows I say: It is good for them to stay unmarried, as I do. But if they cannot control themselves, they should marry, for it is better to marry than to burn with passion."

1 Corinthians 7:32-35: I want you to be free from anxieties. The unmarried man is anxious about the things of the Lord, how to please the Lord. But the married man is anxious about worldly things, how to please his wife, and his interests are divided. And the unmarried or betrothed woman is anxious about the things of the Lord, how to be holy in body and spirit. But the married woman is anxious about worldly things, how to please her husband. I say this for your own benefit, not to lay any restraint upon you, but to promote good order and to secure your undivided devotion to the Lord.

1 Corinthians 7:8: To the unmarried and the widows I say that it is good for them to remain single as I am.

1 Corinthians 7:1-40: Now concerning the matters about which you wrote: "It is good for a man not to have sexual relations with a woman." But because of the temptation to sexual immorality, each man should have his own wife and each woman her own husband. The husband should give to his wife her conjugal rights, and likewise the wife to her husband. For the wife does not have authority over her own body, but the husband does. Likewise the husband does not have authority over

his own body, but the wife does. Do not deprive one another, except perhaps by agreement for a limited time, that you may devote yourselves to prayer; but then come together again, so that Satan may not tempt you because of your lack of self-control.

2 Corinthians 6:14: Do not be unequally yoked with unbelievers. For what partnership has righteousness with lawlessness? Or what fellowship has light with darkness?

Although many married couples are very happy and enjoying every bit of married life, let us not be cynical about marriage. In real life, it is not a tag of married or single that makes one happy or unhappy, a success or a failure - no. What makes you happy or unhappy, a success or a failure is your personal choices, and never a presence or lack of the matrimonial bed.

To those who say that you can't find a woman to marry, this is a true lie. In the world, there are seven billion people. More than half of them are female. Probably, among the fishes in the ocean, you are asking yourself: "Why can't I catch even one?" So, let's start to identify the problems, and once you know, try to remove and dump them!

It is not easy to find a good person; it takes good work of screening. But remember that they are also people not demigods. If you want to find him/her, don't look in the sky, try to search on land. Go out and explore. Don't just wait in a corner of your house. If you want to eat fish you go to the lake.

Acknowledge the fact that half of the population is your rival! People are skeptical about you as you are skeptical about them. They are scared of commitment just as you are.

There is no such a thing as Mr. and Mrs. Perfect. Everyone has flaws. If you insist that there is a perfect person, be ready to be single forever.

In case you see a possible target, do something about it by swinging into action. Show that you are interested. Show your intention and express your feeling. Nothing will happen without doing anything. "A relationship is formed through mutual efforts—it's a two-way process."

Looking for your soul mate is like applying for a position in a company. There should be a job description and qualifications. Have a list of about ten qualities written down which your possible soul mate must have. It may not be easy to get somebody that has all of the qualities on your checklist, but if somebody has seventy percent, it is good enough.

At times people are afraid of approaching people who put their standards high in the sky. They think they are too much to handle. For example men like women who are vulnerable sometimes, like a damsel in distress. They want to be your knight and shining armor that you can lean and depend on. They don't like a superwoman who can literally do everything!

The mirror has an answer for you why you are always single! Use your mirror as much as possible. Always improve on your looks.

The idea of looking for a mate in Church: Most people run to Churches hoping to meet their future spouses. Pray and wait on the Lord rather than moving from your comfort zone and go out to find a partner anywhere. Cedric Pulford a blogger, says the prospects of finding a partner get poorer with age as women increasingly outnumber men in Church.

According to Pastor Bashan Samuel Zziwa of Bajjo Full Gospel Church, as one looks for a marriage partner, they should look for someone who is: God fearing- if he or she puts God first and fears him, they will value you as well; apologetic and teachable among other qualities. I am going to outline the dos and don'ts of getting a spouse at Church:

Dos

- If you are a woman, look good because God gave women the ability to look good. Do not over do it by wearing heavy make up because you might scare someone away. A girl can wear a dress from Owino market (second hand) and look stunning.
- Be available serving the Lord. Do not be inconsistent by changing from one service to another.
- Pray for God's will to be revealed unto you. Do not pray with a biased mindset because then you have already made your decision

Don'ts

- Do not undermine people because some people have great dreams despite their current financial status.
- Do not look for a marriage spouse in a bar or club because out there, people pretend to be what they are not. However even in church, there are some people who are not sincere (hypocrites) pretend.
- Do not pray claiming a man as yours unless God reveals it to you.

March Celebration of the Resurrection of Jesus

Christianity without the resurrection of Christ is void. Paul made the following strong statement: "But if there is no resurrection of the dead, not even Christ has been raised; and if Christ has not been raised, then our preaching is vain, your faith also is vain" (1 Corinthians 15:14). The resurrection of Jesus from the dead is central to the message of the New Testament - it doesn't make sense without it. After a thorough survey of its teaching, Biblical scholar, G. E. Ladd, concludes: The entire New Testament was written from the perspective of the resurrection. Indeed, the resurrection may be called the major premise of the early Christian faith.

The Gospels tell us a lot about the remarkable things that Jesus said and did during his three years of ministry. However, it is interesting to note that in the rest of the New Testament these things are hardly mentioned again. All the emphasis is on his death and resurrection which are referred to about 100 times. Much of the message of the New Testament - our present relationship with the living Jesus, his presence and transforming power in our lives, the final defeat of evil, our future hope - is related to the resurrection. In later Christian writings it is the same. The cross and resurrection are central to virtually all known forms of early Christianity. It follows, therefore, that if the resurrection never happened, we are left with the alternatives of either proclaiming a message that is based on a lie, or radically altering what the early Christians were on about. Michael Ramsey, a former Archbishop of Canterbury, has said: For the first disciples, the gospel without the resurrection was not merely a gospel without a final chapter; it was not a gospel at all. Or as John S. Whale put it in Christian Doctrine: Belief in the resurrection is not an appendage to the Christian faith: it is the

Christian faith. The Gospels cannot explain the resurrection; it is the resurrection which alone explains the Gospels.

The gospel is the life story of Jesus Christ. The gospel is the life that Jesus Christ lived for your sake; the death that He died on your behalf; the resurrected life that became your life that is not subjected to death. Everybody has a story but I want His story to be my legacy!

Without the cross there cannot be the resurrection. The history of the cross: The infallibility of the Scriptures is proven by their prophetic accuracy. King David wrote about how the Messiah would be crucified 1,000 years before crucifixion had even been invented (Psalm 22). The Phoenicians introduced crucifixion to Rome in the 3rd century B.C. And the Romans, always quick to pick up on methods of subjugation to keep conquered countries under their control, embraced the practice with gusto. In their usual efficient manner, they began to mass-produce the structures so they could get rid of as many dissenters as possible. By the time Jesus arrived on the scene, the practice of crucifying criminals was wide-spread.

Before the Romans took over, the Hebrews stoned criminals to death. The significance of the cross, before Jesus was crucified, was its power to subjugate and keep people in fear. It was a cruel and inhumane method of death. Before the victims were crucified they would scourge their bare bodies. Scourging consisted of a cat-of-nine-tails with bones and rocks and/or metal tied to them. The rocks would cause deep contusions while the bones would rip away the skin. After the scourging, if one survived it (because many would die during the scourging alone), the victim would be taken to the site of the crucifixion carrying his own cross. The cross weighed not less than 120 kilograms. Nails were driven in their wrists between the two bones and also in the feet. The victim would hang there barely able to breathe and once in awhile would push up from the platform their feet were on all the while scraping their bleeding backs from the scourging upward on the rough cross. After a period of time the Roman soldiers would come by and break their legs so that they couldn't push up anymore to get a breath and the person would die of asphyxiation. It was a long horrible death. The cross is an instrument of torture. It should never be venerated or worshiped. The significance of the cross after Jesus was nailed to it is that, on the third day, he was resurrected. The tomb is empty! Hallelujah!

The resurrection made the life of Jesus available to all who believe: "And Jesus answered them, saying, "The hour has come for the Son of Man to be glorified. "Truly, truly, I say to you, unless a grain of wheat falls into the earth and dies, it remains alone; but if it dies, it bears much fruit" (John 12:23-24). The new birth experience is the greatest miracle because it is the product of love and grace.

Scrolling through my posted sermons about the resurrection of Jesus Christ:

Wine at the Jewish Passover Meal was symbolic of the atoning power of the blood of Jesus. The Feast of the Passover was instituted and has been practiced in commemoration of the grace of God when the angel of God passed over the first born of the Hebrews but slew the first born of the Egyptians (Exodus 12:14-15). The innocent lamb died in place of the first born (sons) of the Hebrews and the blood was painted at the door posts of their houses.

The word "Pasika" is the Latin translation for Passover. During the Jewish Passover Meal (Seder Meal), there is an obligation to drink four cups of wine. Each cup is connected to a different part of the Seder and represents the four expressions of deliverance promised by God. The 1st cup was connected to sanctification. The 2nd cup was connected to deliverance from Egypt. The 3rd cup was connected to the promise of redemption. The 4th cup was connected to the promise of restoration. Jesus skipped the 3rd cup saying that "I will not drink again from the fruit of the vine until the kingdom of God comes" He reserved it for His Second Coming at marriage feast after our restoration. He picked the 4th cup saying "This cup is the new covenant in my blood, which is poured out for you" (Luke 22:20). The Jews still practice this Passover meal today much like they did nearly 3300 years ago. The fourth part is the climax of the meal where they would conclude with several more prayers, and then they would sing the "Great Hallel", which was Psalms 114-118. Then they would drink the fourth cup of wine and the presiding priest would say the words, "TEL TELESTI" which means "IT IS FINISHED" or "IT IS CONSUMMATED".

The meal is completed. Jesus said that "It is finished" and gave up His spirit (died); He meant that the ransom for our sins is paid in full. Salvation is a onetime event but it is practically experienced in a process of redemption, sanctification and glorification.

****

This Sunday is a commemoration of the triumph entry into Jerusalem (Palm Sunday). Jesus did not sneak into Jerusalem but entered publicly and in triumph. Multitudes paraded applauding and shouting "Hosanna" meaning "save now!" In the secular world no government can be overthrown without capturing the capital city. During biblical times powerful armies matched into the cities to overthrow the incumbent when riding on horses and when armed with spears and swords. But Jesus matched into the city riding on a borrowed young colt (donkey), when dragging His feet on the ground. Perhaps the occupying Roman soldiers ridiculed the conquering King of the Jews as He entered the city. But Jesus was reinstating the heavenly kingdom that is contrary to the secular world. His was the kingdom characterized with the power of surrendering, humbleness and humility. "To become truly great, one has to stand with people, not above them. To be humble to superiors is duty, to equals courtesy, to inferiors is nobleness." In commemoration of this day let us imitate our Lord. Let us crucify the strong will, stubbornness and pride.

****

Normally, we prepare for Christmas months ahead of time. The main way of preparation for Christmas involves exercising our generosity or giving. Next month is Pesach (Pasika) meaning "Passover." The Jewish people celebrate Passover as a commemoration of their liberation by God from slavery in Egypt and their freedom as a nation under the leadership of Moses. Jesus became our ultimate Passover Lamb to liberate us from the slavery of corruption by atoning for our sins. Pasika is definitely the most significant Christian holiday. Spiritually, it is the season of liberation, when we pass over all our obstacles to inner freedom. We are already in the mood of preparation for the Resurrection Day. However, unlike Christmas there are no minimally agreed upon rituals of preparations for this season. Some denominations prepare their hearts by fasting one favorite dish that goes on for one month. Some of us who make it a habit to fast and pray regularly do not participate in this religious ritual. I suggest that all of us prepare for the Resurrection Day in the area of forgiving because the cross stands for the grace. Let this season be for extending grace (forgiveness) to the people that offended us. I am perplexed at the growing discords within the body of Christ. This has been the major cause of the surging moral decay. We seriously need a "moral revival". But it cannot happen unless we come to our senses and revisit the spiritual heritage which our Lord bequeathed to us. It is the perfect will of the Father that we walk as Jesus walked. Let us embrace the standard of "loving unconditionally" as it is set by the Scriptures instead of setting our own standards of love depending on the circumstances. Of course Agape love is the tag that separates us from the world. Pass it on!

****

Jesus entered Jerusalem as a king; but he did not want to be king of earthly things. He wanted to be king of people's hearts. Who is the king of your heart today?

****

Matthew 26:39 - "My Father, if it is possible, may this cup be taken from me. Yet not as I will, but as you will." Jesus foreknew the sufferings He was about to partake of as a result of the wrath of God against sin. His major concern was the separation from the Father after He carried on Himself the sins of the world.

****

"Father, if you are willing, take this cup from me; yet not my will, but yours be done" (Luke 22:42). The scripture portrays the humanity of Jesus. He was very God and very man. In His humanity He is sensitive to the pending burden and the intensity of suffering involved. Nevertheless, He did not allow the suffering to have the last say. He yielded to the will of the Father. He focused at the life beyond the cross. We are the primary beneficiaries of His suffering. We are co-heirs and co-laborers with Christ. "Now if we are children, then we are heirs--heirs of God and co-heirs with Christ, if indeed we share in his sufferings in order that we may also share in his glory" (Romans 8:17). We cannot do the cross but we can share in His sufferings by enduring the suffering involved when preaching the gospel. Every believer has a spiritual cross to carry, the spiritual death to experience and the resurrected life to inherit.

****

When Jesus manifested Himself to the people who were against Him all of them fall on the ground: "When Jesus said, "I am he," they drew back and fell to the ground" (John 18:6). The same thing will happen when Jesus appears at His Second Coming. All those who are against Him will fall down to their knees. The Bible says that "At the name of Jesus every knee should bow, in heaven and on earth and under the earth" (Philippians 2:10).

****

"Then Jesus said to him, "Put your sword back into its place; for all those who take up the sword shall perish by the sword." Or do you think that I cannot appeal to My Father, and He will at once put at My disposal more than twelve legions of angels? "How then will the Scriptures be fulfilled, which say that it must happen this way?" (Matthew 26:53-54) A legion denoted a group of at least 6,000 Roman soldiers, although the total number could be higher. This means that anytime we read about a legion of anything, we can know it always refers to at least 6,000 of something. Jesus said that if He wanted to escape He could call 72000 angels to defend Him. Jesus did not call them but willingly gave up His life in obedience to the Father.

****

Luke 23:28 - "Daughters of Jerusalem, stop weeping for Me, but weep for yourselves and for your children". Scholars comb their minds to interpret the above saying and come up with different interpretations. Jesus said these words to the crowd of mourners that followed Him at His crucifixion. The bible says that at this point of time most of the disciples of Jesus had abandoned Him. The prophetic words say that "Strike the shepherd, and the sheep will be scattered" (Zechariah 13.7). The crowd consisted of sympathetic mourners who were sorry for His imminent fate (death) but were not necessarily His followers. They did not recognize Him as their Messiah because in their Jewish minds they expected the Messiah to be the King delivering them from the Roman occupation, and before them stood a beaten, brutalized man in chains. They expected their Messiah to be the conqueror of the Romans as opposed to the conquered by the Romans. They did not acknowledge the Messiah as the suffering servant of Isaiah 55. Basically these Daughters of Jerusalem wept for the pending death of a great moral teacher but not their Savior. Jesus responded to them that "Don't cry for me, I'm dying for your sins in accordance to the divine plan but cry for yourself and your children who will not accept the divine provision of salvation". In the same manner nonbelievers should be crying for themselves because of rejecting the saving grace of God. They are caught up in the snare of rebellion and they will share the fate reserved for the rebellious fallen angels.

****

Simon the cross-bearer's sons called into the ministry: The centurion noticed him immediately. He was just the man! He barked an order, and the legionnaires grabbed Simon and forced him to pick up Jesus' cross. Who was Simon of Cyrene? We do not know for certain, but we can make some pretty good guesses. Mark tells us that he was the father of Alexander and Rufus. (Mark 15:21, Acts 13:1.) And since the gospel of Mark was directed to the Romans, it is evident that the sons were well known in the Church at Rome.

****

Different cultures have different ways to debase their opponents. The Arabs treated the then president of USA, George W. Bush, in the most contemptuous manner in accordance to their culture by throwing a sandal at him. Spitting and slapping in the face are the ultimate contemptuous acts in accordance to the Jewish culture. Jesus was therefore mocked and insulted in the most disgraceful manner by the Jewish religious leaders when they spat and slapped Him in the face.

****

Today this question was asked in our Bible study "Luke 22:44 - Why did Jesus sweat blood in the Garden of Gethsemane?" Jesus was in agony, most probably greater pain than the nails at the cross. The agony involved being separated from the Father as He took on Himself the sins of the whole universe. The Bible says that: "And being in an agony he prayed more earnestly; and his sweat became like great drops of blood falling down to the ground." He sweated water and then blood. This was the beginning of His atoning work of the blood. The finality of his atoning work was at the cross when one of the soldiers pierced his side with a spear, and forthwith came there out blood and water (John 19:34). John wrote that "This is he that came by water and blood, even Jesus Christ; not by water only, but by water and blood. And it is the Spirit that beareth witness, because the Spirit is truth" (1 John 5:6). The Church is born out of the water and blood of Jesus. We were baptized into His death, buried with Him and raised with Him so that we might walk in newness of life.

****

Judas Iscariot was one of the twelve disciples of Jesus. He was the son of Simon Iscariot. Jesus chose Judas but he was a thief from the beginning. He betrayed Jesus for thirty pieces of sliver coins as prophesied. Judas' life teaches us a lesson that when you lust for something you will never have enough of it. Judas is known for the kiss and betrayal of Jesus. By inverting a symbol of a kiss (perceived as a gesture of good will, holy greeting and intimate) Judah's betrayal of Jesus appears all the more dramatic and despicable. After all he could have opted for another means like just pointing at Him. For over 2000 years the name Judas has been synonymous with betrayal, treachery and shame. "Sometimes the pain and tears are found in the last place you would look for them like from close friends whom you least expect to shatter your heart"

****

Judas was caught in the most jaded times, without hope after betraying Jesus. He ended up committing suicide in bid to reconcile with his conscience. Suicide is when the incestuous sinner could no longer live with his depraved self. Judas ignored the fact that the blood of Jesus, whom he had just betrayed, is powerful enough to take away his sins and guilt. God calls all sinners to repentance. "Say unto them: 'As I live, saith the Lord God, I have no pleasure in the death of the wicked, but that the wicked turn from his way and live. Turn ye, turn ye from your evil ways; for why will ye die?' Ezekiel 33:1"

****

"Behold the man!" (John 19:5): If there be one place where our Lord Jesus most fully becomes the joy and comfort of His people, it is where He plunged deepest into the depths of woe. Come, gracious souls, and behold the Man in the garden of Gethsemane; behold His heart so brimming with love that He cannot hold it in—so full of sorrow that it must find expression. Behold the bloody sweat as it distills from every pore of His body and falls upon the ground. Behold the Man as they drive the nails into His hands and feet. Look up, repenting sinners, and see the sorrowful image of your suffering Lord. Consider Him as the ruby drops stand on the thorn-crown and adorn with priceless gems the diadem of the King of Misery. Behold the Man when all His bones are out of joint, and He is poured out like water and brought into the dust of death; God has forsaken Him, and hell surrounds Him.

Look and see - was there ever sorrow like His sorrow that is done unto Him? All passersby pause and look upon this spectacle of grief, a wonder to men and angels, an unparalleled phenomenon. Behold the Emperor of Woe who had no equal or rival in His agonies! Gaze upon Him, you mourners, for if there is no consolation in a crucified Christ there is no joy in earth or heaven. If in the ransom price of His blood there is no hope, there is no joy in the harps of heaven, and the right hand of God shall know no pleasures forevermore. We need only sit more continually at the cross to be less troubled with our doubts and woes. According to Alistair Begg, we should see our sorrows in His sorrows; we need only to gaze into His wounds and heal our own. If we would live properly, it must be by the contemplation of His death; if we would rise to dignity, it must be by considering His humiliation and His sorrow.

****

In the real world we do not celebrate the death of a person. Why do we celebrate the death of Jesus the man? Jesus died so that we might live forever in the presence of God. Pasika is about the resurrection and the beginning of the new life. Jesus became what we are so that we might become what He is. Our sins separated us from God. At the cross Jesus took on Himself our sins; When Jesus hanged on the cross God saw all the sins of the world at the cross and turned His face away from His Son. The perfect Son of God was temporarily separated from His perfect Father because of our sins. At the cross Jesus said, "It is finished". This is a legal and spiritual term means that it is paid in full. He made it possible for a sinner to stand face to face with God the creator in harmony. In Christ we are one with God. We are complete in Christ because He paid in full the wages for all of our sins (which is death). Also, in Him we take on the very righteousness of God. Jesus took our dirty laundries in exchange for His perfect robe of righteousness. "God extended His grace to you. It is by investing your faith in the finished works of Jesus Christ that makes the benevolences of salvation to be yours." Will you do that today?

****

"The only way the veil is taken away from our eyes is when we understand who Jesus is and celebrate what Jesus has done." The Law pointed to the blood of Jesus Christ. Jesus stated that the Law of Moses, the Prophets, and the Psalms spoke of Him, and that He had come to fulfill them. At the cross when Jesus said that "It is finished" meaning that He has fulfilled the demands of the Law. The first murder given by the Scripture was committed by Cain when he killed his brother (Abel) due to jealous over worshiping God. A mysterious voice went up beyond the skies; it reached the ear of the Invisible, and moved the heart of Eternal Justice, so that breaking through the veil which conceals the Infinite from man, God revealed himself and spoke to Cain and reprimanded him: "What have you done? The voice of your brother's blood cries to me from the ground." (Genesis 4:10.)

When God revealed Himself to mankind in the flesh; it was a dread experiment when they dragged Him before the judgment seat and falsely condemned Him, shouting "Away with him, away with him," they actually took the nails and fastened the Son of God to the accursed tree, to lift up his body between earth and heaven, and there to watch its grieves until it ended in His death. To be certain that He is dead, they pierced his side, and immediately blood and water flowed from it. Abel had chosen an acceptable offering because God had chosen it, and because it was the suitable means for leading his faith to its true object, the Lord Jesus. He saw by faith in the bleeding lamb the memorial of the Lord's great propitiation for sin, which could not be seen in Cain's offering of the fruits of the earth, however tasteful that offering might be. He paid dearly for his act of obedience – His own life was taken by Cain and his blood split on the earth (The first human blood to stain the earth). His blood pointed to the blood of Jesus. The Bible says that "And to Jesus the mediator of the new covenant, and to the blood of sprinkling, that speaks better things than that of Abel" (Hebrews 12:24).

The blood of Abel condemned His brother. But God's grace made the blood of Jesus available to save all (including those who killed Him). In the person and work of Christ is found the true definition of kinsman-redeemer. His blood cries louder: "Oh God, I have carried on my head all the sins the world has ever committed and will ever commit. I have vindicated your law, what more do you demand?" Faith dips the hyssop in the atoning blood and sprinkles it upon the soul, and the soul is clean.

****

Christianity is faith oriented but also it constitutes of a fabric of some religious traditions and values that are highly respected. For example we have the tradition of erecting Christmas trees. The legitimate tree for the Christians to celebrate is not the Christmas tree but it is the cross. The other tradition we have during this time and season is the celebration of Good Friday. One of the principal arguments for Friday is found in Mark 15:42, which notes that Jesus was crucified on Friday, the day before the Sabbath. However, the biblical conclusion drawn from John 19:14 is that Christ was crucified, not on a Friday—the Preparation day for the Sabbath—but on a Wednesday—the Preparation day for the annual ceremonial Passover Sabbath, which that year supposedly fell on a Thursday. The word "Sabbath" simply means resting or holiday. Thus, all the references to the "Preparation day" of Christ's Crucifixion (Matt 27:62; Mark 15:42; Luke 23:54; John 19:31, 42) are interpreted in the light of John 19:14 as meaning Wednesday—the day preceding the Passover Sabbath (Thursday)—rather than Friday—the day preceding the regular seventh-day Sabbath. Wednesday is believed to be a Biblical fact supported by the claim of Jesus that He will be in the heart of the soil (buried) for three days or the sign of Jonah (Matthew 12:39-40).

****

Good Friday is a Christian tradition and not a biblical holy day/feast day. The only occasion whereby we celebrate the death of somebody is Good Friday. This is a Christian tradition and not a biblical holy day/feast day. The official Jewish holiday is the Passover Day when we celebrate Christ's sacrifice on the cross.

****

Matthew 28:5 - There was a violent earthquake, for an angel of the Lord came down from heaven and, going to the tomb, rolled back the stone and sat on it. His appearance was like lightning, and his clothes were white as snow. The guards were so afraid of him that they shook and became like dead men. The angel said to the women, "Do not be afraid, for I know that you are looking for Jesus, who was crucified. He is not here; he has risen, just as he said. Come and see the place where he lay. The angel did not roll away the heavy stone from the entrance of the tomb in order for Jesus to come out because the spiritual body of Jesus could not be restricted by any physical matter. He appeared and disappeared to His disciples who were locked in a room where the windows and doors were closed; Jesus Christ just walked right in. He needed no door. No wall could hold Him out. (See John 20:19 - 31) (Luke 24:39). Jesus is not still a human being a little lower than the angels. He is crowned with glory and honor (Hebrews 2:9) Jesus is no longer in the "days of his flesh." (Hebrews 5:7) He is now a "life-giving spirit". — (1 Corinthians 15:45). Jesus did not need the angel to roll the stone away in order to rise because He was already resurrected. The angels rolled away the stone for the disciples to enter and as proof that Jesus was no longer dead; He is risen!!!

****

Luke 24:5 - "Why do you look for the living among the dead?" The angels had legitimate reason to ask the women who visited the tomb to perfume the dead body of Jesus. The angels reminded them what Jesus spoke to them while He was still in Galilee. Indeed at multiple occasions Jesus did forewarn the disciples of his pending death and resurrection: (Matthew 20:18-19; Matthew 26:1-2, 31-32; Mark 8:31; Mark 10:33-34). But none of them heeded and acted on the truth within the words of Jesus. "It is elusive and awkward for some to wear the label of Christianity when in reality they do not heed to the teachings of their Master. Listening and heeding is an attitude of the heart, a sincere heart has affection for the statutes of God; this is the evidence of the transformed soul."

****

John 20:17 - Jesus said, "Do not hold on to me, for I have not yet ascended to the Father." Some teach that Jesus did not allow Mary Magdalene to touch Him because He had not presented Himself as the sacrifice to His father. But we know that after that He let Thomas touch him. Certainly, Jesus was not objecting to Mary Magdalene's merely touching him, because she was a woman since he allowed other women who were at the grave to 'catch him by his feet.'—Matthew 28:9. The King James Version renders Jesus' words: "Touch me not; for I am not yet ascended to my Father" (John 20:17). However, the original Greek verb, which is usually translated "touch," means also "to cling to, hang on by, lay hold of, grasp, handle." Reasonably, Mary wanted not to let Jesus go but Jesus restrained her from clinging on Him because He had to go to His Father. Jesus was dealing with a misplaced desire to prevent Him from leaving. Jesus said, "Do not hold on to me, for I have not yet returned to the Father. Go instead to my brothers and tell them, 'I am returning to my Father and your Father, to my God and your God." Like Mary we are sent with instruction to take the Good News of the resurrection to the lost world. The Church has an apostolic calling.

****

What did Jesus breath on His disciples after His resurrection? In John 20 the newly resurrected Jesus appears to his disciples. Jesus' activity among them not only includes blessing them and allowing them to examine his wounds, but also breathing on them. Now I can honestly admit that I have never been in a situation where someone was breathing on me and I considered it a good thing. But here in John 20 we can imagine that John is looking back to texts in the Hebrew Scriptures. Texts like Genesis preparation for his mission to be a caretaker of all of God's creation. Or texts like Ezekiel 37:10 where the valley of dry bones regain life through the breath of God and turn into an army of living people. The image of Jesus breathing on his disciples is an image of God new creative action in the world. Here again God is bringing new life into a people to prepare them for his mission.

****

"And Jesus came up and spoke to them, saying, "All authority has been given to Me in heaven and on earth. "Go therefore and make disciples of all the nations, baptizing them in the name of the Father and the Son and the Holy Spirit" (Mathew 28:18). Jesus had been the all powerful eternal Son of God with all powers attributed to His divine nature (second trinity of God). But after resurrection He said that all authority has been given to me. He meant the acquired authority as man and divine to turn around the universe from the mess of Adam. He said "As the Father sent me so I send you" (John 20:21). He rightly acquired the power to change the universe by His obedience to the Father. He made the same power available to those who obey Him. He sends us to evangelize the world so that more worshipers might come in to glorify the Father. God's eternal purpose is to fill this universe with His glory. God puts His Son on display so that His glory may be planted wherever He is worshiped.

****

The significance of the resurrection: At the cross Jesus cried out in a loud voice, "It is finished!" (John 19:30). It means that "paid in full". Jesus paid in full the wages for our sins at the cross. Then on the third day, He rose from the dead. The Bible says that, "He saved us through the washing of rebirth and renewal by the Holy Spirit…" (Titus 3:4-7). Regeneration is the work of God, by which His nature (Spirit) becomes our nature. We are the spiritual body of Jesus Christ of which He is the head. "No one can see the kingdom of God unless he is born again... You must be born again." (John 3:3, 6). The new birth is Christ regenerating your soul. He changes your soul so that with a new mind and a new heart, you love Him, trust Him and follow Him freely. Regeneration is a miracle of such breathtaking proportions that it can only be compared to the re-creation of the heavens and the earth. "I will sprinkle clean water on you, and you will be clean; I will give you a new heart and put a new spirit in you; I will remove from you your heart of stone and give you a heart of flesh." (Ezekiel 36:25-26). Regeneration and renewing is the direct work of the Holy Spirit. He comes to live on the inside of a believer (take up residence in our human spirits) to initiate transformation and the process of our conversion till the resurrection of the bodies when we shall be glorified.

****

When the people of Israel were wandering in the wilderness, God fed them for forty years every morning with manna in a public way. But Moses was also told to take some manna, put it into a golden pot, and place this golden pot in the ark within the Holy of Holies for a memorial before God (Exodus 16:32-34). In Revelation the Lord promised the faithful saints that He would give them to eat of the hidden manna, which signifies that Christ as the special portion allotted to the saints. He was hidden in the grave for three days, then raised from death, and His life became the life of the faithful ones.

****

Jesus said concerning the resurrection of the dead, "Have you not read that which was spoken unto you by God, saying, I am the God of Abraham, and the God of Isaac, and the God of Jacob? God is not the God of the dead, but of the living (Mat 22:31-32). The whole point of Christ telling the Jews that "God is not the God of the dead but of the living" is "now that the DEAD ARE RAISED..." They are "the children of God" only because "they are the children of the RESURRECTION" from the dead.

****

"But we speak God's wisdom in a mystery, the hidden wisdom which God predestined before the ages to our glory; the wisdom which none of the rulers of this age has understood; for if they had understood it they would not have crucified the Lord of glory" (1 Corinthians 2:7-8). Even though Satan did not know that by crucifying Jesus he was signing his extermination order, he tried to stop Jesus' triumph at the cross through Peter. Jesus responded by rebuking Peter that, "Get behind me, Satan," (Matthew 16:23; Mark 8:33). Peter was speaking for Satan.

****

The Bible says that God alone is perfect (Luke 18:19). Again, the Bible teaches us that "without holiness, no man shall see God!" (Heb. 12:14). Holiness therefore is an absolute necessity as a discipline for the believer. But according to the Scriptures, holiness cannot be merited by any human being: "All of us have sinned and fall short of the glory of God" (Romans 3:23). If holiness is of God alone, it can therefore be given by God in order for man to have it. That is why it was necessary for God to put on the human flesh so that we may attain to the bliss of eternal life by regeneration. Jesus, in the human body demonstrated to us the virtues and vices of the perfect life that we can only live by faith in our humanity. He is the Savior that paid the penalty for our sins and bestowed the eternal benevolences to the human race. We are sealed in the eternal fellowship with God beginning from this world. Those who yield to His influences become good; those who obey His impulses do good; those who live under His power receive the goodness of God.

Holiness is a simple concept; it means being set apart by God to reflect His will in this world. Since God is set apart from the evil of this world we must be also. The goodness of God is extended to us in two main ways: Revelation functions in the order of knowledge and grace functions in the order of action, and right knowledge and right action are impossible without revelation and grace. Let us then act in accordance to the divine plan of goodness. "If your understanding cannot comprehend, let your affections apprehend; and if your spirit cannot compass the Lord Jesus in the grasp of understanding, let it embrace Him in the arms of affection" ~ Alistair Begg

****

The atoning work of Jesus Christ projects what Jesus did for us by Himself (alone in his humanity). The story of Abraham projects the Father going together with the Son at the altar of sacrifice. But the story of the crucifixion ends with Jesus going alone without the Father. The Bible says that the Father turned His eyes from the Son and the Son asked "Why have you forsaken me?" It is at the cross that the Father, for the first time turned His eyes from the Son. Christ carried on Himself the sins of the world. His death was the wages of your sins as opposed to His sins. The cup that He was unwilling to drink is a cup of the wrath of the Father poisoned with the filthiness of the world (sin); but He chose to drink it so that you may be saved! If you are a murderer, God saw Christ at the cross as the monster serial murderer; if you an adulterous, God saw Christ at the cross as the most promiscuous sex offender; if you are a liar, God saw Christ as the most professional liar. The Father had no option but to turn His eyes away from the Son. The Father was with Him, yet physically not there. He suffered emotionally, psychologically, physically and spiritually. Jesus did not just offer His blood for atonement but He offered the entirety of Himself so as to purge our sins. He did not just purge some sins from us but He purged all sins from us. By His atonement He said it is finished (this account is paid in full). He Himself was the High priest. He Himself was the sacrifice. He Himself (very God and very man) bore our sins in His body. He didn't die as an example but He died as a substitute. I appeal to you to embrace Christ the redeemer rather than theology; I ask you to believe in the person of Jesus Christ rather than a system or religion; I ask you to believe in Jesus at the cross rather than the cross.

****

God the Father, the Son and the Holy Spirit: The Son "proceeds" from the Father by eternal generation. God, who eternally knows Himself and everything in Himself, begets the Word. Jesus was filled with the Holy Spirit from birth: "He will be great in the sight of the Lord; and he will drink no wine or liquor, and he will be filled with the Holy Spirit while yet in his mother's womb" (Luke 1:15). Yet the Holy Spirit descended on Him at baptism and fused with Him. In His humanity, Jesus went to the desert to be tempted when He was full of the Holy Spirit (Luke 4:1). The Old Testament predicted that the Holy Spirit will rest on Jesus during His ministry on this earth: "The Spirit of the

LORD will rest on Him, the spirit of wisdom and understanding, The spirit of counsel and strength, the spirit of knowledge and the fear of the LORD" (Isaiah 11:2). After resurrection Jesus breathed on His disciples the Holy Spirit (John 20:22) in the same manner God breathed His life (His Spirit) in Adam at creation (Gen. 2:7). Although Jesus had the Holy Spirit without measure, He had to ascend to the Father in order for Him to send the promise of the Holy Spirit to us. The Holy Spirit is "sent" by the Father and Son, as He also "proceeds" from them. For this reason he is called "the Spirit of the Father" (e.g., Mt. 10:20; 1 Cor. 2:11; also John 15:26), but also "the Spirit of the Son" (Gal 4:6), or "the Spirit of Jesus" (Acts 16:7), since it is Jesus himself that sends him (cf. John 15:26).

****

Jesus died a shameful death to pay for our sins (past, present and future sins) and to extend His own righteousness to us. "God was reconciling the world to himself in Christ, not counting people's sins against them" (2 Cor. 5:19). After raising from death Jesus said that "I am ascending to my Father and your Father, to my God and your God" (John 20:17). He restored our communication with the Father. His Father became our Father. He ascended to sit at the right hand of the Father to intercede for us. "Who then is the one who condemns? No one. Christ Jesus who died— more than that, who was raised to life—is at the right hand of God and is also interceding for us" (Romans 8:34). The right hand of God is the place of power, majesty and favor. Our Lord Jesus is our advocate, lawyer and judge. "What, then, shall we say in response to these things? If God is for us, who can be against us? (Romans 8:31)

****

Emptiness is not preferred edifying word. Emptiness means absolutely nothing. There's just something obvious about emptiness, even when you try to convince yourself otherwise. However, the empty tomb became the only hope for Christians. The kingdom message is primarily focused on emptying ourselves. Jesus said that "Whoever finds his life will lose it, and whoever loses his life for my sake will find it" (Matthew 10:39). Jesus fills empty vessels. The Christian life is basically an empty bottle filled with the love of Christ. May you begin this week with the same experience?

****

The angel said to the women that visited the tomb that "Come and see". God's eternal plan for the fallen world is to put His Son on display so that whenever we worship Him the glory of God flashes. "Behold, My Servant, whom I uphold; My chosen one in whom My soul delights" (Isaiah 42:1). This world is basically the theater to exhibit the glory of God. Worshiping is the means of displaying the glory of God. Evangelism is therefore important because it brings on board more worshipers. This is how the glory of God will flood this universe as waters of the sea. God so loved the world and He gave His only begotten Son that He may become a sacrifice for our sins and so that we may become living sacrifices. If Jesus is God and if He lived and died for us, then there is no sacrifice we cannot make for the sake of taking the gospel to the uttermost ends of the world.

****

Salvation is an elaborate system of dialogue whereby God reconciles us who previously were His enemies. To be born again is the supernatural work of God regenerating the soul into the new nature that has affection for the commandments of God. The old nature involves the selfish and corrupt desires inherited from Adam. "The absolute necessity for the regenerating operation of the Holy Spirit in order for a sinner's being converted to God lies in his being totally depraved. Fallen man is without the least degree of right disposition or principles from which holy exercises may proceed. He is completely under a contrary disposition: there is no right exercise of heart in him, but every motion of his will is corrupt and sinful. If this were not the case, there would be no need for him to be born again and made "a new creature." When a person is born again, the old nature does not cease to exist. In fact it becomes more aggressive trying to dominate the new nature. God requires a born again person to feed the new nature with His Word to maturity so that it dominates the old nature. This process is perpetual experience as long as we are living in this corrupt world. This is what it means to be led by the Spirit.

****

1 Corinthians 15:44: "---it is sown a natural body, it is raised a spiritual body. If there is a natural body, there is also a spiritual body. So also it is written, "The first MAN, Adam, BECAME A LIVING SOUL." The last Adam became a life-giving spirit". Blessing is the rule of the game in the kingdom of God but God blesses the second birth as opposed to the first birth. Cain was born first but God blessed Abel. Ismail was born first but God blessed Isaac. Esau was born first but God blessed Jacob. Manasseh was born first but God blessed Ephraim. You are born a natural man but the natural man is supposed to serve the spiritual man (our second birth).

****

"And this is life eternal, that they might know you the only true God, and Jesus Christ, whom you have sent" (John 17:3). Also, "But these are written, that ye might believe that Jesus is the Christ, the Son of God; and that believing ye might have life through his name" (John 20:31). Jesus is the source of life. He is the substance of life. He is the assurance of life. He is the security for life. Certainly, I am heaven born and heaven bound! "It is after you know who you are then you know where you are heading".

****

The Messiah's suffering was foretold by David in Psalms 22. When contemplating what really took place on the cross in the divine transaction between God the Father and God the Son, we must not think of the physical sufferings of Christ, terrible as it was. We must focus primarily on His spiritual suffering. Jesus was not like any of us. He had known no sin but suffered the additional revulsion and destruction of being changed from a perfect man into a loathsome, repulsive creature God could not look upon. He became sin by absorbing evil into his own person.

****

Life goes on after death regardless of one's belief. You see when you plant a seed in ground it must first die (rot) then a new plant comes up with even greater fruits. That is how God designed life to function after the fall of man. We know very little about life the right thing is to trust in the Source and Maker of life (God). But we know everything about our salvation. A soul is restless till it rests in Christ. The shocking truth is that religiosity does not help until you find real spiritual freedom by investing your faith (trust) in Jesus Christ. The cross of Jesus is the only way to return back home to the Father. But Christians have been mistaken to be fanatics and intolerant whenever they proclaim one way to God. "There are two circumstances that lead to arrogance: one is when you're wrong and you can't face it; the other is when you're right and nobody else can face it." — Criss J. Battery loot

****

This world is our spiritual wildness. Jesus told us how to survive in the wilderness. "So they asked him, "What sign then will you give that we may see it and believe you? What will you do? Our ancestors ate the manna in the wilderness; as it is written: 'He gave them bread from heaven to eat.'" Jesus said to them, "Very truly I tell you, it is not Moses who has given you the bread from heaven, but it is my Father who gives you the true bread from heaven. For the bread of God is the bread that comes down from heaven and gives life to the world" (John 6:30-33). The Israelites needed manna to survive in the wildness. Manna was symbolic of Jesus. We need Jesus to survive in this world (wilderness).

April for Overcoming Temptation/Reclaiming Lost Territory:

Temptation will certainly come to us: Temptation is a way of life that is expected to be encountered by each and every believer. God allows temptation to prove our loyalty to Him and our faith. I want to begin by using the temptation of Jesus as my example. Jesus was very God and very man. He was tempted in His humanity and He overcame as a man. Before the testing, He was filled with the Holy Spirit. At His baptism, the Spirit of God descended upon Him and rested on Him. The same Spirit immediately led Him into the wilderness to be tempted (Mark 1:12-13). No sooner had He been endued with the Spirit than He faced the need to rely upon the Holy Spirit to resist temptation.

Here we find the Son of God as truly man as anyone of us, buffeted by temptation, but conquering at every turn. He was led by the Spirit but tested by Satan. The testing was intended to prove that He will not fail like Adam did.

Matthew 4:5 - Then the devil took him to the holy city and had him stand on the highest point of the temple. The "pinnacle" of the temple was the highest place among the "royal colonnade" gallery built by Herod within the area of the temple. The cloisters (porches in the NT) were among the finest architectural features of the entire Temple. Solomon's Porch (only remaining portion of the original temple built by Solomon) was also located here. They were a spectacular sight to behold, overlooking the Kedron valley. The historian Josephus gives an interesting description: "This cloister deserves to be mentioned better than any other under the sun; for, while the valley was very deep, and its bottom could not be seen if you looked from above into the depth, this farther vastly high elevation of the cloister stood upon that height, insomuch that if any one looked down from the top of the battlements, or down both those altitudes, he would be giddy, while his sight could not reach to such an immense depth." -Antiquities, Book 15, Chap.11:5.

Some believe the distance to have been seven hundred feet. It was from here that the Priest on the highest pinnacle had watched, waiting for dawn, to give the signal for beginning the services of the day where he summoned his waiting brethren beneath to offer the morning sacrifice. It is interesting to note that in rabbinic literature, the Midrash (Pesiqta Rabbati, 162a) plainly states the Jewish belief that Messiah would manifest himself standing on the roof of the temple. Not on any roof but "the" roof, as it states in the NT using the definite article "the pinnacle."

No doubt that Satan enticed Jesus with the temptation to fulfill Malachi 3:1 before the designated time. Another interesting note is that the Rabbis believed that the person identified by God in Psalm 91 is none other than the Messiah. This is exactly where Satan misquoted the Scripture about the angels: "He shall give His angels charge concerning you (and) in their hands they shall bear you up..." Jesus was in the wilderness forty days, being tempted by Satan. He was with the wild animals, and angels attended him. But He overcame Satan by rightly dividing, interpreting and acting on the truth of the Scriptures. Regarding the above temptation, Satan took Jesus to the highest point of the temple. Satan is not afraid when you go to Church. He is afraid when you make your body home of God (the Church).

The Bible says that Jesus experienced the temptations for our own sake. He can relate to us and sympathize with us. "For we do not have a high priest who cannot sympathize with our weaknesses, but One who has been tempted in all things as we are, yet without sin. Therefore let us draw near with confidence to the throne of grace, so that we may receive mercy and find grace to help in time of need" (Hebrews 4:15-16).

Jesus overcame where Adam failed. Jesus conquered Satan by defeating death on our behalf. He partook of our sins and was nailed at the cross, this being the most painful experience to save us. There is nothing else that He cannot do for us. He promised to be with us in the trials of life. As Pastor Alistair Begg says that: "He never fails; He is never a dry well; He is never as a setting sun, a passing meteor, or a melting vapor; and yet we are as continually troubled with anxieties, molested with suspicions, and disturbed with fears as if our God were a mirage of the desert."

Isaiah 49:16 – "Behold, I have engraved you on the palms of my hands; your walls are ever before me." "Behold" (see) is a word intended to stir our admiration. Here, indeed, we have a theme for marveling. Heaven and earth may well be astonished that rebels should obtain such a closeness to the heart of infinite love as to be written on the palms of His hands. "I have engraved you." It does not say, "your name." The name is there, but that is not all: "I have engraved you." Consider the depth of this! "I have engraved your person, your image, your circumstances, your sins, your temptations, your weaknesses, your wants, your works; I have engraved you, everything about you, all that concerns you; I have put all of this together here." Will you ever say again that your God has forsaken you when He has engraved you on His own palms? Do not let anything set your heart beating so fast as love for Him. Let this ambition fire your soul; may this be the foundation of every enterprise upon which you enter, and your sustaining motive whenever your zeal would grow cold. Make God your only object.

According to Pastor Alistair Begg, you were called by grace and led to a Savior and made a child of God and an heir of heaven. Doesn't this all prove a very great and super abounding love? Since that time, whether your path has been rough with troubles or smooth with mercies, it has been full of proofs that you are greatly loved. If the Lord has chastened you, it was not in anger; if He has made you poor, still in grace you have been rich. The more unworthy you feel yourself to be, the more evidence you have that nothing but unspeakable love could have led the Lord Jesus to save a soul like yours. The more disapproval you feel, the clearer is the display of God's abounding love in choosing you and calling you and making you an heir of heaven.

In the wildness, God the Rock became the fountain of rivers of water to sustain the life of His children (Israel). It was symbolic of Jesus who is the living water to restore and sustain eternal life in us. He is the water that washes us by regeneration. Paul wrote that, "He saved us, not because of works done by us in righteousness, but according to his own mercy, by the washing of regeneration and renewal of the Holy Spirit, whom he poured out on us richly through Jesus Christ our Savior, so that being justified by his grace we might become heirs according to the hope of eternal life. The saying is trustworthy, and I want you to insist on these things, so that those who have believed in God may be careful to devote themselves to good works" (Titus 3:5-8).

Thus, what is the most evil act of pride in the universe? Thus, what is the evil in God's eyes that He would call the heavens to be shocked at and utterly dismayed? (1) Forsaking God, who is the fountain of living waters (i.e. a double entendre meaning, 'running' and 'life giving' water); and (2) brining out for yourself a cistern (i.e. stagnant and stale water), and even still a broken cistern that could hold no water. So evil is sticking your nose up at God's offer of life and satisfaction (which is an offer of Himself) and saying, "No thanks!" While at the same time, turning to dry cisterns, sticking a shovel in the dirt, putting it up to your mouth, and trying to get satisfaction out of it; which is pride! Someone once said, "The national anthem of hell is, 'I did it my way.'"

C.S. Lewis once said that the problem with evil isn't that our desires are too strong, but that they're too weak; and what he meant by that was that we as people are far too easily pleased. He then gave an illustration of people acting like children who are content to play with mud pies, when they don't know what a day at the beach is like. Or, in the words of John Newton, "Men are like children. Offer a child an apple or a banknote, and he will always take the apple." Therefore, it isn't our desire for satisfaction that displeases God, but rather our attempt at satisfaction in things of far lesser value and satisfaction then Himself. Therefore, "good" is going to the fountain and drinking, drinking, and drinking; being satisfied, and beginning to commend it! John Piper once said, "God is most glorified in me, when I am most satisfied in Him." Thus, the root of all goodness is satisfaction in God. (*Part of the teaching in this paragraph is from the Holy Bible - Desiring God by John Piper*)

God does not tempt us but He tests us. Satan is the tempter. Satan can tempt us to sin, but he cannot make us sin. There are different degrees of temptations. Every Christian has a besetting sin. This is the sin that you are most tempted with. Satan knows your weakest point, and this is where he tempts you most. To have victory over this sin and the other sins in your life, you must learn how to overcome temptation. The grace of God helps us to overcome temptation when we are weak. The Bible says that, "No temptation has overtaken you except what is common to mankind. And God is faithful; he will not let you be tempted beyond what you can bear. But when you are tempted, he will also provide a way out so that you can endure it" (1 Corinthians 10:13). God did not save us to depend on ourselves. You do not need any natural weapon to overcome temptation, set aside your hammer, and pick up God's weapon of GRACE. A secret to having power released in your life and my life to conquer strongholds of sin is God's weapon of GRACE. This weapon – GRACE – is more powerful than a hundred million atom bombs detonated all at one time. This weapon not only has the power to cast a mountain into the sea, but then dry UP the sea!

The grace is of the Father, the Son and the Holy Spirit. We trust in a triune God for our salvation. We believe in the Father that chose us before the foundations of the world; we trust Him to sustain our faith and to protect us until He takes us home. We trust the Son Jesus Christ (very God and very man) to take away our sins. He is seated at the Most High Throne interceding for us to overcome temptation; to present our prayers and desires before His Father's throne. He is our Advocate at the

Day of Judgment to plead our cause, and to justify us. We trust the Holy Spirit that sanctifies us. Sanctification is the process of cleaning our minds and getting rid of sin. The Holy Spirit indwells our bodies; He curbs our temper; He subdues our will, enlightens our understanding and comforts our despondency, to help our weakness, to illuminate our darkness. He dwells in us to rule where Jesus is acknowledged as King. He sanctifies us completely (spirit, soul, and body) till the day of glorification. We are people of hope, not despair!

Jesus defeated Satan and gave us the same power to overcome temptation. Satan is powerless until you yield to sin. It means that a believer surrenders the godly ordained victory and authority at his or her belt to Satan whenever he or she compromises on the truth and yields to sin. When sin steps into your life, the peace of God exits; you can't have both at the same time.

Temptation is intended to empower us as opposed to weaken us. It is the testing of our faith. But in case of sin there must be repentance. A study of Bible characters reveals that most of those who made history were men who failed at some point, and some of them drastically, but who refused to continue lying in the dust. Their very failure and repentance secured for them a more ample conception of the grace of God. They learned to know Him as the God of the second chance to His children who had failed Him—and third chance, too.

The historian Froude wrote, "The worth of a man must be measured by his life, not by his failure under a singular and peculiar trial." Peter the apostle, though forewarned, thrice denied his Master on the first alarm of danger; yet that Master, who knew his nature in its strength and in its infirmity, chose him.

God hates sin but He gets glory whenever we overcome sin. His testing is therefore intended for His glory when we overcome sin. The Bible says that a believer can fail but he or she does not continue in a consistent lifestyle of sinning. Sin is a reproach to God and it should be a reproach to the body of Christ (Church). Sin is a personal issue but every one's business. Paul used the analogy of the human body with different body parts to define the functioning of the Church whereby when one part of the body suffers the rest of the body suffers. There are various stages of accountability in the Church purposely intended to get rid of sin from our midst and to help each of us to stand in perfect communion and fellowship with God.

Scrolling through posted sermons on temptation:

Temptation is not sin until you yield into sinning. If temptation was sin Jesus would have been a sinner. Jesus was tempted and yet He was without sin. "For we do not have a high priest who is unable to empathize with our weaknesses, but we have one who has been tempted in every way, just as we are—yet he did not sin" (Hebrews 4:15).

****

The only person that understands what you're going through is the person that climbed the same mountain you are climbing and he or she overcame. The rest can at best just be sympathetic. The Bible says concerning Jesus Christ that, "Seeing then that we have a great High Priest who has passed through the heavens, Jesus the Son of God, let us hold fast our confession. For we do not have a High Priest who cannot sympathize with our weaknesses, but was in all points tempted as we are, yet without sin" (Hebrews 4:14-16). Adam does not qualify to be our high priest because he failed the test of temptation. Jesus qualifies to be our High Priest because He was tempted in His humanity like any of us and He overcame. He does not ask us to do what He did not do.

****

God does not tempt us but He tests us. Satan is tempter. The objective of Satan is to kill or shoot down your faith in Christ. But God tests purposely to prove our faith. We can therefore not avoid temptation. A study of the Bible indicates that great biblical characters, most of those who made history were men who failed at some point, and some of them drastically. For example Peter the apostle, though forewarned, thrice denied his Master on the first alarm of danger; yet that Master, who knew his nature in its strength and in its infirmity, chose him. But they refused to continue lying in the dust. Their very failure and repentance secured for them a more ample conception of the grace of God. They learned to know Him as the God of the second chance to

His children who had failed Him—and third chance, too. The historian Froude wrote, "The worth of a man must be measured by his life, not by his failure under a singular and peculiar trial.

****

God is omniscient. He does not test us to discover our spiritual level or in order to know us. The testing is intended for us to know who we are and how we respond in times of crisis. "The more I am determined to be holy the more I fail. The more I fail the more I acknowledge my frailty, and the more I need the grace. The more I need the grace the more I know Jesus Christ."

****

Satan is the personification of evil and the architect of treachery. The Bible teaches that the devil – as he works his craft against us – personifies wiles. He is the master of wiles. In order to be ready for this adversary, we must be knowledgeable of his methods and tactics. The Scriptures tell us of the great ability of Satan to tempt us, enumerates his wiles, and then provides antidotes against his deceptions. The good news is that the Lord is able to defend us and to keep us from the evil one.

****

Somebody asked me "What is the greatest sin?" I believe that all sins are equally offensive to God. The laws of God are like a chain whereby when you break one joint off the whole thing falls apart. All sins need to be repented. God forgives whenever we repent. Given the fact, there are different degrees of the intensity of our depravity. The unforgivable sin is rejecting the conviction of the Holy Spirit to receive Jesus Christ as your Lord and personal Savior (Matthew 12:31-32). Jesus said that, "Anyone who rejects the Holy Spirit's convicting influence and does not repent will not be forgiven, 'neither in this world, neither in the world to come'" (Matthew 12:32). Pride is the mother of all sins. The first sin was committed by Lucifer in heaven. It is commonly accepted that the fall of Lucifer (meaning light-bearer) was due to pride (Isaiah 14:12-15). God resists the proud (James 4:6). Lewis said that, "A proud man is always looking down on things and people; and, of course, as long as you are looking down, you cannot see something that is above you."

****

I love this chorus:
When I survey the wondrous cross
On which the Prince of glory died,
My richest gain I count but loss,
And pour contempt on all my pride

****

The happiest state of a Christian is the holiest state. Just as there is the most heat nearest to the sun, so there is the most happiness closest to Christ. Satan does not often attack a Christian who is living near to God. It is when the Christian departs from God, becomes spiritually starved, and tries to feed on lies that the devil discovers his moment of advantage. Satan may sometimes stand foot to foot with the child of God who is active in his Master's service, but the battle is generally brief. He who slips as he goes down into the Valley of Humiliation will find that with every false step he invites the devil's attack. Pray for the grace to walk humbly with our God!

****

Never risk making life-changing decisions emotionally in form of gambling. If deception was so easy to spot, it wouldn't have been very deceptive. The Bible says that Satan is crafty and subtle, and it warns us to be wary (cautious) of his "wiles." Our English word "wiles" is generally used to express deception through trickery and includes all the methods that would be part of that. It has to do with cunning or skill applied to no good purpose. The word ruse is a synonym with stress on the creation of a false impression. For example the devil exaggerates the pleasures of sin while minimizing the true nature and outcome of sin. No human wisdom or even modern electronic device can detect and neutralize Satan's tricks. An enemy as powerful and as potentially harmful as this one requires all the preparation we can make. That is why Jesus gives us His own armor to fight Satan: "Put on the whole armor of God, that you may be able to stand against the wiles of the devil," (Ephesians 6:11). The full armor is required in order to stand against the wiles of Satan. "What you stand against is as important as what you stand for".

****

Jesus said that, "Therefore everyone who hears these words of mine and puts them into practice is like a wise man who built his house on the rock. And the rain fell, and the floods came, and the winds blew and slammed against that house; and yet it did not fall, for it had been founded on the rock. "Everyone who hears these words of Mine and does not act on them, will be like a foolish man who built his house on the sand." The rain fell, and the floods came, and the winds blew and slammed against that house; and it fell-- and great was its fall" (Matthew 7:25-26). Both houses faced storms. It means that believers and nonbelievers face the same trials of life. It is the nature of the foundation that makes a difference. Both houses represent believers of different levels of faith. The house built on the rock is the person whose faith is actively strong and that is not shakable. The house built on sand is the lukewarm believer who cannot stand in times of trials. The purpose of the storms in the lives of the believers is to test their faith; because faith not tested cannot be trusted.

****

Strictly follow your doctor's instructions in order to achieve the full benefit and lessen the possible side effects of your medications. Have patience and allow time for the medicine to work. The uncomfortable words you often hear from doctors are: "It might get worse before it gets better". If you want to get well you cannot afford to ignore any of the doctors' instructions. Spiritually, in order to secure answered prayers, you must obey God's instructions. Here is God's prescription for your spiritual wellbeing: "Obey me, and I will be your God, and you will be my people. Do everything as I say, and all will be well!" (Jeremiah 7:23). Whereas God is responsible for your obedience, you are responsible for your disobedience. Add the virtue of patience to obedience: "It is likely to get worse before it gets better."

****

The Bible warns that, "Be alert and of sober mind. Your enemy the devil prowls around like a roaring lion looking for someone to devour" (1 Peter 5:8). Satan, like a hungry lion is ambushing his prey ready to attack. He uses demons. On the surface, they have advantages over us because they are invisible to our eyes. In addition, they can, without our even being aware, communicate their thoughts and attitudes to our minds through the very air that supports our lives. The devil can use any person close to us to attack. He can use even our family members. Most people in this world do not know they are being used by Satan. They do not know that they are deceived or how they became deceived. Satan and his demons have not sat us all down to tell us, "We are here to deceive you." We know only because God's Word reveals this truth to us, and we believe it. Despite this happening in our lives, deception can still be communicated to us unless we are astute enough to take care that it does not happen again. We must be rooted in God's Word. This is the safest place to be.

****

The ability to synthesize sensory input into a coherent picture of the world is associated with physical regions of the brain. Most critical of all our senses is vision, and the brain devotes more resources to visual perception than to any other sense. The minds significantly control all our five senses by controlling how we act and react (emotions). Spiritually, the mind is the battle field for the control of the will. Every bad act begins as a thought. Evil thoughts infiltrate our minds in a non-restrained manner. But we have the power to decide how long those thoughts can stay. Billy Gram insinuated that "You cannot prevent a bird to stand on your head, but you can prevent it from making nests on your head". Fantasizing on the bad thoughts will eventually result into yielding to temptation. Sin is compared to an erosion process that carries away the richness of life.

****

The world is changing, and it's changing fast. Given the fact, God and His sovereignty over the world is unchanging. Technology makes information more accessible every day but not necessarily wisdom. This changing digital scene brings with it new challenges to maintaining purity as a Christian—for singles, for couples, and for families as a whole, including children. Christians are called to guard their hearts. The answer is not found in abstaining from using the social media but in training ourselves and our children in the discipline of using the digital technology for the glory of God. Reject isolation and embrace accountability that comes with visibility.

****

Every biblical character mentioned in the Bible (apart from Jesus) faced temptation and sinned because we are human beings and we are still in our fallen nature. But God equips the Christians to overcome temptation. "The battle for sin is won or lost in your minds. Whatever gets your attention will get you" - Rick Warren

****

Temptation is ordained by God to prove that we will not fail. In the Lord's Prayer Jesus instructed us to prayer to our Father that "Lead us not into temptation". It does not mean skipping temptation but it means to go into temptation with confidence that God is with us and He will not abandon us there.

****

Luke 22:32-33 - "Simon, Simon, behold, Satan has desired (demanded permission) to sift you like wheat; but I have prayed for you, that your faith may not fail; and you, when once you have turned again, strengthen your brothers." Jesus predicted the dawning of the new day for Peter. "God does not change us so that He may love us but He loves us so that He might change us."

****

Child of God, never contradict your profession. Be ever one of those whose manners are Christian, whose speech is like Jesus, whose conduct and conversation are so reminiscent of heaven that all who see you may know that you are the Savior's, recognizing in you His features of love and His countenance of holiness. Stand fast in the evil day, remembering that you are Christ's.

****

"Nostalgia will work in a situation where hypnotizing fails." One expert in training dogs insinuated that the love of the dog is not expressed when it jumps on your lap when you walk into the house but when you accidentally leave the door open and the dog runs out, but after a while it finds its way back into the house. In the same manner our love for God is manifested when we come back home (to Him) after going astray. We all mess up in one way or the other. The tragedy is for our sins to send us away from God instead of drawing us near to Him in repentance. Our failure to come back is concurrence with the self-righteous view dictating that God accepts us on condition of our works. Self-righteous is the major cause of unabated paranoia. The reality is that we put nothing at table before Christ except our sins. Salvation is of God and by God. It is given by grace and received by faith. The righteousness we have is of Christ, and we live the life of Christ by faith. Without faith nobody can measure up to the life of Christ. If everybody knew this truth it would put an end to self-righteousness.

****

A catalyst is an agent of change. God's grace is the catalyst of change that can bring about hope in a hopeless situation. The Bible says that, "Even when we were dead in sins, has made us alive together with Christ, by grace you are saved" (Ephesians 2:5). The word 'dead' means corpse. The dead person's condition is not expected to improve on its own except to deteriorate. The grace of God brings life into the lifeless situation. The grace is Christ's power that reaches out to us in our weaknesses to make us perfect. The grace restores our fellowship with the holy God and sustains us in our spiritual walk. When we fall down; we get up. "Fallen flowers can't grow back on the tree, but if the root is strong new flowers certainly can. Nothing is permanent in this world, not even our troubles and challenges. You can have a new beginning if you are rooted in Christ."

****

In our Christian walk there are disruptive moments. Such are bumps in the road which can be avoided but not all times do we succeed in avoiding them because they are there for a reason. As long as you are moving chances are you will stumble on something, perhaps when you are least expecting it. Just keep on going without fear of stumbling. I have never heard of anyone stumbling on something when sitting down.

****

We are in a spiritual warfare against our ark enemy Satan. The best fight is the offensive. In boxing, a quick jab to the nose or trachea is always a good option, to momentarily stun your opponent. It is effective, and potentially deadly. It induces excruciating pain, causes blurred vision through teared eyes, allowing you to get more shots at the same spot through the course of the fight. The nose breaks easily too. Our offensive war against Satan is by means of surrendering to Jesus. We fight by our godliness. Defeating your enemy by surrendering may not seem practical for a spur of a brave fighter but remember that we fight from victory to victory. Jesus saves us by separating us for Himself. He separates us from the world and from our comfort zones, and He sends us into the world to display His glory.

****

James 1:2-4: "Consider it pure joy, my brothers and sisters, whenever you face trials of many kinds, because you know that the testing of your faith produces perseverance. Let perseverance finish its work so that you may be mature and complete, not lacking anything". We are called to rejoice in times of temptation because it is the means of building characters (endurance, perfection and maturity).

****

A wretched person asked God why he is traveling the rigid way of life with so many mountains to climb. God replied that: "Mountains are necessary in order to have a better view of life." Trusting in God does not make the mountain smaller, it makes climbing much easier! Moses said to God that, "If your Presence does not go with us, do not send us up from here" (Exodus 33:15). Take God with you everywhere you go, and He will see you crossing to the other end. Where you can't take Him, don't go. Have a blessed week mountain climbers.

****

The Christian life is the life of faith. God gives us the promise of faith and the plan of faith. "Jehovah knows how by the irresistible grace addressed to our understanding, by mighty reasons appealing to the affections, and by the mysterious influence of His Holy Spirit operating upon all the powers and passions of the soul to subdue the whole man". But we must seek to put God at the center of our lives. Before we seek His will, we must be willing to obey His will.

****

Seasons change and are at times unpredictable but we can count on the unchanging character of God. When He instructs you to do something do not hesitate even when His instructions defy logic. Go ahead and jump with your eyes closed rather than resisting with your eyes open. At times obedient is uncomfortable but inevitably you will triumph because a first faint gleam of Heaven is already inside you. "You will know as much of God, and only as much of God, as you are willing to put into practice." To obey is choice that is perpetually necessary and -- let us not forget -- possible. It is a deadly error to fall into the notion that when feelings are extremely strong we can do nothing but act on them. Obedience is an act of the will of the heart involving our faith. When we exercise our faith, the unpredictability becomes exciting. For example Abraham went on the mountain to sacrifice his son most probably a sad man but walked down the mountain the happiest man. Keep up the walk of faith. "Life is like riding a bicycle - in order to keep your balance, you must keep moving" ~ Albert Einstein.

****

Nobody wants to go through trials but at times God ordained you to go through the storms so that you can pull out others who are stuck in the same storms. Jesus entered our world of suffering to redeem us from suffering. Take note that our light never shine brighter than when the environment is dark. Beauty remains beauty even in darkness.

****

It happens every five minutes. On average, a Christian is martyred every five minutes — killed because of their faith. Introvigne told the conference gathered near Budapest the number of Christians killed every year for their faith is about 105,000. And these are only those who were put to death because they were Christians. It does not include those killed as victims of war. Martyrdom is a gift from God to those who die because of their faith. However not all of us are called to die because of our faith but all of us are called to live our faith.

****

Keys for spiritual victory: Knowledge - Hosea 4:6; A life of prayer - Luke 18:1; A person of the Word - Joshua 1:8; Spiritual Mentor – 2 Chr. 20:20

****

When you carry a Bible the devil trembles. When you open it he collapses. When you read it he faints. When you live by it he flees.

****

It is true that underestimating the task at hand can often lead to overestimating our capacity to accomplish it. There are two main things on which Christians can't compromise: faith and family. To these, all things – friendships, and partnerships, gentleman's agreements, name it, must submit.

****

Backsliding is a process of walking in the opposite direction that begins with compromising the Christian moral values. The Christian life is a pilgrimage involving making daily choices. The choices determine the direction and the destiny. Backsliding is not just falling backward, but it is also failing to go forward spiritually. If you are not moving forward in Christ, then you are vulnerable to falling backward. The tragedy is that most backsliders do not readily admit that they are backsliding. The Bible gives serious consequences of backsliding: "For if after they have escaped the pollutions of the world through the knowledge of the Lord and Savior Jesus Christ, they are again entangled therein, and overcome, the latter end is worse with them than the beginning. For it had been better for them not to have known the way of righteousness, than, after they have known it, to turn from the holy commandment delivered unto them. But it is happened unto them according to the true proverb, The dog is turned to his own vomit again; and the sow that was washed to her wallowing in the mire" (2 Peter 2:20-22). In Jeremiah 2:19 God says, "Your own wickedness will correct you, and your backslidings will rebuke you. Know therefore and see that it is an evil and bitter thing that you have forsaken the Lord your God...." Also, Jeremiah 3:22 says, "Return, you backsliding children, and I will heal your backslidings."

****

St. Augustine was born in north Africa, in the town of Tagaste (the present Souk-Ahras in Algeria) that was situated in the north-east highlands of Numidia, some sixty miles from Hippo Regius (the present Annaba [Bone]) the sea-side city. This is where Augustine spent the last 40 years of his life. The people had a taste for wine and women. Augustine was not exceptional. Before he was converted, he lived an immoral life and confessed occasionally buying prostitutes for pleasure. After he was converted, he was walking down the street and one of the girls he used to date approached him calling his name. Augustine ignored the girl and crossed to the other side of the street to avoid her. But the girl followed him yelling that, "Augustine it is me!" Augustine looked straight into her eyes and replied back that, "I know it is you but it is no longer me; I am a new person".

****

Satan is the Tempter but your greatest challenge is not Satan but "you". Sin is when your "will" goes into relationship with the lust of the flesh and the lust of the world. Sin is satisfying the legitimate desires by illegitimate means.

****

Sin attracts demons like garbage attracts rats. No matter how spiritually mature you become you will never outgrow temptation. When you conquer it on one front it attacks you on the other. And the closer you get to God the more Satan will try to tempt you. The flesh (corrupt desires) is the avenue that Satan uses to access the heart of a believer. He is always waiting for a believer to make blunders. Sin weakens the soul from within and allots Satan opportunity to strike when it is strategically viable. This is the general challenge for everyone in this world. The reality is that sin attracts demons like garbage attracts rats.

****

Ephesians 4:22-24 - Leaving your former way of life, you must lay aside that old human nature which, deluded by its lusts, is sinking towards death. You must be made new in mind and spirit, and put on the new nature of God's creating, which shows itself in the just and devout life called for by the truth. Both the putting off and the putting on are equally important.

****

To please God stir your tongue in the right direction. The Bible warns against the lying tongue (Proverbs 25:18). Satan is the father of lairs (John 8:44). The fate of the lairs is everlasting fire (Revelation 21:8). The Bible warns against the proud tongue (Psalms 5:9, 12:3-4). The Bible warns against the swift tongue (Proverbs 18:3, James 1:19). The Bible warns against the cursing tongue (Romans 3:13-14). The Bible says that, "Let no corrupt word proceed out of your mouth, but what is good for necessary edification, that it may impart grace to the hearers" (Ephesians 4:29).

****

Satan has advantage over us because we dwell in the corrupt bodies and in the corrupt world. Our blessed assurance is that Jesus is exalted on high to give repentance and forgiveness of sins. The most crimson sins are removed by the crimson of His blood.

****

In Exodus, Yahweh makes explicit what was understood from the beginning. In spite of our predisposition to sin, there is an intuitive awareness that God's law is right and good. Since we are made in God's image, our souls resonate with commands against idolatry, adultery, thievery, and envy. The Apostle Paul insinuated in his epistle to the Romans chapter one that even pagans understand the right way to live; what about us whose have God's laws written on our hearts? "This is the covenant I will establish with the people of Israel after that time, declares the Lord. I will put my laws in their minds and write them on their hearts. I will be their God, and they will be my people." (Hebrews 8:10; Jeremiah 31:33). God's will on obedience and altar building is bedrock wisdom on righteousness and spirituality.

****

You have history with God. What He did yesterday, He can do today. Such was Jeremiah's experience: in the previous verse memory had brought him to deep humiliation of soul: "My soul continually remembers it and is bowed down within me"; but now this same memory restored him to life and comfort. "But this I call to mind, and therefore I have hope." Like a two-edged sword, his memory first killed his pride with one edge and then slew his despair with the other. As a general principle, if we would exercise our memories more wisely, we might, in our very darkest distress, strike a match that would instantaneously kindle the lamp of comfort.

****

We are most vulnerable to Satan's attacks when we are in our comfort zone. When is the Christian most liable to sleep? Easy roads make sleepy travelers. Another dangerous time is when everything seems to be going pleasantly smooth spiritually. "A Christian did not fall asleep when lions were in the way or when he was wading through the river or when fighting with Apollyon. But when he had climbed halfway up the Hill Difficulty and came to a delightful spot, he sat down and promptly fell asleep." - Alistair Begg

****

The comfort and easy of the world is a great enemy to faith; it loosens the joints of holy zeal and snaps the sinews of sacred courage. "The balloon never rises until the cords are cut; affliction provides this service for believing souls. While the wheat sleeps comfortably in the husk, it is useless to us; it must be threshed out of its resting place before its value can be known" - Alistair Begg.

****

One who sees inaction in action, and action in inaction, is intelligent among men. The tragedy is that at times we spend way too much time looking at what others do when we need to be running to God to find out what He wants us to do. At times God calls us to abstain. The best weapon to fight ambush is retreat; it is wisdom disguised as cowardice.

****

Divided allegiance is wavering faith. Faith is not a feeling because God is bigger than our hurting. God must be the center of your focus. He says "I will deliver you out of the hand of the wicked, and redeem you from the grasp of the ruthless" (Jeremiah 15:21). Notice the personal nature of this promise: "I will." The Lord Jehovah Himself intervenes to deliver and redeem His people. He pledges Himself personally to rescue them. His own arm shall do it, in order that He may have the glory. Not a word is said of any effort of our own that may be needed to assist the Lord. Neither our strength nor our weakness is taken into account, but the lone "I," like the sun in the heavens, shines out resplendent in complete sufficiency. Why then do we allow ourselves to be wounded by calculating our forces and consulting with mere men? God has enough power without borrowing from our puny arm.

Pastor Alistair Begg says that to enjoy peace, our unbelieving thoughts must be stilled, and we must learn that the Lord reigns. There is not even a hint of help from any secondary source. The Lord says nothing of friends and helpers: He undertakes the work alone and feels no need of human arms to aid Him. All our lookings around to companions and relatives are vain; they are broken reeds if we lean upon them— often unwilling when able, and unable when they are willing. Since the promise comes from God alone, it is best for us to wait only on Him; and when we do so, our expectation never fails us.

Who are the wicked, that we should fear them? The Lord will utterly consume them; they are to be pitied rather than feared. As for terrible ones, they are only terrors to those who have no God to turn to, for when the Lord is on our side, whom shall we fear? If we run into sin to please the wicked, we have cause to be alarmed; but if we maintain our integrity, the rage of tyrants will be overruled for our good. When the fish swallowed Jonah, he found him a morsel that he could not digest; and when the world devours the church, it is glad to be rid of it again. In all occasions of fiery trial, let us maintain our souls in patience.

****

One who sees inaction in action, and action in inaction, is intelligent among men. The tragedy is that at times we spend way too much time looking at what others do when we need to be running to God to find out what He wants us to do. At times God calls us to abstain. The best weapon to fight ambush is retreat; it is wisdom disguised as cowardice.

****

Scripture says, "'Be appalled, O heavens, at this, and shudder, be very desolate,' declares the LORD. 'For My people have committed two evils: They have forsaken Me, the fountain of living waters, to hew for themselves cisterns, broken cisterns that can hold no water'" (Jeremiah 2:12,13). C.S. Lewis once said that the problem with evil isn't that our desires are too strong, but that they're too weak; and what he meant by that was that we as people are far too easily pleased. He then gave an illustration of people acting like children who are content to play with mud pies, when they don't know what a day at the beach is like. Or, in the words of John Newton, "Men are like children. Offer a child an apple or a banknote, and he will always take the apple." Therefore, it isn't our desire for satisfaction that displeases God, but rather our attempt at satisfaction in things of far lesser value and satisfaction then Himself.

****

The world is unsafe place to be. Christianity minus worldliness equals to spirituality but Christianity plus worldliness equals to zero. Watch out for Western world madness!

****

Most people pretend to be holier than they are. Others pretend to be fine when deep inside they are hurting. "It is easy in the world to live after the world's opinion; it is easy in solitude to live after our own; but the great man is he who in the midst of the crowd keeps with perfect sweetness the independence of solitude." Ralph Waldo Emerson

****

If you want to succeed in life be a man of value. When you make a one step of trust and integrity, God will accompany you to the next step... Life must be lived by convictions not consensus.

****

Deception is Satan's end time weapon of mass destruction. The effect of deception is delusion. When somebody rejects the truth, the only alternative left is for him to fill the vacuum with lies. Be aware that Satan is not what he makes you think he is, he is what he hides (2 Corinthians 11:14). "There is nothing more deceptive than an obvious fact." ~ Arthur Canan Doyle

****

What kind of heaven do you expect to inherit? The Bible says that "But lay up for yourselves treasures in heaven, where neither moth nor rust doth corrupt, and where thieves do not break through nor steal" (Matthew 6:20). Another appealing scripture says that, "For no one can lay any foundation other than the one already laid, which is Jesus Christ. If anyone builds on this foundation using gold, silver, costly stones, wood, hay or straw, their work will be shown for what it is, because the Day will bring it to light. It will be revealed with fire, and the fire will test the quality of each person's work. If what has been built survives, the builder will receive a reward. If it is burned up, the builder will suffer loss but yet will be saved—even though only as one escaping through the flames" (1 Corinthians 3:11-15). There is heaven to inherit for all those whose foundation is built on Christ. But there are rewards in proportional to our treasures in heaven. Some of the works of the believers which are built on wood and hay will be burnt down and they will suffer loss! Your view of the world changes when you view things from the prospective of the holiness of God.

****

A lady walked into the store to buy a dress and she read the label on it saying "shrink resistance". She asked the shop attendant whether the label implicated that the dress will never shrink. The shop attendant replied that "No, the label simply means the dress does not want to shrink". The same thing applies to believers. We have power to resist sin but it does not mean we do not sin; it means we do not intend to sin.

****

We all worry about what people will think of us (and what we will think of ourselves) if we don't do as well as we should. That's a very human thing. In the real world, our good works are constantly subjected to public scrutiny and Satan's attacks. "A believer never yet had a virtue or a grace that was not the target for hellish bullets: whether it was bright and sparkling hope, or warm and fervent love, or all-enduring patience, or zeal flaming like coals of fire, the old enemy of everything that is good has tried to destroy it. The only reason why anything virtuous or lovely survives in us is this: "The Lord is there (JEHOVAH SHAMMAH)" ~ Alistair Begg

****

2 Corinthians 6:1-6: "As God's co-workers we urge you not to receive God's grace in vain. For he says, "In the time of my favor I heard you, and in the day of salvation I helped you." I tell you, now is the time of God's favor; now is the day of salvation. We put no stumbling block in anyone's path, so that our ministry will not be discredited. 4 Rather, as servants of God we commend ourselves in every way: in great endurance; in troubles, hardships and distresses; in beatings, imprisonments and riots; in hard work, sleepless nights and hunger; in

purity, understanding, patience and kindness; in the Holy Spirit and in sincere love". His first request is not to receive God's grace in vain by rejecting him as God's ambassador (vv. 1-2). There are potentially good reasons for a Church to reject an itinerant evangelist like Paul. Traveling preachers were constantly faced with the temptation to adapt their life and message to what the world expected in order to gain acceptance. Paul, however, emphatically denies being seduced in this fashion (vv. 3-4), and his life of adversity bears witness to his resistance (vv. 4-5, 8-10).

Cor. 6:1-13 - Don't receive God's Grace in Vain. By refusing to hear the admonition of Paul, the Corinthians were in danger of rejecting the grace offered to them. They were choosing comfort over conviction, rhetoric over repentance, and wealth over wisdom. They placed more value in immediate appearances than eternal priorities. The general gist of what I gained from this scripture is that we can't intentionally behave in the manner that contradicts the commitment to live a life for God regardless of the difficulties life or people present. To do so will render receiving God's grace in vain. If we act like we don't know Christ and the power of the Holy Spirit to transform our lives, it nullifies, in the minds of onlookers, the life of Christ we received; we make Him a mockery!

****

The seventy returned with joy, saying, "Lord, even the demons are subject to us in Your name." And He said to them, "I beheld Satan fall from heaven like lightning" (Luke 10:18). The original translation is "I perceive Satan falling from heaven." Heaven in this scripture is not the dwelling throne of God but the third heavens where Satan rules. He is called the prince of the air (Ephesians 2:2). Air is something that surrounds us, we are completely immersed in it; we can't get away from it. Satan's influence in the corrupt world is around us. The corruption of sin you see everywhere is directly linked to Satan. You can't get completely away from it because it surrounds us as if it was air. Satan is the Prince (or ruler) of the "air" because he controls the corrupt system of the world. There is no natural power that can overcome Satan. Jesus defeated Satan and gave us power over Satan. In the above scripture,

Jesus perceived the power structure of Satan crumbling from its power base (air) in form of lightening.

****

Satan will direct his energies against the very virtue for which you are most famous. Just because you have walked consistently with integrity it does not mean that you are not vulnerable. Never brag that no one can challenge your integrity. "If you have to this point been a firm believer, your faith will soon be attacked; if you have been meek like Moses, expect to be tempted to speak unadvisedly with your lips. The birds will peck at your ripest fruit, and the wild boar will dash his tusks at your choicest vines" ~ Alistair Begg

****

David and Solomon knew this law concerning kings: "He must not take many wives, or his heart will be led astray. He must not accumulate large amounts of silver and gold" (Deuteronomy 17:17). But David had many wives and Solomon accumulated concubines on himself and surplus gold. Success did not weaken them but indulgence weakened them. Beyond the examples in Scripture of many people who are warped and destroyed by greed, and its warnings against idolatry, the Bible also lists various dangers of becoming centered on money and possessions. Warning: Don't dismiss this as negativism. On the contrary, if we understand the dangers of materialism, it will help liberate us to experience the joys of Christ-centered stewardship. When we shift from wanting enough stuff to wanting things in excesses, it is a reflection of greed and lustful desires of the flesh. Materialism is a broken cistern that can't hold water. The spirit of materialism will never be satisfied; the more they get, the more they want. Materialism brings us unhappiness and anxiety. Materialism ends in futility.

****

Brother Nsubuga posted an article implicating the biased reporting by the media against the pastors of the Pentecostal movement. My book called "The New Generation of Worshipers" addresses your point Brother Nsubuga. It is true that the media is dominated by liberals who are anxiously and maliciously set to tarnish the reputation of the born again believers. Given the fact, the Pentecost movement has its grey hairs in particular the doctrine of prosperity and the independent structures of the Churches (without proper accountability). These irregularities have become open windows for the quacks (fake preachers/ self seekers) to come in. These windows must be closed. Not to mention that some pastors have the attitudes of the celebrities; they delight whenever their names flash on the front pages of our newspapers. I wish all pastors can read this book. It is very detailed regarding the order of the ordained ministers/laity.

****

The Book of Acts gives an illustrative structure of the early Church of the 1ˢᵗ century. The Christians worked as a community but each showed, in their own way, the relentless and powerful influence of the message of Jesus Christ. They shared everything in common. They worked on building a wall of unity against the adversary. Christians need to be armed with the same attitude today. They need to be always ready, always clothed with the righteousness of Jesus Christ, always wearing the armor of God, functioning as one body of Christ until the final trumpet blast that will gather us together with our LORD.

****

The Savior was "a man of sorrows," but every thoughtful mind has discovered the fact that down deep in His innermost soul He carried an inexhaustible treasury of refined and heavenly joy. He was announced as the Prince of peace. His peace will finally be realized at His Second Coming. As per now His peace does not mean the absence of trials but His presence in midst of trials. He calls us to suffer for His name's sake. If you are suffering, reflect on these questions: Is it because of your own bad decisions? Is it because of your circumstances? Are you suffering for righteousness' sake or is your suffering self-inflicted? Either way God loves you unconditionally. Turn your eyes and focus to Jesus; He will turn things around for you to be in your favor.

****

There are many specific ways of sinning. These all fall generally under two ways; the sins of commission and the sins of omission. All sins fall under one or the other. The first, sins of commission, is a category of sin describing the things we did and shouldn't have. I committed (commission) a sin when I lied and I shouldn't have. The second, sins of omission, are the category that encompasses the sins of not doing what we should have. We don't think as much about the sin of omission even though it is as pernicious and destructive as anything we could commit. For example resolving that you should have testified because you knew he was innocent, but you didn't out of fear. When we know the right thing to do and don't, that's a sin. A sin unto death is the unrepentant spirit; it is deliberately continuing in sin in spite of the conviction. It is the sin that you continue loving to do.

****

Make no friendship with the powers of darkness. Garbage in, garbage out. We dwell in the corrupt world but it is not an excuse to indulge in sin. Remember that all the water in the ocean could never sink a ship unless it gets inside. The life of purity is the narrow way lived at the center rather than at the edge of the street. The main things are the plain things and the plain things the plain things.

****

An African proverb says it is easier to control a herd of cows than one human being. At his best, man is the noblest of all animals; separated from law and justice he is left to the Jungle Law. The Jungle Law is a law without exceptions. Only the strong survives. Animals are following it; human societies at times follow it. It is the law of the beast, and it knows neither reason nor compassion. The truth is that man was at his best way back in the Garden of Eden before the fall. Man needs to be reconnected to the divine in order to be at his best. That is what is called regeneration or to be born again. A regenerated person is of the new nature with God (spirit). His spirit is rejuvenated by the Spirit of Christ. He is guided and controlled by Spirit of God. He has affection for God's statutes and ordinances.

****

Living through a facade puts an incredible burden on your emotional well-being. Looking at life from our own limited view is like seeing the comic strip one frame at a time. Sometimes events in life may look disappointing in particular when your misery is due to other people's negligence. One thing you can't hide - is when you're crippled inside. But never let people dictate your mood. "If you want to get annoyed with people you will be forever an angry man!" The Bible says that, "For we wrestle not against flesh and blood, but against principalities, against powers, against the rulers of the darkness of this world, against spiritual wickedness in heavenly places" (Ephesians 6:12).

****

Emotion is the highway of the devil. Emotions can be positive and negative. For example excitement, crying, stress and etc. Stress may also be a result into passive aggressive behavior - out of sullenness or deliberate or repeated failures in life. We should own our failures gracefully with awareness that we are all mortal and we are not exempted from flaws. C.S. Lewis once said that the problem with evil isn't that our desires are too strong, but that they're too weak; and what he meant by that was that people are far too easily swayed emotionally.

****

How do you separate the voice of God from other voices? In order for something to be of God it must not be in contradiction to the written Scriptures. The voice of God is always convicting rather than condemning. It is that soft voice that yearns to bring you back into righteousness in case of flaw. Jesus said that, "I didn't come to condemn the world, but to save it" (John 3:17). Before our Savior came to save us, there was so much judgment and condemnation by the religious leaders. Jesus came to change a few things to open the eyes of the blind and to blind those that claim to have already seen the truth without His ability. If the world was without sin (condemnation), Jesus would have never been needed to save us. We would have been perfect already.

****

Today I witnessed for the first time to an old lady at my work place. She insinuated that she is a strong Christian but she does not believe in Church fellow-shipping. I told her that attending Church is not an optional; it is an instruction given in the Scriptures to be obeyed (Hebrews 10:25). I explained to her that fellow-shipping and worshiping God here (in this world) is a rehearsal of the endless and timeless fellow-shipping and worshiping in heaven. Those who are not part of the rehearsal here on earth may as well miss it in heaven (eternally). "Do more than belong: participate." Participation is a generic or umbrella term covering a range of activities during Church fellowship like serving, spiritual growth, sharing and etc.

****

Homosexuality is equally a sin as witchcraft, adultery, fornication and etc. People choose the lifestyle fitting to satisfy the lust of their flesh. Jesus said that people are not saved because they chose to love darkness (immorality) than light (John 3:19). Light is the symbol of truth. Paul lamented that "And even if our gospel is veiled, it is veiled to those who are perishing. The god of this age has blinded the minds of unbelievers, so that they cannot see the light of the gospel of the glory of Christ, who is the image of God" (2 Cor. 3-4). We (believers) are privileged to know the truth, not only by the reason, but also by the heart. Those whose minds are blinded by the god of this world (Satan) relentlessly suppress the truth in vain. "Truth is incontrovertible, malice may attack it and ignorance may deride it, but, in the end, there it is" ~ Sir Winston Churchill

****

A believer is conscious of his own failures but he must also know where his gain is. Jesus said that "If anyone comes to me and does not hate father and mother, wife and children, brothers and sisters--yes, even their own life--such a person cannot be my disciple" (Luke 14:26). Jesus used a hyperbole (exaggerated figure of speech) meaning that the love for those whom we care about most must be less than the love for Christ. The love we have for the most important things in this world should appear to be hate compared to the love we have for God. This is what it means to love the Lord your God with all your heart and with all your soul and with all your strength and with all your mind (Luke 10:27). In order for Jesus Christ to be Lord, He must be the object of our supreme devotion.

****

"Every man is more willing to reward injury than benefit, for gratitude is a burden whilst revenge is for pleasure" We (believers) are called to return good for evil. At least we are aware of our losses but also where our gain is.

****

Life is like a swinging pendulum. We have each heard some flash-in-the-pan success stories; tales of people and businesses that skyrocket to fame and fortune, only to plummet back into the pit of nothingness just as quickly as they had emerged from it. Don't stay up there and forget that you could come down. Time is fleeting, and you don't want to miss a thing, but life can become juicy and bitter as well. That is why couples make vows to stay together in good times and bad times. Even Jesus marries us for good and for worse. He does not abandon us in times of trouble. God's covenant with man is forever because God is a faithful partner. God allows us to go through the trials of life just to test our patience and love for Him. Squeezing moments should therefore increase our dependence on God rather than squeezing our faith to bleakness. Remember that winners never quit and quitters never win. Only he who keeps his eye fixed on the far horizon will find his right road!

****

The past weeks have been emotional and exhausting to some. The president of Uganda signed the laws against mini-skirts, pornography and homosexuals. As for those who are playing by the rules they have nothing to worry; they are celebrating. As much as the horizon looks good, rules can at best regulate rather than eliminate evil. Religion without Christ cannot help either. When religion is reduced to fabrications to serve human interests, it invariably moves toward manipulation, bureaucratic control, and complexity. It is absolutely the knowledge of God that is experienced through our intimate relationship with Jesus Christ that can put a remarkable mark on the universe. We need to be reminded that "No one has ever seen God, but the one and only Son, who is himself God and is in closest relationship with the Father, has made him known" (John 1:18). It is important to have your internal appraisal and be honest about your status.

****

Mainstream culture is saturated with pornography. According to Josh McDowell, one in four internet searches is for porn and half of American men are addicted to it. But if you think that means everyone approves of it, think again. A recent survey found that the vast majority of Americans think watching porn is morally objectionable—even those who do it. But without Christian morality, they have trouble explaining why. Some like psychotherapist John Woods describes children and teens he's treated as having a disease that disrupts their lives, even those with convictions for possessing child porn. Others treat porn as a manifestation of sexism. John Stonestreet says that, "But both of these secular objections miss the deeper problem with porn: it turns people into objects and dehumanizes everyone involved. Christians must communicate this fact if we hope to de-saturate our porn-saturated culture."

****

Karl Marx insinuated that Religion is the opium of the people. False religions are equally seductive. They barefaced make a lie appear to be a truth; they make tinsel look so much like gold. Defiant religiosity rejects spiritual transformation. Remember that a chicken will never fly like an eagle. "True contemplation is not a psychological trick but a theological grace" ~ THOMAS MERTON

****

Telling the truth is good and it sets you free....but it also creates enmity because it unveils foes. Never be afraid because at times it is easier to handle foes than hypocrite friends. Hypocrites are self made enemies. They are compared to a spider. A spider's web emerges all from the creature itself. The bee gathers her wax from flowers; the spider doesn't, but still she spins her material to great length. In the same way hypocrites find the reason to hate from themselves in spite of your generosity. They are allergic to the truth because their trust and hope is not in God but from within themselves; their anchor was forged on their own anvil, and their rope twisted by their own hands. They rest upon their own foundation and carve out the pillars from their own house, scorning the thought of being debtors to the sovereign grace of God.

****

Some believers think that the book Revelation is scaring to read because of its prophetic message of the end time catastrophe. There is no need to dread or be intimidated by the future for in a brief moment we will be in it; let's make every attempt, take those risks needed, do all it takes to make sure when we get there we have the muscle and thought power to withstand whatever is in there. Satan does not want people to read the book of Revelation because it predicts his fate in future.

****

The Bible says that, "For the wrath of God is revealed from heaven against all ungodliness and unrighteousness of men, who hold the truth in unrighteousness" (Romans 1:18). This is the Divine and justified wrath targeting unrighteousness. The Law was given not to make man righteous but to reveal the unrighteousness of man before the Holy God. In the Old Testament there are over 25 offences which were subjected to capital punishment (death). In the New Testament there is only one case of treason and that is rejecting the Lordship of Jesus Christ. How long He laid siege to our hearts! How often He sent us terms of surrender, but we barred our gates and built our walls against Him. If that is you, it is not too late to surrender. Jesus took on Himself the justice of God against all of your unrighteousness so that you might be saved from the wrath of God towards all unrighteousness.

****

Our capacity for self-deception is so great that God must resort to what Lewis once called a "severe mercy" to overcome it. All it takes is one bad day to reduce the sanest man alive to lunacy. Developing your feelings vocabulary is a way to experience more of the wonderful person you are becoming. Dense and crooked people should never lead you into stupid actions. Years ago, Gandhi said that the an-eye-for-an-eye policy would leave us all blind. Neither should you let people make you act out of character nor allow their nasty attitudes make you cry. If a person can make you cry they will keep you in tears because their objective is to upset you and drive you crazy. The people surrounding you are never going to be a solution to your predicaments. The old adage is true: "Those that mind don't matter and those that matter don't mind."

****

Psychology has identified two main traits that seem to produce an immensely broad range of benefits to man: self-control and intelligence. Despite many decades of trying, psychology has not found much one can do to produce lasting increases in intelligence. Self-control can be encouraged and strengthened. Self Control is dominance over all desires. Lacking in Self-control is the major cause of all negative behaviors.

****

All the water in the ocean could never sink a ship unless it gets inside.... likewise all the pressure of life can never hurt you unless you let it in.... difficulties in your life do not come to destroy you but to help you to realize your hidden potentials and power. Let the difficulties know that you too are difficult.

****

Humankinds' failure to repent and return to God leads to the multiplication of their problems. Yes, there is no doubt that we cannot by ourselves escape the pressure and the dark shadows of life but we can return to our Savior and have our pressure and the dark shadows of our lives conquered by His spiritual strength. "God is my strength and power: and he maketh my way perfect" (2 Samuel 22:33).

****

Waiting for God is the huddle in the lives of all believers. Waiting for God becomes even more difficult after God has revealed His promise to you.

****

Whenever a person destroys your reputation, he or she steals the most valuable item from you. Never waste your time trying to establish your reputation because it is God's duty to do it. David said that "He only is my rock and my salvation; he is my defense; I shall not be greatly moved" (Psalm 62:2). He meant that God is his defense. God defends His own. We are accountable to God, and His protection is our inheritance.

****

Living through a facade puts an incredible burden on your emotional well-being. Regardless of one's status, we are all accountable to God regardless of our beliefs. Every day in life adds a page of history that you will be accountable for. Accountability means focusing on the creator of life by observing His statutes. Always walk the path of truth and honor. Stand firm in your faith in Christ, and refuse to be corrupted

****

Joseph had a dream that one day he will be someone....he never saw the pit, the slavery, the false accusations or the jail, but those were challenges that made his dream come true. All the challenges you are going through every day, will not deter you but will make you reach your dreams, visions and calling. Don't lose hope trust in God for he will never forsake you; His promises are YES & AMEN.

****

God builds a hedge of protection around His elects as long as they abide in His Word. Trespassing is walking in disobedience to the Word of God and making yourself vulnerable to the evils of the world. All of us can stumble but a Christian does not rejoice in his or her corrupt ways but repents. You will never overcome a habit that you defend. "The chains of habit are generally too small to be felt until they are too strong to be broken." ~ Samuel Johnson

****

To conquer oneself is the best and noblest victory; to be vanquished by one's own nature is the worst and most ignoble defeat ~ Plato

****

Christians across the world grapple with the modern understanding of mental illness. Science suggests several biological disorders including the chemical imbalances. The impetus behind the use of the words "chemical imbalance" is good however, saying "you've got a chemical imbalance" does not go far enough and, paradoxically, can often take us too far in the wrong direction. It is helpful to not only understand what these imbalances are and how medication might address them, but also to challenge a point of view that reduces mental illness to a mere malfunction of biology. Assigning mental illness solely to such imbalances is inadequate firstly because it under-appreciates the complexity of neurobiology. For example, we know very well that people with depression have lower serotonin levels (most potently demonstrated in studying the brains of those who have committed suicide.) When dealing with even more complex illnesses like bipolar disorder (which responds to a wide range of medications that are also effective for epilepsy) or schizophrenia (which involves a greater variety of neurochemical pathways), it is clear that the language of "chemical imbalance" is simply a starting point. Christian suggest broader causes including immoral behaviors like using drugs and demonic possession as influencing factors for mental sickness.

****

A lie told is easily forgotten; tell the truth because it's the easiest thing to remember.

****

Shallow understanding from people of good will is more frustrating than absolute misunderstanding from people of ill-will ~ ML King.

****

Fallen flowers can't grow back on the tree, but if the root is strong new flowers certainly can. Nothing is permanent in this world, not even our troubles and challenges. "Everything that we see is a shadow cast by that which we do not see" ~ Martin Luther King, Jr.

****

Your living is determined not so much by what life brings to you as by the attitude you bring to life; not so much by what happens to you as by the way your mind looks at what happens ~ Kahlil Gibran

****

The burden of Egypt: Behold, the LORD rides on a swift cloud, and shall come into Egypt: and the idols of Egypt shall be moved at his presence, and the heart of Egypt shall melt in the middle of it. And I will set the Egyptians against the Egyptians: and they shall fight every one against his brother, and every one against his neighbor; city against city, and kingdom against kingdom. And the spirit of Egypt shall fail in the middle thereof; and I will destroy the counsel thereof: and they shall seek to the idols, and to the charmers, and to them that have familiar spirits, and to the wizards (Isaiah 19:1-3).

May Defending the Faith (Apologetics)

Apologetic is the branch of Christianity that deals with the defense and establishment of the Christian faith. God is our defense but we are called to defend what was delivered to us in form of scripture. The fierce contest of the end times is not between God and Satan but it is between the truth and the deception of Satan and the world. Even some confessing Christians are being influenced by the world views. Apologetic is something every true believer should be involved in even on a small scale. The Bible says that, "But sanctify Christ as Lord in your hearts, always being ready to make a defense to everyone who asks you to give an account for the hope that is in you, yet with gentleness and reverence" (1 Peter 3:15).

We get the truth from the written Scriptures. Before I open my Bible to minister to you I must be convinced that you believe that the Bible is not just one of many books but it is the only book written by God. The book of the Christians is the Bible. The books of the Bible contain prose, poetry, prophecy, history, type, antitype, sign, symbol, miracle, parable, biography, philosophy, description, travel, exploration, legislation, invitation, exhortation, denunciation, argumentation, commendation, indignation, prayers, blessings, curses, oration, consolation, fierce invective, impassioned appeal, and coolest and calmest logic, letters, hymns, pastorals, romance, tragedy and jubilee, sobbing sighs and shouts of joy, sermons, lyrics, proverbs, epigrams and axioms.

The Bible is a collection of 66 books written by 40 different authors, on three different continents, in three different languages, over a period of 1500 years. Yet all 66 books have a marvelous unity. 40 men have never written with such unity and agreement. The Bible has proven itself to be from God (Scientifically, Archaeologically, Historically, etc.).

Is the Bible authentic? To check if something is Authentic you have to look back at the historical documentation. Like, "Are the writings of Plato authentic?" Plato wrote from 427-347 B.C. Many would argue that "Yes indeed they are authentic." Because there are seven manuscripts, which are very similar, that date back to 900 A.D. Those are old and most people would have no problem believing his writings are authentic. Now take the writings of the Bible. What are the historical documentations? The New Testament was written from 40-100 A.D. and the earliest manuscripts to be uncovered are around 125 A.D., some think earlier. There are also close to 30,000 manuscripts that are 99.5% accurate to each other. Compare that to Plato's writings of which the oldest manuscripts found are 1200 years from the time it was originally written and there are only 7 available to check authenticity with. Is the Bible Authentic? Much more than Plato, Caesar's "Gallic Wars" (10 Greek manuscripts, the earliest 950 years after the original), the "Annals" of Tacitus (2 manuscripts, the earliest 950 years after the original), Pliny the Younger's "History" (7 manuscripts; 750 years elapsed); Thucydides' "History" (8 manuscripts; 1,300 years elapsed); Herodotus' "History" (8 manuscripts; 1,300 years elapsed); Sophocles (193 manuscripts; 1,400 years); Euripides (9 manuscripts; 1,500 years); and Aristotle (49 manuscripts; 1,400 years).

Furthermore, archaeology is a powerful witness to the accuracy of The New Testament documents. Repeatedly, comprehensive archaeological fieldwork and careful biblical interpretation affirm the authenticity and reliability of the Bible. In fact if it weren't a book of religion and it had only recently discovered by archaeologists, it would be proclaimed the most significant find in all history. For its details as to family lines, lands of occupation, life spans, and events should provide positive proof to even the most skeptical observers that its accounts are genuine and accurate, because no one would go into such minute detail if they were simply creating a forged document. Oh, they could if they wished, but that would require a high level of sophistication and some very dark motives. The Bible records predictions of events that could not be known nor predicted by chance or common sense. For example, the Book of Daniel (written before 530 B.C.) accurately predicts the progression of kingdoms from Babylon through Median and Persian empires to the further persecution and suffering of the Jews under Antiochus IV Epiphanes with his desecration of the temple, his untimely death, and freedom for the Jews under Judas Maccabeus (165 B.C.). It is statistically preposterous that any or all of the Bible's specific, detailed prophecies could have been fulfilled through chance, good guessing, or deliberate deceit.

The God of scriptures is revealed in the Bible. The true understanding of God comes from only one source – God's revelation to mankind, the Bible. Unfortunately, the culture of today is anti-truth (rejection of truth). We have exchanged the truth with lies. We have no moral compass because we have rejected the absolute truth. All immoralities like homosexuality, pornography, abortion and etc, are traced back to this point of departure from truth.

One of the defining features of our post-Christian culture is the embrace of what we might call "philosophical relativism." The prevailing view today is that there are no absolute truths. There is only "my truth" and "your truth," but there are no "true truths," to borrow Francis Schaeffer's language. The Scriptures expose the absurdity and self-defeating nature of denying absolute truth, and also point us toward the One who is the Way, the Truth, and the Life (John 14:6).

According to humanism, there is no absolute truth; truth is attained only in a subject, and the truth of personality only in a person rather than in a deity. One of the defining features of our post-Christian culture is the embrace of what we might call "philosophical relativism." The prevailing view today is that there are no absolute truths. There is only "my truth" and "your truth," but there are no "true truths," to borrow Francis Schaeffer's language. The Scriptures expose the absurdity and self-defeating nature of denying absolute truth, and also point us toward the One who is the Way, the Truth, and the Life.

Relativism says that the truth depends on individual preferences. Pragmatism says whatever works is the truth. Mysticism says that the intuition is the truth. Pluralism says that each one has a piece of the truth. Skepticism says no one can know the truth. Humanism says that man is the measure of the truth. Secularism says that the present world is the truth. Hedonism says that feeling is the truth. Positivism says that whatever man confesses is the truth. The reality is that God is the measure of the truth. There is the Moral God and Jesus the absolute truth to know God. Truth is divine and came from heaven to the earth to show us God. There is no truth outside Christ. Truth is the expression of God; it is what God says it is. I want to discuss the reception of truth. Truth is not something that can be gleaned from a book; it can be revealed only by God and believed by receiving Christ. Truth is known by intimate relationship. How you relate to the truth determines your eternal destiny. *(Portions of the above teachings are taken from my books The Miracle at P called "The Spirit is the Crown of the Heart")*

Scroll through my sermons on apologetics:

We live in a very complicated universe. We can memorize the physical features (mountains, lakes, rivers and etc.) which are in our neighborhood or the biggest ones taught in classes but no one can know all of them (big/small) existing worldwide. When many of us grew up, there were nine planets in the Solar System. It was like a fixed point in our brains. As kids, memorizing this list was an early rite of passage of nerd pride: Mercury, Venus, Earth, Mars, Jupiter, Saturn, Uranus, Neptune and Pluto. Today, astronomy discovered that there more than 900 planets not yet discovered. An exoplanet or extrasolar planet is a planet that does not orbit Earth's Sun and instead orbits a different star stellar remnants or brown dwarf. Over 1800 exoplanets have been discovered (1822 planets in 1137 planetery systems including 467 multiple planetary systems as of 12 September 2014). There are also free floating planets, not orbiting any star, which tend to be considered separately, especially if they are free floating gas giants gas, in which case they are often countedas low-mass brown dwarfs. Complicated as it is, the universe is not eternal but God the creator of the universe is eternal.

****

Recently we were witnesses to an eclipse. It is believed that the last time it happened was some 500 hundred years ago. It is not likely to happen again in less than 150 years. It is one of the many wonders of the world. The earth is immense in size, about 8,000 miles in diameter, with a mass calculated at roughly 6.6 x 1,021 tons. The earth is on average 93 million miles from the sun. According to science, as the earth moves farther from the sun in its orbit, the sun's gravitational force on the earth decreases. Gravitational force is inversely proportional to the radius. If the earth traveled much faster in its 584-million-mile-long journey around the sun, its orbit would become larger and it would move farther away from the sun. If it moved too far from the narrow habitable zone, all life would cease to exist on earth. If it traveled slightly slower in its orbit, the earth would move closer to the sun, and if it moved too close, all life would likewise perish. The earth's 365-days, 6-hours, 49-minutes and 9.54-seconds trip around the sun (the sidereal year) is consistent to over a thousandth of a second! Certainly, the earth is not eternal, it will one way or another come to an end. But we worship an eternal God that created the universe and in His wisdom sustains it in right place in space without visible poles.

****

Science says that this universe is expanding. The Bible says that it is God that expands the earth (Isaiah 40:22). It takes faith to believe the very creator of the universe is still working on it to sustain it and to transform it. Everything is subject to change and transformation except the eternal God and His infallible Word. The Bible is not a science book, but a love letter from God to His creation. It is concerned with "why" we are here, and not so much the "how" processes involved. That is why it is great we have science. Science explains the "how" and God explains the "why."

****

The UN Climate Summit 2014 was held this week in New York. UN Secretary-General Ban Ki-moon has invited world leaders, from government, finance, business, and civil society to Climate Summit 2014 this 23 September to galvanize and catalyze climate action. He insinuated that in spite of the threat there is a growing recognition that affordable, scalable solutions are available now that we are able to leapfrog to cleaner, more resilient economies. "There is a sense that change is in the air." But recent survey projects that it is not true that it is warmer now than it has been for thousands of years ago. "The warming we have seen in the late-20th century is not unprecedented," says reader Steve Foster. "There was another peak temperature between 950-1050 AD. However, many people still believe there are not CYCLES."

A new paper looking at the climate of the past two thousand years, published in the journal "Climate of the Past," shows that temperatures during the Medieval Warm Period were higher than today's temperatures. As it turns out, all those atmospheric greenhouse gases that Al Gore and all the other global warming hoaxers have long claimed are overheating and destroying our planet are actually cooling it, based on the latest evidence. The Global warming is a crusade of the World Order Agenda intended to prepare the world for a One World Government. Although we are supposed to be good stewards of this earth, we are not called to fix it because none of us other than God can sustain this universe. We cannot change the earth just as we cannot change day and night. Instead of fighting an anonymous enemy, the United nation should embark on eradicating evil that is apparent on the earth, like the Islamic fanatics chopping off people's heads before the cameras!

****

A humanist made this shocking statement: "It has become appallingly obvious that our technology has exceeded our humanity." Really? Computers can never replace the human brains, for it is humans that created them. Computers can only support man, and hence cannot replace human intelligence. Computers do what we want, and a man does what is needed in the present circumstances; a computer has no mind of its own, man uses computer to get what it wants. Computers are made because of the intelligence humanity possessed and thus they are made to lack the creativity of humanity. Since the brain has 100-trillion-synapses, we can safely say that the average brain can hold about 100 million megabytes of memory! So far, we have never heard of anybody's brain being "overloaded" because it has ran out of memory. So it seems as if, the human brain has no limit as to how much memory it can hold. A computer is a machine but man is a living soul created in the very image of God. "Heaven is not the imitation of earth but the earth is the imitation of heaven."

****

The human brain is the most sophisticated organ. The brain is made up of approximately 100 billion microscopic cells called neurons. They communicate to each other using chemical and electronic sparks. The message zooms from your feet to your brain at the speed of 150 miles per hour; then from your hands to your brain at the speed of 200 miles per hour. We can react to danger in less than a second. Given the fact we stumble all the times because of the influence of our corrupt nature. The Bible says that we need the WORD of God as illuminating light to keep us from stumbling (Psalms 119:105).

****

Scientists are telling us that the Arctic is spinning out of control. As the planet warms, the ice melts, yet, Shell and other oil companies move in unrestrained to drill more oil, which is more likely to warm the planet and melts the ice. If the scientists' discovery was true, then the monopoly acts of the drilling companies should be considered as a vicious circle, insanity and greed at its very worst that must be stopped. Otherwise sincere people see a hidden agenda regarding the Global Warming Theory!

****

During the initial space flights, NASA discovered that biro pens didn't work under zero gravity conditions. Nasa resolved to invent a pen that would work under zero gravity conditions; due to the pressurized ink inside, it would work under sub zero conditions, underwater, on glass and virtually any surface known to man. NASA spent 6 years and $2 million in designing the desired pen suitable for use in space. The way to space is extremely expensive but still affordable to the civilized world. But the way to the heaven of heavens (to the Father) is NOT just too expensive but it is impossible for any man to afford. It is affordable only to the divine. That is why God became man (put on human flesh) in order to pay the same bills on our behalf to get us there.

****

The word "fool" means insane or seer madness. It is spiritually used in reference to a heathen: "A fool says in his heart, "There is no God". They are corrupt, their deeds are vile; there is no one who does good" (Psalms 14:1). Atheism isn't just the denial of any and all gods; it is basically the absence of belief in God. God loves repented sinners but hates sinners who refuse to repent their sins by surrendering their hearts to Jesus Christ. "The arrogant cannot stand in your presence. You hate all who do wrong; you destroy those who tell lies. The bloodthirsty and deceitful you, Lord, detest" (Psalms 5:5-6). God will certainly condemn sinners because of their sins (John 3:16-17). The standard of God's judgment is absolute perfectness that cannot be merited by any human being. God alone is absolutely perfect. By His grace He declares us (believers) to be perfect through Jesus Christ. Jesus was condemned for all of our sins (past, present/future). We cannot be condemned again for the same sins.

****

Atheists, especially those of the "new atheism" variety, are hesitant to put too much stock in any experiential data, and thus they shun any feelings that would indicate that there's something supernatural behind the universe, relying only on what we can observe and prove through science instead. This view is useful to a certain extent: When people decide what's true and what's false based solely on feelings and emotional experiences, they can end up with all sorts of crazy beliefs. Certainly it's good to take the subjective, non-provable aspects of the human experience and balance them with objective, verifiable data. But that view, too, can be taken too far. The universe, like a Shakespearean sonnet, is not meant to be seen through an analysis of its components alone, and to do so would be to miss all of its poetic beauty.

****

An atheist is a person who does not believe in the existence God. In actual fact there is no true atheist because God has revealed Himself to all mankind without exception (Rom. 2:11). God has given man an innate knowledge of Him. None lacks a knowledge of God. Innate knowledge of God is a gift of God to all men. Through it, He has given all an opportunity to know Him. Much of our innate knowledge of God comes through reason, a gift God has given only to man among the creatures. Then God has revealed Himself through His creation. Nature reveals the wisdom of the supernatural designer. Certainly, God has revealed Himself directly through His Word and His Son. Correspondingly, there are different levels of knowing God: bare knowledge of the existence of God, which is attained from our innate knowledge of God; inferred knowledge of our Creator's attributes, which is gleaned from God's revelation through His creation; objective knowledge of His attributes and His plan for the creation, which is learned from the revelation of Himself in the Bible; personal knowledge of Him, which can be gained through Jesus Christ (Hebrews 1:1-3). The knowledge of God is the most important kind of intelligence that we can seek. He is our Creator. It is obvious that those who have an understanding of their Creator and who are acquainted with His purpose and will, from the Creator's point of view, live more wisely here on earth and live in His presence eternally.

****

The unwarranted and puerile vituperation of the ATHIESTS baffles me. You don't have to see God in order to acknowledge His existence. Everything that we see is a shadow cast by that which we do not see. I pay for the doctor's bill, even when I cannot read his prescription. I believe in the sun, even when it is not shining. I believe in love, even when I am alone and I believe in God, even when He's silent. The atheists ridicule faith yet it takes more faith not to believe in God than believing. Atheists choose to embrace the deception of evolution. They ignore the fact that a lizard will never be a crocodile no matter how much you feed it. A young boy asked his mother the origin of the human race. His mother replied that we all came from Adam and Eva. The young boy then asked her why his teacher said that we came from monkeys. The mother replied that your teacher was telling the true story of his family tree.

****

I have no problem with atheists or agnostics. I'm perfectly fine if you have real, tangible and pragmatic reasons not to believe in God. My problem is when this same agnostics or atheist people suddenly believe in witchcraft, mysticism and etc., which belong to some dark occultist group, and visit mediums or sorcerers and those sorts of things. I think that is 'agnostic hypocrisy'! So you can believe in tiny spirits roaming about but not in an all powerful spirit. Oh well. Without trying to sound scientific, whatever created or fashioned humans placed in us an urge to want to believe in something. What you chose to believe in is entirely up to you but your believing or not believing cannot create reality. The truth remains true regardless of one's belief.

****

One writer said that "A theologian is like a black man in a dark looking for a black cat that isn't there and he finds it". I want to say that Christianity is not a blind belief. As Albert Einthien said "Blind belief in authority is the greatest enemy of truth." Christianity advocates for absolute truth, and engages reasoning and faith. Extraordinary claims require extraordinary evidence. Christianity provides evidences of what to believe and how to believe. The burden is not on the Christians to prove that there is God the creator of the universe because the evidence is apparent. The burden is on the atheists to prove that there is no God, no creator, everything we see happened by chance! Christianity states that the fear of God is the beginning of wisdom. Christianity begins with believing. The atheists begin with doubt. Basically, to them doubt is the beginning of wisdom, but to us (believers) faith in God is the beginning of wisdom and of course the end of doubt.

****

These are some of the challenges involved in reaching Millennials (young adults aged roughly 18 to 33) for Christ. While 55 percent of Baby Boomers say they're religious, only 36 percent of Millennials do. "Today," University of Virginia sociologist W. Bradford Wilcox notes, "fully 29 percent of Millennials consider themselves religiously unaffiliated, a record postwar high. They are also much less likely to describe themselves as 'religious' compared with earlier generations of Americans."

Well, how is this rising generation connecting to the Bible? In a word, poorly. According to a new study by the Barna Group, "Non-Christian Millennials hold ambivalent and sometimes extremely negative views about the Bible." How negative? The first thing to know is that a full 62 percent of non-Christian Millennials have never even read the Bible. Friends, that's the kind of world in which we live—one with tremendous ignorance of God's Word. It's no wonder that the nation has gone so far downhill, so fast, because we can't expect people to live like Christians if they aren't Christians, and especially if they don't even have a passing acquaintance with the Scriptures.

Non-Christian Millennials' unfamiliarity with the Bible, however, has not kept them from forming an opinion on it—an extremely negative one. Barna says that nearly half believe "the Bible is just another book of teachings written by men that contains stories and advice." The most common words they use to describe the Bible are "story," "mythology," "symbolic," and "fairy tale." Fully 30 percent of Millennials allow that it's a useful book of moral teachings, but nearly as many—27 percent— agree that the Bible is "a dangerous book of religious dogma used for centuries to oppress people." According to Erick Metaxas, almost one in five says the Bible is "an outdated book with no relevance for today." I don't know about you, but those numbers kind of make me want to weep.

****

The Bible is the Word of God. The Bible gives over 350 prophecies concerning the coming of Jesus Christ. Half of the prophecies were fulfilled in the First Coming; the other half will be fulfilled in the Second Coming. The Bible is true because of the person of Jesus Christ. First is the resurrection of Christ witnessed by over five hundred witnesses. Secondly is that the Word of God does what it claims to do (the transformed lives). The Word of God has disapproved some of the claims of scientific discoveries throughout the centuries yet none of them has ever disapproved the Bible. You either believe that it is or it is not but you don't have the right to add or to take away from it. The burden is on those who don't believe the Bible to be the Word of God to prove that it is not. The Bible begins with the self-existence God creating all things. Darwinism believes in the world apart from the Creator. The story of creation is trustworthy and given in its simplicity. It is repeated over and over throughout the Scriptures. "People who reject the creation account because they don't want the God of Scripture are in the most dangerous position anyone can be in, and the position that all rejectors of the gospel are in."

****

Christ is the Christian maker. "Christianity" is indicative of everything that Jesus Christ came to be and to do. The entirety of the revelation of God to man is constituted and comprised of the person and work of Jesus Christ. Repentance begins with revaluating of one's character in conformity to the mind of Christ. Repenting is not complete until a sinner confesses his or her sins to Christ. Confessing involves seeing things eye-to-eye (agreeing) with God; it is having the same attitude as God towards sin. Salvation is an elaborate system of dialogue whereby we who previously were enemies of God are reconciled with Him. Sin is evidently visible in the evils of the world. Even atheists cannot dispute the existence of evil because it is everywhere. Sin is abomination to the holiness of God. "The Gospel begins with a recalibration of thought - REPENT- repentance is the reframing of mind so that thought can be free to flow to its divine creative potential" ~ Bishop Adonijah

****

Hebrews 1:1-2 : "God, who at various times and in various ways spoke in time past to the fathers by the prophets, has in these last days spoken to us by His Son, whom He has appointed heir of all things, through whom also He made the worlds." The book of Hebrews was addressed to a group of Jewish Christians who had begun to drift from the Christian faith. They had lost all awareness of the relevancy of their faith to the daily affairs of life. They had begun to drift into outward formal religious performance, but to lose the inner reality. Doubts were creeping into their hearts, and some of them were about to abandon their faith in Christ because of persecution and pressure. Paul brought to their awareness that Jesus is the final revelation of God. And the Bible, of course, is filled with this reality. It is not obscure. It is not marginal. It's not even limited in its presentation. It is all over the pages of Scripture, unmistakably. The unforgivable sin of blaspheming the Holy Spirit (Mark 3:28-30) involves rejecting Jesus Christ as your personal Savior.

****

Hebrews 2:7 – "You made Him a little lower than angels; you crowned Him with glory and honor" Jesus was fully God and fully man. The word 'made' does not mean created but it means ordained. Jesus willingly accepted the mission given to Him by the Father. The Bible says that "Let this mind be in you, which was also in Christ Jesus: Who, being in the form of God, thought it not robbery to be equal with God: But made himself of no reputation, and took upon him the form of a servant, and was made in the likeness of men: And being found in fashion as a man, he humbled himself, and became obedient unto death, even the death of the cross. Wherefore God also hath highly exalted him, and given him a name which is above every name: That at the name of Jesus every knee should bow, of things in heaven, and things in earth, and things under the earth; And that every tongue should confess that Jesus Christ is Lord, to the glory of God the Father.(Philippians 2:5-11). Jesus was given the physical body to operate in the physical world. In His humanity He had some limitations and was a little bit lower than angels. Angelic beings are basically ministering spirits, and spirits are connected to the eternal dimension.

****

Fire fighters use water to put out fire. Water molecules (H_2O) are each made of two hydrogen atoms ($H2$) and one oxygen atom ($O2$). Yet hydrogen is highly explosive and oxygen is very good for combustion. Likewise, in case of immunizing measles, smallpox and tuberculosis the live vaccines prescribed involve a common live virus injection - a living virus is injected into you to fight off the related disease. In many cases, the injected organism is a relative to the human disease that is less dangerous. Live vaccines are preferred for healthy adults because the immune response is stronger and the injected organism can sometimes multiply in your system and thus give a greater exposure. According to the Bible the Israelis were bitten by snakes as result of God's judgment. After they repented, Moses interceded for them, and God instructed him to make a snake and put it up on a pole; so that anyone who is bitten can look at it and live (Numbers 21:8). When we were bitten by sin, God made Jesus who had no sin to be sin for us, so that in him we might become the righteousness of God (2 Cor. 5:21).

****

Mohammad Ali was asked to buckle his belt on the plane. He egotistically responded to the flight attendant that "Superman needs no seat belt." The attendant replied that then Superman needs no plane to fly. Even the strongest human being is vulnerable to gravity. God alone can defy the laws of nature. Jesus defied the laws of nature because He is God. Colossians 1:16–17 "For by him were all things created, that are in heaven, and that are in earth, visible and invisible, whether they be thrones, or dominions, or principalities, or powers: all things were created by him, and for him: And he is before all things, and by him all things consist." The Old Testament is clear about this truth; Yahweh is the only God the Jews were to love, fear, worship and revere (Exodus 20:3-6). The scriptures below project the disciples of Jesus worshiping Him (Matthew 2:10-12; 8:2; 9:18-19; 14:32-33; 15:25-26; 20:20-21; John 9:35-38). Jesus never reprimanded any of His disciples for worshiping Him because He is God. The Bible says that "At the name of Jesus every knee should bow, of things in heaven, and things in earth, and things under the earth" (Philippians 2:10). Don't miss to worship Him this weekend.

****

Why would a loving God create hell? God is holy, just and righteous. The Just God must judge righteously. He must reward goodness and judge (condemn) evil. That is why Jesus talked about heaven and hell. Yet He talked more about hell than heaven because without hell, there is no need for the Savior. Hell is the means by which God will finally purge this universe of evil. Evil will be utterly mopped up from the face of the earth. The doctrine of hell is therefore not a rhetorical device designed to scare off people. It is not concocted; it is not another way of finding a bigger hammer with which to swat the fly. Hell is real as heaven is real.

****

Somebody asked that "If Jesus' love is unconditional, why does He send the sinners to hell?" I want to say that Jesus did not come to condemn the world but to save the already condemned world. All people were on the broad way heading to hell BUT His narrow way became an exit for us (believers) to take in order to avert hell. His love is unconditional because He accepts us on condition of His works as opposed to our works. His love is extended to whosoever believes in Jesus Christ and receives Him as a personal savoir. Pastor Gram says that in order to assess how much God loves you, think about what you would do if somebody mistreated your son the way they mistreated His Son to the extent of crucifying Him. He adds that, "------take the intensity of that emotion, multiply it by infinity, and that's a taste of how much God loves you. He allowed His Son to be taken, beaten, broken, and killed just for you." The standard of God's love is given in the person of Jesus Christ. The Love of God is experienced only by those who receive the Son. In order to understand the depth of God's love, you must understand the depth of the depravity of man. It is impossible to acknowledge the depth of God's love without realizing the depth of your depravity.

****

Hell is not meant for eternal torment. It is the second death and the purging of sin from the universe. The Bible tells us that "the wages of sin is" not eternal life in hell-fire, but "death" (Romans 6:23), the same penalty God assured Adam and Eve would be theirs if they ate the forbidden fruit. Ezekiel states clearly that "the soul that sinneth, it shall die" (Ezekiel 18:4), and a plethora of other Bible verses and passages endorse this position. The prophet Malachi wrote that sinners would burn up as "stubble" and would become "ashes under the soles" of the feet of the redeemed (Malachi 4:1, 3). Even the final fate of Satan is explicitly pronounced in Ezekiel 28:18, where the Bible says that the enemy of souls will be reduced to ashes upon the "earth." Compare that with Psalm 37:10 ("For yet a little while, and the wicked shall not be"), Psalm 68:2 ("as wax melteth before the fire, so let the wicked perish at the presence of God"), and other similar verses. Soon you get a clear picture that the purpose of the fires of hell is to eradicate sin and to expunge the universe of its awful presence. Jesus said that, "Do not be afraid of those who kill the body but cannot kill the soul. Rather, be afraid of the One who can destroy both soul and body in hell" (Matthew 10:28). Please read Jude 1:7 God is not speaking about a fire that will burn forever. He is speaking about a fire that have eternal consequences.

****

Marvin Muyanja asked "Why did God created such people like Hitler? I answered him that, God created the perfect angel called Lucifer but he willingly rebelled and became evil (the Devil); also God created a perfect man (Adam) and he willingly rebelled and became corrupt. We are all corrupt because all of us have Adam's DNA. But we are not corrupt to the same degree; some people are absolutely corrupt because of their natural instincts and evil desires. God did not create them that way. They function contrary to God's will in the same manner the world (worldly system) is functioning contrary to God's will. Otherwise if God made them that way He wouldn't have been justified to condemn them for doing the very things He created them to do.

****

Somebody asked me that, "Will there be babies in hell?" I want to say that it is not given to me to decide who will be in hell. We can trust the justice and love of our God. However, I can certainly say that there is no innocent human being born after Adam (Psalm 51:5). Babies are not guilty of specific sins but they have the corrupt nature. As the saying goes, "We are not sinners because we sin; we sin because we are sinners".

The virgin birth of Jesus was intended to put an end to the corrupt nature of Adam by beginning a new nature that is void of corruption.

In the Old Testament, when God judged the world by the floods, all people (including babies) perished apart from Noah and his family. Noah's ark is symbolic of our salvation. Before God judged Sodom and Gomorrah, He told Abraham that He will not destroy the cities for the sake of ten righteous people within the city (Genesis 18:25-32). God destroyed Sodom and Gomorrah because he did not find ten righteous people. We know that thousands of babies perished together with their parents but God saved Lot and his family.

In the New Testament, Paul taught that, "For the Christian wife brings holiness to her marriage, and the Christian husband brings holiness to his marriage. Otherwise, your children would not be holy, but now they are holy" (1 Cor. 7:14). Jesus said, "Let the little children come to me, and do not hinder them, for the kingdom of heaven belongs to such as these" (Matthew 19:14). Jesus did not say that don't bother the little children because they are already clean. He said that allow them or bring them to me. That is why we dedicate our children to Jesus in order not to take chances. On the contrary there are children dedicated to the evil spirits and to the heathen religions of the world; God alone knows their fate! Remember that hell is not just a punishment but it is a means of purging evil from this universe. The justice of God is that nobody goes to hell that does not deserve to go there. Instead of asking why did God not save so and so, the legitimate question should be why God saves any sinner. The justice of God is that nobody goes to hell that does not deserve to go there.

****

Will there be babies or toddlers in heaven? Here on earth we are limited by time and space because of our corrupt nature. Eternity is not limited by time and space. Age is the evidence of our fallen nature. Before Adam sinned, he lived in the perfect environment in Garden of Eden. We do not know how long Adam lived in Eden. But he lived a total of 930 years. Apparently, Adam lived the vast majority of these years after God expelled him from the Garden of Eden. God created Adam a mature being. He is the only person without umbilical cord. My opinion is that in heaven we shall all be as mature as Adam was created. Jesus is called the Second Adam. The Bible specifically says that all of us shall be like Christ when He appears (1 John 3:2). There shall be no babies and no aged in heaven. Babies will be given a resurrection body (1 Cor. 15:35-49) that is "fast-forwarded" to the "ideal age," just as those who die at an old age are "re-wound" to the ideal age. Whatever age we appear to be, we will be gloriously perfect and unchanging. Jesus said that at resurrection we shall be like angels (Matthew 22:30). There is hierarchy among angels but not age differences.

****

Will there be animals in heaven? The Bible does not specifically answer this question except mentioning that Jesus is coming riding on a white horse. Everything we have here on earth is given to us to enjoy but the beauties of the world primarily point to the wisdom of God the creator (Romans 1:20). In heaven we shall see God face to face. The streets of heaven are made of gold but when we go to heaven we shall no longer need gold. All our desires and attention will be focused on adoring the awesome glory of God. So it doesn't matter whether there will be animals in heaven because nobody will need a pet. We rehearsal heaven here on earth by loving the LORD our God with all our heart and with all our soul and with all our strength and with all our minds (Matthew 22:37).

****

Rutherford says, "Heaven and Christ are the same thing." To be with Christ is to be in heaven, and to be in heaven is to be with Christ.

****

On Friday I was at the meat factory on my normal schedule. I was chatting with a young Amish man called Simon that works at the plant. He asked me the following tricky question: "Does God love Hitler?" I replied to him that it depends on how you define the word "Love". God's standard of love is in Christ. He loves all people including Hitler, Idi Amin and etc., and He did something to prove His love by giving His only son to redeem even the worst of the sinners. Those who have received the Savior experience His love and are saved. Abraham and other people of God who lived in past times before Jesus died at the cross had faith in the future deliverance of God. Jesus said that, "Your father Abraham rejoiced at the thought of seeing my day; he saw it and was glad." (John 8:56). We divide time into BC and AD; BC before Christ and AD, Anno Domini - in the year of Our Lord - since the birth of Jesus. This is our way of showing that Jesus is the center of history; Jesus is the most important event in history. Just as we divide time into BC and AD, before Christ and after his birth, the Sacred Scriptures do the same and so we have the Old Testament and the New Testament. In the Old Testament from time to time we get glimpses and hints of Jesus who is to come, in events or people who are pointing the way to Jesus. The New Testament is the continuation of the Old Testament and the fulfillment of the prophetic messages in the Old Testament. The Gospels present not just the words of God but the manifested works of God through Jesus Christ.

God's final judgment of the world is intended to finally purge the universe of evil. Those people who die without receiving Jesus Christ become unwanted damaged good to be dumped in the everlasting flames of hell, most probably as the contaminated meat is thrown in the dumpster; it is not wanted. The word "Gehenna" is of Hebrew origin, from "valley" and "Hinnom." It is the Valley where the fire burned continually. The Greek word for hell is "Gehenna" or "the Gehenna of fire." It is never translated by any other word but it is used as "Hell", and ten of the eleven times the word is used, it is used by the Lord Himself. Here are a list of passages in which the word "Gehenna" appears: (Matthew 5:22, 5:29, 30, 10:28, 18:9, 23:15, 23:23; Mark 9:43, 9:45, 9:47; Luke 12:5; James 3:6). Jesus referred to Hell as the "Gehenna of fire," into which "both body and soul" will be cast. He said that it is "unquenchable fire" and that "the worm (man) dies not" in the flame.

****

An ethical dilemma is a debate between two moral principles, where two sides can argue about what is wrong or what is right. However, there is no real answer to an ethical dilemma. It is simply a matter of what one believes in. In Christianity we do not have dilemmas but we have mysteries. A mystery is something that is true but that is not yet revealed to our natural minds. Yesterday I was at the meat processing plant and the manager told me that they used a very strong chemical to sanitize ending up killing all of the bacteria including the good ones in the water system. One cannot afford to wonder whether there is such a thing as good bacteria. Most people learn about bacteria in the context of disease, so it's easy to think only about the harm they do as opposed to the benefits. In the soil and in the ocean, bacteria are major players in the decomposition of organic matter and the cycling of chemical elements such as carbon and nitrogen, which are necessary for human life. Bacteria also play a role cycling another important substance for human life water. In recent years, scientists from Louisiana State University have found evidence that bacteria represent many, if not most, of the tiny particles that cause clouds to precipitate into falling snow and rain. On and inside the human body, bacteria offer still other benefits. In the digestive system, they help us break down food, like plant fibers, that we're not so good a handling ourselves. Next time before you question the wisdom of God for creating dangerous spices, trust His integrity because He is holy and He makes no mistakes. "And we know that in all things God works for the good of those who love him, who have been called according to his purpose" (Romans 8:28).

****

Yesterday we discussed that the wisdom of God created both the good and harmful bacteria for our benefits. According to psychology we use less than eighteen percent of our brains during our life span. It's not just about the brain, it's about genetics. Unused code is untapped potential. Our brains are only a part of the equation. DNA plays the major role, since it is DNA which constructs our biology. Before the corruption of sin mankind was not vulnerable to death. There were harmful spices in the Garden of Eden but Adam had dominion over the rest of creations (good/harmful). When sin stepped in it corrupted not just the brains of man but also his DNA and other biological functions. For example cancer is caused by DNA damage. Radioactive carbon-14 in our DNA from the food we eat damages our DNA all the time. We get an average of 10 DNA mutations every 3 seconds this way. This makes normal food the most potent cause of cancer by far.

Before the corruption of sin Adam used 100% of his brains but after the fall about 90% was lost in corruption. If your awareness is turned up high, you know things others don't. But it can't be tuned up to the extent of the pre-fall condition. As I wrote in one of my books there is cure of each and every sickness in the world although the cures of some terminal sicknesses are not yet exposed to our natural brains. No cure does not mean nonexistence; it means they just don't know how.

****

Yesterday I had lunch with Simon. As usual we discussed some spiritual matters. This time, he revised his preferred genre to something a little more eccentric. He used God as a spiritual smoke to shield his inadequacies. He came up with a notion that if God was all loving, He shouldn't have created us with free-will, knowing that we shall violate it. I tried my best to apologetically make a case to him by clearly and concisely listing what I consider to be the LOVE of God in connection to the free-will of man. "Free-will involves making choices. Life without choices is absolute bondage." Anyway, he decided to disagree with the provided balance sheet! After he left the table, I thought that I could do a better job to reach-out to him without being critical and theological. I called him and told him that regarding man's freedom without free-will, I was wrong and he is right. His face shined afresh. I went ahead to tell him that a believer that is born again surrenders his will to God; you can't qualify for the grace of God unless you reach the point of saying that "Not my will but your will be done". This is the right way of getting rid of the human free-will! He was receptive to this idea. My friend, Lamont, asked him to surrender, and he said a simple prayer of deliverance over his soul.

****

Psalm 139:14-16 - I praise you because I am fearfully and wonderfully made; your works are wonderful, know that full well. My frame was not hidden from you when I was made in the secret place, when I was woven together in the depths of the earth. Your eyes saw my unformed body; all the days ordained for me were written in your book before one of them came to be. He gave you DNA, which is the code contained in your cells describing your every feature. He created in us a sophisticated

DNA coding for human cells. The nucleus of each cell contains over 30,000 multi-tasking genes, which are the genetic code for the formation of your entire physical structure, with all of its unique features. Your DNA is God's code for your individual features, characteristics, and tendencies. The process of replicating DNA requires so many separate and precisely interacting parts that it is simply impossible - not just very improbable - that it could have evolved by accident. Even just the formation of the proteins which combine to make up DNA has not been explained in an evolutionary context. The more they find out about DNA and living cells the more complex they discover it to be and the more difficult for them to explain.

****

"Who do you say that I am?" Jesus asked His disciples this question shortly before His death, and the same question presents itself to us. It is the most important question any of us will ever face. Dr. R.C. Sproul believes that the coming crisis in the Church is a christological one, and how our fathers in the faith equipped us for the battle. John the Baptist after introducing Jesus as the Lamb that takes away the sins of the world, and after forced to baptize Jesus when he felt he was not worthy to do it, still did not get the Christology in its fullness. Days later he sent his disciples to Jesus asking Him that "Are you the one to come?" (Luke 7:20)

****

When did Jesus become the Son of God? Jesus was the Son of God from eternity. The term Son of God attracts criticism in particular from Muslims, who strongly consider it to be a blasphemy because they equate it with biological birth resulting from sexual encounter. However, the term "Son of God" has everything to do with the same nature and character with God. The Second Trinity (Jesus) has always been the Son of God from eternity because He is of the same nature with God the Father. Also because of His perfect obedience to the First Trinity - God the Father (Philippians 2:5-9). Jesus explained the meaning of son-ship when He confronted the Jewish religious leaders who bragged to be descendants of Abraham. Jesus told them that, "You are of your father the devil, and your will is to do your father's desires" (John 8:41). Spiritual fatherhood depends on whom you obey! We become children of God when we take on the new nature of God (Spirit), and by virtue of the perfect obedience of Christ imputed on us. Jesus made it possible for His Father to be our Father. After resurrection He said that "I ascend unto my Father, and your Father" (John 20:17).

****

Somebody asked that, "Why Jesus is called the Son of God and the Son of man? Why is He not called the Son of woman since He had no earthly father?" The term Son of God is in reference to His deity as truly God. The term Son of man is a Messianic title as given in Daniel 7:13-14. Son of man is also in reference to His humanity. Jesus has one foot in the divine and one foot in humanity. He bridged the gap between God and man. The word 'man' in this case is used in reference to mankind (male/female). The Bible says that "So God created man in His image, in the image of God created he him; male and female He created them" (Genesis 1:26). Also "Male and female created he them; and blessed them, and called their name Adam (Mankind), in the day when they were created." (Genesis 5:2).

****

When Jesus put on the human flesh the omnipotent God who is timeless existence, and who created and sustains all things including time, stepped into this universe that is limited by time and space to change its ontological status. We are assured that the Lord is with us in all our ways and condescends to enter into our humiliations and banishment! Thank God for Jesus our Lord and Savior (Adonai Yahawashai HaMashiach). The Bible might not answer all of our questions concerning the procedure of the universe but it has the only explicit answer regarding our salvation. Our limited ability highlights God's limitless power. What we know of God encourages us to trust Him in all we do not know.

****

Infinite realities exist that are outside the reach of our observation. We know this to be true. Yet, too often Christians are labeled as crazy for making assertions about the spiritual world, God, and heaven. Faith is not just closing your eyes and imagining things that down deep in your heart you don't really think are true. Faith is not mysterious power working in us. Faith is not positive thinking because even New Age movement teaches to be positive. Faith is our obedience by believing in God. God works at the level of man's capability by granting His grace to those who exercise their faith. Faith and grace go together compared to the two wings of a bird, whereby it cannot fly without both wings. Faith is trusting in the abilities and faithfulness of Christ to work on our behalf. The grace connects God to man. Faith connects us to God. Every step of trusting in God diminishes our trusting in self, and increases our access to His grace. Paul said that, "I am crucified with Christ: nevertheless I live; yet not I, but Christ liveth in me: and the life which I now live in the flesh I live by the faith of the Son of God, who loved me, and gave himself for me" (Galatians 2:20).

****

Some people are searching for the remains of Noah's Ark that existed four thousand years ago. They use the missing pieces of ark (wood) to mean never existed. How many billions upon billions of people have died and left absolutely no evidence of their existence and yet this is not an argument for their non-existence. Absence of evidence is not evidence of absence.

****

The Spirit of God has been active on this earth because He is the means through which God accomplishes all things. At first the earth was shapeless and covered in darkness, and God's spirit hovered over the waters to activate creation (Genesis 1:2). At the birth of Jesus the Spirit of God overshadowed the Virgin Mary and what was conceived was called the Son of God (Matthew 1:18-25). It is the Spirit's intervention that resulted into an action that consecrated and made fruitful Mary's virginity. The words "hovered" and "overshadow" have the same meaning. Jesus expressed His work towards humanity when He cried over Israel, how often I have longed to gather your children together, as a hen gathers her chicks under her wings, and you were not willing. In this metaphor Jesus used the same word hovering over your children like the hen hover over her chicks. An honest view will reveal that God has been speaking all along in different times and climes and there has never been a time when he wasn't represented on earth even now!!

****

In the beginning was the Word, and the Word was with God, and the Word was God....And the Word was made flesh, and dwelt among us, (and we beheld his glory, the glory as of the only begotten of the Father,) full of grace and truth (2 John 1:7). "In HIM (JESUS) dwells ALL (not part, 1/2 or some) of the fullness of the Godhead bodily" (Colossians 2:9). The Islamic faith does not understand what the trinity is that is why Christians are often incorrectly labeled as polytheists. The trinity is a way to describe the entire being that is God. In the Holy Bible we see God described in and interacting with His creation in three primary guises: As the Creator, as His Holy Spirit or Holy Ghost, and finally as Jesus Christ. These three essences of the one God are what make God, God. For example, you have a triangle and it has three corners and each corner represents a part of the triangle that makes it a whole. 3 pieces of one shape. It's that simple. Of course Islamists will reject the trinity; they reject the divinity of Jesus, the Crucifixion and Resurrection so Christianity has already been considered null and void by said Islamists. This is why I have a hard time believing that their religion is one of peace or that Christians or Jews (actually any human being who is not Muslim!) are to be treated kindly when elsewhere throughout the Koran is it taught to smite us at our necks, to make us pay humility taxes or to not make friends with us...

****

John 1:1-18 puts it, Jesus is the Word — the Logos who is God and is with God. In Him all things were made, including the lesser principalities and powers whom the Colossian false teachers trusted (Col. 1:16, 2:18). Their hope in angels for spiritual advancement was misplaced because it meant turning from the Creator to creatures. Moreover, if Jesus' identity with the Creator is not enough to convince readers of Christ's sufficiency, the apostle also explains that the Son of God is the great Sustainer. "In him all things hold together" (1:17): Christ, no other being or impersonal force, keeps the universe in order. Without Him, the cosmos would be chaos, and if He has the power to hold everything together, how could anyone believe that he needs to turn anywhere else to find completion?

Colossians 1:18 – "And he is the head of the body, the church: who is the beginning, the firstborn from the dead; that in all things he might have the preeminence." The canticle of the Letter to the Colossians presents another function of Christ: He is also the Lord of the history of salvation, which is manifested in the Church (verse 18) and is accomplished by the "blood of his cross". Through the cross of Christ, the whole of reality is "reconciled" with the Father (see verse 20). He is the source of peace and harmony for all human history. Therefore, not only the horizon that is external to our existence is marked by the efficacious presence of Christ, but also the more specific reality of the human creature, namely, history. The latter is not at the mercy of blind and irrational forces; instead, despite sin and evil, it is ruled and oriented -- by the work of Christ -- toward fullness.

****

The Redeemer of Man, Jesus Christ, is the center of the universe and of history. In the person of Jesus, the love of God entered into time and space redeeming time. Faith is not limited by time. Remember that God is not limited by time and space, so is faith. That is why without faith it is impossible to please God. Faith connects us to the eternal God. By faith we died and we were raised in Jesus Christ, and we are sitting in the heavenly places with Jesus. The Christians look forward to the future Day of the Lord, the day of triumph when the nature of the new creation will finally be revealed to our eyes. But we live in the future glory now by faith.

****

In the person of Jesus Christ, Love entered into the human race and became like one of us (incarnation) and made all things new (Revelation 21:5). Love is not just a magnetic word or a mysterious force but the reality of the real power holding all creations together. Among believers, there is the common sharing in the death of Christ and life of Christ together. We find our identity in Christ. We live in Christ and Christ dwells in us. We are bonded together by God who is the center that holds us together. Jesus loved sacrificially. We live as He lived and love as He loved. Our freedom is relational in nature. We are free eternally but our freedom in this world is for the sake of others. We live together in a communal way of sharing. We live a common life with other believers together. We are a unique community of one....

****

This weekend go and worship Jesus. The Bible says that at the name of Jesus EVERY KNEE WILL BOW, of those who are in heaven and on earth and under the earth (Philippians 2:10). Jesus Christ must be God in order to qualify to be the redeemer. God also in the Old Testament identifies Himself as the Redeemer. In Isaiah 43:14; Hosea 13:14 God says He alone is the Redeemer. Jesus, however, was also considered the Redeemer. Zacharias, the priest, said He was the Redeemer. Anna the old woman in Luke 2 said He was the Redeemer. Paul called Him the Redeemer. Peter called Him the Redeemer. The apocalyptic living creatures in the book of Revelation and the 24 elders in Revelation 5:9 called Him the Redeemer. God alone can redeem. Christ can redeem. God alone is Redeemer. Christ is Redeemer. Therefore unmistakably He is God.

****

I was privileged to talk to a follower of Jehovah Witness who paid a courtesy call to my house. He challenged me to prove the deity of Christ in the Bible. I picked this scripture out of many: "And Thomas answered and said unto Him, 'My Lord and my God!'" (John 20:28). He quickly rebutted my quotation saying that "Thomas never called Jesus God but he simply exclaimed that "Oh my God!" in amazement. He forgot that Thomas, like any other Jew would not take the name of the Lord in vain. I was not surprised by his response because all people that are lost in false doctrines make the Bible say what they want it to say in order to justify their falsehoods. They forget that the Bible means what it says. I want to reprimand the perpetrators that we (humans) hate it when somebody puts words in our mouths; so does God.

****

The God that you can confine in your finite minds is god with a small 'g' not God with a capital 'G'. We cannot fully comprehend the trinity, the grace, the infinity of God and etc. The only way we can know about the Holy Trinity is by divine revelation. You will never understand the Trinity by human investigation, logic, philosophy, or science. Don't get the idea that on your own you "discover" the Trinity. The only way you can know about the Trinity is what God says in His Word. John Wesley, a great man of God, said, "How can a worm understand a man, and how can a man understand God?"

****

The Son of God is God the Son. The uniqueness of Christianity is in the doctrine of the trinity. The Muslims, the Jews, the Jehovah Witnesses, the Mormons, the Unitarians and etc. do not believe in the trinity. The trinity like other Christian doctrines cannot be fully comprehended by our finite minds, partly because God cannot be confined in our finite minds. "Trying to understand the trinity you end up losing your minds; but rejecting the trinity you lose your soul."

****

Though he was in the form of God … emptied himself" (Phil. 2:6-7). This scripture is confusing and is the main cause of many false teaching regarding the nature of Jesus Christ (Christology). Below are some of the heretical teachings of the above Scripture: Says one: "It means Jesus became a man for a time and then went back to being God afterwards." "No," says another, "He only emptied himself of His divine attributes and then He took them up again." "Surely," says another (not pausing to reflect on the miracles of Moses, Elijah, or the Apostles), "He mixed humanity with His deity—isn't that how He was able to do miracles?"

Does it really matter if those views are wrong, indeed heretical, so long as we know that Jesus saves and we witness to others about Him? After all, the important thing is that we preach the gospel. But that is precisely the point—Jesus Christ Himself is the gospel. Like loose threads in a tapestry—pull on any of these views, and the entire gospel will unravel. If the Christ we trust and preach is not qualified to save us, we have a false Christ. Jesus said that, "I said therefore unto you, that ye shall die in your sins: for if ye believe not that I am he, ye ... For unless you believe that I am he, you will die in your sins" (John 8:24).

What is the true doctrine? The true doctrine taught by the early fathers of the Church maintains that our Lord Jesus Christ is to us one and the same Son, the self-same perfect in Godhead, the self-same perfect in manhood; truly God and truly man, acknowledged in two natures, unconfusedly, unchangeably, indivisibly, inseparably. The properties of each nature (man/God) being preserved - The Son's two natures are not united to each other, but they are united in His one person. So in everything He did, He acted appropriately in terms of His deity or His humanity, one divine person exercising the powers of each nature in its own proper sphere.

The Church fathers and later the Westminster divines, stressed that God's Son ever remained "of one substance, and equal with the Father" and yet, in the incarnation, took "upon him man's nature, with all the essential properties and infirmities thereof, yet without sin. So that two whole, perfect, and distinct natures, the Godhead and the manhood, were inseparably joined together in one person, without conversion, composition, or confusion" (WCF 8.2).

****

God designed the human eyes in a unique way. For example the human eyes see things upside down and the brains turn them upright. Animals see better at night because they can't see color as we do. Sight is considered to be the most important of all the 5 senses. Our ability to see is important because it supplements the rest of the senses. For example when you want to exercise your sense of touch you say "Let me see" instead of "Let me touch." The sense of sight helps the sense of touch to get something right. Light sustains life. Spiritually, all of us are born as blind as a bat. Jesus declared that, "I am the light of the world: he that followeth me shall not walk in darkness, but shall have the light of life" (John 8:12). Light is related to righteousness that sustains eternal life. Jesus is the light we need in order to see the invisible things to the natural eyes and minds. Light shines brightest at source. Jesus is the source of light. It means we are not manufacturers but distributors or agents of light. Darkness is the absence of light. Light drives away darkness; the thicker the darkness the brighter the light.

****

"This is the message we have heard from him and declare to you: God is light; in him there is no darkness at all" (1John 1:5). God is light in Him there is no physical and spiritual darkness. When Moses went to meet God, his face shone so bright that he covered it with the veil in order for people to look at him. Jesus appeared to Paul as a blazing flashing light blinding his eyes (Acts 9:3-9). John wrote that, In God there is no deception and vanity. Darkness is not a thing; it is the absence of light. We (humans), unless redeemed we are born in spiritual darkness following vanity as truly in a portfolio as in a theater. Read the stories of the prophets they were called all sorts of names because the society couldn't see what the prophets saw or were seeing. God opened the blind spiritual eyes of the prophets to see what the world cannot see.

****

Most of the ancient pagan religions banded together into the occultism Sun-worship; veneration of the Moon; constellation and star worshiping. The leading ancient cults of the centuries have vanished from the earth but a few have survived the test of ages and their mysterious symbols are still preserved in some religions today. Sun worship played an important part in nearly all the early pagan Mysteries. The Solar Deity was usually personified as a beautiful youth, with long golden hair to symbolize the rays of the sun. Archaeologists have uncovered temples to the Moon-god throughout the Middle East. From the mountains of Turkey to the banks of the Nile, the most wide-spread religion of the ancient world was the worship of the Moon-god. As a matter of fact, everywhere in the ancient world, the symbol of the crescent moon can be found on seal impressions, steles, pottery, amulets, clay tablets, cylinders, weights, earrings, necklaces, wall murals, etc. The zodiac is pagan religion. It is what we see in the horoscope in every weekend newspaper on earth, generally the stuff of amusement. We know this system; it is based on the (extraordinary) assumption that the stars control the earth and that what happens on earth is a result of influences from what happens in the sky. All they need in order to understand the earth (that is, about their destiny) is to understand the stars. The Bible warns that the universe will be shaken at the judgment of God then the Sun-god, Moon-god and star-god shall fall down from the sky: "I looked when He broke the sixth seal, and there was a great earthquake; and the sun became black as sackcloth made of hair, and the whole moon became like blood; and the stars of the sky fell to the earth, as a fig tree casts its unripe figs when shaken by a great wind" (Revelation 6:12-13).

****

One of the defining features of our post-Christian culture is the embrace of what we might call "philosophical relativism." The prevailing view today is that there are no absolute truths. There is only "my truth" and "your truth," but there are no "true truths," to borrow Francis Schaeffer's language. In reality, there is absolute truth because there is the God of truth from where the moral code originates. Truth is objective and authoritative. Jesus is truth incarnate. Jesus said to Pilate that, "In fact, the reason I was born and came into the world is to testify to the truth. Everyone on the side of truth listens to me." Pilate asked Jesus that "What is truth?" (John 18:27-28). Pilate was a sophisticated man of the world and a politician in service to the Roman Empire. I'm quite certain that life had taught him that truth is relative to the conditions in which one lives. He thought that every person can make it to God depending on what they believed. He asked on that basis. But Jesus' reply implicated that truth is single and is immutable. "Right is right, and wrong is wrong depending on God." Truth is not the way we want things to be but the way things are. Truth is sovereign. Truth is whatever God say it is because God is the ultimate measure of the truth. Truth is a person. Truth is divine. Truth is not in man but comes down from heaven to us. Jesus is the truth (John 14:6). Your eternal destiny is determined by the truth.

****

Jesus said that He is the only way to God the Father. Why do we need Jesus to reach God the Father? I compare it to trying to look direct at the sun. When you look up you see the brightness light of the sun but not the sun. I know this because looking directly into the sun is fatal. The sun is not fire, but it does throw out intense ultraviolet light so if you look at the sun directly you will completely go blind. Likewise the Bible says that our God is a consuming fire (Hebrews 12:29). It means a fire that utterly consumes or destroys. God's holiness is the reason for His being a consuming fire, and it burns up anything unholy. Therefore, we (sinners) can only see God by looking at Jesus Christ. There is no need to fear the consuming fire of God's wrath if we are covered by the purifying blood of Christ. The Bible says that "Who being the brightness of his glory, and the express image of his person, and upholding all things by the word of his power, when he had by himself purged our sins, sat down on the right hand of the Majesty on high" (Hebrews 1:3).

****

God is the source of light. According to the Bible before the sun was created, there was night and day. Light does not automatically require the sun. The sun was created to reflect the light of God in order to sustain life on earth. Actually there are many other causes of light apart from the sun. There are also many types of light, not just visible light. Short-wave light includes ultraviolet light, X-rays, and others. Long-wave light includes infrared light, radio waves, etc. Light is produced by friction, by fire, by numerous chemical reactions, as well as the nuclear reactions of atomic fission and fusion, which is what we think is occurring in the sun. God had at His fingertips many options to accomplish His purposes. It is believed that the sun is many thousand times bigger than the earth in physical size. But of course the sun doesn't have a solid or fixed core like the earth does. The sun is made of plasma i.e. super hot gases at extreme temperatures, like Hydrogen, helium etc. In normal sense the sun is like an object compared to looking into the heart of a nuclear reactor.

****

Darkness is not a thing; it is the absence of light. We don't have to battle against the darkness when all we need to do is to turn on the light. Jesus is the light of the world; He is the only bright spot on the universe that deposes the darkness of the world. He is the truth that exposes the deception of Satan.

****

"We are only what we are in the dark; all the rest is reputation. What God looks at is what we are in the dark—the imaginations of our minds; the thoughts of our heart; the habits of our bodies; these are the things that mark us in God's sight." --Oswald Chambers, in The Love of God from the Quotable Oswald Chambers.

****

A hundred years or so ago, we thought that the seconds ticked away predictably. Tick followed tock, followed tick. In spite of the people's naive ideas about time, they managed to control time unlike this age of technology and materialism whereby time controls people. We are time conscience but hyper living too. We are addicted to fast things – fast foods, slim fast, speed micro soft wares and etc. Intriguingly, the faster we move, the faster time slips away from us. In reality none of us can admit having enough time. Newton claimed that time is absolute but Einstein proved that time is relative. For example the person in the spaceship only needs to travel near to the speed of light. The faster they travel, the slower their time will pass relative to someone planted firmly on the Earth. The enigma of time is solved in eternity. God is eternal and dwells in eternity that is not limited by time. In eternity the past and the future meet in the present. Thus the past is simply another "place" or space in time, as is the future—all in a "simultaneous present". The Bible instructs us to seek eternal things. The destiny and direction of our journey toward eternity depend upon how wisely we have invested time or *kairos*.

****

Psalm 85:10-11: Mercy and truth have met together; Righteousness and peace have kissed. Truth shall spring out of the earth, And righteousness shall look down from heaven. The cross a unique spot on the universe. It is a place where the love of God met with the justice of God. The cross of Christ is the climax of all moral truth. If God did not spare His begotten Son when He carried on Himself the sins of the world, what makes you think that He will spare you for your sins? Make a decision today to accept Jesus Christ to die for your sins. Remember that indecisiveness is the worst decision! Not to decide is to decide. Failure to decide is to decide by default. Even when you postpone a decision, you have already taken a decision. Remember that, "It is in your moments of decision that your destiny is shaped."

****

There can be no faith without the promise (Word). Faith obeys the Word on basis of the integrity of God who gave the promise. Faith is not against reasoning but faith goes extra miles where reasoning can't go. Reason deals with logic with limitation but faith deals with expectations without limitations. Faith hears the inaudible, believes the incredible, and receives the impossible. Faith is the evidence of the things not yet revealed to the natural eyes. Angels need no faith because they believe and obey God whom they can see. Our faith is manifested obedience without involving the senses of sight. So hold tightly to the hope that one day, your faith will become sight when you stand before the heavenly throne. In Heaven we shall need no faith because we shall see Christ face to face and stay in His presence for ever. What a glorious day!

****

John 17:17 - Sanctify them through thy truth: thy word is truth. The truth is immutable (never changes). What was true 2000 years ago is true today. There is nothing new; if it is new it is not true. The Bible Is The Infallible Word Of God. When the Bible speaks God speaks. Want to hear the voice of God? Then read the Bible to yourself aloud! His Word is authoritative. The truth is received by the heart with faith. Paul instructed us never to negotiate or compromise the truth. Doctors never let the patients write their prescription. Likewise, we should never allow the world to dictate to the Church the right doctrine. Doctrine is indispensable to Christianity. Christianity does not exist without it. The New Testament repeatedly emphasizes the value and importance of sound doctrine, sound instruction (1 Tim 6:3), and a pattern of sound teaching (2 Tim 1:13-14). "Our obligation is to fill our pulpits with the truth as opposed to the worldliness". Then God will draw in His elects by His irresistible grace.

****

We are living in anti-intellectual era. I am not talking about academic or scientific discoveries but the use of the minds to do what God created it to do. Even some Christians believe that faith replaced thinking. Christians today often do not think. Logic is considered worldly while contradiction is prized as a hallmark of true faith. Some Christians mistake the minds to be part of the physical nature that expire with time. The reality is that we are more than material. The minds are mental as opposed to physical. The brain is material organ that occupies space and can be weighed or measured but the minds are not material. When we die the brain ceases to exist after this earthly body dissolves. But after the body expires we continue to have a conscious awake personal identity that goes on forever. The minds go on with the consciousness of the soul.

There is nothing more vulnerable, nothing more corruptible than the human mind; nor is there anything as powerful, steadfast and ennobling as the human minds. The capacity of our minds should not be underestimated because our actions are the results of our thoughts. There is a strong relationship between the minds and the will. The human will is the mind choosing. Your choices depend on what your mind deems right to do. A moral choice involves a voluntary conscious choice made in accordance to the will of God.

There is the primacy of the heart and the primacy of the minds but there cannot be anything in the heart that is not first in the minds. That is why the change of the minds (repentance) results in the change of the heart. That Christian doctrine of sanctification is about renewing of the minds. God demands that we love Him with all our minds and with all our heart. He demands that we use our best mental faculties to make Him known and to make the truth known to the darkened world.

**************************************.

The story of creation is not a fiction. The story of creation was passed on to different generations by Adam. Remember that Adam died 120 years before the birth of Noah.

****

It is amazing how the Scriptures invoke inspiration by renewing our thinking. The Word fills our emptiness. Christianity is unique and different from other religions of the world. For example the Buddhist idea of EMPTINESS meaning that all that we may think, consider and project is empty of true meaning or of intrinsic awareness. Their philosophies are premeditated to take care of the outside leaving you messed up from inside. We strive hard to keep our religious preferences separated but an honest view will reveal that God has been speaking all along in different times and climes and there has never been a time when he wasn't represented on earth even now! "In the past God spoke to our ancestors through the prophets at many times and in various ways, but in these last days he has spoken to us by his Son, whom he appointed heir of all things, and through whom also he made the universe" (Hebrews 1:1-2). If Christ is anything, He must be everything. Do not rest until love and faith in Jesus are the master passions of your soul! When you read the Bible and act on the truth in it, the center of this book (Christ) becomes the center of your life.

****

Until you know where you want to go, you settle anywhere and end up going nowhere. The path of the just is as the shining light, that shines more and more unto the perfect day. He is like a fired bullet that will destroy anything trying to block him from reaching his intended divine destiny. Jesus was born and brought up in an insignificant place and become the most significant person in history! (John 1: 46 & Luke 2: 52) What matters is not where you grow up but how you grow up. What we become is more important than where we come from. We may be belittled for our lack of sophistication but we know it is not lacking in the basic things pertaining to eternity. Certainly, we are not ignorant of the truth. When the truth is birthed in you it exposes and drives away the lies, allowing you to possess your inheritance. The birth of Isaac exposed Ismail as an illegitimate heir and drove him away.

****

It is important to focus on those sobering facts that draw us closer to God now and for eternity. We tolerantly extend people the dignity of their own beliefs without minimizing the differences between religions. We honor them without compromising. We are allowed to profess our belief without ridicule or venom, or disparagement. The life of Christ produces in us true humility. But it also produces in us true enlightenment. We have come to grasp grace that God works His way down to us, dies for our moral and religious failures and offers us life. We must lovingly, humbly try to persuade others to believe in Jesus, who alone offers the wonderful promise of the way to God, the truth of God and the life of God. The bitter truth is that the choice you make now determines your destiny. "You are today a summation of your past choices. You will be tomorrow and into the future what you choose to do now. Lead Yourself First." ~ David Bernard-Stevens

****

How many ways to God? The cross of Jesus stands alone as the only hope of redemption to mankind. There is only one way to salvation through Jesus Christ. In the Garden of Gethsemane Jesus was faced with the greatest temptation in His ministry on the earth. Satan tried his last chance to bring Jesus down in the Garden of Gethsemane as he did Adam in the Garden of Eden but he failed miserably. The pressure on Jesus was so great that His sweat turned into blood. He withdrew from His disciples and knelt down and prayed to the Father that: "Father if you be willing, remove this cup from me". He made the above prayer out of desperation. The meaning of the prayer is that, if there be another way of redeeming man let this cup pass; if there is another way let this way of the cross become void. The cup that Jesus was about to drink is God's wrath of judgment against the sinners. Then Jesus said that, "Nevertheless not my will, but your will, be done" (Luke 22: 42). Here we see the humanity of Jesus enduring pain. At that moment the Son of God surrendered His will to go through the pain of the cross because it was the only way to redeem mankind. If there was another way to redeem man this was the right time to reveal it in order to spare Jesus from the pain of the cross. Jesus took the roughest way of the cross because it was the only way to save man; there was no any other way but the way of the cross. God reconciled the world to Himself through the death and resurrection of Jesus Christ. Jesus is our only way back home to the Father.

****

Do all ways lead to God? All ways (apart from Jesus) lead to other gods but not to one true God (with capital 'G'). Ironically, if you don't know where you are going, any road will take you there - I mean to the unknown destiny! We (believers) know where we are going as well as the way to where we are going (our destiny). We do not follow any of the ways at random. We chose to follow the way and the truth. Jesus is not one of the ways; He is the only way to God (the Father). He is the truth or means by which God reconciled the world to Himself (2 Cor. 5:18). Before Jesus came on earth, heaven was sealed off to all humanity because there was no one righteous. A sinner (without the grace) cannot see God. Jesus, the only begotten Son of God, was conceived of the Holy Spirit and born of a virgin to open the way to heaven for mankind. Indeed, at His baptism heaven opened up for Him. The Bible says that: "And behold, the heavens were opened, and he saw the Spirit of God descending as a dove and lighting on Him, and behold, a voice out of the heavens said, "This is My beloved Son, in whom I am well-pleased" (Matthew 3:16). I appeal to you to accept Jesus Christ as your Lord and Savior when the way is still open. When you put your trust in Him, you equate your limitlessness with the unlimitlessness of God!

****

Today, at lunch time, I was prevailed to minister to a young man who claimed to be a believer. Brother Lamont asked him the following question: "How will God judge the world?" He answered that God will judge people in accordance to their knowledge which they acquired. I intervened with objection. If it was true that God is going to judge people in accordance to their knowledge then all of other religious people like the Muslims, Buddha and etc. would have hope to be in heaven on account of what they know and what they believe! The book of Revelation says that God will judge the world by His Law as His absolute Standard. Those of us who accepted Christ will not be judged because we were judged in Christ but we shall be rewarded (judged) in proportion to our good works of obedience to God's commandments

(Revelation 22:12-13). But those who are not saved will certainly pay the wages of breaking God's Law. The Bible says that, "Whosoever commits sin transgresses also the law: for sin is the transgression of the law" (1 John 3:4). Also, that the wages of sin is death (Romans 6:23). Death is the eternal separation from the presence of God.

****

Romans 2:14-15: "For when Gentiles, who do not have the law, by nature do what the law requires, they are a law to themselves, even though they do not have the law. They show that the work of the law is written on their hearts, while their conscience also bears witness, and their conflicting thoughts accuse or even excuse them." Although God handed the Moral Law to Moses and made the Jewish people custodians of His statutes, all humanity (Jews/Gentiles) are accountable to the Moral Law because the laws of God were written on their hearts. We were created in the image of God (morality of God) with capability to discern right from wrong.

****

Most religions have an ethical component. Ethics, which is a major branch of philosophy, encompasses right conduct and good life. God is the basic requirement of ethics. However, as religion and faith are being driven out of the public square, the Judeo-Christian ethical foundations that have sustained our country since its beginning, are being lost and are being replaced with a humanistic amorality, a self-centered, pragmatic indifference that will ensure that our moral compasses will fail to point us in the right direction in the future

****

"Political correctness does not necessarily mean moral correctness." The secular governments of the world do not own this world. The Bible prophesied concerning our Messiah that the government will be on His shoulders (Isaiah 9:6). The Bible says that we are joint-heirs with Christ (Romans 8:17). Therefore this world does not just belong to God but it is our Father's property. As His children we have mandate to take care of it by polishing it with the gospel so that it might shine. The old saying goes, "You don't polish brass on a sinking ship," and Christians today might be tempted to see the world as the sinking ship. "But this world was made by our Father and belongs to our Father. The dominion mandate not only abides, but will be carried through, and that this ship will not sink." ~ Dr. Sinclair Ferguson

****

Whenever I have questions concerning the philosophies of life I go to my God who designed my life. But God does not explain Himself; He reveals Himself to convict. I am left with no choice but to fall into His own plan for my life. He gives me what I need not what I want. The want is the philosophy that challenged me but the need is the person (Christ) that changes me. The need is the game changer. "It is neither the strongest nor the most intelligent species that out live time, but it is those that are most responsive to change" ~ Charles Darwin.

****

It is wrong to believe that all Jews rejected Jesus as their Messiah. Jesus was sent to the Jews first then to the Gentiles. His twelve Apostles were Jews. The 120 disciples who waited in the upper room were Jews. The 3000 converts on Pentecost were Jews. Albert Einstein is Jewish scholar. He says that as a child he received instruction from both the Bible and the Talmud. In his own words he says: "I am a Jew, but I am enthralled by the luminous figure of the Nazarene... No one can read the Gospels without feeling the actual presence of Jesus. His personality pulsates in every word. No myth is filled with such life".

****

We naturally grow up responding to the patterns we are exposed to. Adam was created a mature human being. He was never a toddler therefore he was not influenced by any parenting. His only influence was God. The Bible says that God walked in the Garden in the cool of the evening (Genesis 3:8). Adam had contact with God on a level known only by a few other humans. God talked to Adam and instructed him how to stay in the perfect environment forever. Adam's fall into sin was therefore a moral failure as opposed to ignorance. The Garden of Eden was the perfect environment for perfect growth. The challenges he faced were designed to make him succeed as opposed to bring him down. But he willingly rebelled against God well knowing the consequences of his action as many of us do today. After he was corrupted by sin, he was expelled from the perfect environment. He ended up dwelling in the corrupt world. He became absolutely corrupt because the character of a person is defined by his dwelling place (environment). All human beings are born with the corrupt DNA of Adam and our actions are influenced by the corrupt world. By one man (Adam), sin was imputed to the entire human race. But our God is a just God, because by the obedience of one man (Jesus Christ also called the Second Adam) righteousness was imputed to all who believe (Romans 5:18-19).

****

If you read atheist's websites, you will often find complaints that the God of the Bible arbitrarily ordered the destruction of entire cities, such as Jericho, just to allow the Jews to have a homeland in the Middle East. How could a loving God command the destruction of all those "innocent" people? The argument sounds good, but it is utterly false. First of all there is no such a thing as an innocent person born after Adam. The unstated assumption is that the people who God ordered destroyed were morally corrupt as the Jews, who replaced them but these pagan tribes had their cup overflowing with iniquities. "You shall not behave thus toward the LORD your God, for every abominable act which the LORD hates they have done for their gods; for they even burn their sons and daughters in the fire to their gods" (Deuteronomy 12:31). God spared the Jews not for the sake of their own righteousness but because of His plan to bring about the Savior of the whole world as He promised to Abraham. The Bible says about the Jews that: "It is not for your righteousness or for the uprightness of your heart that you are going to possess their land, but it is because of the wickedness of these nations that the LORD your God is driving them out before you, in order to confirm the oath which the LORD swore to your fathers, to Abraham, Isaac and Jacob. (Deuteronomy 9:5). The God of the Old Testament is the God of New Testament, and His attitude towards sin has not changed. His righteousness demands justice. He cannot let sin go un-judged. Certainly, He will purge this universe of evil. The cross is the only escape route from the wrath of God's judgment. The cross makes a difference because it is the place where all believers are judged in Christ.

****

Some people do not believe that Jesus is the only way to God. They say who are we to judge? In fact, many of our friends believe the opposite—namely, there are many ways to God, a view called religious pluralism. Unfortunately no religion teaches that others ways are collect apart from theirs. The claim of the religious pluralist is therefore arrogant because it enforces its own belief on others. Jesus claimed to be the way (not one of the ways) to heaven. If there was another way to reconcile with God, Jesus would not have suffered at the cross. In the Garden of Gethsemane He cried out to the Father that if there is another way, let this cup pass. He partook of the cup of God's wrath on our behalf because this was the only way to save humanity (Luke 22:41-46). God does not take our salvation lightly. He paid for our sins dearly. Remember that it took His Son to come from eternity to the earth in order for us to become His sons. Salvation is when God reaches out to the lost world to save a handful of People who are willing to believe in Him. The truth is that every person has the right to believe what they want; but have you ever asked what God wants you to believe?

****

Truly God loves all His creation including you. But God's unconditional love is extended to the Church alone. God's love motivates Him to save but His love cannot save you. It is His gift of grace that saves whosoever receives Jesus Christ. Receiving is believing (John 1:11-12). Therefore the born again believers, whose sins were atoned for by the blood of Jesus are the only candidates to the saving grace of God. "For by grace you have been saved through faith, and that not of yourselves; it is the gift of God, not of works, lest anyone be found boasting. For we are his workmanship, created in Christ Jesus for good works, which God prepared beforehand that we should walk in them" (Ephesians 2:8-10).

****

We can defile the laws of God even the laws of nature at our peril! I had a Muslim friend whom I invited to Church and he surprised me when he came. He did not receive Jesus as his personal savior. Because he was a heavy smoker, I tried to convince to him to quit smoking. He resisted my efforts and responded that America is a free country whereby people are free to do as they will. Recently I met him in a shopping mall, carrying an oxygen tank to help him breathing. I asked him if he is still smoking. He replied that his doctor gave him an optional of quitting smoking or look for another doctor. He decided to quit smoking. The good news is that he is no longer smoking but the bad news is that he has lung cancer. He had the same power of will to quit before he got cancer but he missed it! No one is autonomous. If you deny God a chance to tell you what to do, then the law of nature, the law enforcement officers and the doctors will tell you what to do.

****

There is an orderliness in the universe; there is an unalterable law governing everything and every being that exists or lives. It is no blind law; for no blind law can govern the conduct of living beings ~ Mohandas Gandhi

****

"The measure of human stupidity is not the failure to establish a city on Planet Mars but the failure to recognize the fact that human civilization will ever amount to nothing irrespective of the innovativeness and inventiveness if the lordship of Christ is not at the pinnacle of all our endeavours" ~ Godfrey Nsubuga

****

Every person even nonbelievers agree that Jesus is the most moral person ever walked on the universe. Because of His integrity, I have no reason to doubt His Words. "See to it that no one takes you captive through hollow and deceptive philosophy, which depends on human tradition and the elemental spiritual forces of this world rather than on Christ" (Colossians 2:8).

Stephen Kyeyune

****

A British philosophy professor who has been a leading champion of atheism for more than a half-century has changed his mind. He now believes in God more or less based on scientific evidence, and says so on a video released Thursday. At age 81, after decades of insisting belief is a mistake, Antony Flew has concluded that some sort of intelligence or first cause must have created the universe. A 'super-intelligence' is the only good explanation for the origin of life and the complexity of nature. "To recant is to make a formal retraction or disavowal of (a statement or belief to which one has previously committed oneself). Repenting is deeper than recanting because it involves moving from previous errors and moving to the righteousness that God alone can provide" ~ Pastor Stephen Kyeyune, New Generation of Worshipers.

****

One critic wrote that "A theologian is like a Black man in a dark room looking for a black cat that isn't there and he finds it". I want to say that unlike Islam, Christianity accommodates all kinds of criticism. I think we do ourselves a huge disservice when our idea of rationalism is blind adulation without criticism. Nevertheless, sycophants never love what they volubly extol. They are perpetually running out of ammunition, with which to sustain their inundated criticisms, and soon they will plummet into intellectual oblivion. Humanism puts man at the center of everything. A spider's web is *a marvel of skill*: Look at it and admire the tricks of this cunning hunter. She spins her material from within her body to set up her snare (web) to a great length. In the same way atheists are seer humanists that find their trust and hope within themselves; their anchor is forged on their own anvil, and their rope twisted by their own hands. They rest upon their own foundation and carve out the pillars from their own house, scorning the thought of being debtors to the sovereign grace of God. "To conquer oneself is the best and noblest victory: to be vanquished by one's own nature is the worst and most ignoble defeat."

****

Open minded people like new things. New experiences teach you new things. I am always excited to read the Bible because the Word is ever new to me and every time I read it I look forward to listen to God speaking to me. The Word is ever new to me though I am not new to it; new in the sense of the divine guidance. You can learn new things at any time in your life if you're willing to be a beginner. If you actually learn to like being a beginner, the whole world opens up to you. God wants to breathe on you so that you can have a new beginning but you must be willing to listen to His Word and heed. No wonder Jesus often said that "Let him that has ears hear": The hearing ears are common but the listening ears are rare!

****

The cult leaders install fear among their followers. The cults do not allow people to reason. The cult leaders apply the bible interpretation differently to suit their interests. The word "cult" comes from the Latin word Cultus which means 'to worship or give reverence to a deity'. Therefore, a cult is a not-so-well-known religion often reflecting deviations from the central teachings and practices of the well-known religions in one or more aspects of spiritual life. Most cults teach ninety percent of the truth of the Scriptures but ten percent falsehood ending into a sharp curve to hell.

****

Truly God loves all His creation including you. But God's unconditional love is extended to the Church alone. God's love motivates Him to save but His love cannot save you. It is His gift of grace that saves whosoever receives Jesus Christ. Receiving is believing (John 1:11-12). Therefore the born again believers, whose sins were atoned for by the blood of Jesus are the only candidates to the saving grace of God. "For by grace you have been saved through faith, and that not of yourselves; it is the gift of God, not of works, lest anyone be found boasting. For we are his workmanship, created in Christ Jesus for good works, which God prepared beforehand that we should walk in them" (Ephesians 2:8-10).

****

The reason you are breathing is not to live but to give God the glory. In all that we do, the driving passion of the Christian must always be Soli Deo Gloria (to God alone be the glory). And the only way for this passion to be realized is to honor God as God, to understand Him as He has revealed Himself in His Word and not according to the mere opinions of fallen creatures.

****

Isaiah began his ministry about 740 B.C. and ended in 680 B.C. God, through Isaiah, gives us a clear picture of what was to happen, not only in the immediate future for Israel, but how He was going to bring the Messiah, His "Suffering Servant," into the world and allow Him to be sacrificed for the sins of the world. Chapters 40 through 66 of Isaiah discuss the Babylonian captivity and the reasons for it, and finally the restoration from it. However, there was going to be a greater deliverance than that from Babylon, and there would be a greater "messiah" than Cyrus, the king of Persia. Isaiah 53 is one of the best-loved passages of Scripture. It was this very passage that caused the Ethiopian to inquire of Philip, "of whom does the prophet say this, of himself or of some other man?" (Acts 8:34). Philip began at Isaiah 53 and "preached Jesus to him" (Acts 8:35). I Peter 2:21 says that you were called to follow Christ's example in suffering. It says that his suffering is the example you ideally follow.

****

Man is a credulous animal, and must believe something; in the absence of good grounds for belief, he will be satisfied with bad ones ~ Bertrand Russell

****

Satan's priority is to undermine the Word of God. He achieves his objectives by underestimating and overestimating the truth. He waters down the Word by taking away from it and adding to it (exaggeration). Half truth is as good as a lie

****

Begin this week with a brand new mindset. Open minded people like new things. New experiences teach you new things. I am always excited to read the Bible because the Word is ever new to me though I am not new to it; new in the sense of the divine guidance. Every time I read the Bible I look forward to listen to God speaking to me. You can seize this moment to learn new things if you're willing to be a beginner. If you actually experience a new beginning, the whole world opens up to you in the physical and spiritual realm. It is the fresh breathe of God on you that opens your minds to understand the mysteries of life, eradicating the limits of your perception. But you must be willing to receive, listen and heed to His Word. No wonder Jesus emphasized that "Let him that has ears hear": The hearing ears are common but the listening ears are rare and practically nonexistence in a non-regenerated soul!

****

We live in the superstitious culture. The more the world goes digital the more the devil gets grip of it through his agents "technology genius/elites". The shocking stories that occasionally flash on the front pages of our newspapers epitomize a growing disintegration of our social fabric. A godless culture glorifies immorality and disgraces morality. The peril comes to someone who does not allow emotions to take control of his or her attitudes. Exchanging one cosmetic blemish for another will begot grief for you in the end. The virtuous person shuns moral turpitude. His or her acts are noble and are motivated by God. Such are distinguished for their loyalty to the Word and the God of the Word. Knowing God is endless process. The more we get to know Him, the more we want to know Him. It is the morality of God that shapes the morality of man. Therefore there can be no morality without the existence of the Moral God.

****

In reference to a published humanistic article propagating man as the source of morality, I can say that his article is noble and is motivated by sympathy but it throws rationality out of the window and enters psychopathy through the door clouding any reasoning. The morality of God shapes the morality of man. Therefore, there can be no morality without the existence of the Moral God.

****

"A new world is not made simply by trying to forget the old. A new world is made with a new spirit, with new values. Our world may have begun that way, but today it is caricature. Our world is a world of things. What we dread most, in the face of the impending debacle, is that we shall be obliged to give up our gewgaws, gadgets, all the little comforts that have made us so comfortable. We are not peaceful souls; we are smug, tumid, queasy and quaky"

****

"The future of our civilization is based on prudence, critical self reflection, belief in higher values, and wisdom in matters of ordinary, everyday life. It is not about grabbing as much as possible, as quickly as possible." ~ Tyler Cowen, Economist

****

Wrong perception of life issues makes man a wrong person. Ironically, the immediate task of the elite, in any social system, is to conceptualize and propagate a comprehensive world view that extend or remake present realities, as imperfect and corrupt as they may seem in accordance with the social demands....In the process, some end up despising the highest moral order. The Bible says that, "And even if our gospel is veiled, it is veiled to those who are perishing, in whose case the god of this world has blinded the minds of the unbelieving so that they might not see the light of the gospel of the glory of Christ, who is the image of God" (2 Cor. 4:3-4). It is possible to have sharp brains but with darkened (blind) minds. You may call it a smart devil. God saves by transforming the heart and renewing the minds. We are called to bear testimonies not in our powers but in His power. It is true that we live under the same sky but we don't all have the same horizon; but the truth is independent of our beliefs. The truth comes from the Scriptures to our heads, not Vice versa. So if it is not sanctioned by Scriptures, please don't do it; this lesson will save you a lot of heartache.

****

Only a fool can say that there is no God. A fool says what he knows, and a wise man knows what he says. Even a fool, when he holds his peace, is counted wise. Albert Einstein said that not everything that can be counted counts and not everything that counts can be counted. God demands more than acknowledging that He is God. Remember that even demons acknowledge the existence of God. Salvation comes to only those who know God in a personal way by virtue of their relationship with Jesus Christ. This kind of knowledge does not depend on feelings but on the surrendered will. Life without Christ is life full of crisis. It is a choice between Christ and crisis! The danger of crisis in the present is the absence of clear consciousness, and in future it is total annihilation.

****

Life is eternal because God who is the source of life is eternal (He was, He is and He will always be). God is eternal and His Word is eternal. Each and every Christian doctrine must be seen within the concept of eternity. The claim that God's Word is bound to time and shackled to the culture of its time does not do justice to God's revelation. He has made everything beautiful in its time. He has also set eternity in the human heart (Ecclesiastes 3:11). God created time and He is not limited by time. God is pleased by our faith because faith is not limited by time. Believers are predestined to live in the presence of God eternally. Nonbelievers are eternally separated from the presence of God. Please place your future in the hands of God. He is God of all creations including time (past, present and future). He never changes but He can change you for the better future!

****

God is self-existence and self-defining but we are not. God defines His creations and determines how His creations function. He is the moral authority above all things. He has a plan and purpose for His creations. It is important to know who you are from God's prospective. Self-awareness and self-esteem begin with your awareness of who you are in Christ. On the contrary, the humanistic perspective is the view that identification with other humans is the most important association. Humanism is the philosophy that advocates a this perspective of the world, and it generally states that human beings have basically the same needs and values regardless of their specific life circumstances. The humanistic identity stands in opposition to the biblical point of view. For example humanism disregards the gender issue. "One cannot hammer a square peg into a round hole. Even to attempt to do such is foolish because the fit is unnatural. All such attempts are by nature doomed to failure. Yet, regardless of how unnatural and abnormal it may be, there are still those who are so detached from the natural reality that they relentlessly continue to hammer away trying to fit something into a place that is just not natural and thus not destined to fit."

****

The Spirit of God has been active on the earth since creation because He is the means through which God accomplishes all things. At first the earth was shapeless and covered in darkness, and God's Spirit hovered over the waters to activate creation (Genesis 1:2). It is the Spirit's intervention that resulted into an action that consecrated and made fruitful Mary's virginity. The Spirit of God overshadowed the Virgin Mary and what was conceived is called the Son of God (Matthew 1:18-25). The words "hovered" and "overshadow" have the same meaning in reference to the work of the Holy Spirit. Jesus used the same word to express His work towards us. He pleaded to Jerusalem, "How often I have longed to gather your children together, as a hen gathers her chicks under her wings, and you were not willing" (Luke 13:34). In this metaphor Jesus used the same word hovering over your children like the hen hovering over her chicks. The work of Jesus to mankind is that of the Holy Spirit hovering over us. An honest view will reveal that God has been speaking all along in different times and climes and there has never been a time when he wasn't represented on earth even now!!

****

Somebody asked: "According to Matthew 10:30, the very hairs of your head are all numbered. Does it mean that God knows the number of hairs on the heads of all people who have ever lived, who are living now and who will ever live on earth?" Answer: God is omniscient. It means He knows all things. He is omnipotent. It means He can do all things apart from the very thing that contradicts His character: God cannot sin, and He cannot cease be God. However, the above scripture is given in form of figure of speech. A figure of speech is figurative language in the form of a single word or phrase. It can be a special repetition, arrangement or omission of words with literal meaning, or a phrase with a specialized meaning not based on the literal meaning of the words. Hairs regularly fall from our heads with or without our notice because it is insignificant to us. Yet, God notices even the least significant things about us. It means God cares about us even more than we care for ourselves. His provision for us depends on the fact that He knows us best. Therefore we need not to worry as long as we put our trust in Him.

****

Question: I have a question for you in the midst of my personal tribulation (I am hanging in there). Could you tell me why the Lord says that he will make his enemies a foot stool, and says elsewhere the earth is his foot stool (Hebrews 1:13 and Isaiah 66:1)?

Response: I believe what we have in both cases are figurative uses. In Isaiah 66:1 it also says "heaven is My throne". On the one hand God exceeds the heavens and the earth by infinity (if He could even be described in these terms); on the other hand He actually has a localized throne in heaven (specifically, the third heaven) for the benefit of His creatures (Rev.4). But it is only in heaven - it is not technically speaking heaven itself. This passage is written in poetry, and this is typical poetic language - not wrong, but rather highly dramatic to make the point. If one were to rephrase this verse in prose it would be something like: "I rule in heaven; and I lord it over the earth". For that is what the throne and throne's footstool are really meant to convey, namely, powerful regal control - God's sovereign control of the heavens is such that it is as if they were His very throne, and His sovereign control over the earth is such that it is as if it were merely the place where He rests His feet.

****

Stella asked that: "Should women work on their hair?" Paul wrote that, "I also want the women to dress modestly, with decency and propriety, adorning themselves, not with elaborate hairstyles or gold or pearls or expensive clothes" (1 Timothy 2:9). Peter who wrote later on after Paul defined Paul's instruction in this way: "Your beauty should not come from outward adornment, such as elaborate hairstyles and the wearing of gold jewelry or fine clothes. Rather, it should be that of your inner self, the unfading beauty of a gentle and quiet spirit, which is of great worth in God's sight" 1 Peter 3:3-4, New International Version (NIV). Peter elaborated that our primary focus should be put on internal cleanness as opposed to external beauty. This means you can take care of your hair but don't waste all the time on the hair and forget your spiritual well-being.

****

Should women work on their hair or dye their hair? Peter who wrote later on after Paul defined Paul's instruction in this way: "Your beauty should not come from outward adornment, such as elaborate hairstyles and the wearing of gold jewelry or fine clothes. 4 Rather, it should be that of your inner self, the unfading beauty of a gentle and quiet spirit, which is of great worth in God's sight" 1 Peter 3:3-4New International Version (NIV)

There are no discussions in the Bible concerning the dyeing of hair because that wasn't an issue until modern times. I know there some wrong teachings denying people to embrace every modern thing. The Bible does not talk about cars; it does not mean that cars are bad but it is because cars did not exist during biblical times. All they had are donkeys and horses.

Regarding hair there are many references that suggest "elders" are wise men and women to be respected; that the "changing seasons" of our lives are normal and natural, and that growing old is basically a badge of honor, including the graying of our hair: Proverbs 16: 31 Gray hair is a crown of glory; it is gained in a righteous life. Since the Bible does not prohibit changing the color of our hair, in this particular case, it is probably safe to say that it's up to each individual to decide what to do to look nice in the glorifying manner to God. "While "abundant" hair is a glory, this does not mean women cannot cut or curl their hair to make it look its best. Not everyone has the good fortune to be born with thick and/or luxurious hair, and there is nothing wrong with cutting it into a nice style that suits our faces and figures. We are simply not to cut our hair into anything resembling a "masculine" style. Our bodies are, after all, God's vessels and we are commanded to take care of them, from top to bottom and the inside-out (1 Cor. 6:19)."

God has always been adamant about the roles and conduct of each gender. He made it very clear that women are to "act feminine" and dress modestly: Deuteronomy 22: 5 "A woman is not to wear men's clothing, and a man is not to put on women's clothing, for whoever does these things is detestable to ADONAI your God. "For so also the Set Apart women of old who trusted in Elohim, adorned themselves and were subject to their husbands...." Paul recommended that wives should respect their bodies and honor their husbands in the manner they dress. The above obviously shows that the wearing today's micro-miniskirts and revealing cleavage, etc., is not allowed or acceptable!

****

Somebody asked is whether cremation is biblical. Cremation comes from Latin word "cremare" meaning "to burn". Some historical reasons for cremating the dead are outlined here: 1) To cope with fear of the dead. 2) To enable easy transportation of bones back to homes or other places. 3) To prevent bodies from being stolen by thieves and miscreants. 4) Belief that fire freed the soul from wandering and searching. 5) Belief that fire purifies the deceased person's soul. In the Old Testament, earth burial was the norm for treating deceased persons. Cremation was used only as punishment and humiliation for those who engaged in grievous, sinful acts as recorded in Joshua 7:15; Leviticus 21:9; 20:14. Cremation was also an instrument of God's wrath as He destroyed certain peoples by fire as recorded in Numbers 11:1-3; 16:35; Joshua 7:15,24-26; 2 Kings 1:10-12 and famously the cities of Sodom and Gomorrah in Genesis 19:24 The Scriptures never instruct people to burn dead bodies turning them into ashes. "Ashes to ashes and dust to dust" is a common phrase we hear associated with funeral practices. This first appeared in the Church of England's Book of Common Prayer in 1549. The phrase "dust to dust" has some biblical origin from Gen. 3:19 and Ecclesiastes 3:20 but the words "ashes to ashes" do not appear anywhere in the Bible. The human body is physical and perishable but it is a vessel that can be clean or unclean depending on the nature of the heart. In a born again (regenerated) person, the body becomes the temple or tabernacle where the Holy Spirit of God is treasured. Upon death the significance of the body ceases to exist because the spirit of man returns to the creator. Therefore it does not matter whether the dead body is buried in the ground or it is cremated. This is my view.

****

When the Bible says that God is love, it means that love is eternal. God sees your situation from eternal prospective. God can be known by revelation. Likewise His love is spiritual and can only be revealed to the transformed hearts and renewed minds.

****

God's Agape love for us could not be stopped even when it meant His only Son to die. Jesus willingly died for us. "Do you think I cannot call on my Father, and he will at once put at my disposal more than twelve legions of angels?" (Matthew 26:53). It is not the nails that held Jesus at the cross but His love for us. God sent His begotten Son to die as a ransom for our sin. The ransom was not paid to Satan or any other person because God does not owe anyone or anything to anybody. The Scriptures say nothing of God having to pay Satan or of Satan requiring payment from God, but the Scriptures do say that the covenant God initiated and made with His people required His life. I mean the only perfect life (perfect sacrifice) on earth.

****

Today the heavy presence of God (Shekhinah) descended during worshipping. The greatest challenge for me has been to maintain experiencing His presence after Church. The Bible says that the Holy Spirit descended on Jesus in form of a dove at baptism. Whenever I think about the symbol of the dove, I recall that it is one of the most nervous birds that will fly away at a slight provocation. I resolved to be conscious of the presence of God; each and every step I take to handle His presence with delicacy like a dove sitting on my shoulder least He flies away. In His presence I am anchored firm and sure, safely anchored on Christ the Rock of my soul, such that I dread not the stormy waves that roll.

****

An idea requires the word. The word "atheist" for the first time used by a Christian describing somebody that did not acknowledge the existence of God. Atheism is the rejection (or absence) of the belief that God, or any other deities, exists. Although the term "atheism" originated in the sixteenth century – based on Ancient Greek ἄθεος "godless, denying the gods, ungodly" – and open admission to positive atheism in modern times was not made earlier than in the late eighteenth century, atheistic ideas, as well as their political influence, have a more expansive history. Over the centuries, atheists have arrived at their point of view through a variety of avenues, including scientific, philosophical and ideological notions.

****

The atheists are so blinded that they have failed to realize that the earth is a better place because of the impact of the Christians. I mean things like former criminals who were converted and denounced their nasty activities. The answer, I respectfully submit, is situated in the bifurcated nature of our ego where any acknowledgement of the positives by the atheists and some of these pseudo individuals would make Christianity look good.

****

I wonder why the secular world chooses the Christians as their punching bag. There are many dishonest criticisms against Christians such as this one: "We should question supposed Christian organizations concerned only with bioethical or so-called moral issues related to life, death and sexuality, without reference to equality, inclusion and a decent and meaningful existence throughout life" writes Moira Byrne Garton. In reality, the majority of churches are more discerning. They articulate policy positions coherent with the 'consistent ethic of life', even if they do not explicitly reference this ethic. This is evident in their comments on palliative care, asylum seekers, employment conditions and more.

****

Stephen Kyeyune

Do all ways lead to God? I would say YES! The Gospel reveals to us the loving Father. Apart from the Gospel, God is known as the merciless judge that righteously condemns the sinner. No one in sound minds would like to know God apart from Jesus because it means condemnation. He is a consuming fire: this is the kind of God all ways (apart from Christ) lead to. The way of Jesus leads to God the Father but all other ways lead to God the Judge. Which way are you taking?

****

Isaiah 54:10 – 17: "For the mountains shall depart, and the hills be removed; but my kindness shall not depart from thee, neither shall the covenant of my peace be removed, saith the LORD that hath mercy on thee. O thou afflicted, tossed with tempest, and not comforted, behold, I will lay thy stones with fair colours, and lay thy foundations with sapphires. And I will make thy windows of agates, and thy gates of carbuncles, and all thy borders of pleasant stones. And all thy children shall be taught of the LORD; and great shall be the peace of thy children. In righteousness shalt thou be established: thou shalt be far from oppression; for thou shalt not fear: and from terror; for it shall not come near thee. Behold, they shall surely gather together, but not by me: whosoever shall gather together against thee shall fall for thy sake." USA was founded on Judoe-Christian values. However, as religion and faith are being driven out of the public square, the Judeo-Christian ethical foundations that have sustained our country since its beginning are being lost and are being replaced with a humanistic amorality, a self-centered, pragmatic indifference that will ensure that our moral compasses will fail to point us in the right direction in the future.

****

"Suppose a nation in some distant region should take the Bible for their only law book, and every member should regulate his conduct by the precepts there exhibited! Every member would be obliged in conscience, to temperance, frugality, and industry; to justice, kindness, and charity towards his fellow men; and to piety, love, and reverence toward Almighty God ... What a Eutopia, what a Paradise would this region be." John Adams, February 22, 1756 (Federer, William

J., America's God and Country Encyclopedia Of Quotations, FAME Publishing, Coppell, Texas, 1994, p.5)

****

Nominalism: The doctrine holding that abstract concepts, general terms, or universals have no independent existence but exist only as names.

****

Definition of secularism (n) sec·u·lar·ism [sékyələ rìzzəm] exclusion of religion from public affairs: the belief that religion and religious bodies should have no part in political or civic affairs or in running public institutions, especially schools rejection of religion: the rejection of religion or its exclusion from a philosophical or moral system.

****

The New Age Movement propagates personal development by believing in yourself. Christianity propagates investing your faith in Christ. Faith is not just positive thinking but it is trusting in God and allowing Him to accomplish all things through you. This is perfect obedience. Half truth is a lie masquerading as the truth. If a purpose of something is misunderstood abuse is inevitable!

****

Naturalism believes that they is nothing beyond the natural realm. The theory denies the supernatural creation and works.

****

Unbelief is a grave sin that can swallow you when you are watching. No wonder the message of the saving grace has been preached, regurgitated over the years, and has become meaningless to some. The culprits come to God with self-righteousness without a need of any spiritual revelation from God. Such cannot receive the deep things of the Word of God which are spiritually revealed. They end up depending on their finite minds for spiritual enlightenment. Unbelief questions the validity of the

Word with prior intention of proving a point from purely humanistic point of reference. Questioning the validity of the Word is questioning the integrity of the writer (God). It is another way of bluntly defending your spiritual bankruptcy in the face of God! It is impossible to overcome a problem or a habit that you jovially defend. I made a resolution never to be comfortable with my natural man even when it means disdaining being comfortable. My earnest prayer is that: "Defend me, God, from myself".

****

Faith is not a virtue but it is the totality of the Christian living. Faith is trusting in somebody's abilities other than your own abilities. We are called to invite Jesus in our lives and to allow Him to manifest His life through our lives. There are people out there still waiting to clean up the mess out of their lives in order for them to receive Jesus Christ. Due to the misconception of salvation they are caught up in a chicken and egg situation, and they are most likely to wait forever and miss the eternal blessings. You are not called to clean up your mess before you come to Christ but to come to Christ as you are (with your burdens) trusting Him to do what you couldn't do (to unburden you). If you were able to clean up yourself God wouldn't have sent His Son to do the job! All you have to do is to surrender your will to Him, and He will take care of the rest. He justifies you, after which, He joins hands with you to sanctify you until the day of glorification.

****

The Vatican and the liberals have a reputation of scratching off some scriptures. They forget that Christianity is based upon the impregnable Rock of Holy Scriptures. The term "sola Scriptura" or "the Bible alone" is a short phrase that represents the simple truth that the Bible is the final authority. The very phrase "It is written" means exclusively transcribed, and not hearsay. The command to believe what is written means to believe only the pure word of God. To believe is to accept the whole counsel of God as given by the Scriptures. What is at stake before the Holy God is His incorruptible truth. To further establish the Authority of the Bible, God ordained that these words be penned near the end of the last chapter of The Book of Revelation. 22:18 For I testify unto every man that heareth the words of the prophecy of this book, If any man shall add unto these things, God shall add unto him the plagues that are written in this book: 22:19 And if any man shall take away from the words of the book of this prophecy, God shall take away his part out of the book of life, and out of the holy city, and [from] the things which are written in this book.

****

Taking away other religious leaders from their respective religions does not make their religions void but taking Christ out of Christianity makes Christianity void. Jesus is not just the center holding this world but He is the center holding the entire universe.

****

Jesus did not point to any one denomination to be true. He simply taught the truth. Denominations are manmade intended to divide and control people. The verse that denominations never read: "God is faithful, who has called you into fellowship with his Son, Jesus Christ our Lord. I appeal to you, brothers and sisters, in the name of our Lord Jesus Christ, that all of you agree with one another in what you say and that there be no divisions among you, but that you be perfectly united in mind and thought." (1 Corinthians 1:9-10).

****

It is important to focus on those sobering facts that draw us closer to God now and for eternity. We tolerantly extend people the dignity of their own beliefs without minimizing the differences between religions. We honor them without compromising. We are allowed to profess our belief without ridicule or venom, or disparagement. The life of Christ produces in us true humility. But it also produces in us true enlightenment. We have come to grasp grace that God works His way down to us, dies for our moral and religious failures and offers us life. We must lovingly, humbly try to persuade others to believe in Jesus, who alone offers the wonderful promise of the way to God, the truth of God and life of God. The bitter truth is that the choice you make now determines your destiny. "You are today a summation of your past choices. You will be tomorrow and into the future what you choose to do now. Lead Yourself First." - David Bernard-Stevens

****

Jesus pointed to Himself as the only way to recover our lost glory that will fully be realized in eternity. Jesus Christ the way without junctions of religious rules and rituals but that is trekked by faith. It is not obeying this, that, and the other; it is a straight road: "Believe, and live." It is a road so hard that no self-righteous man can ever tread it, but so easy that every sinner who knows himself to be a sinner may find his way to heaven by simply confessing his or her sins to Christ. Paul boldly emphasized that, "I determined not to know anything among you except Jesus Christ and Him crucified" (1 Corinthians 2:2). It means salvation from evil and the gift of eternal life.

****

It is common to hear all religions claiming to be the way to heaven. The reality is that if everybody is right, then nobody is right. If every viewpoint is equally valuable, no viewpoint is valuable. If there is a way there must be one true way. But what is this thing called the way? When Adam and Eva sinned God sent them out the Garden. He placed at the east of the garden of Eden Cherubims, and a flaming sword which turned every way, to keep the way to the tree of life. Notice, the Cherubims were just as responsible as the flaming sword to "keep the way." Shamar, Heb., to hedge about, to guard, protect, attend. The main thing in the Garden was the tree of life. The way to the tree of life was closed to Adam but it remained open to man who had credentials to access it. Jesus opened it with the sacrifice of His own blood so that we might obtain mercy and grace (Heb. 4:16). "-----Without shedding of blood there is no remission of sin" (Heb. 9:22). His perfect sacrifice reconciled God with man, opening the Way to the tree of life. Jesus alone is the Door (Way). It is He who the inner "veil" of the O.T. Tabernacle symbolized. When His body was torn, the veil ripped opening the Way to the Throne of Grace. The "Way" was protected that man may come in, but only in God's Way, and that "Way" is by the shedding of blood.

****

Galatians 5:25 - Those who belong to Christ Jesus have crucified the flesh with its passions and desires. Since we live by the Spirit, let us keep in step with the Spirit. Paul says that Christ has set you free, so be free. "If we live by the Spirit, let us also walk by the Spirit." I don't think Paul is using the verbs "live" and "walk" in a technical way here. He means, "If we live by the Spirit, let us live by the Spirit," or "If we walk in the Spirit, let us walk in the Spirit." The indicative grounds the imperative. The imperative always flows out of the indicative. Pastor Tim Keller writes, "Religion operates on the principle 'I obey—therefore I am accepted by God.' But the operating principle of the gospel is 'I am accepted by God through what Christ has done—therefore I obey." This is another way of saying justification is the basis for sanctification. The objective work of Christ is the foundation for the subjective work of the Holy Spirit. It is clear that both the indicative and the imperative are essential but one comes after the other.

****

The problem with African Christianity today is syncretism. It is the combination of different systems of philosophical or religious beliefs or practices in particular traditional religions with Christianity. God's way is not man's way; His way is Yes and Amen. God in his infinite wisdom has demonstrated for us to fully perceive what he would want his people to be.

****

The degree of a fallacy in a human is evident in the tendency and capacity to compartmentalize knowledge by drifting at blurred lines of subjects. Ideas are inter-locked and inter-woven into fragments of knowledge that might not be visible to the simple and unstudied minds. Wisdom is un-broken eternal links that might not be accessible to the natural minds but perceived by the heart. Because of the nature of human capacity and propensity to interpret phenomena according to conceptions, perceptions, interpretations, all of which tend to be influenced by our natural instincts of selfishness, interests, aspirations, and frustrations. Knowledge is the ability to put things apart (dismantle). Wisdom is asking God to put them together. Wisdom is godly idea of fixing broken things. "A mind that is stretched to a new idea will never return to its original dimension" ~ Oliver Wendell Holmes, Jr.

****

The Mormons say we preexisted with God--that God and his goddess wife produced offspring who inhabit human bodies at birth. The reality is that God existed before time and space. Everything was created by God. The universe begins with the story of creation and ends with restoration because it ceased to operate as God intended it to be.

****

When a culture rejects God, it always replaces Him with something else. "For many in our post-Christian culture, the new "god" is science, the new priests (those whom we must not question) are the scientists, and the new religion is a materialistic scientism" ~ Dr. Albert Mohler

****

Science seamlessly interlaces with religion to compartmentalize knowledge. The recent discovery by scientists of massive waters underneath the earth greater than the oceans of the earth combined was predicated some 4000 years ago by the Scriptures: "In the six hundredth year of Noah's life, in the second month, the seventeenth day of the month, the same day were all the fountains of the great deep broken up, and the windows of heaven were opened. And the rain was upon the earth forty days and forty nights" (Genesis 7:14).

****

Illusions can be accepted as a way of life. Movie is moving picture - a form of entertainment that enacts a story by sound and a sequence of images giving the illusion of continuous movement. It involves a sequence of photographs projected onto a screen with sufficient rapidity as to create the illusion of motion and continuity. The camera is the key to the unique power of movies to manipulate our sense of space. No other art form can alter the reality of time and space like film can. It can condense days' worth of action into mere minutes. Film can travel back and forth in time between past, present, and future like no other medium can. Film also has the power to instantly shift locations on opposite sides of the world. A viewer can be in Miami one minute and then Tokyo the next.

****

Ordinary people believe only in the possible. Extraordinary people visualize not what is possible or probable, but rather what is impossible. And by visualizing the impossible, they begin to see it as possible ~ Cherie Carter-Scott Happy week ahead!

****

"It is important to see distant things as if they were close and to take a distanced view of close things" ~ Miyamoto Musashi

****

"To know the mechanics does not mean that we are practicing the Disciplines. The Spiritual Disciplines are an inward and spiritual reality, and the inner attitude of the heart is far more crucial than the mechanics for coming into the reality of the spiritual life"
~ Richard Foster,

****

God gives us His minds to think as He thinks (1 Cor. 2:16). The way you think determines the way you go. At the same time, God expects us to learn from our life experiences. Experience is the best teacher which gives exposure to all aspects of life. "It the endeavor to which you are exposed and your action on it culminates in experience" A decent person is open minded and is ready to learn from the past experiences and from others without being stupid. The tendency to have the same problems, over and over again, is associated with the habitual unwillingness to change. The effective change is demonstrated rather than debated. Saying something one hundred times is not as good as living it once.

****

Today, I had lunch with Simon. As usual our discussion was based on theology. He made a statement that Adam was not created perfect because he had the desire to sin. He went ahead to say that if he was perfect he would have been like God without desire to sin. I disagreed with him. I told him that God created a perfect man (Adam). Simon, like many people confused the wording in the Scriptures. The words we use in our languages dramatically change meaning when they are used in reference to God. For example the word "perfect': God is infinitely perfect without a possibility of sinning. But 'perfect' when used in reference to man means complete or just right to function as intended. Certainly, God did not create evil desires in Adam because evil did not come into the heart of man until Adam sinned. But God created Adam with a free will to choose to obey or to disobey. Choices can be emotional but desires come from the heart. Like Adam, at times the choices we make do not necessarily reflect the desires of our hearts. But we cannot escape the consequences of our choices. "Sin is enticing because it pays the highest wages; but it pays in counterfeit currencies"

****

Adam was in God's breath (Spirit) before God created him. Eva was in God's minds before she ended up in Adam's hands. God separated Eva from the side (rib) of Adam. God created man because He wanted somebody to share with life. After sin corrupted mankind, God redeemed us by restoring His life in us. The redeemed have eternal fellowship with God.

****

We are born with the sinful nature. Even little babies are born with evil intents that gradually manifest as they grow up. Rev. Voddie Baucham said with humor that God made babies so little that they wouldn't kill you, and so cute that you wouldn't kill them.

****

The person closest to the gates of hell is the person who looks in the mirror and says "Look at me I am a good person". The person closest to the gets of heaven is the person who looks in the mirror and says "what a wretched person I am, I need a Savior"

****

God saves us from Himself. Propitiation is a theological term meaning that the wrath of God towards our sins has been satisfied or spent or quenched. It means what God has done for our redemption and what Jesus has accomplished on our behalf.

****

The word "grace" may not appear on the first pages of the Bible but the meaning of Grace is there. From the time Adam sinned, God dealt with the sinful man by His grace alone. However, the first time the word 'grace' appeared on the pages of the Bible is in Genesis 6:8. It says that, "But Noah found grace in the eyes of the Lord". The word grace in this case has the root word of stooping; God stooping down to the lowest of lowness to pick up the filthiness of a fallen man. Man has been on constant run from God but Noah got the favor of God. God picked him up and by His grace declared him to be righteous. In Genesis 9:1-7, God blessed Noah with this benediction: "And as for YOU men, be fruitful and become many, make the earth swarm with YOU and become many in it." From the three sons of Noah came the human races: Shem (Jews/Arabs), Ham (Blacks), and Japheth (Whites). ~ Quotation from my book "Growing in Grace" pg. 449.

****

Why is the divine high-priesthood important? The priests could recognize leprosy but had no power to clean a leper. Jesus recognized leprosy and cleaned the leper. The Law has mandate to show us the righteousness of God but has no power to affect the change of the soul into righteousness. The Old Testament sacrifices had to be repeated over and over because they had no power to take away the sins permanently. But Jesus sacrificed for our sins once for all when He offered himself (Hebrews 10:12). Jesus has the power to clean the physical and spiritual leprosy (sin). That is why He is called the Savior.

****

We must live in harmony with the truth that "Thou art worthy, O Lord, to receive glory and honor and power: for thou hast created all things, and for thy pleasure they are and were created" (Revelation 4:11). We were created for God's pleasure, but all creations give us pleasure, as well. Man was created with the capacity to enjoy them all. His love for us gives us riches beyond measure. Although we have different life stories and legacies, God created us with the same purpose in His mind. We are God's stewards. We should not be afraid of anything as long as we are doing God's will on earth. "A man or woman of God that is in the center of God's will is under God's surveillance; he or she is immortal as long as God is not done with him."

****

Morality is defined by God alone. In the person of Jesus Christ, God in his infinite wisdom has demonstrated for us to fully perceive what He would want his people to be. God reveals His secrets to the despised of the world. In this case the believers have answers to the pending questions pertaining to life because they have the minds of Christ. God calls then qualifies, but man qualifies then calls. The problem is when the envisioned people become ineffective due to doubt while the blind ones are fully saturated with confidence. Laziness is not just resting but neglecting the given assignment. Failure is not our only punishment for laziness; there is also the danger of sanctioning the success of our opponents. Our ineffectiveness in arresting the culture's moral decline has turned out to be the manure for immorality to blossom. I want to pause and ask you that: In case today you were arrested and put on trial for being a Christian, is there enough evidence in your life to convict you (condemn you) for being a practicing believer? If not so, you are cruising in a wrong direction!

****

Though the geophysical catastrophes that frequently ravage our globe today cannot be attributed unequivocally to the direct action of God, they can be traced ultimately to human rebellion, and the *permissive* will of the Creator. Sin corrupted the entire human race and nature.

The Bible says that, "For we know that the whole creation groans and suffers the pains of childbirth together until now. And not only this, but also we ourselves, having the first fruits of the Spirit, even we ourselves groan within ourselves, waiting eagerly for our adoption as sons, the redemption of our body" (Romans 8:22-23).

****

Problems come in different packages. While the majority of us do not want bad things to happen to good people, yet, nobody can say for sure that their choices were absolutely correct. We shall always have moments when we agree that not all our fingers are the same and so do our ways of thoughts! "Your living is determined not so much by what life brings to you as by the attitude you bring to life; not so much by what happens to you as by the way your mind looks at what happens" ~ Kahlil Gibran

****

Socrates said that "The un-examined life is not worth living." I can add that life without trials is not worthy living. We mature by overcoming trials. And no one's life is free from trials. But those who have some sense of who they are in Christ also have a context for understanding how all the elements of their life fit together. God calls us to empty ourselves. The fuller a ship becomes, the deeper it sinks in the water. The trails of life are necessary to increase our dependence on God. "Idlers may indulge a fond conceit of their abilities, because they are untried; but the earnest worker soon learns his own weakness. If you want to feel how utterly powerless you are apart from the living God, attempt especially the great work of proclaiming the unsearchable riches of Christ, and you will know, as you never knew before, what a weak, unworthy thing you are."

****

Life isn't fair. Life isn't maths - it doesn't always add up. Our hope does not depend on the condition of life in which chance has placed us, but is the result of pursuit of the peace that Jesus ushered into this world. In this world we habitually seek justice for ourselves and justice for others; but nobody in the right minds would seek to get justice from

God. The Bible says that "It is a fearful thing to fall into the hands of the living God" (Hebrews 10:31). Regardless, the justice of God will certainly come because He is the Just God; it might delay but will not sleep forever. Thomas Jefferson lamented that "Indeed, I tremble for my country when I reflect that God is just". The unconditional love of God extended to us (believers) the grace therefore breaking the rod of His wrath against our sins.

****

God works in our darkest moment to bring out His goodness in us and to cruise us to our intended potentiality. If Moses was not kicked out of the palace, there would have been no redemption from Egypt. If Joseph was not dumped in the pit, Israel would not have survived the famine. If there was no cross, there would have been no salvation. "How blessed to feel assured that the Lord is with us in all our ways and condescends to enter into our humiliations and banishment! Even at such times we may bask in the sunshine of our Father's love. We need not hesitate to go where He promises His presence; even the darkest valley grows bright with the radiance of this assurance" Alistair Begg

****

The love of God is like an ocean; we may see where it begins but never see its ending. In every desert of calamity God has an oasis of comfort. His mercies are new every morning.

****

Joshua 20 - God instructed Joshua to build the cities of refuge to protect the people who were guilty of homicide. The roads to these cities were straight and clearly marked for everyone to see. As soon as the man seeking refuge reached the outskirts of the city, he was safe; it was not necessary for him to be beyond the walls--the suburbs themselves were sufficient protection. This is a picture of the road to Christ Jesus. It is no roundabout road of the law; it is no obeying this, that, and the other; it is a straight road: "Believe, and live." It is a road so hard that no self-righteous man can ever tread it, but so easy that every sinner who knows himself to be a sinner may by it find his way to heaven. As soon as the sinner confesses his sins to Jesus Christ and receives Him as the Savior, he is safe and secure. He gets immunity for the sins he committed. Christ becomes his sufficient protection.

****

Jesus is called the man of sorrow. He was despised and rejected by men; a man of sorrows, and acquainted with grief; and as one from whom men hide their faces he was despised, and we esteemed him not. God has one Son that is sinless but He has no son that is without sorrow. The first three verses of Chapter 53 describe the Messiah's strange rejection. These words express the feelings of the repentant nation when at last they will recognize him at his return. The prophet cries out as the voice of the nation, Who has believed our report? And to whom has the arm of the Lord been revealed? For he grew up before him like a young plant, and like a root out of dry ground; he had no form or comeliness that we should look at him, and no beauty that we should desire him.

****

I asked one friend of mine, who is a Muslim, and who is known for his critical views of the Scriptures to show me one scripture when Jesus incited violence. The next day he came up with this one: "From the days of John the Baptist until now the kingdom of heaven suffereth violence, and the violent take it by force,"—Matthew 11:12. He was wrong! Jesus said these words in reference to the people who are aggressively striving to enter through a narrow gate to be saved and are aggressively pursuing righteousness to stay saved. There is parallelism with this scripture: "For the kingdom of God is not meat and drink; but righteousness, and peace, and joy in the Holy Ghost" (Romans 14:17). Jesus insinuates that determination and commitment is the key to the spiritual victory. Thomas Calyle once said "The block of granite, which was an obstacle in the pathway of the weak, became a stepping-stone in the pathway of the strong". Be the pacesetter and let others follow!

****

Romans 9:13 - Just as it is written: "Jacob I loved, but Esau I hated." The meaning is that God loved Esau less than He loved Jacob. Why?

The Edomites are the descendants of Edom, i.e., Esau, according to Genesis 36:1-19. And according to Numbers 20:14-21, the Israelites were refused permission to pass inviolate through Edom. This was an instance of religious aversion probably exacerbated by Satan himself. The Herods were the Edomite family that ruled Israel during the time of Jesus' earthly ministry and the first Christian church. The Jewish ruling council, called Sanhedrin, was under the authority of the Herods, who were in turn under the authority of the Roman emperor.

****

Morality is defined by God alone. In the person of Jesus Christ, God in his infinite wisdom has demonstrated for us to fully perceive what He would want his people to be. God reveals His secrets to the despised of the world. In this case the believers have answers to the pending questions pertaining to the world because they have the minds of Christ. God calls then qualifies, but man qualifies then calls. The problem is when the envisioned people become infective due to doubt while the blind ones are fully saturated with confidence. Laziness is not just resting but neglecting the given assignment. Failure is not our only punishment for laziness; there is also the danger of sanctioning the success of our opponents. Our ineffectiveness in arresting the culture's moral decline has turned out to be the manure for immorality to blossom.

****

Love and tolerance does not mean compromising our values. Nowhere is that pattern more evident than in the realm of religious freedom where recent years have seen efforts, both subtle and overt, to squelch diversity of ideas. Preaching the gospel in public places other than the sanctuaries is restricted; speaking against the immoral practices of our times is considered to be hate crime. In the real world that we live in it is the person on the wrong side of the law that is vindicated. Recently, George Zimmerman was acquitted for murdering Trayvon Martin. Millions of people were outraged and some marched on streets to protest. While I do not support violence, I believe the worst scenario is to keep silent. There may be times when we are powerless to prevent injustice, but there must never be a time when we fail to protest. The problem of America is not racism or injustices; it is immorality at rampage. We may not change the procedural events surrounding us but we can change our attitudes.

****

By Associated Press; Tuesday, January 14, 2014 at 1:54 pm: The Judge's ruling - ALBUQUERQUE (AP) — Competent, terminally ill patients have a fundamental right under the New Mexico Constitution to seek a physician's help in getting prescription medications if they want to end their lives on their own terms, a state district judge ruled Monday. Second Judicial District Judge Nan Nash said the constitution prohibits the state from depriving a person of life, liberty or property without due process. "This court cannot envision a right more fundamental, more private or more integral to the liberty, safety and happiness of a New Mexican than the right of a competent, terminally ill patient to choose aid in dying," the judge wrote. Nash also ruled that doctors could not be prosecuted under the state's assisted suicide law, which classifies helping with suicide as a fourth-degree felony. The plaintiffs in the case do not consider physicians aiding in dying a form of suicide. I believe that people who decide to kill themselves misuse the divine authority entrusted to us by God to judge ourselves by judging themselves unworthy to live. Only God has the right to give and to take life.

****

Nature has no laws but the laws of nature belong to God. The laws of nature cannot be broken but can be demonstrated. For example when you jump from the roof, the fractured bone is the demonstration of the law of gravity. Also, it is true that man cannot and will never fly. Man has instead created inventions that allow him to fly in the form of a machine. Man simply found another set of laws that allow man to overcome that limitation through the use of inventions. Thus the basic natural law that man cannot fly remains unchanged. Certainly, broken laws of nature are rarely except by the miraculous intervention of the Creator. The effects of the law of nature can be suspended such as Christ walking on water. The parting of the Red Sea was a suspension of the laws of nature. God gave to us His laws for our own protection; we ignore them at our peril! Likewise, breaking the Moral Law of God is sin (1 John 3:4), the consequence of which is a curse but obedience to His laws means walking into His blessings.

****

As much as we expect miracles, our faith is anchored not in signs and not in wonders but in faith without seeing. We worship the sovereign God that created the Universe. "It is easy to contemplate that we were created to worship. We're flat-out desperate for it. From sports fanaticism to celebrity tabloids to all the other strange sorts of voyeurisms now normative in our culture, we evidence that we were created to look at something beyond ourselves and marvel at it, desire it, like it with zeal, and love it with affection. Our thoughts, our desires, and our behaviors are always oriented around something, which means we are always worshiping — ascribing worth to — something. If it's not God, we are engaging in idolatry. But either way, there is no way to turn the 'worship – switch' in our hearts off."

****

"Science can only talk about what's in this world. But what I discovered and what really blew my mind was that the more science learns…the more science would lead us to believe that there is something beyond the world." Astronomer Fred Hoyle, the scientist who coined the phrase "Big Bang", after years of observation, famously remarked that the universe itself "looks like a put-up job." This led to a realization: Although most people think of miracles as Divine suspensions of the laws of nature— God parting the Red Sea, for example—perhaps the greatest miracle was the creation of those laws in the first place. Maybe the fact that we exist at all is more miraculous than the mightiest wonder recorded by human eyewitnesses in Scripture. "Our existence—the existence of the universe, the existence of life—is itself a crazy miracle, a miracle so astounding that it makes the parting of the Red Sea look like nothing, look like a child's joke," ~ Eric.

****

The word miracle in the Bible is translated as signs and wonders. The African (Luganda) word for miracle is *"Kyamagero"*: which comes out of two words, *Kyama* (Secret) and *Magero* (A Big Story). "The philosophy here is that the more secret the undertaking, the bigger the story when the secret is revealed. The fact that God works in secrecy makes the revelation of the completed work *E'kyamagero!*" (Miracle) ~ Kawesa.

****

We are called to believe in miracles but not to schedule them. Jesus saw an opportunity to teach in everything He did. Jesus did not perform miracles in form of entertaining or magic as portrayed by Hollywood. In fact the word miracle is an English word that does not appear in the original manuscripts; it is represented by the words 'signs and wonders'. It means that miracles were amazing signs pointing to something deeper than the actual miracle. Every miracle performed by Jesus had a moral and theological teaching behind it (John 20:30-31). Satan's priority is to undermine the Word of God. He achieves his objectives by underestimating and overestimating the truth. He waters down the Word by taking away from it and adding to it (exaggeration). Half truth is as good as a lie.

****

How do you separate the voice of God from other voices? The voice of God is always convicting rather than condemning. It is that soft voice that yearns to bring you back into righteousness in case of flaw. In whatever way God speaks, in order for something to be of God it must not be in contradiction to the written Scriptures.

****

When God speaks in a sound voice, the world trembles and things get dire. The voice of God is not necessarily a sound; it is not necessarily a thought or even a feeling. It is a conviction that happens when we meditate on His Word. His voice at times is offensive to our intellect because healing comes after we are offended by the very things that we naturally adore. It takes His Spirit to infuse His voice with deeper meaning. Every believer has an antenna to receive what the Spirit is saying. It is the inner voice that is contrary to human logic. God gave us His written Word to guide us and wrote His Law in our hearts to regulate our desires and priorities. The desires of a person born of God (born again person) become the desires God. Virtue is a condition of the person (creature) that is in the presence of God, reflecting the behaviors of the Creator. The opposite of virtue is vice; it is a habitual, repeated practice of wrongdoing. We have no excuse for vice behaviors because God in his infinite wisdom, through Jesus Christ, demonstrated for us to fully perceive what He would want His people to be.

****

God's dwelling place is called the temple because there is no place that can contain Him (1 King 8:27). Jesus said that He is the true Temple. The Bible says that your body is the temple of God. Jesus said that He is the light of the world. Then He turned around and instructed His disciples to be the light to the lost world. The Bible says concerning the perishing world that, "In whom the god of this world hath blinded the minds of them which believe not, lest the light of the glorious gospel of Christ, who is the image of God, should shine unto them" (2 Cor. 4:2-5). We are the light of the world because we are the body of Christ representing His very presence on the earth. Today, the glory of God is evidently manifested in our lives by the fruit of the Spirit (Galatians 5:22). The Bible says that in heaven we shall shine in the glory of God in its fullness by directly reflecting His light. "And there shall be no night there; and they need no lamp, neither light of the sun; for the Lord God gives them light: and they shall reign forever and ever" (Revelation 22:5).

****

We live in the culture of popular body make-over. It is quite common these days for people to wish to undergo plastic surgery when they are discontented about something in their bodies. The term 'plastic surgery' actually comes from the original Greek word plastikos which means "to mold". The procedure in general basically involves repairing, reshaping or restoring skin, tissue and body parts. The end result is a better appearance or a restoration or enhancement of functions. There are two major types of plastic surgery, reconstructive and cosmetic. "You can change your external appearances as want but the change of character is for a person with a sincere heart and genuine beliefs."

****

The grace is God's power working in our weaknesses. Faith is our positive response to the grace of God. Faith in God is our voluntary assent to God's revelation about Himself. Faith is the most important value of the supernatural knowledge of God. Faith enables us, gives us the capacity, the power, if you will, of reaching our immortal destiny. Faith is not limited by time and space. Faith is the foundation of our hope. No wonder the Bible says that it is impossible to please God except by our faith (Hebrews 11:6). "Anything that cannot stop God cannot stop faith from manifesting..." ~ Pastor Festus Obasohan.

****

Love wants to become like the one whom it loves. What mind boggling truth we believe in when we believe, as we do on faith, that the God of creation, the God of the billowing seas and the towering mountains and the stars millions of light years away, this God became a little child. What more does divine revelation tells us about God that we should never have known by reason alone? That God became man not only to become like us but in order that He might suffer and die for us. Jesus was fully man and He was fully God. When the blood of Jesus was spilled on the cross the blood of the human family and the blood of the family of God were spilled and mingled together establishing the everlasting new covenant in His blood that sealed the covenant between two formerly hostile parties: God and the human race.

****

At the top of the hill, guarding the way to the Highway, stands so gaunt and grim...the Cross. There it stands, the divider of time and the divider of men. ~ Roy Hession: The Calvary road.

****

There is a way that seems good to man but in the end it is destruction. Two roads diverged in a wood, I took the one less traveled by and that has made all the difference. I will never regret why I chose this path...I am glad!

****

"Man's will thinks and says" I will be"...... God's will thinks and says "I am". Enter the state of what you desire to be. God put on the human flesh so that by sharing Himself with us we might want to share ourselves with Him. He alone can save you from your old corrupt self (nature). "Before the truth can set you free you need to realize which lie is holding you Hostage" ~ Angisho

****

When asked what makes us human, many people will say that our large brain is what really sets us apart from the rest of the animal kingdom. Humans are characterized by having a large brain relative to body size, with a particularly well developed neocortex, prefrontal cortex and temporal lobes, making them capable of abstract reasoning, language, introspection, problem solving and culture through social learning. Human are dynamic in nature. The human brain is the most complex organ; more complex than any manufactured device. The human brain has an estimated storage capacity of 256 Exabytes (or 256 billion gigs), the equivalent of 1.2 billion average PC hard drives, enough CDs to make a stack which would reach beyond the moon and 15 libraries for every person on the planet.

Given the fact, it is the conscience that separates us from animals. Conscience is the result of our being made in the image of God and the law of God being implanted in our nature by creation. It either accuses us or defends our actions in light of God's inner law (Rom. 2:15). The conviction of the conscience depends on how it is programmed. Sin polluted the conscience of man but a believer's conscience is programmed in the very righteousness of God. Conviction is the inward perception of the Spirit (Romans 9:1). Paul said that, "I say the truth in Christ, I lie not, my conscience also bearing me witness (is enlightened) in the Holy Spirit" (Romans 9:1). Paul's words mean that his conscience is in agreement with the Holy Spirit. Spiritual maturity is to be guided by the Spirit of God and to live a life that does not violate the principles given by the Scriptures. (*Quotation from my book "The Spirit is the Crown of the Heart"*)

****

Matthew 18:1- "At the same time came the disciples unto Jesus, saying, Who is the greatest in the kingdom of heaven?" The disciples were obsessed with today's spirit projected by celebrities. Today, fans surge around the cars of celebrities asking for autographs (a signature, esp. that of a celebrity written as a memento for an admirer). Jesus referred His disciples to the autograph of serving: "But he that is greatest among you shall be your servant" (Matthew 23:11). The principle of serving puts God in the right place of headship. "The principle of Headship is that if you fail to put God first you won't end with God" ~ Renny Mclean

****

I'm always excited to read the Bible because the Word is ever new to me and every time I read it I look forward to listen to God speaking to me. The Word is ever new to me though I not new to it. New is the sense of divine guidance. No wonder Jesus said that "Let him that has ears hear": The hearing ears are common but the listening ears are rare.

****

Job 38:31 - "Can you bind the chains of the Pleiades? Can you loosen Orion's belt?" If we are inclined to boast of our abilities, the grandeur of nature will quickly show us how puny we are. We cannot move the least of all the twinkling stars or quench so much as one of the sunbeams of the morning. We speak of power, but the heavens laugh us to scorn. When the stars shine forth in spring-like joy, we cannot restrain their influences; and when Orion reigns above, and the year is bound in winter's chains, we cannot relax the icy grip. The seasons arrive by divine appointment, and it is impossible for men to change the cycle. Lord, what is man?

In the spiritual, as in the natural, world, man's power is limited on all hands. When the Holy Spirit sheds abroad His delights in the soul, none can disturb; all the cunning and malice of men are unable to prevent the genial, quickening power of the Comforter. When He deigns to visit a church and revive it, the most inveterate enemies cannot resist the good work; they may ridicule it, but they can no more restrain it than they can push back the spring when the Pleiades rule the hour. God wills it, and so it must be.

****

"You have magnified your Word above all your name" (Psalms 138:2). We are more privileged than Moses who spoke face to face (directly) to God because we have the indwelling Spirit of God and the full revelation of the Word of God (Bible). No wonder Jesus said that "Among those that are born of women there is not a greater prophet than John the Baptist: but he that is least in the kingdom of God is greater than he" (Luke 7:28). Technically speaking, John the Baptist is one of the Old Testament prophets even though his name and works are found in the New Testament. Unlike other Old Testament prophets, John the Baptist did not point to the future coming of the Messiah but he introduced the Messiah by baptizing Him. He pointed to Him saying "Behold the Lamb of God that takes away the sins of the world" (John 1:29). Jesus said that John is the greatest among all natural men who lived before Pentecost. Yet the least of the born again believer (spiritual man) is greater than John the Baptist because on Pentecost God came down to dwell in us and make us His dwelling place (home). We who have experienced spiritual transformation are greater than any of the Old Testament prophet. Jesus emphasized this very fact that many of us tend to ignore!

****

Jesus did not erect any monument (structure or temple) in His honor but made the people His temple because His prime project is people. Christianity is the life of Christ in you. Religiosity focuses on you but faith focuses on Christ in you. Christ is central to Christianity. When you take away the founder of any of the world religions, their religions will flourish. But take Jesus Christ from Christianity, the whole thing will crumble!

****

The horrific attacks in France were sparked by cartoons published by the satirical newspaper Charlie Hebdo. Throughout the years, many of

Charlie Hebdo's cartoons have mocked various religions and religious beliefs, including Muhammad and Islam, something that outraged radical Muslims. On one level, of course, Christians can agree that mocking the religious beliefs of others is deplorable. In fact, we face that kind of mockery ourselves even worse. Who can forget the piece of so-called art produced by Andres Serrano in which a crucifix was immersed in a jar of urine? The massacre in Paris is a perfect example of how Christianity differs from Islam, especially radical Islam. Christians are called to respond to insult—and even blasphemy—in a different way. Christians are called to turn the other cheek, and to love their enemies (Luke 6:27-36). Christians are not called to defend the honor of Jesus but to love Jesus by honoring the dignity of others.

****

Ssenyonjo Brain made this comment on my Facebook home page: "If at all the Muslim fraternity wants to make things right and all this bad repute to be worked on of associating Islam with terrorism, I think the Muslim leadership should go on the drawing board and tackle the issue that has gone viral worldwide".

I replied that: It is the teaching that is wrong; the radicals are the conservatives strictly following the teaching of their book. Quran (2:191-193) - "And kill them wherever you find them, and turn them out from where they have turned you out. And Al-Fitnah [disbelief or unrest] is worse than killing... but if they desist, then lo! Allah is forgiving and merciful. And fight them until there is no more Fitnah [disbelief and worshipping of others along with Allah] and worship is for Allah alone. But if they cease, let there be no transgression except against Az-Zalimun (the polytheists, and wrong-doers, etc.)" (Translation is from the Noble Quran). The Quran contains at least 109 verses that call Muslims to war with nonbelievers for the sake of Islamic rule. Some are quite graphic, with commands to chop off heads and fingers and kill infidels wherever they may be hiding. Muslims who do not join the fight are called 'hypocrites' and warned that Allah will send them to Hell if they do not join the slaughter.

****

When Noah left the ark after the flood with his three sons Shem, Ham, and Japheth, and their wives, there were no others left of the human race. After observing God's provision for them, the family had to have had a strong faith in God. Yet, within a relatively short amount of time and not many generations, the family no longer followed the One True God. Abraham's ancestors were idolaters and polytheists (worshippers of many gods). Joshua reminds the people, "Long ago your forefathers, including Terah the father of Abraham and Nahor, lived beyond the River and worshiped other gods" (Joshua 24:2). Jacob's wife Rachel, who probably grew up with Terah's religion, stole her father's "household gods" (31:32-35; 35:2-4). It is known through archaeology that the city of Haran was a center of moon worship. Archaeology shows that both Ur in Lower Mesopotamia and Haran in Upper Mesopotamia were centers of moon worship. Even the names Terah, Laban, Sarah, and Milcah contain elements that reveal allegiance to the moon-god.

Mohammad, the founder of Islam, picked one of the gods of Terah called Allah. The crescent moon is central to Islamic faith. "Allah was known to the pre-Islamic . . . Arabs; he was one of the Meccan deities" (Encyclopedia off Islam, I:406, ed. Gibb). According to Middle East scholar E.M. Wherry, whose translation of the Quran is still used today, in pre-Islamic times Allah-worship, as well as the worship of Ba-al, were both astral religions in that they involved the worship of the sun, the moon, and the stars (A Comprehensive Commentary on the Quran, Osnabruck: Otto Zeller Verlag, 1973, p. 36).

Abraham's monotheism contrasts sharply with the polytheism of his forebears (Joshua 24:2). He believed God to be the Lord of the cosmos (14:22; 24:3), supreme judge of mankind (15:14; 18:25), controller of nature (18:14; 19:24; 20:17), highly exalted (14:22) and eternal (21:33). Whenever God spoke to him, he obeyed immediately in faith.

****

The menace of secularism: It the world system intended to harden one's heart claiming to exclusively possess the truth and the right of way. All individuals, groups, and states must humble themselves to ensure the collective survival of humankind and its habitat planet earth. Basically, the survival of the earth does not depend on God but depends on mankind. The only thing sacred in secularism is personal autonomy. Following the United Nation resolution that all humans are equal, they maintain that "all religions are alike"; upon this line of reasoning many secularists fail to distinguish between religions. So you hear, as we did in the wake of the Paris terrorist attacks, comparisons between radical Islam and Christianity. I think secularism is primarily about humanism and world domination as opposed to human rights. Regardless of their views, the rocks on which all of their biased ideologies towards God and self-righteous ideologies stand will soon melt like plastics. All forms of theocracies, no matter how much money or how many deadly weapons they may have will collapse sooner or later!

****

Isaiah 45:7 – "I form the light, and create darkness: I make peace, and create evil: I the Lord do all these things". In this verse the word 'evil' means calamity. God created evil means He allows it to take course for His purposes. He gave us immunity and capability to overcome evil. It is like giving you umbrella and sending you out in rain. You have option to put your umbrella up above your head or to put it down and soak in rain.

****

Revelation 21:5 - "Behold, I am making all things new." "Every person born in this world represents something new, something that has never been experienced before, something original and unique and every man or woman's foremost task is the actualization of his or her unique, unprecedented and never-recurring possibilities". You are what you think to be. The battle you are going through is fueled by the mind that gives it importance. Strongholds are built upon deception and lies that we've accepted into our minds. Strongholds are patterns in our minds that are programmed to think contrary to the truth. We tear down the strongholds in our minds by Surrendering to God (2 Corinthians 10:3-5). "The more we let God take us over, the more we become truly to ourselves - because He made us."

End of May Memorial Month

In the earthly life, we are stuck with good and bad Memories. I wish memories were like text messages. I could delete the ones I don't like and lock the ones I love. According to doctors strange diseases like Alzheimer can cause memory loss. A Memory loss, also referred to as amnesia, is an abnormal degree of forgetfulness and/or inability to recall past events. Depending on the cause, memory loss may have either a sudden or gradual onset, and memory loss may be permanent or temporary. Memory loss may be limited to the inability to recall recent events, events from the distant past, or a combination of both.

In our mortality, we are all sick as a result of the curse of sin. The Calvinists call it the doctrine of total depravity, the others might call it the same way too but when it comes down to it, it is all the same. This doctrine of total depravity goes all the way to Augustinian thought and his notion of original sin. The doctrine of total depravity posits that all humanity is sinful, that people possess no goodness that can satisfy God. That last phrase, "that can satisfy God," is very important; they possess no goodness that can satisfy God. So while not all of human nature is depraved, all human nature is totally affected by depravity, meaning, that even the goodness that we do is tainted.

The corruption of human nature affected our capability to use our minds to its full capacity. The human nature is corrupt and therefore human beings are easily corruptible. We can forget things naturally due to the corruption. There is a need to be reminded of those things which matter to us. Memories play a big role in our spirituality. We get people into the Word to get the Word into people. The Word is for our eternal comfort: "But we ought always to thank God for you, brothers and sisters loved by the Lord, because God chose you as firstfruits to be saved through the sanctifying work of the Spirit and through belief in the truth. He called you to this through our gospel that you might share in the glory of our Lord Jesus Christ. So then, brothers and sisters, stand firm and hold fast to the teachings we passed on to you, whether by word of mouth or by letter" (2 Thessalonians 2:13-15).

We have various ways to temporarily bring comfort to us but our ultimate comfort is in Christ. For example there is comfort in music.

Like David's harp, it charms away the evil spirit of melancholy. But nobody can do us like Jesus. In the book of Acts, it was a distinguished honor for Barnabas to be called "the son of encouragement"; it is one of the illustrious names of one greater than Barnabas, for the Lord Jesus is the comfort of Israel. "Eternal comfort"! This is the best of all, for the everlasting nature of comfort is its crown and glory.

What is this "eternal comfort"? It includes a sense of pardoned sin. A Christian man has received in his heart the witness of the Spirit that his iniquities are put away like a cloud, and his transgressions like a thick cloud. If sin is pardoned, is that not an eternal comfort? Next, the Lord gives His people an abiding sense of being accepted in Christ. The Christian knows that God looks upon him as standing in union with Jesus. Union with the risen Lord is a comfort of the most abiding order; it is, in fact, everlasting. Let sickness prostrate us—haven't we seen hundreds of believers as happy in the weakness of disease as they would have been in the enjoyment of blooming health?

If death's arrows pierce us to the heart, our comfort does not die, for we have often heard the songs of saints as they rejoiced because the living love of God was shed abroad in their hearts in dying moments. Yes, a sense of acceptance in the Beloved is an eternal comfort. Moreover, the Christian is convinced of his security. God has promised to save those who trust in Christ. "The Christian does trust in Christ, and he believes that God will be as good as His word and will save him. He feels that he is safe by virtue of his being bound up with the person and work of Jesus. Herein is comfort such as can be found nowhere else and in no one else!" (Alistair Begg).

Scrolling through posted sermons about memorial

Duet 24:18: "Always remember that you were slaves in Egypt and that the LORD your God redeemed you from your slavery." The memorial legacy involves the monument of remembrance. It is remembering where you came from that allows you focusing on where you are going. What would life be like without memory? To find out you only have to find someone with Alzheimer's disease. It is a hideous disease that robs a person of their memory, eventually their memory of literally everything disappears, even their memory of how to swallow food, and finally death. Memory plays one of the most important functions in order for us to be truly human! The inability to remember the past invites chaos into the present and means an uncertain future without meaning. It is for this reason that we find many of the commands and stories in the Bible prefaced with: "Remember …" "Recital" of the past is often a prelude to "revival" in the present with the goal of "renewal" in the future. What He did in the past, He can do it today; and what He did for others, He can do it for you!

****

Whenever somebody dies we are reminded of the wages of sin. Death is the reality of the curse of sin. Levites were not permitted to touch dead bodies if they were serving in the temple, and Jewish people in general are considered to be "ritually unclean" if they touch a dead body (Leviticus 21:1-2; Haggai 2:13). This does not mean that Jewish people are not permitted to touch dead people (during funereal body preparation, for example); but it does mean that a ritual purification is necessary after such incidents. In some or all of Judaism, this has been extended to include graveyards / cemeteries / gravestones, and supposedly this Jewish belief induced Muslims to form cemeteries beneath all of the paths leading up to the Temple Mount in Jerusalem - thereby ensuring that the most devout Jewish people would not be able to enter, they being made unclean by the very attempt of entering the mount and so unable to enter the most holy place in Judaism.

****

1 Samuel 7:12 - The men of Israel went out of Mizpah and pursued the Philistines, and struck them down as far as below Beth-car. 12 Then Samuel took a stone and set it between Mizpah and Shen, and named it Ebenezer, saying, "Thus far the LORD has helped us." Samuel erected a rock, a "stone," he called it Ebenezer, "the stone of help," – We depend upon God in difficult times.

****

Memorial Day is defined as a United States national holiday observed on the last Monday of the month of May. Our fallen soldiers deserve to be honored for defending the freedom we have in America. Our freedom is dictated by our constitution that was drafted from the Ten Commandments. The same freedom is conceptual in most of the third world countries where the constitution is no better than a piece of paper towel that is drafted and later trashed into the dust bin. No wonder African politics has settled into a depressing pattern of ethnic upheavals! In the bifurcated nature of our politics, it is not the prioritizing of democracy, education and health care; it is the prioritizing of wanton corruption, sheer incompetence and mismanagement within the departments of the governments. We should borrow a leaf from the developed countries. Globalization has turned the world into a small village whereby information could be shared at the speed of the lightening. Multiculturalism, philosophy, technology transfer, expertise support, guidance and insights are phenomenal. Let us use the available opportunities to improve on service delivery. "Knowledge is a process of piling up facts; wisdom lies in their simplification" ~ Martin Fischer

****

2014 will be remembered for Ebola epidemic. Ebola has claimed over 4000 lives in West Africa. It is not coincidence that most of the foreign physicians who have volunteered to rescue lives in West Africa happen to be Christian missionaries. Stephen Rowden, who volunteered for Doctors Without Borders in Monrovia, Liberia, was tasked to manage the teams that collected the bodies of Ebola victims. Rowden and his team retrieved 10-to-25 bodies a day. Since close contact with the victims is the chief means by which the usually-deadly virus is spread, Rowden and his team members lived with the risk of becoming victims themselves. Between 250 and 270 A.D. a terrible plague, believed to be measles or smallpox, devastated the Roman Empire. At the height of what came to be known as the Plague of Cyprian, after the bishop St. Cyprian who chronicled what was happening, 5,000 people died every day in Rome alone. The plague coincided with the first empire-wide persecution of Christians under the emperor Decius. Not surprisingly, Decius and other enemies of the Church blamed Christians for the plague. That claim was, however, undermined by two inconvenient facts: Christians died from the plague like everybody else and, unlike everybody else they cared for the victims of the plague, including their pagan neighbors. Candida Moss, a professor of New Testament and

Early Christianity at Notre Dame, notes that an "epidemic that seemed like the end of the world actually promoted the spread of Christianity."

****

Good times make good memories. Bad times make good lessons. Past experiences are a good tutor for future stability. Memories are compared to taking medications; there is a possibility of reacting or responding to medication. A reaction is instinctive and often instantaneous. As human beings, we tend to react while giving little or no thought to the actual circumstances. Responding, on the other hand, involves an actual assessment of the situation so that you can make an informed decision about how best to proceed, based on the particular circumstances that you are faced with. Memories influence our emotional reactions, and emotions can be positive and negative. We can use the memories of the past experiences positively to avoid future vulnerability or we can use them negatively for obstruction. Feelings are normally twisted up in knots of obstructive memories. The bottom line is that we are supposed not to dwell in the past but to learn from the past. It is therefore necessary to separate your feelings from your inferences. "I wish memories were like text messages. I could delete the ones I don't like and lock the ones I love!"

****

Lord help me to build a good character worthy of emulation and to leave behind an adorable legacy for that is what makes a man.

****

Mourning involves deep sorrow. Satan came to steal and to kill. Satan, the killer, is always the prime suspect in particular in tragic incidents involving pre-mature death. Given the fact, we should be aware that Satan is not omnipotent but God is. Hence, the primary objective of Satan is to snatch the glory of God. Satan scores big time whenever he is acknowledged to be the cause of catastrophe. Satan is not hurt by our accusations for causing havoc because that is exactly who he is. He is comfortable as long as his name is constantly mentioned. Naughtiness takes pride in evil. Satan likes any acknowledgement because it takes away our focus from God to him. We should not allow the glory of God to be blanketed by any circumstance. Even in the darkest moments of the darkness, there is a spark of the glory of God, compared to the rough diamond that must be polished, or the luster of it will never appear. Stand warned that we do not retire from preaching the gospel. History projects that most of the Christian giants who died in tragic ways preached to more people after their death than when they were living.

In Memory of Nelson Mandela: Special Tribute to Nelson Mandela

Several other figures have over the week combed corners of their memory to find the right words to describe Mandela, who spent the first half of his life fighting white domination and obnoxious system of apartheid, 27 years in jail, five in power as his country's first black president (from 1994 to 1999) and retired from public life after another 10 years and the last eight suffering increasingly failing health.

Mandela was an icon of freedom. A fresh shoot that sprang forth from the banks of the Mbashe River tracing the lineage of the Thembu royal family, Madiba stayed true to the blood that coursed through his veins; neither turning his back on unfairness nor shying away from intimidation, as he pursued justice for the majority that called South Africa home. Enchanted by the tales of the elders, the love of African history soon struck a chord that reverberated to the utmost depths of his soul. Leadership would soon beckon in the name of the African National Congress Youth League and respond he would. As the knot of racial segregation and open repression tightened, the once peaceful revolutionary, having been pursued and boxed into a tight corner relented, taking on the more radical sabotage and militant excursion. Judgment followed swiftly and a hefty price; a score and seven years, you paid. Your unfazed, unflinching thrust for the ideals of harmony and equal opportunities for all persons inconsiderate of race has flung the lifeline out to all those living in oppression. Your legacy lives on in perpetuity, inspiring countless generations.

Time line magazine wrote concerning Mandela in this way: His imagination and his feelings were always under the control of his intellect. It was said of him that he was half lion and half fox; and that the fox in him was more dangerous than the lion. Living half the time on the battlefield, spending the last decade of his life in civil war, he nevertheless preserved his good humor to end, graced his brutalities with epigrams, filled Rome with his laughter, made 100,000 enemies, achieved all his purposes and died in bed.

After defeating the rebellious army of Marius, the senate appointed him dictator. He then issued a series of edicts designed to establish a permanently aristocratic constitution for he was certain that only a monarch or an aristocracy could administer an empire.

After two years of absolute rule, he resigned all his powers and retired to private life. He was safe for he had killed all who could be suspected of planning his assassination. So he dismissed his guards, walked unharmed in the forum and offered to give an account of his official actions to any citizen who would dare to ask for it.

Then he went to spend his last years at his villa at Cumae. Tired of war, power, and glory; tired perhaps of men, he surrounded himself with singers, dancers, actors and actresses. Then he wrote his commentaries, hunted and fished, ate and drank to his fill. His men called him Sulla Felix because he had won every battle, known every pleasure, reached every power and lived without fear or regret. He married five women, divorced four and made up for their inadequacies with mistresses. Before he died, he dictated his epitaph: "No friend ever served me and no enemy ever wronged me whom I have not paid in full." What a man and what a life he led!!!

By behaving honorably even to people who may not deserve, Mandela believes you can influence them to behave more honorable than they otherwise would. He further says; Control is a measure of a Leader - indeed of all human beings. People want to see that you are not rattled, that you are weighing all the factors and that your response is measured.

Nelson Mandela, former president of South Africa and Noble Price winner has died. During his long life, Mandela inspired countless individuals. Here is a collection of quotes that personify his spirit:

1) "Difficulties break some men but make others. No axe is sharp enough to cut the soul of a sinner who keeps on trying, one armed with the hope that he will rise even in the end."

2) "It always seems impossible until it's done."

3) "If I had my time over I would do the same again. So would any man who dares call himself a man."

4) "I like friends who have independent minds because they tend to make you see problems from all angles."

5) "Real leaders must be ready to sacrifice all for the freedom of their people."

6) "A fundamental concern for others in our individual and community lives would go a long way in making the world the better place we so passionately dreamt of."

7) "Everyone can rise above their circumstances and achieve success if they are dedicated to and passionate about what they do."

8) "I learned that courage was not the absence of fear, but the triumph over it. The brave man is not he who does not feel afraid, but he who conquers that fear."

9) "Education is the most powerful weapon which you can use to change the world."

10) "For to be free is not merely to cast off one's chains, but to live in a way that respects and enhances the freedom of others."

11) "Resentment is like drinking poison and then hoping it will kill your enemies."

12) "Lead from the back — and let others believe they are in front."

13) "Do not judge me by my successes, judge me by how many times I fell down and got back up again."

14) "I hate race discrimination most intensely and in all its manifestations. I have fought it all during my life; I fight it now, and will do so until the end of my days."

15) "A good head and a good heart are always a formidable combination."

16) "I learned that courage was not the absence of fear, but the triumph over it. The brave man is not he who does not feel afraid, but he who conquers that fear."

****

"As I walked towards the gate that will lead to my freedom, I knew that if I did not leave behind my hatred & bitterness, I will forever be in prison" ~ quoting Nelson Mandela

****

Racism whether we realize it or not, influences everyone in some manner each and every day. Sometimes the effects of racism are subtle, other times the effects are profoundly significant and often life changing. Respect for diversity is a fundamental pillar in the eradication of racism, xenophobia and intolerance. "I hate race discrimination most intensely and in all its manifestations. I have fought it all during my life; I fight it now, and will do so until the end of my days." ~ Nelson Mandela

****

A wise person will never claim he is the best for it is a person with limited experience of life that thinks there is none as wise as he is. Arrogance is not simply thinking you are important. Arrogance is thinking others are not important. "One issue that deeply worried me in prison was the false image I unwittingly projected to the outside world; of being regarded as a saint," he said. "I never was one, even on the basis of the earthly definition of a saint as a sinner who keeps trying" ~ Nelson Mandela

****

Life lived in the eyes of others is like being a goal keeper. No matter how many goals you save, people will remember only the one you missed. "Do not judge me by my successes, judge me by how many times I fell down and got back up again" ~ Nelson Mandela

****

Tribute to Some of the Living Heroes (2014-2015):

Tribute to Kiprotich for winning the Gold Medal in Olympic: As I watched Kiprotich make the final ten kilometers, unfazed and with resilience borne out of determination -mainly because of the great love for mother country, I shed tears of joy! I urged the friends I was with at a popular hangout in F/P, to stand in solidarity with our hero as he made the final 5 kilometers. The ululations and chants of praise that followed from everyone -across the political divide, was a prognostic exudation of the patriotism that is inbuilt in all Ugandans - if we rallied them along one common dogma and interest. Methinks; in Kiprotich we could draw lessons on the all elusive patriotism! Wish I had another stronger word to describe ebullient golden boy Kiprotich, other than pedigree and epitome. Never in my life had I ever been on tension like those two hours -as history beckoned, and with it came the enigma... as he ran the final 5 kilometers, we stood with him, none of us sipping at his drink - and the chanting begun, as he begun stretching the lead beyond the Ethiopian's reach. Golden Boy Stephen Kiprotich; Long live!

****

JOHANNESBURG - South African doctors announced March/13th/2015 that they had performed the world's first successful penis transplant, three months after the ground-breaking operation. The 21-year-old patient had his penis amputated three years ago after a botched circumcision at a traditional initiation ceremony. In a nine-hour operation at the Tygerberg Hospital in Cape Town, he received his new penis from a deceased donor, whose family were praised by doctors. The South African team included three senior doctors, transplant coordinators, anesthetists, theatre nurses, a psychologist and an ethicist. "We've proved that it can be done –- we can give someone an organ that is just as good as the one that he had," said Professor Frank Graewe, head of plastic reconstructive surgery at Stellenbosch University. Doctors say the man, whose identity has not been disclosed, has made a full recovery since the operation on December 11 and has regained all urinary and reproductive functions. In 1967, Chris Barnard performed the world's first heart transplant at Groote Schuur Hospital in Cape Town.

In memory of some of my past heroes:

Nelson Mandela will be remembered as the most inspiring leader of the 20th century mostly because of his wisdom. Wisdom is the motivation that gets you started; habit is what keeps you going. Mandela was loved by all because he made it a habit to be wise. Wise men can learn more from foolish questions than fools can learn from a wise answer. Mandela

succeeded in making decisions simpler through knowing what to pay attention to and what to ignore. He has created a positive and lasting legacy for us that doing the right thing is the best legacy any leader can leave to his people; but "right" is never defined in terms of self-interest or expediency. He has successfully honored the past heroes of Africa. His wisdom has not expired with him because he has passed it to our generation. We all need the repetitive guidance to truly get across. We can forsake this cherished-down-the-generations guidance at our peril!
~ Pastor Stephen Kyeyune

****

In memory of the late Sam Njuba: Today we are mourning the death of Brother Sam Kalega Njuba. He was such a man of integrity. As they say integrity is like virginity; once lost it is never recovered. He has lived the honorable life unlike many people living in the vanity of their own mind and end up destroying themselves and bringing destruction to others around them. If one made a Google search about Sam Njuba, accolades about the man's passion for constitutionalism, rule of law, human rights, would stream down the screen. He did not let politics clog up his characters. People respected him and never lost faith in their icon of justice. He was principled and a prominent member that added value to the Uganda Law Society (ULS). Socially, he dearly loved our clan (Nakinsige) and sacrificed a lot to promote our soccer team. When he was still a cabinet minister, he was the first Chairman of Nakinsige football club, and I was the team manager. I enjoyed working with him and I could knock at his door any time without prior appointment. We shall miss your contribution to our clan and the nation at large. RIP

****

ISRAELIS were on Sunday paying their last respects to Ariel Sharon, whose controversial life inspired admiration and provoked revulsion and whose death drew emotional reaction even after eight years in a coma. Celebrated as a military hero at home, recognized as a pragmatic politician abroad and despised as a bloodthirsty criminal by the Palestinians and the Arab world, the former premier was nothing if not a polarizing figure. But Israelis of all stripes acknowledged the burly 85-year-old as a key figure in their nation's history, his death on

Saturday leaving left President Shimon Peres as the Jewish state's last surviving founding father.

****

During the past weeks we mourned the death of three significant figures: Paul Crouch- co-founder of Trinity Broadcasting Network; Nelson Mandela – a humanitarian that was vocal against any injustice; Sam Kalega Njuba – a successful lawyer, farmer and political elite. Money, fame and power are good to the extent that they can make the beholder win prestige, glory and buy everything of his/her choice apart from a few things that can't be bought – like life when your time to die has come. Living the reckless life can cut your life short or make your life span miserable, but none of us can add a moment of life to his or her life. This life can be improved on but can never be extended except by God. The Bible says that it is only the one who has the Son that has life. Life lived outside Christ is life wasted. To such Jesus said that it was better if they were never born (Matthew 26: 24). Jesus insinuated that it is by far worse to be born and enjoy this life to its uttermost then end up in eternal torment in hell. Non-existence is logically preferable to eternal torture.

****

Today, November 10th 2014, the world is mourning the leader of Bahamas Faith Ministries, Myles Munroe and his wife Ruth, who died in the plane crash yesterday. The two were joined in marriage till death separates them but ironically the two have been united even in death. Tragic as it may appear, yet there is a moral love story to tell.

****

Janani Luwum. Archbishop of Uganda, *Martyr*, 16TH February 1977. God's servant *Janani Luwum* walked in the light, and in his death. The late Archbishop Janani Luwum will be remembered as the most straight forward and courageous religious leader that could not be threatened to compromise his Christian values. He was killed by Idi Amin in 1977. Archbishop Janani Luwum's Journey to martyrdom: Amin knew the best way to get Janani was to accuse him of plotting against his government. Janani's official residence was raided by security operatives who searched for weapons and accused him of being part of a group plotting a coup against the government. When this happened, everybody was disgusted and this led to the calling of a meeting for all Anglican bishops.

After the meeting, a small team was set up to draft a response to the raid at Janani's home. Amin accused the Archbishop of treason, produced a document supposedly by former President Obote attesting his guilt, and had the Archbishop and two Cabinet members (both committed Christians) arrested and held for military trial. The three met briefly with four other prisoners who were awaiting execution, and were permitted to pray with them briefly. Then the three were placed in a Land Rover and not seen alive again by their friends. The government story is that one of the prisoners tried to seize control of the vehicle and that it was wrecked and the passengers killed.

Archbishop Janani Luwum, the third Archbishop of Uganda, Rwanda, Burundi, and Boga-Zaire died a sacrificial death. His death brought revival to the Church of Uganda and changed the political climate of Uganda. The following June, about 25,000 Ugandans came to the capital to celebrate the centennial of the first preaching of the Gospel in their country, among the participants were many who had abandoned Christianity, but who had returned to their Faith as a result of seeing the courage of Archbishop Luwum and his companions in the face of death. He was declared the twenty-first saint in the Anglican Communion in 1998. (RIP).

Bakka recalls the day Luwum was arrested: "All religious leaders were called to assemble at the Nile Conference Centre; Catholics, Anglicans and Pentecostals. There is no bishop or priest that did not attend the conference. It was around 10:00am. The government addressed us, saying some religious leaders were suspected of involvement with the rebels."

At that point, Bakka recalls that the security then brought out guns which they claimed had been found in the archbishop's house. Luwum was shocked with the blackmail. It was then that it dawned on him that the earlier search at his home had been a plot to connect him to the rebel movement activities. Those close to the archbishop say the arms had been planted in his house without his knowledge.

Shortly, Bakka says, security then ordered the clergy men to leave the gathering and be locked up in a room at Nile Mansions. "Even Bishop Kivengere was there. We all started singing the Christian hymn I have decided to follow Jesus... We were singing loudly. And our intention was to protest being locked up. Later, the late Cardinal Nsubuga prayed. Luwum was to pray next. Before he did, he said the Church of Uganda was founded by blood, referring to the story of the Uganda martyrs. He said he knew he would die in a similar manner. Luwum said this day should be the same as the Uganda Martyrs' Day.

"He was not afraid of death. The British had contacted him and were ready to rescue the archbishop, but he refused to run away, because 'Jesus himself didn't run away from being crucified'. He said he knew they would hurt us but we needed to be strong. Then he prayed." They had just said "amen", when all hell broke loose. Soldiers, led by Brigadier Isaac Maliyamungu, forcefully banged open the door. "You are under arrest pending investigation over subversive activities. The rest of you are given five minutes to disappear from this room," one of the soldiers said.

The men of God would not budge, saying if the soldiers wanted to, they should kill them. Bakka says: "We were over 50 in the room and there was only one door. They decided to take Luwum away and we heard a car driving off with him. We didn't know the destination. When we came out, we found our cars had been taken. We started singing I have decided to follow Jesus, and marched to Namirembe Cathedral for prayers."

Bakka says later that day, the BBC Focus on Africa programme, broke the news: Janani Luwum had been killed by Amin. Where, when, how, and who actually killed, no one knew. The next day, the government announced that Luwum and two cabinet ministers - Erinayo Oryema and Oboth Ofumbi — had been killed when the car transporting them to an interrogation centre collided with another vehicle. The accident, it was claimed, had occurred when the victims had tried to overpower the driver in an attempt to escape.

Mustapha Edrisi: His story in reference to circumstances surrounding the murder of Archbishop Janani Luwum and two cabinet ministers – Oboth Ofumbi and Erinayo Oryema – in February 1977. The highlight of his interface was his response to queries about the murky Members of the commission, — John Nagenda and John Kawanga — sought to insinuate that Adrisi had countenanced the trio's murder on account of his earlier address to the soldiers assembled at Nile Mansions that February morning.

Adrisi told the commission that contrary to Amin's version that the trio had died in a road accident near Nakasero, they were murdered by Maliyamungu and Lt. Moses Safi Okello on Amin's explicit orders.

Members of the commission, — John Nagenda and John Kawanga — sought to insinuate that Adrisi had countenanced the trio's murder on account of his earlier address to the soldiers assembled at Nile Mansions that February morning.

"Kill them, kill them, kill them," the soldiers had said in unison after Adrisi had asked them three times what the state should do with the trio for allegedly smuggling arms into the country.

Although he acknowledged posing the said question while chairing the morning session, he declined to proffer any apology for Luwum's death, advising the commission to wring it from Maliyamungu "who directly participated in his murder". Adrisi told the commission that contrary to Amin's version that the trio had died in a road accident near Nakasero, they were murdered by Maliyamungu and Lt. Moses Safi Okello on Amin's explicit orders.

On the day of Luwum's death, one-time senior manager of the defunct Radio Uganda, Wod Okello Lawoko, now in his 80s, was among the many Ugandans wasting away in an underground dungeon at the State Research Bureau (SRB) in Nakasero. Luwako, the author of a poignant book about his narrow escape from Amin's clutches, *Dungeons of Nakasero*, Lawoko recalls Luwum's arrival at SRB one Thursday afternoon (February 17, 1977). "Within minutes, more cars arrived, there was commotion and screaming as guards dragged someone downstairs. Lawoko remembers the tension and silence in cell

No.2 as inmates, with trepidation, waited to see whether the next arrival would be pushed into their already overcrowded dungeon. And sure enough, the groans of the new arrival headed for Lawoko's cell. "The heavy door to our cell swung open. And whom do we see? Archbishop Luwum stripped to his underwear and being beaten and mocked by guards led by Hajji Kabugo," Lawoko reminisces. Kabugo who passed away last year was, according to Lawoko, the chief guard at SRB.

According to Apollo Lawoko, Amin spoke to Minawa in Nubian. Luwum and the three ministers were immediately marched to Minawa's office. Lawoko and the other prisoners stayed at the reception. "Immediately they got into Minawa's office, Amin started to shout. We could hear the commotion. The three were being tortured and there was a lot of screaming. They were saying they were innocent. Amin was shouting: 'You were plotting to kill me and topple my government. But before you do that, I am going to kill you!'" Lawoko remembers.

As the beatings, screaming and pleadings of innocence went a notch higher, Minawa rushed out of his office and ordered guards to march Lawoko and the other prisoners at the reception back to their cells. "We shall see them later," Lawoko remembers Minawa saying, before rushing back to his office. But as the disheveled prisoners turned a corner leading to their dark, blood stained dungeons, two gun shots rang out, and then silence descended on the SRB headquarters. That evening, a boisterous guard asked Lawoko and other inmates in cell No.2 whether they knew what had happened to Luwum and the two ministers. "Amin killed them. Tomorrow might be your turn," the guard, according to Lawoko, said in Swahili.

The Archbishop was humiliated and beaten before getting shot in Farouk Minawa's office – most likely by Amin. Minawa was head of SRB. "Soldiers secretly transported his desecrated body to Mucwini (his ancestral home and birthplace), and dumped it in a hurriedly dug grave at the church yard at Wii Gweng on 19 February 19, 1977. This has been St. Janani's resting place ever since," reads a statement obtained from Otunnu, a member of the Janani Luwum memorial committee."

Apparently, the commission's hunch that Adrisi knew more about Luwum's death than he was willing to divulge had been buttressed by

Amin's health minister, Henry Kyemba, who had earlier averred that Amin had told his deputy to prepare the mortuary at Mulago Hospital to receive the three bodies.

The commission, in its conclusion though, did not find Adrisi culpable of any direct participation in those atrocities, something his daughter Mustafa Bako said makes them proud of their late father. Adrisi was an Aringa from Picara clan in Yumbe district, but he acquired a piece of land in Keri in Koboko district during his early years in military service where he was laid to rest.

Luwum is survived by his wife, Mary Luwum, six children (two deceased), four sisters, two brothers, and several grandchildren.

****

Israel Kyeyune, Martyr, 1977: After Idi Amin killed the Archbishop Luwum, there were massive kidnappings and killings of Christians in particular those in leadership of the Church of Uganda (Protestants). My dad, Israel Kyeyune, was the prime target because he was the chairman of the board of elders at Namaliga, Bombo (the birth place of Idi Amin). He was among the victims of Idi Amin who were kidnapped and disappeared without trace.

Israel Kyeyune, you are not just one of many heroes out there but you are my hero too. You died for the truth. You could not be silenced to speak the truth, even the uncomfortable truth. You taught me that the voice of truth, conscience and reason cannot be silenced even by violence. You lived a life that weathered all threats and challenges and soared to dignifying heights, and you died for the right cause. Nixon said that, "To attack people verbally or to threaten them with violence for their reasoned opinions runs counter to maintaining a healthy society. It makes rational discourse impossible. It's knocking at the door of barbarism." Chuck Colson adds that "Barbarism overtakes a society not just because of the bad things that are done, but because of good things left undone." Your legacy lives for us to implement. We miss you always. (RIP).

My late father Israel Kyeyune and
mother Miriam Muganzi Zake

****

In October 1999, Mwalimu Julius Nyerere departed from this world
with a rich legacy in politics and intellectual life behind him. The
trademark of Julius Nyerere (president of Tanzania from 1964 to
1985, with three years as prime minister earlier on), was Ujamaa – in
Kiswahili – or African socialism. After more than two decades in
power, (from 1961 to 1985), Nyerere admitted that his policies of
Ujamaa (African socialism) were unworkable in the contemporary
world outlook. Tanzania has since abandoned socialism as a policy of
governance and economic organization. It appears that in his endeavors,
Nyerere was guided by Christian principles, believing that there is
a divine power behind humankind. This is unlike other Tanzanian
intellectuals such as Abdul Rahman Babu who subscribed to what
is popularly referred to as scientific socialism based on materialistic
interpretation of history. Mwalimu Nyerere's final legacy in power was
about changing leadership peacefully, without recourse to violence. He
served as chairman of the South-South Commission, currently known
as South Centre, which unites the whole of the developing world,
testifying to his international stature. Muwalimu Jurius Nyerere, you
are the father of the revolutionary spirit of the liberation of Africa. You
will always be remembered as a great teacher as your name projects
(RIP).

****

Dr. Justin Kibirige Lwanga was born on the 18th August 1938. His legacy of caring for the needy still lives and Uganda stands to learn from it. Perhaps the right word to describe you is the 'crucible' – given the responsibilities, the accolades, and the persecutions you encountered along the way. Dr Lwanga was everything regarding the dignity and alleviating people's sufferings, be it in form of ignorance, diseases, injustice and abuse of other people's rights. The welfare of people was where his heart lay, and it was this very passion that burned on until the end of his life. Your legacy reminds us that one condition necessary for living together as a people is to treat one another with a certain level of respect and dignity. Our dearest doctor, you taught us the meaning of care and peace and how to imbibe it in our daily endeavors. Death is inevitable, we love you and you are greatly missed. (RIP)

****

October 2014, the world witnessed the demise of Prof Ali Mazrui who is named among the 100 top intellectuals of the world by UK's Prospect magazine and Foreign Policy magazine of the United States. For Mazrui and Nyerere, my analysis is based on their publications and lectures delivered. Equally significant is the fact that the two intellectuals acquired their defining ideologies in the United Kingdom where they attained university education. Mazrui, a product of British education, became a liberal in outlook in the sense that although he advocated capitalism, he was always willing to listen to other points of view. He frequently participated in public lectures in early 1970s before he fled into exile during the days of the military regime led by Idi Amin. (RIP).

****

"Noble Mayombo in his simplicity exuded confidence and deep understanding of societal issues. He cared to know what is affecting society in all spheres even when that seemed to be out of his realm as a military cadre. He confronted every situation however problematic it seemed with solutions and alternative approaches without any form of disorientation. He had clarity of the mind and was never ambiguous both in his speech and actions." (RIP) (Frank Tumwebaze).

****

Qiu Yuanyuan died on Wednesday aged 26, 100 days after giving birth to her child -- a special occasion in Chinese culture. More than 10 million citizens viewed her story on China's Twitter-like Sina Weibo on Friday, but many of those commenting questioned why she had sacrificed her life. The fate of a Chinese television presenter who died of cancer after refusing chemotherapy to save her unborn son has sparked intense online debate like this one: "I don't think it's good to give up on living, even if the mother's love is great," posted one citizen. I want to say that this case is categorically an example of "Agape love of Christ" that would give up His life so that others can live. It is hard for us humans to understand; only God can understand and practice Agape love or sacrificial love. She is a super mum that decided to die so that the baby can live!

****

All those great men of this continent share a common source of education process. Education is the way knowledge, skills and experiences are transferred. Auto-didacticism applying to self taught learners still lacks in Africa. Self taught men like Benjamin Franklin, Abraham Lincoln, Ernest Hemingway, George Bernard Shaw and many others, changed the world. "Original African Intellectual impact that changes Africa is yet to come or be realized. Let there be a promotion of the African intellectual values at all levels." ~ Fiasal Saad

****

He who lives without discipline he will surely die without honor. Character cannot be developed in ease and quiet. Only through experience of trial and suffering can the soul be strengthened, vision acquired, ambition inspired and success achieved. "The tragedy of life is not that it ends so soon, but that we wait so long to begin it." ~ W. M. Lewis

****

June Celebration of Families (Mother's Day/Father's Day.

Earthly families are a reflection of heavenly families. Elohim – A Divine Family includes the Father, the Son and the Holy Spirit. The Bible reveals the Trinity Doctrine. God is the Divine Family as it really is … the Deity called Elohim. Throughout Scripture we come back to the reality that God has chosen to express His personal nature in terms of a family relationship. Elohim is the Hebrew word translated "God" in every passage of Genesis 1 as well as in more than 2,000 places throughout the Old Testament.

When Adam and Eve made the momentous decision to disobey their Creator by eating of the fruit God had forbidden them to eat, the divine reaction was, "Behold, the man has become like one of Us, to know good and evil" (Genesis:3:22). And God cut them off from the tree of life (verses 22-24). The phrase "one of Us," we should note, provides clear evidence that more than one constituted the "Us." Moreover, to "become like one of Us" was actually our Creator's original intention for all humanity.

Elohim is a noun that is plural in form but normally singular in usage—that is, paired with singular verbs—when designating the true God. For a comparable modern expression, consider the term United States. This proper noun is plural in form but singular in usage. It is used with singular verbs. For example, Americans say, "The United States is going to take action," not "The United States are going to take action." The plural form does signify multiple individual states—but, taken collectively, they are viewed as one nation.

It is the same with Elohim. The word Eloah, meaning "Mighty One," is the singular form. Elohim, meaning "Mighty Ones," is plural. And, indeed, there are three Mighty Ones, the Most High, the Son (Word) and the Holy Spirit. But, collectively, as Elohim, the three are seen as one God. Elohim said, "Let Us make man in our image, according to Our likeness" (verse 26). We should note that since Elohim is used of the God family, each family member can be referred to by this word.

Through some rather intense times of study and meditation upon the Hebrew titles for "God," much has been revealed about this. I will try my best to share some of these things with you. There is a Scripture verse in Romans that says: "For the invisible things of Him from the creation of the world are clearly seen, being understood by the things that are made, even His eternal power and Godhead..." (Romans 1:20). Paul was essentially saying here that mysteries (invisible things) even things about the Divine Family (Godhead) itself can be clearly seen and understood by looking at the things that are made (created things). In other words, the things that we see in the natural temporal realm are a reflection of eternal and heavenly realities. Let us take a look at another passage of Scripture: Then Elohim said, "Let Us make man in Our image, according to Our likeness" ...[So] Elohim created man in His own image, in the image of Elohim He created him, male and female He created them (Genesis 1:26-27).

I know that we're all very familiar with these verses, but what does the Spirit desire to show us about the mysteries of the Divine Heavenly Family (the Godhead) through them? Some brief study into the title of "Elohim" will show that it is a very unusual word, for the root of the word is the Hebrew "Eloah," which is a distinctly feminine title for God (like El Shaddai), but then attached to it is a plural masculine suffix that is normally only used on grammatically masculine nouns. This makes Elohim a word of unusual mixed-gender. What does this reveal to us? What could God possibly be saying to us by using such an unusual word as a title for Himself? I believe that this is a clue into the nature of the all sufficient and gender-complete Elohim, Who within Himself contains all of the characteristics of a masculine Father and feminine Mother. This is the reason for the mixed gendered word that also implies plurality. When Elohim created man in His own image, that image was one of gender-completeness, "He created him, male and female He created them..." Adam, created in the image of Elohim, was also gender-complete (contained within him were the full attributes of both femininity and masculinity) until the point where Eve was taken from His side. Within this process of gender separation is revealed God's plan for human reproduction through families upon the earth, and also great mysteries regarding Elohim's plan for the formation of the Family of God and the spiritual reproduction of Himself.

In the Genesis account of creation, we can see that Adam was made complete in the image and likeness of Elohim ... but Elohim chose to separate the female side of Adam from the male side of Adam. This was done for the purpose of bringing them back together again as "one" in conjugal union for the purpose of procreating. In this way "they" (who became distinct personages brought forth from the gender-complete Adam) could become a family... They could "be fruitful and multiply" and their offspring could become very great upon the earth.

Saints, this account of the creation of the human family is a reflection of a very profound spiritual reality. In the eternal moment, gender-complete Elohim brought forth from within Himself distinct personages of El (masculine) and Eloah (feminine) for the purpose of bringing them together again in a conjugal union; one that is way beyond our understanding, and this for the very purpose of bringing forth a Son. He (the Son) would then eventually bring every human being into the Family of God as sons in the Son (new creations in Christ). Because all of this was in the eternal moment and not on a timeline; the Son is eternal, as is El, as is Eloah, and is the spiritual progeny brought forth through the Son.

Beloved, what I am sharing with you is just a brief glimpse into the process and purpose of God creating for Himself a Divine Family, a Family that we also belong to because the Only Begotten Son of the Father has made us holy and blameless as new creations in Christ through His blood. What has been presented to us as a "Trinity" is true but much more than that. There is certainly "triunity" that can be seen in the relationship between El, Eloah, and the Son but in order to see God correctly we must view Him as a Family which the title of "Elohim" clearly implies ... A God Family in subjection to El (The Father).

If we take a look at this Family, we will see that there is a hierarchical structure within it even as there is supposed to be in earthly families. Within this structure we can find Father, Mother, Son, and the Bride-Elect. The structure as I see it is that "EL," the Father, is the "Almighty God" to Whom all others are in complete and total subjection. This makes sense as "El" can be defined as "The Subjector" and "Eloah" can be defined as "one who is in subjection to El." This would then mean that the plural form of Eloah, "Elohim," would now refer to a "Family" in Whom all are in subjection to El and also inclusive of El Himself. Beloved ... this is God.

Brethren, are you able to grasp what is being said here? Can you see that even the creation of man is a picture type of Elohim's plan to bring forth His Own spiritual progeny through a Family? Can you see how all sufficient and fully complete Elohim chose to become distinct personages for the purpose of reproducing Himself through a Family? Earthly families are a reflection of the Eternal Heavenly Family! The invisible things of Him, even the mysteries of the Divine Family (the Godhead) are clearly seen in the created things of this world, even the creation of man himself. God is a FAMILY composed of Father, the Son and the Holy Spirit. The Firstborn Son has the right of inheritance to the Father. "Firstborn" can mean the first born person in a family, and it can also be a title of preeminence which is transferable. He made it possible for all of the believers, beloved Son's brethren who are also His Bride (elect) to be adopted in the divine family.

Beloved saints, there are a couple of Scripture verses that I feel the need to comment on before bringing this article to a close, and that is a statement made by Jesus about the resurrection. Jesus said in Matthew 22:30-31: "You are mistaken, not knowing the scriptures, nor the power of Yahweh. For in the resurrection they neither marry, nor are given in marriage, but are like Yahweh's angels in heaven." This statement by Jesus Himself leads me to believe that after the resurrection, we also will be gender-complete even as Adam was gender-complete when he was created, and therefore there will be no need for marriage as we know it. If this is so, I would imagine that Father, Mother, and Son are and have always been gender-complete in Themselves, for each one of Them is the full expression of God in every way, yet still They each perform Their specific roles within the Divine Family – Elohim.

If any of you thinks that this article might imply that the Holy Spirit could possibly occupy the position of Eloah (Mother) in the Divine Family, there are some reasons to believe that that could possibly be so. Whether or not the Holy Spirit is masculine or feminine seems really insignificant, for I imagine that the Holy Spirit can manifest the full attributes of either one at any time. But, if the Spirit is being revealed in one or the other of these attributes, it is important for us to recognize that, for we must see God as God manifests to us, and not as we want to perceive God to be. Certainly the Holy Spirit is to be recognized as intrinsic to the God-Family, and must not be understood as merely a divine force, but as divine Personhood in internal interaction within that Family. Paul seemed to suggest this by including "the communion of the Holy Spirit" along with "the grace of our Lord Jesus Christ" and "the love of God…" in his benediction.

God is fully God with or without us (children). Likewise, the children in earthly marriages make us parents (father/mother) but marriage is complete with or without children. Although marriage is made up of essentially husband and wife, God created children as the greatest blessing to families. Parents have great influence on the thinking and the spirituality of their children and so is culture. But today we have underestimated the role both parents play to bring up the godly children.

This latest story from our brave new world may blow your mind, so I'll read straight from the Chicago Tribune: "A white Ohio woman is suing a Downers Grove-based sperm bank, alleging that the company mistakenly gave her vials from an African-American donor, a fact that she said has made it difficult for her and her same-sex partner to raise their now 2-year-old daughter in an all-white community."

According to John Stonestreet - Now, I don't doubt the lesbian couple's love for the child. But I find it troubling which challenges the couple was willing and isn't willing to tolerate. They're suing because of the difficulties of raising a black child in a white community, but they were perfectly willing to risk raising the child without a father—a situation that the best evidence suggests poses far greater consequences for the child. Make no mistake: this is one of those stories that's a mirror of our culture's view of sex and children.

There is no doubt that having a mom and a dad in the home is the best situation for healthy development of children. The evidence is overwhelming. Children with fathers in the home tend to do better in school and in life in general. Children from fatherless homes are more likely to succumb to drugs and alcohol, suicide, and a host of social maladies. It's not always the case, of course, but when it's not it should be the exception… not the new rule.

When interviewed, science writer Paul Raeburn about his book "Do Fathers Matter." Raeburn isn't a Christian, and he wouldn't take a position on the issue of same-sex marriage. But there was no doubt in his mind that the overwhelming conclusion of the research is that fathers matter. A lot. Relationally, emotionally, spiritually—even biologically!

Indeed. Whatever the effect of our current social experimentation of intentionally producing children to not have either a father or a mother, I cannot imagine that the child involved in the above case will easily be able to come to terms with such mixed messages inherent in the lawsuit.

On multiple levels, this story illustrates our new and enormous cultural blind spot. Sexual autonomy is now considered the highest good in our society. And it comes as a package deal with so-called "reproductive freedom." To quote my friend and co-author Sean McDowell, we want sex without babies, and babies without sex.

And the great tragic irony is that our so-called freedom means that our children are not free, nor are they seen as the unique creations of God that they are. They're the products of our illusions of autonomy enabled by technological advances.

We now wish to create children on our terms... through science. We choose the traits that make them desirable—eye color, hair color, skin color; athletic prowess; intelligence; and so on—not simply because they are. And if at any time they displease us—either through skin color, disability, or the mere timing of their birth, we feel fully justified in getting someone else to eliminate them, or at least pay us for our inconvenience.

Jesus said, "Let the children come to me." And so ought we. As His Church, those lovingly adopted into His family, may we show our dehumanizing culture, and its children, a better way. Red and yellow, black and white, they are all precious in His sight.

Scrolling through my posted sermons on families:

Mothers' Day:

This weekend we are celebrating Mothers' Day. Moms are super special. A mother is a wonderful combination of warmth, kindness, laughter and love. This should be rewarded with a special message that makes your Mom feel as special as she makes you feel. Mothers are supposed to be the determinant factor in all our endeavors in life. We all have annoying habits and differing preferences but mothers purposefully try to understand the feelings of their children — even when they disagree with them. If your mother is still alive respectfully communicate with her. Show her how important she is not only on Mothers' Day but always. Express how much you appreciate her for bringing you into this world and for working hard to see that you blossom into the prime of life. May all those (who are born of a woman) make this day special, splendid and memorable to their mothers.

****

Dear, God I want to take a minute, not to ask for anything from you but simply to thank you, for my mother. What can I say? What words could I find to express my sincere thanks for the sacrifice made by my mother, so that I could be the responsible person? Home training is paramount in order to exude exceptional and outstanding values! I may not be the best but my mother made me a winner in my own little way. What can I pay back to her? The only way I can show gratitude is to be a blessing to someone else. Maybe a blessing isn't meant to be re-paid, but meant to be passed on. Kind of like the love of God. We cannot repay God for the love and the sacrifice (not to mention the grace). We can only pass along the love of God to someone else. Mother, you are the reason I have high respect for all ladies.

****

To my dear mother: Words are not enough to thank you for all that you did for me. You carried me in your womb for nine months and you carry me in your heart forever. You brought me into this world, then baby-sitting and scooping the filthy and mess I perpetually left behind; you fed me, worked for me, taught me how to walk, protected me from impairment, and picked me up whenever I stumbled. You helped me to make wise decisions - You taught me not to choose my friends for their good looks but to pick my acquaintances for their good characters. They say that a man cannot be too careful in the choice of his enemies but you taught me to turn my foes into friends. Above all you passed on your faith to me. I want to take this opportunity to say a very heartfelt "Thank you". You are the first lady in my life!

****

To some of my friends whose mothers are no longer with us: We share the pain since we are one body of Christ. I like what George Bernard wrote: "Write your Sad times in Sand, Write your Good times in Stone". In reality death temporally ends a life, not a relationship. Let us celebrate their lives in their absence believing that they are in better places with the Lord. We should celebrate while believing in the future family reunion; one day we will join them in eternal presence of God. Certainly, we miss the departed beloved ones and we would rather be with them here on earth, but they on the contrary, would rather have us join them in heaven than be with us here on earth. I am talking about those who died when having intimate relationship with Christ. Not even death can separate them from Christ. "Death is not the greatest loss in life. The greatest loss is what dies inside us while we live. God has not taken them from our natural eyes but not away from us since we are all (dead/living saints) one body of Christ. He has hidden them in His heart, that they may be closer to ours." This is a sour truth to swallow - Sometimes good things fall apart so that better things can fall together.

****

Fathers' Day:

It is a sweet thought that Jesus Christ did not appear without His Father's permission, authority, consent, and assistance. He was sent by the Father, that He might be the Savior of men. We are too apt to forget that while there are distinctions as to the persons in the Trinity, there are no distinctions of honor. We are prone to ascribe the honor of our salvation, or at least the depths of its benevolence, more to Jesus Christ than to the Father. This is a very great mistake. Yes, Jesus came, but didn't His Father send Him? He spoke powerfully, but didn't His Father pour grace into His lips, that He might be an able minister of the new covenant? Whoever knows the Father and the Son and the Holy Spirit as they should know them never sets one before another in his love; he sees them together at Bethlehem, at Gethsemane, and on Calvary, all equally engaged in the work of salvation.

Did you ever consider the depth of love in the heart of Jehovah, when God the Father equipped His Son for the great enterprise of mercy? If not, meditate today on this: The Father sent Him! Contemplate that subject. Think how Jesus works what the Father wills. "In the wounds of the dying Savior view the love of the great I AM. Let every thought of Jesus be also connected with the Eternal, ever-blessed God, for "It was the will of the Lord to crush him; he has put him to grief" (Alistair Begg)

Father's Day is celebrated this weekend. According to statics there are more mothers than fathers who are single parenting. I want to say that all fathers need to be honored regardless of their past mistakes. It is in human nature to point fingers partly because everyone naturally wants to be the righteous one. People have a nature that always try to strive to fulfill the picture perfect of epitome of an ideal and utopia life; yet no one is perfect! "It is easier to be more critical than to be correct. There are negligent fathers out there blaming their failures to their past relationship with their fathers. It is called Projection of Guilt......when you are feeling guilty for something you have done, you tend to put it onto other people. It is passing the blame by pointing a finger away from your-self and sharing the guilt. Such justify their own mistakes by thinking "well, everyone does it". They presume that if everybody does it, then it is not important enough for them to change. "Two wrongs don't make it right." Quit blaming other people for the same things that you are guilty of. If you consider your father to be irresponsible you can pay back by becoming a better father. You can redeem the past inconsistencies by practically putting things in vivid perspective, then watch and see how much you will change, grow and blossom. Happy Fathers' Day to you all!

****

There is an adage: "The Apple Doesn't Fall Too Far From The Tree". It means, "like father, like son" or "like mother, like daughter." Basically, it means children often pick up after their parents. Just as the "apple" is the fruit of the apple tree and falls next to the tree, creating a new apple tree. Usually the adage is used either in a negative or a positive way. The positive way is usually reserved for compliments regarding big accomplishments...like a genius child of a genius parent; then the negative regarding a criminal child of a criminal parent. The reality is that it takes God's intervention (miracle) for a child to have different behaviors from the parents. Stand warned as a parent that you do not live your own private life because your behaviors affect generations ahead of you.

****

Exodus 20:12: "Honor your father and your mother, that your days may be long in the land that the LORD your God is giving you. God did not take the sin of rebellion against parents lightly because it is impossible to give reverence God without honoring your parents. "If a man has a stubborn and rebellious son who will not obey the voice of his father or the voice of his mother, and, though they discipline him, will not listen to them, then his father and his mother shall take hold of him and bring him out to the elders of his city at the gate of the place where he lives, and they shall say to the elders of his city, 'This our son is stubborn and rebellious; he will not obey our voice; he is a glutton and a drunkard.' Then all the men of the city shall stone him to death with stones. So you shall purge the evil from your midst, and all Israel shall hear, and fear" (Deuteronomy 21:18-21). According to Leviticus, the first two witnesses were the first executioners (Deuteronomy 15:9; 17:7; Acts 7:58). In this case the parents were required to cast the first stones to their rebellious children.

****

Did I hear that, "Only a handful of people across the world ever get the chance to know who their real fathers are"! Vague as it sounds, seems to be the painful reality-less painful unknown but excruciatingly hurting brought to birth.

****

PROVERBS 10:9 - "The man of integrity walks securely, but he who takes crooked paths will be found out." Real Integrity is doing the right thing, knowing that nobody's going to know whether you did it or not. Real men do good things not to earn recognition but for others to be recognized. A person who can explain color to a blind man can explain everything in life!

****

There is no such a thing as a perfect father. All fathers are in one club of sinners. There is only perfect Father that gave His Son to die for our sins.

Marriage and the art of communication:

Any relationship is going to be as strong as your knowledge of Christ. The kind of knowledge I am talking begins with justification, continues in sanctification and ends in glorification. It is the progressive knowledge of God that grows with time. God wants us to know Him by knowing Jesus intimately. God progressively works with us to clean our minds to get rid of the pollution of the corrupt desires of the world. It is compared to cleaning your closet. Things are going to look worse before they look better. The house looks messy in the early stages of cleaning the closet but gradually it becomes better. God's redemptive grace transforms us and converts us. God performs the heart surgery opening our minds to know who we are and who we are not. He brings awareness of His image in us and motivates in us the desire to manifest His image.

I am going specifically to talk about marital relationship. Family is the nucleus of Christianity. If we turn to the revelation which the Lord has made to man in the Sacred Scriptures, we find the origin and nature of marriage distinctly declared in the creation of man. "And God said, Let us make man in our image, after our likeness: and let them have dominion over the fish of the sea, and over the fowl of the air, and over the cattle, and over all the earth, and over every creeping thing that creepeth upon the earth. So God created man in his own image, in the image of God created he him; male and female created he them." The sanctity of marriage is emphasized in the very first chapter of the Bible: "Therefore shall a man leave his father and his mother, and shall cleave (join) unto his wife: and they shall be one flesh" (Genesis 2:24).

Do we have mandate to redefine marriage? This general principle running through all, separating all, combining all, gives unity in infinite variety. The union between man and woman, which we call marriage, is only an eminent instance of the universal marriage by which each is bound to all, and all to the Lord. Marriage, therefore, has its origin in the Lord, and its highest and universal form in the union between love and wisdom, or good and truth. Marriage originates, derivatively, in the inmost degrees and principles of man's spirit; in the germs and beginnings of his nature as a human being. God created man male and female. God joined man and woman together as He joined heat and light, affection and thought, heart and lungs, love and wisdom. Marriage has its origin, therefore, in God; its highest, inmost, fullest created form and manifestation in man and woman. Satan's objective to redefine family is therefore an attempt to terminate the only icon of Christianity. The Bible is the Life Instruction Manual (including marriage). The Bible contains necessary information & instructions that we MUST know if we are to get out of this world alive. The Scriptures work for us as they worked for man during biblical times because we serve the Same God; we have the same nature; we have the same basic desires & needs!

Scrolling through posted sermons on marriage:

The LORD God said, "It is not good for the man to be alone. I will make a helper suitable for him" (Genesis 2:18). The word 'alone' does not mean lonely. Adam had company of animals. Above all he had God's company in the cool of the evening. Adam was therefore not lonely because God is the majority. The helper was definitely not a man but a woman (Eva). We can therefore conclude that when God said that it is not good for man to be alone he was insinuating the need for family. It is from the same prospective He blessed them and instructed them to be fruitful and, and, and replenish the earth, and subdue it. God intended the people made in His image to fill the earth with His glory. The sanctity of marriage is for procreation. "Once sex and marriage are disconnected from procreation and our overall human purpose, our biological realities become irrelevant, and our inclinations become authoritative, even over the text itself" ~ John Stonestreet

****

Take your time; never rush into relationship. Watch carefully whom you marry; today's sweetheart might turn out to be your tomorrow's nightmare. Take your time to know each other before you say "I do". Remember that the faster you get into relationship ... the faster you will get out of it. Only God knows the hearts of men. Trust God to scan the heart of your future spouse, and give Him time to show you the hidden things in his or her heart. Also gather information from various sources in particular from people who have known the person you want to marry for a long time.

****

Parents should never forfeit their right to protect their daughters. Whenever a priest that is officiating over a marriage asks that, "Who is giving away this woman?" He is basically asking for one of the parents that has thoroughly well investigated the man that is going to marry their daughter and proved him worthy.

****

Marriage is held together by love. These are six languages of love: Word – Say to the love of your heart that you love him or her. Time – Spend value time with the one you love. Serve – Serve the person you love. Give – Give gifts to the person you love. Touch – Touch them (holding hands) in a nonsexual manner but to show them you care. Sex – Sexual intimacy is the climax of good marriage.

****

Every single day thousands are heartbroken because of broken promises. A relationship founded on virtues of friendship and rooted in the Word of God will stand the test of time. The more you love God the more you want to live by His Word, and the more you love others.

****

A lady's heart should be deeply hidden in God so that prospective suitors will have to seek Him first in order to find her.

****

The kind of marriage that is approved by God is between one man and one woman. Somebody asked me if Abraham, the father of our faith was a polygamist. My answer is that, Hagar, the mother of Ismail was the maid of Sarah and a surrogate under Babylonian law. Hammurabi stated that if a woman can't have children, she's allowed to give a maid as a substitute. Legally, she was not a wife. Abraham married a very young woman Keturah after Sarah died. So he did have two wives but it wasn't polygamy. It is not wrong to re-marry after a death of your spouse. Other biblical characters in the Old Testament like David, Solomon and etc., practiced polygamy but it is a historical truth as opposed to the patent truth for us to implement.

****

The family institution on earth is a shadow of the divine family in heaven. No wonder Satan's priority is destroying families. The earthly father is symbolic of the heavenly Father. That is why in the old covenant dishonoring parents was punishable by stoning. A wife is supposed to respect the husband symbolically of our respect for Jesus, our bridegroom. A husband is called to love his wife as Christ loved us.

****

God works through His established chain of command to establish order on earth. The Bible calls the husband to submit to Christ. The Bible calls the wife to submit to the husband. The Bible calls children to submit to their parents. Submission is individual right and individual responsibility. It is God's instruction for people to submit to each other within their respective groups. It is their responsibility to submit without enforcement in the same manner we submit to Christ. We are called to submit to Jesus but He does not force us to submit. The reason is because submission is an act of free-will.

****

According to survey, freedom is the greatest requirement of humanity. No wonder Jesus is called the Redeemer! Whether it be marriage, location of place to stay, reason for seeking employment and etc., our primary objective is to be free. Ultimate freedom is to be what God created you to be. When God created Adam, He gave him dominion over all creations. Adam in this case was entrusted with stewardship to act on behalf of God. Man's role as the head of family is to secure the freedom of his family members. In this case to help his wife and children to be what God intended them to be. "Whenever there is deterioration in the morals of the culture, it is because men abandoned their calling to lead and to guide". It is unfortunate that men are increasingly becoming culturally irrelevant and even distant from their primary calling and purpose of knowing God and guiding their household into knowing Him.

****

Marriage is the most important and most sophisticated institution on the earth. Marriage is a divine plan for mankind that is supposed to operate on heavenly principles. Like endangered species, we keep on building a wall of protection around the institution of marriage hoping that it will outlive our civilization. A reporter asked an old couple. 'How did you manage to stay together for 65 years?' the woman replied. 'We were born in a time when if something was broken, we would fix it, and not throw it away…' "Broken things can become blessed things if you let God do the mending."

****

Feeling a bond or connection with your significant other is a comforting reassurance of what you share with each other. Love bonds two people in relationship together. Nobody and no natural forces can separate them as long as the bond of love between them is in place. The couples that are meant to be together are the ones who go through everything that is meant to tear them apart, and come out even stronger. "Don't marry the person you can live with, marry the person you can't live without."

****

It is unfortunate that families are increasingly becoming dysfunctional, and people are so heartless. People of the same family recklessly offend each other without caring of the possible ominous repercussions of their actions. It pains me to hear that so many adult siblings today harbor bitterness and hatred against one another. If that describes you, reconcile with your brothers and sisters. Tolerance is a vital tool for conflict resolution. If there is goodwill on one side, there will definitely be goodwill by the other side. The two sides need each other. You need their love and they need your love. That kind of love is so special, so don't lose it! We must establish channels to address the pending family crisis. It means having people whom we can turn to so that they in turn nonchalantly slot our grievances in positive discussions, mending the broken relationships.

****

The three institutions established by God on earth are Church, Family and Government. A family can survive without a nation but a nation cannot survive without families. Our problems do not originate from the White House but in our houses. The families designate values to the nation. God bestows honor to the nation by restoring values in families. Therefore the place to begin sharing God's truth is at home. That's where we're to live authentically by walking with God and showing others the grace He's given us… our spouses, our kids, our parents, and our friends. Start sharing the Gospel at home, testify of the Lord's goodness, and be a living witness of God's grace to your loved ones. They can reject what you say but they cannot dispute what they see in your life.

****

The magnitude of the big problems destroying our marriages could have been reduced to minor solvable issues if at all we mustered the art of communication. Talking is the greatest power at our fingertips. Dialogue is a form of communication in which question and answer continue till a question is left without an answer. "Every discussion which is made from an egoistic standpoint is corrupted from the start and cannot yield an absolutely sure conclusion. The ego puts its own interest first and twists every argument, word, even fact to suit that interest" ~ Paul Brunton

****

The first step to cement your relationship with your spouse is by developing an intimate (and fulfilling) love relationship with God. It is admitting that fulfillment will never be found in another person apart from Christ. This is an internal experience that comes to us from God alone. Never look for fulfillment from your spouse. Remember that some are called to be single and they are fulfilled without a spouse (1 Corinthians 7:7-8). Life is like a puzzle game of broken pieces, demanding fitting them together into one picture with meaning and order that makes sense. We must look at Jesus to find where and how the multiple broken pieces of our lives fit. Shalom is the Hebrew word for "peace". Shalom is the way God intended things to be. Jesus is the Prince of peace. "We are supposed to take the Peace (Christ) with us into marriage in anticipation of experiencing it in our marital relationship." Peace begins in Jesus and continues in His ordained order. God ordained marriage because marriage mirrors God's covenant relationship with His people. The Bible gives us the structure and order of marriage (1 Cor. 7:10; Ephesians 5:21-33). We may ignore the same principles at our peril!

****

Marriage is life, and it will bring ups and downs. Embracing all of the cycles and learning to learn from them and loving each experience will bring the strength and perspective to keep building, one brick at a time. "Never stop courting. Never stop dating. NEVER EVER take that woman for granted. When you asked her to marry you, you promised to be that man that would OWN HER HEART and to fiercely protect it. This is the most important and sacred treasure you will ever be entrusted with. SHE CHOSE YOU. Never forget that, and NEVER GET LAZY in your love."

****

Deep feelings are expressed in words and deeds. I won't say I love you, I will make you feel "I Do". Falling in love is easy but staying in love is a challenge. Couples would be more intimate if only they adhered to this simple rule: "The ingredients of patience and commitment keep the flame of love alive." But when you realize you want to spend the rest of your life with somebody, you want the rest of your life to start as soon as possible!

****

To be ashamed of doing certain things is a virtue. Where there is no sense of shame, decency and dignity exit. Dignity is like virginity, once lost, it can never be regained. A person's upbringing really matters. Family values are never outdated. Modernism has added nothing to the characters of our youth, except to wrench decency from our social values. That is why we are faced with the character crisis. Our ancestors must have been more tenacious in getting problems solved than we currently are, given their rudimentary resources. Their level of achievement outpaces our advances. If you are looking for values and morality, you have to look way back in the past as opposed in the present and future.

****

Have you ever asked yourself why the breakup in God ordained institution of marriage is skyrocketing? It is because we have abandoned our original calling. God did not call us to happiness but to obedience. Unfortunately, hedonism has become the hub motivating everything we do. It is the same reason why some of our Churches have evolved into theatrical entertaining centers and some of our pastors have turned into comedians to arouse excitement. We forget that fulfillment comes from Christ alone not from a Church or your spouse. Avoid going into relationship for a wrong reason. Any relationship can be as strong as the Scriptures projected. If God said it; it is a command not a suggestion. The choice is yours to obey or disobey at your peril.

****

Jesus said that "At the resurrection people will neither marry nor be given in marriage; they will be like the angels in heaven" (Matthew 22:30). Marriage is one of the beauties of this world that you do not want to pass you by! When you Miss enjoying the company of your spouse here on earth you miss it eternally. This is one of the things ordained to be enjoyed to its fullness here on earth. I want to warn that Christians (Unlike the people of the world) are not fulfilled by the temporary joy from the things of this world because the Lord is the source of their joy. The joy deposited within us is supposed to manifest the glory of God in all seasons. Alistair Begg says, "I do not blame ungodly men for rushing to their pleasures. Why should I? Let them have their fill. That is all they have to enjoy." But as for a converted wife, who despaired of her husband, she is always very kind to him for she says, "I fear that this is the only world in which he will be happy, and therefore I have made up my mind to make him as happy as I can in it".

****

Ephesians 5:21 – "Submit to one another out of reverence for Christ." Marriage is a bicycle made for two people to ride. We learn how to ride by falling down over and over. The bruises of one become the bruises of the other. Supporting each other in marriage is celebrating each other daily. Never be ashamed of doing something if it can save your marriage. Spice your relationship to make it more interesting, vibrant and full of love! Remember that marriage is not just a lasting relationship; it is a loving relationship too!

****

1 Corinthians 11:3 – "But I want you to realize that the head of every man is Christ, and the head of the woman is man, and the head of Christ is God." Here we see the chain of command. The Father is the head of the Son, although, the Son is equally God as the Father. In the same way the husband is the head of the wife, although, both of them are equally valued souls before God. God shows no favoritism. He loves all of His children equally. We are all related to Him intimately through Jesus Christ, although, the level of intimacy varies depending on our spiritual maturity.

Submission is a voluntary act. The Son chose to be in perfect obedience to the Father. Christ is the head of the Church but He never forces us into submission. Likewise a husband is not supposed to force his wife into submission. She willingly submits to him in order to be blessed. Any act of insubordinate is offensive to God. The mission of Jesus Christ is to present His bride (Church) without wrinkle. Likewise, the primary objective of a husband is to love, provide and protect his wife so that he might present her without wrinkle (sin/bruise). Spiritually, God created a woman as a weaker vessel to be covered by her husband. Physically, God created a woman with weaker muscles, not to be dominated by her husband, but to be protected by him. The Bible says that, "The husband is to "dwell with his wife according to knowledge, giving her honor as the weaker vessel" (1 Peter 3:7). The word "knowledge" could be translated as "understanding." Both men and women have difficulty understanding their spouses. It takes commitment and surrender to God's order on the part of both partners to come to a place of true understanding. Understanding is the basis for seeing one's wife as a vessel to honor, respect and care for because she is weaker.

****

Ephesians 5:25 – "Husbands, love your wives, just as Christ loved the Church and gave himself up for her". Jesus gave up all of the heavenly glory to save His bride (Church). A husband is supposed to love his wife sacrificially.

****

Therefore shall a man leave his father and his mother, and shall cleave unto to his wife: and they shall be one flesh (Genesis 2:24). The two become one; therefore loving your wife is loving yourself.

****

1 Peter 3:7- You husbands in the same way, live with {your wives} in an understanding way, ... honor as a fellow heir of the grace of life, so that your prayers will not be hindered. Mutual prayer is not possible unless there is mutual love and forbearance. Married life is fellowshipping and worshiping God. We are not called to have bad marriages while praying for the good relationship. We are called to have good marriage so that when we pray for even better relationship, our prayers are not hindered. "Christians do not deliberately act evil in anticipation of becoming better; they act decently in anticipation of becoming better."

****

The sexual revolution of the 1960s has been portrayed as a time of sexual liberation. In reality, this wholesale embrace of moral relativism resulted in a culture that is enslaved to its sexual lusts. Like all revolutions, it has left destruction in its wake. In 1960s there were no divorce laws because divorce was rare. Today we have divorce laws most of them influencing divorce rather than regulating it. The system has grown to effectuate family disintegration, instead of trying to hold families together. Unilateral no-fault divorce has made ending marriages too easy and too one-sided, with children most affected.

Another factor that fueled the sexual revolution is the discovery of contraception. In the twentieth century, all Christian denominations were reluctant to sanction birth control pills also known as contraception and fertility control used to prevent pregnancy. Later on they accepted them on condition that they are supplied to married couples alone. Today, because of the liberation brought about by the sexual revolutions, there are more single people using contraception than married people. In fact today some parents include contraception on the list of essential school supplies to their children.

Sex is no longer a moral issue limited within the context of marriage. There has been unrestricted blossoming of premarital and extramarital sex. It seems that the liberals are disinterested in which appellation sex fits - whether sex is pre-marital, extra-marital or any other prefix of marital. Secularism dictates that sex is legal as long as there is consent between the two adults involved. Moral judgment is no longer made on the basis of the reality of the biding authority of the Scriptures but on the word "consent"! Other consequences of the sexual revolution are abortions, rampant divorce and the destruction of families, gender confusion, acceptance of homosexuality, child molestation, and sex trafficking. All of these are disasters aimed at the destruction of the sanctity of marriage. I call upon all Christians to stand for moral absolutes in the face of evil and persecution.

****

Raising children is compared to flying a kite. A good, experienced kiteflier learns to watch the wind, even though it is invisible, by watching how it affects things around them. He holds a long thread attached to the kite purposely to maneuver its direction as it takes off driven by the winds. Any slight move on his part has great impact on its direction. There is time to hold on the thread while gently releasing it into the wind until it is deemed necessary to let it go on its own. Likewise, children need the controlling and guidance of parents until they reach the adulthood stage to run their own affairs. As long as they are still in your home, never be afraid to exert pressure on them if that is what it takes for them to go in the right direction. Be consistence in anticipation of change. You'll be surprised what a difference it makes. However, when they grow up and start their own lives, it is time to let them go on their own. In Genesis 2:24 we read, "For this reason a man will leave his father and mother and be united to his wife, and they will become one flesh." This principle is repeated in Ephesians 5:31. God's pattern for marriage involves the "leaving" of parents and the "cleaving" to one's mate. Marriage involves a change of allegiance. Before marriage, one's allegiance is to one's parents, but after marriage allegiance shifts to one's mate.

****

Today is the commencement of the family week. Marriage is primarily made up of a husband and a wife with or without children. Children are the greatest blessing to marriage. The Bible instructs children to respect and honor their parents: "Honor your father and mother"--which is the first commandment with a promise---" (Ephesians 6:2). It means children valuing their parents as God intended. "To value is to honor; to respect is to value." The Bible instructs the parents to cater for their children: "Train up a child in the way he should go: and when he is old, he will not depart from it" (Proverbs 22:6). To bring up involve nurturing them into growth in all areas (spirit, soul and body). This is the paramount way whereby parents value their children. It is a process of investing value time into your children allowing them to blossom within the moral values. Parenting is a life time experience. Nobody is too old to be parented. "Parental teaching is a natural duty. Who is better fitted to look after the child's well-being than those who are the authors of his actual being? To neglect the instruction of bringing up our children is worse than brutish" ~ Alistair Begg

****

True, children will follow what you do more than what you say. But don't lead your kids to expect perfection from you. Instead, point them to the One who is truly perfect: Jesus Christ. Exhibit Christlikeness before your children and you'll help build a Christ-like character in them for a lifetime!

****

There are two times when disciplining kids is most essential and yet most difficult—early childhood and the teenage years. In both periods, your children will test you to see how much they can get away with, if you'll actually enforce the rules you've set, and if they can break rules without you knowing. To make these times easier, start by setting a good example early in your child's life. Set rules and be consistent to enforce them. I chuckle inside whenever I hear a parent complaining that a certain child can't take No for an answer. I'm amused because the comment always says more about the parent than it does about the child. A child who can't take No for an answer definitely has parents who can't say No and stick to the No! It is not that the child can't take No, it is that he/she has no reason to believe the No is a definite No. We have a situation whereby children are the recipient of respect instead of parents. It is ridiculous when parents obey children instead of children obeying parents! A parent that allows his/her own child to disrespect him or her indirectly pronounces a curse over his or her child because the Bible says that the blessings of God are reserved for those children that respect their parents. Receiving a blessing from one's parents is a high honor, and losing a blessing is tantamount to a curse. Such a child earns no respect and will hardly respect himself or herself too.

****

Weekend involves resting (Sabbath) and spending time with the family members. The people you love don't just need your quality time. They need quantity as well. Remember that trust increases with intimacy. Quality with very little quantity isn't quality at all. Value time with the family members is the greatest gift you can give them. No spouse or child will tell you in twenty years, "I wish you'd spent more time at work and less at home with us." But the sad reality is that many parents today are absent, spending quality time here and there, but not giving their spouses or kids the quantity of time they need. My greatest regret is spending most of my time traveling instead of sharing it with my children. Let all the decisions be made in the best interest of our people. Give them the gift of your full attention. You will never regret that you did so.

****

Damon Linker called people who are "childless by choice" "hedonists." In other words, they want to enjoy "the fruits of their labor without the constraints, sacrifices, and trade-offs that come with raising kids. Having children is essential; but it is something you do after you arrange your life to maximize your potential well-being.

****

Being a firstborn is not somebody's choice but God's with a purpose! So as a firstborn do what God wanted you to do as a first born, be responsible and a good example to your siblings!

****

The secular world grants children more freedom while reducing parental control. Take extra precaution when granting your children their rights or freedoms least they turn into beasts. Disciplining a child in love is biblical. The Bible says that, "He that spares his rod hates his son; but he that loves him chasteneth him betimes" (Proverbs 13:24). God disciplines His children. Chastisement or punitive punishment is intended to put us in the right way.

****

In case you want to know the spiritual level of your kid, just look at his or her closest friend. I am not talking about the casual friends but I am talking about the intimate friend with whom your kid fellowships and associates.

****

Loving kids unconditionally does not mean giving them what they want but it means giving them what they need. A good parent does not bribe the love of his or her children. A good parent gives gifts to kids to complement them for their good performances and to encourage them whenever they do not meet the required mark. The children should not demand for gifts from their parents. They are expected to appreciate every gift from their parents unconditionally.

****

Kids are supposed to be loved unconditionally by both parents. But you must show your spouse that he or she is the most important person in your life. Never let the kids steal your attention from him or her. Remember that the children are going to be in your house for a moment of time. They are going to leave you with an empty nest when they grow up. Whether you like it or not they are going to get their lovers and start their own lives but your spouse is a life time partner.

****

If you have children remember this, when they leave your house and you are done with them, the rest of the world has to live with them. So please train them in good manners so that they don't become a burden to others. The word 'training' stands for exercising values, preparing for contest and teaching by example.

****

Television and Internet play a major role in shaping the characters of our children. How to protect your children from the pollution of the world: Blacklist some materials/associates you think could threaten the sanity of your child (this includes music, movies and even friends and families). It is a given that the children of an excellent God ought to be excellent in all aspects of their lives. "That our sons may be as plants grown up in their youth; that our daughters may be as corner stones, polished after the similitude of a palace".

****

Now we're asking ourselves why our children have no conscience, why they don't know right from wrong, and why it doesn't bother them to kill strangers, their classmates, and themselves. Probably, if we think about it long and hard enough, we can figure it out. I think it has a great deal to do with 'We reap what we sow.' "It is an illusion that youth is happy, an illusion of those who have lost it; but the young know they are wretched for they are full of the truthless ideal which have been instilled into them, and each time they come in contact with the real, they are bruised and wounded. It looks as if they were victims of a conspiracy; for the books they read, ideal by the necessity of selection, and the conversation of their elders, who look back upon the past through a rosy haze of forgetfulness, prepare them for an unreal life. They must discover for themselves that all they have read and all they have been told are lies, lies, lies; and each discovery is another nail driven into the body on the cross of life."

****

Sadly, in suburban American parenting, the automatic response to an "affront to self-esteem" is more self-esteem. But Pierre and others suspect that the "promotion of unconditional self-esteem of children in more affluent family structures instills a kind of"—here's that word again—"entitlement." Instead of self-esteem being a reward for "good achievement or behavior," feeling good about ourselves comes to be seen as something that the world and our peers owe us. In more extreme cases, "When the happiness and social status that one feels is deserved is not forthcoming, feelings of peer rejection, resentment and blame can become all-consuming."

Also need to shape the expectations of our kids and get them past a sense of entitlement. They need to know that life is filled with pain, sickness, insults, and failures. And overcoming them is often difficult. Anyone who promises them otherwise is lying. Harsh words, but true. Second, they need to know they're not special—at least they are no more special than any other man, woman, or child made in the image of God. But they are loved. And that love—the source of true self-worth and happiness—is found at the foot of the cross.

****

Young people who have been taught high expectations become adults whose character bears fruit regardless of their age. The most rewarding and richest lives are lived on purpose by those who seek out and conquer challenges. As Alex and Brett point out in their book "adolescence" is a recent invention, and history shows just what young people are capable of. President John Quincy Adams, for example, became the U.S. ambassador to Russia at 14, Joan of Arc reclaimed France at 17, Alexander the Great began conquering the world at 16, and the Bible tells us that Josiah, one of Israel's most righteous kings, began his reign at age eight.

****

Speaking to the Italian magazine Panorama, Stefano Gabbana said that the traditional family "is not a passing fashion. It contains a sense of belonging to the supernatural." Domenico Dolce who happens to be a gay surprisingly admitted that "We haven't invented the family." Invoking what he called the "icon" of the Holy Family, Dolce said that "it's not a question of religion or social status, there's no turning over a new leaf: when you are born, you have one mother and one father. At least, that is how it ought to be." He said that he questioned what he called "chemical children" and "synthetic babies," an obvious reference to in-vitro fertilization and its use by the gay community. He asked "how do you tell a child who their mother is" in a world of "rented wombs" and "catalog sperm?" And he added, "Not even psychiatrists are prepared to confront the effects of these experiments." He went on to say that while they would love to have children, he doesn't believe you can have everything in life. "Life has a natural course and there are things you shouldn't modify."

The Art of Communication:

Good communication with others determines the duration of the relationship. "If you want to go fast, go alone; If you want to go far, go with people". Never ignore good manners, or acting appropriate in a way that's socially acceptable and respectful; display respect, care, and consideration for others. Excellent manners can help you to have better relationships with people you know, and those you anticipate to meet. If you want to have good manners, then you have to master the social behaviors like neatness, dining etiquette, phone etiquette, as well as to learn basic etiquette, which includes being polite and holding doors for people, and etc. Good manners convey respect to those you interact with, and also commands respect from those you interact with. "Whosoever desires constant success must change his conduct with the times." - Niccole Machiavelli

Our fallen nature is evidently seen in human ego, which is the garden bed of pride. C.S. Lewis said that, "A proud man is always looking down on things and people; and, of course, as long as you are looking down, you cannot see something that is above you." God resists the proud (James 4:6). It is commonly accepted that the fall of Lucifer (meaning light-bearer) was due to pride (Isaiah 14:12-15). The life of Christ was characterized with humility. He was born in a nasty place (manger) and He died a shameful death at the rugged cross taking on Himself the sins of the whole world. If we don't acquire the virtue (which is the fruit of a habitual way of acting) of humility, we will be forever stuck with the vice of pride. Pride is related with selfish ego and disobedience. Humility, on the contrary is the surrendering of ego in exchange for peace, hope and eternal life (Col. 3:12-13); this being the exaltation of those who humble themselves. "A sense of Christ's amazing love for us has a greater tendency to humble us than even an awareness of our own guilt. May the Lord bring our thoughts to Calvary; then our position will no longer be that of the pompous man of pride, but we will take the humble place of one who loves much because he has been forgiven much. Pride cannot live beneath the cross. Let us sit there and learn our lesson, and then rise and carry it into practice."

I am going to focus primarily on marital relationship. The family is the first fellowship of which the husband is the head (pastor). It is important to discover the divine mission for your family. I mean knowing how you are going to impact the world spiritually. The husband must be kingdom minded. He must pursue the eternal blessings on behalf of his house. Make it a priority to pray together and grow together spiritually. As I said couples that pray together stay together. The spiritual aspect changes the physical.

I want to point out that there is no such a thing as a perfect family. We must take into account that even the first family (Adam/Eva) was a broken family. Marriage brings two different people together. We are all different and we marry people who are different from us. The difference is going to rub your spouse the wrong way. Christ is the common ground where we find unity. That is why it is important to marry a Christian believer. We marry brothers and sister in Christ who share the spiritual DNA.

I want to begin by advising you never seek to change your spouse. The only person you can change on this planet is you. You can give your spouse a new you instead of trying to make him or her new. Never waste calories trying to change others. God reserved the right to change your spouse to Himself. Talk to God about your spouse in prayers.

Many people advise us on how to run our marriage but marriage is not a tool or machine with a manual. I advise couples who are still dating to try to know each other thoroughly well before saying that "I do".

Good communication involves knowing yourself and studying your spouse, and this is a process. No one else can know your partner better than you. Understanding one another is the only means of knowing your partner. Before marriage the two people intending to get married embark on a task of researching each other. They want to know the interests of the person they want to get involved with. They want to know what makes them happy and what makes them angry. When they get married a marriage license is issued compared to a graduation certificate. This should be regarded as certificate at the lower level or a diploma that must be upgraded. You are required to continue researching your spouse to know him or her more and earn an Associate degree, a Bachelor's degree all the way to the doctorate. Knowing yourself and your spouse is basically an endless process. For example it is important to know when to respond. "I don't like acting on the spur of the moment, it is better to speak when one is ready and people are eager to hear you". You need to know when to do things together; need to know when your spouse needs space and the list goes on and on day after day. Knowing each other is therefore an endless process. The more we get to know each other, the more we want to know them.

People respond differently to crisis. Anybody can be nice till they are offended. Solving conflict is the key to the lasting relationship. Again, it is the two of you who must know how to handle conflict without involving the third party. I am not discouraging counseling; I am just saying that it should be the last approach after every effort to solve the conflict between the two people in relationship has failed.

Don't be quick to point fingers. People react differently to accusations and some do not readily admit their mistakes. A sense of guilt might escalate things as opposed to cooling them down. Aggressive defense is a positional element in a group (usually based on selfish motives) based on conflict environment; commonly out of positioning a tactical deployment of similar persons in an unusual but cunning locations. It usually occurs in a situation where a defender is caught in a role reversal anomaly, usually associated with lack of discipline. Aggressive defense is usually out of Guilt & Anger. It results into; Passive aggressive behavior- out of sullenness or deliberate or repeated failure to accomplish requested tasks for which that group is responsible

In case there is a need to fix something in your spouse, you should never be a quick fixer because your fixing might be misinterpreted as controlling. Give it time and correct in love. Be patient and tolerant. Tolerance is about accepting the fact that you cannot have your way in all circumstances in life. It also means you accept that others are different and have different abilities. If you can appreciate these differences, you are said to be tolerant. Patience is the ability to keep cool under trying conditions and not letting self to fly off the handle. It also means not getting discouraged or losing temper when there is a delay. Remember that all of us are vulnerable. "When you're in glass house you don't throw stones."

The two people in marriage (husband/wife) must accept each other. Accepting does not mean agreeing but it means loving a person in spite of who they are. Remember that God intended marriage to be life time (till death separates).

The Bible gives the right way of living in harmony with God and with others. We confess our sins to Christ because He is our High Priest (Hebrews 4:14). But the Bible instructs us to confess our sins to each other because we are a community of priests (1 Peter 2:9). We do not have to go to a priest (clergy) to confess our sins. Sincere confession that is not superstitious makes it right with God and with the neighbor. This is authentically the right way of opening the wound for healing rather than casually covering it with a bandage. "The foundational beliefs of Christianity can essentially be summarized into this one statement: Loving God wholeheartedly and loving others fervent (Matthew 22:37-40). Just as the cross of Christ is comprised of two beams, one vertical and one horizontal, so is your life defined by your vertical love for God and your horizontal love for others." Jesus emphasized reconciliation by saying that He will not accept the sacrifice of the worshiper that holds grudge against his neighbor. "Leave there thy gift before the altar, and go thy way; first be reconciled to thy brother, and then come and offer thy gift" (Mathew 5:24).

Love is a condition of unconditional acceptance of others. Forgiving is vital in any relationship. Forgiveness involves forgiving finally. It is forgiving God's way. When God forgives, He remembers no more what is forgiven. God neither learns nor forgets because He is almighty but when the Bible says that He remembers our sins no more, it means that He never uses the forgiven sins against us.

We should be ready to forgive and ready to apologize. Apologizing doesn't always mean you're wrong and the other person is right. It means you value your relationship more than your ego. Apologizing is sincerely feeling sorry. Sorry isn't good enough when you've done it several times before. That's no mistake; it's a bold and deliberate choice. Apologizing involves true repenting.

As I said, we should not expect our spouses to be perfect but every person should make perfect efforts towards the perfect environment for the perfect relationship to thrive. Perfection should not be expected in actions but rather in efforts. This should be the direction of our daily performance. In real life, all human beings have good and bad portions of deeds, although in some the bad prevails over the good.

The language of love involves knowing the very little things that your spouse likes. Knowing and doing those little things to your spouse put a smile on their face and heart. When your spouse is happy, you are happy too because happiness is contagious. "Let my soul smile through my heart and my heart smile through my eyes, that I may scatter rich smiles in sad hearts."

Focus on the little good things in your spouse as opposed to the bad things. Those little good things might act as sparks to ignite the fire of romance in your relationship. These are little things you say and do to your spouse to make them feel that they are wanted in your life. Never miss such moments because they rekindle the fire of romance in your marriage.

Marriage is a bicycle made for two people to ride. We learn how to ride by falling down over and over. The bruises of one become the bruises of the other. Supporting each other in marriage is celebrating each other daily.

When it comes to matters of Love I don't take chances, my heart must be convinced that I love you. No barrier can regress your feelings for a person you love; not even distance! In love distance is only a test to see how much love can travel. If you love or loved someone, their name is permanently tattooed in your heart. No matter how hard you try to erase it, it'll always remain there. Unfortunately, true love has lost its essence today. "We are all a little weird and life's a little weird, and when we find someone whose weirdness is compatible with ours, we join up with them and fall in mutual weirdness and call it falling in love". The reality is that we do not fall in love but we grow into it.

We are different and we should never try to change others to be like us. But we must learn how to work in harmony in spite of our differences. No relationship stands still; it is either progressively growing better or worse. But somebody has to be initiative to figure out what works in favor of mutual understand. Every spouse must volunteer to be pioneer of unity and peace. There will be problems in married life if there is a lack of mutual understanding and co-ordination between husband and wife or if any of them does not perform his/her duties.

I am going to discuss how to excel in communication skills. The main factor of conjugal happiness & success is communication. Communication leads to the relationship characterized with understanding, intimacy, mutual confidence and valuing. In fact through communication disagreements are minimized, expectations are blended & common courses of action are chosen.

Understanding your partner involves more listening than talking. As one preacher said, "God created us with two open ears and one tongue behind the fence (teeth) purposely so that we can listen more than talking." The more we listen, the more we understand. The more you understand your spouse the more intimate you become. Prove to your spouse that you value what he or she says by listening. Remembering even the little things that your spouse said is good in building trust.

We are emotional animals. But women are emotionally different from men. The fMRI data from 700 participants suggested that women's stronger reactivity to negative emotional images is linked with increased activity of motor regions of the brain. Dr. Annette Milnik explained, "This would suggest that gender-dependent differences in emotional processing and memory are due to different mechanisms."

Previous studies have suggested that women display heightened facial and motor reactions to negative emotional stimuli. Some studies with similar pattern with the fMRI data indicate that one possible explanation would be that women might be better prepared to physically react to negative stimuli than males. Another explanation would be from normative expectations, with women being expected to be more emotional, and also to express more emotions.

We respond differently to gratification as well as to challenges. It is important to study body and your partner. "People who seek psychotherapy for psychological, behavioral or relationship problems tend to experience a wide range of bodily complaints" Generally speaking, the body is most likely to express emotional issues a person may have difficulty processing consciously. Certainly the vast majority of people don't recognize what their bodies are really telling them. Charlette Mikulka suggests that our emotions are music and our bodies are instruments that play the discordant tunes. But if we don't know how to read music, we just think the instrument is defective.

Personal behaviors affect our daily performances. The mood of our contemporary quest is reflected in the manner we tackle issues, for example gambling to make life more meaningful. In course of our pursuits, barriers are inevitable but how we respond in times of trials matter. For many of us, the challenge we face seems to be deeply entrenched in succeeding while enjoying a healthy relationship with the people in the surrounding. It is possible to look good and not do good. But it is impossible to do good and not look good. The bottom line is that you can please all the people some of the time, and some of the people all the time, but you cannot please all the people all the time.

Ralph Waldo Emerson once said "Society is a masked ball, where everyone hides his real character, and reveals it by hiding." Anything you reveal by hiding is evil. Hypocrisy is external performance without internal change. Bad characters never go by hiding but by crucifying them daily to death. The first step toward spiritual transformation is exposing the old corrupt nature to the light. Your destiny in life is tied to the new man that God alone can change you into. This week make a resolution to be influenced by the Holy Spirit. Let Him guide your ways and your dealings with others. Let Him control your tongue.

Scrolling through my posted sermons on communication:

"You may choose your words like a connoisseur, And polish it up with art, But the word that sways, and stirs, and stays, Is the word that comes from the heart" - Ella Wheeler Wilcox

****

We have been discussing the how to excel in our relationship with others. There is the theory that things are destined to happen regardless of our personal input; that is a myth! Good communication requires your personal input. Just start to sing as you tackle the thing that you thought "could not be done," and you'll do it. The plane needs two wings to take off; likewise faith and works are equally important. The noble make noble plans, and by noble deeds they stand. "Finally, brothers and sisters, whatever is true, whatever is noble, whatever is right, whatever is pure, whatever is lovely, whatever is admirable--if anything is excellent or praiseworthy--think about such things" (Philippians 4:8).

****

Ephesians 4:1-3 "I urge you to live a life worthy of your vocation wherewith you are called. Be completely humble and gentle; be patient, bearing with one another in love. Make every effort to keep the unity of the Spirit through the bond of peace". The word 'vocation' also means calling. It is used at least eleven times in the Bible but in this verse it is specifically an invitation requiring our response. It is not a calling to work out unity by human resources but to embrace the unity that is already in place through the Holy Spirit. We are called to train ourselves to respond to the Spirit of God until godliness becomes automatically natural to us.

****

"A good character is, in all cases, the fruit of personal exertion. It is not inherited from parents; it is not created by external advantages; it is no necessary appendage of birth, wealth, talents, or station; but it is the result of one's own endeavors - the fruit and reward of good principles manifested in a course of virtuous and honorable action." - Joel Hawes

****

The way you carry yourself will often determine how you will be treated. In the long run, appearing vulgar or common will make people disrespect you. Adjust your attitude to win others. Sometimes it takes sadness to know happiness, noise to appreciate silence and absence to value presence. A smile doesn't always mean a person is happy. Sometimes it simply means they are strong enough to face their own problems.

****

"Sometimes we need someone to simply be there, not to fix anything or do anything in particular, but just to let us feel we are supported and cared about." TIME is our most precious treasure because it is limited. We can produce more wealth, but we cannot produce more time. When we give someone our time, we actually give a portion of our life that we will never take back. Our time is our life! The best present you can give your family and friends is your time.

****

When you care for people more than they deserve, you get hurt more than you deserve. The people that are the strongest are usually the most sensitive. People who exhibit the most kindness are the first to get mistreated. The ones who take care of others all the time are usually the ones who need it the most. The bitter truth is that no one can innovate by himself or herself; each person needs to work with other. Therefore give people more than they expect and do it cheerfully.

****

Sometimes I get so into myself that I forget there are other people around me. It is pretty easy to get caught up in yourself, especially if you are passionate about what you do. Do nothing from factional motives [through contentiousness, strife, selfishness, or for unworthy ends] or prompted by conceit and empty arrogance. Instead, in the true spirit of humility (humbleness of minds) let each regard the others as better than and superior to himself [thinking more highly of one another than you do of yourselves]. Let each of you esteem and look upon and be concerned for not [merely] his own interests, but also each for the interests of others (Philippians 2:3-5).

****

Acting out: Whatever feelings you have trouble dealing with – jealousy, shame, inferiority, entitlement – transferring them to your spouse and other people and acting out in anger won't just make you and everyone around you miserable, it'll kill your relationship with others too.

****

God created you beautiful. Self-esteem is appreciating who you are. Be yourself, no one is like you. God made you beautiful in His eyes to be you not someone else. "We live in a pathologically dissatisfied world. And I'm going to tell you why. Because we love to compare --- Go around the world and discover that people aren't happy with their bodies. Filipinos want to be fair-complexioned like Westerners, and so buy bleaching stuff. Westerners want to own bronzed bodies like ours, and so purchase tanning lotions. Those with moles have them removed, while those who don't strategically implant beauty spots. "We live in a pathologically dissatisfied world. Some people want to shed a few pounds to look like Ally McBeal, while others want to gain some baby fat to look like Drew Barrymore" ~ Paul Alowo

****

If you act like the world revolves around you, you'd better have the talent to back it up. Even so, being overly self-centered will diminish your effectiveness. Remember that your marriage isn't about you alone; it's about your spouse as well.

****

Living in the past or future: Granted, we can learn from the past, but dwelling on it is self-destructive. Likewise, you can plan for and dream about the future, but if your actions aren't focused on the present, you'll never achieve your plans or your dreams.

****

"----------being the most attractive rarely meant being the most beautiful"
— Alice Walah, A Poker Game of Love

****

Oversensitivity: If you're so thin-skinned that any criticism makes you crazy and every little thing offends you, you're going to have a rough go in the real world. Any good relationship involves people who have a good sense of humor and humility. It's sort of a requirement. Don't take yourself so seriously.

****

Fanaticism: Passion is a big success driver, but when you cross that line and become over-the-top fanatical, that works against you. I've seen it time and again. It leads to a skewed perception of reality, flawed reasoning, and bad decision-making.

****

Do good not for the sake of people but for the sake of your relationship with God. Remember that people will always question the good things they hear about you, and believe the bad ones without a second thought.

****

In Christ, we are not under the written law on tablets of stones but we are under the law of love written in our hearts. A steadily growing desire to be with God results into a steadily growing desire to be with each other. Eric Metaxas says, "--- the law is a poor substitute for prudence, modesty and other virtues." He is reflecting the Apostle Paul's observation in Galatians: "But the fruit of the Spirit is love, joy, peace, patience, kindness, goodness, faithfulness, gentleness, self-control; against such things there is no law." Can you think of ways in which what Paul says applies to our life as a nation? How can we inculcate the fruit of the Spirit in our families and congregations? Search your conscience and emotions.

****

Humility is not to make a list of things about yourself but to make the most of others. "The power of finding beauty in the humblest things makes home happy and life lovely" ~ Louisa May Alcott

****

Love is but the discovery of ourselves in others, and the delight in the recognition. ~ Alexander Smith

****

Love your wife as the cream of everything. Love her as the best the world could offer but love her less than God.

****

Real love does not stop on emotional pleasing but goes deeper into being authentic. It is saying "No" when you mean no, and saying "Yes" when you mean yes. Remember that there are people that will not love you by saying "Yes", and there are people that will never stop loving you even when you say "No". The people in the last category are your true friends.

****

Love of self, in the Christian sense, isn't selfishness; it isn't putting yourself first before everyone and anything else. On the contrary, love for self means that, upon realizing your own worth before God, you seek to live the best possible life, knowing that the results of such a life will be a benefit not just to yourself (which is fine) but also, and even more important, to those with whom you come into contact.

****

We are different but harmonious beings. We can both love and support the best in each other. Wise partners hang onto each other with open hands so that neither suffocates in submission. Love is Acceptance. Love is giving room to grow.

****

There is a thin diving line between pity and sympathy. How far you go in life depends on your being tender, compassionate, tolerant and sympathetic with the striving and hurting. Pity oscillates between pride and ego. Sympathy is sincere responsive, warm wholeheartedness retrieved by the grace. Sympathy does something about the situation but pity feels sorry, condemns and walks away. Sympathy cries with you but pity leaves you to cry alone. Sympathy steps into the shoes of the victim and shares in the pain, acknowledging that today it is you, tomorrow it is me. Sympathy restores hope but pity deepens into hopeless misery. Pitiful people torment the victims with the approval of their own conscience. When unchecked, their tormenting goes on and on......

****

When it comes to matters of Love I don't take chances; for me to confess that "I love you" my heart must be convinced that I sincerely love you! It takes courage to tell somebody that "I love you". But it takes discipline to prove it. A good marriage is not where perfection reigns: it is a relationship where a healthy perspective overlooks a multitude of the irresolvable. They say that it takes moments to fall in love but it takes a mistake, to ruin it all. It is axiomatic that human beings are fallible; the veracity of this assertion is best illustrated within the framework of a conjugal union. In reality falling in love is loving the same person over and over in spite of his or her mistakes. We excel at whatever we think upon regularly. Decide to be an expert in love by practicing love instead of waiting to fall into it!

****

1 Cor. 7:4 – "A wife does not have authority over her own body, but rather her husband, and similarly a husband does not have authority over his own body, but rather his wife." Love is the foundation of marriage. Marriage is held together by love. Love does not begin in bed; it is a noble act of self-giving, offering trust, faith, and loyalty. The more you love, the more you lose a part of yourself, yet you don't become less of who you are; you end up being complete with your loved one. These are six languages of love: "Word" – Say to the love of your heart that you love him or her. "Time" – Spend value time with the one you love. "Serve" – Serve the person you love. "Give" – Give gifts to the person you love. "Touch" – Touch them (like holding hands) in a nonsexual manner but to show them you care. "Sex" – Sexual intimacy is the climax of good marriage.

Remember that marriage is life, and it will bring ups and downs. Embracing all of the cycles and learning to learn from them and loving each experience will bring the strength and perspective to keep building, one brick at a time. Regarding love there is no limit; there is always room to pursue your spouse and discover more love. "Never stop courting. Never stop dating." Never ever take your spouse for granted. When you agreed to marry him or her, you promised to be that person that would own his or her heart and to fiercely protect it. This is the most important and sacred treasure you will ever be entrusted with. You chose each other, never forget that, and never get lazy in your love. As long as there is love there is no external power that can break the bonds uniting the two of you into one. Yet, love without devotion involves serious risks. Never play with the feelings of your spouse because you might win the game but there is the serious risk of losing that person for a life time.

****

The great marriage is made up by two great forgiving couples.

****

"Sometimes the strongest women are the one who love beyond all faults, cry behind closed doors and fight battles that nobody knows about."

****

When a man listens to a woman's feelings without getting angry and frustrated, he gives her a wonderful gift. He makes it safe for her to express herself. The more she is able to express herself, the more she feels heard and the more she understands. Then the more she is able to give her man the love, trust, acceptance, appreciation, admiration, approval and the encouragement that he needs.

****

Any relationship can go sour if one of the spouses brings into the current marriage baggage from the past or previous relationships. "It is difficult for a man to fix the broken heart that he did not break".

****

To love out of duty is doing something for somebody you love out of obligation. A hired servant does the same things for money. True love is motivating; it loving somebody without expectation in return.

****

Even banks don't give loans to people who don't deposit with them...if you ever want a favor from your friends or family deposit your time into your relationship with them not just calling them when you need to be bailed out...It doesn't cost much to call somebody just to say hi. - This is the truth of the matter. "Love me when I least deserve it, because that's when I really need it." ~ Swedish Proverb

****

We all know that communicating about our problems and feelings is the key to a happy relationship, but it's also crucial that you talk about the little things too. The ability to have a good conversation with your partner will enable you to find each other stimulating, interesting and fun to be around, even when the initial fireworks have worn off. Laughing is equally as important because humor is often the glue that keeps people together.

****

Marriage should be a time of bliss not torture. Don't pull the rope too much, it might snap eventually. To love someone is to understand each other, to laugh together, to smile with your heart and to trust one another. In marriage, each partner is to be an encourager rather than a critic, a forgiver rather than a collector of hurts, an enabler rather than a reformer. "May the joy you share today be just the beginning of a life time of happiness and fulfillment of your life".

****

Somebody made this suggestion: "For the sake of accountability, whenever you befriend a person on Facebook, you should invite his or her spouse as well to be friends. Also, whenever you send an e-mail to a married person, you should send a copy of the same e-mail to his or her spouse." Whether you agree or disagree, let me know your opinion please. What do you think about this suggestion?

****

An idle mind is the workshop of the devil. When a husband and a wife are not communicating, it gives the devil uncontested time to talk to each spouse separately, sowing seeds of suspicion, deception, doubt and lies.

****

It's nice to be important but it is more important to be nice. The characters of a good person are a reflection of a clean heart. Your conscience is as clean as what you expose to your five senses (sight, touch, feeling, taste & smell). "Your conscience is the measure of the honesty of your selfishness. Listen to it carefully."

****

The things we do can naturally become part of us. A habit is a recurrent, often unconscious pattern of behavior that is acquired through frequent repetition. It is an established disposition of the mind or character involving things we customary practice even without prior thoughts. People have their little habits even though at times they do not notice that the same habits are offensive to others. Often I tell the members of my congregation that it is not possible to separate somebody from his or her habit. For example I cannot separate a grouch person from his ominous attitude. The habit becomes part of his personality until he decides to change. A habit is an acquired behavior pattern regularly followed until it has become almost involuntary. Self-discipline allows you to be disciplined by others. But the only person that can change your habits is you. A leopard cannot change its spots but people's personalities can change over time just as much as other external factors that affect us in life like aging. Our personalities are the effects of the corrupt nature but the corrupt nature (unlike the personalities) cannot be improved on; it is spiritually crucified.

****

Attitude is a favorable or unfavorable evaluative reaction toward something or someone, exhibited in ones beliefs, feelings, or intended behavior. Self-control aligns our attitude with the divine will. Self-control is solitude at its best. Solitude begins when a man silences the competing voices of the market and mass, and listens to the dictates of his own heart. The mood of our contemporary culture is reflected in fast and easy means (short cuts) towards achievement. But the remedy is in the contrary: Be slow to anger; be slow to make decision. Exercising patience toward all that is unresolved in your heart is rewarding. Never be stressed up by the crucible. Try to appreciate even the mysteries of life for which you have no answers; compare them to locked rooms of treasures or books that are written in a foreign tongue – the access to which may be difficult but inevitable. Self-control is a steadily growing desire to be at peace with others so as to be at peace with God. "The key is to live for everyone else's freedom so that we can have it too."

****

Perception has tremendous emotional power. How people see themselves, their purpose, their beliefs and lifestyle – influence their behaviors. An attitude is the twisted mindset towards others. It is selfish in nature and demeaning to others. "A bad attitude is like a flat tire; you can't go anywhere without changing it."

****

Controlling self is controlling the habits that motivate you. Habits may be the cause of your hard personality. The personality issue may not necessarily be sin but it affects our communication with others. Personality issue is rectified naturally whereas restraining of the flesh (carnality) is of the spirit; it is only possible by taking the full counsel of the Word of God. When the Bible instructs us to die to self, it is in reference to a spiritual death of the old corrupt nature that is not glorifying to God. It is denying the old corrupt nature to be in charge or to control you. God anoints us to help others to grow spiritually but to have a good personality depends absolutely on you. Self-discipline allows you to be disciplined by others. But the only person that can change your habits is you.

****

Selfish means: self-centered, self-serving, self-important. Selfishness is the root cause of conflicts even in families. Selfishness breeds envy. Selfishness is human habit; it is a form of defense and means of survival to some. Selfishness is a lifestyle that puts yourself first. Love of self, in the Christian sense, isn't selfishness. Selfishness is putting yourself first before everyone and anything else. The golden rule is that do to others as you want it be done to you. The cultivation of a uniform courtesy, a willingness to do to others as we would wish them to do to us, would annihilate half the ills of life. The Christian faith calls for death to selfishness. Faith focuses on God's provision. Faith lays hold upon the Lord Jesus with a firm and determined grasp rather than self.

****

Bitterness irritates. Bitter people think that they are mistreated by everyone. Their lives are characterized by never-ending series of unfortunate events — and you can't cure them, either. In fact, you'll be their next excuse for why things are going so horribly wrong in their lives. Bitterness is contiguous. Your real nightmare begins when you start to feel a little like them yourself, and your once-positive nature gets overwhelmed by others' perpetually gloomy outlooks and daily dose of misery. We must love people without allowing their negativity to influence our behaviors. Your behavior is a product of your own conscious choices based on principles, rather than a product of your conditions, based on feelings. Paul wrote in 1 Corinthians 6:12 - All things are lawful unto me, but all things are not expedient: all things are lawful for me, but I will not be brought under the power of any. Again the Apostle wrote in 1 Corinthians 10:23 – "All things are lawful for me, but all things are not expedient: all things are lawful for me, but all things edify not".

****

What a mistake to suppose that the passions are strongest in youth! The passions are not stronger; rather the control over them is weaker! ~ Edward Bulwer-Lytton.

****

"A man who governs his passions is master of the world. We must either rule them, or be ruled by them. It is better to be the hammer than the anvil" ~ St. Dominic

****

Speculation is the major cause of conflicts. In academia, speculation is usually dignified as theory but in practical life it is considered as subversive. In practical life we are compelled to follow what is most probable; in speculative thought we are compelled to follow the truth.

"Every closed eye is not sleeping and every open eye is not seeing" ~ Bill Cosby

****

We cannot change our past. Also, we cannot change the fact that people will act in a certain way. We cannot change the inevitable. Like in course of playing a guitar, the only thing we can do is to play on the one string we have, and that is our attitude. "I am convinced that life is 10% what happens to me and 90% how I react to it" ~ Charles R. Swindoll

****

Don't let your past define you. The past is not a place you can point to on a road map to success. It exists only in your mind. The past is not part of the man you see in the mirror. Love yourself enough to forgive yourself the past faults; be blind to your blemishes, and tell the world about your virtues.

****

Maybe you cannot change the procedural events surrounding you. But you can change your attitude. It is attitude, not aptitude that determines your altitude. Evaluate getting a makeover to diminish the magnitude of your attitude. You will see how much difference it will make in your relationship.

****

"Not everything that can be counted counts, and not everything that counts can be counted." Virtue distinguishes the men from boys, managers from subordinates, the outstanding from mediocre. "It is attitude not aptitude which delivers a person to the altitude.

****

Past experiences are a good tutor for future stability. We can positively use the memories of the past experiences to avoid future vulnerability. Memories end up influencing our emotional reactions. Emotions can be positive and negative. Feelings are normally twisted up in knots of obstructive memories. The bottom line is that we are supposed not to dwell in the past but to learn from the past. It is therefore necessary to separate your feelings from your inferences. "I wish memories were like text messages. I could delete the ones I don't like and lock the ones I love!"

****

"Feelings of worth can flourish only in an atmosphere where individual differences are appreciated, mistakes are tolerated, communication is open, and rules are flexible - the kind of atmosphere that is found in a nurturing family."

****

It's weird how life gathers two people, attaches their hearts and souls together to become one, then in a fraction of a second they are drawn apart, like strangers who had never met. You cannot change your partner by verbal bullets; you will only make him/her cringe.

****

We live in the culture of popular body make-over. It is quite common these days for people to wish to undergo plastic surgery when they are discontented about something in their bodies. The term 'plastic surgery' actually comes from the original Greek word plastikos which means "to mold". The procedure in general basically involves repairing, reshaping or restoring skin, tissue and body parts. The end result is a better appearance or a restoration or enhancement of functions. There are two major types of plastic surgery, reconstructive and cosmetic. "You can change your external appearances as you want but the change of character is for a person with a sincere heart and genuine beliefs."

****

Good manners sometimes have nothing to do with your behaviors but simply mean putting up with other people's bad manners without the possibility of compromising your values. It won't take away anything from you: You are Crucible - hard pressed but not crushed, struck down but not destroyed.

****

Putting on faces or changing the face will change nothing, but facing the change will change everything. Changing location without changing attitude is not a smart move either. When a stone is dropped into a pond, the water continues quivering even after the stone has sunk to the bottom. But it is impossible to squeeze water from the same stone because changing location (from the dry land to the bottom of the pond) does not make it become a sponge! "Our greatest distinction as a species is our capacity, unique among animals, to make counter-evolutionary choices. A man must be big enough to admit his mistakes, smart enough to profit from them, and strong enough to correct them." Sometimes the grass is greener on the other side because you aren't watering your side enough.

****

Life at its best is compared to travelling in the valley. Yet for there to be a valley there have to be higher places. How many times do we focus on the valley instead of the beauty of the mountains that surround us? "I have walked that long road to freedom," Nelson Mandela once said. "I have tried not to falter; I have made missteps along the way. But I have discovered the secret that after climbing a great hill, one only finds that there are many more hills to climb." Life is a journey whereby you meet other travelers. Love them and make someone's life better than you met them so that when you get home they have a reason to miss you.

****

There's nothing that gives us away as much as our speech. Our speech shows where our hearts are. You can't cover up your heart as long as your mouth is open. If there's bitterness in your heart, it will come out through what you say and how you say it. If there's hatred, hatred will come out. If there's anger, anger will come out. The heart is engineering all that the tongue is going to say. The tongue can be tamed by the transformation of the heart and renewing of the minds. The psalmist in Psalm 51 cries "Create in me a clean heart". God can take the foulness of the human heart and make it pure and beautiful and eloquent for His glory. "Withhold no part of the precious truth, but speak what you know and declare what you have seen. Do not allow the toil or darkness or possible unbelief of your friends to dissuade you. Let us rise and march to the place of duty, and there declare what great things God has shown to our soul."

****

Most people do not listen with the intent to understand; they listen with the intent to reply. Argue with passion if you must but always remember to listen to the uncomfortable truths in the opposing viewpoint. "The greatest lesson in life is to know that even fools are right sometimes." ~ Winston Churchill

****

Trust involves faithfulness in all matters. It is your priority to protect your spouse's reputation. You took a vow to stand with him in good and bad times. Never expose your spouse's weakness to the third party unless the situation escalates into life threatening. Even then talk to the person of responsibility like your pastor or a Christian marriage counselor.

****

I am going to discuss the influence of the tongue. James warned that, "For every species of beasts and birds, of reptiles and creatures of the sea, is tamed and has been tamed by the human race. But no one can tame the tongue; it is a restless evil and full of deadly poison". We can tame lions and poisonous snakes but rarely do we control our tongues.

****

These days there are artificial body parts made for almost all of our bodies, but no artificial tongues. The tongue can be only tamed. "He that restrains his mouth is wise" (Proverbs 10:19). David says, "I will guard my ways, that I may not sin with my tongue; I will guard my mouth as with a muzzle." (Psalm 39:1). Solomon says that, "The one who has knowledge uses words with restraint, and whoever has understanding is even-tempered. Even fools are thought wise if they keep silent, and discerning if they hold their tongues" (Proverbs

17:27-28). My professor used to say that "My mother was pretty smart when it came to the tongue. She sprinkled her daily conversation with wise sayings like "Keep your tongue between your teeth" and "Think twice before you speak once."" The Scottish people have some proverbs, too: "Keep your tongue a prisoner and your body will go free" and "A long tongue shortens friendships." Remember, one day you'll answer to God for every idle word you say (Matthew 12:36). Idle words involve reckless saying without seasoning our words with grace to honor the Lord, we have wasted those words!

****

The tongue is like the rudder on a ship. This small moving part can change the direction of a large ship on the sea. Though unmoved by the strongest of winds a ship can be controlled by a tiny rudder (James 3:1-12). You cannot change the direction of the wind but you can control your sails to the right destination. To please God stir your tongue in the right direction. The Bible warns against the lying tongue (Proverbs 25:18). Satan is the father of lairs (John 8:44). The fate of the lairs is everlasting fire (Revelation 21:8). The Bible warns against the proud tongue (Psalms 5:9, 12:3-4). The Bible warns against the swift tongue (Proverbs 18:3, James 1:19). The Bible warns against the cursing tongue: "Their throat is an open sepulcher; with their tongues they have used deceit; the poison of asps is under their lips: Whose mouth is full of cursing and bitterness" (Romans 3:13-14). "Let no corrupt word proceed out of your mouth, but what is good for necessary edification, that it may impart grace to the hearers" (Ephesians 4:29).

****

Until recently, we were pretty much in the dark about the human body. But then came the X-ray with its peeping eye...a marvelous instrument which has saved us much human misery. It was able to show us the human heart, but it couldn't show us the soul or it could show us the throat, but not the voice. The brain, but not the mind. Nevertheless, medical science has done much to help this outward man that perishes. If our eyes are getting dim, we can get glasses. If our kidneys or heart fail, we can have a transplant. But as far as I know, there is one member of the body that has never been transplanted. If we used our arms and legs as much as we use this part, we'd be incredibly stiff and sore. But this member never gets tired, and I've never seen one with a splint on it. As you get older you may get dentures - but you will always have the same tongue you were born with! There are artificial joints made these days, but no artificial tongues.

****

A rhetorical question is a figure of speech in the form of a question that is asked in order to make a point, rather than to elicit an answer. The Bible asks this rhetorical question: "Can both fresh water and salt water flow from the same spring?" (James 3:11). Unfortunately, most us do not adhere to this principle. The same mouth that cursed you yesterday will pile over you shovels of praises tomorrow. "I take no praises from men because whenever you take the praises of men you must be ready to take their blames too." - Billy Gram

****

People would do anything to earn more recognition and praises. Where do you derive your worth? Is it always wrong to seek the recognition of others? For what do you want to be recognized? The world may not recognize you until you are able to solve portions of their problem. However, people's recognition does not last forever. When you seek to please God rather than men things will fall into place in your favor. Recognize this fact and you will establish a lasting legacy that will shine and be remembered even in eternity. Therefore, recognition may turn up to be the greatest motivator. The Bible says that: "Do not withhold good from those to whom it is due, when it is in your power to do it" (Proverbs 3:27).

****

The Bible says that the measure you give to others will be measured to you. "Each nasty word stretches the rubber band further away until finally, one day, it snaps back at you with maximum impact"

****

Nagging is to constantly ask someone to do something that they are unwilling or reluctant to do. It is been persistent on a particular issue even if it is not convenient for the other person. No nagging person can win a partner's love. The Bible says "It is better to live at the roof top than to live with a nagging woman in the house" Nagging is an attitude that can be changed. Nagging is a choice. You can choose to nag or to be quite. Nagging wears out a relationship. I had heard somebody say to me "My wife drilled off the love I had for her through constant nagging".

****

Bragging is a form of weakness, and only those who are unsure of their own success would brag to convince themselves of their false sense success. He who brags is insecure and lacking. Some of the successful stars do brag as a publicity stunt, those are very well orchestrated acting and they know what they are doing - If you done it, it isn't bragging. It is usually those who have had mediocre successes that brag a lot. Let us be honest, bragging is not an attractive trait. A man who catches a big fish doesn't go home through an alley." Positive bragging is when God brags about you. "The Lord said to Satan, "Have you considered...Job? For there is no one like him on the earth..." (Job 1:8).

****

You shall not go around as a slanderer among your people. . . . You shall reason frankly with your neighbor, lest you incur sin because of him. (Leviticus 19:16-17). Slander emits a threefold poison, for it injures the teller, the hearer, and the person who is being slandered. Whether the report is true or false, we are by this precept of God's Word forbidden to spread it. The reputations of the Lord's people should be very precious in our sight, and we should regard it as shameful to help the devil dishonor the church and the name of the Lord. Some tongues need a bridle rather than a spur.

****

Communication reveals the imperfections which reserve concealed. Great minds discuss ideas, average minds discuss events, small minds discuss people. Backbiters are like crickets. Crickets make a lot of noise, you hear it but you can't see them. Then right when you walk by them, they're quiet. Whoever gossips to you will also gossip about you because gossiping is his or her business. Gossiping is a sin like adultery. We are called to gossip the gospel but not to gossip about others.

****

"In life, we must find out things straight from the horse's mouth and not listen to the Jackass spreading the gossip"

****

At the dawn of the Internet age and the explosion of social media, which enable information to be exchanged all over the world at lightning speed, just by just clicking a button, rumor mongering is at its highest rate. People are tempted to go to foolish lengths of exaggeration to make their stories compelling! The Bible warns against gossiping and flattering. "A man who flatters his neighbor spreads a net for his feet" (Proverbs 29:5). Job declared that: "I will not show partiality to any man or use flattery toward any person. For I do not know how to flatter, else my Maker would soon take me away" (Job 32:21-22). If gossiping is talking behind a person what you couldn't say to her face then flattering is saying to her face what you wouldn't say behind her back. You need a match box and fuel in order to make fire. Likewise the fire of the gossiper cannot light without the fuel of the listener to his or her gossiping (Proverbs 26:20). Both the gossiper and the listener share in the sin of malicious damaging of a person's reputation.

****

Don't mingle with idleness, avoid vain vapid verbosity. The reason that dogs have so many friends is because they wag their tails and not their tongues. There is danger when a man throws his tongue into high gear before he engages his brain.

****

Anger: Anger is a strong feeling of extreme displeasure, fury, vexation; it is the inability to control your emotions. Anger is an emotion like any other emotion. There is such a thing as positive anger towards unrighteousness. We have the right to be angry but we should never let anger causes us to sin. Be mad and do good. Negative anger is a secondary emotion usually caused by failed expectation like fear, doubt and hurts. Anger is a dangerous substance to relationship, it is a choice, and you can choose to respond to anger or not. Anger should never be welcome as a heart guest, because it has the ability to destroy love, the carrier and other around.

****

Aggressive defense is usually initiated by Guilt & Anger. It usually occurs in a situation where a defender is caught in a role reversal anomaly, usually associated with lack of discipline. It may also be a result of sullenness or deliberate or repeated failures in life. It can accelerate into passive aggressive behaviors. We should own our failures gracefully with awareness that we are all mortal and we are not exempted from flaws. C.S. Lewis once said that the problem with evil isn't that our desires are too strong, but that they're too weak; and what he meant by that was that people are far too easily swayed emotionally. The sin that is defended and not repented of will definitely explode into a chain of reactions and multiple evils. Learn to accept your faults.

****

It is a scientific fact that your body will not absorb cholesterol if you take it from another person's plate - Dave Barry

****

Stress affects our communication with others because it changes the mood. Emotional stress is mostly caused by our inability to get something that we want badly in time. But even more stressful is the tragedy of after getting what you wanted badly and finds it to be empty: This is the status of the lost people of the world. Believers are called to be anxious for nothing. "Nothing in this world is fulfilling until we find the peace that Christ alone offers". God designed to give us victory over the tyranny of the circumstances we face and to guard our hearts and minds by His peace which surpasses all comprehension (Phil. 4:7). I have learned that no matter what happens in this life, it's not "the end of the world" -- because this world isn't the end. Heather, a recent Stanford graduate, put it this way: "To be in a real-life relationship with God is a staggering and beautiful daily reality. There is 'cosmic companionship' that I won't trade the world for. I am deeply known and loved in a way I can only hope to adequately communicate."

****

To be a leader, be it your family, friends, community or organization, there is one important thing you must be aware of and understand most. 'Self-awareness', this phrase has got three sub dimensions: One, Emotional awareness-first, recognize your emotions and know how it affects you and others. Two, self-assessment- know your strength and weakness and being open to feedback that can help you to develop and build yourself better. Third, self-confident, be aware of your self-worth and capabilities, stand up for what you believe in, even if there are more opponents, defend it with genuine argument. Developing negative emotions, lack of self-assessment and loss of self-confident create big problem in all ways mentioned above.

****

Any good relationship is built on three pillars: Love, trust and respect. Respect is the key ingredient missing in today's generation. Respect is earned by giving it; it is about giving respect in anticipation to receive respect. Respect involves honor and obedience. Honor and obedience is a chicken egg situation. I mean that "A hen is only an egg's way of making another egg." Honor brings obedience; obedience brings honor.

****

Women if you understand Men well kindly watch the animal planet especially the lion family. The dominant male is very poor at providing but very good at protecting and mating. In the event a bachelor male overthrows a married male it first kills all the cubs sired by the deposed male before mating with the females. This is to ensure there is no preferential treatment of the cubs. This is the animal in men.

****

Unrealistic expectations of your spouse are the intoxicated soil where good relationship can be planted and not grow.

****

The word female stands for open to receive. Women are receptacle and emotional. It is possible to think that you love your wife but when she is lacking and not fulfilled in this area. At times men are ignorant about what truly make their spouses feel loved. Review your performance by asking her to point out some areas you need to improve in showing your affection to her.

****

God said to Eva that "Your desire shall be to your husband, and he shall rule over you (Genesis 3:16). God meant that the woman's desire will be to control man instead of being controlled by man. Women use the little opportunities available at their fingertips to manipulate their spouses into submission and controlling them.

****

Good sex plays an important role in cementing the relationship of the couples involved in marriage. Men are more sexual oriented than women. Even among women, their sexual desires are different. Women's bodies produce testosterone, but not nearly at the same level as men and that testosterone production drops significantly if a woman has had her ovaries removed. It also drops after menopause. Dr. Randolph says that testosterone does play a role in women's interest in sex but it may only play a modest role. What plays bigger role in a woman's drive for sex is her emotional well-being. It is therefore important for a husband to study the body of his spouse and also to do what it takes to stimulate her sexual drive instead of forcing it.

****

Love making is supposed to be the product of romantic relationship between the couples. Good sex does not begin at night in bedroom but it is pursued from the very first hour of the day (in the morning) all the way to the bedroom at night. Pornography provides the twisted counterfeit option of inducing sexual desire without necessarily investing romance into the relationship.

****

A comprehensive global study has concluded that abortion rates have sharply shot up in countries where it is legal or illegal to abort. There are 31 abortions for every 100 live births, the study said. Why? The answer is because we have embraced the sexual revolution. Love making (sex) was supposed to be secret. The word 'secret' means something separated that has to be done in privacy. Separate also means sacred. Animals are not moral creatures because they lack such secrecy. For example birds jump on each others' backs anywhere at any time. But human beings are moral because they were created in the image of God. We are therefore supposed to reflect the morality of God. The sexual revolution has been instrumental even in uncovering the sins which used to be considered covered. Today nothing is secret, everything has been uncovered. Immoral people are no longer in the closets. Bedroom privacy has been invaded. The sexual revolution maintains that it is a prestige to expose your private body parts and to aggressively act indecently in seductive manners. The severe consequence is more lustful erotic desires that is quenched by massive casual sex; then orchestrated unwanted pregnancies. No wonder abortion rates have shot up.

****

Forgiving and repenting are the same: both of them must be proven by works. God grants us enough grace to repent but we must receive it and by faith act on the truth that takes away our guilt. Likewise, when we forgive, we must give the culprits the grace by not holding them accountable for their actions. Forgiving is giving up the right to punish the offender and handing him or her to God.

****

Apologizing doesn't always mean you are wrong and the other person is right. It means you value your relationship more than your ego. Saying 'sorry' doesn't necessarily mean you are wrong. I believe it means you are strong, mature and care enough to keep the communication channel open and you probably value your relationship with that person.

****

"There are two circumstances that lead to arrogance: one is when you're wrong and you can't face it; the other is when you're right and nobody else can face it." ~ Criss Jami

****

Irresponsibility and refusing to accept your mistakes is another way of giving your opponents power to torment you. If you always accept and be comfortable for your flaws, no one can use them against you. So the change you need is for your personal benefit as opposed for others.

****

A lie repeated often enough become the truth for some people. Our perceptions or memories of something can be changed or altered over time. This happens naturally or it can be intentionally manipulated. If something is said often enough, not only can you begin to believe it yourself, but other people hear it, or read it, and it merges into the collective consciousness. It is hard to accept the truth once the lies you were told were exactly what you wanted to hear. In this case the lie you want to hear becomes the truth to you. Well, in reality a fact or truth will never change - it is what it is regardless of your perception. The truth is true all the way. Half truth is a lie masquerading as the truth. Living with lies means missing out on life - you are not living in reality but you are cheating and denying yourself the essentials of life. The truth can be as true as the source. The old adage says, "Honesty is the best policy". Honesty begins by being true to yourself. Do yourself a favor and be honest to yourself and then to others.

****

"One of my daddy's favorite sayings was that he would rather hear "the bad truth than a good lie" ~ Matilda Anderson

****

Stephen Kyeyune

Integrity means speaking your truth, even when it hurts; behaving in ways that are in harmony with your morals and values; making choices based on what is morally collect; And, of course, always doing the right thing, even when it's hard, and even when nobody's going to know whether you did it or not. The bitterest truth is better than the sweetest lie.

****

Begin this week with an attitude of gratitude. Never let the bad attitudes of others come in and destroy the greatness that's on the inside of you. "A hero is someone who collects stones thrown to him by the crowd and instead of throwing them back to the crowd; uses those stones to build a castle for himself."

****

True love is knowing a person's faults, and loving them even more for them.

****

Self respect is what you need to get respect from others while self discipline is what determines your attitude in life.

****

"If Jesus was as weak as you are, or as I am, none of us would need Him, because two weak men don't equal one strong man.

****

The need to be appreciated is among the deepest cravings of human nature. You have it. Don't forget that others have it too.

****

Ironically, we marry each other because we are different, and we divorce because we are different!

336

****

If you find someone who makes you smile, who checks up on you often to see if you're ok, who watches out for you and wants the very best for you, don't let them go, keep them close and don't take them for granted, people like them are hard to fine.

****

Ten biblical ways to love:

1. Listen without interrupting (Proverbs 18)
2. Speak without accusing (James 1:19)
3. Give without sparing (Proverbs 21:26)
4. Pray without ceasing (Colossians1:19)
5. Answer without arguing (Proverbs 17:1)
6. Share without pretending (Ephesians 4: 15)
7. Enjoy without complaining (Philippians 2:14)
8. Trust without wavering (Corinthians 13:7)
9. Forgive without punishing (Colossians 3: 13)
10. Promise without forgetting (Proverbs 13:12)

Ten tips to married women; how to keep fire in your marriage:

1. Beauty attracts men but wisdom keeps them.
2. Elegance catches men's attention but intelligence convinces them.
3. Nagging irritates men but 'constructive silence weakens them.
4. The 'boy' in every man pumps out occasionally, your ability to handle this, is a woman's truest maturity.
5. Men have secret struggles and silent pains. Should you ever find them out exhibit the greatest maturity.
6. The power of a woman that humbles a man is in the softness of her tongue. In the long-run your 'words' matters more to a man than your 'looks'. So invest the right words at the right timing.
7. Earn a man's respect and he will consider you the yard stick for all his action.
8. Learn to mold the moods of your man. Never rebuke your man in public.

9. Men will naturally give you their futures if they can recall your maturity in yesterday's issues.
10. Women are everywhere but queens are scarce. Let the queen in you come alive and he will hold you in high esteem.

How to avoid divorce:

Jesus insinuated that marriage is between one male and one female. In the scripture below He used wife in its singular form rather than plural. 4 And he answered and said unto them, Have ye not read, that he which made them at the beginning made them male and female, 5 And said, For this cause shall a man leave father and mother, and shall cleave to his wife: and they twain shall be one flesh? 6 Wherefore they are no more twain, but one flesh. What therefore God hath joined together, let not man put asunder. 7 They say unto him, Why did Moses then command to give a writing of divorcement, and to put her away? 8 He saith unto them, Moses because of the hardness of your hearts suffered you to put away your wives: but from the beginning it was not so. 9 And I say unto you, Whosoever shall put away his wife, except it be for fornication, and shall marry another, committeth adultery : and whoso marrieth her which is put away doth commit adultery. 10 His disciples say unto him, If the case of the man be so with his wife, it is not good to marry. 11 But he said unto them, All men cannot receive this saying, save they to whom it is given. 12 For there are some eunuchs, which were so born from their mother's womb: and there are some eunuchs, which were made eunuchs of men: and there be eunuchs, which have made themselves eunuchs for the kingdom of heaven's sake. He that is able to receive it, let him receive it. (Matthew 19: 4-13)

When God is the foundation of everything we do (including marriage) it cannot be shaken. God works in three main ways in marital relationship: The three are love, submission and respect. Yet these three are the most difficult ones to embrace. A husband is called to love his wife as Christ loved the Church. A wife is called to submit and respect her husband. Then there is neutral submission calling us to submit to each other.

As I indicated in all my books, the key to lasting relationship is the first step in relationship. When you get the first step wrong you are likely to stay in mess the rest of your life. The first step is choosing the right person to marry. God has somebody that will make your marriage work in accordance to His perfect will but you must be patient to meet that person. As one writer said "The only divine and eternal union is that of the "Twin Flames" who are exact geometric energetic matches and halves of the same soul...and opposite in gender. These are created by God/Source, and no man can put these asunder. However, very few of these Twin flame pairs are incarnate on earth at the same time... But a few lucky ones do meet. Everyone has a "Twin!" somewhere in the Universe.

Love is the key element in any relationship. God is Love and He uses love to bind the two together into the non-separatable union. Love knows no barriers. Love is manifested in passion. Passion must create obsession! No ethos, no decisions, just a steady go! We should not ignore other contributing factors which are common illustrations of people that are in love like respect, honesty and straight self-expression, by way of spoken word and mannerism. Unfortunately, the generation of today falls in love with external appearances. "------being the most attractive rarely meant being the most beautiful" ~ Alice Walsh, A Poker Game of Love

Love should be manifested in loyalty. According to Pew Research poll, couples ranked sharing household chores as third most important for a successful marriage, next to faithfulness and fulfilling sex. To this end, keep reading to find out how you can turn burden into blessing in your marriage!

The Bible doesn't specify who has garbage duty. Rather, it encourages each spouse to use their skills to make a house a home. Men are called to manage their household well (1 Timothy 3:12), women to watch over their household (Proverbs 31:27) and both to abstain from laziness (1 Timothy 5:8). In a home with two healthy spouses, each is to actively contribute to the household, whether through paid employment, unpaid housework or both.

There are two dominant definitions of equality regarding marriage: one Biblical, the other societal. One states that man and woman are valued the same, the other suggests man and woman are the same. According to God's perfect plan, He created all humans equally valuable, but not all identically designed. He intentionally created male and female, each distinct and unique (Genesis 1:27).

This complimentary relationship, in which each spouse contributes a specific skill set, cultivates a respectful and supportive marriage. On the other hand, an inflexible pursuit of work equality – or an exact 50-50 split – nurtures selfishness and breeds resentment (1 Corinthians 12:12-26). For a thriving marriage, find strength in your differences!

Review your status and renew your vows always. Most couples who are separated or divorced say that they did not expect the imminent departure of their spouses. Never take things for granted because in the blink of eye, everything can change! So forgive often and love with all your heart. You may never know when you may not have that chance again. "It's not because things are difficult that we don't dare; it's because we don't dare that things are difficult. Therefore never leave something good to find something better, because once you realize you had the best, the best has found better….."

Most couples who are in good marriages acknowledge the fact that they got married to the right people. However, getting the right spouse does not exempt you from marital problems. It is a crucial factor for the two of you to solve your pending problems before they escalate into a hard nut to crack. We must acknowledge this fact, "We all have our own human failings. In marriage there is no sainthood, unless a "saint is a sinner who keeps on trying." Many second chances should be extended to your spouse to make the marriage work through tolerance, forgiveness and reconciliation. Turning the other cheek is saintly, but it should not be emboldened to impunity. Always do anything to keep the fire of love burning in order to keep the flame of hope burning. Never allow that spark of love to be extinguished. Suffice to say it is not worth the effort to spend one's life in a futile marriage devoid of love, trust and faithfulness. Prevention is better than cure. As Robert Greene in his words says: "But men are more ready to repay an injury than a benefit! Because gratitude is a burden and revenge is a pleasure!"

There is no need to play an ostrich game; hiding your head in the sand won't cut it. The Bible says that, "A prudent man foreseeth the evil, and hideth himself; but the simple pass on, and are punished" (Proverbs

27:12). Never speculate or act on rumors before finding out facts. Over exaggeration of facts kills marriage. For example a little spending may be viewed by a spouse as over-spending; less hearing may be mistaken as not listening at all. Socialization may be confused with flirting. Always weigh the facts with considerate minds. Uncle Joe Musalo says that, "It is important that you do a personal and your wife's SWOT analysis. Please be objective. Find out what could have gone wrong. If reconciliation is handled well, lessons out of this experience can lead to strengthening your marriage bond and consolidating your relationship. Guard, against any abuse and face the issue head on."

Women's bodies and emotions change with time in particular when they are in their menstruation or pregnant. The two of you should decide to start having children at an early time. The best reproductive age is between 18 and 25 years, so the children stand a risk of having chromosomal problems such as Down's syndrome when they are being given birth to at age 40 and above. A woman getting pregnant for the first time at age 35 and above could have obstetrics problems or complications, which could lead to still birth!!!

Different cultures have different values but we should never embrace those cultural values that make us embrace the kingdom of darkness. It is considered to be idolatry. American culture resolves around children. It is a self-pleasing culture.

It was published that mothering children from different fathers is common today because there are women out there who are shopping for men related to the scholars of the times hoping that their children will be intellectuals. This statement is quite perturbing because it has been discovered that some women, fed up with tormenting characters of their husbands, discovered later in life, are unwilling to bear children that are likely to propagate similar characters. In fact, others believe that some men are from a cursed lot, and the only way to cut the trend 'without hurting', is to mate with a better gene outside marriage at the most appropriate time and let poor husband believe it was him that did the business. After all, if the resultant child doesn't resemble the "father", it will at least resemble the mother!

All said and done, we must never underestimate the role socialization does to our ultimate being. We've surely seen children born out of supposedly cursed families sprout into world heroes, while those born of so-called upright parents turn into a nuisance. To this level, I believe mothering children from different fathers is merely speculative and serves no other purpose than mere perversion just as does fathering children from different women.

Marriage is not something one tries for size, & then decides whether to keep, it is rather something one decides with a promise & then bends every effort to keep. Marriage is all about companionship. The word commitment means glued together in a non separable manner. Christians commit their lives to Christ. Married couples are supposed to commit themselves to marriage. Commitment means locking yourself in relationship and then throwing away the keys into the sea. Commitment in the face of conflict produces character. Commitment means staying loyal to what you said you were going to do long after the mood you said it in had left.

Surrendering and sacrificing is the key to solving conflicts. Most marital arguments cannot be resolved. Couples spend year after year trying to change each other's mind – but it can't be done. This is because most of their disagreements are rooted in fundamental differences of lifestyle, personality, or values. By fighting over these differences, all they succeed in doing is wasting their time and harming their marriage.

All of us have a choice to make, and it is an attitude choice. Attitudes are contagious. A positive attitude may not solve all your problems, but it is significant in polishing any relationship. Courtship being governed by anger and disagreement will invariably produce marriage that is characterized with strife. "A smile is the best makeup you can wear. Peace is the number one beautiful ornament you can wear."

Value time with your spouse is significant. I like this quotation: "Be present. Give her not only your time, but your focus, your attention and your soul. Do whatever it takes to clear your head so that when you are with her you are fully with her. Treat her as you would your most valuable client. She is."

Infidelity ranks high as major cause of divorce. In case of infidelity, your spouse and your best friend have veered off the trust in the relationship. Initiate a meeting with your spouse, and let him or her know about your findings and discuss the issue exhaustively. In your discussion, open up and give your spouse a chance to explain herself instead of just walking out. I know you might be boiling with anger about the betrayal but it takes two to tango. The grace of God is God's presence purposely given to sustain us amidst trials.

Men are less tolerant of promiscuity than women. This is rather funny to me because men are rather more prone to catch a 'side show' than their female counterparts. Yet, they will not tolerate a similar act from the women...a man's world, right? When asked if she can ever leave her matrimonial home on the bases of infidelity, the pretty actress responded: "In the first place, it will take a lot before my husband can go for another woman. That can only happen when I don't satisfy him in everything, which I do. It is only when a woman does not satisfy her man in everything that he goes in search of other women. I've never caught my husband with another woman, so I don't believe all men are polygamous in nature. I don't think so. There are good men and I married one."

Everyone knows that money problems lead to divorce. Most people think that the stress of living on a tight income is what causes divorce. Sometimes that is true, but typically a tight budget alone does not cause a couple to split. So what types of money issues do cause a marriage to implode? 1) The Financial Roller Coaster: Marriages seem to do better when incomes are stable; extreme highs and lows are devastating to marriages. The Financial Odd Couple-Spenders vs. Savers: Guess who wins in a marriage between a spender and a saver? No one! While common sense seems to suggest that the saver will provide balance to the spender and vice-versa, this is not what occurs in practice. Rather than balance each other out, spenders and savers just come to resent each other's relationship with money.

Control: Divorce attorneys believe this is the Golden Rule: "Whoever makes the gold makes the rules!" Over and over again, family law attorneys watch marriages combust where the major wage earner in the couple (man or woman) attempts to exert solo control over the family income. The irony here is that once the couple divorces over this issue, the controller ends up writing a check every month to the non-wage earning spouse who then spends that money however they choose.

Values: Many couples have different values where money is concerned. Couples have different areas of interest to invest money. Not surprisingly, different values concerning money leads to conflict. Things like gambling are major causes of conflict. Yet this is the issue that no one wants to talk about. This is a far bigger problem than most people think. Many people who are married to a gambler pull the plug on the marriage because they see it as the only way to prevent eventual financial ruin. The sad part in these cases is that frequently the marriage is "good" apart from one spouse's gambling addiction.

Definitely, I'm not an expert in relationship counselor. But there's something about the divorce I am going through that gives me perspective of things I wish I would have done different. After losing a woman that I loved, and a marriage of almost 8 years, here is a list of things from an expert of marriage that would have been done to avoid divorce:

Finance is one of the main causes of conflicts in marriage. If you want to have a long life, let your wife be in-charge of your salary, it will be difficult for her to spend it when she's aware of the home needs and bills to pay but if it's in your care, she will keep you asking even when all has been spent.

Conflicts cannot be avoided but it should never be allowed to escalate into violence. Don't ever beat your woman, the pain in her body is nothing to be compared to the wound on her heart and that means you may be in trouble living with a wounded woman.

Faithfulness must be proven in actions. Now that you're married, if you live a bachelor kind of life with your wife, you will soon be single again.

Never compare your wife to any woman, there are ways she's enduring you too and she has never compared you to any man.

As much as you need your parents, there should be limit to their influence in your marriage. Yes, they should be not monitor what happens in your marriage; try to handle issues without always going to them.

In the end MARRIAGE isn't about Happily ever after. It's about work. And a commitment to grow together and a willingness to continually invest in creating something that can endure eternity. Through that work, the happiness will come.

Marriage is life, and it will bring ups and downs. Embracing all of the cycles and learning to learn from and love each experience will bring the strength and perspective to keep building, one brick at a time.

These are lessons I learned the hard way. These are lessons I learned too late.

But these are lessons I am learning and committed in carrying forward. Truth is, I LOVED being married, and in time, I will get married again, and when I do, I will build it with a foundation that will endure any storm and any amount of time.

If you are reading this and find wisdom in my pain, share it with those young husbands whose hearts are still full of hope, and with those couples you may know who may have forgotten how to love. One of those men may be like I was, and in these hard earned lessons perhaps something will awaken in him and he will learn to be the man his lady has been waiting for.

The woman that told him 'I do', and trusted her life with him, has been waiting for this man to step up.

If you are reading this and your marriage isn't what you want it to be, take 100% responsibility for YOUR PART in marriage, regardless of where your spouse is at, and commit to applying these lessons while there is time.

MEN- THIS IS YOUR CHARGE: Commit to being an EPIC LOVER. There is no greater challenge, and no greater prize. Your woman deserves that from

Be the type of husband your wife can't help but brag about. (Outline from The Enigma of Divorce)

Life after divorce:

I came across this article containing words from a person whose relationship has hit a rock and they are separated: "We are not enemies, but friends. We must not be enemies. Though passion may have strained, it must not break our bonds of affection. The mystic chords of memory will swell when again touched, as surely they will be, by the better angels of our nature." ~ Tewogbade Ts

The above words are for somebody separated from his lover but not necessarily divorced. Separation is healthy means of solving conflicts and avoiding divorce. Never give up on something you really want. It's difficult to wait, but worse to regret. When you really miss someone, you miss the little things the most, like just laughing together. Sometimes, it's not the person you miss. It's the feelings and moments you had when you were with them. Use these fantasies to rebuild a strong relationship.

As I mentioned, love is the key to any relationship. When you love someone, they never get lost; wherever they go, they are still somewhere in your heart and as long as they know that, they will always know that when they find you, they find themselves once again.

When love exits there is no foundation to build on a relationship. In this case it is time to move on. You can't change anyone's opinion about you, but you can prevent their opinion from changing you. It is hard when you still love him or her but when his or her love for you is not there. There is that feeling of betrayal and rejection. Never feel as if the world is coming to an end when someone decides to walk out of your life, let them go. That broken thing you keep trying to put together is beyond repair. Acknowledge the fact that what you are trying build is not comparable to that beautiful thing that is waiting to be built in the near future.

Love once gone in high gear will not reverse. Trying to force someone to love you is like teaching a pig how to appreciate beauty and cleanliness. Don't try to force yourself back into their lives because it will make your situation worse rather than healing. Stop banging on that closed door thinking something good is behind it. At times rejection is God's plan for your protection. An African proverb says that: "He who cannot rest cannot work; he who cannot let go, cannot hold on; he who cannot find Footing, cannot go forward."

It is not good to act as if things are fine when they are actually falling apart. But the strength of a person is the ability to hide their feelings. Sometimes you have to forget what you feel and remember what you deserve. Life is too short to stress yourself with people who don't even deserve to be an issue in your life. Sometimes good things fall apart so that better things can fall together. Giving up doesn't always mean you are weak, it means that you are strong enough to let go.

My dentist told me that letting go is like pulling a tooth. There is pain involved in pulling out the bad tooth in the same way there is pain involved in letting go somebody you love. The reality is that pain will not leave you unless you walk away from it. After the bad tooth is pulled out, you're relieved, but your tongue keeps running over the spot (gap) where the tooth was, probably indicating that you missed it. However you do not want the bad tooth back because of the pain it caused. The same applies to letting go the people we once loved. We miss them but at times we have to let go. People always think that the most painful things in life is losing the one you value. The truth is that the most painful thing is losing yourself in the process of valuing someone too much and forgetting that you are special too.

First and foremost forgive yourself. Never regret anything that has happened in your life, it cannot be changed, undone or forgotten so take it as a lesson learned and move on. In case there is something demanding apology; please apologize sincerely to your ex-spouse. Also be ready to forgive your ex-spouse. Remember that you have been forgiven to forgive. You have been given grace to dispense grace to others. Forgive yourself. Quit blaming yourself because guilt conscience can escalate into self condemnation and eventually into stress. Don't seek to fall in love soon because you are most likely to fall for any person just to cover up the pain or to prove that you are not rejected, even when he or she is not the right person for you.

Look for support groups in your Church. The Church should have open arms for the divorced instead of isolating them. "The wounds have to be treated with mercy. The Church is a mother, not a customs office, coldly checking who is within the rules," Pope Francis said, in an allusion to the many divorced people, cohabiting couples and single mothers within the ranks of the Church. Francis underlined where he stands last month by personally marrying 20 Roman couples, some of whom had been "living in sin" prior to their weddings. The bishops gathered in Rome are certainly not about to embrace gay marriage and few Vatican observers expect much, if any, change on questions such as contraception, another area where Catholic teaching contrasts with the daily practice of millions. But with Francis on the side of reform, the feeling is that the synod process could lead to some highly symbolic changes when it finally reaches conclusions, which is not expected to happen before 2016 at the earliest. The most notable of these could be a change in the rules to make it possible for Catholics who divorce and then remarry to receive communion.

Always choose carefully whom to discuss your affairs with; don't discuss your situation with anybody. Look for a good company to build your morale. A good friend is someone who understands your past, believes in your future and accepts your today just the way you are. Such friend does not deliberately say things to shine in the limelight or to look better than you. He or she knows when and how to criticize without breaking your spirit. I suggest that you keep close company with spiritually mature believers than you. "The best feeling comes when you realize that you're perfectly happy without the people you thought you needed most."

Humor

I don't care how smart and intelligent you are, you can't talk to yourself when you are stressed or sad or whatever. You need somebody to talk to that can identify with you and delight in you. At times we rush to go to therapists. But who talks to the therapist? Who gives advice to the person that gives advice? Who helps the therapist when he/she is stressed out and depressed? Jesus made for us access to God. You can talk to God any time of your choice.

There is a true story about an American lady that had a calling to go on mission to Africa. Before she left, one of the elders handed her a sealed envelope and instructed her to open it only when she reaches a point when she has no body to turn to. The lady spent thirty years on mission in Africa and returned with a sealed envelope. She then gave a testimony that for thirty years she spent on mission, there was no point of time when she had nobody to turn to, because Jesus was ever there for her to turn to. "There is a medicine so powerful that it can cure every sickness and disease known to man. It has no dangerous side effects. It is safe even in massive doses. And when taken daily according to directions, it can prevent illness and stress altogether and keep you in vibrant health; it is the WORD OF GOD and is highly recommended."

Humor is good therapy because it invokes laughter. God created us emotional animals. God loves to laugh too! Paul preached the glorious gospel related to a happy God (1 Timothy 1:11). God's laughter is not like human laughter because He does not smile at sin. Humans laugh at stupid things other humans do. God is described as laughing in derision at the nations, at their boastful words, which come to nothing, and at the confusion their foolish course against Him brings (Psalms 59:8). A wise person surely wants to avoid having Jehovah laugh at him scornfully (Proverbs 1:26). "How long, you simple ones, will you love simplicity? For scorners delight in their scorning, And fools hate knowledge" (Proverbs 1:22). God knows His own power and purposes, and He laughs at the puny, futile opposition they bring against Him and His people (Psalms 2:1-4). While Jehovah has no pleasure in the death of the wicked (Ezekiel 18:23, 32), He is unworried over their plots against his people and laughs because he sees the day of deliverance for the righteous, in which the schemes of the wicked will fail and wickedness will be ended forever.— Psalms 37:12, 13, 20.

The book of Job contains numerous examples of satire and sarcasm. One such use of humor can be found in Job 13:5. The suffering hero of the story, having listened to the self-righteous pronunciations of his friends, utters the biting riposte: "If only you would be altogether silent! For you, that would be wisdom!" Job's retort is perhaps the earliest known expression of the sentiment, "Better to keep your mouth shut and have others think you a fool than to open it and remove all doubt."

Jesus' love of humor is portrayed in some of His parables. The Master could spin a yarn that would have half his audience fuming with anger and the other half doubled with laughter. One of his funniest stories is the often misunderstood story of the friend at midnight (Luke 11:7).

Jesus Christ was the happiest person because he had no feelings of guilt. I want to point out that happiness is not joy because happiness is temporally but joy is eternal fulfillment that come Christ. So never forget who you are and whom you belong to. You are the redeemed of God in Christ and you are a child of God. God defines you and refines you. Your happiness should depend on your internal fulfillment through Christ rather than from the external circumstances.

The power of laughter: Science again says that getting angry and flexing our facial muscles, makes us look haggard and old. And social philosophy tells us that "old age is wisdom". Colombian literature laureate Gabriel Garcia Marquez had earlier said: "People don't stop dreaming because they are old, they grow old because they stop dreaming!" The same applies to laughter. People never stop laughing because they are old but grow old when they ignore laughing.

Don't you and I, in our basic knowledge, know that dreaming and laughing are responsibilities of an active brain? And the late Colombian journalist and great writer, Gabriel Garcia Marquez was not talking of dreaming while we sleep. He was talking metaphorically, dreaming while we are awake —still, not daydreaming. He was talking of the progressive mental activity that uses experiences to synthesize, formulate and coalesce life-experiences into a vision of life. It is discovered that multi-tasks shrink the brain but laughter refreshes the brains.

Scrolling through my posted humor messages

A young boy asked his mother the origin of the human race. His mother replied that we all came from Adam and Eva. The young boy then asked her why his teacher said that we came from monkeys. The mother replied that your teacher was telling the true story of his family tree.

****

If Adam and Eve were Chinese, we would be still in Eden. They would have eaten the snake instead of a fruit.

****

Three teenagers in the Bible class had a discussion regarding the best Bible translation to use. The first one said that King James was the best translation. The second one said that NIV was his favorite translation. The third one said that his mother's translation was the best one. The two asked him if his mother was a theologian. He replied that, "She is not a theologian but she translated the Bible for me by her practical living." Today choose to carry your Bible, read it and act on the truth within it so that those who don't have it may know what it says by just looking at you. Have a blissful Sunday!

****

A tycoon that loved his money more than anything made a deal with his wife to put all his money in the casket when he dies and be buried with it. When they lowered his casket in the grave, the widow came with the money safe box and asked the preacher to bury it with the casket. After burial the preacher asked the widow about the box. The widow explained that her husband asked her to bury him with his money, so she honored his will. The preacher rebuked her saying that he didn't expect her to do such a stupid thing. The widow answered that unfortunately she did exactly that. She went on to explain that it was not hard cash in the box but she wrote to him a check.

****

Girls are funny, they hate it when you ask their age but will kill you if you forget their birthday. Thank you Facebook for reminding me!

****

You can't hold me like a pinch of salt and expect me to carry you like a bag of rice "Value is reciprocal"

****

"When he brings the engagement ring, be sure it doesn't come with a boxing ring or a boiling ring" ~ Amos 3:3

****

If somebody steals your man, it is not worthy to fight for him because a true man will never be stolen.

****

A successful man is one who makes more money than his wife can spend. A successful woman is one who can find such a man.

****

If you marry the right person you are complete but when you marry the wrong one you are finished

****

Two lovers planned to commit suicide. Boy jumped first, Girl closed her eyes & return back saying love is blind. Boy in air opened his parachute saying love never dies.

****

The worst thing next to marriage is a bad marriage. The choice of whom you marry determines the course of the rest of your life. "A wedding cake is the only cake that can give you indigestion the rest of your life."

****

Never explain yourself to anyone. The person who likes you doesn't need it, and the person who doesn't like you won't believe it.

****

Protect her, fight for her, kiss her, love her, hold her, laugh with her. But don't make her fall if you don't plan to catch her.

****

I won't say I love you, I will make you feel "I do".

****

Falling in love is easy, staying in love is a challenge, letting go is hard, and moving on is the hardest.

****

A Wedding Ring is the smallest handcuff ever. So think deep. Choose your prison mate carefully & sentence yourself wisely, to avoid Prison Break"

****

A loud voice of a man may threaten a woman, but the silence of a woman shakes the consciousness of a man.

****

Empty pockets teach you a million things in life but full pockets spoil you in a million ways.

****

Question: "What do alcoholic men and beer bottles have in common? Answer: "They are both empty from the neck up."

****

There is this thing you people call feminism, well, if a woman claim to have equal right with you in the house, divide all the bills into two equal parts, take one part and ask her to start paying the other part.

****

A selfish person will not acknowledge that he has nothing to offer. It is all about his self absorbed attitude even when he is past his sell by date. It is always me me me and no one else!

****

It is not surprising that you do not know the real me. I have been for a long time struggling to know myself.

****

If you doubt that small things can make a difference, sleep with a mosquito in the room

****

Lies get halfway around the world before truth even gets its pant on ~ Churchill

****

Somebody asked his friend how to tell that a politician is lying; his friend answered that "When he is moving his lips".

****

"Politics is the art of looking for trouble, finding it everywhere, diagnosing it incorrectly and applying the wrong remedies."

****

Only the dead have seen the end of war.

****

"In this world of workable democracy, I never heard any government killing its own citizens on its side who hold no guns as well. It only happens in this world of Salva Killer's democrazy government" ~ Chuol Dojiok

****

"I know not what weapons world war III will be fought but I know world war IV will be fought with sticks and stones" ~ Albert Einstein

****

Never pick a fight; but in case you have to fight do so only when you are confidence that you will win.

****

The trouble with being in the rat race is that even if you win, you're still a rat.

~ Lily Tomlin

****

God created us with two ears but with one mouth and one tongue so that we could listen twice as much as we can speak.

****

The phrase "don't be afraid" is written in the bible 365 times. That's a daily reminder from God to live everyday fearless

****

There are only two kinds of people in the end: those who say to God, 'Thy will be done,' and those to whom God says, in the end, 'Thy will be done' ~ C.S Lewis

****

There are three people you can't forget in your life: Somebody that caused you the problem; somebody that left you in the problem; somebody that helped you to come out of the problem.

****

Smartness is not enough. Dumb animals survived a flood that killed "intelligent" people.

****

"Quote me well, I am not saying that you're stupid; I am just saying you've got bad luck especially when it comes to thinking"

****

Stupidity is expensive. If you doubt it ask your insurance company why you pay so dearly for the policy of the car insurance for your teenage boy. It is because kids are more likely to do stupid things than adults.

****

Where do the memories go that have been forgotten? Sometimes I wish I could go to that place, and other times I'm glad I can't find it.

****

"When you are DOWN to nothing.. God is UP to something"

****

"Some newspapers are fit only to line the bottom of bird cages."

****

I strive to speak only words which are truthful and sincere. He who speaks evil of another cannot find the way of peace. Socrates said that "Great minds discuss ideas, average minds discuss events, small minds discuss people."

****

Backbiters are like crickets. Crickets make a lot of noise, you hear it but you can't see them. Then right when you walk by them, they're quiet.

****

Scientific revolution has done wonderful improvements since 17th century. Isaac Newton is well known for scientifically & technically proving the law gravity. But take a minute, what if Newton could come from the dead and find a fully equipped military aero plane flying on top of his head, could he say 'No, this is not the world I lived in or shout out in astonishment?.

****

The only person that has ever pronounced my name correctly is the law enforcement officer after he stopped me. I pleaded to him to help me. He handed me a ticket for speeding and said that "I am helping you."

****

When you marry a woman, you don't marry just one person; you marry even your in-laws.

****

"If we did all the things we are capable of, we would literally astound ourselves."

****

He told me that if everybody can figure it out, I can figure it out too. The problem is that I am not everybody.

****

A bad attitude is like a flat tire: You can't go anywhere until you change it.

****

Make your attitude so expensive that no one can afford it and make your virtues so cheap that people can access them freely.

****

Never chase for love, affection, or attention. If it isn't given freely by another person, perhaps it isn't worth having.

****

The 2005-2007 beauty queen who has been working as the Public Relations Officer of King Fiscal Hospital in Kigali is allegedly to have stolen unspecified amount of money that was meant for orphans. Sources in Kigali have revealed that funds were gathered by the Hospital staff as to help needy orphans living in different areas of Kigali city. "That's what you would call "beauty with long hands".

****

This humor is a true story about the materialism attitude of world: A certain tycoon after conquering money made it serve his appetites without qualm or restraint. He loved his money so much that he made a deal with his wife to put all his money in the casket when he dies and be buried with it. When he died, at the time of lowering his casket in the grave, the widow came with a money safe to honor the pledge she made to her late husband. She knelt down and slid the money safe in the grave beside the casket. After the burial ceremony the preacher asked the widow about the money safe buried with the deceased. The widow explained that her husband asked her to bury him with his money, so she honored his will. The preacher rebuked her saying that he didn't expect her to do such a stupid thing. The widow answered that unfortunately she did exactly that. She went on to explain that it was not hard cash in the box but she wrote to him a check in the full amount.

****

He said it: "How about re-writing the history with a black pen instead of the pale white one that can barely be seen unless it gets a sun tan?"

****

Marriage is the chief cause of divorce ~ Groucho Marx

****

Men of genius are admired. Men of wealth are envied. Men of power are feared, but only men of Character are Trusted.

****

If you marry the right woman, then you are complete but if you marry the wrong woman, then you are finished.

****

A relationship without trust is like a cell-phone without service, all you can do is play games.

****

Girls are like phones, they like to be held and talked to but if you press the wrong button, you will be disconnected!

****

The saddest thing about betrayal is that it never comes from your enemies.

****

Money is not everything but without money, you have nothing.

****

You know you are broke when you start checking your dirty clothes for Money.

****

"Intelligence is more important than strength that is why the earth is ruled by men and not by animals."

****

To whom brain is given, sense is expected.

****

Before you give up .... Think about why you held on for so long.

****

I wish memories were like text messages. I could delete the ones I don't like and lock the ones I love.

****

They wore high heels so that they can touch heaven but I kneeled down and I touched heaven! ~ Juliani

****

When you're happy, you enjoy the music. But when you're sad, you understand the lyrics.

****

I open doors for myself. I do not gate-crash. One reason is because I am careful not to connect to wrong characters. I mingle with the right people and I exercise discernment before I implement their ideas.

****

I always feel bad and sorry when I see animals being killed or slaughtered. But my love of meat won't let me become a vegetarian.

****

Age is just a number, maturity is a choice.

****

If life gives you lemons, politely take them and try and pass them off to someone else as quickly as possible.

****

Experience is not what happens to you; it's what you do with what happens to you.

****

God asks no man whether he will accept life. That is not the choice. He must accept it. The only choice is how

****

"Efficiency is intelligent laziness". Rabbits jump and they live for 8 years. Dogs run and they live for 15 years. Turtles do nothing and they live for 150. "Experience is not what happens to you; it's what you do with what happens to you."

****

All it takes is one bad day to reduce the sanest man alive to lunacy.

****

I hate crocodile tears. The easiest way to tell a wolf in sheepskin is walloping it hard to howl in pain. Real crying cannot be faked..

****

Epistemology teaches that we know nothing for certain, but at least I am certain that I know one thing...and that's the fact that I know nothing for certain.

****

An Opportunist is a person who starts taking bath after he accidentally falls into a river.

****

I am not impressed by girls that go out every night; I am impressed by girls that go to work every morning.

****

A student complained to the professor regarding his grades that he did not deserve a zero in the final paper exams. The professor replied that "I agree with you that you did not deserve a zero but that is the lowest grade I had".

****

It's weird how life gathers two people, attaches their hearts and souls together to become one, then in a fraction of a second they are drawn apart; like strangers who had never met.

****

Love is not a perfect story but a great story.

****

"People are often unreasonable, irrational, and self-centered; forgive them anyway" ~ Mother Teresa.

****

"When you care for people more than they deserve, you get hurt more than you deserve."

****

If you open your heart, someone will open your eyes ......it is not the eyes that are open that see and not the eyes that are shut that can't see!

****

In Genesis 1.1, the Bible says, "In the beginning God". In all your doings make sure God is always at the beginning.

****

Your wisdom runs deep because you live it!

****

Insecure people try to climb up by pulling others down. Their neurotic need for attention makes them parasites on the fortunes and misfortunes of others. But history doesn't reward "Pull Him/Her Downs" (PHDs), only those who graciously lower themselves to uplift & build up others - SKP

****

As soon as you see a mistake and don't fix it, it becomes your mistake ~ Author Unknown

****

Safety means first aid to the uninjured. ~ Author Unknown

****

Chance takers are accident makers. ~ Author Unknown

****

The door to safety swings on the hinges of common sense ~ Author Unknown

****

If you don't think it's safe, it probably isn't. ~ Author Unknown

****

When you are dinning with a devil, you have to use along FORK!

****

Funniest African Proverbs:

1. When a man is stung by a bee, he does not destroy all beehives (Kenya)
2. The man who marries a beautiful woman, and the farmer who grows corn by the roadside have the same problem (Ethiopia)
3. A short man is not a boy (Nigeria)
4. No matter how hot your anger is, it cannot cook

Cassava (Nigeria)
5. *It requires a lot of carefulness to kill the fly that perches on the scrotum (Ghana)*
6. *If the throat can grant passage to a knife, the anus should wonder how to expel it (Seychelles)*
7. *The frown on the face of the goat will not stop it from being taken to the market (Nigeria)*
8. *An old lady feels uneasy when dry bones are mentioned in a proverb (Ghana)*
9. *The same sun that melts the wax, hardens the clay (Niger)*
10. *If you don't know where you are going, any road will take you there (Uganda)*
11. *There is no virgin in a maternity ward (Cameroon)*
12. *A child can play with its mother's breasts, but not its father's genitals (Guinea)*
13. *He who goes to sleep with an itching anus wakes up with smelly fingers (Nigeria)*
14) *A quarrelsome woman is like a house that leaks (S. Sudan)*
15. *The strike of an Arm won't rip the Buttocks (Uganda)*
16. *Thy grow thy bent the head of a baboon became a spoonful (Zimbabwe*

17. It doesn't matter how
many cars you have..still you have to
walk to the toilet (Cote D'vore)
18. A Black man is always a
suspect (Egypt)
19. An ugly person is always the first suspect of passing gas (Uganda)
20. Raise your words, not your voice; It is rain that grows flowers, not
thunder (Kenya). Top of Form Bottom of Form
21. Whoever is up, wait for him or her from down. Literally meaning
"Alioko ju, mgonje chini" (Swahili)
22. "The frown on a goat's face doesn't prevent it to be taken to the slaughter
house"(Uganda)
23. The dance of a millipede does not impress he who has seen the dance of
a snake. (Nigeria)
24. The taste of the pudding is in the eating. (Uganda)

July a Month of Freedom and Liberty

4th July is Independence Day in commemoration of our freedom from Britain. Prior to 1763, we might speak of the international scene being characterized as a bipolar world—that is, France and England were virtually co-equal superpowers, with awesome military and economic resources and vast colonial empires centered in North America and extending elsewhere. But the European balance of power shifted in favor of Britain. Several factors contributed to the emerging of Great Britain: Britain industrialized before the rest of the world creating the largest Navy the worlds ever seen. The monarch also made sure the public received a little bit of what they wanted by creating parliament, this was like letting the steam out of a kettle so it never exploded like in Russia and France with revolution.

History projects that Britain became such great threat to the military crusaders of the time. Napoleon was an ambitious Emperor and wanted to become a world conqueror but Great Britain was a hindrance to his ambitions because they were good at sea war. Out of frustration Napoleon once made the following remark: "Wherever wood can float, you will find the English!" According to history, Napoleon spread the map of the world and pointing at Great Britain said: "Sir if it was not for that red sport I would have conquered the world." Likewise, Satan points at the red spot at Calvary and says "If it was not for the blood of Jesus, I would have conquered the whole world."

Theocracy:

The conquest and liberation of Israel: God made incredible promises to Abraham and his seed about 4,000 years ago … promises of a land for an everlasting possession, an innumerable family, destruction of their enemies, and blessings on all nations of the earth. "And in thy seed shall all the nations of the earth be blessed, because thou hast hearkened to my voice." (Genesis 22:18). God tells Abraham that all the nations of the world would be blessed through him, with the text in Genesis 22:18 stating that this blessing would come through his seed as well.

(Note) the use of the singular seed (spermati) as opposed to the plural here. When we examine God's promise to Abraham the reader will be able to see why the singular was used: The Bible says that promise of blessing was to be fulfilled in Jesus Christ whose earthly descendants are traced in the Israel, from the tribe of Judah and the house of David: "Now to Abraham and his seed were the promises made. He saith not, And to seeds, as of many; but as of one, And to thy seed, which is Christ" (Galatians 3:16).

"Now the LORD said to Abram, 'Go from your country and your kindred and your father's house to the land that I will show you. And I will make of you a great nation, and I will bless you, and make your name great, so that you will be a blessing. I will bless those who bless you, and him who curses you I will curse; and BY YOU all the families of the earth shall bless themselves.'" (Genesis 12:1-3).

Abraham became the father of Isaac. Isaac became the father of Jacob. Jacob became the father of the twelve sons making up the twelve tribes of Israel. God chose Israel as His chosen nation. The Israelites were the people of the covenant; they were custodians to God's laws (Word). Israel was separated and set apart from the rest of the world as an example. The rest of the nations that did not know God were called Gentiles. God's intention was to bless all nations through Israel by producing a Savior. Israel often rebelled against God. God used the heathen tribes to punish Israel. God's people ended in exile but with the promise of the remnants to return to the holy land to worship God in the temple at Jerusalem. This is chronological order of the countries that conquered Israel at different occasions: Egypt, Assyria, Babylon (present Iraq), Persia (present Iran), Greece and Rome (Edom).

ALL the students of the Bible know that in the early period of their history, the children of Israel dwelt in the land of Egypt for a number of years. But how long did they stay in Egypt? Some say 400 years, and quote Genesis 15:13 in support of their claim; this verse reads: "And He (God) said unto Abram, Know of a surety that thy seed shall be a stranger in a land that is not theirs, and shall serve them; and they shall afflict them four hundred years" – (Genesis 15:13). Others say, 430 years and quote Exodus 12, which reads: "Now the sojourning of the children of Israel, who dwelt in Egypt, was 430 years" - Exodus 12:40

God certainly could have chosen a different way or a different time frame for placing the Israelites in their Promised Land, but He chose a particular way to bring glory to Himself. The 400-year sojourn in Egypt included many examples of God's wisdom and might. Joseph's preservation of the Israelites during a famine, Moses' rise to leadership, and God's great miracles such as the crossing of the Red Sea were all part of Israel's time in Egypt. God redeemed Israel as a sign that Israel belonged to God.

The word theocracy is a compound word using theos (Greek for "God") and-cracy ("rule, strength or government"). Israel was supposed to be a theocracy ruled by God. God liberated the Israelites from Egypt and appointed leadership to His people, but not a king, until the people pushed for one. God's original plan was to rule His people through the judges. Israel has not heard from God in decades. The priests are corrupt. The nearby nations threaten the land's safety. Even Eli, the high priest and judge of Israel, is not faithfully serving God and the people. Israel needs more than a judge. Israel needs to hear from God again. Israel needs a prophet. So God gives them Samuel. Samuel serves the people as a prophet and judge. A prophet spoke on behalf of God to the people. A priest talked on behalf of the people to God. A judge implemented the ordinances of God among the people.

But when Samuel grew old and Israel's enemies attacked, the people demanded that Samuel appoint a king. Samuel advised the people to trust in God and not in human leadership, but the people did not listen—they were determined to have a king rule over them and deliver them from the enemy. So God asked Samuel to anoint Saul as the first king of Israel to meet the desires of the people. So the nation of Israel rejected God's rule over them, and God gave them human kings instead (1 Samuel 8:4-9). There will not be a true theocracy upon the earth until the thousand-year reign of Jesus Christ. During the Millennium, the Son of David will rule from Jerusalem in a just and righteous way (Psalms 72:1-11; Isaiah 11; Revelation 20:4-6). At that time, "the dwelling of God is with men, and he will live with them. They will be his people, and God himself will be with them and be their God" (Revelation 21:3).

Saul was a foolish, selfish, cowardly king. He ignored the word of the Lord and craved the approval of men. He disobeyed God several times, overstepped his duties, and put the people at odds with God and each other. King Saul did not keep the Law of Moses, and did not direct the Israelites to live as God's holy people. So God gave the kingdom to David.

David was a "man after [God's] own heart" (1 Samuel 13:14). He was a skilled warrior, musician, and leader of men—a man who trusted in God and encouraged his countrymen to act like God's people. David's famous defeat of Goliath made him a popular, famous figure in Israel. Saul feared that David will seize his kingdom eventually, and spent the rest of his life hunting David down. Israel was united as a nation under King David. But God warned Israel of the pending judgment in case of premeditated disobedience: "Only fear the LORD and serve Him in truth with all your heart; for consider what great things He has done for you. But if you still do wickedly, both you and your king will be swept away." (1 Samuel 12:24-25).

Quick outline of 1 Samuel> God raises up Samuel as prophet and judge (1 Samuel 1-7); Israel demands a king: Saul (1 Samuel 8-15); God raises up David to be king of Israel (1 Samuel 16-20). Saul hunts David out of jealousy (1 Samuel 21-31).

The Kingdom of Israel emerged as an important local power by the 9th century BCE before falling to the Neo-Assyrian Empire in 722 BCE. Israel's southern neighbor, the Kingdom of Judah, emerged in the 8th century and enjoyed a period of prosperity as a client-state of first Assyria and then Babylon (present Iraq) before a revolt against the Neo-Babylonian Empire led to its destruction in 586 BCE. Following the fall of Babylon to Persia (Present Iran), the Persian king Cyrus the Great in 539 BCE, some Judean exiles returned to Jerusalem, inaugurating the formative period in the development of a distinctive Judahite identity in the Persian province of Yehud. Yehud was absorbed into the subsequent Hellenistic kingdoms that followed the conquests of Alexander the Great of Greece. But in the 2nd century BCE the Judaeans revolted against the Hellenist Seleucid Empire and created the Hasmonean kingdom. This, the last nominally independent Judean kingdom, came to an end in 63 BCE with its conquest by Pompey of Rome. With the installation of client kingdoms under the Herodian Dynasty, the Kingdom of Israel was wracked by civil disturbances which culminated in the Jewish Revolt, the destruction of the Temple, the emergence of rabbinical Judaism and Early Christianity.

Israel was ruled by the Roman Empire for a long period of time, and when they rebelled in the year 70 A.D., the Romans laid siege to the city of Jerusalem. They killed many of the occupying Jews, and the rest were forced to leave and spread out to other parts of the world, including Europe. Israel ceased to be a nation. Rome led crusades against the Jews for rejecting Jesus. Through the Crusades, Britain gained control of Israel. Political persecution followed. Hitler killed over six million Jews. After WWII, Britain rounded up all the Jews who were forced from their European countries of residence by Hitler, and offered them Israel (the Jewish holy land). In 1947 the United National voted for a Partition Plan that created the State of Israel. The British agreed to relinquish the mandate it held over Palestine and as a result. They accepted. At the time Israel was ruled by Arabs and it was called Palestine. Britain divided the country into two separate countries, one for the Jews and one for the Arabs. The result being, the chaos that is in the current Middle-East.

Our freedom in Christ:

God told Abraham, "Take your son, your only son, Isaac, whom you love, and go to the region of Moriah. Sacrifice him there as a burnt offering on one of the mountains I will tell you about" (Genesis 22:2). Abraham loaded Isaac with the bundle of wood to burn the sacrifice at the altar and they set off to go to the mountain to sacrifice but without the lamb for sacrifice. Isaac asked his father where the lamb for the sacrifice was. Abraham answered that the Lord would provide the lamb.

When they reached the altar, Abraham bound Isaac with ropes and placed him on the stone altar. He was saddened and confused but trusted in God's provision. Just as Abraham raised the knife to slay his son, the angel of the Lord called out to Abraham to stop and not to harm the boy. The angel said he knew that Abraham feared the Lord because he had not withheld his only son. When Abraham looked up, he saw a ram caught in a thicket by its horns. He joyfully sacrificed the animal, provided by God, instead of his son.

The story of Abraham offering his son Isaac is the Biblical picture of the one-time sacrificial death of Jesus. In that case Abraham pictured Jehovah God and Isaac pictured Jesus. Also it was a supreme test of faith. By passing that test Jehovah made a covenant with Abraham so that the seed of God's woman (Gen 3:15 first prophecy) would come through Abraham's line and all families of man would be sure of the blessing of eternal life when they invest their faith in Christ.

As we have seen, Abraham's faith was involved. God knows us better than we know ourselves. God knew what Abraham would do but Abraham had to know that his faith was strong enough to always do what God instructs him to do. In this case Abraham had a promise that his seed would be like the sands of the sea, and at the same time the commandment to sacrifice his only son of promise. He believed that God would provide a way even though he did not know how. He trusted God even in the things he could not figure out. Likewise, God engages our faith regarding our salvation. We still have such choices like Abraham to obey or not to obey.

An angel was sent to stop Abraham from sacrificing his son (Isaac). A substitute of an innocent Ram was trapped in the bush. In the same manner we are saved from judgment by the substitute of the innocent Lamb of God (Jesus). Mount Moriah, where this event took place, means "God will provide." King Solomon later built the first Temple there. Today, the Muslim shrine The Dome of the Rock, in Jerusalem, stands on the site of the sacrifice of Isaac. This incident foreshadows God's sacrifice of his only son, Jesus Christ, on the cross at Calvary, for the sin of the world. God's great love required of himself what he did not require of Abraham.

We are redeemed because we are saved from the coming wrath of God (Saved by GOD and from God). We are judged now in Christ. The standard of judgment is in Christ: Whether to obey Jesus or not. Those who obey the gospel by receiving Jesus Christ will not be condemned because Jesus was condemned in their place. But those who don't receive the grace of God extended to us by investing our faith in the finished works of Jesus Christ at the cross will definitely pay the wages for their sins (eternal separation from God or spiritual death and suffering in hell).

Certainly, we (believers) are not saved from the trials of this world. It is true that Christians encounter trials here on earth in the same manner as nonbelievers do. But our trials here on earth is hell at its best - In heaven there will be no more suffering. Eternal suffering is reserved for those in hell. If you want Therefore, to a believer the trials of this world is hell at its most. Yet to a nonbeliever whose conscience is separated from God, this world is heaven at its most. Real hell is lingering (waiting) in the background reserved for the children of disobedience (those who are separated from God by their sins). Heaven and hell will be real experience in future.

In Joel 2:32, where the prophet is declaring the terrible judgments of the Day of the Lord, God's offer of deliverance is open to "whosoever shall call upon the name of the Lord." In Isaiah 1:18, God offers the invitation to come, though your sins are as scarlet, and He will make them white as snow. Revelation 22:17 is the invitation in the new Heaven, which says "Come! Whosoever will, let him take the water of life freely." In these and other verses, the clear implication is that, even

371

though we are sinners, God desires us to come to Him as we are, so that He can cleanse us. The Bible says that whom the Son sets free is free indeed (John 8:36).

In the same manner God redeemed the Israelites from Egypt to resettle them in Promised Land, symbolic of our salvation. The same promise of redemption is passed on to the Church by Jesus Christ. "But ye are a chosen generation, a royal priesthood, an holy nation, a peculiar people; that ye should shew forth the praises of him who hath called you out of darkness into his MARVELOUS light . . ." (1 Pet 2:9 (KJV). A quick reading of each passage reveals that the phrase in the King James Bible, "peculiar people," is also translated as "a people for God's own possession" or "a people belonging to God." The actual Greek states, "people for possession." Now we want to ask, "What does that mean?" The answer is found in the words that came before this passage. Verses 1-2 reveal that the passage is written to people who had believed in Jesus Christ. They were encouraged to grow "with respect to salvation."

Jesus carried the heaviest yoke on our behalf. He calls us just to receive by faith what He has already accomplished. There is a popular saying that, "Come as you are". While the concept of "come as you are," if understood correctly, is biblical, the precise phrase "come as you are" is not found in Scripture. But, again, the Bible does have a variety of verses that imply the same message, based on God's amazing grace. We don't take anything to merit our salvation but we must be ready to surrender to His Lordship after we are saved.

As I said, God calls us to come with our sins in anticipation of changing to His image. Therefore the popular saying that, "Come as you are", as for the meaning and application of the phrase, we can go to the examples of how Jesus dealt with the sinners He encountered. Sometimes well-meaning Christians tell people that they have to "clean up their lives" before God will accept them, but that is not what we see in the Scriptures. When speaking to the woman at the well who was living with a man she was not married to (John 4:1-26), Jesus addressed the fact of her sin, then offered her the salvation she needed. Again, when the woman caught in adultery (John 8:1-11) was brought before Jesus, He told her "go, and sin no more." The sin was never excused or ignored, but forgiveness was offered to anyone who recognized the truth of their sin and was willing to confess and forsake it. While God certainly expects us to leave our sin, that comes as a part of our salvation, not as a prerequisite. We are not able to clean ourselves up without God's help.

Therefore "Come as you are" is sometimes misunderstood and misapplied in today's Church. Those Churches which are identified with the Emerging/Emergent Church or Hipster movements, among others, sometimes take the grace of God and turn it into licentiousness (Jude 4) by teaching that it makes no difference how you live, as long as you believe. If you come to Christ in an illicit relationship, they say Christ will accept you just as you are and sanctify that relationship. If you come to Christ as someone who enjoys the night life, you can continue those things, and use them to "reach others for Christ." This may be a popular message, but it directly contradicts the Scripture which clearly says that these things from our past lives should be left behind and that our former friends will think us strange for doing so (1 Peter 4:3-4). Romans 13:13 commands us to walk honestly (or decently) no longer participating in the licentious lifestyle of the world. Galatians 5:13 says that we are called to liberty, but that we cannot use liberty "for an occasion to the flesh," excusing our continued sins.

God is amazing, gracious, loving, and forgiving, so He calls us to salvation, even though we don't deserve it. While we were still sinners, Christ died for us (Romans 5:8), making it possible for us to receive forgiveness. Jesus gave Himself as the perfect sacrifice, acceptable to God for our sins. He saves us and asks us to present our bodies as living sacrifices (Romans 12:1). He requires us to confess and forsake our sins when we come to Him. But He receives us just as we are, then begins to change us as we submit to Him in obedience. He saves us by His grace, and His grace teaches us to obey.

In the book of Hebrews, Paul said, Jesus has already obtained (past tense) redemption for us but in Ephesians he says we are sealed, which means kept or preserved, unto a future time of redemption. In 2 Cor. 1:21-22, we read, "Now he that established us with you in Christ, and anointed us, is God; who also sealed us, and gave us the earnest of the Spirit in our hearts." In Eph. 1:13-14, we read, "in whom ye also, having heard the word of the truth, the gospel of your salvation, -- in whom, having also believed, ye were sealed with the Holy Spirit of promise, which is an earnest of our inheritance, unto the redemption of God's own possession, unto the praise of his glory." Ephesians 4:30 says, "And grieve not the Holy Spirit of God, in whom ye were sealed unto the day of redemption." There is little doubt that the term "earnest," from the Greek "arrabon" originally referred to what we call "earnest money" deposited by a purchaser as a down payment, and to be forfeited if the purchase was not complete, or the agreement broken.

God has put His "stamp of approval" (seal) on us as His children by giving us His Spirit (Rom. 8:9; 1 Cor. 3:16). In the New Testament it is suggested that the Holy Spirit is given to a Christian as a divine pledge or down payment on the future blessings that God has in store for us. Surely every Christian is at least dimly aware that every spiritual blessing he now has in Christ is but a foretaste, a sort of "down payment," of the life and blessings God has reserved in heaven for us "who are kept by the power of God through faith unto salvation reserved in heaven for us, ready to be revealed in the last time" (1 Pet. 1:4-5). Note that we are kept by the power of God, but it is through faith.

"Man without God is never safe from himself". We are our worst enemies. Even the so called advocates of the free world have yet to practice what they never tire of preaching. The only exit from the turmoil eclipsing the universe is by embracing the gospel. Jesus said that "Take my yoke upon you and learn from me, for I am gentle and humble in heart, and you will find rest for your souls" (Matthew 11:29). Jesus promised that He won't lay anything heavy or ill-fitting on your shoulders. On the contrary He carried the burdensome load that you were supposed to carry on His shoulders. If you want not to be burdened or worn out by the burdens of this world you need to take God's yoke. First you need to invite Jesus in your life; then you need to learn from Him. The metaphor of a yoke is in reference to teaming up (union) with Christ. A yoke is wooden bar or frame by which two animals (as oxen) are joined at the heads or necks for working together. In order to yoke two animals: The horns of both animals should be matched in their length, shape and position. They should have a straight back. They should be of the same size. The bones should be healthy and strong. To be yoked with Christ is to be well-matched with His character. Jesus compares us to an untrained ox yoked together with Him (a trained ox) with hope that the untrained ox will learn from the trained ox.

I want to end by saying that the Church hasn't yet experienced the fullness of the Redemption that our Lord purchased for us on the cross. We have experienced it in part; we have had redemption of the spirit and soul since the day of Pentecost, but you and I are not made up of just spirit and soul. God's new creation is spirit, soul, AND body. When God sent his son to redeem fallen man, He didn't send him to save only part of man. But Jesus came to redeem the whole man- spirit, soul, and body: "And the very God of peace sanctify you wholly; and I pray God your whole spirit and soul and body be preserved blameless unto the coming of our Lord Jesus Christ" (I Thessalonians 5:23).

Take a look at the following familiar benedictions as given in the Bible:

"Now God himself and our Father, and our Lord Jesus Christ, direct our way unto you. And the Lord make you to increase and abound in love one toward another, and toward all men, even as we do toward you; to the end he may establish your heart unblameable in holiness before God, even our Father, at the coming of our Lord Jesus Christ with all his saints" (I Thessalonians 3:11-13).

"Now unto him that is able to keep you from falling, and to present you faultless before the presence of his glory with exceeding joy, to the only wise God our Savior, be glory and majesty, dominion and power, both now and ever. Amen" (Jude 1:24, 25).

Scrolling through sermons on my posting regarding our Liberty in Christ:

"I have had trouble with myself than any other man in the world." I felt the rage because it was practically impossible to run away from myself. I would spend the ensuing days beating myself up for every little incident I imagined had exposed the rotten me to the world. Soon I realized that real freedom has to come beyond my humanity and my personal therapy. Indeed I met the same freedom when I was introduced to Christ. Now that I am free it means to be free from myself and to let the life of Christ be my life to live. I am still discovering more and more goodness in Christ, and every discovery brings me even more joy. The more I know Him the more I want to know Him, and the more I want to make Him known!

****

The Bible says that we are redeemed by the blood: "For the life of the flesh is in the blood, and I have given it for you on the altar to make atonement for your souls, for it is the blood that makes atonement by the life (Leviticus 17:11). The blood of the animals was a shadow of the blood of Christ: "For if the blood of bulls and of goats, and the ashes of an heifer sprinkling the unclean, sanctifieth to the purifying of the flesh: How much more shall the blood of Christ, who through the eternal Spirit offered himself without spot to God, purge your conscience from dead works to serve the living God?" (Hebrews 9:13-14 KJV)

****

Jesus was fully man and He was fully God. When the blood of Jesus was spilled at the cross, the blood of the human family and the blood of the family of God were spilled and mingled together establishing the everlasting new covenant in His blood that sealed the covenant between two formerly hostile parties: God and the human race.

****

Hebrews 4:16 - God calls us to draw near to the throne of grace. This is the highest point on the face of the universe where God's mercies and goodness flow infinitely. The unconditional love of God does not indulge in cliques or narrow, exclusive groups of people that only a few can enter. Rather, He extends the hand of friendship to whosoever believes. God is the creator of all things but He is the Father to those born of Him through regeneration. Think of the Lord as an amazing Father of a household of the born again believers, whom He foreknew and predestined to be conformed to the image of His Son, that His Son would be the firstborn among many brothers and sisters (Romans 8:29). Jesus ascended to sit at the right hand of the Father so that all people (whosoever is willing), regardless of the depth of their sins, can boldly approach the Throne of Grace to confess their sins to Him and be forgiven. Jesus came in the category of the Perfect High Priest so that we may go to Him to sacrifice by confessing our sins to Him (Hebrews 4:14). He doubles as the Perfect High Priest that intercedes for us (Hebrews 7:25), and the Perfect Sacrifice that the High Priest gives to atone for our sins (Hebrews 9:12, 25-26; 13:12). We have an amazing Savior!!!

****

Napoleon was an ambitious Emperor and wanted to become a world conqueror. But Great Britain was a hindrance to his ambitions because they were good at sea war. Out of frustration Napoleon once said "Wherever wood can float, you will find the English!" According to history, Napoleon spread the map of the world, and pointing at Great Britain he made the following remark: "Sir if it was not for that red sport I would have conquered the world." Likewise, Satan points at the red spot at Calvary and says "If it was not for the blood of Jesus, I would have conquered the whole world."

****

You were bought by the precious blood of Jesus. When you know your worth others have no choice but to see it in you. Remember that the thoughts that you think and the statements you make regarding yourself determine your mental attitude. You are a legitimate child of God separated from the illegitimate children of the world. The Bible sets a baseline standard for the children of God regarding what is right and acceptable in the eyes of God. Love people with differing opinions but never depart from the truth. One of the truest tests of integrity is the blunt refusal to be compromised.

****

The universe was not made for us because it is too big for us. But it was made to manifest the glory of God; He is much bigger and greater than this universe. The glory of God is ultimate joy that we regain through Jesus Christ. You are an over-comer because Jesus Christ who overcame the world dwells in you. "When you have the life of God in you, in the end, it's not the years in your life that count. It's the life in your years." The life of Christ is the only thing you will take from this world to eternity. The Bible says that "He has made everything beautiful in its time. He has also set eternity in the hearts of men" (Ecc. 3:11). You have such a great treasure; you were not meant for a mundane or mediocre life! You are the child of God because the Spirit of the Son of God dwells in you. Therefore you must believe as one and act as one.

****

Satan goes before the throne of God purposely to accuse the brethren but Jesus sits at the Most High Throne of God to excuse us. The Bible says that, Jesus did not come to condemn the world but to save it by His own blood. "As far as the east is from the west, so far has He removed our transgressions from us" (Psalms 103:12). This analogy is in reference or an example of how far God will put the remembrance of your sins after you ask for forgiveness. The two (East/West) will never meet. When you go West you never come to the East. Same is true with West. However if you could go as far North as the top of the North Pole you would then have to start going South, this is the point, where North and South meet. Basically, when you go South you will come to a point where you are going North. But if you start going East and never turn around, you will always go East. Same is true with West. If you trust that the Lord Jesus Christ died for your sins, God takes your sins from you as far as the East is from the West. You will never meet with your sins again. One thing we need to remember is that we are speaking of the All Mighty God. He never forgets anything because He is God, but because of what was done on your behalf through His Son Jesus Christ, He will forgive you and that Sin will never be mentioned again!!!

****

Spiders have the ability to inject venom in order to kill their prey. A spider kills its prey by trapping it in its net; then in a slow manner it sucks the partially digested fluids from its prey. Sin kills like a spider. Satan traps us by making us comfortable with sin. Sin drinks the juice of your life till you die. Jesus can make your way out of the spider net. He loves a sinner that repents. His love never diminishes; it is enduring. "Precious is the assurance that He does not change! The wheel of providence revolves, but its axle is eternal love." Spiders have the ability to inject venom in order to kill their prey. A spider kills its prey by trapping it in its net; then in a slow manner it sucks the partially digested fluids from its prey. Sin kills like a spider. Satan traps us by making us comfortable with sin. Sin drinks the juice of your life till you die. Jesus can make your way out of the spider net. He loves a sinner that repents. His love never diminishes; it is enduring. "Precious is the assurance that He does not change! The wheel of providence revolves, but its axle is eternal love."

****

Feeling guilty is positive as long as it leads into conviction. Whenever I have guilty conscience, I refrain from doing something sneaky that my significant other wouldn't like. Given the fact, the guilt that leads to condemnation is bad. The power of the blood of Jesus liberates us from guilt. When God forgives, He cleans and remembers no more what is forgiven (Jeremiah 31:34; Psalm 103:12). On the contrary, we occasionally remember the forgiven sins. The part that wants to keep you trapped inside a circle of blame, shame, guilt and fear is essentially the ego part of you that does not want you to be free of it because it does not want to relinquish control. Free yourself from this viscous pattern of behavior for it has the ability to murder your spirit. There is only one solution - you must give yourself the ultimate gift, even the gift of forgiveness.

****

Joshua led the Israelites into the Promised Land. The name Joshua is the Hebrew name for Jesus. The Promised Land is symbolic of our Salvation. It is the promised place of resting. We find our place of resting in Christ. In the Promised Land there were adversaries like the giants but God promised to drive them out in the process of time (not in one day). In the same way in this world we (believers) encounter adversaries but we are not supposed to fear because God promised to fight for us. The good news is that we know how the story will end. The suffering is just for a short time. No wonder the Bible uses the words "fear not" at least eighty times. We should see things from the eternal prospective. We should not see ourselves as grasshoppers in the eyes of the giants but we should see the giants as grasshoppers in our eyes. In one of my books I wrote that there are two major surprises awaiting us in heaven: 1) It is going to be heartbreaking to realize that we ignored the massive power that was entrusted to us in the name of Jesus to overcome our adversaries. 2) We are going to see Satan as insignificant, powerless and less scaring than we regard him to be now. Then we are going to wonder that, "Is this the man that troubled the world?"

****

A slave market resembled a sprawling prison camp. A merchant went to a slave market where slaves were not sold in open market at auction. They were sold singly, or in parties, as purchasers may be inclined to buy. There were classified advertisements of prices placed on individual slaves by the slave traders. Browsing through the merchandise of slaves, a merchant's attention was focused to this young slave girl. He had a remarkable glimpse at this young slave girl on the stall. He then discovered that she was marked by a very high price. The merchant responded by offering the slave trader twice as much as the marked price. The slave trader was astonished because he had never sold a slave at such a huge amount of money. But the merchant waved the money in his hand saying that he wanted to pay the highest price for this slave girl. The slave owner took the money and lowered the girl down the stall to hand her over to her new master. The slave girl spitted in the face of her new master in protest. But when the merchant reached at his office, he ordered his secretary to draft the forms releasing the slave girl immediately. He then signed the forms and after wiping the spit from his face, he handed them to the slave girl saying that "From now you are free". The slave girl was shocked and she collapsed. After gaining her conscience she asked the merchant that, "You mean to say that you paid all that money simply to set me free?" The merchant replied that "Yes, from now you are free to go wherever you want". The girl wept and asked the merchant for just one favor – she requested the merchant to take her as his slave forever. Like this slave girl, all of us were slaves and we spitted in the face of Jesus who came to liberate us. But after liberating us we asked Him to be our Lord and Master forever.

****

Jesus came to liberate the total man. "For you are the God of my salvation." Jehovah is the Author and Perfecter of salvation to His people. Is He the God of your salvation? Do you find in the Father's election, in the Son's atonement, and in the Spirit's quickening all the grounds of your eternal hopes? His First Coming was for our spiritual liberation. The Second Coming is for the liberation of nature. Our bodies are going to be glorified and the corrupt political system will be replaced by the heavenly kingdom.

****

After you are born into this world your connection to your parents is not just biological but it is much more relational. If you are a born again believer (child of God born of God) the main thing that matters to you is your relationship with God. Your new birth (salvation) is of and by God. God purchased you with the precious blood of His Son and sealed your relationship with Him by the promise of the Holy Spirit so that you might be in His presence now and forever (eternally). Both terms - "purchased by the blood" and "sealed with the promise" are legal terms of ownership. God legally owns you! You are reconciled and saved by the death of Jesus Christ at the cross and by His resurrected life. He lives in you, and the life you live is by faith the life of Christ. Child of God, you are called to live His life as opposed to your life. You are called to live for His pleasure as opposed for your own pleasure.

****

Freedom is a simple word....no ambiguity, universally understood yet it is one of the most misunderstood words in the family of vocabularies. Freedom is not just the liberty to do as you will; it is the capability not to do certain things. A person is in bondage of the very things he cannot resist. Something you cannot discard controls you absolutely. For example many people are controlled by certain habits or addicted to certain things whereby it is nearly impossible to say No to those habits or things. We (Christians) were liberated because we have the power to say No to the corruption of the flesh and the world. We become Christlike in the measure that the Word prevails in us.

****

1 John 3:1 - "Behold, what manner of love the Father hath bestowed upon us, that we should be called the sons of God". God's unconditional love is quite above our understanding! It is incredible in view. The One offended loves the offender! In spite of the mass and magnitude of our

sins, yet it is God who is willing to pay the price. To the sinner the love of God means that there is the possibility of reconciliation and forgiveness. No matter how deep our sin and rejection of God, if we repent and turn to Him, He will always accept us and forgive. Here is the shocking truth: The Father loves the repented sinner no less than He loves His Son Jesus Christ. It is His love for His Son that is bestowed upon us.

****

1 John 2:1 - "My little children, I am writing this to you so that you may not sin; but if any one does sin, we have an advocate with the Father, Jesus Christ the righteous; and he is the expiation for our sins, and not for ours only but also for the sins of the whole world." I would summarize the text in three parts: 1) Don't sin. 2) Don't continue to sin. 3) Don't despair when you do sin. Jesus is our advocate (Lawyer) that has never lost a case. The writer of the book of Hebrews said that, "Therefore He is able to save completely those who come to God through Him, because He always lives to intercede for them" (Hebrews 7:25). Salvation is the finished work of Christ. Interceding for us is the unfinished work of Christ that is still in progress.

****

The word joy occurs 16 times in its various forms in the letter to the Philippians. Spiritual joy, rejoicing in Christ, is a major theme. "I will continue to rejoice," Paul writes to concerned believers while he is under house arrest in Rome (Philippians 1:18). Paul wrote in unusual circumstances. He was in no quiet study dictating to some secretary, but in prison where the prospect was either execution or release. Yet he was a cheerful prisoner. He had no worries for himself. Paul maintained this Christ-centered faith during at least four years of suffering as a prisoner of the Roman government, first in Caesarea and then in Rome, possibly in other places as well. During his imprisonment, Paul wrote four letters that survive in our New Testament. They are Ephesians, Philippians, Colossians and Philemon.

****

Philippians 1: 19-24 – "For I live in eager expectation and hope that I will never do anything that causes me shame, but that I will always be bold for Christ, as I have been in the past, and that my life will always honor Christ, whether I live or I die. For to me, living is for Christ, and dying is even better. If he was to be put to death, then he would be with Christ. If he was to be released, then he would be free to continue his evangelical work with the Church of Philippi. He tells us all this, and more, at the beginning of his letter. He forgets what lies behind and strains forward to what lies ahead, the heavenly call of God in Jesus Christ (3:13-14). Meanwhile, as he writes at the end of the letter, whether he had plenty or was in need, whether well-fed or going hungry, he was content (4:11-12). This sort of language resembles that of the Stoic philosophers of his time, but the difference between Paul and the Stoics was Christ. The Stoics depended on their own resources. But for Paul, 'living was Christ' (1:21); he could 'do all things through him who strengthens him', namely Christ (4:13).

****

Philippians 2:1-13 – "So you too, my dear friends, must always obey God. It was important when I was with you. It is even more important now that I am absent from you. Continue to work out your own salvation with fear and trembling. Do that because God is always working in you. He makes you willing and able to obey his purpose". 'Work out your own salvation'. Paul does not mean that the Christians at Philippi must work to earn their salvation. He is writing to those who are already Christians. So they already know Christ's salvation. It was theirs as a free gift from God (Ephesians 2:8). Paul's word that we have translated 'work out' comes in the works of Strabo. He was a Greek who lived in the days of Jesus. Strabo describes how the Romans 'worked out' the great silver mines of Spain. In other words, they were getting all the silver that they could from the mines. So Christians must work hard to get all the wonderful riches that their salvation in Christ has for them. 'With fear and trembling'. This does not mean the terror of a slave in front of a cruel master. It means the honor that we should give to our holy and powerful God.

****

2 Samuel 6:7- "But when they came to the threshing floor of Nacon, Uzzah reached out toward the ark of God and took hold of it, for the oxen nearly upset it. And the anger of the LORD burned against Uzzah, and God struck him down there for his irreverence; and he died there by the ark of God." The Ark of the Lord could not be defiled by falling in the stench mud but could be defiled by falling into the hands of Uzzah that were corrupted with sin. The hands of men are more polluted than any dirt of the world. Unless God intervenes on our behalf, the old nature is adamant to the human race's plight. Until we remove the cancer (sin) from the body, the rot and stench is going to linger. It is only the blood of Jesus that can wash us clean.

****

God sent His people (the Israelites) into exile to Babylon to be far away from the holy city and the temple at Jerusalem. Exile is primarily a state of mind long before it becomes a state of being. Their minds had wondered away from God long before they were physically banished from the holy land. The inner state of exile brought about the outer state of physical bondage (exile). Basically, the first level of exile was not by God but it was the self- inflicted exile from God. While in Babylon, they yearned to go back to Jerusalem to make sacrifices to their God in the temple. The spiritual accomplishment of exile was the restoration of their spiritual hunger, faith and humility. Whatever happened to Israel in the physical is experienced by the Church spiritually. Some of you are already in exile spiritually. The exile is intended to stimulate your spiritual hunger, faith and humility.

****

Humility is the proof of the redeemed person. It is sin to boast in self accomplishment but it is a virtue to boast in God's accomplishments in you. Tell everybody what God has done and brag about it. Jeremiah 9:23-24: "Let not a wise man boast of his wisdom, and let not the mighty man boast of his might, let not a rich man boast of his riches; but let him who boasts boast of this, that he understands and knows Me, that I am the LORD who exercises lovingkindness, justice and righteousness on earth; for I delight in these things," declares the LORD....

****

Human beings are what we are. Being created in God's image, we have free-will to choose what to be that God respects to certain extent. We have considerable freedom to choose how we live, how to express ourselves and even to reject God. We even have freedom to cut ourselves loose from the metaphorical strings that seem to tie us down. Granted, there are false and illusory bonds, from which we really ought to free ourselves, but there are cords of reality too, and if we cut them we will fall. Real freedom is to be who and what God made us to be. Failure to do so is self-deceit, self-deception, self-delusion and succumbing to muted ecstasy and reverie. It is when you come to the point of surrendering your will and committing your life to Christ that you reach the point of grace. Read into your own passion for answers to your Life's Exams. Answers are just right in there!

****

The psalmist declares with joy, "Mercy and truth are met together; righteousness and peace have kissed each other" (Ps 85:10). If you are a believer, you must acknowledge the generosity of Mercy that invaded time and space to find you. But you are not alone because we are a community of believers in fellowship. The ground at the foot of the cross is leveled; we all stand at the same height: There is no Jew, no Greek, no male, and no female. Nobody is no body in the eyes of God. But it is your nothingness before others that makes you something in the eyes of God. The economy of heaven is measured in emptying. Jesus emptied Himself of the glory heaven, and we are called to empty ourselves of the glory of this world. Therefore show some love and humility to those in need and eschew greediness or hypocrisy. Remember that life is not measured by the number of breaths we take, but by the moments that take our breath away. I wish you all a blissful weekend.

****

Psalm 85:10-11: "Mercy and truth have met together; Righteousness and peace have kissed. Truth shall spring out of the earth, And righteousness shall look down from heaven." The cross is a unique spot on the universe. It is a place where the love of God met with the justice of God. If God did not spare His begotten Son when He carried on Himself the sins of the world, what makes you think that He will spare you for your sins? Make a decision today to allow Jesus Christ to die for the consequences of your sins which is eternal death and separation from God forever. Remember that indecisiveness is the worst decision! "It is in your moments of decision that your destiny is shaped."

****

John 15:13 – "Greater love hath no man than this, that a man lay down his life for his friends" In order for the sacrificial love of God (Agape Love) to be ours, it must be must be spiritual and supernatural. No natural man can voluntarily choose to die for the wrongs of His friend. Dave Barry said that "It is a scientific fact that your body will not absorb cholesterol if you take it from another person's plate." But Jesus did not just die in our place but His resurrection secured our victory over death. We were restored to live in the power of His resurrection. We are the spiritual Body of Christ. The moment we are born again we actually begin to usher in this new state of restoration that will be fully experienced when Christ returns. Peter wrote, "By which have been given to us exceedingly great and precious promises, that through these you may be partakers of the divine nature, having escaped the corruption that is in the world through lust." (2 Peter 1:4) God's promises are "exceedingly" great. His promises are precious. All of God's promises are wrapped in the person of Jesus Christ and delivered to us in one package of salvation. It is through Him we become partakers of the divine nature. Jesus is not a mere liberator but He is the Savior to be adored and worshiped.

****

1 John 1:8: "If we say that we have no sin, we deceive ourselves, and the truth is not in us". This is the evolution of deception: First is deceiving yourself; then deceiving others; finally lying to God.

****

"GRACE IS the largess and prodigious outreach of God based on God's intrinsic nature and act without the intervention of man whatsoever, on behalf of Man." We receive God's grace by faith. Grace is receiving what you do not deserve; faith is trusting in someone's abilities other than your own abilities.

****

"My little children, these things write I unto you, that ye sin not. And if any man sin, we have an advocate with the Father, Jesus Christ the righteous" (1 John 2:1). John writes to his children in faith reminding them of their new nature in Christ. A Christian can sin but it should not be deliberate sinning. When a believer sins it is called walking where he or she is not supposed to walk (trespassing). A believer does not make sin his or her lifestyle. The term "sin not" means "do not continue in sin." It is a calling to repent in case of breaking the commandments of God. Jesus (our advocate or lawyer) paid in full the consequences of our sins. Christ redeemed us from the curse of breaking the Law by becoming a curse for us, for it is written: 'Cursed is everyone who is hung on a tree" (Galatians 3:10–13). The curse of the Law fell on Christ on our behalf so that the righteousness of God could fall on us (2 Corinthians 5:21). The curse talked about is the eternal condemnation in hell. Also, we can be free from other related consequences of sin like lung cancer, venereal diseases and etc. as long as we walk in obedience to God's Word. The safest place to be is in Christ.

****

I just read this question on Facebook posting: Why didn't God give out His Law in the Garden of Eden, but instead waited for over 2000 years to give it out to Moses? What do you say? I want to say that the Moral Law (Ten Commandments) portrays the depravity of man. When God handed the Ten Commandments to Moses, it was another way of showing mankind the depth of the depravity of man. When Adam broke the first commandment in the Garden, He broke all of the ten. That is how far man fall from God. The Moral Law is God's demand on man to put right what went wrong (clean up our own mess). It was not necessary for the Ten Commandments to be given to man in the Garden before the fall. After the fall, judgment had to take its course: "The day you shall eat of it you shall surely die" (Genesis 2:17). The Moral Law was given to Moses at God's timing to reconcile with man. Moses was instructed to pass it on to God's chosen people to fix what went wrong in the Garden. In the long run it was another way of awakening man to the fact that he cannot fix it by himself. The only option at the fingertips of man is to run to God who alone can fix it by His grace. In this case the Law is the school master guiding us to embrace the Savior (Galatians 3:24-6).

****

"Wherefore the law was our schoolmaster to bring us unto Christ, that we might be justified by faith. But after that faith is come, we are no longer under a schoolmaster. For ye are all the children of God by faith in Christ Jesus" (Galatians 3:24-26). This text describes how God's Law, brings us to Christ, and how our relationship with Torah changes once we come to Christ. The Law portrays the righteousness of God. In this text Paul shows us that the Torah is like a personal tutor assigned to the child of a wealthy family. Schoolmaster is translated from the Greek word *paidagogos,* from which we get our word pedagogue, which Webster defines as a teacher or schoolmaster. It describes one whose function is to guide and train a young person in order to help them grow up into a healthy, wholesome, well-balanced adult, one who will live in a manner that honors and blesses parents and others. The schoolmaster obtains his authority to train and guide the child from the parents themselves, who entrust the child to him with the understanding that the schoolmaster shares their beliefs and values and that he will faithfully impart their values to the child. At first, when the child is largely untrained, the instruction of the schoolmaster may seem foreign and unnatural to the child.

From the child's perspective much of the discipline may seem arbitrary, harsh, inconvenient and unreasonable. When the child matures into a healthy adult, what was once only on the outside of the child is now permeating his soul and mind from within. The child has grown up to become like his parents by internalizing their value system and standards, not just complying outwardly due to threats of inconvenience and punishment. Now he is not just a biological child, but a child of their hearts and minds as well. "I will put my law in their minds and write it on their hearts. I will be their God, and they will be my people" (Jeremiah 31:33).

****

The Jewish religious leaders made a mess out of the Law of God by breaking it into over six hundred minor laws in accordance to their own interpretations so as to look holier than the people and to control them. Jesus was quick to clean up this mess, and in Matthew 22:37-40, He stunned the religious elite of Israel by summing up God's Word in two profound statements. Christ said, "You shall love the Lord your God with all your heart, with all your soul, and with all your mind. This is the first and great commandment. And the second is like it: 'You shall love your neighbor as yourself.' On these two commandments hang all the Law and the Prophets." The first four commandments of the Moral Law (Ten Commandments) are about loving God, and the last six commandments are about relating (loving) to the neighbor.

****

Growing spiritually is growing in love. Love changes people, for better or for worse. You could look at it as a chance for you to change. Our newly born again nature inclines towards loving God by loving to obey His commandmends. This is the kind of love that helps us to grow vertically (towards God) and horizontally (towards neighbor). If you don't love Jesus today more than you loved Him yesterday, you are most likely to be slipping back (backsliding).

****

The Christian life is warfare. Paul lamented that "For in my inner being I delight in God's law; but I see another law at work in me, waging war against the law of my mind and making me a prisoner of the law of sin at work within me. What a wretched man I am! Who will rescue me from this body that is subject to death? Thanks be to God, who delivers me through Jesus Christ our Lord! (Romans 7:22-25). We see three things in the scripture: The inward delight – delight in obeying the laws of God. The inward dilemma - struggles of overcoming sin (sin is an intruder or unwelcome guest; "the things I want to do I at times fail to do"). Then the inward deliverance – God's restraining grace through Jesus Christ saves me and teaches me to obey. "Conviction is not a one-time event. It is a miracle to get saved; it is even a greater miracle to stay saved. Staying saved is persevering in the sanctified life. It is growing in your new experience without despair."

****

Cor. 6:1-13 - Don't receive God's Grace in Vain. By refusing to hear the admonition of Paul, the Corinthians were in danger of rejecting the grace offered to them. They were choosing comfort over conviction, rhetoric over repentance, and wealth over wisdom. They placed more value in immediate appearances than eternal priorities. The general gist of what I gained from this scripture is that we can't intentionally behave in the manner that contradicts the commitment to live a life for God regardless of the difficulties life or people present. To do so will render receiving God's grace in vain. If we act like we don't know Christ and the power of the Holy Spirit to transform our lives, it nullifies, in the minds of onlookers, the life of Christ we received; basically we make Him a mockery!

****

The Holy Spirit separates us from the corrupt world. The Holy Spirit sanctifies us by the Word of God. It is therefore imperative for us to study the Word for the divine inspiration. In the Old Testament God guided the children of Israel by the cloud in day and by the pillar of fire at night. The pillar of fire and the cloud were not noticeable by the nations (gentiles) because they were signs visible to the children of God alone (Israelites). In the same manner the Holy Spirit reveals Himself to the children of God alone. Jesus said that He will send the Helper (Holy Spirit) from the Father, even the Spirit of truth, whom the world cannot receive, because it neither sees him nor knows him. You know Him, for He dwells with you and will be in you." (John 14:17).

****

When Jesus speaks, God speaks. You can count on His promises because unlike mankind, God cannot deceive. One of His promises is that ""I am the resurrection and the life; he who believes in Me will live even if he dies, and everyone who lives and believes in Me will never die" (John 11:25-26). The other promise is that, "In My Father's house are many dwelling places; if it were not so, I would have told you; for I go to prepare a place for you." If I go and prepare a place for you, I will come again and receive you to Myself, that where I am, there you may be also" (John 14:2-3). Peter wrote, "By which have been given to us exceedingly great and precious promises, that through these you may be partakers of the divine nature, having escaped the corruption that is in the world through lust." (2 Peter 1:4) God's promises are "exceedingly" great. His promises are precious. It is through these promises that we become partakers of the divine nature.

According to the above promises, even when your body expires, the new life of Christ acquired and your destiny will never expire. It is from the same background Paul wrote that, "Blessed be the God and Father of our Lord Jesus Christ, who hath blessed us with all spiritual blessings in heavenly places in Christ" (Ephesians 1:3). Peter emphasized the same point, "Blessed `be' the God and Father of our Lord Jesus Christ, who according to his great mercy begat us again unto a living hope by the resurrection of Jesus Christ from the dead" (1 Peter 1:3). "In Christ" is the spiritual state where life and immortality are brought to light by the Gospel.

****

What can be more astounding than the unfounded doubts and fears of God's favored people? Was not the toil of Jesus for His Church the toil of One who was under obligation to bring every believing one safe to the hand of Him who had committed them to His charge? Look upon toiling Jacob, and you see a representation of Him of whom we read, "He will tend His flock like a shepherd." (Genesis 31:38-40 2 John 18:9 3 Isaiah 40:11). "Behold, I have inscribed you on the palms of My hands" (Isa 49:16). "The Lord's loving word of rebuke should make us blush. He cries, "How can I have forgotten you, when I have engraved you on the palms of My hands? How dare you doubt My constant remembrance when the memorial is carved upon My own flesh?" As Pastor Alistair Begg preached that "O unbelief, what a strange marvel you are! We do not know what to wonder at most-the faithfulness of God or the unbelief of His people. He keeps His promise a thousand times, and yet the next trial makes us doubt Him!"

****

The life we live in this world is the life of faith that is disdained by the world. In the Beatitudes, Jesus pronounced blessings to the poor, the persecuted and those mourning not because He rejoices in our sufferings but because the life of lacking is that of dependence. The sour truth is that people's faith increases at the time of need. That is why the Church is growing faster in China where Christians are hunted down like antelopes. At times the comfort and riches of this world bring temporary fulfillment resulting into sluggish performance spiritually. God warned us that the world is going to hate us not because He wanted us to take precaution of the hostility of the world but because He knew that we are going to fall in love with the world that hates us.

****

"Man's will thinks and says" I will be"...God's will thinks and says "I am". Enter the state of what you desire to be. God put on the human flesh so that by sharing Himself with us we might want to share ourselves with Him. We are called to put off the flesh (corrupt selfish nature) so that we might share in His nature. "Before the truth can set you free you need to realize which lie is holding you Hostage" ~ Angisho

****

Psalms 150:6 – "Let everything that has breath praise the LORD". Everything that has breath can praise God but worshiping is for the redeemed alone. The first song recorded in the Bible is the song of redemption when God redeemed His children from Egypt. Moses led the children of God (Israelites) in singing after they crossed the Red Sea (Exodus 15). It was a song of joy. It was not just of the song of the mouth but the song of the heart. The children of Israel lost the same joy when they lost the presence of God after they were taken into captivity. "For there our captors demanded of us songs, And our tormentors mirth, saying, "Sing us one of the songs of Zion." How can we sing the LORD'S song in a foreign land?" (Psalms 137:3-4). The most miserable person is not the heathen but is the child of God that has lost fellowship with God!

****

Isaiah 49:16 - "See, I have engraved you on the palms of my hands; your walls are ever before me." Consider the depth of this! "I have engraved your person, your image, your circumstances, your sins, your temptations, your weaknesses, your wants, your works; I have engraved you, everything about you, all that concerns you; I have put all of this together here." Will you ever say again that your God has forsaken you when He has engraved you on His own palms? Do not let anything set your heart beating so fast as love for Him. Let this ambition fire your soul; may this be the foundation of every enterprise upon which you enter, and your sustaining motive whenever your zeal would grow cold. Make God your only object.

****

Nobody is no body in the eyes of God. But the nothingness of a believer makes him or her something in the eyes of God. Therefore decrease and be invisible so that He might increase and be visible.

****

Today many people attended our revival. Above all Jesus showed up. The food for the soul (message) by Pastor Kakooza Mulumba from Uganda was good, and so was the food for the body (meals). People kept coming in and at a certain point we lost control of them. Wherever Jesus was, there was commotion. Satan was always not far from where Jesus was in order to counterattack with hostility and venomous response. We had the same experience today. At the end of our revival meeting, it came to our notice that three of our laptops were missing from our small library. Satan tried to steal our joy but failed miserably. At first I contemplated on placing severe restriction on invitations in future meetings like this one. But God rebuked me and instructed me never to retreat but always to be on offensive. God told me that no value of money can purchase a soul from hell. When I discussed the situation with Pastor Kakooza he insinuated that when Jesus delivered the demonic man from the legion of demons, they violently run into 2,000 pigs pushing them off of a cliff and drowning them into the sea. Can you imagine how the owner of the herd of pigs felt? But the deliverance of one man was worthy the loss of

2000 pigs. We should be ready to sacrifice anything for the sake of the salvation of the lost souls. Lives based on having are less free than lives based on doing or being. "Humility is not thinking less of yourself, it's thinking of yourself less" ~ Rick Warren

****

Call me crazy, but it's hard to imagine a better metaphor for salvation than God's gravity snatching us from the void of eternal loneliness. I think that's part of what Jesus was getting at when He likened Heaven to a wedding feast—the ultimate celebration of community and togetherness—and simply called Hell, "the outer darkness."

****

Matthew 10:29 - "God's Eye is on the Sparrow" If His eye is on the sparrow, then I know He watches me. This promise is for somebody that is discouraged, afraid of the future or struggling with the problems of today. The Devine Omniscience knows what you are going through and has already provided an exit. "----for "we know that all things work together for good to those who love God, to those who are the called according to His purpose" (Romans 8:28). Most important is the fact that He has already secured your salvation all the way to the end (Romans 8:29-30). You are under the divine surveillance. "God is always thinking about us, never turns His mind from us, always has us before His eyes; and this is precisely how we would want it, because it would be dreadful to exist for a moment outside the observation of our heavenly Father" ~ Alistair Begg

****

In the days of our Lord sparrows were sold for a very low price -- two of them for a copper coin (Matthew 10:29). A copper coin, an *asarion*, was a very small Roman coin, was worth about 1/16 of a silver denarius, and was therefore worth less than a quarter in U.S. currency today. Those who were poor and could not afford to sacrifice a sheep or a goat might bring a sparrow to the Temple (cf. Lev. 14:1-7). So insignificant were these little birds that if you bought four sparrows the seller would throw in one more for free (Luke 12:4-7). It was most probably this extra sparrow of which Jesus said, "and not one of them is forgotten before God." His care for His creation is so great that even this extra sparrow is noted and observed by God! The point our Lord was making is this: if God is concerned about the tiny sparrow and notes its fate, how much greater must His concern be for man, who is immeasurably greater in value than the sparrow!

****

Believing is knowing the path and walking the path. Jesus came to show us the way back home to the Father. We have no excuse of not believing. But we live in a culture that has, for centuries now, cultivated the idea that the skeptical person is always smarter than the one who believes. Today it is the skeptics who are the social conformists, but because of powerful intellectual propaganda they continue to enjoy thinking of themselves as wildly individualistic and unbearably bright. Real scholars are looked down upon while Crowd Pullers are eulogized and honored. "When you judge the truth by "man" instead of judging man by "the truth", you inadvertently equate affluence with righteousness; truth is exchanged with falsehood .... The difference between the apparent and the reality is consciously or unconsciously blurred. Passivity is automatically actuated in man instead of activity".

****

Hebrews 10:23 - "So let us seize and hold fast and retain without wavering the hope we cherish and confess and our acknowledgement of it, for He Who promised is reliable (sure) and faithful to His word." We are liberated from the wavering faith. We are called to have the faith that does not weaken in spite of the circumstances. Ask God to help you to see your circumstances with the "eye of faith," instead of through your own natural eyes. I mean the kind of faith that doesn't turn back. Faith has two positions: Going forward or standing firm. Faith has one direction-and that's forward. James 1:6-7 says, "When you ask for something, don't have any doubts. A person who has doubts is like a wave that is blown by the wind and tossed by the sea. A person who has doubts shouldn't expect to receive anything from the Lord."

****

Stephen Kyeyune

We don't see things as they are; we see things as we are. Life is in the process of becoming, and it expands into truth beyond self. The truth that sets man free does not come from man but comes beyond humanity, from God. "The big challenge is to become all that you have the possibility of becoming. You cannot believe what it does to the human spirit to maximize your human potential and stretch yourself to the limit." ~ Jim Rohn

****

Jesus taught that there were two things that caused people to go into error: Not knowing the Scriptures, and Not knowing the power *"dunamis"* of God (Matthew 22:29).

****

Allowing man to fund your life is letting him mortgage it and fiddle with your liberty as you become his puppet! Any wall built on trusting man is wobbly and subject to collapse. Strong walls shake but they never collapse. You standing of a solid rock (Christ). Such foundation may be shaken but cannot collapse.

****

Galatians 2:20 – "I have been crucified with Christ. Nevertheless I live; yet not I but Christ lives in me". A Christian having received Christ, he is to this world as one who is utterly dead. Yet, while conscious of death to the world, he can at the same time exclaim, "I live." He is fully alive to God. "The Christian's life is a matchless riddle. The unconverted cannot comprehend it; even the believer himself cannot understand it. Dead, yet alive! Crucified with Christ, and yet at the same time risen with Christ in newness of life! "Union with the suffering, bleeding Savior and death to the world and sin are soul-cheering things. May we learn to live evermore in the enjoyment of them!" ~ Alistair Begg.

****

The derivative of a function is determined only when a variable tends towards zero. Until the self in a man is crucified, his full potential can never be realized. The very reason John the Baptist said, "He must increase, but I must decrease." John.3:30. "How do you rate yourself now? Can we really say the variable is tending towards zero or, infinity? Examine that differential now" ~ Olajide Victor

****

Our liberty in Christ does not mean free from persecution. "The best way to weaken "real Christianity" is to give it all freedom that can be offered" ~ Godfery E N Nsubuga

****

Can a Christian be possessed by demons? A Christian is the one that is delivered and saved. He is the true follower of Jesus. His body is the dwelling place (temple) of God. Jesus said concerning them that, "My Father will love them, and we will come to them and make our home with them" (John 14:23). Jesus cannot occupy the same temple (body) with demons. He cleans the house before He occupies it. Jesus said that, "In fact, no one can enter a strong man's house without first tying him up. Then he can plunder the strong man's house." (Mark 3:27). Jesus said in the Parable of the Perils of an Empty Heart that demons cannot come back into the house unless He (Jesus) vacates it: "When the unclean spirit has gone out of a person, it passes through waterless places seeking rest, and finding none it says, 'I will return to my house from which I came.' And when it comes, it finds the house swept and put in order. Then it goes and brings seven other spirits more evil than itself, and they enter and dwell there. And the last state of that person is worse than the first" (Luke 11:24-26). Demons can oppress a Christian but they cannot possess him or her until Jesus surrenders him or her. Judas was tormented by demons; he was a thief from the beginning but Satan did not enter him until Jesus surrendered him: "So when He had dipped the morsel, He took and gave it to Judas, the son of Simon Iscariot. After the morsel, Satan then entered into him. Therefore Jesus said to him, "What you do, do quickly" (John 13:27).

****

People always find justified reasons to hate. It is almost impossible for a person to hate another person without a valid reason to himself. Jesus is the only person that is hated without a valid reason. He is symbolic of love, compassionate, forgiveness and healing. Yet, some people of His time and of this time hate Him. None of them can give you one reason why they hate Jesus. But I know the reason why. The reason is because our corrupt nature is hostile to the holiness of God. People are going to hate you because they hate Christ in you.

****

Christian, are you serving your Master with all your heart? Remember the earnestness of Jesus! Think what heart-work was His! He could say, "Zeal for Your house has consumed me." "When He sweated great drops of blood, it was no light burden He had to carry upon those blessed shoulders; and when He poured out His heart, it was no weak effort He was making for the salvation of His people. Was Jesus in earnest, and we are lukewarm?" ~ Alistair Begg

****

As we advance in life we learn the limits of our abilities. Certainly, we are limited in what we can do but growth has no limit and it is not instant. It takes time to grow and there is no time when growth ceases. There are no such things as limits to growth, because there are no limits to the human capacity for intelligence, imagination, and wonder. We need to grow physically, mentally and spiritually. Spiritual growth is necessary as we stroll through the journey of this life because it liberates us from an enslaved mindset to the corruption of the flesh and the world. In actual fact refusing to grow is sin.

****

Romans 8:28 says that all things work for good to them that love God. God turns our mess into a message. The Bible says that we are troubled on every side, yet not distressed; we are perplexed, but not in despair; Persecuted, but not forsaken; cast down, but not destroyed (2 Corinthians. 4:8, 9). Life is a journey that never stops no matter how bad things seem to be. So look at your adversity in life positively allowing yourself to get better rather than bitter. Always live your life to the fullness of satisfaction and look forward for a better tomorrow because the happiest people don't have the best of everything, they make the best of everything. "You will never be happy if you continue to search for what happiness consists of. You will never live if you are looking for the meaning of life" ~ Albert Camus

****

Wrong perception of life issues makes man a wrong person. You are not shaped so much by your environment as you are by your perception of your environment. The impact of culture on people's behaviors cannot be ignored. Different cultures have transformed with time. We keep on changing our values depending on the circumstances. Eventually, we seem to have lost appreciation of culture hence our societies are currently undergoing a state of gross moral decadence. The virtues of the Bible never change with time. Our challenge as Christians is to counteract the ever changing culture of the world with the non-changing Word of God. The metaphor of salvation is God's gravity snatching us from the void of eternal separation of the corrupt world. Christians are able to resist religious mixtures, syncretism, and the effects of the weakness of the culture of the world. We live under the same sky, but we don't all have the same horizon, so if it doesn't feel right before God, don't do it. To be 'UPRIGHT' means to be right with God; it is to be up and to be right. You can't be right and not stand up for what is right!

****

If Jesus could exchange His elect bride for all the queens and empresses of earth, or even for the angels in heaven, He would not, for He puts her first and foremost! Like the moon she far outshines the stars. Nor is this an opinion that He is ashamed of, for He invites all men to hear it. He sets a "behold" before it, a special note of exclamation, inviting and arresting attention. "Behold, you are beautiful, my love, behold, you are beautiful!" (Song of Sol. 4:1).

****

The Death of superman: The fall from grace in less than a month of two icons of Sport - Lance Armstrong and Oscar Pistorius (both men who seemingly overcame unbelievable adversity) has disproved once and for

Stephen Kyeyune

all that sacred Nietzscheian canon: there is no superman. Man cannot rise above his base limitations. In other words, we may have wings of the finest gold, diamond hands and platinum heads, but these will always rest on feet of clay. No one can survive the storms of life until he or she finds his or her feet standing on the Solid Rock which is Christ.

****

Sicknesses are due to the corruption of our bodies and the corruption of the world. Psychological disorder can partly be fully understood when a careful attention is paid to psychological processes such as learning, perception and cognition while considered the influence of environmental and hereditary factors on the behavior. Likewise sin is traced all the way back to the first human being. Sin is the corruption of minds inherited from Adam. Jesus came to set the total man (spirit, body and soul) and nature free from corruption (Luke 4:18-19).

****

We have an answer to the hopeless world. The child who asks questions where there are no answers the same child becomes a non-entity and hopeless. We were saved from hopelessness. The way to heaven is the way of the cross. If you change your minds (repent) God will change your heart and change your destiny. Will you do that?

****

Into each life some rain must fall, some days must be dark and dreary. These experiences are fleeting; they come and go. Bear them patiently. Difficult and painful as it is, we must walk on with an audacious faith in the future. ... When our days become dreary with low-hovering clouds of despair, and when our nights become darker than a thousand midnights, let us remember that there is a creative force in this universe, working to pull down the gigantic mountains of evil, a power that is able to make a way out of no way and transform dark yesterdays into bright tomorrows. Let us realize the arc of the moral universe is long but it bends toward justice. Certainly, joy will overtake sorrow and sadness will fly on the wings of time.

400

****

The Messiah's suffering was foretold by David in Psalm 22. When contemplating on the suffering of Jesus at the cross we should not focus just at the physical torment that He encountered from the time He was arrested to the time He died. Jesus was not like us in another sense: He had known no sin and suffered the additional revulsion and destruction of being changed from a perfect man into a loathsome, repulsive creature God could not look upon. He became sin by absorbing evil into his own person.

****

"If Jesus undertook to bring me to glory, and if the Father promised that He would give me to the Son to be a part of the infinite reward of the travail of His soul, then, my soul, until God Himself shall be unfaithful, until Jesus shall cease to be the truth, you are safe."

****

Jesus said that, "You are the salt of the earth. But if the salt loses its saltiness, how can it be made salty again? It is no longer good for anything, except to be thrown out and trampled underfoot" (Matthew 5:13). Jesus tells those wishing to follow him that they must make a difference in the world. The difference made is "the flavor" or the good works believers are to do that are to shine like a light on a lamp-stand and offer a witness for Christ. According to the apostle Paul, we must also use our words like salt to season or benefit those we talk to (Colossians 4:5 - 6). Christians, like salt, have the ability to maximize their "flavor" or bless the earth through their good works. Christ working in and through us is the only hope for the perishing world.

****

David was impressed by God's care for us: "When I consider Your heavens, the work of Your fingers, the moon and the stars, which You have ordained, what is man that You are mindful of him, and the son of man that You visit him? For You have made him a little lower than the angels, and You have crowned him with glory and honor. You have made him to have dominion over the works of Your hands; You have put all things under his feet, all sheep and oxen -- even the beasts of the field, the birds of the air, and the fish of the sea that pass through the paths of the seas. O Lord, our Lord, how excellent is Your name in all the earth!" (Psalms 8:3-9). Among all creations, man has a special place in the eyes of God. Angels are spiritual being operating in the spiritual realm higher than our physical realm but God never gave them a second chance as He did to us. The fallen angels were cast down from heaven. When God wanted to redeem man, He did not send an angel but became like us by putting on a human body.

****

Psalms 121:4 -- "Behold, he that keepeth Israel shall neither slumber nor sleep." "The keeper of Israel," and how delightful to think that no form of unconsciousness ever steals over him, neither the deep slumber nor the lighter sleep. He will never suffer the house to be broken up by the silent thief; he is ever on the watch, and speedily perceives every intruder. This is a subject of wonder, a theme for attentive consideration, therefore the word "Behold" is set up as a way-mark. Israel fell asleep, but his God was awake. Jacob had neither walls, nor curtains, nor body guard around him; but the Lord was in that place though Jacob knew it not, and therefore the defenseless man was safe as in a castle. In after days he mentioned God under this enchanting name -- "The God that led me all my life long": perhaps David alludes to that passage in this expression. The word "keepeth" is also full of meaning: he keeps us as a rich man keeps his treasures, as a captain keeps a city with a garrison, as a royal guard keeps his monarch's head. If the former verse is in strict accuracy a prayer: It is worthy of mention that the Lord is spoken of as the personal keeper of the chosen nation and the individuals within. The pledge of protection and mercy to one saint is the pledge of blessing to them all. Happy are the pilgrims to whom this psalm is a safe conduct; they may journey all the way to the celestial city without fear.

****

God has no comfort to the ungodly mind, but to the child of God it overflows with consolation. God is always thinking about us, never turns His mind from us, always has us before His eyes; and this is precisely how we would want it, because it would be dreadful to exist for a moment outside the observation of our heavenly Father. His thoughts are always tender, loving, wise, prudent, far-reaching, and they bring countless benefits to us: It is consequently a supreme delight to remember them. The Lord always thought about His people: hence their election and the covenant of grace by which their salvation is secured. He will always think upon them: hence their final perseverance by which they shall be brought safely to their final rest.

****

Go to Church but be sincere regarding your faith. This world is like a garden - as a man sows, shall he reap. But the heat of the battle is as sweet as the victory. The sweetest words everybody wants to hear when we stand before our Lord Jesus Christ are "Well done, good and faithful servant!" (Matthew 25:21). However some will be disenchanted when they receive a rebuke instead of a compliment: "I never knew you: depart from me, ye that work iniquity" (Matthew 7:23). Playing Church, religiosity without intimate relationship with Christ and hypocrisy won't cut it! They say that truth has rough flavors if we bite it through: The heart of the matter is that what goes around comes around, you'll reap what you sow, what you give is what you get...You have a choice, make the right one. Do what God created you to do rather than what you want to do. "The whole point of getting things done is knowing what to leave undone" - Lady Stella.

****

The Bible instructs us to pray for our enemies. I choose this prayer for my enemies today: "So Haman was hanged on the gallows that he had built for Mordecai" (Esther 7:10). My prayer for my enemy is that he falls into the same trap he sets for me. Today, I declare in the name of Jesus that every expectation of your enemy over your life be cut short. May their sharp allows aimed at you become void. May they fall in the very snares they set before you. I declare the promise of God to Israel over your life: "Fear ye not, stand still, and see the salvation of the LORD, which he will shew to you today: for the Egyptians whom ye have seen today, ye shall see them again no more forever" (Exodus 14:13).

****

Into each life some rain must fall, some days must be dark and dreary. When our days become dreary with low-hovering clouds of despair, and when our nights become darker than a thousand midnights, bear them patiently. These experiences are fleeting; they come and go. Walk on in the days ahead with an audacious faith in the future. ... Remember that there is a creative force in this universe, working to pull down the gigantic mountains of evil, a power that is able to make a way out of no way and transform dark yesterdays into bright tomorrows. The injustices of this world will not last forever. We should realize that the arc of the moral universe is long but it bends toward justice; even the justice of the Just God that cannot be eroded. Joy will overtake sorrow and sadness will fly on the wings of time.

Scroll through some interesting political statements:

Matthew 22:15-22: "Then Jesus said to them, "Give back to Caesar what is Caesar's and to God what is God's" This scripture is partly tailor-made to affirm the "separation of Church and State"; the relegation of religion into a private sphere while civic life inhabits the public. What is rightfully Caesar's? What is rightfully God's? I would suggest that things fall under the latter category. As William Cavanaugh likes to say when quoting this scripture: "The earth is the LORD's, and all that is in it" (Psalms 24:1; 1 Cor. 10:26). If the whole earth belongs to God, then what does that leave for Caesar? The only thing Caesar gets is his own image thrown back in his face, the symbol of his non-reality that cannot stand up to the truth of God's reign and the coming kingdom. Be careful of the Caesars of our times who confine all powers upon themselves! O that we had boldness to say to such emperors that they are naked!

****

Religion is pure and spotless but when it mixes with politics, it becomes corrupt. Political power corrupts because it seeks authority, when the authority is denied it infers conflict. Conflict is defined as any antagonistic interaction based on scarcity of power or position. When a religious power seeks political power it contaminates its purity and becomes polluted like in the case of Islamic religion.

****

One critic of conservative Churches called Moira Byrne Garton said that we should question supposed Christian organizations concerned only with bioethical or so-called moral issues related to life, death and sexuality, without reference to equality, inclusion and a decent and meaningful existence throughout life. I don't think he is right. In reality, the majority of Churches are more discerning. They articulate policy positions coherent with the 'consistent ethic of life', even if they do not explicitly reference this ethic. This is evident in their comments on palliative care, asylum seekers, employment conditions and more.

****

We're living in an era of deception that denies truth. We talk about postmodernism, we talk about relativism and etc. Paul Copan insinuated that in the past, maybe two generations ago, if someone said 'The Bible says,' we'd perk up and listen, or we'd show at least a respect for the Scriptures. Whereas today, if someone says on a TV show or in a panel discussion, 'Well the Bible says,' he's basically lost the debate, he's lost the discussion, he's lost his audience. He's appealing to a book that at least the audience thinks is irrelevant, and is of no authoritative claim upon them!

****

With Globalization, the world has come too close. This has however aggravated and influential to the fast growing economies of the Developing world. Technology transfer, multilingualism, multiculturalism, multilateralism, technology transfer, spirituality phillosophism, expatriate support, guidance, and insights are phenomenal. As a mental health service user, performing artist, Development Specialist Worker and Advocate I am grateful to these changes for they are changing service provision, treatment, care and rehabilitation of service users. This has availed visible opportunities for service user recovery journeys.

****

They say that, "A little knowledge is danger." I want to add that the greater danger is not knowing how little one's knowledge is. The problem with the world is that the stupid are cocksure and the intelligent are full of doubt. Today, I did myself a favor. I decided to amputate my ego by questioning my mindful throbs and focusing on my inadequacies. I decided to concentrate on analyzing other people's opinions differing from mine. I am glad I did so because I discovered how little I knew. "He that never changes his opinions, never corrects his mistakes, and will never be wiser on the morrow than he is today". Do something today that your future self will thank you for.

****

Psalm 90:12 - "Teach us to number our days, that we may gain a heart of wisdom". The scripture instructs us to account for each and every day that we live. Life is a great bundle of little things, yet it is too sweet to be little. Life is a teacher. The more we live, the more we learn. The difference between school and life is that in school, you are taught a lesson and then given a test but in life, you are given a test that teaches you a lesson. This life when lived in accordance to the sovereign choices of God is exceedingly rewarding. Remember that you have a choice to run your life the way you want but you have no choice regarding the consequences of your choices.

****

2014 was a fun and challenging year personally, but on a cultural level, it was a loaded with conflict. In light of the issues we faced, Christ-followers must pursue two things. First: clarity. Christians need to be more careful than ever to avoid what Chuck Colson called the political illusion. Our cultural divisions are being drawn today on almost completely political lines, and Christians very often find themselves using their faith to justify political divisions rather than seeing each issue, first and foremost, through Scripture and historical Christian teaching. We have to be careful. Though historic Christian teaching on many issues points us to one side of the political aisle, our allegiance belongs to Christ, not the singular platform of a political party. "We must pursue hope. The truth of our culture, and any culture, is that Christ has risen from the dead. And nothing in 2015 can change that" ~ John Stonestreet

****

Inequality had come about when classes started to emerge in society. When you had the slave master and the slave; the feudal lord and the serfs, or peasants on feudal lands; that was when problems started in society. Which direction should we go? "Marx said that we should try to go back to some form of equality by abolishing private property. These are the arguments that have been going on, especially in the last millennium." (*Weekly Observer*)

****

Liberty and freedom do not mean autonomous. Man was created as dependent. We depend on God as well as on our neighbors. This is the perfect will of God. When personal autonomy is greater than your willingness to depend on the will of God, you are doomed because sin is encroaching at your door.

****

Freedom is a simple word....no ambiguity, universally understood yet it is one of the most misunderstood words in the family of vocabularies. Freedom is not just the liberty to do as you will; it is the capability not to do certain things and choosing to do the very things pleasing to the creator. A person is in bondage of the very things he cannot resist. In reality, something that you cannot discard controls you absolutely. For many people it is nearly impossible to say No to certain habits like addiction. We (Christians) were liberated because we have the power to say no to the corruption of the flesh and the world. We become Christlike in the measure that the Word prevails in us.

****

Human rights are God given, including the freedom of expression. Oppressors live on our sweat – and treat us with undeserved contempt. We must never cease to react, for if we do, we are doomed to be driven elsewhere. We are justified to physically protest peacefully; after all, it is a sacred provision enshrined in our sovereign constitution.

****

Human Rights are God given. If you do not know your rights you do not have the same rights. It is important to know your rights and stand for them. Remember that all it takes is one bad day to reduce the sanest man alive to lunacy. Assertive communication is about expressing your feelings, thoughts, and wants in a way that allows you to stand up for your rights without infringing on the rights of other people. Don't let somebody deny you the same rights. Remember that all it takes is one bad day to reduce the sanest man alive to lunacy.

****

Human Rights are God given. Human rights are not given by any presiding government. God created mankind and gave him dominion to rule over other creations (Genesis 1:26). Adam (mankind) was created to be a king by virtue of the image of God in him (mankind). First comes the Creator, who then endows his creatures with "certain unalienable rights," and then the creatures form governments to "secure those rights." Our rights, contained in the Bill of Rights, do not come from the Constitution. They come from God. The Declaration of Independence by the Founding Fathers states that: "We hold these truths to be self-evident, that all men are created equal, that they are endowed by their Creator with certain unalienable Rights, that among these are Life, Liberty and the pursuit of Happiness." And "That to secure these rights, Governments are instituted among Men . . ." Chuck Colson said that human rights are "based on our most fundamental beliefs about humans being created in the image of God." Our "rights are not conferred by government, and so they cannot be denied by government."

****

The Holocaust during the World War II was a watershed event in the 20th Century. A shaken western world sought to banish forever the extreme nationalism and racism that they believed had caused such catastrophic human suffering. The UN, a new body founded in 1945 as a successor to the weak League of Nations, put at the centre of its charter and policy a new Universal Declaration of Human Rights in 1948. Mankind was one and the UN believed in creating a world of dignity of all regardless of creed, color, gender or race. The only thing that separated us was the fortune or misfortune of social, economic and political circumstances.

****

Today I had discussion with one Christian lady. She was agitated when I called her African American - a title that is popularly admired by many because it connects them to their mother land. She asked me to call her Black American because she was born in America. I politely respected her wish. I want to say that God created variety because He likes variety—more variety than we can fully appreciate, even if we had multiple lifetimes to investigate His creation! However, originally God created man in his own image, in the image of God created He him; male and female created He them (Genesis 1:27). Originally, the diversity God designed for humanity did not go beyond gender. After corruption, the diversity was extended to different races, tribes, nations, and genetic-ethnic groups. These varied backgrounds are defined and recognized by myriads of details, including language and appearance, setting the stage for a choir of redeemed humans (in the image of God), selected from multifarious people-groups: "And they sung a new song, saying, Thou art worthy to take the book, and to open the seals thereof: for thou wast slain, and hast redeemed us to God by thy blood out of every kindred, and tongue, and people, and nation. (Revelation 5:9). I want to conclude by saying that it is good to celebrate our differences in love. But we must admit that God alone can define who we are because God alone can create, redeem and save life. Spiritually, there is only one human race of the redeemed. Redemption is provided in the person of Jesus Christ. If your philosophy of life does not begin with Christ, you are outside salvation!

****

"An individual has not started living until he can rise above the narrow confines of his individualistic demands to the broader concerns of humanity" ~ M.L King Jr.

****

It's not the ability to dominate others that makes one strong; it's the strength one has in helping them rise.

****

"The possibility of recognizing common rationality in solving global conflicts has been unique to the thought of humanity contrary to being submissive to the doctrine of power and domination to protect a political interest" ~ Odeke Olira

****

In order to advance in our respective undertakings and set ourselves on the right path we have to learn and draw abundantly from the great spiritual heritage which our fathers and forefathers have bequeathed to us. This can give us strength and a sense of continuity which are essential for progress and development ~ H.I.M. Qadamawi Haile Selassie.

****

"When the power of love, will overcome the love of power; the world will know peace."

****

1 Corinthians 10:12 – "So, if you think you are standing firm, be careful that you don't fall!" Precaution isn't just a slogan; it is a way of life. Even the bravest take evasive action. True soldiers don't foolishly venture into arch-enemy territory. Like it would not have been the finest hour had Churchill stood in the middle of a Berlin street market and challenged Hitler head-on. It'd have been carnage - blood, tears and sweat because the Nazis would have ensured that the necks of insolent were wrung

like a chicken. "The torment of precautions often exceeds the dangers to be avoided. An Ounce of prevention is better than Pounds of cure!"

****

I know men and I tell you that Jesus Christ is no mere man. Between Him and every other person in the world there is no possible term of comparison. Alexander, Caesar, Charlemagne, and I have founded empires. But on what did we rest the creation of our genius? Upon force. Jesus Christ founded His empire upon love; and at this hour millions of men would die for Him ~ Napoleon

****

If you are neutral in situations of injustice, you have chosen the side of the oppressor. If an elephant has its foot on the tail of a mouse and you say that you are neutral,

the mouse will not appreciate your neutrality ~ Desmond Tutu

****

"Law and order exist for the purpose of establishing justice and when they fail in this purpose, they become the dangerously structured dams that block the flow of social progress" ~ Martin Luther King Jr.

****

Locking civilians in army barracks is strange, degrading and a sign of retrogression in civility. If prisons are there why then do this? Criminals are everywhere in the world but institutions are established to settle such deviance.

****

Threatening the media is "barking under the wrong tree"! It is directing your cause in the wrong direction. Experience should have taught you what the media is for in different parts of the world, on different issues and situations.

****

"You have 'Freedom of Speech' but 'Freedom after Speech', that I cannot guarantee" ~ Idi Amin

****

Idi Amin the worst dictator the world has ever known: Worse than Pol Pot of Cambodia, Augusto Pinochet of Chile, Saddam and Hussein of Iraq. He mastered the qualities of deadly dictator and became a perfect liar, evil, greedy, glutinous, psychotic, paranoid, sadistic, controlling, delusional and useless thinker seeking pleasure in other pains. His continue narcissistic personal disorder and delusional behaviors caused us memorable sufferings. No body dared to point a finger in the eye of the bull because all people lived in absolute fear. Thomas Jefferson said that "When the people fear the government, there is tyranny. When the government fears the people, there is liberty."

****

How sweet when the politicians who installed oppressive laws, in future get ensnared, humiliated and destroyed by the nefarious system that they so ably helped put in place.

****

Politicians are the only people I know who create problems and then campaign against the same problems they created!

****

The youth are like "misguided missiles" that have a tendency of being everywhere and end up being nowhere ~ President Y K Museveni

****

The peasants are the poorest but they are the majority and the reserved force for hatching revolution. The soldiers of an army are rarely composed of the intellectually astute. Flavius Vegetius Renatus, who lived around 380 AD, was the author of the most influential military book ever written for the Roman Empire. Look at the type of person he says makes the best soldier: "Peasants are the most fit to carry arms.... They are simple, content with little, inured to fatigue, and prepared in some measure for military life by their continual employment in farm work, in handling the spade, digging trenches and carrying burdens."

****

How sweet when the politicians who installed oppressive laws, in future get ensnared, humiliated and destroyed by the nefarious system that they so ably helped put in place.

****

Reckless disregard. It's a phrase in legal writing that means "gross negligence without concern for danger to others." And it's a phrase that characterizes much of the attitude toward law of an administration headed by a man sometimes described as a constitutional scholar ---- ------ There is a continuum between lawful exercise of discretion and unlawful suspension of the law. Time and again, Obama has lurched toward the wrong end of it.

****

"In politics we're always in departure lounge and can leave anytime" ~ PM Nsibambi

****

"He is just an organized criminal who used elections rigging as a conduit to capture power so that he can enjoy the loot." ~ Remase

****

"Remember never to play a martyr, for dead people don't liberate their nation. We need everyone safe" ~ Tom Okwalinga

****

We do ourselves a huge disservice when our idea of patriotism is blind adulation without criticism. Want to know my experience of sycophants? They never actually love what they volubly extol. "For a real friend, give me a critic any day."

****

Before you put in efforts to free others you must free yourself. We need to free ourselves in order to free others. In order to experience real freedom, we must put in effort to set everyone and everything around us free otherwise we will still live in bondage. The key is to live for everyone else's freedom so that we can have it too.

****

Time hides many things and Time establishes everything. When a man is chewing his food awkwardly you can tell there is sand in it. The personal dynamics required to counter the extreme forces of a bad government are far too great for a human frame. Our leaders should know that what goes around comes around. One day in this century the hunter will become the hunted and he will realize the comfortabilty of degraded life – bad food, fleas, bedbugs and name it...............cry the beloved country.

****

Uganda, fifty years after independence one would have expected development but they have been years of massive siphoning of the resources firstly by the supposed people to lead patriotically. It all boils down to a citizenry that have their country at heart.

****

Why is Africa poor? In Uganda, we suffered misrule of our past rogue rulers, Obote and Amin, but for all their sins, they did not steal the country's wealth. It is said that during his first exile in Tanzania, Obote lived in poverty and survived only as a guest of the Tanzanian government. We also know that Idi Amin lived in poverty in Saudi Arabia until his death. On the other hand, Mobutu of Zaire (now DRC) stole massively and hid his loot in banks abroad, but it is unlikely that what he took was even 1% of his country's wealth. So, who took or who takes the rest?

****

Leaders must develop social policies to address disparities among groups. It is easier for communities to mobilize along ethnic lines than for development in a polarized society. The leaders should inspire in the public sets of civic values and attitudes like participation, social trust and respect for divergent positions. Our fate on earth is not conjoined by common descent, race or nationality, but by the mutual duty we owe one another for the common purpose of peace and progress without which none can survive, let alone thrive, in the world today. Life doesn't get better by chance, it gets better by change. Every change is possible if you are truly sincere, committed and willing to persevere. "If I had my time over I would do the same again. So would any man who dares call himself a man" ~ Nelson Mandela

****

The US was founded as a democratic republic, yet our chief export (other than jobs, thanks corporate wunderkind) is militarism and empire. We stated that "all men were created equal" but counted blacks as 3/5 human and consented to slavery early on and institutional racism that rivaled that of Apartheid South Africa.

****

God exalts a nation that exalts Him. This week the citizens of USA exercised their right to vote for the Congress. People voted for those people who share their values to represent them. As for those who are celebrating for being elected, you should not focus on being re-elected in future. Your priority should be to do what is right because when you do what is right, re-election will take care of itself.

****

In politics there is no traditional enemy. Politicians will work with even with their enemies for their advantage. Somebody can suggest that such gesture means that the politicians are very forgiving. But it can also mean that they are cynical political players who know that once you bring back people who had been dumped, they will offer you maximum loyalty. Although this might be self-deception taking into account the proverb stating that no amount of rain can wash away a leopard's spots.

****

'Destiny called upon me to change the face of the world', Napoleon once remarked. No one could deny that Napoleon was a man of destiny. His illustrious career spawned admiration from the world's French government greatest writers, artists and statesmen; his legacy still leaves its imprint on Europe to this day. When the time came to change the incompetent Directory, the impetuous Corsican undoubtedly felt touched by the hand of history. "Some people dream of success. Others stay awake to achieve it!"

****

Intellectuals do not prove their intellectually through sporadic anecdotal utterances in the media. They engage in research and publish evidence based papers that contribute to the body of knowledge!

****

African politics is dangerous! One minute you're the favorite within the inner circle, another minute you are in exile; you can't even return to your own mother land. This sends a clear message out to all those in politics.....It's not all rosy and it's not all about chauffeur driven bullet proof limousines and police led convoys....There's always a dark spooky side to it."

****

History like experience is the best teacher. One major problem is that this generation has not learnt anything from history. We have not actually and seriously learnt anything from our past experiences. The old adage says that those who forget history will undoubtedly repeat the errors of history. A generation that isn't focused will rarely learn from the errors and good of their ancestors.

****

Tribalism is killing slowly our country. This reminds me of a Runyankole proverb – "*otaryeebwa omuhanda gwakuretsire*"; literally meaning - (never forget where you came from). That is not all; some prominent leaders are now hell bent on churning out hate and sectarian statements. If these short-sighted and irresponsible statements are not stopped, there is no doubt that the horrific past which some people are beginning to deceive themselves that it is passed but it may be repeated again and it would be disastrous.

****

It is regrettable that prejudice seems to be an enduring characteristic of the human race and it is observed in education, business, politics and sports. ~ It's a vice!

****

Honesty saves a country but ego and denial don't. Denial and tribal ego will disintegrate Africa into mini-tribal-warlord controlled territories. The love for a tribe must match with the love for one's country. Differences are not intended to separate, to alienate. We are different precisely in order to realize our need of one another.

****

Leaders must develop social policies to address disparities among groups. It is easier for communities to mobilize along ethnic lines than for development in a polarized society. The leaders should inspire in the public sets of civic values and attitudes like participation, social trust and respect for divergent positions. Our fate on earth is not conjoined by common descent, race or nationality, but by the mutual duty we owe one another for the common purpose of peace and progress without which none can survive, let alone thrive, in the world today. Life doesn't get better by chance, it gets better by change. Therefore live simply. Love generously. Speak truthfully. Pray daily. Leave everything else to God."

****

Chuck Colson was a disciplined Christian thinker: He did his level best, and I would say succeeded, to harness his political and geopolitical instincts, and examine them through the lens of a Christian worldview. And when it came to war, he talked frequently about what is called "just war theory." That might sound a bit academic, but it isn't. It's critical—not only because, as its name implies, justice depends on it. That intent, in this case, is to stop the slaughter of hundreds of thousands of innocent people and to prevent terrorist groups like ISIS from, to use the current term, metastasizing. Equally important we've got to know that there's a reasonable chance that we will succeed. Also there are other criteria for a just war: proper governing authority, proportionality, not targeting civilians, etc. Thomas Aquinas applauded those who wielded the sword in protection of the community. John Calvin called the soldier an 'agent of God's love,' and called soldiering justly a 'God-like act. Because "restraining evil out of love for neighbor" is an imitation of God's restraining evil out of love for His creatures. A world where Christians refused to fight just wars wouldn't be peaceful, and it certainly wouldn't be a more just world. It would be a world where evil would be unchecked by justice and where the strong would be free to prey on the weak.

****

People imitate their leaders. We are like cheerleaders picking up their little pitches. Every leader must be conscious of this very fact. Yet not all leaders can question themselves and have their own mindful throbs; unless one explored this wisdom and adjusted his or her position he/she is a ruler rather than a leader.

****

We are instructed to obey the authorities until the authorities tell us to disobey the authorities above them. The cultural values that are not in contradiction to the Scriptures must be promoted. We should make a habit out of living by the same values. African cultures are rich in values. Africans were torn away from their past, propelled into a universe fashioned from outside that suppresses their values, and dumbfounded by a cultural invasion that marginalizes Africans. Today's Africans are the deformed image of others. The Westernized Africans despise and scorn their indigenous values including language. The saying that 'none is so blind as he who will not see' is applicable to persons of such ilk and disposition. In other words, they see the world and view reality through the prism of hate and prejudice towards their own culture. We need to fall in love with our values (which are not in contradiction to the scriptures) and be proud of who we are because God created the variety of cultures each beautiful in its own way.

****

"Civilization is neither Westernization nor exclusive to other climes. It is building a society on values and institutions designed to protect not the strongest but the weakest as we are only as strong, as honorable, as respected and valued as the sum of our weakest parts." ~ Funmi Iyanda

****

In my culture there are no rules! All there is in my culture is a self-governing ideology through which each individual governs self within the collective. We call this community system *"Obuntu Bulamu"*. A system, according to an Austrian Biologist, "is an entity that maintains its existence through the mutual interaction of its parts": And so is Buganda: it is a system that does not depend on a written law but rather on internally in-built software that is written in the hearts and DNA of our *lulyo*.

****

We are planted in our cultures. Within culture there are bad and good traditions. Any culture is compared to eating a fish; you eat the meat and dump the bones. As precaution, at times some traditions become chains holding us in bondage. "If you cut your chains you free yourself. If you cut your roots, you die." ~ Nnaabagereka Sylivia Nagginda.

****

In Africa, ethnic cannot be separated from politics. African politics is compared to a torn ethnic fabric that urgently needs re-stitching. Unfortunately, many politicians apparently have adapted to a lifestyle that includes cognitive dissonance. They end up promoting the same things they condemn. "Those living in glass houses refraining from throwing stones" Here's the deal. Things on this planet could be a whole lot better for most folks. Perhaps, instead of indulging in infantile primate pooh-slinging, we'd all do well to look around, close to home, and see what we can do to make our little corner of the world a better place, and see, clearly, how that can do a lot more good a lot further afield than any of us might suspect.

****

Civilization began with the discovery of fire. Homo erectus' range of habitats thus increased and enabled them to live in colder climates for the first time. With the invention of fire, they also acquired a weapon for scaring away predators. Later, home sapiens were to use fire to clear forests and bushes for agriculture and to make more advanced tools out of metals. Civilization then started when human beings started living in organized societies — this is what civilization means. Our ancestors were human beings all right, but they were not civilized. They were hunting in small groups — each one looking for survival. First of all what do we mean by civilization? It is the development of the cooperative instinct. The activities controlled by the conscious parts of the brain are the ones that build up civilization. Human civilization has been in existence for about 10,000 years. However, when I talk about civilization, it is a higher possibility that all human life started in Africa. The Europeans and Asians all came from Africa about 100,000 years ago. Before that, human life existed only in Africa. No wonder modern science has recently discovered that all races have their DNA linked to Africans.

****

The generation of unborn children in this country will not forgive this present generation of Nigerian youths for their complacent and docile disposition to the national political and social - economic misdeeds that has pervaded and ravaged every sphere of our national life-this unconcerned disposition is a heinous crime against Posterity!!

****

Laws are enacted to suit different societies and their aspirations. If the West find the anti-homosexuality law repugnant, our society looks at it as a treasure to guard against an abnormal way of living. I am sure that homosexuality is a habit just like smoking, drinking, fornication and adultery. These are learnt and not inborn. With concerted efforts, the vice can be fought and eliminated.

****

"Although I support gay rights, I am aware that 90 percent of Ugandans find homosexuality abominable. Law is (and must be) a reflection of the values, norms, attitudes, beliefs and traditions of the society that it GOVERNS. No state, democratic or authoritarian, can force a lifestyle on a society, which 90 percent of the population sees as an abomination".

****

Was God not scientific enough when He created us in His image with the dual male and female characteristic? He also created the animals, with the same male and female dual characteristics; for purposes of procreation! Even plants have the male & female characteristics (stamen & pistil) in the flowers). I love the Nigerian because they have signed the law without the Western pressure that Museveni is under. They don't need to beg and sell their morals like other pauper leaders. History must be erased if a true African people are to ever emerge on the earth; lest we remain caricatures and cartridges of a false tradition or humanity forever.

****

"Do you not know that the unrighteous will not inherit the kingdom of God? Do not be deceived. Neither fornicators, nor idolaters, nor adulterers, nor homosexuals, nor sodomites, nor thieves, nor covetous, nor drunkards, nor revilers, nor extortioners will inherit the kingdom of God. And such were some of you. But you were washed, but you were sanctified, but you were justified in the name of the Lord Jesus and by the Spirit of our God" (1 Cor. 6:9-11). Paul wrote to the born again Christians reminding them of the nature of the corrupt world from which they were redeemed. He said that in the past they were habitually obsessed with the above sins but now (after embracing the grace of God) they abhor the above lifestyle. They envy the righteousness of God as opposed to the corruption of the world.

****

We have a rich culture therefore we must not compromise on those values which are not in contradiction to the Scriptures. Copying everything from the West at the expense of our values has been identified as the major bottleneck which frustrates morality in Africa. There are things which make us Africans which we cannot afford to give up. Stand warned that it is because of the Cultural Revolution (Westernization of Africa) that many Africans became sucked into a mechanism which facilitates the continued exploitation of Africa and the African people.

****

We are instructed to obey the authorities until the authorities tell us to disobey the authorities above them. The politicians who advocate Westernization at the expense of Africanization must be shunned. The cultural values that are not in contradiction to the Scriptures must be promoted. We should make a habit out of living by the same values. African cultures are rich in values. Africans were torn away from their past, propelled into a universe fashioned from outside that suppresses their values, and dumbfounded by a cultural invasion that marginalizes Africans. Today's Africans are the deformed image of others. The Westernized Africans despise and scorn their indigenous values including language. The saying that 'none is so blind as he who will not see' is applicable to persons of such ilk and disposition. In other words, they see the world and view reality through the prism of hate and prejudice towards their own culture. We need to fall in love with our values and be proud of who we are because God created the variety of cultures, each beautiful in its own way.

****

According to Ngungi wa Thiongo, Africans are truly becoming trees without roots, the way we are increasingly confused about what is and what isn't African. Cultural imperialism is domination of African culture by Western imperialist culture. Cultural imperialism is mother to the slavery of the mind and the body. It is cultural imperialism that gives birth to the mental blindness and deafness that persuades people to allow foreigners to tell them what to do in their own country, to make foreigners the ears and mouths of their national affairs, forgetting the saying: "Only he who lives in the wildness knows what it is like. Hence a foreigner can never become the true guide of another people."

****

Not all democracies are REALLY fully functional. In Africa, tyrants are still more likely to be elected into office; because those are the kind of people that current African culture allows and has respect for. Here is one way to differentiate. In functional democracies, National Problems are expected to become the Personal Problems of the elected representatives. However in corrupt dysfunctional democracies (democracies that exist only in constitutional theory), it is the exact opposite; the Personal Problems of the elected are made to become National Problems of the citizens, who already have too many crushing problems of their own to bear with...

****

The concept of Equality has been conveniently adopted over and over by many causes that had nothing to do with Equality and although many people want to pursue this ideal much confusion makes it much too blurry to materialize. It is not possible to Respect a concept that is not understood. For Equality to spread all over, it would take a Plan based on the most solid principles and one strategy led by a new and clear definition of the concept of Equality. The journey toward Equality would be like entering a labyrinth with the confidence to find the way out because of one compass that will help us to navigate and to reach the destination. Revolution offers that compass to navigate in that labyrinth which is our reality. Like in a "domino effect" the doors will open one after another and a mirrored light will show the exit.

****

African leaders are responsible for the sufferings of the native people. Illiteracy can be eradicated by improvement of the education sector. But it is not the prioritizing of education; it is the prioritizing of wanton corruption, sheer incompetence and mismanagement in government departments.

****

The generation of unborn children in this country will not forgive this present generation of Nigerian youths for their complacent and docile disposition to the national political and social - economic misdeeds that has pervaded and ravaged every sphere of our national life - this unconcerned disposition is a heinous crime against Posterity!

****

Why road carnage is on increase in the third world? Politics is nothing more than a contest of egos, or the domain of special interests. It is pursuing self aggrandizement. The ugliness of politics is that it involves more talking and less action. Politicians think that if you repeat the lies over and over, people will eventually accept it as truth. The main duty of any presiding government should be the welfare of the citizens. As for the civil servants and politicians occupying the sensitive positions - the writing is on the wall in black and white for you to read: If you cannot deliver be honest and change people's expectations of you. Unfortunately, such honest search for decency, paradoxically in the same way as the screaming media headlines, is most likely to end up obscuring the tragedies, turning them into chaotic convulsions in the primeval mud.

****

"May the labors of our past heroes never be in vain. Today, in most African governments we have vagabonds and thieves in power. ... Those who loot the treasury of an entire nation and still insult our common intelligence ... All we need are visionary, dedicated and inspiring leaders and not the shameless rogues and incorrigibly kleptomaniac bandits who lie, rob, cheat, rig and kill their way to power." ~ nigeriacamera.net

****

Revolutions are usually started by a discontented population. The French Revolution was started with the help of peasants who were enslaved to work on lands they could not call their own.

****

"Freedom means choosing your burden." No one is free when others are oppressed.

****

Idi Amin divided the country into religious and tribal ethnical groupings, setting one against the other. By then, Ugandan politics had settled into a depressing pattern of ethnic upheavals. Amin was another gun totting fellow. It was a matter of time before he tried the patience of Tanzanians, and Uganda was saved by Muwalimu J Nyerere's powerful guns. Tanzania stopped Amin and kicked him out. Thank God for our liberators. "Occasionally the tree of Liberty must be watered with the blood of Patriots and Tyrants"

****

"Shall a man go and hang himself because he belongs to the race of pygmies, and not be the biggest pygmy that he can?" ~ Henry David Thoreau

****

It is regrettable that prejudice seems to be an enduring characteristic of the human race; and it is observed in education, business, politics and sports ~ it's a vice People are by nature narrowly selfish and ethically flawed.

****

Of all people's evil ways, none are more prevalent or dangerous than their instinctive lust for power and their desire to dominate others. The possibility of eradicating these instincts is a utopian "pipedream".

The truth of subjectivity is attained only in a subject, and the truth of personality only in a person. In a constitution which has become mature as a realization of rationality, each of the three moments of the concept has explicitly actual and separate formation.

****

Dictators like Idi Amin have illusions that this country is full of peons and idiots, who must be herded and controlled like cattle.

****

Power concedes nothing without a demand. It never has and it never will. People will submit to any amount of injustice imposed on them; and these will continue until they get courage to resist either words or blows; or with both. "The limit of tyrants are prescribed by the endurance of those whom they oppress" ~ Frederick Douglass.

****

Ongwen, now in his mid-30s, surrendered this week in Central African Republic to US forces, and may face trial at the International Criminal Court for crimes against humanity and war crimes. Abducted by gunmen as a 10-year old boy on his way to school, Dominic Ongwen rose to become one of the most feared commanders in Uganda's brutal Lord's Resistance Army (LRA). Ongwen led quick and lethal raids -- carrying out massacres, rapes, mutilations and abductions -- before disappearing into the bush. Mark Kersten, a London-based academic focusing on international justice, described Ongwen as "both a victim and a perpetrator of international crimes" and said efforts to prosecute him could raise difficult questions. "When is a victim a perpetrator and a perpetrator a victim? The line is much more murky than we tend to assume," he said.

****

The freedom you enjoy today is the result of the split blood of the past heroes. Some fought for it with arms, some with their brains and others with the ballot. They chose liberty even when it meant to die. "Nothing is more difficult, and therefore more precious, than to be able to decide."

These were men and women of destiny. Napoleon whose illustrious career spawned admiration from the world's French government, greatest writers, artists and statesmen once remarked: "Destiny called upon me to change the face of the world" When the time came to change the incompetent Directory, the impetuous Corsican undoubtedly felt touched by the hand of history. Our independence is a reminder to us that those who expect to reap the blessings of freedom, must, like men, undergo the fatigue of supporting it. "Some people dream of prosperity. Others stay awake to achieve it!!"

****

"Twelve people shot by terrorists in Paris." Indeed, the responses from our own president, French President Hollande and British Prime Minster David Cameron all spouted the same empty pabulum in asserting that the Paris attack had nothing to do with Islam or any religion for that matter. But the hollow comments coming from our own leaders are steeped in the stench of appeasement and cowardice. Islamic extremism cannot be confined to groups we don't like. Islamic extremism is now a movement, just like fascism and communism; it spans a spectrum from Hamas to Al Shabab to the Muslim Brotherhood. And to ignore the common denominator in the motivation behind 75% of the world's annual terrorist attacks carried out by Islamic terrorists is a sure guarantee that Wednesday's attacks in Paris will be repeated over and over again. Phrasing the problem of "violent extremism," as the Obama administration has done repeatedly, of being a problem exclusively of only Al Qaeda and now ISIS, is intellectually spurious and truly dangerous to our national security.

****

Already this year, we've seen a lot of evil: suicide bombings, the attacks in Paris, religious persecution, Boko Haram and ISIS. These have all outraged the world—and rightly so. But here's a question worth pondering: will our kids be able to recognize evil when they see it? In order to know the answer we must revisit today's worldview regarding what is evil. Our children must know the difference between "fact and opinion." Fact is something that is tested and proven to be true. Opinion is what someone thinks regardless of its authenticity. Opinions,

427

of course, can be true or false. In our public school students are taught that claims are either facts or opinions. McBrayer writes. "They are given quizzes in which they must sort out claims into one camp or the other but not both." A little digging reveals that public schools today teach, as a matter of course, that all value claims are opinions, not facts. Moral claims are labeled as mere opinions that are not true, or are true only in a relative sense. "But if value statements are always opinions, why should anyone believe them? For that matter, why should kids believe a teacher who tells them that hitting is wrong? Or a college ethics professor who tells them murder is wrong?" ~ John Stonestreet

****

1 Corinthians 10:12 – "So, if you think you are standing firm, be careful that you don't fall!" "Precaution is better than cure". Even the bravest take evasive action. True soldiers don't foolishly venture into arch-enemy territory. Like it would not have been the finest hour had Churchill stood in the middle of a Berlin street market and challenged Hitler head-on. It'd have been carnage - blood, tears and sweat because the Nazis would have ensured that the necks of insolent were wrung like a chicken. The torment of precautions often exceeds the dangers to be avoided.

****

Today, those who have plundered and accumulated enormous resources are free to rove about and use their stolen wealth to influence events in the country. Looters of yesterday have become heroes of today.

****

My grandmother used to say "…. *tunayogela birungi byereere?*" We have got praise singers like yourself …. to sing the praises. Allow others to state the obvious … that a government that for 30 years has demonstrated an aptitude for kleptomania cannot really be put in charge of the granary! "Neither can a pedophile be put in charge of a day care centre nor a hyena in charge of the market!"

****

Change will not come if we wait for some other person or some other time. We are the ones we've been waiting for. We are the change that we seek….. ~ Barack Obama

****

Change is inevitable. Effective people accept the inevitability of change and consciously decide how they will embrace and manage it when it arrives. Prepare to take advantage of every change.

****

Many people have ideas on how others should change; few people have ideas on how they should change ~ Tolstoy

****

As we look ahead into the next century, leaders will be those who empower others ~ Bill Gates

****

Opportunities have expiration date; that date is today. Make up your mind to act now in order to avoid to be broken by the very things of which you have not made up your minds. "Life is not a reaction, it is an action. People who are highly effective in life are people who are proactive. They do not wait for things to happen, they make things happen" ~ By Sam Adeyemi

****

A bit of an irony: the three biggest and best-run economies of the world are prone to natural disasters, earthquakes, typhoons, tsunamis. On the flip side, the worst economies (mainly in Africa) are under the siege of man-made disasters: civil wars, ethnic cleansing, ritual killings and epidemics.

****

"Throughout history, it is the inaction of those who could have acted, the indifference of those who should have known better, the silence of the voice of justice when it mattered most that has made it possible for evil to triumph" ~ Haile Salassie

****

"You can choose to be silent and that too is not neutrality. Those of us who have chosen the vocal path in the conflict are happy for what our instinct told us. We will not swap paths nor choose to be silent as long as the conflict continues to threaten the existence of all of us."

****

Far better it is to dare mighty things, to win glorious triumphs, even though checked by failure, than to take rank with those poor spirits who neither enjoy much nor surfer much, because they lie in the gray twilight that knows not victory nor defeat.

****

"When leaders don't stand for something, their people will fall for anything." The problem is not getting new, innovative ideas into our minds but getting the old ones out. We need to revisit our old values lest we remain caricatures and cartridges of a false tradition or humanity forever.

****

What frightens me most is my inability to care or lack the capacity to act. That is when I just become an armchair warrior, a paper tiger. Some people have become so religious and sanctimonious that they can no longer speak in public forum in a language the common people can understand. They hardly touch any issue they consider 'sensitive', their repose is always the myriads of platitudes and religious clichés they have learnt over time. "Anyway, I used to be like that before but I have changed because I know that style of communication can't work in the 21st century" ~ Abiodun Jemiloh

****

People spend their lives in the service of their passions instead of employing their passions in the service of their lives. Service doesn't start when you have something to give; it blossoms naturally when you have nothing left to take ~ Nipun Mehta.

****

France has its Bastille Day and if the central government continues to push unemployed youth into a blind alley with no recourse, Uganda will have Luzira Day ~ Betty Long Cap

****

Can we trust politicians? "Is this the guy who referred to some Ugandans as biological substances? Has he changed his views so that he can serve all Ugandans? Or some of us who are biological substances can begin to hide in the crevasse reserved for cockroaches."

****

"In the eyes of politicians we are nothing compared to the pencil in the eyes of an artist." So goes the saying: I would like you to reflect or assimilate this and later inter-plate using the maker's book.

****

"You can fool some of the people all of the time, and all of the people some of the time, but you cannot fool all of the people all of the time." ~ Abraham Lincoln

****

"It is absurd that those few who genuinely ask pertinent issues are gagged. Although this doesn't mean that everything you said is wrong. But such kind of mind programming can only appeal to the gullible and blind. The fact is that your ego blurs your proper view of things. You have ignored the real causes of the sufferings experienced by the masses. Dealing with symptoms is like filtering the water without stopping the influx of pollution!"

****

"The surest means for attaining immortality, for the commoner, is to commit an act of spectacular failure. My life you may take, but my integrity never! No sacrilege, no secret, no sacrifice!" ~ Unknown author

****

"Having a swollen stomach does not mean you have a baby. A tenant cannot be more important than the landlord" ~ Tamale Milundi

****

The life of a non-believer cannot possibly be cold and lonely and without feelings because it is based on their affection, their devotion, their dedication to their beloved. And who, you ask, is their beloved? I will show you now. A non-believer is a natural man that is connected to the world; he or she love's the world. They embrace this enormous earth. The earth knows that they love it and it bestows on them its care. That's why their life is filled to the brim and their state, wherever they'll be, will be plentiful of materialism. They roam on the paths of their love and, wherever they are, they are longing for it without a possibility of fulfillment. This earth, and this world embraces them, and Satan anoints them and bestows upon them inconceivable gifts. This is the predilection of a nonbeliever.

****

Psalm 68:2-3, 22-23 – "Let the wicked perish at the presence of God… But let the righteous…rejoice before God: yea, let them exceedingly rejoice". The vast majority of people are living their lives as though they don't believe there is going to be an eternity. Ignoring the fact does not make it void. Regardless of our opinions, there is everlasting (eternal) Heaven and Hell (Matthew 25:46). "Let us be adventurers for another world. It is at least a fair and noble chance; and there is nothing in this worth our thoughts or our passions. If we should be disappointed, we are still no worse than the rest of our fellow-mortals; and if we succeed in our expectations, we are eternally happy" ~ Gilbert Burnet

****

It is important to focus on those sobering facts that draw us closer to God now and for eternity. We tolerantly extend people the dignity of their own beliefs without minimizing the differences between religions. We honor them without compromising. We are allowed to profess our belief without ridicule or venom, or disparagement. The life of Christ produces in us true humility. But it also produces in us true enlightenment. We have come to grasp grace that God works His way down to us, dies for our moral and religious failures and offers us life. We must lovingly, humbly try to persuade others to believe in Jesus, who alone offers the wonderful promise of the way to God, the truth of God and life of God. The bitter truth is that the choice you make now determines your destiny. "You are today a summation of your past choices. You will be tomorrow and into the future what you choose to do now. Lead Yourself First." ~ David Bernard-Stevens

****

It appears that our civic culture places greater values on ethnic identity and material gains. Perhaps, because of social mistrust communities don't believe that without one of their own in the system, nothing good can come their way.

****

Leaders must develop social policies to address disparities among groups. It is easier for communities to mobilize along ethnic lines than for development in a polarized society. The leaders should inspire in the public sets of civic values and attitudes like participation, social trust and respect for divergent positions.

****

A president is not expected to be at each and every little function. He must assign duties to his ministers to represent him. "------ for a whole president to posture at every petty function is a malaise of inferiority complex, which is substituted with overt superiority complex." (Weekly Topic)

****

With my little observation, I am forced to advise that the latent conflict in our country can only be confronted by candid discussion. The business community, the Church and all stakeholders need to realize the need to let the steam out. The current approach of pretending that all is well and deliberately blocking open debate might affect us all indiscriminately in the future.

****

Today most politicians are driven by aggressive, ego-centered ambitions, delusions about ends and means, doctrinaire prejudices and ideas. They may not say it but they communicate it to others in their actions. "He who attempts to act and do things for others or for the world without deepening his own self-understanding, freedom, integrity and capacity to love will not have anything to give to others."

****

In the world at large, all human being are born free and equal in dignity and rights, they are endowed with reason and conscience and should act towards one another in a spirit of brotherhood, but I don't know why South Sudanese are having a very diluted hatred to each another.

****

How possible is it for unknown gunmen to consistently cause havoc in Kenya over and over without a trace. I am very skeptical. Seems Kenyans have entrusted state power in the hands of rogues. I can't stop thinking that Kenyans seem to have a green snake somewhere in the grass.

****

Pray for peace in Sudan. The gloves are off now that Egypt is directly involved in the Southern Sudan war. The former natives of Egypt (Negros) and the colonizers have decided to lock horns, instinctively, something tells me that the wheel has finally gone full circle. Dinka and Nuer were the original owners of Egypt who built the pyramids. King "Tut" was a Negro. Osiris and Thudmosis were black gods. May be it is the fighting over the gods!

****

"Egypt is as much my country as is Kenya. For what are these boundaries but a continuation of colonialism and imperialism in Africa! The fight for Egypt is also a fight for the black Egyptians. Who are the black Kemetians if not you and I?" ~ Unknown

****

Quoting Senegalese scholar Cheikh Anta Diop (1923-86), a historian, anthropologist, physicist and politician, the Atlanta Blackstar feature presents 10 arguments that prove ancient Egyptians were black. Evidence presented includes physical anthropology, melanin dosage test results, blood types tests and osteological measurements (analysis of bones). There are other links promoting the same argument like the evolvement of King Tutankhamun and so on.

****

It's been one month since Boko Haram militants abducted almost 300 girls. Fanatic religions apply brute force to convert others. A brute force is a method of accomplishing something primarily by means of natural strength - in this case without the use of supernatural capabilities and without strategic planning or tactics. It is a method of computation wherein all permutations of a problem are tried manually until one is found that provides a solution. Religious fanaticism contradicts the teaching of Christ: "A bruised reed shall he not break, and smoking flax shall he not quench, till he sends forth justice unto victory" (Isaiah 42:3). This was prophetically talking about Jesus Christ (Matthew 12:20). Jesus did not have an agenda of politics; He did not come to wage a military campaign; he was a contradiction of what the Jewish religious leaders expected. They wanted a great fanfare - but here comes this gentle Messiah riding on a colt of an ass, with meekness and humility - even declaring righteousness to...an unthinkable thought... the Gentiles. Spiritual transformation is a willful act of the heart.

****

Youth placed two pigs at parliament in protest against unemployment. "That is why the symbolism of 'Pigs in Parliament' is indeed an interest for literature students. You see, pigs cannot have a Parliament, simply because they do not need to deliberate about the laws that govern them." ~ Dimas Nkunda

****

All people deserve respect in their capacity. However, inferiority puts rightful self-love beyond reach. Inferiority creates a person broken and humiliated inside but dominant from outside. That is probably why less prominent and powerful people always burst in the limelight even surpassing their superiors: An office cleaner more vocal than the office manager; a morgue cleaner arrogant than a Pathologist; a taxi driver's pretentiousness is noticeable exceeding the owner of the taxi; a house-girl presumptuously louder than a house wife. The sour truth is that if the domination is by an inferior, the resentment grows stronger. It is a shredding of dignity and respect to the perpetrators.

****

"Whoever goes to the bush, would turn into a dictator and ensure that he 'superglues' himself in power ----------Unfortunately Ugandans are often so gullible and excitable!" ~ Pius Muteekani Katunzi

****

In essence, Dr Ramphele says that in order to have a vibrant and fair society, we need to adopt the model of servant leadership, where leaders in public service are agents of citizens, servants of the people. And this model, according to her, is not novel to Africa. For there are some Africans saying that the king is only a king with the consent of the nation. And this thinking is well articulated in our Constitution. We are a continent that articulates most elegantly the concept of Ubuntu (humanity) – our belief in the notion of a common humanity as an essential pillar of being human. Ubuntu captures the essential truth that "our humanity is affirmed by our connectedness to one another….. However, the Ubuntu has been eroded by a new virus called Affluenza. According to Ramphele,

Affluenza tempts the leaders to "place a high value on acquiring money and possession, looking good in the eyes of others and wanting to be famous".

****

Of a truth we live in a very trying time. And there is the tendency for us to overreact to the myriads of irritations and absurdities around us and lose focus if we are not careful and disciplined enough. We must not lose sight of the fact that every generation of human race, irrespective of their location, face certain challenges that are peculiar to them. The onus is therefore on them to be rational, bold, strong and courageous to responsibly deal with and resolve such challenges in their time without having to cowardly pass them over to the next generation unresolved. So I say to the men and women of my generation- less display of passion, less anger, less reaction; more logic, more wisdom, more action. Strength and Honor to you all!

****

They say that power corrupts absolutely. Political power is in positions not in a person. That is why most politicians strive to prove that they have it by dominating others. Whereas the corrupt are corrupted by power, we (believers) are absolutely perfected by power. The power of the Christians is not outside them but is inside them. We (believers) have control over power rather than using power to control people. Jesus demonstrated the unique type of power that is in contradiction to the expectations of the world. The Jews expected their Messiah to be a warrior riding on a horse but Jesus entered Jerusalem on a young donkey and conquered by surrendering to His enemies. Likewise, we get eternal power by surrendering ourselves to Him. We overcome the world by perpetually surrendering our ego (old self or nature). Our power is instigated by our brokenness. Psalm 27:4 (NIV): "The sacrifices of God are a broken spirit; a broken and a contrite heart–these, O God, You will not despise." God uses life circumstances to instigate brokenness. The way up is down. God releases His power to the humble. With His power we are robust and groomed to withstand the harshest situation.

August Dedicated to Evangelism

The Bible says that we are the holy temple that God is building. At the same time we are royal priests called to build bridges between man and God by preaching the gospel. The gospel must be proclaimed in word (vocally) and in deeds (good works). Unfortunately, the believers have been criticized for being unnecessary loud. Never apologize for being loud when proclaiming the gospel. Jesus was so gentle that a bruised reed He did not break, and the smoking flax He did not quench (Matthew 12:20). Yet, wherever He went, there was always a commotion. At the Triumphal Entry in Jerusalem, Jesus was asked to instruct His disciples to keep quite. He replied that, "And he answered and said unto them, I tell you that, if these should hold their peace, the stones would immediately cry out" (Luke 19:40).

We make joyful noises when praising God. Also, our voices when proclaiming the gospel become sweet aroma like the smell of incense to God. God created voices to communicate with others for His glory. Well, we might have expected that it would be so—the analogies of Nature would teach us to look for that. When the morning sun arises, without sound of drum, or tramp of armed men, straightway it causes confusion among the doers of darkness! With a roar the lion goes back to his den and the wolf and the hyena flee before the eyes of light. I daresay, too, that the owl and the bat have a very strong aversion to the rising of the sun. If they could speak their minds, they would hoot or hiss out their opinions which would probably be found to be very much opposed to anything like daylight and noontide glory!

The Pentecost experience: God is accompanied by the mighty wind. Acts 2 records that the coming of the Holy Spirit was accompanied by "a sound like the blowing of a violent wind" (verse 2). Also, God spoke to Job "out of the whirlwind" (Job 38:1). Let us look at an interesting parallel: From Genesis 3:8 God's approach in the garden was heralded by a "sound" or a "voice." The verse begins by stating, "They heard the sound" of the Lord God. Whatever form God took, it certainly allowed for the physical production of sound. His walk was audible; He was making noise. The Bible says that God walked in the Garden in the cool of evening. According to the theory based on the Hebrew phrase translated "the cool of the day." This could be literally translated "the wind of that day." Some think this might refer to a strong wind. If so, Adam and Eve's reaction makes more sense. They heard God's approach as a terrible wind lashed the trees of the garden, and they took cover. God called (using a Hebrew word that also means "to summon") Adam to face judgment.

We are called to be on our toes doing the will of God every day. Every day may not be good, but there's something good in every day. Every day is a divine appointment for us; we have a date with the divine purpose every day. The moment you are born again, God reveals His purpose for you in this world. The purpose is to do His will wherever you are. Jesus calls us to be fishers of men. He knows where the fishes are and He drives the fishes into our nets.

Have you ever wondered why the early Church believers used the symbol of fish? It's an Acrostic: Yes, the first letters of a variety of words form the letters in the word "ICHTHUS" (ikh-thoos), a Koine Greek word for "fish." The acronym, when spelled out, translates into English as "Jesus Christ, God's Son, Savior," all words which represent Jesus as defined by the Christian faith. The Greek words used are: Iesous (Iota), Christos (Chi), Theou (Theta), Uios (Upsilon), and Sotor (Sigma). The English translation, in the Greek letters (IXOYE), is often seen on Church furniture to this day.

The Historical Background of the Symbol: Early Christians were not a well-assimilated group, and they were often persecuted for their religious beliefs by both the Jewish leaders and the Roman Empire. In the first few centuries after Christ's death, his followers were said to have used the fish symbol to mark meeting places and tombs so other believers would recognize them - sort of like a password.

In the first days of Christianity, Roman soldiers were stationed everywhere, serving as a sort of police force for the Empire. Often, when a soldier recognized a Christian, he would report it to his superiors. Generally, the Christians were then arrested and tortured in an effort to force them to recant their new faith and affirm their belief in the polytheistic religions of Rome. In most cases this imprisonment ended in death.

Aware of this possibility, many Christians would draw a fish symbol in the dirt or on the wall to let other believers know where it was safe to talk about their faith. The symbol consisted of 2 intersecting arcs, with the ends on the right side extending farther to resemble the profile of a fish. The fish was also used to safely identify another Christian when strangers met. One person would draw the first arc, and if the other completed the shape, each knew the other was a Christian, without alerting the Roman authorities.

Since the fish symbol was already a pagan symbol, Christians were safer using it than the cross to announce their faith. Greeks and Romans had joined the outlines of two crescent moons to make the same symbol, but with a reference to fertility gods, not Jesus.

Jesus said that we can do nothing without Him. We manifest His life by our godliness. But it is our faith that pleases God. Faith lays hold upon the Lord Jesus with a firm and determined grasp. It knows His excellence and worth, and no temptation can induce faith to place its trust elsewhere. And Christ Jesus is so delighted with this heavenly grace that He never ceases to strengthen and sustain that faith by the loving embrace and all-sufficient support of His eternal arms.

Everything apart from faith is vanity. There are various kinds of vanity. The cap and bells of the fool, the merriment of the world, the dance, and the cup of the dissolute--all these men know to be vanities; they wear upon their chest their proper name and title. Far more treacherous are those equally vain things--the cares of this world and the deceitfulness of riches. A man may follow vanity as truly in a portfolio as in a theater. If he is spending his life in amassing wealth, he passes his days in a vain show. Unless we follow Christ and make our God the great object of life, we only differ in appearance from the most frivolous. It is clear that there is much need of the prayer of our text: "Give me life in your ways." The psalmist confesses that he is dull, heavy, all but dead.

Perhaps, dear reader, you feel the same. We are so sluggish that the best motives cannot quicken us, apart from the Lord Himself. What! Will not hell quicken me? Shall I think of sinners perishing, and yet not be awakened? Will not heaven quicken me? Can I think of the reward that awaits the righteous and yet be cold? Will not death quicken me? Can I think of dying and standing before my God, and yet be slothful in my Master's service? Will not Christ's love constrain me? Can I think of His dear wounds, can I sit at the foot of His cross, and not be stirred with fervency and zeal? It seems so!

No mere consideration can quicken us to zeal, but God Himself must do it; hence the cry, "Give me life in your ways." The psalmist breathes out his whole soul in vehement pleadings; his body and his soul unite in prayer. "Turn my eyes," says the body. "Give me life," cries the soul. This is a fit prayer for every day. O Lord, hear it in my case this night.

We need to evangelize in this century more than ever. In order to make my case, I am going to use the following statics: It is estimated that nearly 50% of Americans have no church home. In the 1980s, membership in the Church had dropped almost 10%; then, in the 1990s, it worsened by another 12% drop-some denominations reporting a 40% drop in their membership. And now, over half way through the first decade of the 21st century, we are seeing the figures drop even more!

What is going on with the Church in America? The United States Census Bureau Records give some startling statistics, backed up by denominational reports and the Assemblies of God U.S. Missions: Every year more than 4000 Churches close their doors compared to just over 1000 new church starts! There were about 4,500 new Churches started between 1990 and 2000, with a twenty year average of nearly 1000 a year. Every year, 2.7 million Church members fall into inactivity. This translates into the realization that people are leaving the church. From our research, we have found that they are leaving as hurting and wounded victims-of some kind of abuse, disillusionment, or just plain neglect!

God's marvelous Church has become culturally irrelevant and even distant from is prime purpose of knowing Him, growing in Him, and worshipping Him by making disciples! This is evidenced by what is going on in our culture and in our Churches as indicated above. Most believers have lost the first love; they have replaced faith with fantasy.

Stephen Kyeyune

Scrolling through my posted sermons on evangelism:

"And Jesus came up and spoke to them, saying, "All authority has been given to Me in heaven and on earth. "Go therefore and make disciples of all the nations, baptizing them in the name of the Father and the Son and the Holy Spirit" (Mathew 28:18). Before He put on human flesh, Jesus had been the all powerful eternal Son of God with all powers attributed to His divine nature (second trinity of God). But after resurrection He said that all authority has been given to me. He meant the acquired authority as man to turn around the universe from the mess of Adam. He said "As the Father sent me so I send you"(John 20:21). He rightly acquired the power to change the universe by His obedience to the Father. He made the same power available to those who obey Him. He sent us out to the uttermost ends of the earth. He did not call us to sit and warm the pews in our Churches. Church fellowship is for believers alone. But He sends us to evangelize the world so that more worshipers might come in to glorify the Father. God's eternal purpose is to fill this universe with His glory. God puts His Son on display so that His glory may be planted wherever He is worshiped.

****

Charles Finney is remembered for the greatest revivals of the century. Harry Conn wrote a Foreword to Finney's Systematic Theology. He commented upon the revivals of Charles Finney: "Students of revivals agree that the greatest evangelist since apostolic times was the tenderhearted and devoted Charles Grandison Finney, 1792-1875. His revivals were known for the presence of the Holy Spirit, great enlightenment of the human mind with the truth of God, deep conviction of sin and sinners having a saving subjective experience based upon objective truth."

John 17:17: "Sanctify them through thy truth; your word is truth". Finney believed that God drew men through truth (his Word) John 17:17). He based his belief on John 6:44-45, where Jesus said: "No one can come to me unless the Father who sent me draws him, and I will raise him up at the last day. It is written in the Prophets: 'They will all be taught by God.' Everyone who listens to the Father and learns from him comes to me. It is the last sentence that I had never noticed in that

442

way before. And it does not say it is the Holy Spirit acting, but everyone who listens to the Father comes to Jesus. We'll see if this understanding has corroboration elsewhere in Scripture and whether we can observe the objective truth of it.

"When you have lifted up the Son of Man, then you will know that I am the one I claim to be and that I do nothing on my own but speak just what the Father has taught me" (John 8:28). "I did not speak of my own accord, but the Father who sent me commanded me what to say and how to say it. . . . So whatever I say is just what the Father has told me to say" (John 12:49-50). "Don't you believe that I am in the Father, and that the Father is in me? The words I say to you are not just my own. Rather, it is the Father, living in me, who is doing his work" (John 14:10). "These words you hear are not my own; they belong to the Father who sent me" (John 14:24). "The world must learn that I love the Father and that I do exactly what my Father has commanded me" (John 14:31).

****

The gospel is the good news. Ironically, the good news when preached for the very first time sounds as bad news because it begins with the calling to repent. John the Baptist baptized calling people to repent. Jesus preached that repent for the kingdom of God is here. It is a calling to rebel against the corrupt kingdom of the world of which the corrupt man is closely attached. This calling does not sound well in the ears of a non-repented sinner; not until there is conviction brought about by the Holy Spirit. Repentance cuts loose the only rope connecting a sinner to corruption. People that reject the gospel will not be judged for the multiple sins they committed during their life time but will be condemned for only this one sin – 'Of refusing the eternal life.' The Bible says that "For God did not send his Son into the world to condemn the world, but to save the world through him. Whoever believes in him is not condemned, but whoever does not believe stands condemned already because he has not believed in the name of God's one and only Son" (John 3:17-18). Rejecting the gospel is rejecting the saving grace. There is no pardon for a person who dies in unbelief (disbelieve).

****

Pray to the God of the harvest to send in more harvesters. We all called to evangelize. But we have a wrong perception that it is the pastor's job to evangelize the community and pull the strays back in. The congregation points fingers to the pastor whenever the Church does not experience growth numerically. Thus pastors are leaving in mass too! According to recent survey, 1500 pastors are leaving the church every month due to moral failure, burnout, or strife. The fact that only 2.2% of Churches are experiencing growth via conversion is the real problem. Most mega congregations grow by taking converts from other Churches instead of winning the lost souls of the world. It is a recycling of believers from one congregation to the other. We are so focused on growth but most of the Church growth is actually Church cannibalism. People see that and get sickened so they leave the Church which is a constant battle for pastors.

****

Every believer is given a seed of Word to plant. Wise sayings often fall on barren ground, but a kind word is never thrown away. You are a spiritual father because you are required to reproduce spiritual children. Until a spiritually mature man reproduces and disciples Christlike maturity in others, he has no spiritual children and cannot be considered a spiritual father. A spiritual father reproduces spiritual children who have a passionate and intimate relationship with God the Father. The spiritual growth process of these children must continue so that they also become spiritual fathers who reproduce other spiritual children too.

****

Musician George Adams said, "We are made up of thousands of others. Everyone who has ever done a kind deed for us, or spoken one word of encouragement to us, has entered into the makeup of our character and of our thoughts, as well as our success."

****

Acts 17 is the famous passage in which the Apostle Paul addresses the intellectuals of Athens, is the most important scriptural example of evangelism in an alien culture. Paul is speaking in a cross-worldview setting. He serves as a model for us in Athens because he is communicating the Gospel without quoting Scripture. He quotes pagans to build bridges with his audience. What we need to do is develop a vocabulary that better connects with people, not compromising theological rigor, not compromising biblical understandings and categories, but we need to communicate the Gospel not just using a lingo that kind of goes over the heads of people. And unfortunately a lot of people engaged in evangelism today kind of presuppose this two-generations-ago thinking. Like Paul, our duty is to reach our culture for Christ by keenly observing its features. As Christians, we should be asking ourselves what the defining characteristics of the West in 2014 are.

****

The Lord is not slack concerning his promise, as some men count slackness; but is longsuffering to us-ward, not willing that any should perish, but that all should come to repentance. True repentance is not just being sorry. According to the above scripture, true repentance involves moving from one spot to another. That is why the scripture uses the term "come to repentance". We go to God to repent. The journey of repentance begins with conviction. It involves brokenness and remorse. Then confession, surrendering and restitution by allowing God to put right what went wrong. Confession is denouncing your sins and saying what God says you are and accepting to be what God wants you to be.

****

And He is full of grace. If He had not been, I would never have been saved. He drew me when I struggled to escape from His grace; and when at last I came trembling like a condemned culprit to His mercy-seat He said, 'Take heart, My son; your sins are forgiven.' And He is full of truth. His promises have been true; not one has failed.

****

I think a lot of times people think that as we engage with people, that we can just give them the same twenty-minute presentation and then we've done our job. Paul Copan says that, "We need to remember that evangelism is a process rather than an event. It's a long process to help people move by God's grace from skepticism about the truth to saying 'I want to embrace Jesus Christ,' and even beyond that to helping them become disciple-makers."

****

Is there something worse than blindness? It is having the sight without having a vision. Jesus called His disciples that, 'Follow me and I will make you fishers of men" (Mark 1:17). You can't follow without fishing souls, and you can't fish the souls without following. Jesus calls us to serve. The calling brings the vision. A vision is a progressive revelation of what God wants us to do. A Vision is the bridge between the present and the future. Vision is what we see, but it is also the way in which we see. Vision is the lens that interprets the events of our life, the way we view people and our concept of God. The vision transfers things from the unseen world and bring them into the natural realm.

****

We are sent to preach the full gospel in anticipation of the power of the gospel to transform people. Yes, we need persuasive language but the power to save is not in our persuasive techniques but in the gospel. I'm amazed how most preachers today have reduced the gospel to a matter of begging and entertaining hoping that the people will zone in on it like bees to a flower. We are missing the point. Paul said that, "My message and my preaching were not with wise and persuasive words, but with a demonstration of the Spirit's power" (1 Cor. 2:4). No one baptized more people than John the Baptist. But when he saw many of the Pharisees and Sadducees coming to where he was baptizing, he said to them: "You brood of vipers! Who warned you to flee from the coming wrath?" (Matthew 3:7). He called them exactly what they are! Jesus used the same tough language calling them brood of vipers (Matthew 12:34). The reason is because in order for there to be conviction, people must be offended of their current life styles. The people were astonished at [Jesus'] teaching, for he taught them as one having authority and not as the scribes (Mk 1:21-28). Jesus is the Word that became flesh (human). He had confidence in the right interpretation of the Word and the power of the Word to transform. He taught important matters of the highest importance and which are necessary for salvation without sugarcoating. While the scribes sought their own glory and the praise of men, our Lord taught solely for the glory of God and the salvation of the souls.

****

Jesus did not erect any monument (structure or temple) in His honor but made the people His temple because His prime project is people. Christianity is the life of Christ in you. Religiosity focuses on you but faith focuses on Christ in you. Christ is central to Christianity. When you take away the founder of any of the world religions, their religions will flourish. But take Jesus Christ from Christianity, the whole thing will crumble!

****

When the religious leaders challenged Jesus to silence His disciples, He replied that, "I tell you, if they keep quiet, the stones will cry out" (Luke 19:40). Jesus was most probably referring to the temple stones. If the stones were to speak, they could tell of their breaker, how he took them from the quarry and made them fit for the temple. In the same manner we are called not to be silent but to proclaim our Maker. The Bible says that we are the living stones making up the true Temple of God (1 Peter 2:5). We are created for good works to testify of the handiwork of God who made us in His very righteousness. We are called to know Him and to make Him known!

****

God calls us to do seemingly impossible tasks because He makes a way where there is no way. We are not exempted from hardship. Struggle and success are bedfellows. For every success there is a corresponding struggle. Never be frustrated when things are not working out smoothly for you. Never doubt your calling because of hardship. Most probably that is where God wants us to be. We have been redeemed from hopeless despair. We are in the process of becoming what God wants us to be. God used Paul astoundingly: He wrote one third of the New Testament, but his life was characterized with turmoil. Paul walked on the sharp edge throughout his ministry. He was always on his toes heading to the synagogues where he was not wanted and often ended up in prisons. It is from the same prospective he wrote that, "We are hard pressed on every side, but not crushed; perplexed, but not in despair; persecuted, but not abandoned; struck down, but not destroyed. We always carry around in our body the death of Jesus, so that the life of Jesus may also be revealed in our body" (2 Corinthians 4:8-10).

****

1 Peter 3:15-16 - "Always be prepared to give an answer to everyone who asks you to give the reason for the hope that you have. Most times this scripture is used to appeal to us to be ready to defend the Christian faith apologetically. However, the apologetic ministry is only for those who are well advanced and rooted in the scriptures. Yet in the above scripture Peter is appealing to all believers. Therefore the scripture should be used as an appeal to all of us to be ready to testify to the lost world the saving grace of Jesus. Be ready in season and out of season to tell the non-believers how you were saved. The Great Commission is about preaching the gospel rather than defending the faith.

****

The character of people is defined by what makes them laugh and what makes them cry. The cry of the transformed heart should be to win the lost soul.

****

2 Timothy 4:5 - The four-fold directive that the Apostle Paul gave to Timothy provides a clear perspective: always be sober-minded, endure suffering, do the work of an evangelist, and fulfill your ministry.

****

2 Corinthians 2:15 – "For we are unto God a sweet savor of Christ, in those who are saved and in those who perish". The sweet aroma of the knowledge of Christ is supposed to be manifested through all believers: The fragrance of Christ to God; an aroma of death to the non-believers and an aroma of life to the believers.

****

This world does not just belong to God but it is our Father's property by virtue of creation. As His children we have the mandate to take care of it by polishing it with the gospel so that it might shine. The old saying goes, "You don't polish brass on a sinking ship," and Christians today might be tempted to see the world as the sinking ship. "But this world was made by our Father and belongs to our Father. The dominion mandate not only abides, but will be carried through, and this ship will not sink." ~ Dr. Sinclair Ferguson

****

Somebody sent to me this message, "If you want to change somebody, don't preach to him. Set an example and shut up." I think the Gospel is the Good News that must be preached and lived. It ceases to be news when it is not proclaimed. So it is not biblical to preach to somebody by example of living alone without proclaiming it. Preach it and live it. "I reckon him a Christian indeed that is neither ashamed of the Gospel nor a shame to it" ~ Peter Toba.

****

The Gospels contain the words and works of Jesus Christ. I asked my students that, "How many Gospels do we have?" All of them replied that four (Matthew, Mark, Luke and John). They were partly correct because they missed the fifth Gospel. The Bible says that, "You yourselves are our letter of recommendation, written on our hearts, to be known and read by all" (2 Corinthians 3:2). You are the fifth Gospel for people to read.

****

More than one pulpit has had the phrase, "Sir, we would see Jesus" posted where the preacher can see it as he proclaims the Word of God. It is a good reminder. One thing we learn from church history is that preachers must always fight the temptation to preach their opinions, current events, popular culture- anything but Christ and Him crucified. Today we are facing a dire need for the church to recapture the centrality of Christ in its preaching and life. From many pulpits people hear messages that do not emphasize the gospel, or they hear no gospel preached. This weakens the church's witness, does not provide spiritual food to those who are hungering and thirsting after righteousness, and it turns us into a people who wander about like sheep without a shepherd.

****

The summary of God's law is given in the two great commandments of loving God and neighbor. The Scriptures direct us how to love God and men. We are commissioned to love others by ministering to them. Our evangelistic duty is not to be viewed as an 'extra' but rather as part of our duty to love God and our neighbor. The love of Christ for His elects is the basis of our love for the neighbor even our enemies. God's redeeming love is non-selective. Jesus came to seek the lost. Therefore evangelism is the crucial manifestation of our union with Christ. We are sent to proclaim salvation through Jesus Christ who produces transformed life.

****

"A time-honored, effective method of evangelism is your personal testimony. Just telling about your spiritual pilgrimage. The skeptic may deny your doctrine or attack your Church, but he cannot honestly ignore the fact that your life has been cleaned up and revolutionized" ~ Chuck Swindle

****

Testimony is an affirmation of facts, an aggregate of truth and the story you have to inspire others. Your testimony is the work of the Holy Spirit in you and through you. Testimony time during Church services is time for accountability. It is telling the body of Christ how God used you throughout the week. We walk into the four walls of the sanctuary to be motivated to serve, and we walk out with a promise to deliver. A testimony is like an offering that you cannot miss to have whenever you walk into the sanctuary to fellowship. The awaited testimony is not the new pair of shoes that you got but how God used you to have impact on the lives of others. The hallmark of a spiritually mature believer is his testimony of living. Spiritual maturity is locating God's will and getting aligned to it, and not bending God to our own plans. As long as your heart is right with God, you must always have a testimony to give. Remember that Cain knew God and went to worship but his sacrifice was rejected because His heart was not right with God. Your heart is right with God when you do what Christ did and what He instructed you to do. Our Savior came to change the world, so do we.

****

God called you to be an instrument of peace. There are two primary choices in life: to accept conditions as they exist, or accept the responsibility for changing them. We are called to be world changers. You may not be able to change the world you see around you but you can change the world within you. A Jewish scholar Abraham Heschel challenged the Christians he was debating that, "It has seemed puzzling to me how greatly attached to the Bible you seem to be and yet how much like pagans you handle it."

****

Paul wrote that "As God's co-workers we urge you not to receive God's grace in vain" (2 Cor. 6:1). The culprits rejected the gospel of an itinerant evangelist like Paul. Paul declared to them that, "I tell you, now is the time of God's favor, now is the day of salvation". Also, some believers were taking salvation for granted without actively participating in the works of the ministry. Paul's concern is that God's grace will not have any meaningful impact on their lives. Paul then defended the paradoxical character of his ministry (vv. 3-10). "The humblest individual exerts some influence upon others." Throughout history, some notable characters have done so much with too little at their disposal whereas others have done so little with too much. It is the divine calling to show in our lives the relentless and powerful influence of the message of Jesus Christ.

****

Creativity is when the messenger influences the message: God anoints us and uses our natural resources to bring home the lost souls. You can't preach what you don't have. You don't need too much preaching when your life is a testimony of what you are preaching. It has come to my notice that most times when we preach the gospel of the Kingdom of God, the response of those listening to us depends on the stature of the preacher of the message. When a Charismatic and well-to-do man preaches Christ, he gets more positive response than a not-so- buoyant fellow. A rich preacher of prosperity wins more souls than a poor preacher of prosperity. A preacher from the foreign developed country attracts bigger crowds than a local preacher from the neighborhood. So, I began to wonder, whether it is possible many of those calling themselves Christians today really never met Christ, they just want the kind of life the preachers have. If he is rich, they want to be rich also; if he is a foreigner, from a developed country, they tend to believe the gospel in his mouth because his country represents everything good they want. "Once the center of gravity is lost, you can expect catastrophic accidents. The purpose of witnessing (testifying) is to share what you have personally experienced and draw men to the source of your experience NOT to keep them at the level of your own experience."

****

We are called to preach the gospel in its simplicity. But what is the gospel? The person of Jesus, His sinless life, His accomplished works at the cross and His resurrected life must be emphasized in order for the people to respond.

****

Come as you are in anticipation to be cleaned. Don't wait to clean up your mess in order to come to Christ. "Holiness is not the way to Christ but Christ is the way to holiness".

****

The people who heard the gospel and rejected it will be not be judged for their sins but will be judged for rejecting the eternal life in Christ.

****

The majority of people that see no need for salvation consider themselves to be good enough to be accepted by God. The first step towards salvation is admitting that you are a sinner and acknowledging the problem of sin. Abandoning or side stepping the hard reality of sin misses the very reality to which the gospel of Christ responds. Without sin, there is no desperate need. Without desperate need, there is no glorious salvation.

****

The gospel does not separate good people from bad people but it separates humble people from proud people who take pride in their sins. Have ever asked yourself why the true gospel is sometimes offensive to people. It is because it tells them that they cannot save themselves apart from the grace. Most people are comfortable with trying their best to earn salvation. It is within human instinct to expect compliments regarding their own achievements. But the grace denies them such opportunity. The story of salvation is not what we must do to be saved but what God has done to save us. Our own works even when at their best cannot save us because they are within the limitation of our fallen nature. It is within the context of the perfect works of Jesus Christ that our works are perfected. This means everything done outside Christ is as filthy as the dirty rags and is unacceptable to God (Isaiah 64:6).

****

Jesus pointed to Himself as the only way to recover our lost glory the finality of which will be fully realized in eternity. Jesus Christ is the way without junctions of religious rules and rituals but that is trekked by FAITH. It is not obeying this, that, and the other; it is a straight road: "Believe, and live." It is a road so hard that no self-righteous man can ever tread it, but so easy that every sinner who knows himself to be a sinner may find his way to heaven by simply confessing his or her sins to Christ. Paul boldly emphasized that, "I am determined not to know anything among you except Jesus Christ and Him crucified" (1 Corinthians 2:2). It means salvation from evil and the gift of eternal life received by faith. You can't earn your way into heaven but you can do fruitful deeds with the new found faith (Jer. 17:10). Our good works are not necessary for our salvation but they are evidences that we are saved.

Goodness is of God and comes to us after we are saved. Jesus said that no one is good but God (Mark 10:18; Luke 18:19).

****

Our relationship with God begins by crossing over. The Hebrew word for a "Hebrew" person is עברי (eevriy) and comes from the root word עבר (ever) which means "to cross over." A Hebrew was one who had "crossed over" into a covenant relationship with God, which begun with Abraham. It is important to have a concept of the Abrahamic covenant because of its unconditional nature; God implemented the covenant in spite of the flaws of man. Abraham was not the first man to be declared by God as righteous because there are other people like Enoch and Noah who walked upright with God. The LORD said concerning Job that there is none like him in the earth, a blameless and an upright man, one that fears God, and turns away from evil (Job 1:8). However, Abraham is unique because God chose to bless the entire universe with His own righteousness through his seed (Jesus Christ). God instructed Abraham to move from his birth place and go to a distant place in order to initiate the covenant relationship. "No one meets God and remains the same."

****

Abraham is called the father of the faithful ones because he obeyed God even when God asked him to offer his son as a sacrifice. He took God by His word even when it did not make sense. "Apart from God every activity is merely a passing whiff of insignificance" ~ Alfred North Whitehead

****

God often visits us, but most of the time we are not at home. If you are not as close to God as you used to be, it is because you moved. "God is a circle whose centre is everywhere and circumference nowhere" ~ Timaeus of Locri

****

Statics by mortality rate shows that one out of every 113 people died last year; there are about 107 deaths every minute, 6390 death every hour, and 56.0 million deaths every year. Every Sunset gives us one day Less to Live. Every minute, hour and day that passes project the time you will never be able to see again. While we are postponing, life speeds by. Those who wait to seek God on the eleventh hour always die at 10:59, one minute to the eleventh hour. There is no time like the present for you to receive Jesus. Postponing won't cut it. The Bible says that, "Now is the time of God's favor, now is the day of salvation." (2 Corinthians 6:2).

****

The principle of Headship is that if you fail to put God first you won't end with God!

****

Spiritual discipline is when your intimacy with God is translated into intimacy with others (neighbor).

****

Then the LORD said, "My Spirit will not contend with humans forever, for they are mortal; their days will be a hundred and twenty years" (Genesis 6:3). Before God judged the world by the floods people used to live beyond five hundred years. God acted purposefully to shorten human life spans. Genesis 6:5 and 11 imply that the shortening of human life spans at the time of the Flood served a specific spiritual purpose of purging the world of evil by limiting the spread of wickedness. Christians need not to be worried by the shortening because they can move on to a life far more wonderful and blessed than anything possible on Earth (1 Corinthians 2:9). Therefore, believers can rejoice that God has shortened humanity's race toward the heavenly prize. But as for nonbelievers, your spiritual destination is by far the most important decision you will ever have to face and make. God allows you to live on Earth long enough to recognize and choose where you are going to be eternally. If you think that this earthly life is miserable or long, eternity is over a million times longer than 120 years!

****

It's not the law of religion nor the principles of morality that define our highways and pathways to God; only by the Grace of God are we led and drawn, to God. "It is His grace that conquers a multitude of flaws and in that grace, there is only favor. Favor is not achieved; favor is received" ~ C. JoyBell C.

****

Think about the leper who told Jesus, "If you will it, you can make me whole." After healing him, Jesus told him to present himself to the priest. Why? So that the priest could declare him "clean" and restore him to his community. So he could live as a whole man and not as an outcast. The Church's mission is to restore outcasts to their communities as whole men. Some outcasts, like lepers and men in jumpsuits, are easily identifiable. Others, like the rest of us, are not. But to all of us, Jesus' message is the same: "I will it. Be made whole."

****

HABAKKUK 2:2-3 write down your vision that whoever reads it runs with it. Having a vision begins with being insightful about the lives with whom we come into contact. It is seeing people in the eyes of Jesus. A ministry begins with people and the vision begins with seeing people in the eyes of Christ. Jesus had unfailing compassion on people. Naturally we see things the way our minds have instructed our eyes to see but an insightful person looks far beyond the surface when viewing others. A visionary person sees people in their intended destiny (in Christ) as opposed to their current status. "The only thing worse than being blind is having sight but no vision" Helen Keller ~ American Author (1880-1968)

****

Any vision must involve winning the lost soul. The vision provides the cause to die for. Our vision is pursuing the prophetic promises of God. Every moment is a golden one for him who has the vision to recognize it as such. The vision is broken down into goals. Setting a goal is deciding how you will go about achieving a vision and staying with that plan. The tragedy of life doesn't lie in not reaching your goal but in having no goal to reach. A man without a goal is like a ship without a rudder.

****

I am looking for a spouse with whom I share the common vision. I mean that is consumed with the passion to serve the Lord, so that can work together, and at the end of the day we hug each other and rest.

****

If someone asks about your educational background, proclaim boldly that: Church is my college. Heaven is my university. Father God is my counselor. Jesus is my principal. Holy Spirit is my teacher. Angels are my classmates. Bible is my syllabus. Temptations are my exams. Overcoming Satan is my hobby. Winning souls for God is my assignment. Receiving eternity is my degree. Praise and Worship is my college slogan (*Posted on my Facebook home page by David Bradford*).

****

"As they ministered to the Lord, and fasted, the Holy Ghost said, Separate me Barnabas and Saul for the work where unto I have called them" (Acts 13:2). God call us to go to people rather waiting for people to come to us. God calls all believers to preach the gospel but we should send to missions the most qualified disciples to teach the Scriptures. Paul and Barnabas were the cream.

****

George Whitefield was a man whose extraordinary evangelistic fervor was marked by remarkable piety and deep theology, and whose unswerving devotion to his God led him to risk all that he had to preach the name of Christ - Sr. Steven J. Lawson

****

The apostle Paul shaped history. Yet Paul would die in the jail of a despot. No headlines announced his execution. No observer recorded the events. Doesn't look like a hero. The fellow who changes the oil in your car could be a hero. Maybe as he works he prays, asking God to do with the heart of the driver what he does with the engine. Max Lucado narrated a story about John Egglen, a deacon that stepped in and gave the sermon for a few folks who had arrived before a snowstorm that prevented the pastor from getting there. He gazed straight in the eyes of a boy man who by chance happened to be there. With unusual courage in he said to the young man that "Look to Jesus. Look!" Guess who this young boy was? Charles Haddon Spurgeon, England's "prince of preachers." You never know… tomorrow's Spurgeon may be in your Church or be your neighbor. And the hero who inspires him might be in your mirror!

****

A holy anointing is the soul and life of godly devotion, its absence is the most serious of all calamities. "To go before the Lord without anointing would be like a common Levite thrusting himself into the priest's role—his religious services would be sins, not sacrifices. May we never embark upon holy tasks without sacred anointings." ~ Alistair Begg

****

A lady was going on mission to Africa, one of the elders handed her a sealed envelope and instructed her to open it only when she reaches a point when she has no body to turn to. The lady spent thirty years on mission in Africa and returned with a sealed envelope. She then gave a testimony that for thirty years there was no point of time when she had no body to turn to because Jesus was ever there for her to turn to.

****

God does not use the most talented but the most available. We preach the gospel out of compassion rather that obligation. "Love is a fruit in season at all times, and within reach of every hand." Mother Teresa ~ Missionary (1910-1997)

****

"Every day is Christmas when you let God love others through you" ~ Mother Teresa

****

Joshua 20:3: It is said that in the land of Canaan, cities of refuge were so arranged that any man might reach one of them within half a day at the most. The roads to the city of refuge, we are told that they were strictly preserved, every river was bridged, and every obstruction removed. The streets leading to the city were clearly marked and there were volunteers on the side of the streets to help the criminal to escape and find an easy passage to the city. In the same way there are evangelists everywhere helping the sinners to escape the wrath of God. Jesus is a present Savior, and the way to Him is marked clearly by the gospel for all to see.

Once a year the elders went along the roads of the cities of refuge to check on their condition, so that nothing might impede the flight of anyone and cause them, through delay, to be overtaken and slain. How graciously do the promises of the Gospel remove stumbling blocks from the way! Wherever there were junctions and turnings, there were signposts clearly stating, "To the city of refuge!" As soon as the man seeking refuge reached the outskirts of the city, he was safe; it was not necessary for him to be beyond the walls--the suburbs themselves were sufficient protection

****

God speaks through the prophet Hosea, pleading, "How can I give you up, Ephraim?...all my compassion is aroused" (Hosea 11:8). This is the heart cry of God. His patient concern is inexhaustible. The divine light of compassion has always shone across the wasteland of dark years. Compassion, mercy, forgiveness – a rolling tide of kindness, an inner driving force for men like Moses, Micah, Hosea and then the apostles and on to us. "Christ's love compels us," said Paul (2 Corinthians 5:14). What a wonderful God. God bless you.

****

Revival refers to a spiritual reawakening from a state of dormancy or stagnation in the life of a believer. It encompasses the resurfacing of a love for God, an appreciation of God's holiness, a passion for His Word and His Church, a convicting awareness of personal and corporate sin, a spirit of humility, and a desire for repentance and growth in righteousness. The revival is necessary in order for the transforming power of God in us (believers) to be fully realized by the world. In fact some of us need to repent to the people of the world for embracing their life-style instead of the life of Christ.

****

True revival begins with you. The tragedy is that the demons are more dedicated to the mission of their master (Satan) than many of the believers are dedicated to the mission of their Master (Jesus Christ). The quality of a person's life is in direct proportion to their commitment to Christ. He perfects our works regardless of our flaws. Therefore the first and greatest victory is to conquer yourself. To be conquered by yourself is of all things most shameful and vile. "Either you conquer the flesh or the flesh conquers you."

****

It is possible to trust God without glorifying Him. Some trust God for purely selfish reasons. Trusting is proven by our good works. Jesus was stripped naked so that we might be dressed and adorned in His very righteousness. Jesus gave a parable of a wedding feast. During the feast the king noticed a man "who was not wearing wedding clothes" (Matthew 22:11-12). When asked how he came to be there without the furnished attire, the man had no answer and was promptly ejected from the feast. He is abandoned "outside, into the darkness, where there will be weeping and gnashing of teeth" (verses 12-13). Jesus then ends the parable with this statement: "For many are invited, but few are chosen" (verse 14).

****

Turkey once had the largest Christian auditorium in Europe called Hagia Sophia in Constantinople. The Hagia Sophia (once largest

Church in Europe) was taken over by Muslims and converted to a mosque for over 400yrs and later used as an Islamic

Museum. Mary the mother of Jesus was taken to Turkey by Apostle John and till date, her room has become a tourist centre. Why Christianity collapsed in Turkey? Emphasis on doctrinal differences weakened the Turkish Church; Rivalries amongst denominations; Petty politics in Church coupled with ethnic bias. Osman Ghazi discovered the disunity amongst Christians and used it to fight a Jihad that led to a mass genocide of the Armenians, the Hellen and Turks of that day. In fact, the weapon of war used was designed by a Turkish Christian. Many Christian women converted to Islam to save their lives and some were raped. The other mistake was that Turks were building big cathedrals instead of building men. Virtually all the mistakes the Church in Turkey made, the Church of today has made it.

****

If the gentleman has ability, he is magnanimous, generous, tolerant, and straightforward, through which he opens the way to instruct others. Marcus Tullius Cicer said that "The wise are instructed by reason, average minds by experience, the stupid by necessity and the brute by instinct." The root word for disciple is discipline. To be disciplined is to operate as commanded not as convenient! Confucius, a Chinese philosopher (551–479 BC), said that "By three methods we may learn wisdom: First, by reflection, which is noblest: Second, by imitation, which is easiest: and Third, by experience, which is the bitterest". Therefore be wise and give the gift of self-reflection to yourself. Be even wiser and allow God to be reflected in you.

****

Deception is Satan's end time weapon of mass destruction. The Bible predicted such great deception of the end times (today). Satan uses deception to destroy the faith of many. Yet God uses deception to sift the chaff from the wheat. In ancient Israel the process of sifting the wheat was the last stage in preparing the harvest. As the bride (Church) is getting ready to meet the Bridegroom (Christ), the lukewarm are most likely to be blown away in the whirlwind (hearken to the voice of the false prophets). When somebody rejects the truth, the only alternative left is for him to fill the vacuum with lies. The effect of deception is delusion. Be aware that Satan is not what he makes you think he is, he is what he hides (2 Corinthians 11:14).

****

Have you wondered why in this century the Pentecost Movement has the highest number of converts and also the highest number of people leaving the Church? It is because some people are manipulated to join our Churches. They end up coming to Church for wrong reasons. Remember that what you win them with is what you win them to. If you win them by manipulation you end up with a congregation of manipulators. We need to preach the gospel in its simplicity without manipulations. Paul said that "And my speech and my preaching was not with enticing words of man's wisdom, but in demonstration of the Spirit and of power" (1 Corinthians 2:4).

****

"People can offer God plenty of reasons why He shouldn't call them to spread the gospel. But His call is not issued for our consideration; He expects a response of obedience and surrender" ~ Charles Stanley

****

Often I hear people claiming to own the truth but their contemplating of the truth is vague. Truth is not just having facts but it is the very object that constitutes the facts. Truth is deeper than knowledge because truth precedes knowledge. For example Africa existed before the explorers discovered it. America existed before Columbus discovered it. Truth is equated with vision: "Where there is no vision, the people perish: but he that keeps the law, happy is he" (Proverbs 29:18). The primary interpretation of this passage is that where there is no Word of God, where there is no message of life, the people perish. That is why David Livingstone spent thirteen years in the jungles of Africa, not to make the Dark Continent known to the outside world but to make the Dark Continent know the God of the light. The vision involves establishing the glory of God in places where none exists. It is a prestige to acknowledge that the vision provides the cause to live for and to die for. Setting goals is deciding how you will go about achieving the vision and staying with that plan. The tragedy of life doesn't lie in not reaching your goal but in having no goal to reach. A man without a goal is like a ship without a rudder. He is left at the mercy of fate!

****

We are called to preach the gospel in season and out of season: With money or without money; in peace and in persecution. Christians are the pioneers of religious freedom but unfortunately we are the targets of persecution by the violators of religious freedom. And certainly we today are the most persecuted faith on the earth. We aren't allowed to profess our belief without ridicule or venom, or disparagement. Christians clearly project that human rights grow out of the whole notion of people having a dignity, of being made in the image of God. But so does religious freedom. Roger Williams, says that granting the free exercise of religion, which is the right to adopt a faith, to exercise freely faith, to share a faith, and of course to change your faith—those are all four crucial things that are foundational for the Gospel. So believing in and supporting religious freedom is important not just because we Christians want to protect ourselves but to protect all people's freedom and rights. Freedom is critical to the spread of the gospel itself because for Christians, conversion isn't a matter of birth, heritage or coercion; it's a matter of freely-exercised faith in Jesus. And in order for such faith to thrive, the sword of government must not oppress anyone for their beliefs—including those who choose to reject the gospel. Given the fact, the gospel has flourished much more in hostile environments. The famous observation of Tertullian is that, the blood of the martyrs is the seed of the Church.

****

It is important to focus on those sobering facts that draw us closer to God now and for eternity. We tolerantly extend to the people who disagree with us the dignity of their own beliefs without minimizing the differences between religions. We honor them without compromising. We are called to profess our belief without ridicule or venom, or disparagement. The life of Christ produces true humility in us. It also produces true enlightenment in us. We have grasped the grace by which God works His way down to us, dies for our moral and religious failures and offers us life. We must lovingly, humbly try to persuade others to believe in Jesus, who alone offers the wonderful promise of the way to God, the truth of God and life of God. The bitter truth to the lost world is that the choice you make now determines your destiny. "You are today a summation of your past choices. You will be tomorrow and into the future what you choose to do now. Lead Yourself First." ~ David Bernard-Stevens

****

Sometimes I wonder whether same sex marriages are natural rights or human rights and if they are human rights why impose them on people who are conscious of natural laws? Are we supposed to love the homosexuals? I want to answer this with a question, What would Jesus do? Jesus ate with sinners. We can love them but loving them does not mean compromising our values. We must love them and tell them the truth that homosexuality is a sin like fornication is. The Bible says that, "Or do you not know that wrongdoers will not inherit the kingdom of God? Do not be deceived: Neither the sexually immoral nor idolaters nor adulterers nor men who have sex with men nor thieves nor the greedy nor drunkards nor slanderers nor swindlers will inherit the kingdom of God" (1 Corinthians 6:9-11).

****

When Abraham interceded for Sodom, the LORD said, "If I find fifty righteous people in the city of Sodom, I will spare the whole place for their sake" (Genesis 18:26). God's judgment for this liberal, humanist and pagan generation is past due. God postpones His judgment for the sake of the few righteous who are striving to walk the narrow way. Yet, the world does not acknowledge the spiritual role of the Christians as the preservative of world. The Christians are the voice to the voiceless, like millions of the unborn babies aborted. Politically, the Christians stand against tyranny and oppression. That is why all dictators hate Christians.

****

"But if it is by the Spirit of God that I drive out demons, then the kingdom of God has come upon you" (Matthew 12:28). Satan is the prince of this world because he initiated the corrupt system by which the world operates. It is a system that is in direct opposition to the Word of God. The world John 2:16) and is headed for destruction. Jesus came to dethrone Satan by establishing on earth the Kingdom ruled by Yahweh. Such kingdom is demonic free. It is the kingdom without Violence; a Kingdom without War; a Kingdom without Deception; a Kingdom without Corruption; a Kingdom without Nepotism; a Kingdom without Arrogance; a kingdom without Chaos, Disorder, and Hatred; a Kingdom characterized with Peace and Judicial order. In the Kingdom of God His Will is done earth as it is already being done in the heaven.

****

Napoleon was an ambitious Emperor and wanted to become a world conqueror. But Great Britain was a hindrance to his ambitions because they were good at sea war. Out of frustration Napoleon once made the following stunning comment: "Wherever wood can float, you will find the English!" According to history, Napoleon spread the map of the world and pointing at Great Britain said: "Sir if it was not for that red sport I would have conquered the world." Likewise, Satan points at the red spot at Calvary and says "If it was not for the blood of Jesus, I would have conquered the whole world."

****

The Bible tells us to judge ourselves so that we may not be judged. Judging yourself is discerning the evil intents of your heart and articulate that you are unworthy to dwell in the presence of God unless redeemed by Christ. It is being sincere to God without allowing your judgment to be perverted by error or your will to be led in chains of iniquity. The Bible says that, "We all, like sheep, have gone astray, each of us has turned to our own way; and the Lord has laid on him the iniquity of us all" (Isaiah 53:6). It is a confession of sin that is shared by all the elect people of God from the first who entered heaven to the last who shall arrive; they all say, "All we like sheep have gone astray and we all need the Savior to bring us home."

Stephen Kyeyune

****

If the gentleman has ability, he is magnanimous, generous, tolerant, and straightforward, through which he opens the way to instruct others. Marcus Tullius Cicer said that "The wise are instructed by reason, average minds by experience, the stupid by necessity and the brute by instinct." The root word for disciple is discipline. To be disciplined is to operate as commanded not as convenient! Confucius, a Chinese philosopher (551–479 BC), said that "By three methods we may learn wisdom: First, by reflection, which is noblest: Second, by imitation, which is easiest: and Third, by experience, which is the bitterest". Therefore be wise and give the gift of self-reflection to yourself. Be even wiser and allow God to be reflected in you.

****

I don't think that this younger generation is savvy enough to really think deeply enough about what Church is really all about. According to survey, sixty percent of the young generation of today who don't believe in God have never been to Church or even read the Bible. They are ignorant of the very things they oppose. "Truth is rejected while Falsehood is bought.... The difference between the apparent and the reality is consciously or unconsciously blurred. Passivity is automatically actuated in man instead of activity."

****

"I testify that no servant ever had such a master as He; no brother ever had such a relative as He has been to me; no spouse ever had such a husband as Christ has been to my soul; no sinner ever had a better Savior, no mourner a better comforter than Christ has been to my spirit" - Alistair Begg

****

If Jesus had received justice from this world He could have been exonerated of all the charges against Him but His mission of saving the world could have flipped. Jesus got injustice from the world but justice from God so that we could be exonerated by God.

****

Scriptures instructing to be born again and acquiring a new nature:

I tell you the truth, no one can see the kingdom of God unless he is born again. (John 3:3)

I tell you the truth, no one can enter the kingdom of God unless he is born of water and the Spirit. (John 3:5)

Flesh gives birth to flesh, but the Spirit gives birth to Spirit. (John 3:6)

But if Christ is in you, your body is dead because of sin, yet your spirit is alive because of righteousness. (Romans 8:10)

He who has the Son has life; he who does not have the Son of God does not have life. (1 John 5:12)

Therefore, if anyone is in Christ, he is a new creation; the old has gone, the new has come! (2 Corinthians 5:17)

September Signifying Resting in Christ

The Bible says that Christ became our resting place. The word resting means Sabbath. The various elements of the Sabbath symbolized the coming of the Messiah, who would provide a permanent rest for His people. Once again the example of resting from our labors comes into play. With the establishment of the Old Testament Law, the Jews were constantly "laboring" to make themselves acceptable to God. Their labors included trying to obey a myriad of do's and don'ts of the ceremonial law, the Temple law, the civil law, etc. Of course they couldn't possibly keep all those laws, so God provided an array of sin offerings and sacrifices so they could come to Him for forgiveness and restore fellowship with Him, but only temporarily. Just as they began their physical labors after a one-day rest, so, too, did they have to continue to offer sacrifices. Hebrews 10:1 tells us that the law "can never, by the same sacrifices repeated endlessly year after year, make perfect those who draw near to worship." But these sacrifices were offered in anticipation of the ultimate sacrifice of Christ on the cross, who "after He had offered one sacrifice for sins forever, sat down on the right of God" (Hebrews 10:12). Just as He rested after performing the ultimate sacrifice, He sat down and rested—ceased from His labor of atonement because there was nothing more to be done, ever. Because of what He did, we no longer have to "labor" to earn our salvation. We don't labor in law-keeping in order to be justified in the sight of God but we keep the commandments of God in obedience to God because we are already justified.

We (believers) are not condemned by the Law. There is no longer enmity between us and God because of our relationship with the Prince of Peace (Jesus Christ). This is not a temporally ceasefire but a permanent reconciliation that God made with man. Jesus was sent so that we might rest in God and in what He has provided. The Bible appeals to sinner to respond to what He has done. To make the point, Paul quotes Psalm 95:7-11: "Today, if you hear his voice, do not harden your hearts as you did in the rebellion, during the time of testing in the desert, where your fathers tested and tried me and for forty years saw what I did. That is why I was angry with that generation, and I said, 'Their hearts are always going astray, and they have not known my ways.' So I declared on oath in my anger, 'They shall never enter my rest'" (Heb. 3:7-11).

"Therefore, since the promise of entering his rest still stands, let us be careful that none of you be found to have fallen short of it" (4:1). We can paraphrase the thought in this way: God makes it possible for us to enter his rest, so we need to make sure that we accept his offer. If we do not keep our faith in him (the main exhortation of this book), we will fail to enter. How do we enter? Verse 2 tells us, "For we also have had the gospel preached to us, just as they did; but the message they heard was of no value to them, because those who heard did not combine it with faith." The author of the book of Hebrews urges us to be diligent, then he talks about the gospel. This implies that we enter God's rest by means of the gospel.

Another element of the Sabbath day rest which God instituted as a foreshadowing of our complete rest in Christ is that He blessed it, sanctified it, and made it holy. Here again we see the symbol of Christ as our Sabbath rest—the holy, perfect Son of God who sanctifies and makes holy all who believe in Him. God sanctified Christ, just as He sanctified the Sabbath day, and sent Him into the world (John 10:36) to be our sacrifice for sin. In Him we find complete rest from the labors of our self-effort, because He alone is holy and righteous. "God made him who had no sin to be sin for us, so that in him we might become the righteousness of God" (2 Corinthians 5:21). We can now cease from our spiritual labors and rest in Him, not just one day a week, but always.

Jesus can be our Sabbath rest in part because He is "Lord of the Sabbath" (Matthew 12:8). As God incarnate, He decides the true meaning of the Sabbath because He created it, and He is our Sabbath rest in the flesh. When the Pharisees criticized Him for healing on the Sabbath, Jesus reminded them that even they, sinful as they were, would not hesitate to pull a sheep out of a pit on the Sabbath. Because He came to seek and save His sheep who would hear His voice (John 10:27) and enter into the Sabbath rest He provided by paying for their sins, He could break the Sabbath rules. He told the Pharisees that people are more important than sheep and the salvation He provided was more important than rules. By saying, "The Sabbath was made for man, not man for the Sabbath" (Mark 2:27), Jesus was restating the principle that the Sabbath rest was instituted to relieve man of his labors, just as He came to relieve us of our attempting to achieve salvation by our works. We no longer rest for only one day, but forever cease our laboring to attain God's favor. Jesus is our rest from works now, just as He is the door to heaven, where we will rest in Him forever.

Are Christians supposed to keep the fourth commandment (Sabbath)? The Moral Law consists of Ten Moral laws which are equally relevant to our sanctification. Again, we don't keep them to be saved but to prove that we are saved. According to the new covenant, God transferred the Moral Law (Ten Commandments) from the tablets of stones and wrote them in our hearts. The Hebrew word for "seventh" comes from a root meaning, "to be full, complete, entirely made up." God "blessed" the seventh day of setting it apart as different from the others. Part of bearing the image of God involves resting as He did. God established the Sabbath as part of the Ten Commandments (Exodus 20:8–11). In Genesis 2, we learn that God instituted the 7-day cycle of work and rest pattern for us to live by the divine principle underlying the institution of the Sabbath at creation as a day set apart for the worship of God is still observed. Since the concept of Sabbath and the 7-day cycle of work and rest pattern were instituted before the Mosiac law, they are therefore still applicable to Christians.

It is a sad fact that for many today what God intended to be a day of rest for man's body and soul has become a day of restlessness; a day of hectic activity. Our is a neurotic age in which people are living on their nerves and they do themselves no great service by passing up this God-given opportunity to pause and bring a little quiet into the turmoil of their noise-rocked lives. Abraham Heschel has wisely said, "Six days a week we live under the tyranny of things in space; on the Sabbath we try to become attuned to holiness in time. It is a day on which we are called upon to share what is eternal in time, to turn from the results of creation to the mystery of creation; from the world of creation to the creation of the world.

Scrolling through my posted sermons on resting in Christ

I am the door. If anyone enters by me, he will be saved and will go in and out and find pasture. (John 10:9). Jesus, the great I AM, is the entrance into the true Church and the way of access to God Himself. He gives to the one who comes to God by Him four choice privileges.

1. He will be saved. The fugitive entered the gate of the city of refuge and was safe. Noah entered the door of the ark and was secure. None can be lost who take Jesus as the door of faith to their souls. Entrance through Jesus into peace is the guarantee of entrance by the same door into heaven. Jesus is the only door, an open door, a wide door, a safe door; and blessed is he who rests all his hope of admission to glory upon the crucified Redeemer.

2. He will go in. He will be privileged to go in among the divine family, sharing the children's food and participating in all their honors and enjoyments. He will go into the rooms of communion, to the banquets of love, to the treasures of the covenant, to the storehouses of the promises. He will go in to the King of kings in the power of the Holy Spirit, and the secret of the Lord will be with him.

3. He will go out. This blessing is much forgotten. We go out into the world to work and suffer, but what a mercy to go in the name and

power of Jesus! We are called to bear witness to the truth, to cheer the disconsolate, to warn the careless, to win souls, and to glorify God. And as the angel said to Gideon, "Go in this might of yours," even so the Lord would have us proceed as His messengers in His name and strength.

4. He will find pasture. He who knows Jesus will never lack. Going in or out will be equally helpful to him: In fellowship with God he will grow, and in watering others he will be watered. Having made Jesus his all, he will find all in Jesus. His soul will be like a watered garden and like a well of water that never runs dry.

The Old Testament proclaimed the coming Christ—explicitly in the Messianic prophecies and implicitly in numerous types and shadows. In the old covenant the priest temporarily transferred the sins of God's people (Israelites) to the bullock. The laying of the hand was symbolic of our sins permanently transferred to Jesus Christ (Isaiah 53:5). At the cross, the wrath of God towards our sins was melted heavily upon Him. God made all the offenses of His covenant people rest upon the Substitute Lamb that was slain before the foundation of the world. We enter into the new covenant by investing our faith in the finished works of Christ at the cross.

Surely this is the very essence and nature of faith, which not only brings us into contact with the great Substitute, but also teaches us to lean upon Him with all the burden of our guilt. Jehovah made all the offenses of His covenant people rest upon the Substitute, and each one of the chosen is brought personally to confirm this solemn covenant act, when by grace he is enabled by faith to lay his hand upon the head of the Lamb that was slain before the foundation of the world.

****

One of my friends told me that he chooses any day he wants to go to Church; it doesn't have to be the Lord's Day. Well, there is nothing wrong with going to Church any day or even every day. I highly recommend it. However God created all days and gave them to us to enjoy but He reserved one day (Sabbath) and He separated it for Himself. In fact the word holy means separated from others. God is holy because He is separated from all creation. This reminds of the home where I grew up. There were a couple of sets of chairs in our seating room but this one chair was separated for my dad as a place of respect and honor. We could jump and step on the rest of the chairs except for this one chair. The same thing applies to the Lord's Supper. It is unique, uncommon and separated from the rest of the meals served at other tables. The Lord's Day is unique and uncommon reserved to honor God. Fellowshipping every day should therefore not take away from our obedience to God but should add to our obedience to the commandments of God.

****

"Therefore I urge you, brethren, by the mercies of God, to present your bodies a living and holy sacrifice, acceptable to God, which is your spiritual service of worship" (Romans 12:1). Our bodies are sacrifices of dedication and thanksgiving. They are consecrated for the service of God. It means that the body is not yours but belongs to God. You do to it as God says and as He wills. This is a token of sacrifice compared to the sacrifice Jesus made for us.

****

Romans 8:37 – "--in all these things we are more than conquerors through him who loved us." The scripture is a comparison between us (believers) and Christ. Jesus conquered death by physically experiencing suffering: It is His body that hanged on the cross. He became sin yet He was never a sinner. He conquered but we are more conquerors than Him because we are the primary recipients of the benefits of His sufferings. In Christ we are eternal conquerors.

****

What is the difference between doubt and unbelief? Doubt is an error of the mind but unbelief is the hardening of the heart which is sin. The 'doubt' that does not discredit the capability of God is not sin. At times it is safer to test the waters before jumping in. But we should not allow doubt to escalate into unbelief. Doubt can be constructive as in the case of self-examination and can be instrumental to conviction. Thomas confessed Jesus as my "Lord and my God" after doubting (John 20:28).

Jesus did not rebuke Thomas for his confession, rather Jesus accepted the confession, and blessed Thomas. David lamented: "Say to my soul, 'I am your salvation!'" (Psalm 35:3). The text informs me first of all that David had his doubts—for why should he pray, "Say to my soul, 'I am your salvation',' if he was not in doubts and fears? David was not content while he had doubts and fears, but he refurbished at once to the mercy seat to pray for assurance. He could not rest unless his assurance had a vivid personality about it: "Say to my soul, 'I am your salvation.'" The Bible instructs us to examine our faith and make sure that it is rooted in Christ (2 Cor. 13:5).

****

The Psalmist said that "The Lord is my strength". It means that no one can stand without His grace. The moment Satan makes you believe that you can make it by your own strength he has got you where he wants you. We are redeemed spiritually but we are still in the corrupt bodies and the corrupt world. God alone is immortal and He alone is perfect. Faith is trusting in God's abilities other than our own abilities. Our union with God through Jesus Christ qualifies us to be as perfect as God positionally: "God made him who had no sin to be sin for us, so that in him we might become the righteousness of God" (2 Corinthians 5:21). We are declared to be the very righteousness of God but we are still fragile vessels used by God. There is always work in progress until glorification. God is working in us and He works through us to impact the world (sanctification). But we must set ourselves apart from the world (consecrate ourselves) in order to be usable.

****

What is truth? Truth is reality and actuality as determined by God. The truth is not conditional, not relative but it is absolute. The truth is the means that we need to go back to God. The truth is not an idea but the person of Jesus Christ (John 14:6).

****

Think of the Lord as an amazing Father of a household. We should fear him, but that fear stems from love. And from that Love we will want to please him. We cannot please Him unless we invest our faith in Christ. It is our faith alone that lets Him welcome us back into His home, no matter how many times we screw up. We have a comforting assurance, that when we take refuge in Christ we cannot be moved. You can't earn your way into heaven so don't bother trying. God has already provided for your way back to Him through Jesus Christ. But you can do good works and fruitful deeds pleasing to God with the new found faith (Jeremiah 17:10).

****

Jesus said that nobody goes to the Father without Him. Why do we need Jesus to reach God the Father? Hebrews 1:3 – "Who being the brightness of his glory, and the express image of his person, and upholding all things by the word of his power, when he had by himself purged our sins, sat down on the right hand of the Majesty on high". When you look up you see the brightness light of the sun but not the sun. I know this because looking directly into the sun is fatal. The sun is not fire, but it does throw out intense ultraviolet light so if you look at the sun you will completely go blind. Likewise the Bible says that our God is a consuming fire (Hebrews 12:29). It means a fire that utterly consumes or destroys. God's holiness is the reason for His being a consuming fire, and it burns up anything unholy. We (sinners) can only see God by directly looking at Christ. There is no need to fear the consuming fire of God's wrath if we are covered by the purifying blood of Christ.

****

"Now if we are children, then we are heirs—heirs of God and co-heirs with Christ, if indeed we share in his sufferings in order that we may also share in his glory" (Romans 8:17). Within this scripture is the promise of inheritance given to all God's children now (in the present) rather in future. We are heirs to God through Christ. We are promised not to inherit stuff but to be heirs to God that owns all stuff. The condition is if we share in His sufferings now ------ we shall share in His future glory also. By entrusting yourself fully to the Spirit of truth, therefore, you entering into the rich inheritance that only God can fathom.

****

Jesus primarily came to die for our sins. He did not look upon his calling as drudgery but He entered upon it with intense delight. Likewise, we are called to be partakers in His suffering. Yet, none of us can do the cross; it is the corollary of the ministry of the Anointed One (Messiah). The only way we can share in His suffering is by suffering for the righteousness sake. "----For it is better to suffer for doing good, if that should be God's will, than for doing evil" (1 Peter 3:17). Paul wrote that we partake in Christ's suffering by dying to the old nature so that the life of Jesus might be revealed in us (Romans 6:3-4).

****

Life is about choices. It is a choice of either to be for God or against Him. Any person without Christ is against God. Reconciliation with God means trusting in His Son. Trust is not a passive state of mind. It is a vigorous act of the soul by which we choose to lay hold on the promises of God and cling to them despite the adversity that at times seems to overwhelm us.

****

Romans 8:23 - We ourselves... groan inwardly as we wait eagerly for adoption as sons, the redemption of our bodies. This groaning is common among God's people: To a greater or lesser extent we all feel it. It is not the groan of murmuring or complaint: It is a note of desire rather than of distress. Having received a deposit, we desire the rest of our portion; we are sighing that our entire manhood, in its trinity of spirit, soul, and body, may be set free from the last trace of the Fall; we long to discard the rags of corruption, weakness, and dishonor and to be clothed with incorruption, immortality, glory—the spiritual body that the Lord Jesus will bestow upon His people. We long for the manifestation of our adoption as the children of God. "We . . . groan," but it is "inwardly." It is not the hypocrite's groan, by which he would make men believe that he is a saint because he is wretched. "Our sighs are sacred things, too holy and too personal for us to broadcast. We keep our longings for our Lord to ourselves." ~ Alistair Begg

****

Romans 5:3-4: "Suffering produces endurance, and endurance produces character, and character produces hope" The kind of suffering propagated involves our suffering for the Lord's sake or righteousness'. Paul connects such suffering with the promise: "If indeed we suffer with Him in order that we may also be glorified with Him" (Romans 8:17d). "If" does not denote a question or uncertainty, but would better be translated as "because" or "inasmuch". Paul shows here one of the best proofs of a believer's belonging to his Lord: that is our suffering for the Lord's sake. It is suffering for righteousness sake.

****

A newly born again person is like a man that has been blind since birth and has just regained his sight. He is fascinated with exploring everything in the spiritual realm. His performance is fabulous, compared to the new bloom that sweeps fast. Unfortunately, the same passion diminishes as time goes by. I suggest that there should be in you, always, a nostalgic yearning for regaining the lost fire. Nostalgia comes from two Greek words: The Greek word for "return" is nostos. Algos means "suffering." So nostalgia is the suffering caused by an unappeased yearning to return." Recall your earliest days of salvation and build on that momentum. The good old experience could be an inspiration to defeat the deplorable experience today. Remember that any time you choose not to do what you used to do you are taking a step backwards. Backsliding is not a onetime event but a process of retreating in a slow manner. The truth is that if you are not progressing you are regressing. Quit driving in reverse-gear. Burn your bridges behind you – and say no to retreat. "God did not call us to start the race with enthusiasm but to finish the race passionately."

****

Why battle against darkness when all we need to do is turn on the light? Darkness is not a thing; it is the absence of light. Jesus is the light of the world; He is the only bright spot on the universe that deposes the darkness of the world.

****

The Bible instructs that, "Quench not the Spirit". It means don't put out the fire of the Spirit. When we allow the fire of adversity to burn we end up putting off the fire of the Holy Spirit. We can extinguish the odd fire by throwing the waters of life (Word) over our soul.

****

The Bible is the only book whose author is always present when one reads it. Read the Word of God everyday so that when you go through the valley, you have deposits of joy to draw from. The Christian life is like running a marathon: You keep running while drinking water in order to avoid dehydration. Keep refreshing your soul from spring of life in order to keep on going. A spiritual person lives even beyond the grave. The physical heart may lose its strength to beat, but the spiritual heart never loses its power to glow. Eternal life begins now and continues forever and ever......

****

The truth on earth is determined by the Bible! The knowledge in all other books should be backed by the knowledge of God. "Zeal without knowledge is like a sword in the hands of a fool" ~ John Calvin

****

Perseverance and endurance are virtues. The reason we fail to endure is because we settle for the little things offered by this life. We forget that the pleasures of the world are temporary but God gives us eternal pleasures.

****

Hebrews 4:14 – "Nothing in all creation is hidden from God's sight. Everything is uncovered and laid bare before the eyes of him to whom we must give account. Jesus the Great High Priest. Therefore, since we have a great high priest who has ascended into heaven, Jesus the Son of God, let us hold firmly to the faith we profess." There is no creature hidden from His sight, but all things are naked and open to the eyes of

Him to whom we must give account. The Bible calls us to hold on our confession but not on our salvation because it is His work to secure our salvation. We are safe and secure in the hands of our Lord. "Precious is the assurance that He does not change! The wheel of providence revolves, but its axle is eternal love.'

****

Jesus is God manifested in the flesh. It was necessary for God to manifest in the flesh so as to make His grace available to mankind. The Grace of God is enormously great; much greater than we can comprehend. The grace allows the Holy God to inhabit our corrupt bodies (your body is the temple of God). The grace makes it possible for the infinite God who is much bigger than the universe to indwell our tinny hearts. The grace extends love to those who least deserve it. The grace of God is God's influence on our hearts teaching us to obey His commandments. We are called to grow into His grace perpetually by growing into obedience.

****

The grace connects God to a sinner. Faith connects a repented sinner to God. Faith can move mountains but it is Love that made mountains. In this sense, love is the greatest power in the universe. Love is an action word. Jesus summarized the Ten Commandments into two commandments of 'loving God and loving neighbor with all your mind and heart.' These two are the evidence of the born again person. Though love is a crucial element in everything God does, the two commandments are not the gospel. The primary requisition of God to be perfect as God is. The gospel is the power of God unto salvation because it gives us access to the perfect works of Jesus. The gospel is the historical facts concerning the life, death and resurrection of Jesus. The gospel reveals God's love extended to us unconditionally - but to come into a relationship with this love is conditional. You must repent in order to qualify for His love. One commentator writes, Love can offer neither grace nor mercy until the full truth concerning the evil which is to be forgiven has been laid bare. That is why God is worshiped by only a sincere heart.

****

God called Abraham a friend (Genesis 18:20-33). The relationship that Abraham enjoyed with God was a remarkable one by human standards – but tremendously encouraging for us. God is not a partial God. He is not a respecter of persons. If we follow the example of our spiritual forefather Abraham by being in agreement with God, displaying loyalty and dependability towards God, and freely confiding in Him in all matters, then we too will be called the friends of God. It is important therefore for us to focus on those sobering facts that draw us closer to God now and for eternity.

****

The intents of the heart determine the purity of our actions. "God made man to go by motives, and he will not go without them, any more than a boat without steam or a balloon without gas." Our intents determine our actions. When the intents are clean, the actions are considered to be clean. Bad intents make good actions evil. The human heart is compared to a fountain that cannot produce both salt and fresh water at the same place. That is why the Bible says that salt and fresh water cannot come from the same fountain (James 3:11). The intents or motives of the conscience that is cleaned by the blood of Jesus are considered to be clean regardless of the flaws in the actions. But the motives of the seared and unclean conscience of the unbelievers make even their seemingly good works to be as filthy (dirtiest) rugs before God (Isaiah 64:6). A believer's faith is pleasing to God because it involves trusting in the abilities of Jesus (the only one that is holy); his intents are to manifest His works. The grace of God covers for our failures, rendering everything we do as perfect before God.

****

You can have a new beginning! Faith is the beginning of the progressive journey of walking with God. Faith is trusting in someone's abilities. But we are not saved by our faith except that faith connects us to the righteousness of Jesus Christ (His accomplished works at the cross) of which we are saved. Faith is looking at reality through the flame work of the cross. In order for faith to be valid there must be on object of faith. Faith is no better than its object. Also, there can be no faith without a promise (Word) to activate our faith. Faith is acting on the truth in the

Word. Faith is the confidence that the unseen promises will actually happen; it gives us assurance about things we cannot see (Hebrews 11:1). The Word of God is the very place where faith is initiated. Faith is confessing as God decreed. In this case it is to see eye to eye (to be in agreement with God). Therefore, faith must be in God rather than in self. Faith in faith is nothing but positive thinking. Anybody (including a nonbeliever) can think positively but the grace motivated positivity of life is a prerequisite virtue of the redeemed alone. If your faith is invested in positive thinking, you are going to be disappointed compared to entering a jewel mine and coming out with empty hands. Hope I am helping somebody.

****

Infinite realities exist that are outside the reach of our observation. We know this to be true. Yet all too often, Christians are labeled as crazy for making assertions about the spiritual world, God, and heaven. Faith is not just closing your eyes and imagining things that down deep in your heart you don't really think are true. Faith is not mysterious power working in us. Faith is not positive thinking because even New Age movement teaches to be positive. Faith is trusting in the abilities of Christ to work on your behalf. God works at the level of man's capability to grant His grace to those who exercise their faith. Faith is our obedience by believing in God. Faith is trusting in the faithfulness of Christ to work on our behalf. Faith and grace go together compared to the two wings of a bird whereby it cannot fly without both wings. Every step of trusting in God diminishes our trust in self, and increases our access to His grace. Paul said that, "I am crucified with Christ: nevertheless I live; yet not I, but Christ liveth in me: and the life which I now live in the flesh I live by the faith of the Son of God, who loved me, and gave himself for me" (Galatians 2:20).

****

A non-repented sinner is a fugitive; he is on run in rebellion without taking on the responsibility for his sins until Jesus catches him or her. The first thing that happens after God opens the eyes of the sinner to see Jesus is to take on the responsibility for his or her sins by acknowledging that, "I am a sinner." You see, it takes a revelation for somebody to admit that he is a sinner. The first gift that God grants to His elect is the responsible heart that is big enough to absorb blames. There is a true story concerning a king that visited a jail to address the grievances of the prisoners. Apart from one man, all of the prisoners in jail complained to the king that they were convicted of the crimes they did not commit. The king commanded the Prison Warden that "Release that rascal who admitted that he is guilty least he spoils the innocent ones". Ironically, the one that pleaded guilty went home a free man! Placing the blame where it does not belong leaves you powerless to change your experience; but taking responsibility for your faults liberates you. Today decide that your heart is the factory where your problems are manufactured and look for the solution that God alone can provide.

****

God called you to be an instrument of peace. There are two primary choices in life: to accept conditions as they exist, or accept the responsibility for changing them. We are called to be world changers. The Word of God is a two edged sword that cuts from inside to the outside; it changes you in order to change the surrounding. You may not be able to change the world you see around you but you can change the world within you. Embracing the Truth is the key to genuine change. The truth on earth is determined by the Bible! Today rest in the promises of our faithful God, knowing that His words are full of truth and power; rest in the doctrines of His Word, which are consolation itself; rest in the covenant of His grace, which is a haven of delight.

The knowledge in all other books should be backed by the knowledge of God. Satan's priority is to cause rebellion among us by twisting the Scriptures. Satan tempted Eva by twisting God's words. God commanded that: "But of the fruit of the tree which *is* in the midst of the garden, God hath said, Ye shall not eat of it, neither shall ye touch it, lest ye die" (Genesis 3:3). Satan appealed to Eva in this way: "Now the serpent was more crafty than any of the wild animals the LORD God had made. He said to the woman, "Did God really say, 'You must not eat from any tree in the garden'?" Satan knows that any slight change in the Scriptures is likely to lead you astray. A Jewish scholar Abraham Heschel challenged Christians, "It has seemed puzzling to me how greatly attached to the Bible you seem to be and yet how much like pagans you handle it." The reason is because most Bible thumpers love less, give less and live like pagans. "Zeal without knowledge is like a sword in the hands of a fool" ~ John Calvin

****

Believing is knowing the path and walking the path. Jesus came to show us the way back home to the Father. We have no excuse of not believing. But we live in a culture that has, for centuries now, cultivated the idea that the skeptical person is always smarter than the one who believes. Today it is the skeptics who are the social conformists, but because of powerful intellectual propaganda they continue to enjoy thinking of themselves as wildly individualistic and unbearably bright. Real scholars are looked down upon while Crowd Pullers are eulogized and honored. "When you judge the truth by "man" instead of judging man by "the truth", you inadvertently equate affluence with righteousness; truth is exchanged with falsehood .... The difference between the apparent and the reality is consciously or unconsciously blurred. Passivity is automatically actuated in man instead of activity."

****

This weekend go to the full gospel Bible teaching Church. Our works reveal our fallen nature. Headstrong, self-esteem and arrogance are the physiognomies of the fall of man. Pride is the adversity causing prejudice against the Word of God. A man who has such a swollen ego won't submit to authority figures. Also, he has difficulty acquiescing to the authority of the Scriptures. Our communities are permeated with egocentric people who believe that truth is what they make it to be rather than what God predetermined it to be. Concerning the Word of God, we do not need to be tactical because it is all powerful compared to the lion in the cage: Just let it out of the cage and it will rip the enemy to shreds!

****

Obedience is our highest calling yet the most difficult thing to all of us. Any sincere believer will tell you that "Self" is the greatest hindrance to this precious calling. The reason is because the outward man and the inward man are not in harmony, for both are tending toward opposite directions. There is a tendency of the inability of the outward man to submit to the spirit's control, rendering us incapable of obeying God's highest commands. The situation worsens when we are faced with the trials of life. Definitely, the trials could not kill the spirit of man. Your body and mind can be broken, but your spirit is unbreakable, and unchangeable by any natural means, except supernaturally by the divine intervention through transformation. God allows the trials of life purposely to draw us towards Him. God created the human spirit in such a way that it responds with brokenness to the tragedies of life therefore letting God in. "Obedience is not reached by making resolutions but by dying to "the old self" and allowing the new life of Christ to be your life"

****

Researchers say that Multi-tasking shrinks the brains. You can avoid the dilemma by prioritizing. Putting your priorities in the right order involves ethics and timing. Ethics determine choices and actions, and at times suggest making strenuous choices. Jesus said to His critics "Give back to Caesar what is Caesar's and to God what is God's" (Mark 12:17). What did Jesus mean? We know that the earth and everything in it belongs to God. Basically what belongs to Caesar belongs to God. This leaves Caesar with nothing other than what is given to him by God. Jesus determined what belonged to Caesar by looking at the image of Caesar on the coin. Then He determined what belonged to God by virtue of the image of God on man. Jesus basically instructed his critics to put things in their right order: To give the taxes to Caesar but to give themselves to God. Jesus extends to us opportunity to purge, rethink priorities, and be sincere regarding our belief. "True contemplation is not a psychological trick but a theological grace" ~ Thomas Merton

****

Our beauty is in Christ. The beauty of God is His unchanging character manifested in His glory. It is too beautiful for a sinner to see and perceive. In the beginning, the entire universe was void until God activated its beauty by His Spirit. The Garden of Eden was the original temple where God met with Adam. After the corruption of sin, God instructed Moses to build the tabernacle so that He can meet with man again. It is significant that the first individuals in Scripture said to be filled with the Holy Spirit were Bezalel and Oholiab (Exodus 31:1-11), craftsmen tasked with executing God's plans for building and furnishing the tabernacle. The tabernacle was a mobile tent symbolic of our mobile bodies (temple). Our God loves beauty, and He is beautifying the saints through sanctification by the Holy Spirit. The Holy Spirit played a significant role in creation, and is actively involved in recreation. The ministry of the Holy Spirit is that of restoration and preservation of order, harmony and beauty.

****

Do you know that your body is not who you are but a house that you occupy? Yes, you move in it and with it; you are the sole landlord that owns it but also a tenant that can be evicted upon death. A wise tenant arranges for a better house to occupy in case of eviction. Jesus has pre-paid reservations in His Father's house for all of His followers. Don't be like the earthly landlords of rental properties who call themselves landlords but when they travel to other places, they become tenants there. "The only people I recognize as landlords in the whole universe are turtles and snail. They are the only creatures that move about with their houses" ~ Davies Offor (Clarius).

****

2 Cor. 6:1-13 - Don't receive God's Grace in Vain. By refusing to hear the admonition of Paul, the Corinthians were in danger of rejecting the grace offered to them. They were choosing comfort over conviction, rhetoric over repentance, and wealth over wisdom. They placed more value in immediate appearances than eternal priorities. The general gist of what I gained was that we can't behave in any manner that contradicts the commitment to live a life for God regardless of the difficulties life or people present. To do so will render receiving God's grace in vain. If we act like we don't know Christ and the power of the Holy Spirit to transform our lives, it nullifies, in the minds of onlookers, the life of Christ we received.

****

We are children of God. When you look at your family you notice the stark differences between every person in it. Each of your children looks different, has a distinct personality, and likes different things than the others. Yet, despite the diversities they all belong. The same is true of the family of God. When we come together with other believers from different backgrounds, ethnicity and walks of life, there's going to be some differences between us. But the unity we share in Christ is so much stronger than what divides us. Together we form the spiritual body of Christ. We are not human beings going through spiritual experiences. We are spiritual beings going through human experiences. Think about this as you go to Church today.

****

I came across this humor that the brain of a cockroach is located inside its body. It speculated that if a cockroach loses its head, it could live up to nine days. That a decapitated cockroach will not easily die because of frailty of its thinking. On the contrary, man cannot survive with amputated head because man cannot last a minute without thinking. According to the doctors, the EKG may indicate death in the rest of the body when the brains are still alive. Our brains remain active even when we are asleep. The brain is the most sophisticated organ and device in the world. My philosophy of life is that we make up our mind what we are going to make of our lives. Repentance is the change of minds. We cannot change our hearts but when we change our minds (repent) God changes our hearts. The grace of God bridges the gap between the heart and the minds to present to God a perfect man without any contradiction of values from within. The conscience is the voice of the heart and the intuition is the power of the minds. Intuition involves knowing without evidence. Faith involves believing without seeing. The conscience convicts depending on the truth it is exposed to. It is possible to be sincerely wrong. A believer's conscience is cleaned by the blood of Christ and is programmed in the righteousness of God as long as he abides in His Word. God receives the words of our conscience only, and He is pleased by He is pleased by His works in and through us (our faith).

****

Somebody made this humorous statement: "Every morning for about 20 years God has made a beep by my ear waking me up: Has anyone ever heard of this happening to someone?" and the Moderator answered, "Yes, it is called an alarm clock." I want to say that if you think it's your clock's alarm that wakes you up every morning; try putting it next to a corpse and see if it will wake up! Hope this will help you to understand the Grace of God. The reality is that without the living God that gives life, everything in the universe is void and lifeless. God created the universe and He is in control of it. The Bible says that He waters the grass and makes it grow. Always thank God for waking you up. It is by the grace of God that we breathe in and out.

****

Life is a sleazy stranger of which we are vaguely familiar. Vanity is the frustrated condition of the heart after investing all your efforts in this world in search for fulfillment but then end up wanting. Every step we take when we are separated from God is like walking around a slippery slope towards a bottomless pit. Life is like a coin. You can spend it any way you wish, but you only spend it once. The purpose of life is a life of purpose lived in Christ. Certainly, we (believers) are not exempted from the trials of this world. However, our trials (here on earth) is hell at its best we shall ever experience because after this life there is eternal heaven to inherit. Yet for a nonbeliever, whose conscience is separated from God, this world is his heaven at its best; real hell lingers in future. The goodness of God extends to us a choice to make while still living in this world regarding where to dwell eternally. Choose Christ; choose life forever in the presence of God.

****

Galatians 2:20 "I have been crucified with Christ." Alistair Begg says that the Lord Jesus Christ acted in what He did as a great public representative person, and His dying upon the cross was the virtual dying of all His people. In Him all His people rendered justice its due and made expiation to divine vengeance for all their sins. The apostle of the Gentiles delighted to think that as one of Christ's chosen people, he died upon the cross in Christ. He did more than believe this doctrinally—he accepted it confidently, resting his hope upon it. He believed that by virtue of Christ's death, he had satisfied divine justice and found reconciliation with God.

Beloved, what a blessed thing it is when the soul can, as it were, stretch itself upon the cross of Christ and feel, "I am dead; the law has killed me, and I am therefore free from its power, because in Christ I have borne the curse, and in the person of my Substitute all that the law could do by way of condemnation has been executed upon me, for I am crucified with Christ."

But Paul meant even more than this. He not only believed in Christ's death and trusted in it, but he actually felt its power in himself causing the crucifixion of his old corrupt nature. When he saw the pleasures of sin, he said, "I cannot enjoy these: I am dead to them." Such is the experience of every true Christian. Having received Christ, he is to this world as one who is utterly dead. Yet, while conscious of death to the world, he can at the same time exclaim with the apostle, "I live." He is fully alive to God. The Christian's life is a matchless riddle. The unconverted cannot comprehend it; even the believer himself cannot understand it. Dead, yet alive! Crucified with Christ, and yet at the same time risen with Christ in newness of life! Union with the suffering, bleeding Savior and death to the world and sin are soul-cheering things. May we learn to live evermore in the enjoyment of them!

****

God did not call us to start the race but to finish the race. God sees what you are becoming as opposed to what you are. Gideon was cowardly hiding from the threat of the huge invading Midianites force when an angel of the LORD appeared to him and addressed him this way: "The LORD is with you, O valiant warrior" (Judges 6:12). Consequently, Gideon with 300 brave men, each carrying an empty pitcher with a burning torch hidden inside the pitcher and the trumpets in one hand marched down the mountain-slope toward the enemy's camp and defeated thousands of them. "Sometimes you need a little crisis to get your adrenaline flowing and help you realize your potential." — Jeannette Walls, The Glass Castle

****

The kingdom of God is in you and will come to you. The kingdom of God is God's image established on the earth. The kingdom of will finally be established by the coming of the King of kings but right now it is established wherever Jesus is worshiped and His name revered.

****

In Christ we fight from victory to victory. Never be dismayed when you fail. Get up and approach the throne of grace in repentance. Consider the Apostle Paul's words in the seventh chapter of Romans: "I find it to be a law that when I want to do right, evil lies close at hand. For I delight in the law of God, in my inner being, but I see in my members another law waging war against the law of my mind and making me captive to the law of sin that dwells in my members."

****

"Yea, though I walk through the valley of the shadow of death, I will fear no evil: for thou art with me; thy rod and thy staff they comfort me" (Psalms 23:4). Worry looks around circumstances but Faith looks up with expectations. Those who live with expectation will never be ashamed. Failure, fear and procrastination are results of not sticking with the Promises of God. Man despises instructions due to their perception that they know how things ought to work. God demands that we believe in His Word even when the situation projects contrary.

September the Month of Laboring/Harvesting

On Monday 1st we shall be celebrating Labor Day in recognition of workers. God ordained mankind to labor from the time He created him. The curse of sweating to labor was added after the fall of man. Before the curse of sin labor did not involve toiling and sweating. Given the fact, God is looking for an opportunity to bless His people as opposed to curse them. God created Adam and instructed him to labor in the Garden of Eden. God called men to serve him who were busy working. For example Moses was a shepherd. Simon Peter, Andrew, James and John were fishermen. Matthew was a tax collector. One was a political zealot. Simon, called the zealot, is referred to in Luke 6:15, "Matthew, Thomas, James son of Alphaeus, Simon who was called the Zealot…"

Paul was a tent maker and etc. Jesus' disciples had jobs that described them as ordinary men of the day. None of them were theologians! They were prone to mistakes, faults, misstatements, and lapses in faith. In a sense, these men were remarkably unremarkable!

Labor Day is also a pivotal time to take stock of where our families, our economy, and our democracy are heading. Today, America finds itself in a position of incredible challenge. Half of all Americans now make less than $15 an hour. The families are worst hit by the economic crisis. Only 15% of American kids have one staying home parent to take care of them. The rest of the kids belong to homes whereby both parents work full time jobs to meet the financial demands. We must take notice that the family institution matters most to God. The children need their parents more than we need money. We must have value time with our children in anticipation of securing a strong nation of tomorrow.

A good case can be made for Shavuot being the most important of all the Jewish festivals. The revival of its observance is of particular concern to Reconstructionist Jews because our understanding of the nature and task of the Jewish people in the world and of what God should mean to us cannot be separated from our reinterpretation of the meaning of Torah. Shavuot is the festival of the giving and the receiving of Torah — of Torah as revelation, as law and as study. The word "Torah" means teaching, guidance, instruction, orientation. It is actually synonymous with Judaism itself and it has been used as such through the centuries.

In the Pentateuchal Torah (the Five Books of Moses), the Jewish people is told to count off seven weeks from the second day of Passover: "Start to count the seven weeks when the sickle is first put to the standing grain. Then you shall observe the Feast of Weeks for the Eternal your God, offering your freewill contribution . . . You shall rejoice before the Eternal your God with your son and daughter . . . and the stranger, the fatherless and the widow in your midst" (Deuteronomy 16).

Shavuot originated as an agricultural festival. It celebrates the beginning (the "first fruits") of harvest in Eretz Yisrael which continues throughout the summer and ends with Sukkot in the fall. "On the day of the first fruits, your Feast of Shavuot, when you bring an offering of new grain to the Eternal, you shall observe a sacred occasion: you shall not work at your occupations" (Numbers 28). "Then you shall observe the Feast of Weeks for the Eternal your God, offering your freewill contribution according as the Eternal your God has blessed you. You shall rejoice before the Eternal your God" (Deuteronomy 16).

Harvest festivals are universal, and Israelite farmers probably observed their harvest festival in ways not much different from those of their neighbors. What transformed Shavuot into something more than an agricultural celebration was the fact that our forbears gradually came to thank God not only for the harvest of their fields, orchards and vineyards, but also for the laws and traditions of the harvest which they had developed during the centuries. Israelite law, for example, insisted that even during the busy planting and harvesting seasons the Sabbath be observed as a day of rest for people and animals alike (Exodus 34). Indeed, the original reason for counting the days of the seven weeks may have been to keep track of the Sabbaths. Israelite law also ordained that the edges of the field and the gleanings of the harvest belonged exclusively to the poor and unfortunate. "When you reap the harvest of your land, you shall not reap all the way to the edges of your field, or gather the gleanings of your harvest. You shall not pick your vineyard bare, or gather the fallen fruit of your vineyard; you shall leave them for the poor and the stranger" (Leviticus 19).

Since the Israelite saw God's gift in the laws of the harvest as much as in the harvest itself, the book in which those laws were eventually recorded (the Torah) also came to be regarded as divine and the feast of the harvest became the holiday of revelation (the Season of the Giving of the Torah). With time, the agricultural aspect of Shavuot became secondary and the festival was observed primarily as a celebration of the revelation of the written and oral Torahs (the Pentateuch together with the Talmud and the Mid-rash). Two thousand years ago, the Pharisees, the primary shapers of Judaism as we know it today, championed this view. That the laws of nature and the ethical laws by which people should live are all derived from the same divine source is beautifully expressed in the 19th Psalm:

Scrolling through posted messages on labor/harvest:

"Give not that which is holy unto the dogs, neither cast ye your pearls before swine, lest they trample them under their feet, and turn again and rend you" (Matthew 7:6). God blesses you according to what is in your heart. If you are being kind, giving, loving and sharing it is the nature of your heart, and you should do everything without looking for anything in return. God blesses a cheerful giver that does not expect rewards from the world. However, at times we are hurt by the same people whom we help. Never let the culprits change your heart because it would be changing the very thing that God wants to bless. It is not worthy to lose your blessings because of other people's flaws. Just guard your heart and divert your works of charity from the manipulators to others who are in need of your service. In the parable of the marriage banquette, Jesus instructed His disciple not to beg those who turned down His invitation. He instructed them to go to the intersections of the highways, and invite as many as they can find (Matthew 22:2-14). Happy Labor Day to you all that labor in the harvest of souls.

****

Focus on the eternal blessings. In our world, reward systems are designed to recognize people who distinguish themselves in a particular field of human Endeavour. Nobel Prizes winners and Oscars are rewarded after specifying the niche. At the judgment seat there are promises of crowns to be handed to the overcomers in Christ. But this is the most humbling promise in the Scripture: "Blessed are those servants, whom the lord when he comes shall find watching: truly I say to you, that he shall gird himself, and make them to sit down to meat, and will come forth and serve them" (Luke 12:37). I know that during His earthly ministry, Jesus washed the feet of His disciples and served them at the Last Supper. But that was then and this is now! By then His glory was veiled in human flesh. This scripture insinuates that He will wait on His faithful servants at table when He is in His utmost glory. The degree of the glory makes it fascinating; it makes me addicted to serving. And the Bible says "The Glory of your latter days shall be greater than the Glory of your former". Let your past be history and strive towards the prize that is ahead!

****

Begin this week with prayers. "Pray as though everything depended on God. Work as though everything depended on you." Remember that prayer is not the substitute of work. Pray for the daily bread and go to work for it. Pray for good health and take precaution to live and to eat healthy. Pray for a spouse and work on improving your manners and your general physical appearances. The Bible warns that, "Sluggards do not plow in season; so at harvest time they look but find nothing." (Proverbs 20:4).

****

Genesis 8:22 - "As long as the earth endures, seedtime and harvest, cold and heat, summer and winter, day and night will never cease." The word season is traced all the way in Genesis rendering to planting and harvesting. Jesus told them, "The harvest is plentiful, but the workers are few. Ask the Lord of the harvest, therefore, to send out workers into his harvest field.(Luke 10:2). Spiritually Jesus is the chief harvester. "I sent you to reap what you have not worked for. Others have done the hard work, and you have reaped the benefits of their labor" (John 4:38). "Let both grow together until the harvest: and in the time of harvest I will say to the reapers, Gather ye together first the tares, and bind them in bundles to burn them: but gather the wheat into my barn." (Matthew 13:30).

****

Thus saith the Lord, and I will make thee exceeding fruitful, and I will make nations of thee, and kings shall come out of thee (Genesis 17: 6).

****

God's shalls must always be understood in their largest sense. From the beginning of the year to the end of the year, from the first gathering of evening shadows until a new day dawns, in all conditions and under all circumstances, it will be well with the righteous. It is so well with him that we could not imagine it to be better, for he is well fed—he feeds upon the flesh and blood of Jesus; he is well clothed—he wears the imputed righteousness of Christ; he is well housed—he dwells in God; he is well married—his soul is knit in bonds of marriage to Christ; he is well provided for—for the Lord is his Shepherd; he is well endowed— for heaven is his inheritance. It is well with the righteous—well upon divine authority; the mouth of God speaks the comforting assurance.

****

Go to Church knowing that you are the blessed of God. It bothers me whenever a believer confesses that he or she is not blessed. Real blessing is the salvation of your soul. Of all nations, Israel was called the blessed of God because they alone knew God. The believers are more blessed because God dwells in the eternity of their hearts. Without the cross you could have been alienated from the grace. The cross stands between you and eternal condemnation. All altars in the Old Testament (prepared by Abel, Noah, Abraham and the Leviticus priesthood) and billions of gallons of blood split from animals' sacrifices were typologies of the cross of Christ. God reconciled the world to Himself through Christ. We were adopted into the divine family and we became co-heirs with Christ to God's riches. The Bible instructs us to seek the eternal blessings: "Seek you the kingdom of God first and the rest shall be added to you." The word 'first' means alone or only. Salvation is the real blessing; the rest of things are tokens added to the main blessing. We are blessed to bless others. We have the answer to the hopeless world. The child who asks questions where there are no answers the same child becomes a non-entity and hopeless. We were saved from hopelessness. This week walk in the sanctuary with a reason to praise Him rather than looking for a reason to praise Him.

****

God does not call you to nothing but He calls you to something. When God calls you to accomplish a certain task, you are safe and secure in spite of the challenges of life. Believer, if your inheritance is meager, you should be satisfied with your earthly portion; for you may rest assured that it is best for you. "Some plants die if they have too much sunshine. It may be that you are planted where you get only a little, but you are put there by the loving Farmer because only in that situation will you produce fruit unto perfection" ~ Alistair Begg

****

This is a résumé of all believers: "For you see your calling, brethren, that not many wise according to the flesh, not many mighty, not many noble, are called. But God has chosen the foolish things of the world to put to shame the wise, and God has chosen the weak things of the world to put to shame the things which are mighty" (1 Cor. 1:26-27). God perfects us in our weaknesses. We are all called to be disciples regardless of our titles. Every person needs two types of people in his or her life: The first one is the mentor that teaches you. The second one is whom you mentor (the one you teach). All my friends fall in one or both of the above categories. The Bible says that all believers will stand before the Bema Seat (judgment seat of Christ), to receive rewards for the good works done while in the body (2 Corinthians 5:10). It is going to be double victory for us to see the people whom we encouraged and those who encouraged us standing next to us to receive their crowns. I want to say to all my friends on Facebook "Thank you for mentoring me and for choosing me to be your mentor."

****

We are guilty of embracing the worldly mentality propagating that success in life solely depends upon power, fame, and riches. We forget that our yardstick of measuring the rich and the poor is lacking; for a man without a clean conscience cannot swim above the vanity that only this world could offer. He puts on vain airs yet he is counted among the dead still breathing. The Bible says that, "Now if we are children, then we are heirs—heirs of God and co-heirs with Christ, if indeed we share in his sufferings in order that we may also share in his glory" (Romans 8:17). Here is the promise of inheritance given to all God's children now (in the present) rather in future. We are heirs to God through Christ. We are not promised to inherit stuff but to be heirs to God that owns all stuff. It means viewing all the land and its fullness as though they belong to you, and yours belonging to all mankind. The condition is that if we share in His sufferings now --- we shall share in His future glory also. Therefore, by entrusting yourself fully to the Spirit of truth, you are entering into the rich inheritance that only God can fathom. Our success is measured in our spiritual influence on others (serving). We were bought by the blood of Jesus such that the life we live is not ours but it is His life that we live for His own pleasure. The new life demands that we become servants to God and servants to each other. No man is an island to himself. This gives us a reason never to feel guilty to testify that the God we worship is the one that others must accept. So help us God!

****

To be a soul-winner is the happiest thing in the world. With every soul you bring to Christ, you get a new heaven on earth. But who can conceive of the bliss that awaits us above! How sweet is the sentence, "Enter into the joy of your Master!" Do you know what the joy of Christ is over a saved sinner? This is the very joy that we are to possess in heaven. Yes, when He ascends the throne, you shall ascend with Him. When the heavens ring with "Well done, well done," you will have a part in the reward. You have worked with Him; you have suffered with Him; you will now reign with Him. You have sown with Him; you will reap with Him

****

Watch out for those people who testify that everybody hates them but God loves them. It is impossible to love God and hate your Christian Brother and Sister. One of the fathers of the early Church said that it is impossible to have God as your Father without having the Church as your mother. The Church is the mysterious body of Christ. The ones who are born of the Father must be in communion with other believers. Fellowshipping is rehearsing heaven on earth. Ironically, we fellowship and accommodate the same people with whom we will fellowship with in heaven. If you can't put up with them here on earth how are you going to put up with them eternally? Within fellowshipping are the elements of communion, sharing and partnership. We do not have a choice regarding whom to love because God made that choice for us. We must love our neighbors. God has chosen a person next to you to love regardless of their mistakes.

****

Nobody is no body in the eyes of God. But the nothingness of a believer makes him or her something in the eyes of God. Therefore decrease and be invisible so that He might increase and be visible. Remember that everything that belongs to Jesus is given for your inheritance. His increase is your increase.

****

Christian, do you doubt whether God will fulfill His promise? Will the fortresses of rock be swept away by a storm? Will the storehouses of heaven fail? Do you think that your heavenly Father, even though He knows that you need food and clothes, will forget you?------ We whom God has fashioned after His likeness, dishonor Him by unbelief and tarnish His honor by mistrust. Shame on us for this! Our God does not deserve to be so poorly treated; in our past life we have proved Him to be true and faithful to His word, and with so many instances of His love and of His kindness as we have received and are daily receiving at His hands, it is base and inexcusable that we allow a doubt to lodge within our heart. From now on let us resolve to wage constant war against doubts of our God—enemies to our peace and to His honor—and with an unstaggering faith believe that what He has promised He will also perform. "I believe; help my unbelief!" ~ Alistair Begg

****

In his book, What Money Can't Buy, Michael Sandel notes that whereas a market economy is a tool for organizing how resources are allocated in society, a market society is where everything is for sell. The behavior of laborers demanding for payraise today should not be seen as an isolated case. It is systemic and characteristic of a market society. It is prevalent in all spheres of life – Churches, schools, lawyers, medics, MPs, and even homes. Children today are paid either to take medicine or to read! No wonder some see children as consumers that come with liabilities.

****

"Yes, it's vital to make lifestyle choices to mitigate damage caused by being a member of industrialized civilization, but to assign primary responsibility to oneself, and to focus primarily on making oneself better, is an immense copout, an abrogation of responsibility" ~ Derrick Jensen

****

Today, after my morning devotion, God put the following scripture on my heart: "The poor you will always have with you, but you will not always have me" (Matthew 26:11). The scripture is literally about Christ but with deeper meaning. As I was contemplating on the interpretation, I watched this one program where it was mentioned that American Churches are worthy 230 billion dollars in real estates. I remembered that I have been always praying for a multi-million fancy Church building. The Holy Spirit convicted me that I need to have the attitude of Christ, caring most for those things that matter within their time setting. Jesus cared for the poor but He was also time conscious. He was conscious of His imminent departure. I remembered that God's idea of the place of worship for the children of Israel who were on the pilgrimage was a mobile tent that could be easily pulled down. I started to ask myself who will occupy the multi-million Church facilities which we are constructing after we are ruptured? Wouldn't it have been advantageous if we spend the portion of the money that we are investing in constructing the fancy Church buildings on winning the lost souls and caring for the needy. The people of God are the real Church. I mean the un-churched, the hungry, the homeless, those who can't afford to buy a Bible and etc.

****

We, as Christians simply have to rethink this whole emphasis on prosperity gospel that seems to create hope for the poor and hapless, while providing jets and unspeakable comfort to Pastors. Last I checked the forerunners of the modern Church sold all they had to keep the gospel alive and they as well lived extremely simply and rustic lives. Yet, the impact of their lives and message of Jesus Christ has survived well over 2000 years! Now, just a little food for thought on what Gandhi said over half a century ago: Although Hindu, Gandhi had a very close connection with Christianity and admired Jesus very much, often quoting from his favorite 'Sermon on the Mount' chapter in Mathew 5–7. When the missionary E. Stanley Jones met with Gandhi he asked him, "Mr. Gandhi, though you quote the words of Christ often, why is that you appear to so adamantly reject becoming his follower?" Gandhi replied, "Oh, I don't reject Christ. I love Christ. It's just that so many of you Christians are so unlike Christ." "If Christians would really live according to the teachings of Christ, as found in the Bible, all of India would be Christian today," he added.

****

Romans 8:28 says that all things work for good to them that love God. God turns our mess into a message. The Bible says that we are troubled on every side, yet not distressed; we are perplexed, but not in despair; Persecuted, but not forsaken; cast down, but not destroyed (2 Corinthians. 4:8, 9). Life is a journey that never stops no matter how bad things seem to be. So look at your adversity in life positively; it will help you to get better rather than bitter. Always live your life to the fullness of satisfaction and look forward for a better tomorrow because the happiest people don't have the best of everything, they make the best of everything. Remember that success is not a destiny; it is a process. You will never be happy if you continue to search for success beyond now.

****

"You will never be happy if you continue to search for what happiness consists of. You will never live if you are looking for the meaning of life"

~ Albert Camus

****

At times God speaks in the language you know best, not through your ears but through your circumstance. "It is funny when we ask God to change our situation not knowing that He puts us in that situation to change us".

****

Failure and procrastination are evidences of not following instructions. Man despises instructions due to their perception that they know how things ought to work. If you doubt what I am saying just watch people when they buy appliances. Many don't follow the attacked instructions on the guidebook assuming that they already know how they work. God's word is our manual of instruction to successful living. God expects us to be doers of the Word. "Take fast hold of instruction; let her not go: keep her; for she is thy life" (Proverbs 4:13).

****

Tomorrow is an old deceiver, his cheat does not grow stale... "I've never met a poor man who puts value on his time. I've never met a rich man who did not" ~ Dr. Mike Murdock

****

Live life with a great Expectation, Regret looks back, Worry looks around but Vision and Expectation looks up. Those who live with expectation will never be ashamed. If you want to be instructed, put your expectations in Christ. Fear is opposite of Faith, and yet it is the false evidence appearing as real.

****

Life is not a reaction, it is an action. "There are three kinds of people you will meet in life: 1) The Critics: They're the first to point an accusing finger and the last to extend a helping hand. 2) The Cautious: When you're in trouble they'll distance you lest they become tainted by your perceived liabilities. These people are not bad, they're just self-serving. Don't put your trust in them. 3) The Committed: A friend loves at all times, and a brother is born for adversity. Recognize such people and build your life around them because they are a gift from God.

****

Nobody succeeded without being a beginner at some point. Remember the quotation "you don't have to be great to start, but to be great you must start". Don't attempt to build a skyscraper on the foundation for a bungalow. Dig deep and wide and do things right from the outset knowing you're building a giant edifice. Nothing is more beautiful than a real smile that has struggled through tears!!

Stephen Kyeyune

****

High achievers will gain the most out of situations where the probability of success is relatively low and that success becomes a challenge. However a low achiever may see losing in such a scenario as one that promotes a feeling of personal shame from a loss.

****

One who sees inaction in action, and action in inaction, is intelligent among men- Bhagavad Gita

****

"Don't be afraid if things seem difficult in the beginning. That's only the initial impression. The important thing is not to retreat; you have to master yourself" - Olga Korbut

****

A fish will grow to the size of its environment. You cannot grow a shark or any big fish in a small pond. So sometimes the reason why people do not do well is because of the environment they found themselves in. So people want to be big fish but in a small container (environment).

****

Don't depend on anyone in this world, even your own shadow leaves you when the lights go off (in the darkness).

****

High achievers are open- minded. Learn from successful people and those who fail as well. Don't laugh at someone who has fallen because the road ahead of you it's slippery

****

When we work with competent people, we're confident and trusting, knowing they'll deliver quality. Competency begets excellence and builds a strong team. Competency erases any cause for needless anxiety and is good for our mental health, as well as the health of the team.

****

Chickens can't fly like the eagles. My belief about life is that you can make the best out of it regardless of the limitations. Tough time never last but tough people do.

****

God may not have sent that problem, but He wouldn't have allowed it unless He had a purpose for it. God can use disappointments, closed doors, pain and rejection to move you toward your destiny.

****

Want to know the characters of a person, just check on the books they read and their mentors.

****

Amnon the son of David had a friend whose name was Jonadab the son of Shimaeh...and he was a bad influence to him (2 Samuel 13:3). Who is your friend? What kind of counsel does he give when you are not thinking right? Pray that friends like Jonadab in your life's journey shall leave your life. "Your mentor is not necessarily your best friend. Your best friend loves you the way you are, but your mentor loves you too much to leave you the way you are" ~ Dr Sola Fola

****

Hebrews 11:6- "And without faith it is impossible to please God, because anyone who comes to him must believe that he exists and that he rewards those who earnestly seek him." God rewards those who diligently or faithfully seek Him. The Greek word pistis can mean either faith or faithfulness, and many people have noticed that Hebrews often uses it in the sense of faithfulness, or obedience, and it is sometimes hard to tell whether the author is focusing on belief or behavior. (Although Paul occasionally uses the same word in the sense of faithfulness, he usually refers to belief.) Obedience is evidence of belief, and both are needed. To be Obedient is a progressive ongoing requirement (passive). It is unwavering (steadfast) faith. Wisdom is making God's choice your choice perpetually. God demand nothing more or less than our faith. Faith involves trusting the finished works of Jesus Christ. But the evidence of faith is obedience. "Fear God, and keep his commandments: for this is the whole duty of man" (Ecclesiastes 12:14).

****

The secret of success is working hard plus contentment. Be ready to seize the opportunity when it comes. Contentment is the key to ultimate happiness and peace. When you get little, you want more. When you get more, you desire even more. But when you lose everything, you realize little was enough...always remember, greed will bring you nowhere in life...

****

When blessings spring to you from God, you must be creative enough to diversify them into different other channels. As usual, a river sprang from Eden to water the Garden, but right there, it was redistributed into four other channels. "The blessings of God should not be hoarded, but redistributed (Genesis 2:10-14). You are that distribution center from today, in Jesus name!" ~ Olajiede Victor

****

Fulfillment comes from eternal things. Everything in this world is vanity. Vanity is emptiness and frustration at time wasted without fulfillment; it is life apart (separated) from the purpose and conscience of God.

****

Success is different from development. China one of the most populated nation is considered to be developed yet lagging behind.

****

Gloomy seasons of religious indifference and social sin are not exempted from the divine purpose. "When the altars of truth are defiled, and the ways of God forsaken, the Lord's servants weep with bitter sorrow, but they need not despair, for even the darkest eras are governed by the Lord and will come to an end at His command. What seems defeat to us may be victory to Him" ~ Alistair Begg

****

October: Known for Halloween

Halloween (or Hallowe'en ... but also known as Samhain, Summer's End, All Hallow's Eve, Witches Night, Lamswool, and Snap-Apple), is a holiday that's celebrated annually on the night of October 31. It originated in Ireland, and is celebrated in quite a few countries including Ireland itself, the United States, Canada, the United Kingdom, Japan, New Zealand, Australia, Sweden among others. It's celebrated in a variety of ways and activities including trick-or-treating, ghost tours, bonfires, costume parties, "haunted house" tours, carving pumpkins (Jack-o'-lanterns) and reading / watching scary stories / movies.

The many customs we have today in relation to Halloween have their origin in the religious practices of the Romans and the Druids, therefore dating back many centuries. The Romans worshiped various gods, and on October 31, a special feast was held in honor of Pomona, goddess of the fruit trees. Later the Druids, an ancient order of Celtic priests in Britain, made this feast an even more extensive celebration by also honoring Samhain, lord of the dead. This was normally done on November 1 and it was therefore decided to conveniently honor both Pomona and Samhain on October 31 and November 1.

These Druids believed that on the night before November (October 31), Samhain called together wicked souls or spirits which had been condemned to live in the bodies of animals during the year which had just transpired. Since they were afraid of these spirits, they chose October 31 as a day of sacrifice to their gods, hoping they would protect them. They really believed that on this day they were surrounded by strange spirits, ghosts, witches, fairies, and elves, who came out to hurt them. In addition to this, they also believed that cats were holy animals, as they considered them to represent people who lived formerly, and as punishment for evil deeds were reincarnated as a cat. All this explains why witches, ghosts, and cats are part of Halloween today.

Should Christians celebrate Halloween?

Is it OK to allow our kids to participate in HALLOWEEN? The October 31st holiday that we today know as Halloween has strong roots in paganism and is directly connected with worship of Satan. It is the second most celebrated day in America, just next to Christmas. Some Christian families justify participating in it as having fun. I want to warn that Hedonism is the highest form of worshiping. Hedonism a philosophical doctrine that holds that pleasure is the highest good or the source of moral values. All people that worship the false gods do it for their own pleasure. They simply enjoy doing it!

Today, when I went to work on my daily routine, I was surprised by an unusual welcome by managers dressed in costumes handing out apples dipped in chocolate as Halloween treatment. I was aware that it is Halloween Day but I did not expect any special treatment since I do not celebrate this pagan holiday. I was tempted to reject the gift but refrained because it would have been such great embarrassment to the managers. I remembered Paul's teaching on meat sacrificed to idols in 1 Corinthians 9. Idol worship is always wrong, but eating meat sacrificed to idols is a matter of conscience. Halloween is the second most commercialized day in America, just next to Christmas. It is popularly called Satanic Day but the very name "Halloween" means "holy evening"—a throwback to when Catholic Christians prepared for the Feast of All Saints on November 1st. The history of the spooky costumes is unclear. Some sources say they date back to when Christians would dress up like demons—not for fun, but to disguise themselves from the marauding forces of darkness hoping to crash their celebration of their church's heroes. Other sources say the costumes were originally about mocking Satan and his minions. There are plenty of other things to celebrate this time of year: Reformation Day - on November 1, the beauty of fall's changing colors, and as always, the sovereignty of God over everything.

November is dedicated to praying:

The National Day of Prayer is an annual day of observance held on the first Thursday of May, designated by the United States Congress, when people are asked "to turn to God in prayer and meditation". Each year since its inception, the president has signed a proclamation, encouraging all Americans to pray on this day. On June 12, 1775, the Continental Congress called on the colonists to set aside July 20, quote, "as a day of public humiliation, fasting and prayer; that we may, with united hearts and voices ... confess and deplore our many sins; ... humbly beseeching him to forgive our iniquities, to remove our present calamities." It even called for everyone to "abstain from servile labor and recreations."

George Washington later proclaimed a national day of prayer "as a day of fasting, humiliation and prayer ... to deprecate deserved punishment for our Sins and Ingratitude, to unitedly implore the Protection of Heaven." And during the Civil War, President Lincoln, designating "a day for National prayer and humiliation," wrote, "it is the duty of nations as well as of men, to own their dependence upon the overruling power of God, to confess their sins and transgressions, in humble sorrow, yet with assured hope that genuine repentance will lead to mercy and pardon; and to recognize the sublime truth, announced in the Holy Scriptures and proven by all history, that those nations only are blessed whose God is the Lord." These are powerful words! What's that noise? Oh, sorry—I'm just imagining the shrieking if a president today uttered such beliefs!

Lincoln. He continues "We have been the recipients of the choicest bounties of Heaven. We have been preserved, these many years, in peace and prosperity. We have grown in numbers, wealth, and power as no other nation has ever grown. But we have forgotten God. We have forgotten the gracious hand which preserved us in peace, and multiplied and enriched and strengthened us; and we have vainly imagined, in the deceitfulness of our hearts, that all these blessings were produced by some superior wisdom and virtue of our own. Intoxicated with unbroken success, we have become too self-sufficient to feel the necessity of redeeming and preserving grace, too proud to pray to the God that made us! It behooves us, then, to humble ourselves before the offended

Power, to confess our national sins, and to pray for clemency and forgiveness." Now those were words of substance!

As we discussed, In 1952 Congress proclaimed an annual National Day of Prayer, and in 1988 it was assigned to be on the first Thursday in May. So now it's on the annual calendar: Presidents make lofty proclamations, and religions promote it with diverse events. Here's the problem: When a call to devote ourselves to prayer becomes routine, based on designated dates, then we have institutionalized spiritual form and sacrificed spiritual substance. Humbling ourselves, praying in sincerity and truth, seeking God's face, and turning from wicked ways is the stuff of substance. It's deeply personal; it's from the heart; it's genuinely repentant and ready to change. It's not form, and it's not done by formula—an annual routine on a designated date.

A word of warning about the National Day of Prayer coming up this week: Not all things religious impress God, and not all things religious are spiritual. Don't get me wrong—we desperately need to turn to God in prayer! The shocking truth is that God receives only the prayers from sincere hearts. As for the skeptical people the Bible clearly says that, "These people draw near to Me with their mouth, and honor Me with their lips, but their heart is far from Me. And in vain they worship Me, teaching as doctrines the commandments of men" (Isaiah 29:13). Can we be in the same boat?

It always makes me uncomfortable whenever we jointly unite with the false prophets of the worldly religions to pray on the National Day of Prayer. The Bible instructs not to equally be yoked with the nonbelievers. It is wrong when we fellowship with them and sacrifice at the same altar. Jeremiah 2:11: "Hath a nation changed their gods, which are yet no gods? but my people have changed their glory for that which doth not profit" Although the word "nations" is often used in reference to heathen nations, in this scripture it is used in reference to God's chosen people who were custodians of the ordinances of the true living God. During biblical times the heathen nations protected their gods without a possibility of exchanging them. In fact regarding any war, victory was not declared until the gods of the nation were captured and taken as trophies. Exchanging the true God with the heathen gods is an issue of moral decadence. One way we commit this grave sin is when we join the false prophets in joint prayers. But, in a lapse of faith, and no doubt in condescension to pressure from the masses we have compromised our values and watered down the demands of covenant worshiping. It is like acknowledging their false gods. Tolerance does not mean compromising our values. We are priests to the Most High God that commanded us to sacrifice to Christ alone through repentance. It is His perfect blood alone that can sanctify us before God. The world religions are not specific regarding their sacrifices but we are! We are called to sacrifice by repenting our sins to Christ. It is His blood alone that atones for our sins.

The Bible says that "If my people, who are called by my name, shall humble themselves, and pray, and seek my face, and turn from their wicked ways; then will I hear from heaven, and will forgive their sin, and will heal their land" (2 Chronicles 7:14). Look carefully... God requires FOUR things from His people: Humble themselves; Pray; Seek My face; Turn from their wicked ways. And if God's people will do these four things, then and only then will God do these three things: Hear from Heaven; Forgive their sin; Heal their land. *"If my people"*..... Can the church be considered to be God's people. Of course, Yes. *"who are called by my name"*..... Is the church called by God's name? Undoubtedly. *"shall humble themselves, and pray, and seek my face, and turn from their wicked ways"*.....Are there any New Testament teachings that would indicate the church should not "humble themselves" or "pray" or "seek God's face" or "turn from our wicked ways"? Certainly not. These admonitions are ALL repeatedly taught throughout the New Testament epistles.

The calling to pray is for the spiritual body of Christ alone. Joining the false prophets on the National Day of Prayer is not biblical. It is akin to recognizing their sacrifices before their gods. Then we feel good about ourselves thinking we've done something very spiritual! Jesus Himself warned of having a false sense of spiritual security based on form without substance. It's not to say that calls to national prayer cannot be of substance.

The Bible says that we are in this world but not of this world. It means that our new nature is not compatible to this world. The world is not what we are fighting for but it is what we are fighting against. We are constantly in a spiritual battle which we can only win when we are on our knees. Jesus Christ fights for us but our commitment to our relationship with Christ can only be strengthened by praying. There can be no effective communication with God without praying.

Praying is communicating with God. Our intimate relationship with God is proven by our direct communication with God. According to Pastor Alistair Begg, distance and separation were marks of the old covenant. When God appeared even to His servant Moses, He said, "Do not come near; take your sandals off your feet"; and when He revealed Himself on Mount Sinai to His own chosen and separated people, one of the first commands was, "You shall set limits for the people all around." In the sacred worship of the tabernacle and the temple, the thought of distance was always prominent. The majority of the people did not even enter the outer court. Into the inner court none but the priests might dare to intrude, while into the innermost place, or the holy of holies, the high priest entered but only once in the year. It was as if the Lord in those early ages was teaching man that sin was so utterly loathsome to Him that He must treat men as lepers put outside the camp; and when He came closest to them, He still made them feel the extent of the separation between a holy God and an impure sinner.

The Tabernacle was a place of worshiping and praying. The holy of hollies was separated from the rest of the tabernacle because that is where the presence of God was encountered. When the Gospel came, we were placed on quite another footing. The word "Go" was replaced with "Come"; distance was replaced with nearness, and we who previously were far away were brought near by the blood of Jesus Christ. Incarnate Deity has no fire wall around it. "Come to me, all who labor and are heavy laden, and I will give you rest" is the joyful proclamation of God as He appears in human flesh. He no longer teaches the leper his leprosy by setting him at a distance, but by Himself suffering the penalty of the leper's defilement.

When worshiping the holy God, it's not just the altar that is important but also the sacrifice. "Oh let thy blessed sacrifice be mine, And sanctify this altar to be thine." This scripture captures the meaning of the unadorned altar. Examine it carefully to see if it is the expression of your heart. Divine initiative is the theme. A prayer for mercy seeks the redemption to be found in Christ's atoning sacrifice. A prayer of consecration asks the Lord to set apart our lives for His purpose.

What a state of safety and privilege is this proximity to God through Jesus! Do you know it by experience? If you know it, are you living in the power of it? This closeness is wonderful, and yet it is to be followed by a greater nearness still, when it shall be said, "The dwelling place of God is with man. He will dwell with them, and they will be his people."4 Lord, haste the day!

1) Exodus 3:5 2) Exodus 19:12 3) Matthew 11:28 4) Revelation 21:3

Scrolling through my daily sermons about Praying:

Lord's Prayer: Luke 15:18 - This prayer begins where all true prayer must start, with the spirit of adoption: "Our Father." There is no acceptable prayer until we can say, "I will arise and go to my Father."1 This childlike spirit soon perceives the grandeur of the Father "in heaven" and ascends to devout adoration, "hallowed be your name." The child lisping, "Abba, Father" grows into the cherub crying, "Holy, holy, holy." There is but a step from rapturous worship to the glowing missionary spirit, which is a sure expression of filial love and reverent adoration-"your kingdom come, your will be done, on earth as it is in heaven."

Next follows the heartfelt expression of dependence upon God - "Give us this day our daily bread." Lord's Prayer: Next follows the heartfelt expression of dependence upon God- "Give us this day our daily bread." God's provision is guaranteed for our daily meals. This is a prayer of gratitude and thanksgiving. Gratitude unlocks the fullness of life. It turns what we have into enough, and more. God's guidance and provision is the mechanism that sustains our very existence. Prayer is not a "spare wheel" that you pull out when in trouble, but it is a "steering wheel" that directs the right path throughout the journey.

Being further illuminated by the Spirit, the one praying discovers that he is not only dependent but sinful; so he cries for mercy, "Forgive us our debts, as we also have forgiven our debtors". The man who is really forgiven is anxious not to offend again; the possession of justification leads to an anxious desire for sanctification. "Forgive us our debts"- that

is justification; "Lead us not into temptation, but deliver us from evil"-
that is sanctification in its negative and positive forms. Forgiving is the
condition of being forgiven. And being pardoned, every man should have
a fair sized cemetery in which to bury the faults of his friends. And being
pardoned, having the righteousness of Christ imputed, and knowing his
acceptance with God, he humbly prays for holy perseverance, "Lead us
not into temptation." It is God testing us to prove that we can pass the
tests, and God protecting us from the snares of the enemy. David prayed
that "Search me, O God, and know my heart: try me, and know my
thoughts" (Psalm 139:23). The word "Try" was used in the context of a
metallurgist who would take impure metal and remove the impurities.
David is asking God to test him and remove anything that is impure
in order to be stronger when the testing is over.

As the result of all this, there follows a triumphant ascription of praise,
"For yours is the kingdom and the power and the glory, forever. Amen."
We rejoice that our King reigns in providence and shall reign in grace,
from the river even to the ends of the earth, and of His dominion there
shall be no end. So from a sense of adoption, up to fellowship with our
reigning Lord, this short model of prayer conducts the soul. Lord, teach
us then to pray.

Lord's Prayer: As the result of all this, there follows a triumphant
ascription of praise, "For yours is the kingdom and the power and the
glory, forever. Amen." We rejoice that our King reigns in providence and
shall reign in grace, from the river even to the ends of the earth, and of
His dominion there shall be no end. So from a sense of adoption, up to
fellowship with our reigning Lord, this short model of prayer conducts
the soul. Lord, teach us then to pray.

Doxology is a usually liturgical expression of praise to God. Ephesians
3:20, 21 is referred to as a doxology. "Glory to God whose power,
working in us, can do infinitely more than we can ask or imagine:
Glory to him from generation to generation in the Church and in Christ
Jesus forever and ever. Amen." God gave you 86,400 Seconds Today.
Have you taken just a second to say 'Thank You God'? __ We rejoice
that our King reigns in providence and shall reign in grace, from the
heaven to the ends of the earth, and of His dominion there shall be no
end. Praising moves us from glory to glory: From a sense of adoption,

up to fellowship with our reigning Lord. There is only one way to maintain intimacy with God; it is by remaining in His presence. I want to conclude this subject by saying that when the disciples of Jesus asked Him that "Lord, teach us to pray." He gave them the Lord's Prayer as a model of prayer. Praying works; but it is also a work. You must therefore pray.

****

As a Christian, what do you think of not praying? Old Testament Samuel considered not praying as a sin against God. Do you think he was right? Think about it: to live a life without praying is to be disobedient to the command of God, for the attitude and habit of prayer is encouraged and even commanded throughout the Bible. Praying is the practical expression of the existing relationship between the Creator and His creation. We approach the heavenly throne and experience heaven on earth when we communicate with God through prayers. Not praying reveals a sick, tragic condition of that Christian's heart and life. It indicates an ego problem, reveals a smug, "I'm in control" attitude, a moral laziness, even a spirit of unbelief and a preoccupation with worldly things.

****

Matthew 5:45 – "For he makes his sun to rise on the evil and the good, and sends rain on the just and the unjust." The just are the sons of God who were justified by Christ. The unjust are the non-repented sinners. God answers the prayers of the just because they are entitled to the things of God. But when God answers the prayers of the unjust, He does it out of His mercy. I compare it to the bank giving out money. When a customer comes to withdraw the money he is entitled to the money because he deposited it into the account. But the same bank may give money in form of donations to charities and other people who are not under obligation to receive money from the bank.

****

Satan is called the accuser of the brethren. He accuses us by stealing our testimony of Christ. But we have we have the concrete partnership in the person of Jesus Christ interceding for us. He knows our weaknesses but he wants us to join Him in intercession by praying. Satan can only succeed when you let him steal your spiritual potentials and powers embodied in your prayers. Peace eludes those who do not pray. Today's prayer is against the evil devices of the adversary. We pray to the Father, in the name of the Son, against the enemy.

****

We confess our sins to Christ because He is our High Priest (Hebrews 4:14). Alternatively, the Bible instructs us to confess our sins to each other because we are a community of priests (1 Peter 2:9). We do not have to go to a priest (clergy) to confess our sins. Sincere confession that is not superstitious makes it right with God and with the neighbor. This is authentically the right way of opening the wound for healing rather than casually covering it with a bandage. "The foundational beliefs of Christianity can essentially be summarized into this one statement: Loving God wholeheartedly and loving others fervent (Matthew 22:37-40). Just as the cross of Christ is comprised of two beams, one vertical and one horizontal, so is your life defined by your vertical love for God and your horizontal love for others." Jesus accentuated the necessity to reconcile by saying that He will not accept the sacrifice of the worshiper that holds a grudge against his neighbor. "Leave there thy gift before the altar, and go thy way; first be reconciled to thy brother, and then come and offer thy gift" (Mathew 5:24).

****

We worship before the throne of God in heaven. Isaiah says that, "In the year that King Uzziah died, I saw the Lord, high and exalted, seated on a throne; and the train of his robe filled the temple" (Isaiah 6:1). Isaiah was not alone in seeing God's throne. Almost everyone in the Bible who had a vision of heaven, was taken to heaven, or wrote about heaven spoke of God's throne. The prophet Michaiah saw God's throne (1 Kings 22:19), Job saw God's throne (Job 26:9), David saw God's throne (Psalm 9:4 and 7, 11:4), the Sons of Korah saw God's throne (Psalm 45:6, 47:8), Ethan the Ezrahite saw God's throne (Psalm 89:14), Jeremiah saw God's throne (Lamentations 5:19), Ezekiel saw God's throne (Ezekiel 1:26, 10:1), Daniel saw God's throne (Daniel

7:9), and the Apostle John saw God's throne (Revelation 4:1-11). In fact, the book of Revelation may as well be called "the book of God's throne," because God's throne is specifically mentioned more than 35 times in that book!.

****

Sacrifice is the highest form of worshiping. Worshiping benefits us spiritually and emotionally. When Abraham went on the mountain to sacrifice his son, he was most probably a sad man. But he walked down the mountain the happiest man!

****

This weekend choose to go to a full gospel teaching Church. A Christian that does not fellowship with other believers at Church is compared to a person whose relationship is limited to texting and phone conversation only. Such relationship lacks an essential element of physical contact that can be obtained only by talking face to face with a person that you claim to love. God wants to have value time with us and with others whom we share the body of Christ. The Bible warns us against the danger of forsaking the assembling of the saints as the habit of some is (Hebrews 10:25).

****

Weekend is Church time. It is not just socializing but it is like the break after the first half of the football game whereby the players correct the mistakes made in the first half in order to turn the tables against the opponents in the second half. The resting on the Sabbath is time-out intended to correct our failures in the past week in preparation for a new week. We do it by meditating on the Word in search for obedience. The end is not in meditating but rather in obedience. The Sabbath is an opportunity of renewing our minds and getting us back on the right track. Yesterday I was reading about golden eagles that winter in West Virginia and summer in Canada. They migrate along the mountain ridges in Pennsylvania to take advantage of very distinct, airborne pathways with buoyant updrafts. This allows them to soar and glide with little effort. But those eagles had to find and choose the right track for them.

****

One of the visible evidences of a born again person is Church fellowship. Although not all people that attend Church services are born again, it is impossible to be born again and lack the passion of fellowshipping with other believers with whom you share the same body (body of Christ). A born again person feels missing the other part of himself or herself whenever he or she is away from other believers. It is not a yearning that one expects to be fulfilled because we are fulfilled in Christ. It is that sorrow brought about by the longing to be among the faithful. Perhaps the right word to use is 'nostalgia'. "The Greek word for "return" is nostos. Algos means "suffering." So nostalgia is the suffering caused by an unappeased yearning to return." Not to mention that Church fellowship is the key to our spiritual discipline and serving. The Bible instructs us that: "Not forsaking the assembling of ourselves together, as is the manner of some, but exhorting one another, and so much the more as ye see the Day approaching" (Hebrews 10:25).

****

Worshiping is praying but praying is broader than worshiping. God chose the nation of Israel and instructed them how to approach His most holy place (holy of hollies). Whatever happened to Israel in the physical is experienced by the Church spiritually. God is connected to a fallen man by grace, and we are connected to God by our faith. The Church is spiritual but functions in the natural world with supernatural capabilities. The Church is made up of the departed saints in heaven and living saints on earth. When we worship God on earth we join the saints in heaven to worship God at the heavenly throne. If you do not fellowship, chances are you are not part of the Church.

****

Today, people's choice of the place of worship depends on its magnificent. But God instructed Moses to build for Him an altar that is not superlative: "Make an altar of earth for me and sacrifice on it your burnt offerings and fellowship offerings, your sheep and goats and your cattle. Wherever I cause my name to be honored, I will come to you and bless you. If you make an altar of stones for me, do not build it with dressed stones, for you will defile it if you use a tool on it. And do not go up to my altar on steps, lest your nakedness be exposed on it.'" (Exodus 20:22-26). This is intriguing and seldom command that broadens the prohibition against idolatry. Does the divine stipulation against dressed stones and a raised platform apply only to the Israelites in the wilderness or is there a principle implied in this command that applies to our worship of God today? At times God's presence is experienced in despicable places. The manger and the rugged cross are not coincidental. Have a blissful Sabbath please.

****

No man meets God and remains standing upright on his feet. When Jesus revealed Himself to the people who were against Him all of them fall on the ground: "When Jesus said, "I am he," they drew back and fell to the ground" (John 18:6). The same thing will happen when Jesus appears at His Second Coming. All those who are against Him will fall down to their knees. The Bible says that "At the name of Jesus every knee should bow, in heaven and on earth and under the earth" (Philippians 2:10).

****

Praise God for His wonderful works. Psalm 139:14-16: I praise you because I am fearfully and wonderfully made; your works are wonderful, know that full well. My frame was not hidden from you when I was made in the secret place, when I was woven together in the depths of the earth. Your eyes saw my unformed body; all the days ordained for me were written in your book before one of them came to be. He gave you DNA, which is the code contained in your cells describing your every feature. He created in us a sophisticated DNA coding for human cells. The nucleus of each cell contains over 30,000 multi-tasking genes, which are the genetic code for the formation of your entire physical structure, with all of its unique features. Your DNA is God's code for your individual features, characteristics, and tendencies. "You cannot change your body very much positively, only negatively"

****

Jesus said that, "We worship what we do know, for salvation is from the Jews." (John 4:22). Worshiping God begins with salvation: In the Old Testament the presence of God dwelt in the mobile tent (Tabernacle). The Bible says that we are the (Temple) tent of God: "Do you not know that you are God's temple and that God's Spirit dwells in you?" (1 Corinthians 3:16). When a person is born again, God moves in and God is at home in the temple (tent) He made with His own hands. Like a mobile tent (Tabernacle), we move with Him wherever we go. He is in us purposely to guide us to places where He wants to be. His glory is established wherever He is and that place is marked by His name. What you worship determines where you go and what you do. We are caught up in worship wherever we are because God is worshiped wherever He is!

****

Worshiping is ascribing all worthiness to God. It is surrendering all our nature to all that is valuable. Idolatry is ascribing worthiness to the valueless. The word worship is used about 158 times in the Bible. The first time the word worship was used in the Scriptures it was in reference to sacrifice in Genesis 22:5. Abraham thinking to sacrifice takes all he had (his son of promise Isaac) and lays him down on the altar before God in an act of worship. Life is all about worshiping. Sacrificing makes worshiping worthwhile. It is not just praising but the sacrifice of praises; it is not just loving but loving sacrificially; it is not just giving but giving sacrificially and etc. Paul said that "I beseech you therefore, brothers, by the mercies of God, that you present your bodies a living sacrifice, holy, acceptable to God, which is your reasonable service" (Romans 12:1). Everything including our lives belongs to God but God accepts only a perfect sacrifice. A sacrifice dies at the altar. We are living sacrifices but called to die to our old nature constantly. We do not change into a perfect and holy sacrifice overnight. It is a process of persevering with all steadfastness to present our bodies holy and acceptable to God. Begin transforming your body today by the renewing of your mind in Christ Jesus our Lord.

****

Worshiping takes place before the highest heavenly altar of the throne God. Singing prepares us to go there. Praising takes us there.

****

Paul writes to concerned believers while he is under house arrest in Rome (Philippians 1:18). The word joy occurs 16 times in its various forms in the letter. Spiritual joy, rejoicing in Christ, is a major theme. "I will continue to rejoice," "There will be always a need to rejoice when the greatest feeling of happiness and prosperity is in the dimension of our eternity" ~ Olirah O.B.

****

Everything you are going through is much smaller than your God. The question is do you know how big your God is? The most important thing is what comes in your minds whenever you think about God. Every spiritual breakthrough hinges on your understanding of God. No believer can rise any higher than their worthy thoughts of God. High view of God leads to higher worship of God. God is worshiped because of who He is: I mean His sovereign will, His infinite knowledge and wisdom, His majesty and power, the splendor of His glory, His holiness and His inexhaustible grace. Many people embrace what has been called "moralistic therapeutic deism," a view of God that says He exists to make us feel good about ourselves, and that He involves Himself in our lives only to affirm us and solve our problems. "As long as we do not properly grasp the transcendent majesty and holiness of God, our light will not pierce the darkness." ~ Dr. Steven J. Lawson

****

Worshiping is rendered to God alone. A good worshiper does not seek to impress people but motivates them to worship. When you are worshiping God you do not have an audience but God.

****

Worshiping God is to know Him and to make Him known. Worshiping is for saved people who are washed by His blood. Worshiping and working for Christ go together. When I see the believers that do not work for God, I do not doubt their salvation but for sure I doubt if they truly worship God. I pray that you ask God to teach you to truly worship Him.

****

The unseen and invisible victory of Jesus over cosmic evil on the cross is yet another reason why Jesus alone is qualified to receive from the Father all honor and power and glory. Jesus is the Lamb of God crucified from eternity. The Bible says that "All people living on earth will worship the beast, except those whose names were written before the creation of the world in the book of the living which belongs to the Lamb that was killed" (Revelation 13:8). God is not limited by time. The people whose names had been written in the Lamb's book of life before the creation of the world are those whom Christ foreordained and predestined to redeem by his blood (Revelation 5:1-14; 1 Peter 1:17-20). Satan's destruction, too, was accomplished on the cross, outside of time. What happened at Calvary is basically in the eternal time-frame. God's plan for salvation therefore cannot be swatted by any natural means because it originates from eternity, though it is revealed to us at God's appointed time on our earthly calendars.

****

Isaiah 53:2 – "When we see him, there is no beauty that we should desire him." According to Alistair Begg, the superlative beauty of Jesus is all-attracting; it is not so much to be admired as to be loved. He is more than pleasant and fair--He is lovely. Surely the people of God can fully justify the use of this golden word, for He is the object of their warmest love, a love founded on the intrinsic excellence of His person, the complete perfection of His glory. Our love is not as a seal set upon His heart of love alone; it is also fastened upon His arm of power, nor is there a single part of Him upon which it does not fix itself. We worship His whole person with the sweet fragrance of our fervent love. We would imitate His whole life and character. All earthly suns have their spots: This fair world has its wilderness; we cannot love the whole of the most lovely thing. But Christ Jesus is gold without alloy, light without darkness, glory without cloud.

****

This weekend go to Church with an attitude of thanksgiving. If you think it is not worthy to be thankful for the little you have received; be thankful for what you escaped. Thank God for what could have happened but didn't because of His swift grace. "The talent for being happy is appreciating and liking what you have, instead of what you don't have" ~ Woody Allen

****

Begin the week with enthusiasm. Pray about everything. There is no little thing that does not require prayers. After praying, quit worrying. An intimate man with God is never intimidated by man. When you kneel before God, you can stand tall before any man and against any situation. Praying invites God on board to tackle your adversity on your behalf. Remember that there is no failure more disastrous than the success that leaves God out.

****

Jesus defeated Satan and gave us the same power to overcome temptation. Satan is powerless until you yield to sin. It means that whenever the believers compromise on the truth and yield to sin, they surrender their godly ordained authority that is already at their belt to Satan. When sin steps into your life, the peace of God exits; you can't have both at the same time. There are different levels of temptations. At times we need the covering of God in order to overcome certain temptations. That is why praying is very important. Praying is admission of one's weakness. Prayer is putting oneself in the hands of God's protection.

****

The Bible says "In the same way, the Spirit helps us in our weakness. We do not know what we ought to pray for, but the Spirit himself intercedes for us through wordless groans" (Romans 8:26-27). Praying is seeking understanding even concerning the very things that we assume to know. It is in your best interest to pray in order to be filled with the knowledge of his will in all spiritual wisdom and understanding.

****

Neglecting to pray makes a Christian poorer, but also not praying robs others of blessings. The sins we commit can be avoided by praying. It is impossible to perpetually overcome temptation without praying. Satan knows our weaknesses and he has a habit of attacking us at our weakest points. But God turns our weaknesses into strength. God moves in to change us when we are broken. Unfortunately, some believers pray less or even abandon praying when things are moving on well with them. Ironically, this is exactly the right time when we are most vulnerable to satanic attacks. This is the time we should run to God but not away from God.

****

1 Kings 8:28 - "Yet have thou respect unto the prayer of thy servant, and to his supplication, O LORD my God, to hearken unto the cry and to the prayer, which thy servant prayeth before thee today". Make an agony of prayer, and before long a blessed answer will be sent from heaven because God is in the business of answering each and every prayer of His children. The rewarding may be contrary to our expectations but it is the best answer to our prayer. Most of us do not readily accept "NO" as an answer to our prayer requests, yet in accordance to God's infinite wisdom, judgment and foreseeing, it is the greatest answer we need. We can count on this truth that God answers all of the prayers for His children. In the economy of God, there is no such a thing like unanswered prayer.

****

We are called to pray even over those prayers which are already rewarded. The greatest work that Jesus came to do is to die for our sins with assurance of resurrection. Yet He prayed that, "For thou wilt not leave my soul in hell; neither wilt thou suffer thine Holy One to see corruption" (Psalms 16:10). One third of the prophetic scriptures concerning the coming of Jesus focus on His Second Coming. Yet Jesus asked us to pray for His Second Coming. There must be praying in progress regarding everything that God accomplishes on earth. Therefore you must pray.

****

Talking to God in prayers should neither be complex nor complicated because the power is not in the words we use but in God who listen to our words.

****

God is omniscient. He knew what we are going through long before we went through them. Praying is therefore not informing God what He didn't know. Praying is asking God to intervene on our behalf in accordance to His will.

****

How you pray and when you pray matter. It is good when praying becomes a tradition but we should never let it escalate into a ritual. Rituals have certain elements that make them spiritual and supernatural - like sacredness, magic and ancestral worship. A ritual is actually a sequence of activities involving words, gesture, objects and performances, which are designed to influence preternatural entities or forces on behalf of the actors' goals and interest. Ritual practices include ghost dance, myths and exhuming the remains of dead persons. These are usually prescribed by the traditions of a community in respect for the entities. But praying is not a ritual; it is the voice of our conscience that God alone can hear.

****

1 Kings 17 - The Early Ministry of Elijah. And Elijah the Tishbite, of the inhabitants of Gilead, said to Ahab, "As the LORD God of Israel lives, before whom I stand, there shall not be dew nor rain these years, except at my word." The drought Elijah prayed for indeed came. He did not pray for rain to come again, even for his own survival. He kept the purpose of God first, even when it adversely affected him. "Elijah was a man with a nature like ours, and he prayed earnestly that it would not rain, and it did not rain on the earth for three years and six months. Then he prayed again, and the sky poured rain and the earth produced its fruit" (James 5:17-18). The name Elijah means, Yahweh is my God.

We see the prayers of a man with integrity. Also, we see the intensity of prayer with persistence.

****

James 5:16 – "The effectual fervent prayer of a righteous man avails much". James says that the effective, fervent prayer of a righteous man avails much; first we need to know the make-up of this type of prayer for it to avail much and there are three; effective, fervent and righteous. Righteousness is of God. Righteous before God means to stand right with God through Jesus Christ. A person with a sincere heart is committed to please God by his faith. Such man that is regularly on his knees and that is rooted in the Word of God can stand against any situation and against any person. "If God is for you no one can stand against you".

****

"Even now," declares the Lord, "return to me with all your heart, with fasting and weeping and mourning." Rend your heart and not your garments. Return to the Lord your God, for he is gracious and compassionate, slow to anger and abounding in love" (Joel 2:12-14). Fasting in accordance to the new covenant is required but it should not be done out of show (bragging), legalism, extremism, ritualism, and bargaining to win God's favor.

****

We find Jesus articulating the three pillars of His faith. In Matthew 6:1–18, Jesus outlines three spiritual disciplines: righteousness (almsgiving), prayer, and fasting (repentance). With each practice, He warns not to practice before people, but rather before "your Father, who sees what is done in secret" (verses 4, 6, 18), who is the one who rewards: "Be careful not to do your acts of righteousness before men (verse 1). ... But, when you give to the needy. ... Then your Father, who sees what is done in secret, will reward you (verses 3,4). And when you pray. ... But when you pray. ... Then your Father, who sees what is done in secret, will reward you (verses 5,6). ... When you fast. ... But when you fast ... and your Father, who sees what is done in secret, will reward you" (verses 16–18).

****

"Every moment of prayer is an investment in eternity and true prayer is a romance of righteousness"

****

The Bible instructs us to pray for our enemies. Today, I chose this prayer for my enemies: "So Haman was hanged on the gallows that he had built for Mordecai" (Esther 7:10). My prayer for my enemy is that he falls into the same trap he sets for me....

****

1 Kings 17 - The Early Ministry of Elijah. And Elijah the Tishbite, of the inhabitants of Gilead, said to Ahab, "As the LORD God of Israel lives, before whom I stand, there shall not be dew nor rain these years, except at my word." The drought Elijah prayed for indeed came. He did not pray for rain to come again, even for his own survival. He kept the purpose of God first, even when it adversely affected him. "Elijah was a man with a nature like ours, and he prayed earnestly that it would not rain, and it did not rain on the earth for three years and six months. Then he prayed again, and the sky poured rain and the earth produced its fruit" (James 5:17-18). The name Elijah means, Yahweh is my God. In the personality of Elijah, we see the prayers of a man with integrity. Also, we see the intensity of prayer with persistence.

****

Solitude is loneliness at its best. Loneliness is a sense of feeling of isolation but solitude is separating from the world in order to be connected with God. Solitude is what you run to as opposed to what you run from. Solitude is silencing the noises of the world in order to listen to God.

****

Stephen Kyeyune

Always talk to God that understands everything you are going through. Most people will tell you that they understand what you are going through even when they had never experienced the pain you are experiencing. "There is the solitude of suffering, when you go through darkness that is lonely, intense, and terrible. Words become powerless to express your pain; what others hear from your words is so distant and different from what you are actually suffering." — John O'Donohue, Anam Cara: A Book of Celtic Wisdom

****

There is nothing like unanswered prayer. God is in the business of answering prayers. The answer may not be compatible to our emotional desires but it is what we need. There are three answers to prayer: yes, no, and wait awhile. It must be recognized that no is an answer. "God is the Master of all things, even the wills that resist His. He always reserves the right to be God and answer our prayers not our way, but His way... When He says "no" it often means He has planned a greater "Yes"." (Commentary from Zondervan Prayer Devotional Bible, NIV, 2004).

****

God is omniscient. He knows everything about us before we pray. The reason we pray is to honor Him with invitation to participate.

****

Our Prayer is not supposed to be directive but direction prayer. Praying aligns our will with God's will. God's generosity is unlimited. He provides in accordance to our needs even before we ask. Don't think of the things you did not get after praying but rather think of the unlimited blessings God gave you without asking.

****

Heaven is synonymous with the unlimited benevolences of God. The word "illimitable," as its root suggests, refers to something without limits, something boundless. "Empyrean" is much the same kind of word. It refers to the celestial, ethereal or heavenly. In the Lord's Prayer, Jesus instructed us to pray that "Your kingdom come. Your will be done on earth as it is done in heaven" (Matthew 6:10). "One can imagine the original creation as a hyper-dimensional realm in which heaven and earth were not separate, but adjoined, overlapping and interlocking, allowing God, a hyper-dimensional Being, to be manifestly present for man to experience in complete intimacy." The Bible says that "For this purpose the Son of God was manifested, that He might destroy the works of the devil" (1 John 3:8). In the last two chapters of Revelation we see heaven coming down to us so that once again God can have intimate fellowship with His children. When heaven comes down, God's children will experience a renewed inhabitance (Isaiah 65:17; Revelation 21). Currently, we experience the renewal of the new heaven and new earth by thirsting for God and overcoming through faith in Jesus.

****

There is a thin diving line between pity and sympathy. How far you go in life depends on your being tender, compassionate, tolerant and sympathetic with the striving and hurting. Pity oscillates between pride and ego. Sympathy is sincere responsive, warm wholeheartedness retrieved by the grace. Sympathy does something about the situation but pity feels sorry, condemns and walks away. Sympathy cries with you but pity leaves you to cry alone. Sympathy steps into the shoes of the victim and shares in the pain, acknowledging that today it is you, tomorrow it is me. Sympathy restores hope but pity deepens into hopeless misery. Pitiful people torment the victims with the approval of their own conscience. When unchecked, their tormenting goes on and on......

****

Praying is asking God what you want others to have. We do pray for mercy; And that same prayer doth teach us all to render the deeds of mercy. – "He prayeth best, who loveth best. All things both great and small; For the dear God who loveth us, He made and loveth all" – Samuel Taylor Coleridge

****

Prayer works because God works. An effective prayer is the one that comes from heaven, and goes back to heaven. It is the prayer that proceeds from the heart of the Father and comes down into the heart of man and then goes back to the Father through the cross. Such prayer is aligned with the will of the Father. Jesus instructed us to pray that, "Your will be done on earth as it is done in heaven".

****

On March 19th 2015, Thursday morning before I wake up, I had a dream when Jesus was visiting His people of all ages with massive healings. He appeared in His spiritual resurrected body. He moved like sweeping winds among His people and He was in control of the situation. Multitudes of people of all ages were receiving their healings. He moved swiftly covering all people could not see Jesus because He was moving everywhere in form of wind spreading to all people at the same time but the people could not see Him. He manifested in a physical form whenever He touched somebody. He identified with whoever He touched; He looked like them. If He touched a young kid, He would appear to be young; if He touched a black person He would appear to be black. I have been pondering about the dream. The Lord convicted me that He wants us to pray so as not to miss our visitation. Every move of God on earth is preceded by people praying intensively. Before the birth of Jesus, Simeon and Anna waited praying in the temple daily for the coming of the promised Messiah. Anna was a widow. Anna had been married for 7 years and her husband died. After her husband died she began serving God in the temple. She was now 84 and was known as a prophetess. She stayed in the temple praying and fasting every day and night. Because she had a close relationship with the Lord, she knew that God had promised a Savior and as she heard Simeon's praises she was available in the temple to see her redeemer (Luke 2:22-28). Before the outpouring of the Holy Spirit 120 faithful believers waited in the upper room praying.

****

At times we are tempted to ask God to give us something even when we know that what we want is in contradiction to the Scriptures. It is a tragedy when God grants to us something that is in contradiction to

His will. God will let us have that thing plus the severe consequences attached to that thing. We all know the story of Abraham when he took Hagar, Sarah's Egyptian slave girl, as his concubine to give him a son instead of waiting for God's promise to have the son by his legitimate wife Sarah (Genesis 16). The mistake of Abraham is still haunting the Israelites today. The Israelites are descendants of Isaac (Sarah's son) whereas the Arabs are descendants of Ishmael (Hagar's son). The Arabs are the traditional enemies of the Israelites up to today. Yes, God forgave Abraham but the scars (being the consequence of his choices) are still fresh.

****

Praying makes a difference. "As it is the business of tailors to make clothes, so it is the business of Christians to pray" ~ Martin Luther

****

Do you know that praying means begging. Begging is the lowest act in our social settings because it is a sign of despair and dependence. Yet, spiritually, praying is the noblest cause because it portrays our dependence on God. I am a certified beggar because I beg from God what man cannot give but what God alone can give supernaturally.

****

If God wanted to mock you, He will grant each and every prayer request you made, and step aside to watch you destroying yourself. Thank God that He did not answer some of my petitions.

****

Praying is like a soldier reporting to duty for instructions. Praying does not change things but God changes things when we pray. Effective prayer is when you allow God to be God.

****

Repenting is turning from your ways to God's way. Surrendering your will is surrendering your life to Christ. It saying that, "Not my will but your will be done". Christ moves in to transform the heart allowing you to see things from eternal prospective. Paul called us to put on the helmet of salvation (Ephesians 6:17). The armor of Christ is for believers. We need the helmet to protect our heads because this is the place where the spiritual battles are fought. Renewing your minds is acquiring the minds of Christ by abiding in His Word perpetually. God anoints the renewed minds to protect us from the snares of the enemy.

****

My philosophy of life is that we make up our mind of what we are going to make of our lives. It is when you come to the point of commitment that you reach the point of grace. We can change our minds but we cannot change our hearts. God alone can change our hearts but after we change our minds. Repentance is the change of the minds.

****

Praying is reporting on duty to be instructed. Meditate on His Word in prayers. If Gods word guides your conscience let your conscience be your guide. Meditation is knowing about God, whereas, acting on the truth is knowing God.

****

Singing to God is a high form of praying. From the songs of Moses and Miriam after the exodus to the songs of the angels and the saints in John's vision of heaven (Exodus 15:1-21; Rev. 5; 15:1-4), the Bible is filled with songs unto our Creator and exhortations to sing His praises. David started praising with instruments at the early age of thirteen. He wrote and composed at least 74 out of 150 Psalms. The book of Psalms is the Jewish book of praising. Music is for meditation, comforting and evangelism. The musician's vocation and the musical arts are part of the dominion mandate. Musicians are regularly and actively engaged in praising and worshiping God. Worshiping is our first obligation. Music brings us together to achieve our obligation to sing, praise and worship God.

****

This weekend go to Church. This weekend go to Church. I often ask people to tell me the most important thing that God required of Adam. Most people say that: "Not to partake of the forbidden tree." Well, it is true but we must not forget that this restriction was given for the benefit of Adam as opposed to God. The most important thing God required from Adam is that simple walk with Him in the evening times (Genesis 3:8). That is why when Adam sinned, his fellowship with God was severed. Walking with God suggests closeness and intimacy and fellowship. Fellowshipping is not a minor thing but the main thing that God requires of you. Don't' miss this weekend to fellowship with other members of the body of Christ (Church).

****

The key to the anointment is brokenness. God's power works in our weaknesses but not apart from our weaknesses. God does not use the mighty but the humble. Never be disillusioned when people fault you. God sees beauty in your humbleness and humility rather than failure. (James 4:6). We approach God humbly when we are on our knees.

****

Not everyone will be happy when you begin to better yourself. Those who are for you will not just celebrate in your triumphs, but they will also pray with you through your tribulations. "Intercession is a calling to all believers."

****

Always talk to God that understands everything you are going through. Most people will tell you that they understand what you are going through even when they had never experienced the pain you are experiencing. "There is the solitude of suffering, when you go through darkness that is lonely, intense, and terrible. Words become powerless to express your pain; what others hear from your words is so distant and different from what you are actually suffering" ~ John O'Donohue

****

Every challenge has an expiry date, but God's blessings do not expire. Real heroes are champions of peace and are judged by their perseverance in tough times when adversity meets integrity. Our dignity is not in what we know but in what we implement. God tests our patience in times trials. Questioning the integrity of God when you are faced with tough times is fatal; it is like testing the depth of the river with both your legs. Never be tempted to do so.

****

"Prayer is not a "spare wheel" that you pull out when in trouble, but it is a "steering wheel" that directs the right path throughout the journey." Praying is counting on the faithfulness of God. "If Jesus undertook to bring me to glory, and if the Father promised that He would give me to the Son to be a part of the infinite reward of the travail of His soul, then, my soul, until God Himself shall be unfaithful, until Jesus shall cease to be the truth, you are safe."

****

Prayer should not be mistaken for grumbling, but a deep heart groaning.

****

Every time is praying time. Certain thoughts are prayers. There are moments when, whatever be the attitude of the body, the soul is on its knees ~ Victor Hugo

****

There is a need to pray even when the body feels reluctant to pray. Look at the reluctant prayer of Jesus: "If it is possible, let this cup of suffering be taken away from me. Yet not my will, but yours be done" (Luke 22:42). God receives our prayers even when we are reluctant to pray. The bottom line is that when you wait to pray only when you want to pray, you might end up not praying at all (prayerless) because the body often inclines towards the old nature(flesh).

****

Praising is reminiscing on the beauty of God. Words can barely describe the goodness of God because of the limitations of our languages. Peter tells us that Jesus is precious, but he did not and could not tell us how precious, nor could any of us compute the value of God's unspeakable gift. Words cannot convey the preciousness of the Lord Jesus to His people, nor fully tell how essential He is to their satisfaction and happiness. "As all the rivers run into the sea, so all delights center in the Lord Jesus. The glances of His eyes outshine the sun: the beauties of His face are fairer than the choicest flowers; no fragrance is like the breath of His mouth. Gems of the mine and pearls from the sea are worthless things when measured by His preciousness." True praises are the overflowing of a transformed heart.

****

As all the rivers run into the sea, so all delights center in the Lord Jesus. The glances of His eyes outshine the sun: the beauties of His face are fairer than the choicest flowers; no fragrance is like the breath of His mouth. Gems of the mine and pearls from the sea are worthless things when measured by His preciousness. Peter tells us that Jesus is precious, but he did not and could not tell us *how* precious, nor could any of us compute the value of God's unspeakable gift. Words cannot convey the preciousness of the Lord Jesus to His people, nor fully tell how essential He is to their satisfaction and happiness. (Alistair Begg)

End of November Month for Thanksgiving:

Thursday, November 28th 2014, is Thanksgiving Day. It is the day that the Christian settlers in America set aside to demonstrate their attitude of gratitude towards God in 1621. In the middle of the American Civil War, President Abraham Lincoln, prompted by a series of editorials written by Sarah Josepha Hale, proclaimed a national Thanksgiving Day, to be celebrated on the final Thursday in November 1863.

We owe so many thanks to God for the blessings He has bestowed upon us and our nation. I am going to quote Dr. Schweikart's thoughts concerning Thanksgiving. His views represent something we have a duty, as heirs of these blessings, to understand and preserve. We're excited to have him here to help set us straight on Thanksgiving's true history.

Dr. Schweikart, who has authored numerous books, including "A Patriot's History of the Unity States" "Seven Events that Made America America," and "48 Liberal Lies About American History," has spent years dispelling distortions about the motives, actions and beliefs of key figures in our nation's past, not the least of which are the Separatists who landed at Plymouth Bay in 1602.

For the typical public school student today, says Schweikart, the story goes something like this: A band of incompetent Englishmen, driven to colonize the New World by the promise of self-enrichment land in Massachusetts and largely die off under the wrath of a North American winter. Only under the generous tutelage of the Native American population, who selflessly assist the invaders, are they prepared for another winter. Thus, the first Thanksgiving was held as a celebration to thank the native population for their life-saving contribution.

The real account, says Schweikart, looks little like this fiction. It involves a people determined to create a profoundly faith-centered society modeled after the Puritan view of life. In pursuit of that end, they instituted an economy based on collectivist principles. It was this substantially communist system, rather than a lack of understanding or competence, which led to Plymouth's "starving time," not unlike that experienced at Jamestown several years prior. Bad economics and public policy, not inability to care for themselves, was what cost the pilgrims so dearly during their first days in the New World, says Schweikart.

By the same token, it was the institution of four previously uncombined tenets, what Schweikart calls the "pillars of American exceptionalism," which led to subsequent prosperity in the upstart colony, and would shape the civilization which soon inhabited the American continent. This unique combination included a people who held to the Christian worldview, specifically its Protestant variation, exercised English Common Law, permitted private property and relied on a free market economy. Nowhere else in the world had these four pillars come together in the way they did at Plymouth. And that combination in this tiny colony of Anglican Separatists largely laid the foundation for the nation to come.

Ironically, the role played the Native Americans resulted from a Christian influence as well, in the person of Tisquantum (commonly called "Squanto"), a Patuxet Indian captured for slavery as a youth, but liberated by Christians and converted to the faith. William Bradford, governor of Plymouth colony, hailed the Christian, English-speaking Squanto as providentially sent to assist the pilgrims in their endeavors and relations with the natives. BreakPoint co-host Eric Metaxas has written the full account of how God used Squanto in "Squanto and the Miracle of Thanksgiving" which you can find at the Colson Center store.

We (believers) have a lot to thank God for. Not just for creating us but for choosing us to be His dwelling place. At best we are but clay, animated dust; but viewed as sinners, we are monsters indeed. As one preacher said that the natural mind unless tamed is compared to a wild beast. A wild animal may be greedy, fierce, or filthy, but it has no conscience to violate, no Holy Spirit to resist. Let it be published in heaven as a miracle that the Lord Jesus should set His heart's love upon people like us. Dust and ashes though we be, we must and will magnify the exceeding greatness of His grace. "Could His heart not find rest in heaven? Does He need to come to these tents for a spouse and choose a bride from the children of men? Let the heavens and earth break forth into song and give all the glory to our sweet Lord Jesus." Alistair Begg

Scrolling through posted sermons on Thanksgiving

Tomorrow we are celebrating the much awaited Thanksgiving Day. Sometimes we have fallen so suddenly and hard that when we try to sing a song of praise -- all the wind has been taken from our lungs. We need to breathe in the fresh air of the Spirit to take that next "breath" and expel a sound that only a loving God hears as beautiful and right to His ears. Every person has a reason to thank the creator of the universe for the gift of life. We who are born again expressively thank God for saving us from His wrath against our sins. The person closest to the gates of hell is the person who looks in the mirror and says "Look at me I am a good person I need no Savior". The person closest to the gets of heaven

Stephen Kyeyune

is the person who looks in the mirror and says "What a wretched person I am, I need a Savior". We are all in this wilderness together BUT some are already in "deserted places" because they rejected God's only offer of salvation. Repentance is an act of surrendering to the Holy Spirit. Jesus conquered by surrendering to the will of God, so do we. The bitter truth is that all of us shall one day stand face to face before Him who created us to answer for all our evil deeds. Jesus died on the cross to pay for the faults of those that put their trust in Him. Are you one of them?

****

America is the richest country in the world because it was founded by settlers who were looking for spiritual freedom unlike the rest of the countries which were founded by self-seekers. The settlers spent nine long weeks on boat on their way to America. And after they reached here, half of them died because of the bad winter climate. They suffered so that we might have freedom to worship. The pilgrimages set up a day to thank God for their safe trip. As for us, Thanksgiving Day is to thank God for using our founding fathers for the spiritual harvest we see today.

****

Good idea to set aside a day of Thanksgiving because we live in the generation of unthankful people who are always complaining. I was introduced to the following teaching that challenged me personally and that has drastically changed me: God equally hates all sins but God did not tolerate the sins of pride and complaining. Satan was kicked out heaven because of pride. The whole generation of the Israelites who were redeemed from Egypt passed away before they could settle into the Promised Land. They had the wilderness experience without experiencing the Promised Land because of complaining. Pride and complaining dethrone God as the Supreme Master. When the Israelites complained it was reported in Hebrew that, "They have equated a servant with his master" (vayedaber ha'am be'elohim uve'moshe – hishvu eved lekono). Pride and complaining are the major causes of rebellion. "If you spend five minutes complaining, you have just wasted five minutes. If you continue complaining, it won't be long before they haul you out

534

to a financial desert and there let you choke on the dust of your own regret." ~ Jim Rohn

****

Hope you all had a great Thanksgiving Weekend. "In the economy of God, none is more impoverished than the one who has no gratitude. Gratitude is a currency that we can mint for ourselves, and spend without fear of bankruptcy."

****

"You've no doubt heard of "Black Friday," the day after Thanksgiving that features, along with countless sales, the more-than-occasional trampling of shoppers by their frenzied peers. In many ways, "Black Friday" has become a bigger deal than Thanksgiving. So much so that many major retailers have announced that they are opening their doors on Thursday. The hope is that the possibility of buying something you don't really need for a little less than you would pay a few weeks later will help people work off the turkey and pumpkin pie and get down to some serious Christmas shopping. The problem is that it isn't Christmas yet—at least not for Christians.

****

"Enter His gates with thanksgiving." It does not please the Lord to see our sad faces. A Christian ought to be of a courageous spirit, in order that the Lord may be glorified when trials are bravely endured. In fact it was the law of Ahasuerus that no one should come into the king's court dressed in mourning. Given the fact, this is not the law of the King of kings, for He said that "Blessed are they that mourn" (Matthew 5:4). We come to Him mourning in anticipation of being comforted. He would rather we put off the spirit of heaviness and put on the garment of praise, for He inhabits our praises (Psalms 22:3).

****

"Joy to the world the Savior is come". Redemption is the central message of the Bible. Joy is synonymous with redemption because it is the restoration of what we lost in Adam by Jesus Christ. Joy is the longing of the soul. Rejoicing is the response of the soul to what God has done. Indeed we who have spiritual insight have a reason to rejoice. Thanksgiving is simply acknowledging our inadequacies that have been filled with the sufficiency of God... Be Thankful

****

"Gratitude is a vaccine, an antitoxin and an antiseptic" ~ John Henry Jawed

****

This week I am determined to be cheerful and happy in whatever situation I may find myself. For I have learned that the greater part of our misery or unhappiness is determined not by our circumstance but by our disposition. Life is not about waiting for the storm to pass. It is about learning to dance in the rain. Let gratitude be the pillow upon which you kneel to say your night prayer. Counting sufferings to be a blessing can transform melancholy into massive cheerful joy and hope. "Hope is like the sun, when you march towards it the shadow you are burdened with will be left behind".

****

"Joy is the serious business of heaven" ~ C. Lewis

****

Weekend is about going to Church. Worshiping is the basic response of the soul towards God's sovereignty and holiness; we worship Him because of who He is. Praising is the sacrifice of thanksgiving because of what He has done > Chorus:

"When I survey the wondrous cross
On which the Prince of glory died,
My richest gain I count but loss,
and pour contempt on all my pride"

****

Chorus: Great is Thy faithfulness, O God, my Father,
There is no shadow of turning with Thee;
Thou changest not, Thy compassions they fail not,
As Thou hast been Thou for ever wilt be.
Great is Thy faithfulness!
Great is Thy faithfulness!
Morning by morning new mercies I see;

All I have needed Thy hand hath provided, Great is Thy faithfulness,
Lord unto me.. .. ..!

December: Celebrating the First Coming of Jesus, in anticipation of His Second Coming.

Advent (from the Latin word adventus, meaning "coming") is considered to be the beginning of the liturgical year also known as the Church or Christian Year for most Churches in the Western tradition. It begins on the fourth Sunday before Christmas Day, which is the Sunday nearest November 30, and ends on Christmas Eve (Dec 24). The weeks leading up to Christmas day are properly called Advent in Western Christianity, from the Latin word adventus, meaning "coming." Adventus was the Latin translation of the Greek word parousis, which the New Testament most often used to refer to Jesus' second coming. In antiquity, parousia, was nomarally associated with the arrival of royalty: that is when the leaders of a city went outside the city gates to meet the Emperor and escort him back into the city as a gesture of honor.

This is in conjunction with our yearning for His Advent (Second Coming). Specifically, yearning for God to fulfill His promises to His people and to set right what has gone terribly wrong. It is the yearning for His appearing in the fullness of His glory as Titus 2 calls it "our blessed hope". This yearning permeates perhaps the greatest of all Advent hymns, "O Come, O Come Emmanuel." This hymn is to commemorate the birth of our Savior (First Coming) but the meaning of the lyrics can be best suited for the Second Coming. The hymn is a paraphrase of parts of the liturgy dating back to at least the Middle Ages. Each verse invokes biblical titles for Christ—Emmanuel, Root of Jesse, Day Spring, etc.—and then rehearses why His people yearn for His presence among them.

Another Advent hymn, "Creator of the Stars of Night," which dates from the seventh century, captures the season's emphasis on both Christ's first and second comings. After expressing the yearning at the heart of the season, it proclaims "Thou, grieving that the ancient curse, should doom to death a universe, hast found the medicine, full of grace, to save and heal a ruined race."

Although we do not believe that Jesus was born on December 25th but the season puts us in mood to proclaim the gospel, taking into account that the nonbelievers celebrate the day equally as the believers. The secular media, radios and television broadcast openly the story of the birth of Christ and play Christmas carols whose lyrics are composed of the gospel.

Scrolling through sermons of the First Coming of Jesus

Luke 1:28 – "The angel appeared to Mary and said, "Hail, you are highly favored, the Lord is with you: blessed are you among women". Mary the mother of Jesus is an important figure in the Christmas story because she is the earthly mother of Jesus Christ. Mary helps us understand modesty and teaches us honesty and piety; but her role should never be over-exaggerated. The Catholics pray through Mary although Jesus specifically instructed us to pray directly to the Father in His name (John 14:13-16; Matthew 6:9). The Catholics and Orthodox Christians claim that Mary remained a virgin all her life, even when the two Gospels and two of the Pauline letters tell us specifically that Jesus had siblings. His four brothers are named and his (unnamed) sisters are mentioned. Mary is so important in Islam that the faith's holy book, the Quran, has a chapter (called sura Mariam) named after her. She is one of the few people mentioned by name in the Muslims' book. The Muslims' prophet, Mohammed, is said to have called her the most blessed of all women. Muslims view the virgin birth of Jesus as a miraculous event and consider him to be an important prophet but not divine. The story of his life is included in the Quran, and Muslims pray for him but not to him, and not to his mother. But Jesus claimed that He is God. "Therefore I said to you that you will die in your sins; for unless you believe that I am He, you will die in your sins" (John 8:24). He claimed to forgive sin, which is a reserved duty for God alone (Mark 2:1-12). In fact, He claimed to be God, and the Jews were ready to kill Him right there! Why? "Because you," they said, "a mere man, claim to be God" (John 10:33). Let every man be a lair but God be true!

****

John 1:46 - "Nazareth! Can anything good come from there?" Nathaniel asked. "Come and see," said Philip. Nazareth was known for immorality. In such an increasingly hostile and secular culture, it was a miracle to find a virgin young lady.

****

The word reincarnation was hijacked by Satan in particular the religious sects in Asia to mean a person or animal in whom a particular soul is believed to have been reborn. Reincarnation is the rebirth of a soul in a new body. It is a Christian doctrine concerning God putting on human flesh. Jesus' existence didn't begin with His birth or conception, but He pre-existed. In the beginning was the Word, and the Word was with God, and the Word was God. He was with God in the beginning (John 1:1-3). Through Him all things were made, and without him nothing was made that has been made. This Word is also called God the Son— in Hebrews 1:8, God Himself addresses "the Son" as "God". To back up "the Word was God" in John 1:1, the Son likewise has all the attributes of Deity (Colossians 1:15-20, Philippians 2, Hebrews 1:3). In Jesus, God took on human nature, so He could die for our sins as a fellow human, taking the penalty we deserve for our sins. One whose birth is celebrated at Christmas was none other than the One who brought the whole universe into existence! Our Creator took on the nature of one of His creatures, a helpless infant.

****

The conception and birth of Jesus are important not because it was the beginning of His life like any of us. Jesus is God, and He has no beginning and no end. The reincarnation marked the beginning of the humanity of Jesus to live among us like one of us. "His name Emmanuel, which being interpreted as God is with us" (Matthew 1:23). He did not cease to be God but He lowered Himself to be contained in the physical body that is subjected to physical limitations to save us. The uniqueness of Christianity is not the reincarnation because by the time of his birth, the concept of God becoming man was widely practiced by other heathen religions in particular in the east. The uniqueness of Christianity is the love of God manifested in His grace. The God who came to save us demanded nothing from us but became the ultimate sacrifice on our behalf.

****

Among the Evangelicals, Joseph is almost a forgotten character that is rarely mentioned in the Christmas story. Although he was the step-father of Jesus, we should not ignore his role as a father figure in the mainstream conservative Jewish community that had zero tolerance for pregnancy outside marriage. He looked beyond the social norms and taboos. He reacted and acted with humility, and God empowered him with much grace as truth. Joseph continued to love in spite of the mystery of the incarnation. In Joseph's response we trace the love of God for the imperfect, as the situation projected. His response demonstrated the inherent dignity of a godly man with a big heart. "Our identity and worth are based on who we are and how we react. We must continue to uphold the truth of Christ while speaking and acting with humility, love and grace." Love came down at Christmas, and Love was born at Christmas to settle in the hearts of all men of goodwill. I mean sacrificial love that takes focus off 'self' and focuses on others. The proclamation of "peace on earth and goodwill to all" is synonymous with the Christmas spirit, conveying an implicit hope, a spirit of generosity and a kindly disposition toward others.

****

The word reincarnation was hijacked by Satan. The Eastern ideas of reincarnation and mysticism are drawing converts from every walk of life. They teach that reincarnation is a person or animal in whom a particular soul is believed to have been reborn. Reincarnation is the rebirth of a soul in a new body. It is a Christian doctrine concerning God putting on human flesh. Jesus pre-existed. His existence didn't begin with His conception and birth. One cannot easily disassociate the doctrine of the pre-existence of Christ from that of his deity, as they are part and parcel of the same teaching. In the beginning was the Word, and the Word was with God, and the Word was God. He was with God in the beginning (John 1:1-3). The 'Word' is capitalized because it is a person. The first phrase clearly presents the eternity of the Word and hence His pre-existence. The second phrase presents the inter-personal relationship of the Logos and God. The Greek phrase pros, translated "with," refers to the existence of communication and fellowship between the Logos and theos. Verse 3 links the eternity of the Word with creatorship. "Through him all things were made; without him nothing was made that has been made." A point that Paul will reiterate in his Epistle, "For in him all things were created: things in heaven and on earth, visible and invisible, whether thrones or powers or rulers or authorities; all things have been created through him and for him. (Colossians 1:16). This Word is also called God the Son—in Hebrews 1:8, God Himself addresses "the Son" as "God". To back up "the Word was God" in John 1:1, the Son likewise has all the attributes of Deity (Colossians 1:15-20, Philippians 2, Hebrews 1:3).

Why did God put on human flesh? Because the entire human race was polluted by the corrupt DNA of Adam. The virgin birth was necessary so that God can take on a human nature in order to provide the perfect sacrifice on our behalf. Since God cannot die, the perfect human nature of Jesus died for our sins, taking the penalty we deserved (wages of sin). One whose birth is celebrated at Christmas is none other than the One who brought the whole universe into existence! Agape Love compelled our Creator to take on the nature of His creatures, a helpless infant!

****

Muslims have a problem with the virgin birth yet they have no problem in believing that Sarah, childless until the age of ninety, is the first matriarch of the Hebrew people. Abraham and Sarah Humanly, biologically, and physically there was no way they could have a son. In the same way the virgin birth was a purely divine act. Grace is the prodigious outreach of God based on God's instinct and act without the intervention of man whatsoever, on behalf of Man. Christmas is a true story about the King stepping off His throne and taking off His kingly royal robes to save His people. This is not an ordinarily king but God putting on human flesh to teach us to be holy and to pay for our sins.

****

This covenant is divine in its origin. "He has made with me an everlasting covenant." Oh, that great word "He"! My soul, consider-God, the everlasting Father, has positively made a covenant with you; yes, the God who spoke the world into existence by a word; He, stooping from His majesty, takes hold of your hand and makes a covenant with you. Isn't this act so stupendous and such an example of condescension that it would overwhelm us forever if we could really understand it? "He has made with me an everlasting covenant." A king has not made a covenant with me-that would be something; but the Prince of the kings of the earth, El-Shaddai, the Lord All-sufficient, the Jehovah of ages, the everlasting Elohim - "He has made with me an everlasting covenant."

****

Grace is the prodigious outreach of God based on God's instinct without the intervention of man whatsoever, on behalf of Man." We receive God's grace by faith; faith is trusting in someone's abilities other than our own abilities. God, the Jehovah of ages, stepped out of eternity to make it possible for me to be adopted in the divine family. The Son of God is God the Son.

****

Mary said to the angel, "How can this be, since I am a virgin?" The angel replied that, "For with God nothing shall be impossible" Mary answered that, "Behold, the bond-slave of the Lord; may it be done to me according to your word." (Luke 1:34-37). God supernaturally opened the minds of Mary to believe the words of the angel. The power God gives to the believers to understand the Bible is on the level of the miraculous. No amount of natural aptitude or scholarship can bestow that ability. God provides to us the ability to understand what the world cannot understand. The problem with the skeptics concerning the virgin birth is their prospective of God. God can do everything except that which is contrary to His nature. For example God cannot cease to be God and He cannot sin. God has the power and ability to perform any act which is consistent with the application of logic and He can defy the laws of gravity. Our human capabilities are a result of His delegated power—the capacity, aptitude, authority, and active effectiveness—for it to be done. Sometimes God works through a person's natural ability or supernaturally bestowing additional power for miracles.

****

Think about the birth of Jesus. It is true that we are born into this world crying and we leave this world crying. We are born crying because of the trauma felt during childbirth and that is to follow in course of travelling the ambiguous journey of life in this world. Our bodies are prisons for our souls until liberated by death. In the same manner we left the wombs of our mothers, we leave our bodies and this world crying because of unfulfilled life lived and the torment of physical and spiritual death that separates a sinner eternally from the presence of God. Jesus was born as a little baby but in Him was wrapped the two natures (divine/human). He cried at birth like any other baby but also for other different reasons: 1) For leaving the heavenly throne and putting on the human flesh that is limited by time and space. 2) The unexpected conception. 3) The fatigue of His parents travelling the ninety miles journey to register according to the decree of Caesar Augustus. 4) At His birth there was no good place to accommodate Him except the manger. 6) He was born as the perfect sacrifice (Lamb of God); he was born condemned with a death sentence hanging around His neck. 7) He came to this world rejected and He left this world rejected. People celebrate our birth and mourn our death but the uniqueness of Jesus is that the world did not celebrate His birth but celebrated His death. By reincarnation He obtained the body to atone for our sins so that we might be reunited with the Father eternally. The lyric of the popular Christmas song: "Joy to the world, the Lord is come! Let earth receive her King" is about His Second Coming. This time He is coming not coming as a little tinny baby in the manger but as the King of kings. The world rejoices in anticipation of His return as King of kings.

****

Luke 2:10-14 - "And, lo, the angel of the Lord came upon them, and the glory of the Lord shone round about them: and they were sore afraid. And the angel said unto them, Fear not: for, behold, I bring you good tidings of great joy, which shall be to all people. For unto you is born this day in the city of David a Savior, which is Christ the Lord. And this shall be a sign unto you; Ye shall find the babe wrapped in swaddling clothes, lying in a manger------And suddenly there was with the angel a multitude of heavenly hosts praising God and saying, Glory to God in the highest heaven, and on earth peace to those on whom his favor rests." Christianity was born as a result of one huge event when heaven invaded earth. Eternity invaded time; truth and justice meet on earth. The shepherds had a glimpse at God veiled in human flesh, with limitations as a little baby because they were positioned near the manger. They were at the right place at the right time. They were the first witnesses to this historical event. They saw the angels and the heavenly hosts descending down worshiping the little baby. This was not just another little baby but the Savior sent from the Father to adopt us into the divine family. The shepherds became part of the Christmas story, but much more the Christmas story became part of them. Christmas is not about a season but it is the peaceful mind set in anticipation of receiving. Child of God, the shepherds were specific recipients of the promise of Christ's First Coming, as we are the specific recipients of the promise of Christ's Second Coming. Are you well positioned to receive? Therefore be you also ready and lift your eyes up: for in such an hour as you think not the Son of man returns (Matthew 24:42-51). In the twinkling of an eye your face will be bright with heaven's splendor as is His countenance and your soul will be filled with heavenly joy just as His soul is.

****

The four songs of nativity: The song of Zacharias Luke 1:67-79; the song of Mary after she received the news (Luke 1:46-55); the song of the angels at the birth of Christ (Luke 2:13-14); the song of Simeon when he took the baby in his arms (Luke 2:28-35)

****

Love, both God's for us and ours for Him, is the subject of the Christmas carols. "Love Came Down at Christmas." Love was born at Christmas. God did Hs part. The only fitting response to this act of love is to return it however imperfectly: "Yet what I can, I give Him—Give my heart."

****

We have been celebrating the earthly birthday of Jesus. Do you know that angels in heaven celebrate birthdays? Angels celebrated the birth of Jesus: "Suddenly a great company of the heavenly host appeared with the angel, praising God and saying, 14 "Glory to God in the highest, and on earth peace to men on whom his favor rests." (Luke 2:13-14). Angels in heaven rejoice when the soul is born in heaven (born again): "In the same way, I tell you, there is rejoicing in the presence of the angels of God over one sinner who repents." (Luke 15:10).

****

We have been in holidays in commemoration of the birthday of Jesus. It is good to celebrate birthdays. Every believer has a second birthday when he or she was born again. But remembering the day you were saved is not a guarantee to salvation. The reason is because God saves in the present rather than in the past. The evidence of those who are saved is their current status of obedience. The Bible says that, ""If you love Me, you will keep My commandments------Whoever has my commands and keeps them is the one who loves me. The one who loves me will be loved by my Father, and I too will love them and show myself to them--- Jesus replied, "Anyone who loves me will obey my teaching. My Father will love them, and we will come to them and make our home with them." (John 14:15-23)

****

The Magi at the time of Christ were aware that a special star would be used by God to announce the Savior's birth to this world. The phrase "wise men," in Matthew 2:1, 7, is Magi (or Magoi) in the Greek original, and applies to members of a special group of men. A class of scholars called the Magi (from which our modern word "magic" is derived) may originally have come from a certain tribe in Media, and may even have later become a part of the governing body of Persia. This is uncertain, but what does appear to be well established is the fact that they were especially interested in astronomy and the prophetic "wisdom" that this talent seemed to give them. They eventually became a sort of priestly caste, and were attached to the royal courts of Babylonia and Persia and even those of more distant lands such as Arabia and India, as consultants and advisers to the nobles of those lands. There is even an ancient tradition that Balaam, the notorious prophet from Mesopotamia, was an early member of the Magi, and perhaps their founder. It was Balaam's prophecy, of course, as recorded in the Bible, that spoke of this future star. Thus Balaam's reluctant, but divinely inspired, prophecy, revealed that a unique Star associated with Israel would accompany a future Sceptre (that is, King) who would eventually rule the world. Here is his prophecy, actually constrained by God to be uttered against the prophet's own will. "I shall see Him, but not now: I shall behold Him, but not nigh: there shall come a Star out of Jacob, and a Sceptre shall rise out of Israel, and shall smite the corners of Moab, and destroy all the children of Sheth, and Edom shall be a possession. Seir also shall be a possession for his enemies; and Israel shall do valiantly. Out of Jacob shall come He that shall have dominion, and shall destroy him that remaineth of the city" (Numbers 24:17-19).

The Magi were quite confident that this coming King was already in the land and that His presence had been announced by God Himself through a star in the heavens. They did not visit the baby Jesus in the manger as portrayed by Hollywood but visited a young kid. We actually do not know the actual number of Magi that came searching newly born king but we know that they came with three kinds of gifts and worshiped Him (Matthew 2:10-12). Gold is a symbol of divinity and is mentioned throughout the Bible. The gift of gold to Jesus the child was symbolic of His divinity—God in flesh. Frankincense is a white resin or gum. It is obtained from a tree by making incisions in the bark and allowing the gum to flow out. It is highly fragrant when burned and was therefore used in worship, where it was burned as a pleasant offering to God (Exodus 30:34). Myrrh was also a product of Arabia, and was obtained from a tree in the same manner as frankincense. It was a spice and was used in embalming. It was to prepare Him for His pending death at the cross as the perfect sacrifice. The newly born King was a threat to Herod. Herod had been appointed "King of the Jews" as his official title by Rome, but here was a delegation from a powerful enemy empire demanding information about someone "born King of the Jews". Herod asked the Magi to show him where the King was born. The Magi were warned in the dream not to go back to Herod as he had requested them. They returned to their country by another route.

****

Isaiah 9:6 - "For to us a Child is born, to us a son is given, and the government will be on his shoulders. And he will be called Wonderful Counselor, Mighty God, Everlasting Father, Prince of Peace." A child is born is in reference to His humanity. A Son is given is in reference to His divinity.

****

Jesus was born in a manger and was first seen by the despised people in the community (shepherds) because humility is integral to His mission. Jesus came to reach out to the people of all classes including the poor. According to Micah 6:8 walking humbly before the Lord is as much a requirement of God as seeking justice and showing kindness. True humility is seeing the poor as those who represent God. God gives us an opportunity to know Him more through the poor and those suffering. Humility is primarily the model we have been given by God. In 1 Corinthians 4 Paul says the Apostles are 'at the end of the procession'. They are 'the scum of the earth'. This is authentic Christian leadership. If you choose to be irrelevant you are not out of touch. You are where most of the world is because the majority of the people are poor and they are not relevant. When we become the scum of the world we become what the poor already are. We must see the poor not as objects of charity, but people from whom we can learn.

****

The Magi never saw the baby Jesus in the manger but visited the young kid Jesus, and took gifts to Him and worshiped Him (Matthew 2:10-12). They missed the manger occasion because they were waiting to be led by the star instead of searching the Scriptures. Sometime between 750-686 BC, Micah prophesied revealing that Bethlehem would be the birthplace of the Messiah (Micah 5:2). And throughout the span of the past 27 centuries, from the days of the prophet Micah up through the present time, Bethlehem is credited as being the birthplace for only one person who is widely known throughout the world. And that person is Jesus Christ. But the shepherds saw the baby Jesus in the manger because they went to search for the baby as instructed by the angels.

They did not sit down and wait for a star. Passion is evidence of faith. People who are highly effective in life are people who are proactive. They do not wait for things to happen; they make things happen. In Christ, God provided everything you need to excel. But you must capitalize on your strengths and take advantage of each and every opportunity out there, and at the same time it is vital to make moral lifestyle choices to mitigate damage caused by your old corrupt nature (flesh). Yes, you are under the divine provision and monitoring but He assigns the primary responsibility to you of making your situation better; it is an obligation. "The safest way to get what you want is to deserve what you want." ~ Charlie Munger

****

"She will bear a Son; and you shall call His name Jesus, for He will save His people from their sins" (Matthew 1:21). It was not left for Mary and Joseph to name the Baby. God named Him Jesus (Yoshua) meaning Savior. He saves us from sin and its consequences. There are at least eight different terms in the Hebrew Old Testament reflecting some aspect of sin. Like "wickedness," "iniquity" and etc. Some thirteen different words in the New Testament similarly depict various shades of sin, e.g., "evil," "unrighteousness," "transgression" and etc. Sin is the breaking of God's laws the consequences of which is death. The human sufferings and the geophysical catastrophes that frequently ravage our globe today cannot be attributed unequivocally to the direct action of God, but they can be traced ultimately to human rebellion, and the permissive will of the Creator. Jesus saves us from the wrath of God against sin. His nature is the new nature regenerated in a believer. It is the resurrected life of Christ that overcame death; it is not subjected to judgment and death. Our new nature is in Christ. This is what it means to be born again. Our bodies (like the whole earth) groan waiting for their redemption (Romans 8:21-22). Even we ourselves, having the first fruits of the Spirit, groan within ourselves, waiting eagerly for the redemption of our bodies.

****

Jesus is the center of time. The Resurrection of Jesus Christ is most certainly the hinge on which the doorway of history swings. History is divided Anno Domini (AD or A.D.) and Before Christ (BC or B.C.). These are designations used to label or number years used with the Julian and Gregorian calendars. The term Anno Domini is Medieval Latin, translated as In the year of the Lord, and as in the year of Our Lord. It is sometimes specified more fully as Anno Domini Nostri Iesu (Jesu) Christi ("In the Year of Our Lord Jesus Christ"). This calendar era is based on the traditionally reckoned year of the conception or birth of Jesus of Nazareth with AD counting years from the start of this epoch, and BC denoting years before the start of the era. There is no year zero in this scheme, so the year AD 1 immediately follows the year 1 BC. The Sacred Scriptures do the same and so we have the Old Testament and the New Testament. In the Old Testament from time to time we get glimpses and hints of Jesus who is to come, in events or people who are pointing the way to Jesus. The New Testament is the fulfillment of the Old Testament. There is one gospel narrating the life of Jesus but presented to us by four writers (Matthew, Mark, Luke and John). The life of Jesus is the hinge on which the doorway of so many lives swing. The destiny of over seven billion people living on the universe today and those who have ever lived on this universe depends on this one man Jesus Christ!

****

The New Testament words for time include one for duration and the other for a point in time. For duration, length of time, the word is chronos. For a point in time, a special day or hour, the word is kairos. Scripture speaks much more about kairos – special times, than about chronos, time itself. 'When the fullness of the time (chronus) was come, God sent forth his Son made of a woman'. Galatians 4:4. God came into time at a special time and brought time to the full. The Timelessness One entered time and made one ordinary day the greatest in the history of the human race. That's the birthday to celebrate! We can relate to it. His coming involves us in greatness. He gives sparkling life to our drabbest days, and makes them occasions. He gave the fishermen of Galilee the greatest fishing day of their lives, and then piloted them in new fishing grounds – the nations of the world. He swept them along in His own victorious and redeeming manifestation. So be it in 2014.

****

None of us can purge (clean) himself or herself of sin. Forgiving sins is God's business. "If our greatest need had been information, God would have sent an educator. If our greatest need had been technology, God would have sent us a scientist. If our greatest need had been money, God would have sent us an economist. But since our greatest need was forgiveness, God sent us a Savior"- Max L Lukado

****

Last Friday I was in a food processing factory with the one of the supervisors when we were surprised by an expected visitor. A glossy black bird (raven) was flying above our heads bumping into the light bulbs, pipes and AC appliances at the ceiling. This was a sensitive area of food processing which required high standard of hygiene. Our heads were covered, our hands sanitized and our closes covered under gown before entering. The bird was most probably running from a very cold climate outside that was below seven degrees and seeking sanctuary inside the food factory. The supervisor out of fear of the contamination of the food by the bird called the quality control dept. for help. They responded by sending a man with a rifle to shoot down the bird because the ceiling was very high. I tried in vain to convince him instead of killing the bird to find other means of getting rid of it. The bird was flying none stop and at time hiding in sensitive areas where it was hard to shoot. I wanted the bird to live but I had no way of communicating to it to stay in the safe zone where it was hard to shoot. I realized that the only way I could have communicated to it was if I was a bird. The same thing applies to us. God had to become like us in order to communicate to us and save us.

****

The unfinished story of Christmas is that Jesus is coming again. He is coming in His sovereign as the King of kings. He is coming to glorify those lives in whom He is glorified now. Only the skeptics doubt the Second Coming of Jesus Christ: "The Bible says that in the last days many scoffers will say, "Where is the promise of His coming? For since the fathers fell asleep, all things continue as they were from the beginning of creation" (II Peter 3:4). A true believer has confidence in the promise of God. No Christian enjoys comfort when his eyes are fixed on falsehood—he finds no satisfaction unless his soul is quickened in the ways of God.

****

The Second Coming of Jesus:

An apocalypse (Ancient Greek: ποκάλυψις apocálypsis, from πó and καλύπτω meaning 'un-covering'), translated literally from Greek, is a disclosure of knowledge, hidden from humanity in an era dominated by falsehood and misconception. The Bible allows us to have a glimpse into the spiritual world that cannot be seen by our natural eyes. 1 Timothy 4:1 - "Now the Spirit speaketh expressly, that in the latter times some shall depart from the faith, giving heed to seducing spirits, and doctrines of devils". The word "some" is not confined to backsliders alone but includes even the active Church goers who will depart from faith by embracing the false doctrines of men inspired by the evil spirits and end up with false hopes. The true doctrine of Christ must be scriptural, clear, evangelical, and practical; well stated, explained, defended, and applied. But these duties leave no leisure for worldly pleasures, trifling visits, or idle conversation. May every believer be enabled to let his profiting appear unto all men; seeking to experience the power of the gospel in his own soul, and to bring forth its fruits in his life.

The Bible allows us to have a glimpse into the spiritual world that cannot be seen by our natural eyes. 1 Timothy 4:1 - "Now the Spirit speaketh expressly, that in the latter times some shall depart from the faith, giving heed to seducing spirits, and doctrines of devils". The word "some" is not confined to backsliders alone but includes even the active Church goers who will depart from faith by embracing the false doctrines of men. Paul warned that in the end times many are going to embrace the doctrines inspired by the evil spirits and end up with false hopes. The true doctrine of Christ must be scriptural, clear, evangelical, and practical; well stated, explained, defended, and applied. But these duties leave no leisure for worldly pleasures, trifling visits, or idle conversation, and but little for what is mere amusement, and only ornamental. May every believer be enabled to let his profiting appear unto all men; seeking to experience the power of the gospel in his own soul, and to bring forth its fruits in his life.

The Bible says that the secret things belong to the LORD our God, but the things revealed belong to us and to our children forever, that we may follow all the words of this law. (Deuteronomy 29:29). God revealed all things pertaining to our salvation but not all things regarding the end times. "But you, Daniel, roll up and seal the words of the scroll until the time of the end. Many will go here and there to increase knowledge." (Daniel 12:4). The Bible deals with the history of man's world from the beginning, across historical time and into our present time and forward until the very end of time as we understand it. You are living RIGHT NOW in Biblical days. The great "I AM" of Exodus 3:14, who spoke to Moses from the burning bush, STILL IS and speaks to us today through His written Holy Word and the Holy Spirit. And, today, that ancient malignant spirit of Satan is also still whispering in the ears of modern man, "Yea hath God said?" (Genesis 3:1)

Scrolling through my posted sermons about Eschatology

Eschatology i/ˌɛskəˈtɒlədʒi/ is a part of theology concerned with what are believed to be the final events of history, or the ultimate destiny of humanity. This concept is commonly referred to as the "end of the world" or "end time". The end of times should not be confused with the end of the world. The end of times began at the ascension. The Bible predicts the ending of this corrupt world and the coming of a new world that is not subject to corruption.

Biblical prophecy provides some of the greatest encouragement and hope available to us today. Just as the Old Testament is saturated with prophecies concerning Christ's first advent, so both testaments are filled with references to the Second Coming of Christ.

About one-third of the Bible is prophecy—history written in advance. Over 80 percent of this future history is yet to be fulfilled. One scholar has estimated that there are 1,845 references to Christ's Second Coming in the Old Testament, where 17 books give it prominence.

We are living in the Church age whereby 95% of the prophecies have already been fulfilled. Fulfilled prophecy is one of the most powerful proofs that the Bible is the Word of God. In the 260 chapters of the New Testament, there are 318 references to the second advent of

Christ—an amazing 1 out of every 30 verses. Twenty-three of the 27 New Testament books refer to this great event. For every prophecy in the Bible concerning Christ's first advent, there are 8 which look forward to His second!

The next event in the series of prophecies is the rapture of the Church. Although the word rapture does not appear in the Scriptures, its meaning is there. In fact some of these 318 references are specific and refer to the Rapture. The rapture is the catching away of the faithful believers. It is compared to having different types of metals (copper, zinc, iron and etc.) on the ground and swing a magnet above the metals. The magnet will attract only the iron because it is of the same kind as the magnet. Jesus is going to take away only those people who share the same nature with Him. They are going to meet Him in the air.

The Second Coming is when Jesus Christ will return to earth in fulfillment of His promises and to fulfill the rest of the prophecies made about Him. Jesus Himself promised, "At that time the sign of the Son of Man will appear in the sky, and all the nations of the earth will mourn. They will see the Son of Man coming on the clouds of the sky, with power and great glory" (Matthew 24:30). Revelation 19:11-12 proclaims this about the Second Coming, "I saw heaven standing open and there before me was a white horse, whose rider is called Faithful and True. With justice he judges and makes war. His eyes are like blazing fire, and on his head are many crowns. He has a name written on him that no one knows but he himself."

I want to share my testimony concerning the rapture. This year (2014), at night, I had this dream concerning the rapture. In my dream it was the seventh day (Sabbath). I saw the cloud coming down and eventually breaking into individual angels. I realized that it was the awaited rapture of the Church. One of the angels came down to talk to me. I told him that thank God it is Sabbath and the day of rapture. The angel instead warned me that I need to be ready and put my house in order if I expected to be raptured. I saw some Christians left behind at rapture for reasons like abandoning their spouses and children and greed for earthly gains. One of the angels insinuated that the greedy materialistic Christians were too loaded with the world stuff to be raptured. The Christians left behind had branches in their hands most probably they were anxiously waiting to be raptured; they were singing "hosanna" but they missed the appointed time because they were not spiritually ready. Some of them relentlessly ministered the gospel to the non-believers left behind but it was a very tough task to preach the gospel because the Holy Spirit (Restrainer) was removed from the earth (2 Thessalonians 2:6). They looked very exhausted and worn out. The nonbelievers who were left behind were preoccupied with fighting for the properties of the believers who were raptured. "Materialism is the great deception of the end times." Then there was severe movement of clouds predicting bad weather (storms, Tornadoes, lightning and other phenomena) but the nonbelievers left behind did not heed in spite of the warnings of judgment by God.

The following Sunday, after I had the dream on the Sabbath (Saturday), was Women's Day at our Church. The pulpit is set aside for ladies but I am humbled to teach Bible study on their day. I decided to give the testimony of the dream I had recently concerning the rapture. But I kept it to myself because I wanted it to be a surprise to my congregation. To my surprise Sister Nancy read "Matthew 13:38-39" as the opening scripture. My eyes opened wide when she read the last portion of the scripture: "---- the harvest is the end of the world; and the reapers are the angels". I never saw it as I did after my experience (dream). In my dream the cloud descended down and broke down into numerous angels. The angels were divided in two groups: The angels in one group were gathering Christians from all corners of the earth whereas the angels in the other group were sorting them out, taking only those who were spiritually ready. According to the Bible (Acts 1:9-11), Jesus will return in the same manner he ascended: "while they beheld, he was taken up; and a cloud received him out of their sight". He was received by the cloud of angels, and He will return with the cloud of the angels. Angels are clothed with a cloud (Rev.10:1).

Those who witnessed Christ's ascension into heaven after his death and resurrection heard the angels declare in Acts 1:11, "Men of Galilee...why do you stand here looking into the sky? This same Jesus, who has been taken from you into heaven, will come back in the same way you have seen him go into heaven." The Second Coming is the literal return of Jesus Christ to earth as King in power and glory to rule for a thousand years (Revelation 20:1-6). The Old Testament prophets did not seem to fully understand this distinction between the two comings of Jesus (His birth and His Second Coming) as seen in Isaiah 7:14; 9:6-7); and Zachariah 14:4. Those who argue that Jesus was not the Messiah because He did not fulfill all the Old Testament prophecies about the Messiah, fail to take into account the Second Coming of Christ, in which He will fulfill all the prophecies about the Messiah. Christ's first coming was to fulfill the Law in the following ways: By observing the Moral Law without breaking any part of it (sinless); by defining to us the meanings of the Moral Law (Ten Commandments); by standing in our place and receive the penalty exacted for sin (wages of sin is death). His Second Coming will defeat sin for all eternity.

The Second Coming should also not be confused with the event referred to as the Rapture. The Rapture refers to a time when Jesus Christ will come to remove all of the believers that are ready for their bridegroom from the earth (1 Thessalonians 4:13-18; 1 Corinthians 15:50-54). The Bible also foretells a supernatural event where many Christians will disappear from the earth and be taken by Jesus to Heaven. This is expected to be just before or during the tribulation and could even begin the tribulation. Some say it could be at the end of the tribulation. (Matthew 24:40, 41, 1 Thess. 4:15-17) The Church holds many positions on the rapture, but the Second Coming is undisputed. The Second Coming is the event when Jesus Christ returns to the earth to defeat evil and establish His reign of justice and peace.

The Bible declares, "No one knows about that day or hour, not even the angels in heaven, nor the Son, but only the Father" (Matthew 24:36). The Bible does not give the specific day of the Second Coming of Jesus but it gives signs and events pointing to His imminent return to the earth. The Bible describes several events which must occur before the Second Coming (Matthew 24:4-29; 2 Thessalonians 2:1-12; Revelation chapters 6-18). So, we are to anticipate the Second Coming, but have a biblical understanding of it. We are not to set dates and times, but live our lives as if it could happen any day, any moment.

Those who are left behind after the Rapture of the Church will be faced with an excruciating choice—accept the mark of the beast in order to survive or face starvation and horrific persecution by the Antichrist and his followers. But those who come to Christ during this time, those whose names are written in the Lamb's book of life (Revelation 13:8), will choose to endure, even to martyrdom.

Signs of end times:

<u>*The Rebirth of Israel*</u>: We know that the Jews were scattered throughout the planet as a result of the Roman conquest, but amazingly they kept through tradition their own people group and their own identity and because they never did merge into the societies they lived in very well. Always anti-Semitism chased them out of country after country. Finally, with the Balfour Declaration in 1917 and then UN Resolution 181 issued in 1947, Israel was allowed to come and take back at least a small part of their land, though not all of the land God promised them, and become a nation once more.

The blossoming of the climate of Israel is prophetic. There is more fruit growing there than you can imagine. Israel is one of the world largest exporters of fruits and vegetables. I think there are over six million people living now in Israel. Supposedly there is actually more rain in Israel than ever before; it is because of the amount of trees and plants they planted which has increased the moisture content. Just as Bible prophecy predicted in Ezekiel 36:34-35, the land has been restored along with the people.

The Bible says that God through the coming Gog-Magog Battle of Ezekiel 38-39 will continue to bring the Jews back into Israel from all the corners of the earth. The persecution will get really bad and anti-Semitism will continue to rise around the planet and force all the Jews into returning back to Israel. This return is a major, major sign that proves to us that we are in the season of the Lord's return.

The controversy over Jerusalem: The return of the Jews to Israel and their control of Jerusalem is what so many in the Bible prophecy community call the "Super Sign." It is what the Bible told us to look out for. When we see this happen, we can know the Lord's return is coming soon. Jesus in the Parable of that Fig Tree said that the generation that sees this return — that's you and me — when we see this we can know that Jesus is coming back very soon. So, wow, we are living in exciting, exciting times! We have discussed that the nation of Israel was reborn in 1948.

That nation completed a generation of forty years in 1988. Second, the Jews now control all of Jerusalem and have since 1967. Right now the fighting between the Palestinians and Israel is mainly over who can control Jerusalem. The Arabs want Israel to withdraw from Judea and Samaria. Much more they want to share control of Jerusalem. They say that they will not rest until Israel withdraws from the old city of Jerusalem. Yet it appears that the Government of Israel is unwilling to let Jerusalem go. The eyes of the whole world are set towards Jerusalem. The Bible prophetically said that, "Behold I will make Jerusalem a cup of trembling unto all the people round about, when they shall be in the siege against Judah and against Jerusalem (Zechariah 12:2-3). This verse assumes that in the final Great War, all nations will be engaged at Jerusalem, but the Lord will defend his people (Israel).

****

The Bible says that in the end times there will be an increase in tribulations. "And ye shall hear of wars and rumors of wars: see that ye be not troubled: for all these things must come to pass, but the end is not yet. For nation shall rise against nation, and kingdom against kingdom: and there shall be famines, and pestilences, and earthquakes, in divers places. All these are the beginning of sorrows" (Matthew 24:6-8).

The Church is the light of the world. After the Church is taken away, the world will be left in absolute darkness. The Church is the life in this world. After the Church is taken away, the world will languish in death. Famine will follow wars as night follows day. Jesus warned that there have never been a time as bad as this. God's judgments during the tribulation are pictured as seven seals, opened one at a time. When Christ breaks the first seal off his scroll, the seven year Tribulation period will commence down on Earth.

****

Massive deception: The Bible prophesized that in the end times many false prophets will come pretending to be Christ. "Then many false prophets will rise up and deceive many," states Jesus (Matthew 24) about the signs of the end times. I don't think Jesus meant to exclude anyone who was false in their approach or motive regarding the things of God. Here He uses the word prophet, but I believe He includes in that word anyone who falsely represents Christ for their own self-interest, or on behalf of the interest of the devil. Here he also refers to anyone who is false in their motives, not only as a prophet but in any of the five-fold ministry office-gifts listed in Ephesians 4. Here is the rest of what Jesus said in Matthew 7:21-23 "Not everyone who says to Me, 'Lord, Lord,' shall enter the kingdom of heaven, but he who does the will of My Father in heaven. Many will say to Me in that day, 'Lord, Lord, have we not prophesied in Your name, cast out demons in Your name, and done many wonders in Your name?' And then I will declare to them, 'I never knew you; depart from Me, you who practice lawlessness!'

One thing the world's religions seem to agree on is that God is immortal. So when mortal man claims divinity, he is seen as challenging the authority of God, being a heretic or just crazy. But every now and then someone will still rise and make the claim and incredibly convince enough people to have a following. The false prophets are not prophetic, they are pathetic!

One of the final end times signs involves the revival of the Roman Empire.

Many theologians and Bible scholars believe that Europe will play an especially important role in end time prophecy, and for good reason too. John Walvoord, one of the most respected evangelical theologians of end time prophecy, anticipated the: "formation of the revived Roman Empire composed of a ten-nation confederacy."

Daniel said the head of the statue, made of gold, represented Babylon, the first Kingdom of Gentile Dominion. The chest and arms of silver represented a kingdom that would rise after Babylon, to be followed by a third one, the belly and thighs of bronze, and finally the legs of iron with feet of iron mixed with clay, which spoke of the final kingdom. After that God will set up a kingdom of His own that will never be destroyed or given to another people (Daniel 2:36-44).

Most scholars agree on the identities of the two kingdoms that followed Babylon. In Daniel 8 we can read of a vision Daniel saw just before Babylon was conquered, where they were made known to him. Daniel was told in effect they would be Medo-Persia and Greece (Daniel 8:20-21). He lived to see the Medes and Persians conquer Babylon, and knew from the vision that Greece would conquer Persia. This is confirmed by the historical record, which shows that events unfolded just as Daniel's vision had indicated. That left only the fourth kingdom unknown to Daniel.

Daniel 2 described Gentile Dominion from man's perspective, a bright, shiny statue constructed mostly of precious metals. Before looking at the 4th Kingdom, lets skip forward to Daniel 7 and see God's view of these kingdoms, which is a series of voracious beasts. By laying it alongside Daniel 2 and using Daniel 8 for further clarification, we can see what Daniel saw. Daniel 7:4 depicts Babylon as a lion with the wings of an eagle. It morphed into a man that represents Nebuchadnezzar, Babylon's most powerful king. Daniel 7:5 tells us the next beast was a bear, representing Medo Persia. In Daniel 7:6 the third kingdom appeared to Daniel in the form of a winged leopard with four heads. This is a model of Greece under Alexander and the four generals who succeeded him.

The Empire that followed Greece was Rome, and that's how the identity of the 4th kingdom, represented by the legs of iron in the statue and the terrifying, frightening beast of Daniel 7:7, was determined in the Roman view. Proponents say Rome was never conquered, but transformed itself into the Holy Roman Empire that finally became the Catholic Church, which is still a powerful force in the world with over a billion members and wealth beyond measure. During that time, various components of the old Roman Empire (Portugal, the Netherlands, Spain, France, and especially Great Britain) were recognized as having worldwide influence. They say an end times version of the Roman Empire will appear again at the end of the age to preside over world affairs. This empire is represented by the feet and toes of the statue.

The spreading of the Gospel to the entire world: And this gospel of the kingdom will be preached in the whole world as a testimony to all nations, and then the end will come (Matthew 24:14). When this prophecy was given the known world was not as huge as today. Also, the means of preaching was not as simplified as today whereby we have modern technology. Today we have instant communication around the world. We can use internet, satellites, radios, televisions and etc. to preach the gospel. But God anoints people. He sent us to preach, teach and baptize those who believe in the name of the Father, Son and Holy Spirit. Then teach them to obey all things. He promised that He will be with us up to the uttermost ends of the earth (Matthew 28:20).

The Antichrist: Antichrist means against or instead of Christ. Jesus warned that, "I am come in my Father's name, and ye receive me not: if another shall come in his own name, him ye will receive" (John 5:43). The Antichrist is the personification of evil.

Revelation 12 indicates many important facts about Satan. Satan and one-third of the angels were cast out of heaven during a rebellion before the world began (Revelation 12:4). The Archangel Michael and the other angels will make war with Satan and his demons, and Satan will be excluded from heaven forever (Revelation 12:7-9). In his attempt to prevent God's fulfillment of His earthly kingdom, Satan will attempt to annihilate the Jews, but God will supernaturally protect a remnant of the Jews in a location outside of Israel for the last 42 months of the Tribulation (Revelation 12:6,13-17; Matthew 24:15-21).

"What is the unholy trinity in the end times?" Answer: A common tactic of Satan is to imitate or counterfeit the things of God in order to make himself appear to be like God. What is commonly referred to as the "unholy trinity," described vividly in Revelation 12 and 13, is no exception. The Holy Trinity consists of God the Father, the Son Jesus Christ, and the Holy Spirit. Their counterparts in the unholy trinity are Satan, the Antichrist, and the False Prophet. The Holy Trinity is characterized by infinite truth, love, and goodness, the unholy trinity portrays the diametrically opposite traits of deception, hatred, and unadulterated evil.

The second member of the unholy trinity is the Beast or Antichrist described in Revelation 13 and Daniel 7. In his apocalyptic vision in the Book of Revelation, the Apostle John sees the "beast," also called the Antichrist, rising out of the sea having seven heads and ten horns (Revelation 13:1). Combining this vision with Daniel's similar one (Daniel 7:16-24), we can conclude that some sort of world system will be inaugurated by the beast, the most powerful "horn," who will defeat the other nine and will begin to wage war against Christians. The ten-nation confederacy is also seen in Daniel's image of the statue in Daniel 2:41-42, where he pictures the final world government consisting of ten entities represented by the ten toes of the statue. Whoever the ten are and however they come to power, Scripture is clear that the beast will either destroy them or reduce their power to nothing more than figureheads. In the end, they will do his bidding.

The ten horns indicate ten seats of world government that will provide power to the Antichrist, three of which will be totally yielded to or taken over by the Antichrist (Daniel 7:8). The number ten also indicates completion or totality, in other words, a one-world government. The one-world government will be blasphemous, denying the true God. The final kingdom will possess traits in common with the former "beast kingdoms" of Babylon, Medo-Persia, Greece, and particularly Rome (Revelation 7:7, 23).

Revelation 13:3 seems to indicate that the Antichrist will be mortally wounded about halfway through the Tribulation, but Satan will miraculously heal his wound. (Revelation 13:3, 17:8-14). After this wondrous event, the world will be totally enthralled by the Antichrist. They will worship Satan and the Antichrist himself (Revelation 13:4-5).

John goes on to describe the ruler of this vast empire as having power and great authority, given to him by Satan himself (Revelation 13:2), being followed by and receiving worship from "all the world" (13:3-4), and having authority over "every tribe, people, language and nation" (13:7). From this description, it is logical to assume that this person is the leader of a one-world government which is recognized as sovereign over all other governments. It's hard to imagine how such diverse systems of government as are in power today would willingly subjugate themselves to a single ruler, and there are many theories on the subject. A logical conclusion is that the disasters and plagues described in Revelation as the seal and trumpet judgments (chapters 6-11) will be so devastating and create such a monumental global crisis that people will embrace anything and anyone who promises to give them relief.

Once entrenched in power, the beast (Antichrist) and the power behind him (Satan) will move to establish absolute control over all peoples of the earth to accomplish their true end, the worship Satan has been seeking ever since being thrown out of heaven (Isaiah 14:12-14). One way they will accomplish this is by controlling all commerce, and this is where the idea of a one-world currency comes in. Revelation 13:16-17 describes some sort of satanic mark which will be required in order to buy and sell. This means anyone who refuses the mark will be unable to buy food, clothing or other necessities of life. No doubt the vast majority of people in the world will succumb to the mark simply to survive. Again, verse 16 makes it clear that this will be a universal system of control where everyone, rich and poor, great and small, will bear the mark on their hand or forehead. There is a great deal of speculation as to how exactly this mark will be affixed, but the technologies that are available right now could accomplish it very easily.

The beast comes out of the sea, which typically in the Bible refers to the Gentile nations. He also has seven heads and ten horns, indicating his connection to and indwelling by Satan. The Antichrist is also called the man of sin. Ironically, the Bible begins with the sin of man and ends with the man of sin. The Antichrist becomes emboldened and, dispensing with all pretenses of being a peaceful ruler, he openly blasphemes God, breaks his peace treaty with the Jews, attacks believers and the Jews, and desecrates the rebuilt Jewish temple, setting himself up as the one to be worshiped (Revelation 13:4-7, Matthew 24:15). This particular event has been called the Abomination of Desolation.

The final personage of the unholy trinity is the False Prophet, described in Revelation 13:11-18.

Jesus expressly warned believers to watch out for false prophets that may look innocent but actually can be very destructive (Matthew 7:15). They have no prophecies but they are prophetic because they were predicted to come. The False Prophet speaks like a dragon, meaning that he will speak persuasively and deceptively to turn humans away from God and promote the worship of the Antichrist and Satan (Revelation 13:11-12).

The False Prophet speaks like a dragon, meaning that he will speak persuasively and deceptively to turn humans away from God and promote the worship of the Antichrist and Satan (Revelation 13:11-12). The Bible reveals the number of the beast as 666. The Bible reveals the times of the beast: 2 Thessalonians 2:3-4; Daniel 9:27.

Politically, the Anti-christ will rule over an organized New World Order System. The Bible does not use the phrase "one-world government" or "one-world currency" in referring to the end times. It does, however, provide ample evidence to enable us to draw the conclusion that both will exist under the rule of the Antichrist in the last days.

****

Additional posting about the end times:

Revelation 12 and 13 contain prophetic passages that describe some of the main events and the figures involved during the second half of the seven-year Tribulation period. Although many Bible passages allude to Satan in various forms, such as a serpent or an angel of light, he is described in Revelation 12:3 as a "great red dragon, having seven heads and ten horns, and seven crowns upon his heads" (Revelation 12:3). The color red indicates his vicious and homicidal personality. The seven heads symbolize seven evil kingdoms that Satan has empowered and used throughout history to attempt to prevent God's ultimate plan from coming to fruition. Five of the kingdoms had already come and gone—Egypt, Assyria, Babylon, Medo-Persia, and Greece.

All these kingdoms severely oppressed and persecuted the Hebrews, killing many of them. Satan's intent was to prevent the birth of Christ (Revelation 12:4). The sixth kingdom, Rome, was still in existence during the writing of this prophecy. Under Roman rule, King Herod murdered Hebrew babies around the time of Christ's birth and Pontius Pilate ultimately authorized the crucifixion of Jesus. The seventh kingdom, which is more fierce and cruel than the others, will be the final world kingdom that the Antichrist forms during the end times. These kingdoms were also prophesied in Daniel, chapters 2 and 7. The seven crowns represent universal rule, and ten horns represent complete world power or authority.

****

Somebody asked me that, "What is the greatest promise in the Bible for a believer?" I quickly pointed to this one: "Behold, I am coming quickly!" (Revelation 22:12). The reason is because the world is operating contrary to God's original plan. When Jesus returns He will fix everything that went wrong (spiritually, socially and politically). During the Kingdom Age, the heavenly throne will become the throne of the earth. The statutes of God will become the constitution of the earth. The King will rule over kings (King of kings). In democracy the majority rules over their elected leaders. But in the Kingdom of God the King rules over His elects. But we (that will return with the Lord on the earth) shall be seated in high places because we are members of the Royal Priesthood. What a moment of time!

****

Christ's Second Coming on earth is not the end of things. The scope of the Savior's work in bringing beauty to the world through recreating all things, undoing the damage of the fall, and beautifying His bride, all of which is work He does as the Son to honor His Father. After He has done what He is supposed to do, He will hand over the kingdom to the Father: "Then comes the end, when he delivers the kingdom to God the Father after destroying every rule and every authority and power. 25 For he must reign until he has put all his enemies under his feet. 26 The last enemy to be destroyed is death. 27 For "God[a] has put all things in subjection under his feet." But when it says, "all things are put in subjection," it is plain that he is excepted who put all things in subjection under him" (1 Corinthians 15:24-27).

****

Seeking Wisdom

The Bible does not say that wisdom is God but it says that Jesus Christ is the sole proprietor of wisdom. He takes credit and glory for every good thing that we do. The pursuit of wisdom is the pursuit of our Lord Jesus Christ. The Bible is the source of wisdom and our study of Scripture is our means of pursuing wisdom.

The Book of Wisdom (sometimes called the Wisdom of Solomon) doesn't mention any women by name. (You can find the Book of Wisdom in the Apocrypha of Protestant Bibles or in the Deuterocanon of Catholic and Eastern Orthodox Bibles.) What it does do, however, is refer to Wisdom, in concept, as a feminine entity. Personification is attributing personal qualities and characteristics to abstract ideas or inanimate objects. The Book of Wisdom uses personification. In this case, wisdom is spoken of as a woman, even beyond using simple feminine grammatical endings. The Hebrew wordchakmah, like its Greek (sophia) and Latin (sapientia) equivalents, is a noun with feminine gender.

Even outside the Book of Wisdom, this device is employed — Proverbs 1–9 not only uses the word wisdom but also speaks of wisdom as if it's a she. "The beginning of wisdom is the most sincere desire for instruction, and concern for instruction is love of her" (Wisdom 6:17).

Wisdom is presented as more than an abstract concept like justice. By personifying wisdom as a woman, the abstract idea becomes more immediate and attainable. And the description, beautiful and poetic as it is, makes Lady Wisdom someone you want to know and know well. Bride and bridegroom is an image used heavily in the Bible, not just at a realistic level, as in the case of Adam and Eve, but also in the typological sense. For example, the relationship between God and the Hebrews — the "Chosen People" — is described as a spousal union. Even when the people become unfaithful by experimenting with idolatry, the covenant is not dissolved, and the union is intact. Later, when Paul uses the same image, both bride and groom are portrayed as faithful partners in this covenant of love. Similarly, the Word and Wisdom are faithful partners — the ultimate biblical bride and groom.

Wisdom as described in the Book of Solomon is a type of lady suitable to become the bride of an equally honorable, virtuous, intelligent, and respected groom. (Type refers to someone or something in the Old Testament that prefigures someone or something in the New Testament.) Who's the lucky guy? Christ. Wisdom was intended to be the image of the future bride of Christ — the Christian Church. The image of Christ as groom and of the Church as His bride is first used by Paul and later by many of the fathers of the Church. In this scenario, wisdom is united to Christ but distinct and separate from him. Wisdom is considered created by God and endowed with the highest authority and respect.

Again, the Bible does not deify wisdom. The Gnostic sect of the ancient Church did in fact deify wisdom to the level of a goddess, or at least a demigod. For Gnostics, salvation was secret knowledge (gnosisin Greek), which only the few and elite could possess. Logos (Greek for "word" and often used in reference to Christ as the Word of God) and sophia (Greek for "wisdom") were seen as complementary powers that only the learned could appreciate. This teaching is erroneous and heresy.

As described, wisdom becomes someone whose company you enjoy and look forward to. She is approachable to anyone and everyone. The goodness of your heart and purity of your spirit — not your I.Q. — is what attracts wisdom. The desire and resolve to do what is right and just in the eyes of God are the first steps toward wisdom that anyone and everyone can take, if they so choose.

In the Christian sense, wisdom isn't the same as truth or knowledge. Wisdom isn't just intellectual insight or book learning, either. Wisdom is the ability to make good judgments. A wise person doesn't have to be the most intelligent or the most accurate but does have to be someone who knows what to do with the knowledge he or she has, where to find more, and how to apply it. The author of the Book of Wisdom underscores the connection of wisdom with righteousness. Righteousness is of God whereas wisdom can be naturally acquired in her right order by knowing God intimately.

Logos, the Word, often used to identify Christ: "And the Word became flesh and dwelt among us"(John 1:14). Christ is given the name Logos, which denotes knowledge of truth: "I am the way, and the truth, and the life" (John 14:6). Wisdom (sophia) is a little different, however, because it's considered to be the bride of the Word made flesh, or Jesus Christ.

Basically, wisdom is putting knowledge into practical application in the manner glorifying God. Wisdom is acquired from God but knowledge is searched either by reading or instruction. We get wisdom by looking up in heaven but we get knowledge by looking down on the earth. Knowledge is improved on depending on one's passion to know. To be conscious that you are ignorant is great step towards knowledge.

Wisdom is given by God after knowing God intimately through your personal relationship with Christ. Wisdom is our blessing tied up in our relationship with God. The knowledge of God deepens by perpetually being rooted in the Word of God. Wisdom is a virtue: "The fear of the LORD is the beginning of wisdom: a good understanding have all they that do his commandments: his praise endureth forever" (Psalm 111:10).

There is the richness of wisdom: "How much better to get wisdom than gold! To get understanding is to be chosen rather than silver" (Proverbs 16:16). There is the power of wisdom: "Then said I, Wisdom is better than strength: nevertheless the poor man's wisdom is despised, and his words are not heard" (Ecclesiastes 9:16).

Scrolling through posted nuggets of wisdom:

To seek wisdom is to seek understanding. The Bible says that "Get wisdom; get insight: do not forget, nor turn away from the words of my mouth" (Proverbs 4:5). In Jewish tradition, it was passed per the oral tradition way with each succeeding generation. If even only one generation did not obey this tried and tested method for guaranteeing the safety of the spiritual genome disaster could hit the nation of Israel - all that moral virtue of the ancients finished in one or two foolish generations. "When we boil life down strictly to the race for only one thing, Proverbs' parent is saying godly Wisdom is all there is - the be all and end all of life itself. GET IT!"

****

Proverbs 1:20-23 – "Wisdom crieth without; she uttereth her voice in the streets: She crieth in the chief place of concourse, in the openings of the gates: in the city she uttereth her words, saying, How long, ye simple ones, will ye love simplicity? and the scorners delight in their scorning, and fools hate knowledge? Turn you at my reproof: behold, I will pour out my spirit unto you, I will make known my words unto you." Wisdom is personified. The voice of Wisdom is God. The invitation of Wisdom is by God. The cry of Wisdom is the tear of God. Rejecting Wisdom is rejecting God.

****

Proverbs 3:5 - "Trust in the LORD with all your heart And do not lean on your own understanding. In all your ways acknowledge Him, And He will make your paths straight...." This is a conscious decision to live in accordance to the ways of God in spite of your natural instincts. Jesus Christ must be the reason you live. "Yet for us there is but one God, the Father, from whom all things came and for whom we live; and there is but one Lord, Jesus Christ, through whom all things came and through whom we live" (1 Corinthians 8:6)

****

God uses not the wise people but people with humility and tender heart. "For ye see your calling, brethren, how that not many wise men after the flesh, not many mighty, not many noble, are called: But God hath chosen the foolish things of the world to confound the wise; and God hath chosen the weak things of the world to confound the things which are mighty" (Cor. 1:18-31).

****

If you see yourself as weak, feeble, or unskilled, don't let that bother you too much. God has been calling feeble and unskilled people from the beginning of time. Few of those whom God has called have been the "cream of the crop" according to the flesh. Again and again, God has chosen people who were ill-esteemed in the eyes of the world when He needed a candidate or a group of people to do a job. So if you have ever thought you weren't good enough for God to use, it's time for you to renew your thinking! God is looking for people no one else wants or deems valuable. When great victories are won through ordinary folks, there's no question as to who should receive the glory! As First Corinthians 1:29 says, "That no flesh should glory in his presence." The Bible (Old and New Testaments) is filled with illustrations of people who were considered to be the rejects of the world but whom God wanted to use. "God's choice is not based on beauty or ugliness, talent or lack of talent, education or lack of education, a diploma or lack of a diploma. If a person has a right heart toward God, he is qualified to be used by God" ~ Rick Renner

****

All of us exert some influence, either good or bad, upon others. But those who truly influence the earth positively are the ones who are influenced by heaven. They are the ones with the wisdom of the ages because 'Ancient of days' is a title in reference to God (Daniel 7:9, 13, 22). God is the eternal One or the ancient of days; He alone is uncreated and unending. Since God is infinite and wise, He must be infinitely wise. He alone is naturally and entirely and invariable wise. Therefore the godly wisdom, when used by godly men, always carries a strong moral connotation. D.L. Moody once said that "If you partner with God, Make your plans big!" I encourage you today to make God your partner.

****

Wisdom is passed on from older people to the young generation. "When I first visited the homes of whites, I was often dumbfounded by the number and nature of questions that children asked of their parents — and their parents' unfailing willingness to answer them. In my household, questions were considered a nuisance; adults imparted information as they considered necessary" ~ Nelson Mandela.

****

Always have a book at hand, in the parlor, on the table, for the family; a book of condensed thought and striking anecdote, of sound maxims and truthful apothegms. It will impress on your own mind a thousand valuable suggestions, and teach your children a thousand lessons of truth and duty. Such a book is a casket of jewels for your household ~ Tryon Edwards

****

The old adage is true: "Wise men can learn more from foolish questions than fools can learn from a wise answer". You see, a wise person learns from even the foolish people but a foolish person ignores the wise because he or she is allergic to wisdom!

****

Wisdom is like money. You can only spend/give as much as you have and you can multiply it by putting it in the right place(s). It's a wrong thing to be in the company of wrong people in wrong places. Equally wrong is to be in the company of right people in wrong places. Think about it!

****

It is important to see distant things as if they were close and to take a distanced view of close things. "A blind man's world is bounded by the limits of his touch, an ignorant man's world by the limits of his knowledge, and a great man's world by the limit of his vision" ~ Paul Harvey

****

Absolute truth exists, and it is immutable. Those who do not believe it are blind; they simply can't access it. You need both light and sight in order to see. Blindness is not the absence of light but it is the absence of sight. Not seeing something does not mean its non-existence. Read the stories of the prophets; they were called all sorts of names because the Society couldn't see what they saw or were seeing. No wonder whenever Christians claim to have custody of the truth they are ridiculed by the worldly people!

****

Humanity regardless of their age or state of physical frailty fight their own battles otherwise they cease to be considered humans. Life is a continuous learning without a possibility of graduation. It is not the years that you live in the life that matter but rather the life that you live in the years. Reflect before you act because it is the quality of the quantity that matters. They say that age is gold. As time chases us and age is stepping in, one of the advantages of aging is wisdom. Indeed, life is a wheel of fortune; it is your time to spin it.

****

A dynamic life is always fired by the vision built on the word of God. It is important to see distant things as if they were close and to take a distanced view of close things. "A blind man's world is bounded by the limits of his touch, an ignorant man's world by the limits of his knowledge, and a great man's world by the limit of his vision" Paul Harvey

****

"Even a fool, when he holdeth his peace, is counted wise." The English people say that, "Empty vessels make the loudest noise whilst loaded ones make little or none." You see, 'quiet' and 'sage' are attributed to a wise man. They are parallel; they both fall into the same line justifying the truism of the proverb.

****

A teacher affects eternity; he can never tell where his influence stops. I am grateful to God for being a teacher.

****

You don't attract people to you because of what you want but because of who you are.

****

Kindness is a language understood by the blind and the deaf.

****

Never fear shadows. They simply mean there is a light somewhere nearby. - Ruth E. Renkee

****

Life is like a camera focus on what is important. Capture the good time. Develop from the negative. And if things don't work out just take another shot.

****

You wouldn't worry so much about what others think of you if you realized how seldom they do.

****

People rarely talk about the good you do but, always about the bad because "Good deeds never leave home; bad ones echo for a thousand miles"

****

If there is nobody working out for your downfall, think twice because you could already be down.

****

At best man is the noblest of all animals; separated from law and justice he is the worst ~ Aristotle

****

Friendship is a prized gift that gives our heart a lift, a blessing we just can't do without because friendship is what living is all about! But many friends are not true friends. When you rise in life, your friends know who you are, but when you fall in life, you know who your friends are... Everybody wants to be your sun to shine on you when you are in down but a true friend wants to be your moon to shine on you during your darkest hour. What you are driving is not as important as what drives you, if you are driven by lust you will soon get lost, if you are driven by status you may soon become a statue. What you are driving is not as important as what drives you.... What is the driver of your dear life?

****

People spend their lives in the service of their passions instead of employing their passions in the service of their lives. "Service doesn't start when you have something to give; it blossoms naturally when you have nothing left to take" ~ Nipun Mehta

****

You can dodge a responsibility but you cannot dodge the consequences. You make your bed you must now lay in it. The truism - you reap what you sow - is a universal law. God forgives us, absolutely, and He can turn the worst things in our lives into good if we seek Him. But, we will suffer the consequences of our choices and actions. That's just the way it is. You might not be able to change the outcomes of previous choices but you can change the course and direction of your life.

****

"Do I take any pleasure in the death of the wicked?" declares the Sovereign LORD. "Rather, am I not pleased when they turn from their ways and live?" Ezekiel 18:21-23. (Hell) is a doctrine which the heart revolts from and struggles against. The doctrine of hell is a doctrine to which the heart submits only under the stress of authority. The Church believes the doctrine of hell because it must believe it or renounce faith in the Bible and thereby give up all the hopes founded upon its promises.

****

"The tragedy of life is not that it ends so soon, but that we wait so long to begin it." ~ W. M. Lewis

****

Many have longed for change in the physicals by spraying of expensive perfumes, creams, deodorant and etc,... But the true change comes when a man changes his library, value systems, friends... Invest in the man in you!

****

"Christianity is not an escape system for us to avoid reality, live above it, or be able to redefine it. Christianity is a way that leads us to grasp what reality is and, by God's grace and help, to navigate through it to our eternal home." ~ RZIM

****

Experience is the best teacher. "But one of the great misconceptions of modern life is the assumption that by the magic age of twenty-one we are jelled, dreams in place, ready to tackle the adult world and leave childhood behind. All we lack, according to this myth, is experience. The reality is that many of us lack quite a bit more: a psychic passport to adulthood" ~ Victoria Secunda.

****

Past mistakes or missteps are water under the bridge... You can walk over them by focusing on the future today.

****

"The greatness comes not when things go always good for you. But the greatness comes when you're really tested, when you take some knocks, some disappointments, when sadness comes. Because only if you've been in the deepest valley can you ever know how magnificent it is to be on the highest mountain." ~ Richard M. Nixon

****

God forgives and forgets. He deals with a sinner by His grace. He deals with you not because of you but in spite of you. God never gets glory from sin but He gets glory from the victory over sin.

****

A person touched by His grace, who lives according to His Spirit, automatically exudes a lot of good works! The Law of Christ is the Law of Love. Bear one another's burdens, and fulfill the law of Christ.

****

In our world today, we are always eager to broadcast any little thing/ achievement that's not even worth knowing about. Not that I am innocent of this. But when we know better, we are expected to do better! Whatever we achieve in His name is about Him and not us. Let's make His name not our name popular like never before.

****

Fulfillment eradicates the void within us and the longing for worldliness, creating space for eternity to over flow our hearts. To such Jesus pronounced the benediction that "Blessed are those who hunger and thirst for righteousness, for they will be filled" (Matthew 5:6). Fulfillment comes by emptying ourselves to Nothing. Nothingness is a state of nonexistent (dying to self) and humility. The more we empty ourselves of the corrupt desires the more He fills us. My prayer is that: "Lord, bring me to that place I can say 'I have Nothing to Prove, Nothing to Lose and Nothing to Hide' in life." Nothing to prove is a state of deep security in God, Nothing to lose is a state of absolute surrender to God and Nothing to hide is a state of transparency and integrity before God. Hope this is your prayer too. Happy weekend to you all!

****

You know you're lazy when you actually get excited about canceled plans. - Ace Wise

****

"Champions aren't made in gyms. Champions are made from something deep inside them - a desire, a dream, a vision, a goal."

****

Our actions began as ideas. Ideas reflect our innermost feelings, therefore we cannot separate ourselves from what we habitually admire to do because "As a man thinks so he is. So we are our thoughts".

****

Bread of deceit is sweet to man, but afterwards his mouth shall be filled with gravel; embrace the wisdom of God & be diligent in your work, riches will come to you.

****

The profound beauty of life is not to become a man of success but rather a man of value. The true value can be found in the degree to which man's attains liberation from himself, thus true value lies in his deeds, honesty and kind precepts ~ Odeke Olira

****

We all know that tiny drops of water make mighty oceans. But you can never cross the ocean unless you have the courage to lose sight of the shore. Make an effort to constantly think positively making the best out of the seemingly bad situation. High achievers will gain the most out of situations where the probability of success is relatively low and that success becomes a challenge. However a low achiever may see losing in such a scenario as one that promotes a feeling of personal shame from a loss. The heart of the matter is always to know the right thing to do. The hard part is doing it.

****

The things you run into occasionally may be just illuminating your path to what God is calling you to do. "Seek you the kingdom of God first and the rest will be added to you". When first things are put first, second things are not suppressed but they are increased.

****

"To a brave man, good and bad luck are like his left and right hand. He uses both."

~ St Catherine of Siena

****

Unless we learn to do small things right in this country we will have problems getting the big and "important" issues right. No issue is too small. Have a blessed week.

****

Life is like a swinging pendulum. We have each heard some flash-in-the-pan success stories; tales of people and businesses that skyrocket to fame and fortune, only to plummet back into the pit of nothingness just as quickly as they had emerged from it. Don't stay up there and forget that you could come down. Time is fleeting, and you don't want to miss a thing, but life can become juicy and bitter as well. That is why couples take vows to stay together in good times and bad times. Even Jesus marries us for good and for worse. He does not abandon us in times of trouble. God's covenant with man is forever because God is a faithful partner. God allows us to go through the trials of life just to test our patience and love for Him. Squeezing moments should therefore increase our dependence on God rather than squeezing our faith to bleakness. Remember that winners never quit and quitters never win.

****

Life is a journey; the journey of a thousand miles begins with one step. The patient people are privileged to achieve their goals. The impatient ones are struggling and most times they give up due to frustration. The best thing to do with frustration is to turn it into positive motion. When you feel like giving up, remember why you held on for so long in the first place. Others are Jack of all trades, master of none. They jump from one thing to another without mastering any particular one thing. They are constantly on their heels in search for greener pastures. Remember that sometimes the grass is greener on the other side because you aren't watering your side enough.

****

Life at its best is compared to travelling in the valley. Yet, for there to be a valley there have to be higher places. How many times do we focus on the valley instead of the beauty of the mountains that surround us? "I have walked that long road to freedom," Nelson Mandela once said. "I have tried not to falter; I have made missteps along the way. But I have discovered the secret that after climbing a great hill, one only finds that there are many more hills to climb."

****

Life is a journey whereby you meet other travelers. Love them and make someone's life better than you met them so that when you get home they have a reason to miss you.

****

Sometimes in life, a fog sets in and you don't know which way is the right direction. No matter what comes your way in life you've got to believe it's not over until God says it is over. It is a new day for you to match forward because God knows how to make up for lost time.

****

Some people are born great, some achieve greatness, and some have greatness thrust upon them. Great people are over-comers. Overcoming a certain challenge does not mean no more challenge. It means graduating to confront even tougher challenges. "Life is either a daring adventure or nothing at all." The challenged life is the best therapist. An over-comer is simply one who understands much because he has been tested and graduated. He displays a greater simplicity of character than one who understands little. He is positioned to be a heavy weight lifter. Overcoming is the art of being wise - it is about knowing what to overlook and how to respond in time of crisis. The ultimate measure of a man is not where he stands in moments of comfort and convenience, but where he stands in times of challenge and controversy. "Character is the only secure foundation; the man of character falls back upon himself."

****

Problems come in a wide variety of shapes and sizes. Regardless of who you are or what you do, you will face obstacles. Know that problems are there to be solved. "You don't drown by falling in the water. You drown by staying there." Problem solving is one of the most essential skills in life. Acknowledge that your current experience is not exceptional; you are not alone because whatever problem you have in your life, someone has faced it and overcome it. If you going through hardship, you can get bitter, or you can get better by seeing your situation as soil that needs fertilizers for upgrading to promote you to the next level.

****

The existence of problems is the reality of the fact that life has no smooth road for any of us. However, a problem is a problem if you refuse to look for a solution. The tormenting problem you have demands a solution. Real difficulties can be overcome; it is only the imaginary ones that are unconquerable. "Every problem has in it the seeds of its own solution. If you don't have any problems, you don't get any seeds." Disgusting as it may sound, without a problem there can be no solution. Likewise, without an odd situation, we cannot anticipate for a miracle. The need in your life necessitates the divine provision. Therefore, see your problem as a challenge to triumph. There may be more than one solution to your problem; identify all of your options and implement the best option for a solution. Start by getting the right diagnoses in order to avoid putting bandages on headaches instead of prescription of Aspirin Tablets. "Erroneous assumptions can be disastrous." Knowing what the problem isn't is just as important as knowing what it is.

****

Problems come in a wide variety of shapes and sizes. Problem solving is one of the most essential skills in life. Regardless of who you are or what you do, you will face obstacles. Acknowledge that your current experience is not exceptional; you are not alone because whatever the problem we have in our life, someone has faced it and overcome it.

****

Fear is from the devil not God (2 Timothy 1:7). Our forefathers were never fearful people. That is why they lived far better than us in terms of customs and values. 'Fear' today has robed our country (the generation of today) the power and sound minds. It is absurd that grandparents, their sons and grand-children are all caught up in this cycle of fear. My prayer is that we overcome fear. It is going to take the same power demonstrated by Paul in the scripture to overcome fear. I mean choosing to speak out and doing things differently with a sound mind in order to maintain integrity. Nobody has control over our mind expect us!

****

There is a saying that misfortunes never come single. It means that just because you are experiencing one big problem it does not make you immune to other problems. In such situation prioritizing is important when solving your problems. Some things need immediate attention than others. "Never try to solve all the problems at once — make them line up for you one-by-one". Be persistent and seek out all information before tackling your problem. Understand why the problem exists. Seek a lasting solution to your problem even when it requires great sacrificing. Choosing the path of least resistance is most likely to yield to temporally solution. It is ridiculous when the problem of last year becomes the problem of this year. For better results the change of attitude is necessary: For you cannot solve your problem with the same level of thinking or consciousness that created it!

****

When you badly wanted something and it is gone, don't spend too much time or energy mourning what has happened. Let a broken relationship, romance or friendship go. It is time to move on. There is much to learn from the story of David when he lost his son. David asked them point blank, "Is the child dead?" The servants verified that the child was dead. Then David arose from the earth, and washed, and anointed himself, and changed his apparel, and came into the house of the Lord, and worshiped: then he came to his own house; and when he required, they set bread before him, and he did eat. Then said his servants unto him, "What thing is this that thou hast done: thou didst fast and weep for the child, while it was alive but when the child was dead, thou didst rise and eat bread. And David said, "While the child was yet alive, I fasted and wept: for I said, 'Who can tell whether God will be gracious to me, that the child may live? But now he is dead, wherefore should I fast? can I bring him back again? I shall go to him, but he shall not return to me.'" (II Samuel 12:20-23). I feel energized this evening; I could lift a mountain!

****

The "foolish things" he used to tell me while I was growing up have become things of great wisdom. He used to say that, "you will only ever be as great as the people you surround yourself with".

****

The task of leadership is not to put greatness in humanity, but to elicit it, for the greatness is already there ~ John Buchanan

****

No man under heaven will connect you and put you in a position higher than where he is. You need God to get you to the top most position in this world; because He is above all powers, authorities and principalities on the earth.

****

"Moving on doesn't mean you forget about things. It just means you have to accept what happened and continue living..."

****

"If they're holding onto their pride, their ego and their excuses instead of holding onto you, it's time to let go."

****

Cutting people from your life doesn't mean you hate them, it simply means you respect yourself.

****

"The frown on a goat's face doesn't prevent it to be taken to the slaughter house" Putting on faces or changing the face will change nothing, but facing the change will change everything. Changing location without changing attitude is not a smart move either. When a stone is dropped into a pond, the water continues quivering even after the stone has sunk to the bottom. But it is impossible to squeeze water from the same stone because changing location (from the dry land to the bottom of the pond) does not make it become a sponge! "Our greatest distinction as a species is our capacity, unique among animals, to make counter-evolutionary choices. A man must be big enough to admit his mistakes, smart enough to profit from them, and strong enough to correct them" .

****

Celebrate the gift of life. "No matter how good or bad you have it, wake up each day thankful for your life. Someone somewhere else is desperately fighting for theirs." Be motivated with enthusiasm; it is a new day for you to match forward. No matter what comes your way in life you've got to believe it's not over until God says it is over. Remember that God knows how to make up for the lost time. God gives us hope so that in whatever we do, we look for an excuse to win rather than to fail.

****

Those who live in glass houses don't cast stones for fear of retaliation especially when the fragile glass cannot protect one from insults returned.

****

The problem with the rat race is that even if you win you are still a rat. I would rather be a lion; the pride and king of the jungle.

****

"Whispers ignored do not become shouts." It is only through labor and painful efforts, by grim energy and absolute courage that we move unto better things.

****

The decision you make today is an exit out of tomorrow's problem and a door for you to access tomorrow's blessings. Therefore use discernment when choosing your door. When one door swings open it is most likely to lead you into various rooms even those you didn't anticipate. Feel adventurous, look on every exit as being an entrance to somewhere else. Choosing effectively begins with faith. Faith is patience, wise and persistence. Choose your battles wisely. Don't fight a battle if you don't gain anything by winning. If you are in hole today, stop digging. Above all, remember that even if you have the keys to the doors of your tomorrow, you are not the author and finisher of your faith, God is. The greater the object of your faith is, the greater is your faith!

****

My prayer today is: "Lord, help us to build a good character worthy of emulation for that is what, makes a man and that is what we leave behind when we depart." I entice you to join the winning team of the believers by receiving Jesus Christ as your Savior. Whoever walks with the wise becomes wise, but the companion of fools will suffer harm" (Proverbs 13:20)

****

Genesis 25:8 - "Then Abraham breathed his last and died at a good old age, an old man and full of years; and he was gathered to his people." Abraham learnt to live the sacrificial life when he offered Isaac to be sacrificed. God intervened to save his son by giving a replacement of a ram. Abraham lived a happy man the rest of his life, knowing that God will never withhold anything from him. He learned to pause and wait until God says that, "This is it".

****

Uncertainty is one of the most unpleasant experiences. Life is a puzzle such that it is hard to learn - which bridge to cross and which to burn. That is why anthropology agrees that, man, regardless of the degree of civility is obsessed with paying allegiance to a certain known or unknown deity. During biblical times people looked for ultimate peace in Jewish Legalism, Greek Philosophies and Eastern Mysticism. Whenever I have questions concerning the philosophies of life I go to my God who designed my life. But God does not explain Himself; He reveals Himself to convict me and illuminate my path. I am left with no choice but to fall into His own plan for my life. Basically, He gives me what I need as opposed to what I want. The want is the philosophy that challenged me but the need is the person (Christ) that changes me. The need is the game changer. To change is to live and to live is to keep on changing. Ultimate peace is not discovered in the changed world but in the transformed heart. "True contemplation is not a psychological trick but a theological grace" ~ Thomas Merton

****

The ultimate measure of a person is not where he/she stands in moment of comfort and convenience but where he/she stands at times of controversy and challenge.

****

The Bible says that, "Christ Jesus who died—more than that, who was raised to life is at the right hand of God and is also interceding for us (Romans 8:34). When a person is touched by His grace, he is supposed to live by His Spirit. He is not in the state of rebellion. He automatically exudes good works. Given the fact, no one can stand on his or her own without the intercessory prayer of our Lord. We are all vulnerable to the schemes of Satan. We may not be weak in the same areas but every person has a weakness. It's not necessarily the big sins that bring us down but the small sins, those simple things we excuse, tolerate or compromise. The missiles of the enemy are aimed at shooting down our faith. Without the covering of the intercession of our Lord, we are all obvious targets, as vulnerable as exposed ducks.

****

What hinge does the doorway of your life swing on? Put God in your schedule in order for the door to swing open so that you may have access to the reserved treasures of your life. He will help you surmount the mountains lining up at the entrance of it and to lock your adversaries outside. May God have the final say in all endeavors of your life this week.

****

God still speaks to us in various ways. But it is creepy to stay around people who claim that God told them to do even the things that they can figure out by their natural brains - like choosing an outfit to wear. Most probably the culprits try to convince their audiences regarding their spirituality but in the long run they end up hurting themselves. I believe that God can speak to us supernaturally, but He also created us with different body organs including the brains to use them for His glory. He does not control us because He gave us the freewill to determine things in the glorifying ways to Him. The reality is that God wants us to love Him with our heart and minds. He did not call us to trash our minds but to renew our minds.

****

All men dream, but not equally. Those who dream by night in the dusty recesses of their minds, wake in the day to find that it was vanity: Day-dreamers are dangerous because they may act on their dreams with open eyes, to make them come to pass.

****

If you do not build your dreams, someone else will hire you to build theirs... Your time is limited, so don't waste it living someone else's life. Great dreams come from great discipline and inspiration. You can be inspired all day long, but if you don't have the discipline to advance your vision the inspiration is void. This week quit sailing in the sea of imagination and wishes; start dreaming big time. "There is only one thing that makes a dream impossible to achieve: the fear of failure." ~ Paulo Coelho

****

When you study the lives of those who are moving their dreams into reality, you find that it isn't because they are more gifted or talented; rather, they shrink the gap between the amount of time it takes them to formulate their ideas, put them into practice, and begin taking real solid action.

****

The tragedies of life help you to discover who you ought to be, where you ought to be and how you should be there. Give thank to God for everything in life. God is at work in your life even in times of trials. Even when we experience tough times, He is at work to bring about His purposes in us. Whatever is happening in your life is linked to your destiny. Your circumstances are not a series of random uncoordinated events. God is orchestrating events & circumstances; moving people in & out of your life to prepare you & to position you for your next higher assignment. Trust God. He knows what He's doing. He will fulfill His purpose for your life in the best possible way. Believe!

****

Happiness cannot be traveled to, owned, earned, or worn. It is the spiritual experience of living every minute with love, grace & gratitude. ~ Denis Waitley

****

Stop telling God about the size of your problems, rather, tell your problem the size of your God (I Sam 17: 45).

****

"Qualities die for want of attention, so the unlovely states might best be rubbed out by imagining "beauty for ashes and joy for mourning" for yourself-----"

****

Being a male is a matter of birth, being a man is a matter of age, but being a gentleman is a matter of choice. A great man is always willing to be little ~ Ralph Waldo Emerson

****

A leader is identified by his followers. He who thinks he is leading and no one is following him is only taking a walk.

****

One tree makes a million match sticks but it takes only one match stick to burn a million trees. All things including time and circumstances are subject to change. Those who think that they are heroes and feel invincible today may be unknown tomorrow. What is urgent today may be irrelevant tomorrow; nothing but history! If you are in the position of authority never devalue or hurt anyone because power changes like the outfits we wear. You may be powerful today but powerless tomorrow....

586

Your subordinate today may be your superior tomorrow. A great man shows his greatness by the way he treats little men.

****

Some people are born great, some achieve greatness, and some have greatness thrust upon them. Great people are over-comers. Overcoming a certain challenge does not mean no more challenge. It means graduating to confront even tougher challenges. Child of God, the moment you were born again, you promoted yourself from light weight lifting to heavy weight lifting. The Bible says that to whom much is given, much is required of him. One who understands much displays a greater simplicity of character than one who understands little. Our mutuality spiritually is tested in times of crisis. The art of being wise is knowing what to overlook and how to respond in time of crisis. The ultimate measure of a man is not where he stands in moments of comfort and convenience, but where he stands in times of challenge and controversy. The man of character falls back upon himself. Have a great day fellow graduates.

****

We are all held to a high standard of conducts like not getting involved in sloppy behaviors. It takes courage either to comply or to do the opposite. Spiritually, the courage to embrace the truth is a virtue. Courage is not the absence of fear; it is pressing forward even when you feel afraid. It doing what is pleasing to God regardless of our emotions. Courage is persistently getting comfortable with being uncomfortable. "Courage is the most important of all the virtues because without courage, you can't practice any other virtue consistently" ~ Maya Angelou

****

The stubbornness in us blinds our capability to see and to listen. A stubborn person is unpredictable and irresponsible. The strength of character fluctuates stubbornness. A person of character takes full responsibility for his actions. "Taking responsibility for your failures is scary, no doubt. It places a big bull's eye on your ego, and exposes your ego to shudder failure." Certainly, unless you accept responsibility for your failure, you are not qualified to accept responsibility for success. One of the powers at your belt is the ability to accept your mistakes and take on the blame instead of passing on the blame to others. Desist from giving your powers away. You can do it by taking responsibility for your life including your failures. One preacher insinuated that failing to take on responsibility for your mistakes and accusing others for your mistakes is akin to eating poison and expect someone else to die!

****

The way you carry yourself will often determine how you will be treated. In the long run, appearing vulgar or common will make people disrespect you. Always take a stand concerning what you believe. Own up your fault. All the praying, fasting, Bible study, etc won't do you any good, unless YOU admit YOUR failings and stop passing the buck (the blame game). God sees through the lies, all the time.

****

Learn from the past, set vivid, detailed goals for the future, and live in the only moment of time of which you have any control: now. ~ Denis Waitley

****

"When you feel like giving up, remember why you held on for so long in the first place."

****

The words you don't want to hear from your doctor, yet often used: "You will get worse before you starting feeling well" The intensity of pain does not mean the termination of hope.

****

When we were young we responded to life's challenges emotionally. Controlling emotions is evidence of mutuality. Growing old is compulsory but GROWING UP is optional...

****

Every person goes through dark times. The reality is that if you are not going through a crisis, you just come out of it or it is stalking you. When you are going through something, critics are always fast to point fingers. The last thing you need when you are going through something is a good lecture regarding what could have been done to avert the problem, instead of what should be done to rectify the defect. On the positive side, over-comers know how to use the dirt of critical comments to manure their paths to significance. Antagonism can either make you bitter or better, never both. The great news is that you choose which… Don't be captured by your circumstances; rather let your obedience to God subdue your circumstances.

****

Do you realize that one of the first things people notice about you is your aura or that distinctive atmosphere that surrounds you? You create that aura and you are responsible for what it says about you and whom it attracts. There is nothing more truly artistic than to love people. God is Love. Love must be central in order for God to be at the center of everything we do. Determine the center and the circumference will establish itself. Have a Blissful Weekend.

****

It is our responsibility to create an atmosphere that is conducive for the flow of the Holy Spirit. That is what we are told in the following scriptures: "Do not quench (suppress or subdue) the [Holy] Spirit;" (1 Thessalonians 5:19 Amplified); "For this reason I remind you to fan into flame the gift of God, which is in you through the laying on of my hands. For the Spirit God gave us does not make us timid, but gives us power, love and self-discipline." (2 Timothy 2: 6, 7 NIV).

****

We love all believers because we are one body in Jesus Christ, and we love all nonbelievers because of Jesus Christ. God chose for us two types of friends to behold. The vertical friends are those with whom we share the body of Christ. The horizontal friends are the nonbelievers whom we love dearly but with prudence lest they dent our relationship with God. The vertical friends cannot be substituted by any natural means. They are our closest friends in whom we can freely confide. We can communicate to them with our deepest feelings and convictions, knowing we have a supportive listener and that we won't be betrayed. With real friends we can discuss what is on our mind, we can share our joys, our observations, our plans, and even our sorrows and regrets. When there is deep and intense friendship, nothing needs to be held back. Jesus described this dimension of friendship in this way: "No longer do I call you servants, for the servant does not know what his master is doing; but I have called you friends, for all that I have heard from my Father I have made known to you (John 15:15). Therefore when you choose your close friends from the friends, don't be short-changed by choosing personality over character.

****

William Shakespeare said, "love me or hate me" both are my favorite because if you love me that means I am in your heart, if you hate me that means I am in your mind.." Do you agree with him? ~ Lawrence Raul

****

"Love is a decision, it is a judgment, it is a promise. If love was only a feeling, there would be no basis for the promise to love each other forever. A feeling comes and it may go. How can I judge that it will stay forever, when my act does not involve judgment and decision." ~ Erich Fromm

****

True love is expressed emotionally but it is never emotional; In fact it is difficult to know at what moment love begins. The reason is because it is planted in the inner chambers of the heart that is out of bound to emotional excitement. True love awakens the soul making you yearn for more. True love brings peace to the heart and leaves the minds in wondering. You simply realize that you are in love but cannot explain how. That's what I hope to give you forever.

****

Selfish means: self-centered, self-serving, self-important. Selfishness is the root cause of conflicts even in families. Selfishness breeds envy. Selfishness is human habit; it is a form of defense and means of survival to some. Selfishness is a lifestyle that puts yourself first. Love of self, in the Christian sense, isn't selfishness. Selfishness is putting yourself first before everyone and anything else. The golden rule is that do to others as you want it be done to you. The cultivation of a uniform courtesy, a willingness to do to others as we would wish them to do to us, would annihilate half the ills of life. The Christian faith calls for death to selfishness. Faith focuses on God's provision. Faith lays hold upon the Lord Jesus with a firm and determined grasp rather than self.

****

Sometimes I find it difficult to convince myself to accept the reality of real life issues. The reality is that this life is a bundle of unlimited wants. The more we grow the bigger the challenges become. When we were young our parents helped us to solve the riddle of life. An open mind gives chance for someone to drop a worthwhile thought in it. The more input you have from divergent perspectives the better position you are in to make good decisions.

****

Strive to make your dreams come true but acknowledge the bumps in the highway to your destiny. "I was taught to strive not because there were any guarantees of success, but because the act of striving is in itself the only way to keep faith with life." ~ Madeleine Albright.

****

Everyone wants to live on top of the mountain, but without encountering the hardship involved in climbing it.

****

Respect yourself enough to walk away from things that don't add value to your life.

591

Laziness is the habit of unnecessarily resting even before one gets tired. Respect yourself enough to walk away from anything that no longer serves you, grows you, or makes you happy. But never give up on people because God uses other people to bless us. Whenever somebody closes a door against you, God will open even a wider door to accommodate you. "Sometimes our light goes out, but is blown again into instant flame by an encounter with another human being" ~ Albert Schweitzer

****

It is so hard to trust someone for a 2nd time after they have already given you 1 reason not to trust them . . . integrity is like virginity, when you lose it, you lose it once and for ever.

****

The stupid neither forgive nor forget; the naive forgive and forget; the wise forgive but do not forget ~ Thomas Szasz

****

Forgiving is a bitter pill but it heals the heart and sets the soul free. Joseph named his first born Manasseh meaning, 'God has made me forget.' This shows us that Joseph had tried to forget what his brothers did to him but it was hard but God came in and gave him the grace to forgive. He then had a second son and named him Ephraim meaning, 'God has made me fruitful'. You only become Fruitful after you Forgive. Bitterness makes a person Barren. Forgiving releases the blessing. Jesus plainly said that those who forgive are the candidates of receiving forgiveness from God (Matthew 6:12).

****

I learnt the hard way never to make promises to God because I find myself often failing to keep the same promises. Jesus said that the spirit is willing but the body is weak (Matthew 26:41). Paul said that "For that which I do I allow not: for what I would, that do I not; but what I hate, that do I" (Romans 7:15). Therefore, I decided to depend on the promises of God rather than making promises to God because God will never back out on His promises. He said that "My covenant will I not break, nor alter the thing that is gone out of my lips" (Psalms 89:34).

****

God is willing to save you. The Bible says that, "The Lord is not slack concerning His promise, as some count slackness, but is long-suffering toward us, not willing that any should perish but that all should come to repentance. Repentance is the changing of minds and attitude from yourself to God. It is acknowledging that God alone can save you. It is putting your faith in Christ to save you. The only thing you need to be saved is to bring your sin to Him. He takes your filthy rugs (sins) in exchange for His white robe (righteousness).

****

Remembering the day you were saved is not a guarantee to salvation. The reason is because God saves in the present as opposed in the past. The evidence of those who are saved is their current obedience. The Bible says that, ""If you love Me, you will keep My commandments-----Whoever has my commands and keeps them is the one who loves me. The one who loves me will be loved by my Father, and I too will love them and show myself to them---- Jesus replied, "Anyone who loves me will obey my teaching. My Father will love them, and we will come to them and make our home with them. ." (John 14:15-23)

****

I've been thinking retrospectively at the scenario of life. I realized that there are a lot of things I could have done differently if only I could turn back the hands of time. My greatest regret is delaying receiving the gift of salvation. I often ask myself, "Why did it take me so long to acknowledge the truth?" One thing I don't ever regret is that I am saved. The Bible says that there is a way that seems good to man but in the end it is destruction. Two roads diverged in a wood, I took the one less traveled by and that has made all the difference. I will never regret why I chose this path...I am glad I did!

****

Irresponsible persons always have lame excuses for what they do. Ability is what you're capable of doing. Motivation determines what you do. Attitude determines how well you do it. In everything you do, try to be yourself in a world that is constantly trying to make you to be something else other than what God intended you to be. Stand firm in faith because not doing so means not standing at all!

****

To begin a race is not as tough as to finish it. The last push is often the most difficult one. I have seen people giving up at the eve of their victory. God answered your prayer but at times the manifestation takes longer than our expectations. Your restoration (elevation) is already complete though it has not yet manifested in the physical. The tough times you are experiencing are the final touches to usher in the long awaited results in the tangible manner. Never quit because of the hardship involved. Consider your situation as a woman in labor that goes into intensive pain but rejoices at the birth of the baby. Success is compared to going to the gym -- it takes massive work-outs to secure a breakthrough. Therefore have the tenacity to push on all the way to the end no matter how daunting it may seem to be. Remember that God is at work even when you cannot see results. No pain, no gain -- Your setback was just a setup for your comeback! "I am prepared to go anywhere, provided it be forward. I determined never to stop until I had come to the end and achieved my purpose" ~ David Livingstone

****

I am determined to be cheerful and happy in whatever situation I may find myself. For I have learned that the greater part of our misery or unhappiness is determined not by our circumstance but by our disposition. Life is not about waiting for the storm to pass. It is about learning to dance in the rain. Let gratitude be the pillow upon which you kneel to say your night prayer. Counting sufferings to be a blessing can transform melancholy into massive cheerful joy and hope. "Hope is like the sun, when you march towards it the shadow you are burdened with will be left behind".

****

Respect yourself enough to walk away from anything that no longer serves you, makes you happy, build you up or grows you. But never give up on people because God uses other people to bless us. Whenever somebody closes a door against you, God will open even a wider door to accommodate you. "Sometimes our light goes out, but is blown again into instant flame by an encounter with another human being" ~ Albert Schweitzer

****

Mind how you spend each day, and with whom you spend it. To redeem your time, you may have to prune off relationships that are not adding value to your life. Pull down every force that is working against you to sprint to your destiny.

****

My dentist told me that letting go is like pulling a tooth. After it is pulled out, you're relieved, but your tongue keeps running over the spot (gap) where the tooth was, probably indicating that you missed it. However you do not want the bad tooth back because of the pain it caused. The same applies to letting go the people we once loved. We miss them but at times we have to let go.

****

Virtue distinguishes men from boys, managers from subordinates, the outstanding from mediocre. Yearn to do what is right in spite of others' opinions. When you please others in hopes of being accepted, you lose your self-worth in the process. "I prefer to be true to myself, even at the hazard of incurring the ridicule of others, rather than to be false, and to incur my own abhorrence." ~ Frederick Douglass

****

However beautiful the strategy, you should occasionally look at the results. "I think there is a profound and enduring beauty in simplicity, in clarity, in efficiency. True simplicity is derived from so much more than just the absence of clutter and ornamentation. It's about bringing order to complexity" ~ Menton Kronno

Stephen Kyeyune

****

Any man who admits his limitations is most likely extremely good and so is what he does. No one can make you feel inferior without your consent. "A man can't ride on your back unless it's bent" ~ Martin Luther King Jr.

****

When you care for people more than they deserve, you get hurt more than you deserve. The people that are the strongest are usually the most sensitive. People who exhibit the most kindness are the first to get mistreated. The ones who take care of others all the times are usually the ones who need it the most. Yet the less interested mostly carries the day and the most interested are mostly ignored or used as floor mats.

****

The bitter truth is that no one can innovate by himself or herself; each person needs to work with other. Therefore give people more than they expect and do it cheerfully. Remember what goes around comes around----

****

"Regarding everything that you do, try to be yourself in a world that is constantly trying to make you something else; making you something other than what God intended is the greatest accomplishment of the world."

****

I have been having serious reflections concerning success. Life is worthless if you stand for nothing. In order to stand for something you must stand against the contradictory principles of what you stand for. When something bad happens you have three choices: You can let it define you, let it destroy you, or you can let it strengthen you.

****

Your critique and criticism is always welcome. Small keys can unlock big locks; simple words can express great thoughts. The major cause of strife is taking the wrong side of an argument because your opponent has taken the right one. The disciplined minds accept defeat on basis of logic. "Affirmation without discipline is the beginning of delusion" ~ Pastor. Don Matheny

****

Disappointment is the major cause of discouragement. The set back you are experiencing is most likely to be caused by discouragement. Peter denied Jesus because he was disappointed by Jesus. He rebuked our Lord for His intentions to die on the cross, and Jesus responded to Him that "Get behind me Satan". He fought the soldiers that came to arrest Jesus by cutting off the ear of the servant of the high priest but Jesus restored the ear and reprimanded him that everyone who uses a sword will be killed by a sword. Disappointment comes dressed in different fashions but most times we are disappointed by the unknown; by the hard things to figure out and get a grip on. At times the things we oppose are the very things intended to benefit us. All things are only transitory. Things are most likely to become worse before they become better. "There are a good many ugly things there and the ugliest are the most pretentious. You have three choices: You can let the ugliness define you, or let it destroy you, or you can let it strengthen you."

****

A man saw a tiger in the bush, instead of praying to God while taking precaution, he knelt down and closed his eyes and prayed to God for protection. When he opened his eyes he saw the tiger kneeling in front of him thanking God for today's meal. The Bible says that, "What does it profit, my brethren, if someone says he has faith but does not have works? Can faith save him?" (James 2:14).

****

Fear is the greatest weapon that our adversary uses to steal our blessings. In the Bible the angels introduced themselves to mankind with the slogan "Fear not". Everything you've ever wanted is on the other side of fear. Faith is the opposite of fear. Faith is putting your boldness to test. Faith is trusting in God's abilities to deliver.

****

Today's African proverb from Ethiopia: Do not blame God for creating the tiger. Be thankful He didn't give him wings.

****

Never manipulate people because of their external appearance because you may be surprised how fast they counter-react. Africans have a proverb saying that, "Never ever under estimate the speed of a Cheetah while it is lying down. Wait until it gets an opportunity to exercise the sprint." In Swahili they say If you see a lion rained on never assume it's a small cat. Baganda people say just because a sheep looks down, never underestimate its capability to see you and to knock you down.

****

The ultimate measure of a man is not where he stands in moments of comfort and convenience, but where he stands in times of challenge and controversy. It is good to follow your instincts. Let yourself be caught up in the mood every once in a while. Sometimes the consequences are worth it. The ultimate measure of a man is not where he stands in moments of comfort and convenience, but where he stands in times of challenge and controversy. A life without regret isn't worth living. The challenges of life motivate desperation to succeed, even when it means taking risks.

****

They say that "ignorance is bliss". Meaning that what you don't know cannot hurt you. I say that knowing something is often more comfortable than not knowing it. It is always impossible to hide the truth from a person who has above average intelligence. Our psyche demands for the truth of the matter, for that matter, the hidden truth becomes as good as a lie. The open enemy can be less dangerous than the enemy disguised as a friend. Ignoring the truth is like seeing a lion rained on and assumes it is a small cat. Your imagination will not diminish the danger. "Never

ever underestimate the speed of a Cheetah while it is lying down. Wait until it gets an opportunity to exercise the sprint."

****

God does not save us by grace so that we may live in disgrace. Therefore, do not let sin reign in your mortal body. Get more from Romans 6:1-14.

****

Doctors temporarily save lives but Jesus saves life eternally.

****

Do you know that your body is not who you are but a house that you occupy? Yes, you move in it and with it; you are the sole landlord that owns it but also a tenant that can be evicted upon death. A wise tenant arranges for a better house to occupy in case of eviction. Jesus has pre-paid reservations in His Father's house for all of His followers. Don't be like the earthly landlords of rental properties who call themselves landlords but when they travel to other places, they become tenants there. "The only people I recognize as landlords in the whole universe are turtles and snail. They are the only creatures that move about with their houses" ~ Davies Offor (Clarius).

****

Some people claim that they want to go to heaven but in reality they are walking in the opposite direction. Plant your feet in the direction where your heart want to be. "It is easier to cry over one thousand sins of others than to kill one of your own." The principle of Leadership is that if you fail to put God first you won't end with God.

****

It's better to be an optimist who is sometimes wrong than a pessimist who is always right. And the pessimists will continue to run out of ammunition, with which to sustain their inundated criticisms..and soon they will plummet into intellectual oblivion - and into the epithets of frustrations (having failed to leave a mark) on their downward journey towards the annals of history -whence they belong – An optimist has a vision that leads to the Promised Land.

****

Sometimes divulging your vulnerabilities without any kind of filter can make you more human, but then again, it can also provide material that can be used against you." ~ Tonya Hurley, Lovesick

****

Wisdom is making moral choices. That is why Jesus is the most wise man ever lived.

****

"Wisdom never kicks at the iron walls it can't bring down" ~ Olive Schreiner

****

"What counts is not necessarily the size of the dog in the fight - it's the size of the fight in the dog" ~ Dwight D. Eisenhower - 34th U. S. President (1890-1969)

****

"Common sense is like deodorant. The people who need it the most never use it. "~

Unknown

****

Whatever affects one directly, affects all indirectly. I can never be what I ought to be until you are what you ought to be. This is the interrelated structure of reality. ~ Martin Luther King, Jr.

****

One thing I've learned over the years is that the more intimate we are with Him, the more powerful our lives will be. That's because we begin to resemble and act like those we spend time with. So, if we "hang out" with Christ, we will eventually become more like Christ. The trouble is many of us don't spend a whole lot of time with Him ~ Joyce Wade Meyers

****

"Take a survey of those whose lives count for much at home, in Church, in business, career, leadership and society. You will find each one without exception, learnt to use the dirt of critical comments to manure their paths to significance. Antagonism can either make you bitter or better, never both. The greater news is, you choose which" Footprints of Grants.

****

Real heroes are champions of peace and are judged by their perseverance in tough times when adversity meets integrity. Our dignity does not depend on what we know but on what we implement. Every challenge has an expiry date, but God's blessings do not expire.

****

God tests our patience in times trials. Questioning the integrity of God when you are faced with tough times is fatal; it is like testing the depth of the river with both your legs. Never be tempted to do so.

****

"A conference is a gathering of important people who singly can do nothing, but together can decide that nothing can be done" ~ Fred Allen, American comedian

****

"Let gratitude be the pillow upon which you kneel to say your nightly prayer. And let faith be the bridge you build to overcome evil and welcome good, and literally those who have the ability to be grateful are the ones who have the ability to achieve greatness".

****

Character is power; it makes friends, draws patronage, support and open the way to wealth, honor and happiness. Never make a promise when you are excited. Never take a decision when you are angry. If your foot slips, you can recover your balance but if your tongue slips, you can never recall your words. Your words are your assets, be careful how you dispense them. Many people talk themselves out of their destiny. In such way their words become liabilities as opposed to assets.

****

Character is power; it makes friends, draws patronage, support and opens way to prosperity, honor and happiness. Your true characters are judged in times of trials. Our moral sufferings are as much a requisite element as our genteel manners and our cosmopolitanism. Good mannered people care more about their legacy. We are called to uplift each other.

****

If all people truly measured their lifestyle to that of Jesus, I believe that would have been the end of self righteousness. You have not grasped the gospel until you acknowledge that we live the life of Christ by faith, and that without the grace we cannot stand even one minute!

****

Humility: Our culture says, believe in yourself! Assert yourself! But we should not be surprised to learn that the Bible tells us to do the opposite of what the world advocates. We read over and over in the Bible that God pulls down those who exalt themselves and lifts up those who are humble (1 peter 5:6). The Lord highlights humility throughout Scriptures, but the culmination of true humility is the attitude of submission to God that Jesus Himself displayed, and that we are called to imitate Him (Philippians 2:4)

****

We live in a culture that has, for centuries now, cultivated the idea that the skeptical person is always smarter than one who believes. You can be as stupid as a cabbage, as long as you doubt. The old adage is true: "Wise men can learn more from foolish questions than fools can learn from a wise answer".

****

It's hard to be a hypocrite in the vortex of a crisis. There isn't time to paste on a mask or worry about what other people think. When you're confronted by a crisis, the true character of your faith will emerge—unvarnished and unannounced. Among hypocrites faking will not last forever "Glory is fleeting, but obscurity is forever." - Napoleon Bonaparte (1769-1821)

****

A wise person will never claim he is the best for it is a person with limited experience of life that thinks there is none as wise as he is. "Arrogance is not simply thinking you are important. Arrogance is thinking others are not important" ~ Dr. Mike Murdock

****

"Things may come to those who wait, but only the things left by those who hustle" ~ Abraham Lincoln

****

God puts people in your life for reasons. Some to learn lessons from, others to help you along your way, and others to make you realize how strong you really are..... Best endeavors...

****

Ignorance is bliss definition: Not knowing something is often more dangerous than knowing it. What you don't know cannot hurt you ~ (Thomas Gray)

****

Many people are not bold enough to identify with their divinity because either they are not fully aware of it or they are not ready for the responsibility that comes with it; In Christ is the greatest revelation and awareness one should embrace boldly and unapologetic-ally. Jesus said that "I and my Father are one". He then prayed that we may be one with Him (John 17:21). He promised us to do greater works than He did! Stand up to your divine self and Christ will stand in you, through you and for you!

****

"Leadership is lifting a person's vision to high sights, the raising of a person's performance to a higher standard, the building of a personality beyond its normal limitations" ~ Peter Drucker

****

Let's not look back in anger, nor forward in fear but around in awareness" ~ James Thumber.

****

"The tortoise is not tall, but it is taller than the frog; the frog is taller than the lizard; the lizard is taller than the snail; the snail is taller than the fly; the fly is taller than the ant; the ant in turn is taller than the ground on which it claws. Everything has its own place, its own level, its standing."

****

Things are tough but there are never too tough to be solved. Human beings are powerful than any other thing in the world because human beings can communicate. They can solve the seemingly impossible problems by sharing information.

****

One who sees inaction in action, and action in inaction, is intelligent among men ~ Bhagavad Gita

****

There are no two people even identical twins that are 100% alike

****

There are three kinds of people: The activists that make things happen, the uninvolved who watch things happen, the uncaring who wonder what happened. Who are you?

****

Courage and compassion are two sides of the same coin. Compassion without courage is not genuine. You may have a compassionate thought or impulse, but if you don't do or say anything, it's not real compassion.

****

Life is like photography. You need the negatives to develop the obscure things into manifestation.

****

The greatest Victories in my life are in the near future. The best is just starting to unveil itself. But the sum total of my future victory depends on what I do today.

****

If it is worth it, you won't give up. If you give up, you're not worth it.
****

The soul is placed in the body like a rough diamond, and must be polished, or the luster of it will never appear ~ Daniel Defoe

****

I don't have gray hairs; I have highlights of wisdom

****

The more I study the Bible the more it reveals my ignorance rather than knowledge

****

Those who think to SEEK GOD ON THE ELEVENTH HOUR always DIE at 10:59 one minute to the ELEVENTH HOUR... so always be with him. Don't think of seeking him at the eleventh hour

****

James 4:17 - "So whoever knows the right thing to do and fails to do it, for him it is sin." Neglecting what you are supposed to do is sin. You don't have to sow weeds; all you have to do is neglecting to cultivate the land, and the weeds will grow up.

****

Through Christ you have the capability to bring all things under subjection (Philippians 4:13).

****

God will never let you down but will provide exceeding your expectations (Philippians 4:19)

****

Faith is not just believing that God will do what He promised to do but also trusting in His timing that He will deliver when it is appropriate.

****

"The universe may not only be stranger than we suppose, it may be stranger than we CAN suppose" ~ J.B.S. Haldane

****

Today, we have more technology than the past centuries but we are generally not better off than them because we have substituted wisdom with intelligence.

****

Wisdom is making God's choice your choice perpetually.

****

"A wise man does not test the depth of a river with both legs together"

****

"The real measure of our wealth is how much we'd be worth if we lost all our money." ~ Benjamin Jowett

****

"People rarely succeed unless they have fun with what they do" ~ Ap. Tumwine Willy

****

"Sometimes we need someone to simply be there, not to fix anything or do anything in particular, but just to let us feel we are supported and cared about."

****

Vision is a picture of the future that produces a passion for the future ~ Bill Hybels

****

Matthew 7:16 ~ "By their fruit you will recognize them." Your belief doesn't make you a better person, your behavior does.........The fruit of the Spirit marks the Christian not the rhetoric jargon!

****

Life is compared to running a marathon whereby you need to drink water occasionally due to thirsty. Don't wait too long to take a drink, lest you slide into dehydration. Water is symbolic to the Word of God. You need the Word for direction otherwise you will get lost into this world.

****

The only difference between a good day and a bad day is your attitude"
~ Dennis S. Brown

****

Anyone can make you smile, many people can make you cry, but it takes someone special to make you smile with tears in your eyes.

****

"Commitment means staying loyal to what you said you were going to do long after the mood you said it in had left." ~ Unknown

****

Patience is a virtue because it is one of the fruits of the Spirit. It involves persevering in times of trials. Therefore, before you pray for patience be ready to handle trials.

****

I can't write a book commensurate with Shakespeare, but I can write a book by me ~ Sir Walter Raleigh

****

"To share your weakness is to make yourself vulnerable; to make yourself vulnerable is to show your strength" ~ Criss Jami

****

Jesus said that He is the light of the world. He then turned to us and said we are the light of the world. He finally instructed us that "Let your light shine" (Matthew 5:16). In order for there to be light there must be burning. The fire of God has to burn the impurities within us in order for the light of Christ to glow (blaze) through us. The moral lesson is that God will never ask us to do something without providing to us the means of implementing it.

****

Righteousness is an outcome of Faith in Christ. The Bible says Abraham believed God and it was imputed to him as righteousness. Righteousness is a gift to men by God through the death of Christ. Righteousness is the state in which man finds himself accepted by God.

****

Thank you for preaching the gospel of the kingdom. We have a lot of prophets preaching material prosperity and turning the Scriptures upside down. They don't have that servant hood- heart of God. You are a blessing.

****

Putting on faces and/or changing the face will change nothing, but facing the change will change everything. Changing location without changing attitude is not smart either.

****

"Things may come to those who wait but only the things left by those who hustle."

****

Your breaking point may just be your turning point (Genesis 50:20).

****

And, when you want something, all the universe conspires in helping you to achieve it." ~ Paulo Coelho

****

Time never stops for you, therefore never wait for it. There is never a wrong time to do any right thing.......... So get up and do it now!

****

They say that age is gold. As time is evaporating in thin air age is stepping in. One of the advantages of age is wisdom.

****

If you want to live under the shadow in your old age, plant a tree now!

****

'A society grows great when old men plant trees whose shade they know they shall never sit in' ~ Greek proverb

****

Forgiveness is not what we do to other people. We do it for ourselves to get well and move on.

****

Inspiration without information leads to frustration!

****

Wise men can learn more from foolish questions than fools can learn from a wise answer

****

The biggest fool is the one that believes there is God but lives as if there is none

****

A man can fail many times, but he isn't a failure until he begins to blame somebody else ~ John Burroughs

****

Develop a habit of speaking words, thinking thoughts and cultivating desires that activate, sustain and increase on virtue. The operation of the Holy Spirit in your life is the manifested virtue of Christ in your life.

****

"Do not pray for easy lives. Pray to be stronger men" ~ John F. Kennedy

****

Psalm 145:13 – "The Lord is faithful to all his promises and loving toward all he has made". The Bible says concerning God that His love and faithfulness endures forever. It means that God will never stop loving and He will never stop being faithful because these are His very attributes. He blesses and chastises out of love. He keeps His promises and He never walk away from His covenants. Unfortunately at times we view God differently. We often blame Him for our own mistakes, and we take credit for the good things He does! We need to be careful and make sure that we are not digressing into a situation where we are questioning the integrity of God or even touching His glory.

****

This is the enigma of life - fulfillment is not in material things. Life is not what we think it is. We crave for the things of this world and after we get them we find that they are not as good as we expected. Then comes the stress associated with the passion of controlling and protecting the same things at our fingertips out of fear of losing them, regardless of the fact that we cannot keep them forever. "To crave and to have are as alike as a thing and its shadow." The reality is that craving for the things of this world drives our worst behavior. Yes, God created all things for us to enjoy but it is foolish, selfish and cruel wish to make your heart ache for them without letting your heart ache for the God of the things first. The Bible warned that it does not profit a man to gain the whole world and lose his or her soul (Matthew 16:26). "Let me lose everything on earth and the world beyond, but let me not lose my soul." So help me God.

****

If you have never made a mistake you have never tried anything new. Jesus said that, "If anyone be in me behold he is a new creation". When you are in Him you are new but you are also prone to mistakes. But be resilient; be quick to repent and ask Him to dust off your mess and to pick you up.

****

As we look at the Characteristics of wise people – not only are they Good Listeners, they are open to Correction. There are two kinds of listening: The passive listener attentively listens but picks nothing. The purposeful listener attentively listens purposely to pick something. The fools may not listen to advice until they suffer the consequences of their actions. The good news is that Jesus died for the fools because we are all recovering fools to a certain degree.

****

Opportunity dances with those who are already on the dance floor

****

Remember that you have two arms: One for helping yourself; one for helping others

****

When you reach the end of your rope, tie a knot on it and hang on.

****

Money may buy titles but the value of a good name is worth its weight in gold

****

Courage is what it takes to stand up and speak; courage is also what it takes to sit down and listen

****

The first to apologize is the bravest, the first to forgive is the strongest, and the first to forget is the happiest.

****

Service doesn't start when you have something to give; it blossoms naturally when you have nothing left to take ~ Nipun Mehta.

****

Intriguingly, some people get judged for being real while some are getting loved for being fake!

****

A woman marries a man hoping he's going to change, but he doesn't; a man marries a woman hoping she doesn't change, but she does.

****

"Love me when I least deserve it because that is when I most need it".

****

It is one thing to try to be better for someone who loves you and quite another to try to be something different so someone will love you ~ Michael

****

Knowledge is a process of piling up facts; wisdom lies in their simplification. ~ Martin Fischer

****

Those with the dirty desks are most likely to come up with new ideas

****

How you schedule your life determines how live

****

Strive to have face-value. Your posture speaks volume. A look of confidence on your face impresses everybody. You can't command respect if you look dejected or frustrated # personality tips

****

"The Average woman would rather have Beauty than Brains... The Average man Can See Better than He Thinks" - David Opito

****

The ultimate leader is one who is willing to develop people to the point that the eventually surpass him or her in knowledge and ability. - Fred A. Manske Jr.

****

The seed of truth exposes the seed of deception. When Isaac was born, he exposed Ishmael as illegitimate heir.

****

The distance between you and God is the distance between your knees and the ground; always be prayerful. "Prayers can move mountains," the good book says.

****

Be convinced that God has already baked your bread for today because He promised you daily bread; so receive it with thanks and remain faithful to him.

****

Faith dictates that no matter what lies ahead of me, God is already there

****

"Your beliefs become your thoughts. Your thoughts become your words. Your words become your actions. Your actions become your habits. Your habits become your values. Your values become your destiny" ~ Mahatma

****

The value of the believers begins with Jesus Christ. Our Lord, Jesus Christ preached the message of the kingdom of heaven involving dying to ourselves and vanishing so that we might manifest Him. But the New Age advocates for the most part, vain phantoms; and to confidence in one's self, and become something of worth and value is the best and safest course.

****

Save me from the temptation of making a poor, albeit necessary, decision.

****

One of the truest tests of integrity is the blunt refusal to be compromised

****

"People demand freedom of speech to make up for the freedom of thought which they avoid." ~ Soren Aabye Kierkegaard (1813-1855)

****

"Writing fiction is the act of weaving a series of lies to arrive at a greater truth."

~ Khaled Hosseini

****

Obstacles and delay are part of the journey in life. But don't let them you to doubt God.

****

Integrity is like virginity, when you lose it, you lose it once and for ever.

****

The fragrance of flowers spreads only in the direction of the wind, but the goodness of a person is supposed to spread in all directions.

****

Men of genius are admired. Men of wealth are envied. Men of power are feared, but only men of Character are Trusted.

****

Wisdom is like money. You can only spend/give as much as you have and you can multiply it by putting it in the right place(s)

****

The Prince of Preachers, Charles H. Spurgeon, once said, "Visit many good books, but live in the Bible."

****

The Bible is a classic for a reason, and even if you've read it before, it has a richness that will reward you again and again. As C.S. Lewis said, "I can't imagine a man really enjoying a book and reading it only once." And if you've never had the pleasure, you'll have a real treat in front of you ~ Eric Metaxas

****

Psalms 90:12 - So teach us to number our days, that we may apply our hearts unto wisdom.

****

"To be humble to superiors is duty, to equals courtesy, to inferiors is nobleness"

****

"You know more than you think you know, just as you know less than you want to know".

****

See clearly where the road is leading, and you won't be bothered by the rocks and pebbles over which you must travel.

****

Life is like a multiple choice question. Sometimes the choices confuse you, not the question itself.

****

We need never be ashamed of our tears except for crocodile tears. The easiest way to tell a wolf in sheepskin is walloping it hard to howl in pain. Real crying cannot be faked.

****

An appeaser is one who feeds a crocodile – hoping it will eat him last ~ Sir Winston Churchill

****

In a relationship, distance is only a test to see how much Love can travel.

****

It's weird how life gathers two people, attaches their hearts and souls together to become one, then in a fraction of a second they are drawn apart like strangers who had never met.

****

"It's not because things are difficult that we don't dare; it's because we don't dare that things are difficult.

****

Emancipate yourselves from slavery mentality. Slavery is an attitude of the minds.

****

People living in the vanity of their own mind not only destroy themselves, but far too often, they bring destruction to others around them.

****

"When you care for people more than they deserve, you get hurt more than you deserve."

****

"People are often unreasonable, irrational, and self-centered; forgive them anyway" ~ Mother Teresa.

****

You will be remembered for two things: The problem you solved and the problem you created.

****

When you have a casual approach to life, you become a casualty.

****

"Never let kindness and loyalty leave you, bind them around your neck!"

****

Show me your check book and I will tell you whom you worship. "You can sing all you want about how you love Jesus, you can have crocodile tears in your eyes, but the consecration that doesn't reach your purse has not reached your heart" Adrian Rogers

****

If you open your heart, someone will open your eyes…….. It is not the eyes that are open that see and not the eyes that are shut that can't see!

****

Whatever you have power to do, you have power not to do also.

****

------ for this thing that we call "failure" is not the falling down, but the staying down.

****

It is not the mountain we conquer but ourselves.

****

Meekness is restrained strength. It is not weakness because it takes more strength not to defend yourself than to defend yourself.

****

Every setback that you face is a setup for a comeback.

****

Yesterday's regret and the fear of tomorrow are the tragedies of life. Life can only be understood backwards but it must be lived forward.

****

When a bird is alive, it eats ants. When the bird dies, ants eat it.

****

One tree can be made into a million matchsticks but only one matchstick is needed to burn down a million trees. Circumstances can change at any time so don't devalue or hurt anyone in this life.

****

"We can't change the world but we can change the way we live in it one subscriber at a time"

****

Restricting the Kid from playing with fire propels him to want to touch it. The reason is because it is within human nature to be fascinated with doing the forbidden.

****

Wisdom of warfare: The art of war: It is only a mad man that fights many battles at the same time. No smart man becomes the aggressor in a war he expects to lose.

****

"You must not fight too often with one enemy, or you will teach him all your art of war" ~ Nyamwezi proverb.

****

"If we encounter a people of rare intellect, we should ask them what books they read" ~ Ralph Waldo Emerson

****

Common sense is a flower that does not grow in every person's garden

****

You may put fruits on the tree but you cannot change the nature of the tree!

****

It is possible to look good and not do good. But it is impossible to do good and not look good.

****

"When I was young, I used to admire intelligent people; as I grow older, I admire kind people" ~ Abraham Joshua Heschel

****

Why is it very easy for some people to borrow something but returning it back becomes somebody's hustle? My suggestion is that, you should live within your budget lines. Don't live a life you will never sustain or else, you will become endogenously depressed.

****

There is no deeper calm than that which follows the storm.

****

Great minds discuss ideas, average minds discuss events, small minds discuss people

****

People who are informed are much more difficult to manipulate. It doesn't take brain surgery to figure out this but common sense.

****

Procrastination is the grave in which opportunity is buried.

****

Two rams cannot drink from the same bucket at the same time, they will surely lock horns! ~ Ola Rotimi

****

Never do something that you will regret later. A man is powerful when he controls power and powerless when power controls him.

****

Selfishly motivated anger turns into sin but divinely motivated anger turns against sin.

****

The truth is that we live under the same sky, but we don't all have the same horizon, so if it doesn't feel right, don't do it, that is the lesson that will save you a lot from grief.

****

People are often unreasonable and self-centered. If you are kind, people may accuse you of ulterior motives. Be kind anyway. If you are honest, people may cheat you. Be honest anyway

****

Laziness is the habit of unnecessarily resting even before one gets tired

****

The truth becomes tremendously hard to swallow when you are choking on your pride.

****

I am thankful for all of those who said NO to me. It's because of them I'm doing it myself.

****

Whenever you say 'Yes' you are not just saying yes to one thing but to other things that come with yes.

****

I reminisce the old youthful tough days; happiness is not in future but behind.

****

"Everyone starts from scratch, but not everyone keeps on scratching!"

****

We are what we repeatedly do. Excellence, therefore, is not an act but a habit.

****

"Good times make good memories. Bad times make good lessons."

****

Stretch towards your dreams. Dress towards your dreams. Think towards your dreams. Walk towards your dreams. True dreams are inspired by God. They are not wishful thinking and gambling with the world.

****

Destiny is not a matter of chance; but a matter of choice. It is not a thing to be waited for; it is a thing to be worked for.

****

"Do not pray for easy lives. Pray to be stronger men." - John F. Kennedy

****

Never doubt in the dark what God has shown you in the light.

****

"People can offer God plenty of reasons why He shouldn't call them to spread the gospel. But His call is not issued for our consideration; He expects a response of obedience and surrender" ~ Charles Stanley

Stephen Kyeyune

****

Sometimes you will never know the value of a moment until it becomes a memory ~ Dr. Seuus

****

"It is generally acceptable that there are only two possible outcomes to the flipping coin – heads or tails. In reality there is a small possibility of the coin landing on its edge."

****

If you can't change the outside, change the inside. If you can't change the situation, change the attitude

****

We are naturally generous but because our generousness is focused on 'self' we need to be taught how to be generous to God.

****

"Those who mind don't matter, and those who matter don't mind" ~ Bernard Baruch

****

We are masters of the unsaid words, but slaves of those we let slip out ~ Winston Churchill

****

A vocabulary of truth and simplicity will be of service throughout your life ~ Winston Churchill

****

People who fail to plan, plan to fail

****

I consider looseness with words no less of a defect than looseness of the bowels ~ John Calvin

****

The more the words, the less the meaning, and how does that profit anyone? (Ecclesiastes 6:11)

****

Bitterness is self-inflicted torment

****

Let your speech be always with grace, seasoned with salt, that ye may know how ye ought to answer every man (Colossians 4:6)

****

Sorrow looks behind, worry looks around but hope looks up. Our blessed hope is the Second Coming of our Lord Jesus Christ.

African proverbs:

If the crocodile tells you that there is no more fish in the lake, believe it because that is where it lives ~ (Nigerians have a proverb)

****

Pick up a bee from kindness, and learn the limitations of kindness ~ (Sufi proverbs)

****

Teeth and tongue do fight every often. But they never forget to live in peace for once and pursue their one goal: crush the bite by any means ~ (Southern Sudan)

****

When arguing with a stone, an egg is always wrong ~ Afroverb

Stephen Kyeyune

****

Do not judge by appearance, a rich heart may be under a poor coat ~ Afroverb

****

When you have spoken the word, it reigns over you. When it is unspoken you reign over it (Egyptian Proverb)

****

"He that lies in a dog's den should expect to rise-up with fleas". Meaning that staying close to a corrupt character may result in learning some of their bad traits. ~ (Baganda)

****

"A fool says what he knows, and a wise man knows what he says." ~ Yiddish Proverb

****

"A blind person knows his environment better than a sighted stranger" ~ Uganda

****

Beauty is just a color but character is a virtue ~ Uganda.

****

Whatever level of familiarity, never test your friendship with a leopard by putting your fingers in its mouth ~ Baganda

****

You become wise when you begin to run out of money (Tanzania)

****

Alexander's craziness: On His Death Bed Alexander summoned his generals and told them his three ultimate wishes.

1. The best doctors should carry his coffin;
2. The wealth he had accumulated (money, gold, precious stones) should be scattered along the way to his burial, and
3. His hands should be left hanging outside the coffin for all to see.

Surprised by these unusual requests, one of his generals asked Alexander to explain. Here is what he said -

1. I want the best doctors to carry my coffin to demonstrate that in the face of death, even the best doctors in the world have no power to heal;
2. I want the road to be covered with my treasure so that everybody sees that the wealth acquired on earth, stays on earth.
3. I want my hands to swing in the wind so that people understand that we come to this world empty handed and we leave empty handed after the most precious treasure of all is exhausted –

Typically, in life, we think we need to treat everyone the same. But the Bible gives some very specific instructions on how to treat 3 different groups of people: The wise (Prov. 12:15), The foolish (Prov. 10: 8), and the Evil (**Proverbs** 17:4). Whoever corrects a mocker invites insults; whoever rebukes the wicked incurs abuse (Proverbs 9:7).

9:8 Do not rebuke mockers or they will hate you;
rebuke the wise and they will love you.
9:9 Instruct the wise and they will be wiser still;
teach the righteous and they will add to their learning.
9:10 The fear of the Lord is the beginning of wisdom,
and knowledge of the Holy One is understanding.
9:11 For through wisdom your days will be many,
and years will be added to your life.
9:12 If you are wise, your wisdom will reward you;
if you are a mocker, you alone will suffer.
This instructs me to not treat people the same way – This is not about favoritism, it is about discernment.

Printed in the United States
By Bookmasters

Printed in the United States
By Bookmasters